Christmas 1985

D0229145

To Diane

Love & Best wishes

From Bill & Liz

the Creative Cook

The complete guide to kitchen techniques with over 850 recipes

Collins
London · Glasgow · Sydney · Auckland · Johannesburg · Toronto

Editorial concept: Hans Belterman
Photographer: Henk van der Heijden
Editors-in-chief: Joy Langridge, Arlene Sobel
Deputy editor: Lewis Esson
Home economists: Sarah Bush,
Alison Granger
Book editor: Julie Thompson
Art directors: Jack Botermans, Carol Collins
Designers: Shirley Hunter, Sue Lee,
Martin Lovelock

Published in 1985 by
William Collins Sons & Co Ltd
London · Glasgow · Sydney · Auckland ·
Johannesburg · Toronto
Designed and produced for
William Collins Sons & Co Ltd
by Eaglemoss Publications Ltd
Most of this material was first published in
The Creative Cook partwork.
© 1985 Eaglemoss Publications Limited
© 1981, 1982, 1983, 1984
Kluwerpers/Utrecht. Holland
Printed in Spain by Cayfosa. Barcelona
Dep. Leg. B - 14485-1985
Typesetting by Grange Filmsetting Limited

ISBN 0 00 411220 2

INTRODUCTION

For me, cooking is a challenge and a pleasure. When I want to relax, there's nothing I like more than cooking for my family and friends – sometimes a traditional roast shoulder of lamb with a potato gratin (fortunately my husband is good at carving). Other times, it's fun to invent delicious surprises, like a Baked Alaska topped with three sparklers for my daughter.

As a cookery writer, though, much of my time is spent in developing and writing recipes, and also in demonstrating them on TV. Over the years I've developed my own reliable ways to handle most cookery techniques. If you want to be a creative cook, it's no good just following recipes through slavishly. You need to understand the underlying principles. Once you know how and why the basic methods work you can try *any* new recipe with confidence. You can adapt recipes to use in-season ingredients (fresher and

cheaper), or ring the changes with your own choice of seasonings. And you can usually save a dish if something goes wrong.

What I like about this book is that it gives a thorough and up-to-date rundown of all the current kitchen techniques, illustrated with dozens of both familiar and unusual recipes from all over the world. Particularly valuable are the practical tips on almost every page. Did you know, for example, that a two-egg omelette should ideally be made in a six-inch pan, while four eggs need nine inches? You'll find everything from roasting times for the Sunday joint to how to tell a hard-boiled egg from an uncooked one without breaking either of them (on page 38). And, if you're conscientious about providing healthy meals, every recipe carries a fat-content symbol so you can always plan well-balanced menus.

At the moment I'm intrigued by the

way Far Eastern influences are filtering into everyday cooking – with kiwi fruit and Chinese leaves coming on to our supermarket shelves, and more and more people using woks. *The Creative Cook* includes them all, which makes it one of the most welcome 'cook's bibles' around.

So – whether you want to learn more about sauces or cakes, discover how to steam or pot roast – here's a book I can thoroughly recommend. It provides a fresh source of inspiration and should make every meal a success.

Mary Berry

How to use this book

The Creative Cook has been designed for everyone who enjoys good food and is looking for more imaginative ways to cook and present dishes. In it you will find a reliable guide to modern cooking techniques, particularly those which enhance the flavour of ingredients and maintain their goodness.

The key to creative cooking This book is about the how and why of cooking, because once you understand the underlying principles, you'll know how to succeed with every sort of dish.

Each chapter starts by explaining a particular cookery technique, followed by a range of step-by-step recipes which show how to adapt the method for different ingredients and different dishes. There are also chapters for specialized techniques such as 'Cake, pastry and bread-making' and 'Stock, soup and sauce-making'. And, for when you're feeling particularly creative, topics like pasta-making and cooking with gelatine are included in the chapter called 'Extending your repertoire'. Throughout, the side columns provide helpful advice, with diagrams (as left) showing how to cope with any tricky stages.

Choosing your recipes You'll find the 850 recipes and variations in *The Creative Cook* arranged according to the cooking method used. For example, some chicken recipes appear in the chapter on 'Cooking in hot water or steam', others come in the chapters on 'Cooking in hot fat or oil', 'Cooking in the oven' and so on. To find all these chicken recipes at a glance, just turn to the Index at the end of the book, where all the recipes and techniques are clearly listed under 'Chicken' with their page references.

Where basic recipes such as stocks or sauces form part of a dish, they are referred to by name only – just consult the Index to find where the full instructions appear. (For example, when a recipe lists Chicken Stock among the ingredients, the Index shows that the recipe for Chicken Stock is on page 239.) For convenience, page references for all the main basic recipes are listed together on page 456.

What the symbols mean

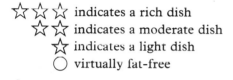 Hundreds of useful hints and tips from experienced cooks are given throughout, indicated by this symbol. Many of these 'tricks of the trade' will save you time, money and effort.

Preparation and cooking times

To help you plan ahead, every recipe gives times for preparation and cooking. These timings are of course intended only as a general guide.

At-a-glance menu planner

To help you create well-balanced meals that are satisfying but not over-rich, every recipe has a star rating.

☆☆☆ indicates a rich dish
☆☆ indicates a moderate dish
☆ indicates a light dish
○ virtually fat-free

The richness of a dish is based on its fat content – butter, oil, cream or the fat content of meat. Often this fat content will not be obvious, as in a cake or casserole.

✳ This symbol shows where information on freezing has been given.

Measures

Every recipe has been worked out in both imperial and metric measures. You should follow one set or the other as the two are not interchangeable in a given recipe. The metric quantities are based in general on the 1oz:25g measure. However, these metric equivalents are likely to vary between recipes.

All spoon measures are level, unless otherwise stated. Where teaspoons are given, a standard 5 millilitre measure has been used. Where tablespoons are given, a 15 millilitre measure has been used.

Flour

In all the recipes where flour is indicated among the ingredients, plain flour is indicated unless self-raising flour is specially mentioned.

Butter/margarine

In all cake recipes where butter is used, block margarine may be substituted unless otherwise stated.

CONTENTS

In *The Creative Cook* the recipes are arranged according to their method of preparation. By showing what makes each recipe 'work', this helps you to cook more confidently and creatively. Each section starts by explaining a cookery process, and is followed by a wide variety of recipes using that technique.

Cooking in hot water or steam

Cooking in hot fat or oil

Cooking by direct heat

Cooking in the oven

Covered cooking

Stock, soup and sauce-making

Cake, pastry and bread-making

Making preserves

Extending your repertoire

COOKING IN HOT WATER OR STEAM

Boiling • Poaching • Steaming

Boiling

Boiling, the transmission of heat from water that is kept at 100C (212F) to food, is one of the most versatile cooking methods. It needs the minimum of equipment–a saucepan–and heat. Water itself provides the simplest, purest cooking medium. Yet it accomplishes all the good cook's aims, producing palatable food in the shortest possible time which is minimally affected by the process.

Fast boiling, the classic method of cooking food in a large quantity of vigorously boiling water until tender, only applies to foods which need sustained high-temperature cooking to break down and soften their structure such as root vegetables and potatoes and grains like rice and pasta. Fast boiling is also used for eggs and shellfish which are protected by their shells.

As boiling is a cooking method with particular relevance to vegetables, these will be considered first in some detail.

Boiling spinach in the minimum water.

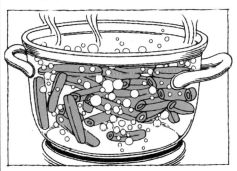

Boiling beans in a panful of water.

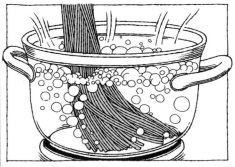

Softening pasta before boiling it.

Most foods, especially vegetables other than the more resistant roots and tubers, are cooked by a partial boil which is gentler and less turbulent than a full, rolling boil. In the following pages the world of vegetables is thoroughly covered. Grouped by families you will find leafy vegetables such as spinach, chicory and endive, the cabbage family (brassicas), stalks and shoots, legumes (peas and beans), vegetable fruits (including aubergines), the onion family, wild and cultivated mushrooms as well as roots and tubers (such as carrots and potatoes).

Starting in cold water
Follow this general rule: start vegetables that grow above ground–the leaves, legumes, stalks and shoots–in water that is already boiling. This ensures the shortest cooking time and maximizes colour, flavour and nutrient retention. Also start young root vegetables and new potatoes in boiling water because they are small and tender enough to cook evenly.

Mature roots and tubers are starchy, their plant cells thicker and less digestible in the raw state. Start them off in cold water so that heat penetrates gradually to the centre and cooks the vegetables to the same degree throughout.

The quantity of water
Here again, there is a simple rule of thumb–if you are cooking vegetables whole you can safely use as much water as you like. A large quantity of water has the virtue of speed and whole vegetables have fewer cut surfaces from which to lose nutrients.

When vegetables are cut up or when they have thin leaves with a large surface area (spinach, Swiss chard or endive, for instance), they are vulnerable to nutrient loss and should be treated differently. The precise amount of water depends on the size of the pan and the amount of the vegetable. But use enough water to cover the bottom of the pan by at least $\frac{1}{2}$ inch (1cm). Too much and you risk having to throw away water that contains valuable nutrients; too little and the vegetable will stick or not cook through evenly. Moist, soft leaves with a high water content–spinach or chard–which have been well washed in plenty of cold water, need only the water that clings to their large leaves in order to cook successfully. Any water left over can be used in stocks or sauces.

Thickening boiled milk for a dessert.

Preserving nutrients

Valuable minerals and vitamins such as C and the B vitamins dissolve in water. The briefer and faster the cooking, the less dissolves and the smaller the loss. It is equally important to buy vegetables that are fresh and unwilted with their vitamin content intact and to prepare vegetables just before you boil them. Leaving them to soak for lengthy periods or washing them *after* you have cut them up, all result in vitamin loss since, by exposing the cut surfaces to air or water, you accelerate their destruction.

Coring chicory

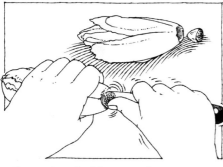

Removing the bitter-tasting core.

Boiling leaf vegetables

Fresh leaf vegetables, whether from spinach, Swiss chard, endive or chicory, boiled for the minimum amount of time and served immediately, are among the most underrated delights of vegetable cuisine. Serve them simply with butter or dress them up in the variety of ways shown below.

Boiled Chicory

Chicory is at its best when the heads are compact and straight and the colour pale and bright.

Serves 4:
Preparation: 3 minutes
Cooking: 12 minutes

1-1¼lb (450-575g) chicory
salt
a little melted butter to serve

Trim the base of the chicory and remove any damaged leaves.

☐ Use a small knife to remove the bitter-tasting core from the base as shown on the left.

☐ Rinse and place the chicory in a saucepan of salted boiling water. Return to the boil, then cover and cook for 10-12 minutes, until tender.

☐ Drain and serve immediately with melted butter and, if you like, a sprinkling of cayenne.

Chicory au Gratin

Serves 4   ☆☆☆
Preparation: 5 minutes
Cooking: 15 minutes

1-1¼lb (450-575g) chicory

The sauce:
1oz (25g) butter
2 tablespoons flour
½ pint (300ml) milk
salt and pepper
3oz (75g) grated cheese (optional)

The topping:
2oz (50g) grated cheese
1oz (25g) breadcrumbs
1oz (25g) butter

The stages involved in making Chicory au Gratin.

Prepare the chicory as left.

☐ Cut each head into thin, even slices.

☐ Cook the slices in salted boiling water—they will only take 5 minutes. Drain and transfer to a serving dish.

☐ Make a roux with the butter and flour and gradually add the milk to make a smooth, thick sauce. Season to taste with salt and pepper. Stir in the cheese.

☐ Spoon the sauce over the chicory. Combine the grated cheese and breadcrumbs. Sprinkle the mixture over the sauce, dot with butter and brown under a hot grill.

Boiled Endive

Endive and Batavian endive (sometimes sold as Batavia), look a little like curly-leaved lettuce. The leaves are firmer and more bitter than lettuce.

Serves 4   ◯
Preparation: 5 minutes
Cooking: 8 minutes

1½lb (700g) endive
salt and pepper
a little butter (optional)
a sprinkling of nutmeg

Discard any damaged leaves and trim the base.

☐ Plunge the endive head first into a bowl of cold water to dislodge sand and grit.

☐ Shred the leaves by holding the endive firmly and slicing through the leaves as shown on the right.

☐ Put the slices into a large pan with just the water that clings to the leaves.

☐ Add salt, cover the pan, and cook gently for 8 minutes. Drain well.

☐ Serve with a little butter, if liked, and season to taste with salt, pepper and a little nutmeg.

Tip: The heart of endive is often eaten as a salad with the outer leaves discarded. Instead of wasting them, try cooking the outer leaves as described above or combining them with other leaf vegetables such as chicory.

Endive with Bacon and Tomato

This recipe makes a meal in itself. To give body to the final dish, the cooking liquid is thickened with a little arrowroot.

Serves 4   ☆
Preparation: 10 minutes
Cooking: 15 minutes

1½lb (700g) endive
5-6oz (150-175g) streaky bacon
2 teaspoons arrowroot
1 tablespoon cold water
pepper
3 tomatoes, skinned, deseeded and diced

Prepare and cook the endive as in the previous recipe. Do not drain.

☐ Cut the bacon into thin strips and fry until crisp.

☐ Blend the arrowroot with the water and stir into the endive in the pan.

☐ Simmer over a low heat until the cooking liquid thickens, then season with pepper. Stir in the bacon and diced tomatoes and serve immediately.

Endive in Cheese Sauce

Serves 4   ☆☆
Preparation: 5 minutes
Cooking: 8 minutes

1½lb (700g) endive

The sauce:
1oz (25g) butter
2 tablespoons flour
½ pint (300ml) milk
3oz (75g) grated cheese
salt and pepper
a sprinkling of nutmeg

Prepare and cook the endive as in Boiled Endive.

☐ Make a cheese sauce as for Chicory au Gratin. When the sauce has thickened (3-4 minutes) season to taste.

☐ Stir the sauce into the cooked endive.

Preserving colour
Cook green vegetables uncovered for the first few minutes. Heat releases volatile chemicals which can turn vegetables an unappetizing grey colour. By plunging the vegetables into boiling water then leaving off the lid until the pan returns to the boil, you allow these chemicals to escape in the steam. You can then safely cover the pan for the rest of the cooking time.

Washing endive

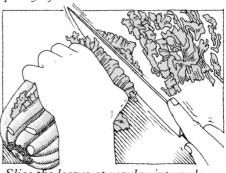

Wash endive heads upside down in plenty of cold water.

Slice the leaves at regular intervals.

Washing spinach

Leafy vegetables such as spinach are often grown in sandy soil and sand remains trapped in their leaves. To prepare, pick over the spinach leaves and remove the tough stems by holding the closed leaf with its underside towards you and stripping off the stem towards the tip. Wash the leaves in plenty of cold water in a large bowl or a clean sink. Lift the leaves out with your hands to prevent sand and grit resettling on the leaves. Wash them twice more in fresh water.

Seasoning spinach

Spinach and other green vegetables are often seasoned with a little grated nutmeg and pepper. Both spices enhance the natural flavour of the vegetables.

Spinach à la Crème variation

Heat ¼ pint (150ml) double cream over a low heat until thick. Stir into the cooked drained spinach.

Chard

The fragile green leaves of chard take less time to cook than the firmer, nutty-flavoured ribs. The two are therefore treated as separate vegetables, the leaves prepared like spinach, the ribs like stalks and shoots.

Chopping spinach

To chop spinach finely use two matching knives as shown. Spread the spinach on a chopping board and, working rapidly with simultaneous strokes in opposite directions, chop steadily until it's as fine as you want it.

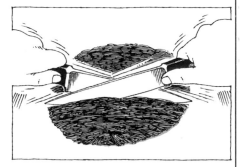

Chopping with alternating strokes.

Boiled Spinach

One way to boil spinach is in a large pan of salted, rapidly boiling water. Cook for 1-2 minutes, keeping the leaves immersed. Drain the moment they are ready. Alternatively, use *only* the water that clings to the leaves after washing. This method, not strictly boiling, is given below.

Serves 4 ☆
Preparation: 10 minutes
Cooking: 8 minutes

1½lb (700g) spinach
salt and pepper
1oz (25g) butter

Remove the stems and wash the spinach.

☐ Pile the spinach into a large pan with only the water that clings to the leaves. Add a little salt.

☐ Cover the pan and cook over a moderate heat for 7-8 minutes or until the leaves are wilted.

☐ Shake the pan two or three times during cooking to make sure the spinach cooks evenly.

☐ Drain well in a colander.

☐ Melt the butter in the rinsed pan, and toss the spinach in it. Season to taste and serve.

Spinach with eggs and cheese sauce.

Spinach with Eggs and Cheese Sauce

This classic way of serving spinach, Oeufs à la Florentine, makes a delightful supper dish.

Serve 6 ☆☆
Preparation: 10 minutes
Cooking: 25 minutes

1½lb (700g) spinach
6 eggs

The sauce:
1oz (25g) butter
2 tablespoons flour
½ pint (300ml) milk
3oz (75g) grated cheese

To finish:
1lb (500g) potatoes, boiled and mashed

Chop cooked spinach as shown on the left and pile into a large, shallow ovenproof dish.

☐ Make six hollows in the spinach with the back of a spoon. Poach eggs and place into the hollows.

☐ Make a white sauce with the butter, flour and milk. Reserve 2 tablespoons of cheese and stir the rest into the sauce. Spoon the sauce over the eggs and spinach.

☐ Pipe or spoon the potato round the dish, sprinkle with cheese and brown under a hot grill.

Brassica leaves and florets

Cabbages are among the best known members of the brassica family. Of the firm-headed varieties—green, white and red—choose compact ones with unblemished outer leaves. Red cabbage should never be boiled in plain water—the alkalinity of it turns the leaves blue. To counteract this, add an acid, such as wine or vinegar to the cooking water, or an acidic fruit such as apple.

Brussels sprouts, really cabbages in miniature, should be bought fresh, with their colour a vivid green, and cooked for a very short time.

Boiled Cabbage

Serves 4   ☆
Preparation: 5 minutes
Cooking: 10 minutes

1½lb (700g) white or green cabbage
salt
1oz (25g) butter
freshly ground pepper

Remove the outer leaves of the cabbage and cut the head into four, trimming the stalk as shown.
☐ Plunge the quarters into a saucepan half-filled with salted boiling water.
☐ Return to the boil, cover and cook for about 10 minutes until tender when pierced with a skewer. Drain well in a colander.
☐ Melt the butter in the rinsed pan and toss the cabbage in it. Warm the cabbage.
☐ Season to taste with freshly ground pepper.
Note: Shred cabbage according to the method shown on the right. It will take less time to cook—allow 3 to 4 minutes. Try to keep to the cooking times given—under or overcooked cabbage can taste unpleasant. Adding bicarbonate of soda will destroy the vitamins. Preserve colour by putting on lid.

Boiled Red Cabbage

Red cabbage should be shredded, and cooked in a large pan of salted boiling water to which 1-2 tablespoons of vinegar is added. This recipe adds apples and cloves to complement the distinctive flavour of the cabbage itself.

Serves 4   ☆
Preparation: 5 minutes
Cooking: 12-15 minutes

---

red cabbage weighing about 1½lb (700g)
salt
4-6 whole cloves
1 cooking apple, peeled, cored
    and coarsely grated
1oz (25g) sugar
1oz (25g) butter

Quarter and core the cabbage, then slice it thinly.
☐ Bring ½ pint (300ml) salted water to the boil.
☐ Add the cabbage, cloves and grated apple.
☐ Cook, covered, for 12 to 15 minutes—the cabbage should still be crisp.
☐ Stir in the sugar and butter. Cook for a further 2 to 3 minutes over a medium heat just to melt the sugar before serving.

Boiled Brussels Sprouts

Serves 4   ☆
Preparation: 10 minutes
Cooking: 5 minutes

1½lb (700g) brussels sprouts
salt and pepper
1oz (25g) butter

Cut a small cross in the base of each trimmed sprout.
☐ Plunge them into a saucepan half-filled with salted boiling water.
☐ Return to the boil, cover and cook for 5 minutes—the sprouts should be barely tender when tested.
☐ Drain, dot with butter, season to taste with pepper and serve.

Cabbage variations
The traditional flavourings for red cabbage are sugar with cloves, apples or vinegar. For white or green cabbage, add a sprinkling of caraway seeds. Alternatively, grate some well-flavoured cheese (Cheddar, Parmesan or Gruyère) and stir it into the shredded leaves just before serving

Perfect brussels sprouts
Cutting a small cross in the base of each sprout allows heat to penetrate more evenly so that the core cooks in the same time as the more tender head. The result is sprouts that are tender but crisp, with more of their nutritional value intact.

Slicing cabbage

Quarter cabbage and remove stalk.

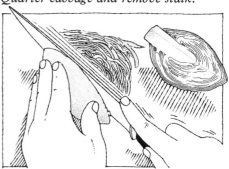

Slice each quarter into strips.

Curly kale with Cheese Sauce

Make a cheese sauce. Boil the kale, drain it well and stir it into the sauce just before serving.

Chinese leaves variation

To make a more substantial dish, fry 3-4oz (100g) diced bacon and add it to the leek or onion mixture before stirring in the cabbage.

For a hearty one-pot meal based on Chinese leaves, briefly boil the leaves, then mix them with a mixture of fried leeks and bacon.

Boiled Curly Kale

Two popular members of the cabbage family are curly kale, a strong-flavoured brassica often sold as 'winter greens' and Chinese leaves—crisp and pale with a delicate flavour all their own.

Serves 4 ☆

Preparation: 3 minutes
Cooking: 25-30 minutes

Boiled and Fried Chinese Leaves

Serves 4 ☆☆

Preparation: 5 minutes
Cooking: 8 to 10 minutes

Chinese leaves, weighing about 1½lb (700g)
2oz (50g) butter
1 medium onion, finely chopped, or
1 leek, sliced
salt and pepper

For a hearty one-pot meal based on Chinese leaves, briefly boil the leaves and combine them with fried leeks and bacon.

1½lb (700g) curly kale
salt and pepper
3 tablespoons single cream or
1oz (25g) butter

Wash the kale and cut away the tough ribs. Finely chop the leaves.

☐ Cook in salted boiling water until tender—25-30 minutes.

☐ Drain the kale and serve it immediately with a little cream or butter, seasoned with plenty of pepper.

Note: spring greens cook in 15 minutes. Chinese leaves takes 10-12 minutes.

Trim the base of the cabbage and remove discoloured leaves.

☐ Wash the leaves and slice them thinly, as shown on the left.

☐ Plunge the Chinese leaves into a large pan of salted boiling water and blanch it for about 2 minutes.

☐ Drain and rinse immediately under a running cold tap.

☐ Heat the butter in a large frying-pan. Add the onion or leek. Cook, stirring, over a moderate heat until tender, about 5 minutes. Stir in the cabbage and season to taste.

Preparing Chinese leaves

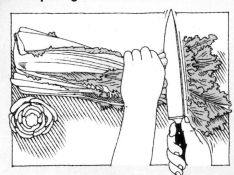

Trim the base and slice the leaves.

Boiled Cauliflower

Serves 4 ☆
Preparation: 2 minutes
Cooking: 15 minutes

---

1 cauliflower, weighing about 1½lb (700g)
2 tablespoons chopped parsley (optional)
salt
1oz (25g) butter

Remove the outside green leaves and trim the stalk.

☐ Cut away a conical section from the base of the central core so the heat can penetrate evenly through the whole head.

☐ Place the cauliflower, stalk side down, into a saucepan half-filled with salted boiling water.

☐ Return to the boil, cover and cook for 15 minutes. The centre should feel tender when tested with a skewer. Drain well.

☐ Melt the butter, pour it over the cauliflower and serve immediately, sprinkled if you like with a little chopped parsley.

Boiled Broccoli

Both purple-sprouting and green broccoli (calabrese) take the same time to cook.

Serves 4 ☆
Preparation: 2 minutes
Cooking: 5 minutes

1½lb (700g) broccoli, larger stems
split lengthways
salt
1oz (25g) butter

Trim the ends of the stems and remove damaged or discoloured leaves.

☐ Cut a cross in the base of each stem with a sharp knife.

☐ Cook, covered, in salted boiling water for about 5 minutes: the pieces should be slightly under-cooked.

☐ Melt the butter in a pan and toss the drained broccoli in the hot butter just before serving.

Variation: boil the broccoli until slightly undercooked, following the method given above.

☐ Heat 2 tablespoons olive oil in a frying pan; add 2 finely chopped garlic cloves and cook until slightly browned.

☐ Gently toss the broccoli in the mixture and add salt, pepper and finely chopped parsley to taste.

Boiled Cauliflower with Prawn Sauce

Serves 4 ☆☆
Preparation: 10 minutes
Cooking: 20 minutes

1½lb (700g) cauliflower or broccoli
salt

The sauce:
1oz (25g) butter
1oz (25g) flour
½ pint (300ml) milk
3oz (75g) peeled prawns
1 tablespoon tomato purée
freshly ground pepper

Trim and boil the cauliflower, following the instructions on the left. Meanwhile, make the sauce.

☐ Melt the butter in a pan. Stir in the flour to make a roux.

☐ Over a medium heat, gradually add the milk, stirring continuously until the sauce thickens—3-4 minutes.

☐ Reserve a few of the prawns for a garnish.

☐ Purée the prawns in a blender, adding a little of the sauce if necessary.

☐ Stir the prawn purée and the tomato purée into the sauce and season to taste.

☐ Pour the sauce over the cauliflower and garnish with the remaining prawns.

Tip: Plain boiled cauliflower can be given a simple last minute addition which also provides a contrast in texture. Finely chop 2 hard-boiled eggs. Melt some butter and gently brown about 1oz (25g) of breadcrumbs. Sprinkle over.

Cauliflower with Cheese Sauce
Boil the cauliflower whole or as florets. Make a Cheese Sauce and pour it over the cooked cauliflower. Sprinkle grated cheese on top and brown the surface under a hot grill or in a hot oven (450F, 230C, gas 8).

Cauliflower and broccoli
Cauliflower, green and purple-sprouting broccoli belong to the cabbage family. You can either cook the vegetable whole as explained or divide it into individual florets.

Combined vegetable dishes
Green or purple broccoli and cauliflower are attractive when combined. Divide into florets. Cook the cauliflower (which takes slightly longer) for one minute, then add the broccoli, taking care not to overcook it. Arrange the drained vegetables in a serving dish and serve with melted butter.

A dash of lemon
To keep cauliflower white, add a little lemon juice to the cooking water.

Broccoli in salads
Cold boiled broccoli makes a good addition to rice or pasta salads It's also good in salads based on prawns, crab or lobster.

Cutting broccoli stems

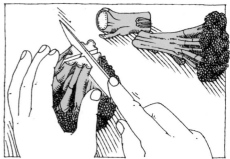

To help the heat penetrate, cut a cross in the base of each broccoli stem.

Boiled celery in sauce

Cut trimmed celery into 2 inch (5cm) lengths. Cook, covered in salted boiling water for 10 to 12 minutes. Drain and reserve the cooking liquid. Use it to make a white sauce. Stir in the celery pieces, season to taste and serve immediately.

Fennel au gratin

Cut fennel into ¼ inch (5mm) slices. Boil for 8 minutes. Drain. Arrange the slices in an ovenproof dish. Cover with a cheese sauce. Sprinkle grated cheese and breadcrumbs on top. Dot with butter and bake in a pre-heated oven 425F (220C) gas 7.

Preparing fennel

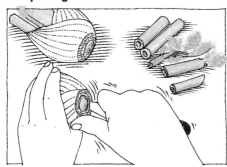

Trim off the stems and leaves, then remove a conical section from the base.

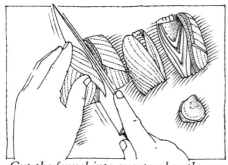

Cut the fennel into quarters lengthways.

Stalks and shoots

Stalks and shoots are prized—each kind quite different in taste and texture. Cooking them is easy and there are few rules to follow—the most important one simply being not to overcook them.

Asparagus is seasonal, available in spring and early summer. Cultivated asparagus should be plump, with tightly formed buds (the tip of the shoot). Expect wild asparagus, if you can find it, to be much thinner—it will still taste delicious. White, green or purple-tinged asparagus is all cooked in the same way.

Celery is a versatile vegetable, used as a flavouring and also as a vegetable in its own right. Stalks should be crisp and unblemished and white or pale green. Dark-coloured celery usually tastes bitter.

Fennel (also called bulb or Florence fennel) should be round and swollen, rather like a bulbous head of celery.

Seakale, available in spring and summer, has long white stalks that are similar to chard ribs. Use the leaves raw in salads.

The cardoon looks a little like celery but is really related to the thistle family like the globe artichoke. Discard the leaves and prepare as for celery.

Boiled Fennel

Fennel is at its best served boiled and unadorned. Its mellow aniseed flavour complements fish dishes, or bland meats like veal or chicken. Serve it on its own for an elegant first course.

Serves 4   ☆
Preparation: 10 minutes
Cooking: 10 minutes

---

4 fennel bulbs, each weighing about 5oz (150g)
salt
1oz (25g) butter
a sprinkling of paprika

Wash the fennel bulbs, cut off the upper stems and leaves. Discard the stems but retain the feathery leaves to use as a garnish.

☐ Trim the base, and cut away the conical core as shown on the left.

☐ 'String' the fennel by cutting part-way through the inside edge of each stalk at the top. Pull each partly detached piece of stalk towards the root.

☐ Halve or quarter the bulbs, depending on size.

☐ Half fill a saucepan with salted boiling water and add the prepared fennel.

☐ Cook, covered, for about 10 minutes, or until tender when tested at the thickest part with a skewer.

☐ Drain, and serve hot with butter and a light sprinkling of paprika. Garnish with the fennel leaves.

Fennel as an Hors d'Oeuvre

You can prepare this appetizer one or two days in advance, then keep it in the refrigerator until needed.

Serves 4   ☆☆
Preparation: 5 minutes
Cooking: 15-20 minutes

---

4 small fennel bulbs

For boiling:
½ pint (300ml) dry white wine
3 tablespoons olive oil
grated rind and juice of half a lemon
1 bay leaf
1 teaspoon crushed coriander seeds
1 teaspoon chopped rosemary
  or ½ teaspoon dried rosemary
salt
½ teaspoon green peppercorns

Put all the ingredients except the fennel into a saucepan and bring to the boil.

☐ Add the fennel, cover, reduce the heat and cook for 10 minutes or until the bulbs are tender.

☐ Remove the fennel, boil the strained cooking liquid until reduced by about half.

☐ Pour on sauce and chill.

Boiled Asparagus

The tips of asparagus are more tender than the stems. To prevent the tips knocking against each other and breaking, tie the stalks in bundles of 6 or 8, using kitchen string. You can also boil small bunches of asparagus in clean preserving jars, placed upright in the water.

Alternatively, put crumpled foil in half of the pan as a prop for the tips to cook in the steam.

Serves 4 ☆☆☆
Preparation: 5 minutes
Cooking: about 10 minutes

1¼lb (700g) asparagus
salt
7oz (200g) butter

Peel the asparagus as shown.
☐ Tie in bundles and lower into a large pan of salted, boiling water.
☐ Return to the boil, cover and cook for 5-10 minutes depending on the thickness of the stems.
☐ To drain, open the bundles and spread the stems on kitchen paper.
☐ Meanwhile, melt the butter, then pour it over the asparagus. Serve immediately.
Tip: hard-boil eggs, shell and halve them. Serve them with the asparagus. Serve asparagus with plain boiled new potatoes garnished with chopped chives or parsley.

Pieces of tenderly boiled asparagus served in a sauce that is garnished with finely chopped cooked ham and chives. The sauce is a basic white sauce made with the cooking liquid and enriched with egg yolks and cream.

Peeling asparagus

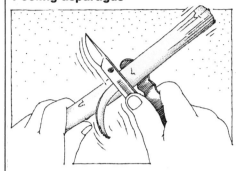

Remove a thin paring from each stem.

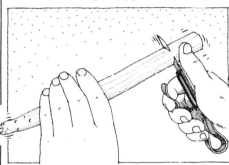

Trim off the woody base.

Cooking artichokes

Avoid overcooking artichokes—they are ready to eat when the centre feels tender when pierced with a skewer or when a single leaf can easily be pulled away from the centre.

For serving cold

Drain the artichokes, allow to cool and serve them with a Hollandaise sauce or Vinaigrette.

Stuffed artichokes

Remove the choke and fill the centre of the artichoke with prawns, crab or lobster mixed with a little vinaigrette or mayonnaise.

Preparing artichokes

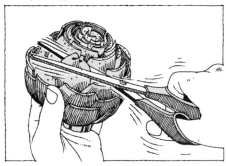

Trim off the top third of the leaves.

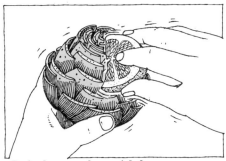

Rub the cut edges with lemon.

Asparagus in Quick Ham Sauce

Serves 4
Preparation: 10 minutes
Cooking: about 20 minutes

1¼lb (700g) asparagus
salt

The sauce:
1oz (25g) butter
1oz (25g) flour
¼ pint (150ml) milk
at least ¼ pint (150ml) asparagus cooking liquid
5oz (150g) cooked ham, finely chopped
salt and pepper
1 egg yolk
3 tablespoons single cream
1 tablespoon finely chopped chives

Cut trimmed and peeled asparagus into 1½ inch (4cm) lengths.

☐ Set aside the tips. Cook the stem pieces, covered, in salted boiling water for 7-8 minutes.

☐ Add the tips and cook for a further 4-5 minutes until tender but still crisp.

☐ Drain, reserve the cooking water.

☐ Melt the butter in a saucepan over a moderate heat and stir in the flour.

☐ Gradually stir in the milk and enough asparagus cooking liquid to make a fairly thin sauce.

☐ Cook, stirring, for 3-4 minutes until smooth.

☐ Stir in the ham and asparagus. Season to taste.

☐ Mix the egg yolk and cream in a small bowl.

☐ Stir in a little of the hot sauce, then stir the mixture back into the pan. Serve immediately, garnished with chopped chives.

Tip: turn Asparagus with Ham Sauce into a buttered ovenproof dish. Sprinkle with grated cheese. Brown in the oven, pre-heated 425F (220C) gas 7, or under a hot grill.

Variations

● Slice asparagus thinly. Parboil and sauté gently in melted butter.

● Asparagus with Ham Sauce makes a quick, supper dish served with buttered toast, rice or pasta.

Boiled Artichoke

Globe artichokes belong to the thistle family. Each leaf has a fleshy edible base and together they surround an inedible choke (the unformed flower.) This rests on a fleshy base (fond).

Serves 4
Preparation: 10 minutes
Cooking: 20 to 40 minutes

---

4 large artichokes
½ lemon
salt
2 tablespoons lemon juice
6oz (175g) butter, melted

Thoroughly wash the artichokes by plunging them head downwards in a basin of cold water.

☐ Trim the stalks level with the base. Immediately rub the cut surfaces with a half lemon to prevent discolouration.

☐ Pull off and discard the tough leaves at the base, and trim off the top third of the remaining leaves with scissors. Rub the trimmed edges with lemon.

☐ Half fill with boiling water a pan large enough to hold the artichokes in a single layer.

☐ Add the salt, 2 tablespoons of lemon juice, and artichokes, stem side down, to the pan.

☐ Cover, and cook until tender—20-40 minutes depending on size. Test by piercing the centre with a skewer.

☐ Lift out and drain well.

☐ Serve immediately with melted butter or a sauce.

Serving artichokes

Place the cooked artichokes on individual plates. Provide a separate dish for the discarded leaves and chokes. To eat the artichoke, remove the leaves one by one from the outside and dip their bases into the butter or sauce—only the fleshy base is eaten. Discard the green parts. When all the leaves have been removed, scrape away and discard the central hairy choke with a knife or teaspoon. The fleshy base can then be savoured.

Boiling roots

Root vegetables include carrots, swedes, beetroot, turnip, salsify and celeriac. By enlarging its root the plant lays down a food supply that provides us with a nutritious and colourful vegetable source throughout the year. Large, mature root vegetables are more starchy and should be put into cold salted water to begin cooking. Start timing when the water boils.

Boiled Carrots

Tender young carrots are best scrubbed and cooked whole, quickly, to preserve their fresh flavour. Peel and slice older carrots.

Serves 4 ☆
Preparation: 2 minutes
Cooking: 10 minutes

1¼lb (700g) carrots, topped and tailed
salt
1oz (25g) butter
1 tablespoon chopped herbs (tarragon or
    chervil)

Scrub or peel the carrots.
☐ Put into a saucepan with ½in (1cm) salted, boiling water. Cover and cook for about 10 minutes, until tender. If necessary, add more boiling water to prevent them from boiling dry.
☐ Add the butter and herbs and serve.

Coring carrots
Mature carrots sometimes have cores that are woody and paler than the rest of the carrot. Cut out and discard the cores before cooking—they are tough and flavourless.

Cooking in stock
Cook carrots in a little veal or chicken stock for a delicious variation. Alternatively, some cooks prefer to emphasize the delicate flavour of fresh, young carrots by boiling them in bottled spring water. Serve them with butter and herbs such as chives or tarragon.

A brimming pan of tiny young carrots, boiled until tender.

Ways to preserve colour

The flesh of both salsify and celeriac discolour easily when exposed to air. Either boil them whole with the skins on as instructed on the right, then peel them, or cook them peeled in acidulated water or a 'blanc'.

● acidulated water—add the juice of half a lemon to each pint of water.

● blanc—cook the vegetables in water to which you have added a tablespoon of flour, oil and lemon juice.

● the pan—cook salsify and celeriac in pans that are chemically neutral—enamelled or made from stainless steel or glass.

Celeriac

Boil strips of celeriac; allow them to cool, then serve them with a mustard-flavoured mayonnaise.

Cold Beetroot Salad

Boil and skin beetroot; cut into strips or cubes. Grate an apple and finely chop the shallot or spring onion—add these to the beetroot. Mix together 3 tablespoons of oil and 2 teaspoons of wine vinegar. Add salt and pepper to taste and use as a dressing for the beetroot.

Boiled Salsify

The salsify resembles an elongated white carrot. White salsify or the black-skinned scorzonera are both cooked in the same way.

Serves 4 ☆
Preparation: 5 minutes
Cooking: 25-30 minutes

1½lb (700g) salsify or scorzonera
salt
1oz (25g) butter
a sprinkling of nutmeg
¼ pint (150ml) soured cream—optional

Scrub the salsify in cold water and cut off the tops and tails. (Cook whole or add the juice of half a lemon to the cooking water and cut the salsify in half.)
☐ Cover and cook in salted, boiling water for 25-30 minutes, depending on size. The salsify should be tender but still crisp.
☐ Drain and rinse in cold water.
☐ Scrape off the skins, then cut the salsify into 2in (5cm) pieces.
☐ Melt the butter, add the salsify and nutmeg to taste.
☐ Stir in the soured cream and heat through but do not boil.
Variation: Parboil salsify for 15 minutes. Peel it, then cut it into even pieces and sauté lightly in butter. Serve with lemon wedges. You can also coat parboiled pieces in a batter and deep-fry them.

Buttered Celeriac

Serves 4 ☆
Preparation: 10 minutes
Cooking: 10 minutes

1½lb (700g) celeriac
salt
juice of ½ lemon
1oz (25g) butter
freshly ground black pepper

Peel the celeriac and cut it into strips as shown on the opposite page.
☐ Immediately plunge it into a saucepan half-full of boiling salted water. Add the juice of half a lemon to keep the celeriac white.
☐ Cover and cook for about 10 minutes or until tender.
☐ Drain and serve with butter and black pepper.

Beetroot in a Piquant Sauce

Boil beetroot in its skin to preserve the colour, and peel it before serving. Small young ones served whole with firm butter and lots of coarse black pepper make one of the best of vegetables. On into the winter, the larger ones are better sliced or cubed. They may be served hot (best), or cold with mayonnaise or vinaigrette.

Serves 4 ☆
Preparation: 2 minutes
Cooking: 20-50 minutes

1½lb (700g) beetroot, washed
salt
1 tablespoon cornflour
1oz (25g) sugar
3 tablespoons vinegar
1oz (25g) butter

Trim off the tops and put the beetroot into a large saucepan half-full of salted, boiling water.
☐ Cover and cook until tender. Small beetroot take 20-30 minutes; larger ones 45-50 minutes.
☐ Drain and reserve the cooking liquid. Run cold water over the cooked beetroot, trim them and rub off the skins. Dice or slice the flesh.
☐ Measure out 8 fl oz (250ml) of the cooking liquid, making up the amount with cold water, if necessary. Blend the cornflour and sugar with a little of the liquid. Bring the rest to the boil; add the cornflour mixture, and cook, stirring, for 2-3 minutes until smooth and thickened. Add the vinegar then stir in the beetroot. Remove the pan from the heat, cover and set aside for 30 minutes to allow the flavour to develop. Re-heat before serving.

Boiled Swedes

Serves 4
Preparation: 10 minutes
Cooking: 20 minutes

☆

1¼lb (700g) swedes
salt
1oz (25g) butter
1 teaspoon soft brown sugar
freshly ground black pepper

Boiled Kohlrabi, Turnips and Mooli

Kohlrabi is a swollen, edible stem with a flavour reminiscent of cabbage. Mooli (also called white or icicle radish), is a plump white relative of the radish. Both are cooked in the same way as the turnip.

Serves 4
Preparation: 5 minutes
Cooking: 10-12 minutes

☆

Kohlrabi, turnips and mooli
Instead of butter, finish the cooked vegetables with a generous spoonful of soured cream or yogurt.

Mixed vegetable purées
Root vegetables can be combined to make wonderful mixed purées: carrots, swedes and mooli, for instance, or turnip and celeriac. The flavours will merge to make new and exciting dishes.

Tender fingers of peppered, boiled swede and slices of mooli, finished with a knob of butter.

Peel, slice and dice the swedes or prepare them according to the method for celeriac.
☐ Put them into a saucepan with not more than ½in (1cm) salted, boiling water and the sugar. Cover and cook for about 20 minutes (add a little more water if necessary to prevent them boiling dry). Drain well. Dry them off briefly by cooking them in a little butter. Season with freshly ground black pepper.
Variation: Boil and drain swedes, then purée them with a little cream and a pinch of nutmeg.

1¼lb (700g) kohlrabi, turnip or mooli, or a
**   mixture of vegetables**
salt
1oz (25g) butter

Wash, peel, and slice the vegetables. Cook in a covered pan with about ½in (1cm) salted, boiling water until tender; 10-12 minutes.
☐ Drain well, then dry off briefly in the hot saucepan, tossing them in the butter. Serve.

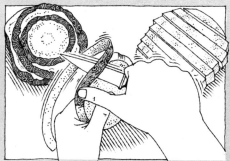

Cut celeriac into even slices.

Peel, then cut slices into strips.

Cooking potatoes in their skins

Potatoes have vitamin stores under their skins. Simply scrub well and boil them as usual. Drain and dry off over a low heat, then serve them with butter and freshly ground black pepper. Alternatively, sauté briefly in a little hot oil or butter and serve with chopped chives or parsley.

Golden potatoes

Add a lightly beaten egg or egg yolk to mashed potatoes for a delicious flavour and golden colour.

✳Freezing

Make a quantity of Duchesse Potatoes (see right), dry off a trayful without browning them, then cool and put into the freezer. Remove the potatoes and store in freezer bags for up to 2 months. To serve, put in an oven pre-heated to 375F (190C) gas 5, for 10 minutes to brown and heat.

Tubers

Potatoes are the underground fleshy tubers from which both the stem and the root of the new plant develop. The recipe below is for old potatoes which should be started off in cold water allowing heat to penetrate and cook them evenly. If started in boiling water, the outside becomes soft and floury before the centre cooks. New potatoes are smaller and less starchy than old potatoes: plunge them straight into boiling water.

Boiled Potatoes

Serves 4 ☆☆
Preparation: 5 minutes
Cooking: 15-20 minutes

1¼lb (700g) potatoes
salt
3oz (75g) butter
chopped parsley or chives

Wash and thinly peel the potatoes.
☐ Cut into even-sized pieces.
☐ Put into a pan and cover with salted, cold water. Bring to the boil, cover, and cook for about 15 minutes until the centres feel tender when pierced with a skewer.
☐ Drain well, and return to the saucepan to dry off by shaking them over a low heat. Serve with butter and parsley or chives.
Note: Peeled potatoes discolour when exposed to air so keep them covered with cold water before cooking.

Creamed Potatoes

Serves 4
Preparation and cooking: 25 minutes, including cooking potatoes

1¼lb (700g) boiled potatoes
4 tablespoons hot milk
2oz (50g) butter
pepper and salt
a sprinkling of nutmeg (optional)

Mash or purée the potatoes.
☐ Bring the milk to the boil, add the butter. Beat the mixture into the potatoes. Season to taste with salt, pepper and nutmeg if liked.

Duchesse Potatoes

Creamed potatoes make a splendid garnish for many dishes: pies, poultry, meat or fish. Piped from a forcing bag fitted with a large rose nozzle and finished off in the oven with an egg glaze, they become Duchesse Potatoes. Mash the potatoes with butter and 1 or 2 egg yolks instead of the milk. Pipe the potatoes into small mounds on to a baking sheet. Alternatively, use a spoon to form the mounds. Dry out in an oven pre-heated to 375F (190C) gas 5, for 5 minutes. Remove, brush with lightly beaten egg and return to the oven for 5-10 minutes to brown.

Leeks and onions

Onions, leeks and garlic all belong to the onion family–alliums–and are among the greatest assets of good cooking, as flavourings and as vegetables in their own right. Leeks and onions can be served plain with butter –or with a white or cheese sauce. Leeks make excellent cold hors d'oeuvre.

Boiled Leeks

Serves 4
Preparation: 5 minutes
Cooking: 5-7 minutes

1¼lb (700g) leeks
salt
1-2oz (25-50g) butter

Trim off the root and the tops of the leaves. Wash thoroughly as shown on the right. Cut into 1½in (4cm) lengths.

☐ Put the leeks into a saucepan half-filled with salted, boiling water. Cover and cook until tender but still crisp, about 5 minutes.

☐ Drain, serve hot, tossed in a little butter.

Tip: For a simple hot hors d'oeuvre, cook whole leeks (choose slender early season ones). Serve them with a Hollandaise Sauce, or with a tomato-flavoured Hollandaise. If early season leeks are not available, use larger leeks. Trim and slice them as shown.

Boiled Onions

Simply cooked, and served with butter and paprika, onions make a delicious accompaniment to serve with roast meats or game. Choose onions of even size, each weighing about 2-3oz (50-75g). If large onions are used, they must be cut into halves or even quarters, and they tend to separate during cooking.

Serves 4
Preparation: 5 minutes
Cooking: 10-15 minutes

1½lb (700g) even-sized onions
salt
2oz (50g) butter
a sprinkling of paprika

Peel the onions and trim the tops. Leave the roots on to help keep the onions whole as they cook.

☐ Put into a saucepan half-filled with salted, boiling water.

☐ Cover and boil until tender– about 10 minutes.

☐ Drain, slice off the roots and serve the onions with melted butter and a sprinkling of paprika, nutmeg or grated cheese.

Variation: To make a caramel glaze for small onions, boil the onions, then drain them. Add a generous knob of butter and about a tablespoon of sugar to the pan. Continue to cook the onions for a few minutes over a low heat. When the butter and sugar mixture begins to colour, add a few tablespoons of water or stock, then swirl the pan to coat the onions in a syrupy glaze.

Quick way to wash leeks
After trimming the root and the leaf tips, use a sharp knife, blade towards the green part, to pierce the leek through at the point where the white part joins the green. Draw the knife through to the top end to split the leaves. Make a second cut at right angles to the first. The leek will hold together but the more gritty leaves will open out to allow you to wash the vegetable thoroughly.

Leek Vinaigrette
For a cold hors d'oeuvre, cook sliced leeks in white wine. Reserve the cooking liquid and add olive oil and seasonings to make a wine vinaigrette. Pour over the leeks and leave to chill before serving.

Peeling small onions
Top and tail the onions. Cover them with boiling water for about a minute to loosen their skins. Drain and when cool enough to handle, peel them.

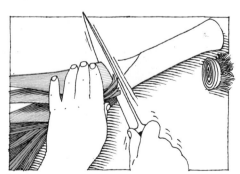

Slice the trimmed leek through to separate white and green.

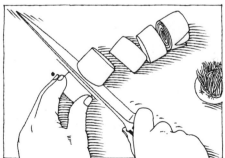

Cut the white part into neat, even-sized slices for cooking.

Petits pois

The youngest and most tender peas—petits pois—are also the sweetest. As the pea matures, its natural sugar is stored as starch. To heighten the flavour of mature peas, add a pinch of sugar to the cooking water.

Vegetable combinations

Combine mangetout peas with lightly sautéed button mushrooms. Dust with a little cayenne before serving. Serve petits pois with boiled small onions.

Broad beans in a sauce

Serve the beans with a cheese sauce or Velouté Sauce garnished with finely chopped ham or leftover cooked bacon or gammon.

Corn on the cob

Cook whole cobs for 5-7 minutes in boiling water without salt, until the kernels are tender and slightly translucent. Serve with butter, salt and pepper. Corn on the cob is equally good served cold.

Cooking corn

Don't add salt to the cooking water as this toughens the skins during cooking. Season when serving the cobs or kernels.

Pods and seeds

The fresh seeds of leguminous plants—peas and beans—and of corn, are compact stores of nourishment and respond well to boiling. Many seed-bearing plants have edible pods too, such as mangetout peas, slender French beans and runner beans.

Boiled Peas

Serves 4 ☆
Preparation: 20 minutes
Cooking: 10 minutes

2lb (1kg) fresh peas
salt
sprig of fresh mint
1oz (25g) butter

Shell the peas and barely cover with salted, boiling water, add the mint.
☐ Cook, covered for about 10 minutes.
☐ When tender, drain and discard the mint.
☐ Serve immediately with butter.

Boiled Mangetout Peas

Mangetout are also called sugar peas. They are small flat pods with tiny, barely developed seeds.

Serves 4 ☆
Preparation: 5 minutes
Cooking: 5 minutes

1¾lb (700g) mangetout peas
salt
1oz (25g) butter

Cut partway through the pea's stem. Pull off the stem together with the string running along the pod.
☐ Wash carefully and cook, covered, in as little salted, boiling water as possible for 4-5 minutes—they should still be crisp. Drain and serve immediately with butter.

Petits Pois à la Francaise

In this recipe canned or frozen petits pois can also be used.

Serves 4
Preparation: 25 minutes
Cooking: 15 minutes

2lb (1kg) petits pois
2oz (50g) butter
4 tablespoons water
1 bunch of spring onions, cleaned and chopped
1 small lettuce, washed and shredded
1 teaspoon sugar
salt and pepper

Shell the petits pois.
☐ Melt the butter in the water, then add the remaining ingredients.
☐ Cover the pan and cook for 10-15 minutes, stirring occasionally, until the peas are tender. Older peas may take a little longer.
☐ If there is any liquid left, this can be thickened by stirring in some kneaded butter (equal quantities of butter and flour worked together) a little at a time over moderate heat until it thickens to a sauce.

Boiled Broad Beans
Cook broad beans in the same way, giving them 10-12 minutes depending on their size and age. Peel older beans first, using your thumbnail to split the skin at the indentation. If you like, replace some of the cooking liquid with skimmed milk—this flavours the beans and helps to keep them white. Vary the flavouring herbs too—sprigs of winter savory, thyme or borage are all suitable. Remove and discard herbs before draining and serving.

Boiled corn kernels

Strip husks and silk down to the stem. Use a sharp knife to slice off kernels close to the central cob. Boil for 2-5 minutes in plenty of slightly sugared, boiling water. Drain and serve with butter, salt and pepper.

Boiled French Beans

French beans (haricots verts), also called green, bobby, or stringless beans, are the smallest whole bean type. Yellow varieties are also available. Leave the smallest ones whole, cut larger ones into shorter lengths. The larger or coarser varieties, such as bobby beans, obviously take longer to cook than delicate French beans.

Serves 4 ☆
Preparation: 5 minutes
Cooking: 2-10 minutes

1lb (500g) French beans, topped and tailed
salt
1oz (25g) butter
freshly ground pepper

Cook the beans in as little salted, boiling water as possible for 2-10 minutes depending on size—they should still be crisp.

☐ Drain; add butter and seasoning to taste.

Variation: For a contrast in colour and flavour, serve the beans with chopped tomatoes. Skin and de-seed the tomatoes and cut the flesh into small dice. Stir the tomato into the drained beans just before serving and sprinkle with 2 tablespoons chopped parsley.

Boiled Runner Beans

Serves 4 ☆
Preparation: 10 minutes
Cooking: 5-8 minutes

1lb (500g) runner beans
salt
1oz (25g) butter

Top and tail the beans; string them if necessary.

☐ Cut them into 1in (2.5cm) long diagonal pieces as shown.

☐ Cook, covered, in salted, boiling water for 5-8 minutes, until tender.

☐ Drain and serve with butter.

Variation: Sauté chopped onion in oil or butter. If you like, add a little fried chopped bacon. Stir into the cooked beans.

Variation: Make a white sauce using the beans' cooking water or a Velouté Sauce using chicken stock. Add the beans and stir gently until heated through.

Note: Both French and runner beans are sometimes called string beans because of the fibrous strings that run along the length of some older varieties. Many modern varieties are stringless.

Sweet and Sour Beans

This makes an interesting change of flavour for any type of green bean, and is useful for adding flavour to runner beans from the freezer.

Serves 4 ☆
Preparation: 5-10 minutes
Cooking: 5-10 minutes

1lb (500g) green beans—runner or French—washed and cut into 1in (2.5cm) lengths
salt
4 rashers streaky bacon, cut into small strips
1 tablespoon wine vinegar
1 tablespoon brown sugar

Boil the beans until tender but still crisp. Drain well.

☐ Fry the bacon pieces until very crisp, then remove from the pan and add to the beans.

☐ Put the vinegar and sugar into the frying-pan and stir to loosen any bacon juices.

☐ Add the beans and bacon to the pan and stir to coat with the sauce.

Runner beans, cut into diamond shapes for quicker cooking, boiled and served in a Velouté Sauce made with chicken stock.

Lentils hors d'oeuvre

Mix olive oil, finely chopped onion and thyme into the drained lentils and allow to cool. Use this simple dressing with white beans too, varying the flavour: try garlic, spring onion, chives, parsley or fresh sage. Alternatively mix cooked white beans into a salad.

Storing pulses

Although pulses keep well for up to a year, they harden and dry out with age, taking longer to soak and cook as well as becoming less interesting to eat. Buy in small quantities from a shop with a fast turnover.

Soaking pulses

Pick over the pulses and wash them. Soak them in cold water—split peas and small beans take 1 hour, other beans can take up to 7-8 hours. Discard the soaking water. Alternatively, put washed pulses in a pan with about twice their volume of cold water. Bring slowly to the boil, turn off heat and leave to soak for about an hour, drain.

Cooking dried red kidney and soya beans

It is important to fast-boil red kidney beans and soya beans for at least 10 minutes before further cooking to destroy a potentially dangerous enzyme.

Naked Children in the Grass

A traditional Dutch bean dish made with two kinds of beans: haricots for the children, runners for the grass. Cook the haricot beans as for the main recipe. The method for runner beans is given on page 25. Mix and serve with butter, seasoned to taste.

Naked Children in the Grass.

Boiling pulses

Pulses are the dried seeds of leguminous (pod-bearing) plants—lentils, peas and beans. Split pulses have had their skins removed.

Boiled Lentils

Larger beige lentils or the mottled green variety (Puy) keep their shape if boiled with care. Red lentils are better boiled and served as a purée. Don't add salt to the cooking water as this toughens them.

Serves 4　　　　　　　　　　☆
Preparation: 2 minutes
Cooking: 25-30 minutes

6oz (175g) green lentils
1oz (25g) butter
salt to taste

Pick over the lentils to remove any grit and rinse well.

☐ Put into a saucepan, cover with water and boil. Cover and cook gently for 25-30 minutes or until tender.

☐ Drain, stir in the butter, add salt and serve hot.

Boiled Red lentils

Cook the lentils for 25-30 minutes until softened—add onion, carrot, an unpeeled clove of garlic and herbs. Drain, reserving the cooking liquid, and purée with a little cooking liquid. Reheat with butter.

Boiled Red Kidney Beans

The kidney bean family includes large beans such as butter and cannellini beans, medium-sized Dutch brown, borlotti, haricot, black and flageolet beans and the tiny mung and aduki beans. Cooking times vary slightly—1 hour for aduki and mung beans; 1-2 hours for the others. The cooking method is the same. Do not add salt to the cooking water or the skins will toughen.

Serves 4　　　　　　　　　　○
Preparation: soaking time, see left
Cooking: 1-2 hours

8oz (225g) dried beans
salt to taste

Cover ready-soaked beans with twice their volume of fresh water.

☐ Cook, covered, until tender.

☐ Add salt about 10 minutes before the end of cooking. Drain well.

☐ Serve with butter or a sauce. Cooking time for peas: green, yellow or black eyed peas take 1-1½ hours to cook. Green or yellow split peas, 45 minutes to 1 hour.

Boiled Mussels with Leeks.

Boiling Mussels

Mussels are boiled not only to cook them but to open their shells. Serve them as a main course or add them at the last minute to fish soups or casseroles. Smaller shellfish—winkles, cockles or whelks—are usually sold cooked. If you buy them raw, cook them in the same way—they will take 2 to 3 minutes.

Serves 4   ☆☆
Preparation: 15 minutes
Cooking: 5-6 minutes

---

3 pints (1.75 litres) mussels in their shells
2oz (50g) butter
1 large onion, roughly chopped
2 sticks celery, chopped
1 small leek, sliced
1 clove garlic, crushed
2 teaspoons salt
½ teaspoon freshly ground pepper
7 fl oz (200ml) dry white wine

Rinse the mussels thoroughly in cold, running water to get rid of sand.

☐ Tap any open ones; if they do not close, discard them.

☐ Trim the beards or cut them free with scissors.

☐ Heat the butter in a large pan. Add the vegetables and cook gently for about 3 minutes; do not allow to brown.

☐ Add the salt, pepper, and wine and bring to the boil.

☐ Add the mussels, cover, and boil briefly, shaking the pan so that all the mussels come into contact with the heat.

☐ When the mussels are cooked the shells open. Remove from the heat and discard any mussels which are still shut.

☐ When cool enough to handle, transfer them—still in their shells—to a large serving dish along with the vegetables.

☐ Strain off the cooking liquid, boil vigorously to reduce it slightly and pour it over the mussels. Serve with fresh bread.

Variations: After reducing the mussel cooking liquid, cut 2oz (50g) butter into pieces; whisk them into the liquid one by one. Finish the sauce with 2 or 3 teaspoons of lemon juice.

● Alternatively, melt the butter in a pan, stir in 1oz (25g) flour; cook to a light golden colour. Stir in the strained mussel cooking liquid, season with salt, pepper and a little chopped garlic and simmer, stirring, for 10 minutes. Combine an egg yolk, 6 tablespoons of cream, 1 tablespoon of lemon juice and a teaspoon of curry powder in a bowl. Slowly stir in the hot sauce, pour over the mussels in their shells.

Spaghetti with mussels

Cook spaghetti, drain it and keep it hot. Cook the mussels as described in the main recipe, using 2 cloves of garlic. Reduce the cooking liquid and spoon some of it over the spaghetti. Shell the mussels, heat them through gently with the rest of the cooking liquid. Transfer to a warmed bowl or a large sauceboat and sprinkle with chopped parsley. Serve with the spaghetti.

Preparing mussels

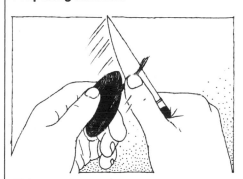

Trim off the beards with a knife.

Mussels open their shells when cooked.

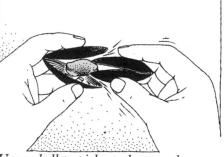

Use a shell to pick up the mussels.

The fish stock (fumet)

Put the bones and trimmings such as heads and tails into a large pan. Add 1¾ pints (1 litre) cold water, pieces of leek, carrot and onion, sprigs of parsley and thyme and a strip of orange peel. Add salt and bring the contents slowly to the boil. Skim the liquid with a spoon to remove any scum that rises to the surface. Reduce the heat and simmer, covered, for about 30 minutes. Strain through a colander, pressing with a wooden spoon to extract flavour.

Rouille

The fiery red sauce known as Rouille is the traditional sauce served with fish stews. Seed red chilli peppers and purée them or pound them to a paste with peeled garlic cloves, salt and pepper. Add enough breadcrumbs and olive oil and if necessary some of the fish stock to make a smooth sauce. Transfer to a bowl and serve it with the stew so that a spoonful can be added to each serving.

For a traditional serving

The traditional method of serving Bouillabaisse is to serve the cooked pieces of fish and shellfish separately on a serving dish with some of the cooking liquid spooned over them. The garlic bread slices are placed in the bottom of soup bowls and the rest of the liquid is poured over them to be served as a first course before the fish.

✳Frozen stock

Condensed fish stock is very useful to keep in the freezer, it provides a handy base for sauces and stocks.

Bouillabaisse

Bouillabaisse and the many other famous Mediterranean fish stews are among the most outstanding products of the technique of boiling. They consist simply of a variety of fish, boiled vigorously with olive oil and flavourings to produce delicious chunks of fish surrounded by their own semi-thickened sauce. Boiling not only breaks up the softer fish and emulsifies the olive oil to give the dish its characteristic textures, the process also blends the flavours of the ingredients so that each variation of the dish has a unique flavour.

The fish used should be a selection of locally caught varieties. But in fact you can include any fish with the exception of oily fish such as herrings or sardines, as the flavours would be too strong. The more varieties you choose the better so it is not worth making Bouillabaisse for a few people. The quantities given in the recipe alongside will serve 8 to 10.

Making Bouillabaisse also gives you a chance to become familiar with some of the more exciting and unusual fish you may come across at your fishmonger. Choose from delicate-fleshed fish such as whiting, brill, mullet or John Dory and combine them with firm-fleshed varieties such as angler-fish, conger eel, sea bass or squid. You can also include whatever shellfish you like: mussels, prawns, spiny lobster or crayfish.

Have the fish cleaned but trim them yourself, removing heads, tails and bones for a quickly-made reduced fish stock known as a 'fumet'. You then simply cook the fish in the fumet with added flavourings such as garlic and tomato.

It is traditional to serve Bouillabaisse over baked or toasted bread croûtes, spread or sprinkled with garlic. Sometimes the toasted French bread is rubbed with garlic, sprinkled with salt and handed separately. For a truly Mediterranean dish, make the fiery hot Rouille sauce too.

Serves 8-10
Preparation: 30 minutes
Cooking: 30 minutes

4-5lb (2-2½kg) assorted fresh fish, and shellfish
3 medium onions
4 tomatoes, skinned
4 fl oz (100ml) olive oil
6 garlic cloves, peeled and chopped
a pinch of ground saffron
1 bay leaf
1 teaspoon fennel seeds
2 teaspoons sea salt
1 teaspoon black peppercorns
1 long French loaf

Clean the fish, if not already done; scrape off scales if necessary.

☐ Keep small fish and shellfish whole, cut up larger ones into even-sized pieces.

☐ Put the bones and trimmings such as heads and tails in a large pan and make the fish stock.

☐ Peel and coarsely chop the onions, cut the tomatoes into wedges.

☐ Heat the olive oil and sauté the garlic, onion and tomato wedges. Add the saffron, bay leaf and fennel seeds, salt and peppercorns.

☐ Put the firmer fish and the shellfish into a large pan with the onion and tomato mixture; set aside the more delicate fish to add later.

☐ Stir the ingredients together and pour in the prepared stock and enough water to cover generously.

☐ Bring back to the boil and boil rapidly for 10 minutes to combine the oil and stock.

☐ Add the rest of the fish and continue to boil, stirring, for a further 5 minutes.

☐ Cut the bread into slices.

☐ Dry the slices in a low oven or under a low grill. Rub them with a cut clove of garlic.

☐ Serve the fish stew by arranging the bread in the bottom of a large serving dish. Lay the large pieces of fish on top and spoon the juices over.

A classic Bouillabaisse.

Suitable cuts for boiling
Beef–silverside or brisket
Veal–neck or knuckle
Mutton and Lamb–breast, middle, scrag or leg
Pork–hand, leg, knuckle or belly
Ham–forehock, collar, gammon

Cooking times for fresh meat
Beef, veal, mutton, lamb and pork: 20 minutes per lb (500g) plus 20 minutes.

Cooking times for salted meat
Beef, pork and ham: 25 minutes per lb (500g) plus 25 minutes.

Oatmeal dumplings for boiled beef
Mix 8oz (225g) oatmeal with finely chopped chives, salt and pepper. Use the fat skimmed from the beef to mix to a smooth dough. Roll the dumplings into balls. Allow to stand for 20 minutes to firm up. Add to the pan 15 minutes before the end of cooking.

Cumberland Sauce–reminder recipe
Put 4oz (100g) redcurrant jelly into a saucepan. Add the shredded rind and the juice of an orange, a squeeze of lemon juice and a glass of port or red wine. Simmer gently for 5 minutes. Pour into a sauceboat.

Boiling Meat

All kinds of meat can be treated in this way: fresh and salted beef, mutton and lamb, fresh and salt pork and gammon. With salt meat, ask your butcher if the meat is very salty, and soak it accordingly. Heavily salted meat will need soaking in cold water for 2-3 hours or possibly overnight. Bring the meat to the boil in fresh water. Discard this water–it will contain most of the salt. Replace with fresh water to start the cooking. The cooking method is the same for fresh or salt meat. It is weighed, covered with cold water and brought slowly to the boil before simmering for the required length of time. Any vegetables or accompaniments such as dumplings you want to add are put in to cook an appropriate length of time from the end.

Boiled Gammon

For extra flavour, replace some of the cooking liquid with cider or apple juice.

Serves 4-6 ☆ ☆
Preparation: about 12 hours soaking
Cooking: 1½ hours

3lb (1.5kg) gammon joint
1 onion, peeled and quartered
1 carrot, peeled

Soak the joint to get rid of excess salt.
☐ Put the soaked gammon, onion and carrot into a large pan; add enough cold water to cover.
☐ Bring slowly to the boil; remove the scum that will rise to the surface as the liquid comes to the boil.
☐ Reduce the heat to a simmer; cook, covered, for 1¼ hours.
☐ Remove the pan from the heat, leave the gammon to cool slightly and when it is cool enough to handle, remove it and carve or slice it.
☐ Serve the gammon slices with

baked potatoes, a vegetable such as broccoli and parsley or Cumberland Sauce.
Variation: You can give a delicious glazed finish to boiled ham by finishing it off in the oven. Slit the rind, separate it from the fat beneath and peel it away. Use a knife to make diagonal cuts in the fat to form a diamond pattern. Stud the surface with cloves and rub on brown sugar or honey. Bake in an oven preheated to 400F (200C) gas 6 for about 15 minutes, until brown.
Tip: To serve ham cold, allow it to cool in the cooking liquid. Remove the rind as described above. Grill fresh breadcrumbs, turning them frequently, until they are a light golden colour; spread them out on a work surface. Press them firmly on to the surface of the ham before carving.

Boiled Beef and Carrots

Serves 4-6 ☆
Preparation: 5 minutes
Cooking: 1 hour 40 minutes

3lb (1.5kg) salt silverside or topside
6 allspice berries
bouquet garni
6 onions, peeled
12 small carrots, peeled

Put the meat into a large saucepan with water to cover. Bring to the boil and remove any scum.
☐ Add the allspice and bouquet garni. Cover the pan, reduce the heat and simmer for 1 hour 40 minutes. Top up the water as necessary.
☐ Twenty minutes before the end of the cooking time, add the vegetables. Dumplings (recipe given on the left) can also be added at this point.
☐ When the meat and vegetables are cooked, remove them from the pan, drain and keep warm.
☐ Serve the skimmed cooking liquid separately.

Boiled Ox Tongue

Cooking an ox tongue at home is much more economical than buying it sliced by the portion. Cooking it yourself also means you can flavour it as you wish and serve it hot or cold. A cake tin may be used to shape a cooked tongue, or you may serve it hot, sliced, with a caper sauce.

Serves 12
☆☆☆
Preparation: 10 minutes
Cooking: 2½-3 hours

1 ox tongue, weighing about 5lb (2.5kg)
1 tablespoon salt
1 large onion, chopped
1 large carrot, chopped
1 bay leaf
6 black peppercorns
4 cloves
a large sprig of parsley
a sprig of fresh thyme

Rinse the tongue, put it into a large pan and cover it with cold water. Bring to the boil, discard the water and rinse the tongue again.

☐ Cover with fresh water, add the other ingredients, cover the pan and bring the water to the boil.

☐ Lower the heat to a simmer and cook the tongue until tender, about 2½-3 hours. The tongue is cooked when a skewer easily pierces the thickest part.

☐ Remove the tongue from the pan. Trim away any fat or gristle from the base of the tongue and remove any small throat bones.

☐ Use the tip of a sharp knife to free the skin—it will then strip away easily.

☐ Slice the tongue thinly and serve it hot with a caper sauce, creamed potatoes and peas, or cold with a salad.

Caper Sauce

Melt 2oz (50g) butter in a pan; stir in 3 tablespoons flour to make a roux. Gradually add ¾pt (450ml) of the strained tongue cooking liquid—the rest of the liquid can be used for other soups and sauces. Cook, stirring, until the sauce thickens—about 15 minutes. Season with salt and pepper and add 2 tablespoons drained, chopped capers.

Using leftovers

Slice the tongue thinly and use as a sandwich filling, topped with mustard-flavoured mayonnaise. Or cut leftovers into strips and toss them in a mixed salad.

A whole boiled tongue is ready for skinning and slicing. Adding vegetables to the cooking liquid, and keeping it at a simmer, flavours the tongue and makes it moist and tender.

Cooking lambs' tongues

Cook these (and calves' or pigs' tongues when available) as ox tongue, but adjust the flavourings and allow about 45 minutes to an hour's cooking time. Lambs' tongues are smaller than ox tongues and you may want to cook several at a time.

Pressing smaller tongues

Instead of one large ox tongue, you can use smaller lambs', pigs' or calves' tongues. Curl 2 or 3 of the smaller tongues around one another and press into a mould as described in the main recipe.

Skinning and trimming tongue

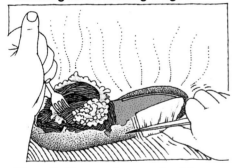

Use a knife to peel away the skin.

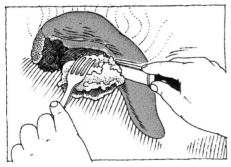

Remove fat and gristle from the base.

Pressed Ox Tongue

A pressed tongue set in jelly makes an impressive buffet-party dish, especially if decorated as described below. However, a plain pressed tongue is just as acceptable and can be accompanied by cold boiled vegetables or a salad, or as part of a platter of cold meats with pickles and sauces. A 9in (23cm) round cake tin should take an ox tongue of average size.

Serves 12   ☆☆☆
Cooking tongue: as for previous recipe
Pressing: at least 12 hours

---

1 ox tongue, cooked as previous recipe and left to cool in its liquid

---

Remove the tongue from the cooking liquid, drain and trim away the skin and gristle as shown on the left.
☐ For a plain pressed tongue, curl it into a circle to fit inside a round cake tin or deep soufflé dish.
☐ Cover the top with a double thickness of foil, then cover with a plate that fits neatly inside the mould.
☐ Add kitchen weights or even-sized cans from the store cupboard to a weight of at least 7lb (3.25kg). Leave overnight in a cool place to set.

Tongue and Vegetable Platter

Serves: 12   ☆☆☆
Preparation: 45 minutes

---

1 ox tongue, cooked and pressed as above

The accompaniment:
1lb (500g) baby carrots, peeled
1 small cauliflower, divided into florets
8oz (250g) broccoli, heads divided into florets, stalk cut into fingers
8oz (250g) French beans, topped and tailed
2lb (1kg) broad beans, shelled
1lb (500g) very small beetroot, rinsed
1 lemon, thinly sliced
fresh bay leaves

Choose very young, fresh vegetables, and boil them separately in salted water until only just cooked. Drain and cool rapidly in cold water to preserve the colours.
☐ Place the tongue in the centre of a large platter. Arrange two bands of lemon slices across the top, and between them place a band of bay leaves.
☐ Around the tongue carefully arrange the vegetables in small alternating mounds, adding the beetroot last so that its colour has least chance of discolouring the other vegetables.

Jellied Tongue

Serves 12   ☆☆☆
Preparation: 12 hours including setting

---

1 ox tongue, cooked and left to cool in its cooking liquid
½ pint (300ml) of the tongue cooking liquid
2 teaspoons powdered gelatine
1 lemon, thinly sliced
fresh bay leaves to garnish

Drain the tongue and measure out the ½ pint (300ml) cooking liquid. Sprinkle the gelatine over the cooking liquid and dissolve it by heating gently and stirring until no grains remain. Do not boil.
☐ Pour just enough of this liquid into a 9in (23cm) round cake tin to coat the base and chill until set.
☐ Arrange the lemon slices on the jelly in two equal rows and arrange a row of bay leaves between them, remembering they will be seen from the other side when turned out.
☐ Curl the tongue into the tin and pour in the remaining liquid. Weight down and leave to set.
☐ To remove the tongue from the mould, submerge the tin to the rim in warm water for a few seconds. Invert a serving plate over the top, grasp both firmly and turn the mould so it sits on the plate. Shake mould and remove the tin.
☐ Serve with vegetables or salad.

Boiled Shin of Beef

Shin is well-flavoured, economical and needs little preparation. Boiling is the ideal cooking method, as it keeps the meat moist throughout the long cooking time. Both beef and veal shin are suitable, and the bone marrow is an added nutritional bonus.

Serves 6 ☆ ☆
Preparation: 10 minutes
Cooking: 2-3 hours

---

about 3lb (1.5kg) shin of beef, cut into
    6 pieces
2 large onions, roughly chopped
3 large cloves of garlic, crushed
1 bay leaf
8 peppercorns
2 teaspoons salt

The sauce:
a 15½oz (430g) can of tomatoes
2-3 tablespoons port
salt and pepper

Arrange the pieces of shin in the bottom of a large pan; cover with water and bring to the boil.

☐ Lower the heat so you can remove the scum that rises to the surface.

☐ Add the rest of the ingredients, return to the boil, then reduce the heat to a simmer, cover and cook for 2-3 hours, or until the meat is tender.

☐ Transfer the shin to a serving dish, cover and keep warm.

☐ Strain the cooking liquid; skim off the fat that rises to the surface as it cools.

☐ Boil the liquid rapidly for 2-3 minutes to reduce it; sieve in the tomatoes and add port and seasoning to taste. Simmer for 6-8 minutes.

☐ Spoon the sauce over the meat and serve with fresh bread, warmed in the oven, or plain boiled rice.

Boiled Shin of Beef, ready to serve with a rich tomato sauce.

Serving marrow
Both beef and veal shin contain marrow. Use a teaspoon to spoon out the marrow and spread this on the bread, if served.

Serving suggestion

Cooked joints of chicken or duck, with or without a sauce, are delicious served on a bed of boiled rice. Garnish the rice with cooked peas, diced red pepper and sweetcorn kernels, and moisten it with some of the reduced cooking liquid. Sprinkle with parsley if liked.

Chicken Joints with a Rich Tomato Sauce

Simmer the chicken joints with vegetables—as described in the main recipe—for about 15 minutes. Strain the cooking liquid and reduce it by about half. Stir in 2 tablespoons of single cream, 2 teaspoons of tomato purée, a pinch of sugar and finally whisk in 2oz (50g) of butter, a piece at a time, to make a sauce.

Chicken joints with Parsley Sauce.

Chicken Joints with Parsley Sauce

Serves: 4-6
Preparation: 5 minutes
Cooking: 40 minutes

☆☆☆

8-10 chicken drumsticks
6 small carrots, sliced
2 celery stalks, chopped
1 onion, cut into wedges
small piece of mace
1 bay leaf
8 peppercorns
1 teaspoon salt
2 small leeks, sliced

The sauce:
2oz (50g) butter
3 tablespoons flour
¾ pint (450ml) cooking liquid, strained
salt and pepper
3 tablespoons finely chopped parsley

Put the drumsticks into a large pan with boiling water to cover.
☐ Bring to the boil, remove any scum, then add the carrots, celery, onion, mace, bay, peppercorns, and salt.
☐ Reduce the heat to a simmer and cook, covered, for 10 minutes.
☐ Add the leeks and continue to cook for a further 5 minutes, or until the drumsticks are tender.
☐ Transfer the chicken joints and vegetables to a serving dish; cover and keep warm while you make the sauce. Strain off ¾ pint (450ml) cooking liquid for the sauce.
☐ Melt the butter in a pan, stir in the flour to make a roux.
☐ Gradually whisk in the strained cooking liquid and simmer until the sauce is smooth and thickened—about 10 minutes—stirring constantly.
☐ Season to taste, then stir in the parsley just before serving.

Chicken Joints with Ginger and Garlic

Serves 4
Preparation: 5 minutes
Cooking and infusing: 4¼ hours

☆

8 chicken joints, skinned
salt
1oz (25g) fresh ginger root, grated
3 cloves garlic, crushed

Bring the joints to the boil in enough salted water just to cover, then simmer, covered, for 10 minutes.
☐ Remove from the heat, add the ginger and garlic, and leave to infuse and cool in the liquid for at least 4 hours before serving.
☐ Serve cold with a salad.

Rice

Rice is a grain, available complete with the germ and bran layers as 'brown' rice or with the outer layers removed as 'pearled' rice. There are two basic types: long-grain (Patna) rice is used for dishes where you want the grains to remain separate, for plain boiled rice or classic pilafs. Round-grain (risotto or Carolina) rice has grains that are more glutinous and it is used for risottos and for sweet dishes.

Cooking methods

Whatever the variety, rice must absorb twice its own volume of water to become plump, tender and digestible (the heat and moisture of the cooking process softens the uncooked starch within the grain). There are basically two boiling methods. The simplest uses an unlimited amount of water, the excess is then drained off and the grain is allowed to dry and swell in its own steam. The second method uses a measured amount of water (both brown and white rice need approximately twice their own volume). The rice absorbs all the water and no draining is necessary. Both methods should give perfect results.

Plain Boiled Rice

Method 1

Serves 4 ⬭
Preparation: 2 minutes or less
Cooking: 18-20 minutes (white rice)
40-45 minutes (brown rice)

8oz (225g) long-grain rice
18 fl oz (500ml) boiling water
1 teaspoon salt

Rinse the rice under the cold tap to remove any surface starch.
☐ Bring the salted water to the boil and stir in the rice.
☐ Reduce the heat to maintain a gentle boil. Cook, covered for 18-20 minutes (40-45 minutes for brown rice), or until the water is absorbed and the rice is tender to the bite.
☐ Rinse the cooked rice with boiling water to remove any starch residue.
☐ Season to taste.
Note: If the rice starts to boil dry before it is tender, add a little more boiling water.

Plain Boiled Rice

Method 2

Put the rinsed rice into a pan that is almost filled with salted boiling water. Boil, covered for the same length of time as for Method 1. Drain the rice, return it to the rinsed pan and dry it briefly over a low heat, tossing with a fork to separate the grains.

Risotto

Serves 4 ☆
Preparation: 5 minutes
Cooking: 30 minutes

---

1 tablespoon oil
1oz (25g) butter
1 large onion, finely chopped
8oz (225g) round-grain rice
½ pint (300ml) veal or chicken stock
salt and pepper

Gently heat the oil with the butter in a large frying-pan.
☐ Add the onion and cook, stirring, for 3-4 minutes.
☐ Add the rice and cook, stirring, for a further 2-3 minutes.
☐ Meanwhile, bring the stock to the boil.
☐ Keep the rice at a light boil and add the stock, a cupful at a time, stirring in each addition until completely absorbed before adding more. Season to taste.
☐ Continue cooking and stirring the rice until tender and moist—about 20 minutes.

Cooking rice
Always start cooking rice in boiling water otherwise the grains will stick to each other—and the pan.

Pilaf Rice
To serve four, heat 3-4 tablespoons oil in a pan and stir in 8oz (225g) long-grain rice. When the rice is translucent and coated with oil, add 18 fl oz (500ml) boiling water or stock. Add salt, stir once, and simmer, covered, for 18-20 minutes. The liquid should all be absorbed. Flavourings such as mushroom, dried fruit, onion, herbs or cooked meat can be added, together with nuts and spices, such as turmeric.

Risotto
For a Risotto, the usual aim of cooking rice to produce completely separate grains is abandoned. This dish is moist and creamy, with the rice grains lightly bound together. Round-grain Italian rice is the best to use (it is stickier than long-grain).
Risotto is usually served with butter and grated Parmesan cheese, but there are many other flavourings, such as mushrooms, prawns, ham, beef marrow and saffron. It is best to keep to only one or two at once.

Risotto variation
While the rice cooks, prepare a colourful vegetable garnish. Sauté skinned, seeded tomatoes, leeks, parboiled French beans or carrots, or a mixture, in oil or butter. Gently cook the vegetables until heated through. Add them to the Risotto at the end of cooking. Finish with butter and grated cheese. Alternatively, add cooked bacon or ham.

Pasta cooking times

Fresh pasta will cook in from 2 to 5 minutes; dried pasta takes twice as long. But the precise cooking time depends on the size and thickness of the individual pieces. Time the cooking accurately by removing a sample at regular intervals towards the end of cooking. Lift out a few strands or pieces with a fork and pinch the dough—it should feel tender but not too soft.

Keeping pasta separate

To avoid pasta clumping together, cook it in a large pan with plenty of water. Add oil to the water—as in the recipe. Cooking without a lid also helps prevent pasta pans boiling over.

How much pasta

Allow about 3oz (75g) dried pasta per person, double the quantity for fresh pasta—when it is the main basis of the dish.

Boiling Pasta

Spaghetti and the enormous variety of small shapes, flat sheets and noodles that make up pasta are made from grain—the hard (durum) wheat that is ground into flour or semolina. The pasta dough, plain or enriched with egg and sometimes flavourings is shaped before being dried. Pasta can also be made from other grains—oriental rice noodles, for instance—or from soya or other bean flours.

All pasta, fresh or dried, is cooked in the same way, by boiling in plenty of salted water. The only difference is in the cooking time; dried pasta will take at least twice as long.

Serves 4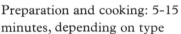
Preparation and cooking: 5-15 minutes, depending on type

---

5 pints (3 litres) boiling water
2 tablespoons olive oil
2 teaspoons salt
8oz (225g) dried pasta

Bring the water, oil and salt to a vigorous boil—the movement of the water and the oil both help to keep the pasta separate.
☐ Add the pasta—if you are cooking spaghetti, push the bundle of long strands gently against the base of the

pan until they soften and curl.
☐ Stir once, then leave to cook for about 10 minutes. Do not cover the pan.
☐ Drain the pasta in a colander and transfer it to a heated serving dish.
☐ Serve with a coating of olive oil or butter and seasoning to taste.
Tip: All pasta is delicious served simply with freshly grated Parmesan or other hard cheese such as Gruyère.

Pasta with Walnut and Anchovy

This can be made with any type of pasta. Unsalted butter is best to use with anchovies.

Serves 4 as a starter
Preparation: 30 minutes, including cooking pasta

2oz (50g) unsalted butter
8oz (225g) pasta, boiled and drained
2oz (50g) anchovy fillets, chopped
2oz (50g) chopped walnuts
2 tablespoons single cream (optional)

Heat the butter in a pan, add the cooked pasta, anchovies and walnuts and stir over a moderate heat. Stir in the cream before serving.

Long strands soften in boiling water.

Cook at a steady boil with no lid.

Cooked pasta is firm to the bite.

The perfect boiled egg

Eggs should be 'boiled' at a temperature more akin to a simmer. The water should just bubble gently, as a vigorous boil overcooks the white that's directly underneath the shell, making it tougher than the rest. This may cause the shells to crack as they bump against one another.

Do not boil eggs straight from the refrigerator. Few shells can withstand such a change in temperature. Forgetful cooks can warm cold eggs in the hand or run them under hot water from the tap. Another remedy is to start the eggs off in cold water: bring the water to a simmer and calculate the time from the moment the water starts to bubble (see Timing guide).

Take the eggs from the fridge at least 20 minutes beforehand to bring them to room temperature. Bring a saucepan of water to the boil—there should be enough water to cover the eggs in a single layer.

☐ Lower the eggs gently into the water with a tablespoon or slotted spoon.

☐ When the water returns to a simmer, start timing. Gently stir the water to rotate the eggs if you want to be sure the yolks are centred.

☐ Follow the Timing guide below and remove the eggs when they are done to your taste.

Timing guide

(Starting in boiling water.)

soft-boiled:
sizes 1-3	3¾ minutes
sizes 4 and 5	3 minutes

set white, soft yolk:
sizes 1-3	5 minutes
sizes 4 and 5	4 minutes

hard-boiled:
sizes 1-3	12 minutes
sizes 4 and 5	10 minutes

If starting in cold water, subtract 1 minute from the above timings.

Top row, left to right: 3, 4 and 5 minute eggs.

Bottom row, left to right: 6, 7 and 10 minute eggs.

Shelling eggs neatly

If you want to shell the eggs immediately after cooking to serve cold, start them off in water that is below boiling point. You can then remove the shells without tearing the whites. Hold them under the cold tap or plunge them into cold water, then tap the shells on a work surface to crack them and release the steam. Peel.

Breakfast eggs

● Boiled eggs will keep hot for some time if they are covered—they will also continue to cook in their own internal heat. To enjoy an egg that is perfectly timed, crack open the shells immediately.

● For a change, scoop an egg out of the shell into a cup or glass. Add butter and a pinch of fresh chives or parsley with seasoning to taste.

Pricking the shells

As eggs age, an air pocket forms beneath the shell at the broad end. Air expands when the egg is put into boiling water and may crack the shell. You can avoid this by carefully making a pin prick through the broad end before boiling the egg.

Is it hard boiled or uncooked?
It is impossible to tell by the look of an egg whether it is raw or a hard-boiled egg which has been allowed to cool completely. If your picnic eggs have been mixed with uncooked eggs, lay each on its side and spin it. The hard-boiled egg will twirl merrily, the raw egg will hardly turn at all, due to the liquid inside.

Quails' eggs, hard boiled and ready to be shelled, resting on a bed of cress. A large hen's egg set alongside gives some idea of relative size.

Quails' eggs

Quails' eggs are now widely available throughout the year. They can be soft- or hard-boiled but since they are small, they require a shorter cooking time than hens' eggs.

Starting in boiling water, allow $2\frac{1}{2}$ minutes for a soft-boiled egg (the yolk soft, the white set), or $3\frac{1}{2}$-4 minutes for a hard-boiled egg. Shelled and arranged on a bed of cress or shredded lettuce, they make a rich-tasting first course. Serve with hot buttered toast and a dish of salt or celery salt to dip them into.

Quails' egg garnish Lightly boil 1 to 3 eggs per person, shell and use them as a garnish for soups such as a vegetable or fish broth or cream of chicken.

Quails' egg toasts Lightly boil the eggs; dip them in cold water, peel and halve. Cut out neat rounds of buttered toast with a biscuit cutter. Add a round of cheese, ham or smoked salmon and arrange the quails' eggs on top. Sprinkle with chopped parsley.

Gulls' eggs

The sale of most wild birds' eggs is prohibited by law, but gulls' eggs are available from 1 April to 22 May. Pheasants' and mallards' eggs may also be found: pheasants' from April to mid-May and mallards' from mid-March to June, though the weather affects the breeding season and the number of eggs laid. Eat them hard-boiled.

Ducks' eggs

Ducks' eggs are larger and richer than hens', each weighing about 3oz (75g). They are often laid by muddy river banks so should be boiled for at least 10 minutes for perfect safety. Ducks' eggs are not suitable for making meringues.

Other eggs such as those of turkeys, geese and guinea fowl may be found in specialist food shops when they are available, although turkey eggs tend to be used only in catering.

Poaching

Poaching is gentle simmering in a liquid, a cooking method that can be adapted to suit a surprising variety of foods. The temperature is sufficiently high to cook the food quickly yet gentle enough to conserve most of its flavour. This fact alone makes poaching a favourite technique with today's top chefs. It is easy to master, it preserves the nutrients in food and it is also economical: the poaching liquid itself—water, wine, milk or stock depending on the food being cooked—often forms the basis of a sauce to serve with the finished dish.

Apart from the need to choose good quality raw materials, the only essential step to success is to control the temperature of the poaching liquid. Always keep it below boiling point so that the food cooks indirectly, in heat transferred through the barely moving liquid. The protein in egg whites, for instance, actually begins to set at around 150F (70C). Boiling over-cooks it and turns it rubbery as well as distorting its shape. And this rule applies to anything you poach: fish, fruit, meat, fresh pasta such as Gnocchi, as well as eggs. The secret is to poach food just enough to make it tender but to ensure it still retains its shape.

Most foods are suitable for poaching. For fish, shellfish and delicate offal, such as sweetbreads, it is one of the most perfect cooking methods, for maximum moisture is retained and you can use the fish liquid as the basis of seafood soup. Fruits such as apples and pears or stone fruits, such as apricots, plums or peaches, will disintegrate if rapidly boiled, but when poached they will hold their shape and are deliciously tender. Foods such as poultry, meat and game are equally suitable for poaching, and well worthwhile for the extra succulence.

The poaching liquid

The simplest poaching liquid is water, lightly seasoned with a little salt. It is suitable for eggs, certain fish and shellfish, and discarded after use. Other poaching liquids are made by adding flavourings such as herbs and aromatic vegetables (onion, shallot, leek or carrot) to the basic liquid. These enhance the flavour of the food as it cooks. If the liquid is boiled to

reduce it it concentrates the flavour, and also provides a flavourful base for the final sauce. Choose appropriate herbs and vegetables, ones that complement rather than mask the natural flavour of the food: the following recipes have been chosen to give you a very good idea of combinations to use.

Court bouillon

The standard poaching liquid for fish is a delicately flavoured stock made by simmering vegetables in water to make what is called a court bouillon. Small whole fish such as trout or mackerel, or fish steaks and fillets are then lowered into the simmering, ready-flavoured liquid to poach for the required time. With larger, whole fish such as salmon, sea trout or turbot, it's best to start them off in a court bouillon that has been allowed to get cold, otherwise the surface flesh will be cooked before the inside is done.

Court bouillon is made from vegetables such as onion or shallot, carrot and herbs such as parsley and bay—all

The poaching liquid

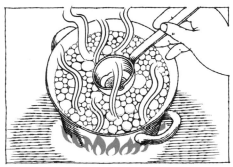

Boiling liquid is too hot for a gentle cooking method such as poaching; bubbling just breaks up the food.

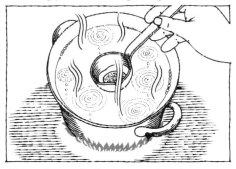

Turn down the heat to maintain a gentle simmer where the surface of the liquid barely moves. Only a few small bubbles should be visible, rising from the base of the pan to the surface of the liquid.

Fish such as the salmon shown here in a court bouillon is ideal for poaching, either whole in a fish kettle, or as fillets or steaks. You can poach almost any food: shellfish such as oysters or scallops, delicate offal such as sweetbreads, or whole chicken, in a liquid flavoured with onion, carrot and herbs all take on a greater succulence with poaching. Fruits, ranging from the peaches shown here, to plums, apricots, cherries, apples or pears, are equally tasty poached.

aromatic enough to lend flavour to any fish without overwhelming its delicacy. As the following recipes show, many subtle and delicious variations are possible, both in the vegetables used and in the liquid itself. Fish particularly benefit from the addition of an acidic liquid such as white wine, or a little lemon juice. Both these firm up the delicate flesh and help preserve its colour.

For meat and poultry

Meat and poultry are poached in liquid which has flavouring vegetables added at the start of cooking. By the time the food is tender, the liquid, too, will be permeated with flavour, making a light stock that can be strained and stored or used immediately to make a sauce.

Poaching in stock or syrup

Homemade stock makes a wonderful poaching medium. Fish stock is easily and rapidly prepared from all the trimmings left over from filleting, particularly the gelatinous bones from fish such as turbot, sole or plaice. Simply simmer the trimmings with a few vegetables and herbs then strain and freeze the cooled stock until you need it. You can then add some of this stock to make up some—or all—of the poaching liquid. For meat and poultry dishes, use meat or chicken stock (page 238 and 239). Offal can be poached in either chicken or veal stock (page 239). Fruits are cooked in light syrup made by boiling water and sugar, then adding the fruit with flavourings such as lemon or orange peel, spices, wine or spirits.

The poaching pan

For foods that require little space such as eggs, scallops, oysters or whole fruits, or for small pieces of

food, use a saucepan or deep frying-pan for poaching. Small whole fish can also be cooked in a relatively small saucepan if you coil the fish around the inside of the pan.

To keep whole fish or fillets flat, or to poach larger fish, you must use a pan that will accommodate the fish comfortably. Either use a specially designed pan known as a fish kettle (shown below), or improvise by using a rectangular roasting tin and covering it with a lid of foil. True fish kettles have removable racks which fit into the bottom for the purpose of lifting whole fish in and out of the poaching liquid without breaking. If you don't have a fish kettle, you can make a 'rack' for an ordinary pan or roasting tin out of foil.

Fold 2 or 3 thicknesses of foil into a long rectangle and arrange this in the bottom of the pan with the ends projecting up and over the sides by a couple of inches (6cm). The two projecting ends can then be used to lift out the food when cooked.

The amount of liquid

Choose a pan that is big enough to accommodate the food comfortably. Apart from fruit where you can pack it loosely to come slightly more than halfway up the pan, arrange the food in a single layer. If you are going to reduce the liquid later to make a sauce, it makes sense to use as little as possible. You must, however, make sure there's enough to at least half-cover the food, then poach it covered with a lid so that it cooks partly in the steam. To keep large items like a whole chicken moist during longer cooking, add liquid to barely cover.

Keep the goodness in

Because poaching is a remarkably quick as well as a gentle cooking method, all the food's natural nutrients and flavour are preserved and it can be regarded as one of the healthiest cooking methods. The fact that the food cooks in liquid, flavoured appropriately, without any added fat, also adds to its healthy appeal. Any water-soluble vitamins that do leach out into the cooking liquid can be recaptured when you make the final sauce to accompany the dish.

Salmon steaks

Instead of cooking a salmon whole, you can poach it in individual pieces as steaks or fillets.

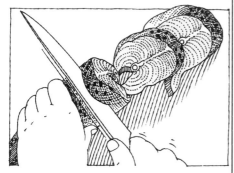

Cut into 1½ inch (4cm) thick slices.

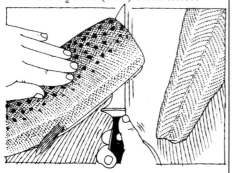

Cut fillets following the backbone.

Poached Salmon with Hollandaise Sauce

To complement its sumptuous natural flavour, serve poached salmon with the simplest of accompaniments: boiled new potatoes and a fresh vegetable such as carrots or broccoli, or a simple green salad.

Serves 4   ☆ ☆ ☆
Preparation: 10 minutes
Cooking time: about 15 minutes
Sauce: 15 minutes

4 salmon steaks weighing about 1½lb
    (700g) altogether
1¾ pints (1 litre) water
7½ fl oz (200ml) dry white wine
6 parsley stalks, chopped
½ bay leaf
small piece of lemon peel
6 white peppercorns, crushed
1 tablespoon sea salt

The sauce:
½ pint (300ml) poaching liquid
3 tablespoons white wine vinegar
2 tablespoons onion, chopped
9oz (250g) cold butter cut into about
    10 pieces
salt and white pepper
1 teaspoon lemon juice, strained
1 tablespoon chives, finely chopped

Bring the water and wine to the boil in the poaching pan.

☐ Add parsley, bay leaf, lemon peel, peppercorns, and salt and simmer gently for 5 minutes.

☐ Lower the fish into the pan, reduce the heat and poach the salmon for 8 to 10 minutes.

☐ Transfer the fish to a warmed dish, spoon over some of the poaching liquid, cover and keep warm.

☐ To make the sauce, put 3 fl oz (100ml) of the poaching liquid into a saucepan with the vinegar and onion. Boil rapidly to reduce to a thick syrup.

☐ Remove the pan from the heat and cool it by dipping it into a sink of cold water; the liquid should be only as hot as the finger can stand.

☐ Gradually whisk the cold butter into the liquid, a piece at a time, to form a smooth, thickened sauce. Season with salt, pepper and lemon juice.

☐ Remove skin and bones from the fish steaks. Place on to a serving dish with the sauce, and garnish with chopped chives. Spoon some sauce on to individual serving plates, arrange the steaks on top and serve the rest of the sauce separately.

Poached Salmon with Butter Sauce

This is one of the great classics of the fish repertoire. The flavour of the sauce is enhanced by a final addition of parsley and poaching liquid.

Serves 4 ☆ ☆ ☆
Preparation: 10 minutes (including fish)
Cooking time: 15 minutes
Sauce: 15 minutes

1¾ pints (1 litre) water
6¼ fl oz (200ml) dry white wine
small piece of lemon peel
6 parsley stalks, chopped
½ celery stick, chopped
6 white peppercorns, crushed
1 tablespoon chopped onion
1 tablespoon sea salt
4 salmon steaks or fillets (about
    1½lb (700g) total weight)
½ pint (300ml) Quick Hollandaise
1 tablespoon parsley, finely chopped
parsley sprigs for garnish

Moist salmon steaks poached in a wine court bouillon and served with a simple Butter Sauce.

Bring the water and wine to the boil in the poaching pan.
☐ Add the lemon peel, parsley stalks, celery, peppercorns, onion and salt and simmer gently for a few minutes.
☐ Reduce the heat and lower the salmon pieces into the pan. Poach the fish for 8-10 minutes, depending on the thickness of the pieces.
☐ Meanwhile, prepare the Quick Hollandaise and stir in 2 tablespoons of the poaching liquid and the finely chopped parsley at the very end.
☐ Remove the fish from the pan, drain well. If you are using steaks, remove the skin and bones. Spoon a little sauce on to a heated serving plate and arrange the fish on top. Garnish with parsley.
☐ Serve the remainder of the sauce in a sauceboat.

❋**Cooking frozen salmon**
Poaching times given in these recipes are for fresh salmon; add 2 minutes to the cooking time if you are using frozen steaks.

The ideal pan

Whole small fish, steaks and fillets can be poached in any pan broad enough to hold them flat; a rectangular roasting pan is ideal. Use a rectangular sheet of foil as a lid.

Special pans such as fish kettles are only necessary if you intend to poach large fish whole.

Note: If the pan you are using is too long to fit on to a hotplate, you can poach in the oven instead. Simply cover the pan and place it in an oven preheated to 180C (350F) or Gas 4 for the same amount of time.

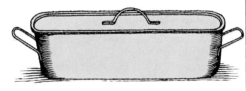

Two common forms of fish kettle, one long and narrow, the other an oval turbotière. Both shapes will accommodate large fish such as whole turbot or salmon. All fish kettles have removable racks so that the fish can be lifted in and out without breaking.

Poached Sole with White Wine Sauce

This simple fish dish produces tender sole fillets served with a delicious sauce made from the poaching liquid. Serve it with creamed potatoes or whole new potatoes and baby carrots or courgettes.

Serves 4
Preparation and cooking time:
   1 hour 10 minutes

2 sole (about 1lb (500g) each) cleaned

Poaching liquid:
¾ pint (450ml) white wine
¾ pint (450ml) water
3 carrots, sliced
1 tablespoon chopped onion
6 parsley stalks, chopped
small piece of lemon peel
6 white peppercorns, crushed

Sauce:
1oz (25g) butter
3 tablespoons flour
1 egg yolk
3 tablespoons single cream
salt

Bring the white wine and water to the boil in a pan that is large enough to hold the fish.
☐ Add the carrot, onion, parsley, lemon peel and the crushed peppercorns. Reduce the heat and simmer gently for 20 minutes. Strain the liquid, return to the pan and bring back to the boil.
☐ Gently lower both the sole into the boiling poaching liquid. Reduce the heat to a simmer. Cover and cook for 10 minutes until the fish are tender, then remove them with a fish slice. Drain on kitchen paper then transfer them to a heated plate and cover with foil to keep warm.
☐ Strain the poaching liquid, return it to the pan and boil rapidly until reduced to about half.
☐ In a saucepan, melt the butter over a medium heat. When the foam has subsided add the flour and stir it in well. Continue to cook, stirring continuously, for a minute or two without letting it brown.
☐ Remove it from the heat and stir

in a little of the poaching liquid. Return to the heat, and cook, stirring, until all the liquid is added. Continue to cook the sauce for a further 2 to 3 minutes until smooth and glossy.
☐ In a small bowl mix together the egg yolk and cream. To prevent the egg yolk curdling, stir in 3 tablespoons of the hot sauce, then pour the egg yolk mixture (liaison) into the pan and stir. Immediately remove the pan from the heat and season the sauce to taste.
☐ To serve the dish, use a fish slice or a broad knife to lift off the upper fillets. Pull away and discard the backbone to release the two lower fillets.
☐ Arrange the fish on a warmed serving dish. Spoon a little sauce over each fillet and serve the rest separately in a warmed sauceboat.
☐ Garnish the dish with wedges of tomato or lemon, and sprigs of parsley and, if you like, a little chopped parsley or chives as a topping for the sauce.

Poached Turbot with Caper Sauce

You can serve this dish either with a Velouté Sauce garnished with capers, or with the 5-Minute Caper Sauce given on the next page.

Serves 4
Preparation: 10 minutes
Cooking time: about 50 minutes
   (Velouté), or about 40 minutes
   (5-Minute Caper Sauce)

4 turbot steaks each weighing about 6oz
   (175g)
salt

Poaching liquid:
¾ pint (450ml) dry white wine
¾ pint (450ml) water
6 parsley stalks, roughly chopped
1 tablespoon onion, finely chopped
6 white peppercorns, crushed

Rub the turbot steaks lightly with salt.
☐ Bring the wine and water to the boil in a pan or fish kettle. Add the parsley, onion and peppercorns.

Lower the turbot steaks into the hot liquid, reduce the heat to a simmer. Cover and cook the steaks until tender:
10-12 minutes for thin steaks,
12-14 minutes for thicker ones.
Follow the shorter time if serving the fish with Velouté Sauce.

☐ Lift the fish steaks from the poaching liquid and allow them to drain slightly over the pan. Remove the skin and as many bones as possible, being careful not to break up the steak. Place the fish on a heated serving plate. Cover and keep hot while you make the sauce.

Velouté Sauce with Capers

poaching liquid, strained and
    reduced to ¾ pint (450ml)
2oz (50g) butter
3 tablespoons flour
3 tablespoons single cream
1 egg yolk
3 tablespoons drained capers
1 tablespoon chives or parsley, finely
    chopped
salt and pepper

Use the reduced poaching liquid to make a Velouté Sauce. Add capers and herbs and season to taste.

☐ Spoon a little of the sauce on to each steak and serve the rest in a warmed sauceboat.

5-minute Caper Sauce

3 egg yolks
2 tablespoons poaching liquid
2 tablespoons white wine
1 tablespoon liquid from caper jar
3oz (75g) softened butter
1 tablespoon capers
1 tablespoon chives or parsley, finely
    chopped
salt and pepper

Whisk together the egg yolks, poaching liquid, white wine and caper liquid. Add the butter and continue whisking; the butter will separate into small pieces.

☐ Set the bowl over a pan of hot, but not boiling water. Over a low heat, whisk until the sauce begins to thicken.

☐ Remove from the heat. Stir in the capers and herbs. Season to taste.

☐ Either pour the sauce over the fish or serve it separately in a warmed sauceboat.

Variation: Lemon Sauce also makes a delicious accompaniment for Poached Turbot.

Varying the poaching liquid

If you like, omit the wine from any of these recipes and make up the amount of liquid with water. Add some extra flavourings to compensate: a handful of parsley stalks, a sliced carrot or two, a bay leaf and perhaps a squeeze of lemon juice.

Remember that if you have fish stock in the freezer you can use it to give a richer, fuller flavour to both fish and final sauce. Substitute the stock for some of the water and proceed as usual.

Carrots, onion and parsley are the usual flavourings to add to a court bouillon for delicate fish like sole. But you can include more strongly aromatic additions like leek or celery for other fish.

Poached turbot steaks served with a sharply contrasting caper sauce. You can garnish the dish with sprigs of parsley as here, and serve it with potatoes and courgettes mixed with dill pickles, or with a vegetable such as broccoli.

Stuffed Sole Fillets with 5-minute White Wine Sauce

Fillets of sole folded around a contrasting vegetable stuffing and served with a quick sauce. You can vary the stuffing to taste: leeks, spring onions or pieces of cooked carrot or celeriac are all suitable. Serve the dish with new potatoes and some boiled spinach.

Serves 4 ★★☆
Preparation: 10 minutes
Cooking time: 35 minutes
Sauce: 10 minutes

8 sole fillets (1½lb (700g) total weight)

Poaching liquid:
2 medium leeks, cleaned
1½ pints (900ml) water
1 tablespoon sea salt
4 white peppercorns, crushed
½ bay leaf
4 parsley stalks, chopped
salt and white pepper

Sauce:
3 egg yolks
1 teaspoon lemon juice
3oz (75g) softened butter
4 tablespoons dry white wine
4 tablespoons reduced poaching liquid

Cut the white part of each leek into four equal pieces, each as long as the sole fillets are wide.

☐ Slice the rest of the leeks thinly and use to flavour the poaching liquid.

☐ Bring the water and sea salt to the boil in a poaching pan. Add the eight pieces of leek, reduce the heat to a simmer and cook gently for 5 minutes or until just tender. Remove with a draining spoon and immediately plunge them into cold water to stop the cooking. Drain well.

☐ Add the sliced leeks, peppercorns, bay leaf, and parsley to the cooking liquid, bring to the boil then reduce the heat and simmer gently for 20 minutes.

☐ Dust each fillet on the skin side with a little salt and pepper. Place a piece of leek on each fillet, roll it up, and tie it securely with one or two pieces of kitchen string.

☐ Strain the poaching liquid, return to the pan and bring back to the boil. Reduce the heat to a simmer and lower the rolled fillets to stand upright in the liquid.

☐ Poach the fillets gently for 6 to 8 minutes until they are tender. Remove the strings and transfer the fish to a warmed dish. Spoon a little of the poaching liquid over the fillets to keep them moist. Cover and keep warm.

☐ Make the sauce by putting the ingredients into a bowl and whisking them.

☐ Set the bowl over a pan of hot, but not boiling, water and continue whisking. As the sauce cooks, scrape down the sides of the bowl with a spatula.

☐ As soon as the sauce thickens— about 5 minutes—remove it from the heat. If you like, garnish with a sprinkling of chopped chives. Spoon the sauce straight on to serving plates and arrange the fillets on top.

Tip: To vary the sauce and give it an unusual flavour suited to the combination of sole and leeks, you can stir in a little vermouth (about a teaspoon), before serving.

Sole fillets, rolled and tied around a section of partly cooked leek and poached, then served with a buttery white wine sauce. Remove the strings before serving.

Tuna with Red Wine and Tomato Sauce

Fresh tuna is seasonal but can be found in markets or specialist fish shops in spring and summer. The dense-textured, meaty flesh goes particularly well with red wine. Serve the dish with boiled rice or macaroni or with a mushroom risotto.

Serves 4 ☆
Preparation: 10-15 minutes
Cooking time: about 30 minutes
Sauce: 20 minutes

4 even-sized tuna steaks or fillets
    (about 1½lb (700g) total weight)
¾ pint (450ml) red wine
1¼ pints (750ml) fish stock
1 tablespoon onion, chopped
1 garlic clove, peeled
½ bay leaf
sprig of fresh thyme or ½ teaspoon dried
    thyme
1 celery stalk, chopped
¾ pint (450ml) Basic Brown Sauce
    made with fish poaching liquid
2 tomatoes, skinned
1 tablespoon parsley, finely chopped

Bring the wine and the fish stock to the boil in the poaching pan.

□ Add the onion, garlic, bay leaf, thyme and celery. Simmer the mixture for 20 minutes.

□ Strain the liquid and return it to the pan. Lower the fish into the stock and bring it back to boiling point. Reduce the heat to a simmer.

□ Poach the fish, covered, for about 10 minutes or until it yields when gently pressed with a finger. Drain the fillets and keep them warm.

□ Measure out ¾ pint (450ml) of the strained poaching liquid. Make the Basic Brown Sauce substituting the liquid for the brown stock.

□ Halve the tomatoes, squeeze them gently to remove the seeds and juice, and dice the flesh. Stir the tomato flesh and the parsley into the sauce just before removing it from the heat.

□ Arrange the fish on a heated serving dish. Spoon over a little of the sauce and serve the rest separately. Garnish with lemon wedges and serve immediately.

Garlic with tuna
Garlic gives a distinctive, subtle bite to the poaching liquid and to the sauce that is eventually made from it. Leave the clove whole so that it contributes a delicate perfume that is not too powerful.

Tuna with red wine and tomato sauce.

For mackerel

Mackerel, like tuna has flesh that contains a higher proportion of oil than white fish. The usual practice of poaching mackerel in an acidic liquid containing lemon juice makes a perfect foil for this richness. If you like, omit the lemon and replace ¼ pint (150ml) of the water with white wine.

Seasoning a whole mackerel

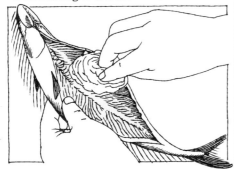

Use kitchen paper to blot the inside.

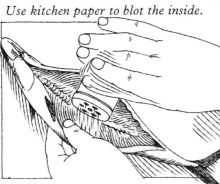

Season it inside with salt and pepper.

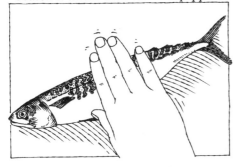

Roll the fish gently back into shape.

Poached Mackerel with Leek Sauce

A leek sauce with a touch of lemon makes a very good complement to the richness of mackerel. Buy the fish whole, but have them gutted.

Serves 4
Preparation: 8-10 minutes
Cooking time: 35 minutes
Sauce: 10 minutes

---

4 mackerel (about 2lb (1kg) total weight)
salt and white pepper
1 large leek, cleaned
1½ pints (900ml) water
6 lemon slices
2 onions, sliced
Sprig of fresh thyme or ½ teaspoon dried thyme
1 tablespoon sea salt
Quick Hollandaise Sauce

Season the inside of the mackerel with salt and pepper.

☐ Cut the leek into fairly large pieces. Finely chop about 1oz (25g) of the white part and reserve it to use in the sauce.

☐ Bring the water to the boil in a poaching pan. Add the leek, lemon and onion slices, and the thyme and sea salt and simmer for 20 minutes.

☐ Strain the liquid then return to the pan and bring it back to the boil.

☐ Lower the fish into the poaching liquid. As soon as the liquid returns to the boil, reduce the heat and poach the fish for 14-16 minutes, depending on size. To test whether the fish is done, pierce the thickest part with a small skewer; the flesh should feel tender and have lost its translucency.

☐ Use a fish slice to remove the mackerel from the pan and drain it.

☐ Cover the fish with a heated plate and keep it warm.

☐ Use some of the strained poaching liquid to make a Quick Hollandaise Sauce. Stir the leek into the sauce just before serving.

☐ Transfer the fish to a heated serving dish. Spoon a little of the sauce over and serve the rest separately in a sauceboat.

Haddock Fillets with Mustard Sauce

Rolled haddock fillets are quick and easy to prepare and look very attractive. Choose fairly thin fillets so that they are easier to roll.

Serves 4
Preparation: 10 minutes
Cooking time: 10 minutes (fish);
    20 minutes (sauce)

---

8 haddock fillets (about 1½lb (700g) total weight)
1½ pints (900ml) water
2 tablespoons lemon juice, strained
6 parsley stalks, chopped
2 celery stalks, chopped
2 small carrots, sliced
1 tablespoon sea salt
¾ pint (450ml) Mustard Sauce
4 tomato slices, skinned
salt and pepper
1 tablespoon chives, chopped

Lay the fillets flesh side down. Starting with the tail, roll them up firmly and secure each end with a wooden cocktail stick.

☐ Put the water, lemon juice, parsley, celery, carrot and sea salt into a poaching pan. Bring the liquid to the boil and simmer for a few minutes.

☐ Reduce the heat to a simmer, lower the rolled fillets into the pan and poach for 6 to 8 minutes depending on size.

☐ Remove the fillets, spoon a little of the poaching liquid over them to keep them moist, cover them with a heated dish and keep them warm.

☐ To accompany the fish, make the Mustard Sauce. Strain off about ¼ pint (150ml) of the poaching liquid and substitute it for ¼ pint (150ml) of the milk used in the recipe.

☐ Arrange the fillets on a serving dish. Spoon a little of the sauce over them and serve the rest separately in a sauceboat. Garnish the dish with tomato slices, each slice sprinkled with finely chopped chives.

Note: Peppercorns have not been included in this recipe as the mustard gives sufficient sharpness.

Poached Calves' or Lambs' Liver

A whole piece of liver remains deliciously moist when poached. To prepare the piece, use a knife to cut away any fibrous tissue and carefully peel away the surface membrane. Slice the liver just before serving and serve it, accompanied by plain boiled rice and a green vegetable such as peas or courgettes.

Serves 4
Preparation: 10 minutes
Cooking time: 25 minutes
Sauce: 25 minutes

Calves' or lambs' liver weighing about 1lb (500g)

The poaching liquid:
1½ pints (900ml) veal or chicken stock
1 bay leaf
1 onion, peeled and sliced
4 parsley stalks, chopped
salt
¾ pint (450ml) Fresh Tomato Sauce
1 tablespoon finely chopped chives

Rinse the liver in cold running water and pat it dry with a kitchen towel.

☐ Bring the stock to the boil in the poaching pan. Add the bay, onion, parsley, and salt.

☐ Lower the liver into the pan and bring the liquid back to the boil. Reduce the heat to a simmer and poach for 20 minutes, until the juices are no longer pink. Transfer to a warmed dish, cover and keep warm.

☐ Prepare Fresh Tomato Sauce. Drain the liver and cut it into fairly thin slices. Arrange the slices on a hot serving dish. Spoon a little of the sauce over the slices; garnish with chopped chives. Serve the rest of the sauce separately in a sauceboat.

Variation: to heighten the flavour of the liver and the final sauce, add a few tablespoons of port or sherry to the poaching liquid.

Poached Brains with 5-minute Caper Sauce

You can use either calves' or lambs' brains for this dish. Lambs' brains are usually served whole; calves' brains which are larger, are cut into slices. Brains are delicious if served very simply–here, they are accompanied by a sharp Caper Sauce. If you like, prepare some croûtons–cubes of bread fried in butter –for a contrast in texture.

Serves 4
Preparation: 10 minutes
Cooking time: 45 minutes
Sauce: 10 minutes

2 calves' or 4 lambs' brains weighing about 1lb (500g)

The poaching liquid:
1¾ pints (1 litre) water
1 onion
5 cloves
2 tablespoons strained lemon juice
6 peppercorns, crushed
salt

5-minute Caper Sauce
1 tablespoon finely chopped herbs–parsley, chives or chervil

Remove skin from brains, soak them in several changes of cold water, then drain and cut out any arteries.

☐ Bring the water to the boil in the poaching pan. Add the onion, cloves, lemon juice, peppercorns, and salt.

☐ Lower the brains into the hot liquid, reduce the heat to a simmer and poach until tender–35 to 40 minutes. Transfer the brains to a warmed dish; cover.

☐ Prepare a 5-minute Caper Sauce.

☐ Drain the brains well and pat them dry on a kitchen towel. Cut them into thick slices and arrange them on a warmed serving dish.

☐ Pour a little of the sauce round and garnish the dish with the finely chopped fresh herbs. Serve the rest of the sauce separately in a sauceboat.

Soup from poached liver
Save the poaching liquid left over from poaching liver. Simmered with aromatic vegetables such as onion, celery and carrot, they form the basis for a light soup. Thicken the soup with cream and garnish with a sprinkling of fresh herbs.

Slicing calves' brains

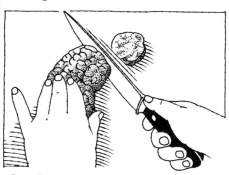

Cut the poached brains into fairly thick slices.

Arrange the slices on individual plates and coat them with sauce.

Poached Veal Medaillons

Poaching is quick and delicate, so it is only suitable for tender meat such as these boneless loin slices, called medaillons.

Serves 4 ☆☆
Preparation: 10 minutes
Cooking: 14 minutes
Sauce: 5 minutes

4 veal medaillons, each about 4oz (125g)

The poaching liquid:
1 pint (600ml) veal or chicken stock
12 parsley stalks, chopped
small piece of lemon peel
6 peppercorns, crushed

2 tablespoons chives, finely chopped
2 tablespoons parsley, finely chopped
½ teaspoon lemon peel, finely grated
white pepper
2oz (50g) cold butter cut into 4 pieces

Bring the stock to the boil in the poaching pan and add the parsley stalks, lemon peel, and peppercorns.
☐ Lower the pieces of veal into the pan. Bring the liquid to the boil, reduce the heat to a simmer. Poach until tender, about 8 minutes.
☐ Remove and drain the veal, blotting it dry with kitchen paper. Arrange the pieces on a warmed serving dish; cover and keep warm.
☐ Strain the stock into a small saucepan and boil vigorously until reduced to about ½ pint (300ml). Season to taste with salt and pepper.
☐ To make the sauce, remove the pan from the heat; whisk in butter one piece at a time. Whisk for a few minutes to make a smooth, thickened sauce. Stir in the chives, parsley and grated lemon peel, spoon the sauce over the veal slices and serve.

Sweetbreads, poached in stock, served with a herby Velouté Sauce.

Poached Sweetbreads with Herb Sauce

Blanched sweetbreads have a firmness and delicacy that makes them ideal for poaching. Serve with boiled rice and any seasonal vegetable.

Serves 4 ☆☆☆
Preparation: 10 minutes
Cooking time: 30 minutes
Sauce: 15 minutes

1lb (500g) calves' sweetbreads

The poaching liquid:
1½ pints (900ml) veal or
**   chicken stock**
4 parsley stalks, chopped
small sprig of fresh thyme, or a
**   pinch of dried thyme**
1 celery stick, chopped
2 small carrots, sliced
piece of leek, chopped
small piece of lemon peel

The sauce:
¾ pint (450ml) Velouté Sauce
salt
1 tablespoon finely chopped chives
1 tablespoon finely chopped parsley
2 teaspoons finely chopped chervil

Soak the sweetbreads in several changes of cold water until the water is clear.
☐ Blanch them by bringing to the boil in a large pan of cold water with a squeeze of lemon juice. Simmer for 2-3 minutes, then plunge into cold water. Peel off membrane.
☐ Bring the stock to the boil in the poaching pan. Add the parsley stalks, thyme, celery, carrots, leek, and lemon peel.
☐ Lower the prepared sweetbreads into the stock, reduce the heat to a simmer and poach until tender.
☐ Transfer them to a warmed serving dish, cover and keep warm.
☐ Using some strained poaching liquid, make a Velouté Sauce.
☐ Remove the sweetbreads from the pan when the sauce is ready. Slice and arrange them on the serving dish. Stir the chopped fresh herbs (chives, parsley and chervil), into the sauce and spoon some over the sweetbreads. Serve rest separately.

Chicken Breasts with Prawn Sauce

Chicken breasts fillets, bought separately, make a quick and delicious supper dish. Try them with other sauces from the Sauce section.

Once cooked, prawns may toughen and lose their flavour if kept hot for too long. Stir them into the sauce just before serving and do not bring the sauce back to the boil.

Serves 4 ☆☆☆
Preparation: 5 minutes
Cooking time: 14 minutes
Sauce: 15 minutes

1 pint (600ml) chicken stock
12 parsley stalks, chopped
piece of leek, finely chopped
4 chicken breast fillets, together
  weighing about 1½lb (700g)
¾ pint (450ml) Velouté Sauce,
  thickened with egg yolk and cream
4oz (100g) shrimps or prawns, peeled
salt and white pepper
2 large tomatoes, skinned
1 tablespoon chives, finely chopped

Bring the stock to the boil in the poaching pan.
☐ Add the parsley and leek and simmer for 5 minutes. Reduce the heat to a simmer, add the fillets and poach for 6-8 minutes, or until tender.
☐ Using a fish slice or a slotted spoon, remove them from the pan. Cover and keep warm.
☐ Strain the poaching liquid and use to prepare the Velouté Sauce. Stir in the peeled prawns or shrimps.
☐ Lightly season the chicken fillets with salt and pepper. Coat them with a little of the sauce and serve the rest separately in a sauce boat. If you like, garnish the dish with tomato wedges or a few chopped chives.
Variation: you can prepare a turkey breast, sliced in half lengthways, in the same way. If you like, leave out the prawns and add a little curry powder to the final sauce.

Pigeons in Mushroom Sauce

Pigeons are available all year. As they are so small they cook quickly so long as you choose young birds, known as squabs. Young birds have a fat breast with a supple breastbone, and a flexible beak.

Serves 4 ☆☆☆
Preparation time: 3 minutes
Cooking time: 15 minutes
Sauce: 20 minutes

4 pigeons each weighing about 8oz (225g)
1 pint (600ml) brown stock
¼ pint (150ml) red wine
3oz (75g) cold butter
2oz (50g) button mushrooms, sliced
3 tablespoons flour
2 tablespoons sherry
salt and pepper
squeeze of lemon juice

Choose a pan that accommodates the pigeons comfortably.
☐ Pour in the stock and wine and bring to the boil.
☐ Lower the pigeons into the hot liquid and reduce the heat to a simmer.
☐ Cover the pan and cook for 15-20 minutes or until the pigeons are tender.
☐ Transfer them to a warmed serving dish, cover and keep warm.
☐ Boil the stock to reduce it to about ¾ pint (450ml). Over a moderate heat melt a third of the butter in a sauté pan.
☐ Add the mushrooms to the pan just as the butter begins to change colour. Cook, stirring, until lightly coloured.
☐ Stir in the flour, then gradually stir in the reduced stock. Cook the sauce for 5-7 minutes until it thickens.
☐ Add sherry, seasoning and lemon juice to taste.
☐ Cut the remaining butter into small cubes. Whisk it piece by piece, into the sauce. Remove the pan from the heat and thoroughly whisk in the last addition. Spoon the sauce over the pigeons and serve.

Last steps in preparing the mushroom sauce

Whisk in the butter piece by piece.

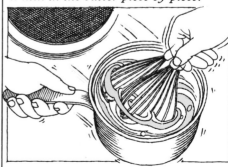

Off the heat, thoroughly whisk in the last of the butter.

Stuffed Chicken with Grape Sauce

Chicken stays juicy and succulent when cooked by this method. A sauce made from the poaching liquid, garnished with grapes, complements the finished dish.

Serves 4 ☆☆☆
Preparation: 15 minutes
Cooking time: 1 hour
Sauce: 15 minutes

---

3 rashers streaky bacon
2 chicken livers
7oz (200g) veal or pork, minced
1 tablespoon parsley, chopped
1 oz (25g) fresh breadcrumbs
1 egg
salt and white pepper
½ teaspoon paprika
1 oven-ready chicken
    weighing about 2lb (1kg)
1¾ pints (1 litre) chicken stock
¾ pint (450ml) Velouté Sauce
3 tablespoons sherry
7oz (200g) white grapes

Mince or finely chop the bacon and chicken livers.

☐ Combine minced meats, parsley, breadcrumbs, egg and seasonings and knead well together. Stuff the chicken with the mixture.

Stuffed Chicken with Grape Sauce.

☐ Using kitchen string and a needle, sew up the vent as shown, then truss the bird.

☐ Choose a pan large enough to hold the chicken comfortably.

☐ Pour in the chicken stock and bring to the boil. Lower the chicken into the stock, reduce the heat to a simmer, and poach until tender; about an hour, depending on size.

☐ To test for doneness, pierce the thickest part of the flesh on the inside of the leg with a skewer.

☐ Transfer the cooked chicken to a warmed serving dish, closely cover with foil to keep warm.

☐ Strain the poaching liquid into a saucepan and boil vigorously to reduce it by about half.

☐ Peel the grapes and remove the pips with the eye of a large needle.

☐ Using the reduced poaching liquid, prepare the sauce as described on page 262. Stir the sherry, grapes and grape juice into the sauce.

☐ Remove the trussing strings, spoon some of the sauce over the chicken and serve the rest separately.

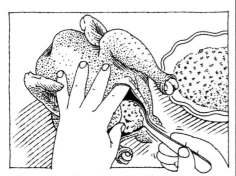

Spoon stuffing into the bird's cavity.

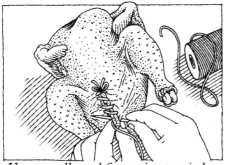

Use a needle and fine string to stitch up the vent.

Stuffing birds for poaching
Buy an untrussed chicken so that you can stuff it. To keep the bird in a compact shape for poaching, stuff it according to the method shown above. Poussin, duck, quail and pigeon can be stuffed and poached in the same way.

Perfect Poached Eggs

The best eggs for poaching are also the freshest. If the eggs are more than about a week old, the whites go thin. Whites of fresh eggs will gather compactly around the yolk, making a neater shape.

1¾ pints (1 litre) water
½ tablespoon salt
1½ tablespoons white vinegar (optional)
4 fresh eggs

☆

Bring the water to the boil with the salt and the vinegar if used.
☐ Reduce the heat to maintain a simmer—no more bubbles should be visible in the water.
☐ Gently break the eggs into the water or use a cup or soup ladle as shown on the right.
☐ Poach medium eggs for 3 minutes, large eggs for 4 minutes. Use a perforated draining spoon to remove them from the pan.
☐ Dip them into warm water to rinse them if they are to be served immediately, or into cold water (to halt the cooking process) if they are to be served later. Drain the eggs on kitchen paper and trim them with a small knife to remove any loose strands of egg white.
Variations:
Poached eggs form the basis of many light first courses or supper

Cold poached eggs on a bed of chopped salad and set in pastry shells.

dishes. By serving the eggs on a bed of vegetables and coating them with a sauce, you can transform them into meals.
Cold poached eggs Half fill cooked pastry cases with chopped, mixed salad. Place the eggs on top and spoon over a little flavoured mayonnaise. Serve as a first course or a light lunch dish.

Poached Eggs Soubise

Serves 4   ☆☆☆
Preparation and cooking: 15 minutes

Simple Tomato Sauce
½lb (225g) onions, sliced
3oz (75g) butter
4 eggs

Melt the butter in a large frying-pan and, when bubbling and foaming, add the onions.
☐ Stir over a low heat for about 10 minutes until the onions are softened and translucent.
☐ Transfer to a shallow serving dish and keep warm.
☐ Poach the eggs, using the method described in the previous recipe. Arrange the eggs on top of the onions. Spoon the sauce over the top and serve immediately.

Poaching eggs
If you are poaching a lot of eggs at once, choose a large pan to avoid a sudden drop in the temperature of the poaching liquid when the eggs are broken into it. Remove the eggs from their cooking liquid as soon as they are done—about 3 minutes—and immediately dip them into a bowl of cold water to stop them overcooking.

Poaching pans
Special 'poaching' pans with small metal cups to contain the eggs are often used for poaching. These cook the eggs by steam rather than by the immersion that is true poaching.

Serving eggs hot
Poached eggs are ideal for a light lunch or supper dish. Serve them on hot buttered toast or on hot toast spread with a little cream or cottage cheese. You can also serve the eggs on a bed of cooked vegetables such as mushrooms or spinach and coat them with a little warmed cream or a Quick Hollandaise Sauce.

To poach eggs

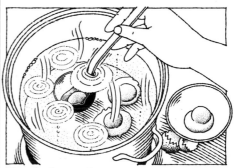

Break the egg into a soup ladle and lower it into the pan.

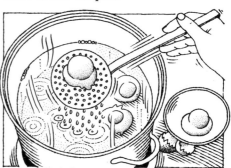

Use a draining spoon to remove the cooked egg from the water.

Poaching fruit

The exact cooking time depends on the fruit being poached and the size of the pieces; peaches and other stone fruit will take less time than firmer-textured apples and pears.

Preparation

Apples and pears

Firm fruit like apples and pears can be cut into wedges or quarters. If you prefer, cut apples into thick slices. Smaller fruits can be poached whole. Choose a pan that holds the fruit comfortably and peel the fruit, leaving on the stems, and poach them in sugar stock until tender. Pears are particularly delicious when poached in a syrup with a cupful of red wine and a stick of cinnamon added. Remember to add 2 or 3 minutes to the cooking time when poaching whole fruit.

Rhubarb

Rhubarb, cut into short lengths, retains its shape perfectly when poached. Add lemon peel or a piece of preserved or root ginger to the poaching liquid. Be careful not to overcook the fruit.

Plums and apricots

Stone fruits such as plums and apricots should be halved so you can remove the stones. If you have a cherry or olive pitter, you can remove the stones from cherries and poach them whole. Prunes need longer cooking to soften their tough skins. Flavour the poaching liquid with lemon peel or a little orange juice.

Skinning peaches

Place the fruit in a pan of boiling water for 15 to 20 seconds—immediately plunge them into cold water then use a small, sharp knife to peel away the skins carefully.

To serve

Home-poached fruit can be stored in the refrigerator to be served with cream or ice cream and perhaps a sprinkling of chopped or flaked toasted nuts. It provides an instant and elegant dessert for family and friends.

Poached Apple Wedges
served with creamy custard.

Poaching Fruit

Poached fruit, sweetened with a little sugar, makes a superbly simple dessert. Poached fruits such as apples or poached dried fruit such as prunes, left unsweetened, make delicious accompaniments to dishes based on meat or game.

Almost any fruit can be poached, so that you can extend your dessert repertoire throughout the year, choosing whatever fruit is plentiful and in season.

Poached fruit is really the home-cooked variety of canned fruit but by doing it yourself, you can have more control over the finished result, adding more—or less—sugar to taste. You can also add a variety of flavourings: liqueurs, spices, wines and spirits to make desserts that are all subtly different.

Once you have learned the technique of poaching fruits, you need never follow a recipe. The method is the same for all fruits and the suggestions given here are simply a guide to help you experiment and create your own special recipes.

It is essential to maintain a gentle simmer when poaching fruit—to stop it becoming mushy.

Poached Apple Wedges

For all fruit, the simplest poaching liquid is water, made into a syrup with sugar. Wine is an optional extra.

Serves 4

Preparation: 5 minutes
Cooking time: 10 minutes

3-4 cooking apples, weighing about 1¼lb (600g) altogether

The poaching liquid:
½ pint (300ml) water
7 fl oz (200ml) white wine
4oz (100g) sugar

Bring the water and wine to the boil in the poaching pan, then stir in the sugar until dissolved.

☐ Peel and core the apples and cut them into even-sized wedges.

☐ Add them to the poaching liquid, reduce the heat to a simmer and poach for about 8 minutes.

☐ Pierce with a small skewer; they should be tender but not too soft.

☐ Remove them from the pan with a slotted spoon; cover and keep hot.

☐ Boil the poaching liquid vigorously until reduced to a thin syrup, then pour over the apples. Serve immediately, or chill and serve cold with custard or cream.

Steaming

This is one of the most simple of cooking methods. Food is cooked not in water, but in the steam created by boiling water. Because the food remains clear of the water's agitation it is an excellent means of cooking delicate food, such as fish. Again because the food is not immersed, there is less leaching out of nutrients, flavour and colour – a distinct advantage for cooking vegetables, in particular. Granular foods such as rice and couscous benefit especially from steaming as the grains remain separate and dry, and the flavour is brought out fully.

Steaming is also an immensely practical cooking method in that more than one tier of ingredients can be handled by one hotplate or burner, giving not only a saving of fuel, but the facility for producing more food in a limited space.

Since food is not in direct contact with the water, steaming is usually a slower method of cooking, and prolonged steaming allows development of good full flavours – as in steamed puddings.

Suitable equipment

There are various types of pans designed for steaming but it is also easy to improvise your own.

Collapsible steaming baskets can be adjusted to stand in any medium-to-large saucepan and there are steamers with perforated bases which can be set one on top of another inside saucepans. Stacking bamboo baskets and other exotic equipment can be bought from specialist kitchen shops for cooking items such as rice, Chinese dumplings and couscous. For cooking fish, elongated pans with trivets are readily available.

In the absence of a steamer, try any of these easy make-do alternatives:

For rice or couscous; cook in a wire sieve or an ordinary colander lined with a piece of muslin. Use foil to cover it if without a suitable lid.

For vegetables: use a sieve, colander, or chip basket, without any muslin. For small vegetables like peas, line with muslin or foil and pierce with a skewer in several places.

For fish: use a deep, covered roasting tin. In the absence of a trivet, use the rack from a meat tin or grill pan, and stand it on empty enamel mugs, or cans, to keep it above the water.

For puddings: use any of suggested 'steamers', or simply boil. Crumple a large piece of foil in the bottom of the pan and set the pudding basin on that.

How to steam

Have on the burner or hot-plate a deep pan containing the required amount of water, or a stock flavoured with herbs and seasonings – which may be used later to make a sauce – at a good, rolling boil. Set the food on its trivet or in its container in the pan. Cover tightly and cook for the stated time. Remember to:

● keep the steamer tightly covered
● keep the water boiling rapidly
● keep the food clear of the water
● make sure the pan doesn't boil dry during long cooking, and top up with boiling water at intervals.

Modified steaming

Some vegetables, such as peas, which cook quickly can be wrapped in a foil parcel and dropped straight into boiling water. This method preserves most of the flavour and nutrients, and more than one vegetable can be cooked in one pan at a time.

Small cutlets or fillets of fish can be placed between two plates, or on a plate covered with foil and set over a pan of boiling water.

Steaming equipment

Collapsible steaming basket; place the closed basket on the bottom of the pan, feet down. Add water to come just up to the bottom of the basket – but not through it. Open the basket out and add the food. Cover the pan tightly to steam.

Tiered Steamers may be oval but are more commonly round. They are usually made of aluminium and designed to fit over standard saucepans.

Each tier can be used to cook a different item, perhaps several, each wrapped in a foil parcel, with potatoes boiling in the water below.

Collapsible steamers adjust to size.

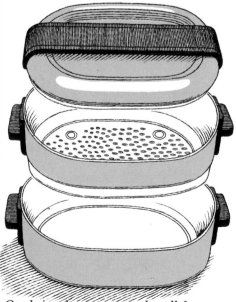

Oval tiered steamers work well for fish.

Brill Fillets with Dill

Substitute Fish Stock for the water, if available. Alternatively, add the fish skins and any bones, cracked, to the steaming water for extra flavour.And 2-3 tablespoons of dry vermouth added with the cooking liquid will enhance the flavour of the dill sauce.

A few stems of cooked asparagus or cooked carrot strips may be used as garnish in place of tomatoes.

To make a tomato rose

Cut at intervals from the top to about two-thirds down, as shown.

Ease cut sections apart to form flower.

Sole Fillets with Herb Butter

Dover sole is renowned for its firm texture and fine flavour but both lemon sole and witch are good cooked this way. Serve it with herb butter, new potatoes and a salad.

Serves 4   ☆☆☆
Preparation: 20 minutes
Cooking: 15 minutes

2lb (1kg) sole fillets, skinned
7 fl oz (200ml) dry white wine
3 fl oz (100ml) dry white vermouth
3 fl oz (100ml) water
a large sprig of parsley
1 celery stick, roughly chopped
1 small bay leaf, crumbled
1 teaspoon sea salt
6 black peppercorns

The herb butter sauce:
5oz (150g) butter, softened
1 tablespoon finely chopped parsley
1 tablespoon finely chopped chives
juice of ½ a lemon
salt and freshly ground black pepper
sprigs of parsley to garnish

Wash the fillets under cold running water and pat dry with kitchen paper. Fold or roll them skinned-side inwards and secure with wooden cocktail sticks.

☐ Put the wine, vermouth, water, parsley, celery, bay leaf, sea salt and peppercorns into a steamer or saucepan. Bring this to the boil, then let it simmer gently for 5 minutes. Place the fish in a steamer basket and set it over the steaming liquid.

☐ Cover the pan tightly and steam for 5-6 minutes or until the fillets are white and opaque. Transfer to a warmed serving dish and keep hot.

☐ Strain the cooking liquid into a saucepan and boil it over high heat until slightly reduced.

☐ Beat together the butter, parsley and chives until well blended, then gradually whisk in 3 fl oz (100ml) of the reduced liquid. Season to taste with lemon juice, salt and pepper.

☐ Remove the cocktail sticks from the fish. Garnish with parsley sprigs and serve with herb butter sauce.

Brill Fillets with Dill

Serve with boiled new potatoes and glazed cucumber sticks or a mixed salad with a mustardy dressing.

Serves 4   ☆☆☆
Preparation: 20 minutes
Cooking: 20 minutes

4 fillets of brill, together about 1¼lb (700g) skinned
7 fl oz (200ml) dry white wine
7 fl oz (200ml) water
1 teaspoon dill seeds
1 teaspoon sea salt
6 black peppercorns
2 egg yolks, size 2
3-4oz (75-125g) unsalted butter, softened
a sprig of fresh dill weed, finely chopped
salt and freshly ground black pepper
4 tomatoes
sprigs of parsley to garnish

Wash the fish under cold running water and pat dry.

☐ Put the wine, water, dill seeds, salt and peppercorns into a steamer. Bring the liquid to the boil, then simmer it gently for 5 minutes.

☐ Fold the fish fillets in half, skinned-side inwards, and secure with cocktail sticks. Place them in a steamer basket and set over the liquid. Cover the pan tightly and steam the fillets for 7-9 minutes, or until the flesh is firm and opaque. Transfer to a warmed serving dish and keep hot.

☐ Strain the cooking liquid into a saucepan and boil briskly until slightly reduced.

☐ Beat together the reduced liquid and the egg yolks in the top part of a double boiler, or a mixing bowl set over some warm water in the steamer or any suitably sized pan.

☐ When slightly thickened, gradually add the butter, beating constantly, until the sauce is smooth, glossy and stiff. Remove from heat, stir in dill and season.

☐ Cut tomato roses as shown. Remove the cocktail sticks from the fish. Garnish with the tomato roses, topped with tiny sprigs of parsley, and serve the sauce separately.

Mackerel with Fennel

The mild aniseed flavour of fennel blends particularly well with the richness of mackerel. Serve with baked potatoes and mangetout peas.

Serves 4
Preparation and cooking: 40 minutes

8 mackerel fillets, together about 1½lb (700g)
7 fl oz (200ml) dry white wine
7 fl oz (200ml) water
1 lemon, sliced
1 teaspoon sea salt
6 black peppercorns

The sauce:
1 fennel bulb
salt and freshly ground black pepper
4 tablespoons double cream
4oz (125g) ice-cold butter, cubed

Rinse the fillets under cold-running water and pat dry.

☐ Put the wine, water, lemon, salt and peppercorns into a steamer. Bring to the boil, then simmer gently for 5 minutes. Put the fish in a steamer basket and set it over the cooking liquid.

☐ Cover the pan tightly and steam the fish for 7-8 minutes or until the flesh is opaque and flakes easily. Remove the steamer from the heat and leave the fish in it to keep hot.

☐ Trim the fennel, reserving the tender fronds. Finely chop the bulb and cook it for 5 minutes in boiling, salted water until just tender.

☐ Purée it in a liquidizer or food processor and return it to the rinsed-out pan with the cream and 2 tablespoons of the cooking liquid. Bring it to the boil.

☐ Gradually whisk in the butter, one piece at a time, removing the pan from the heat for the final addition. Season to taste.

☐ Remove the skin from the fish and arrange on a hot serving dish. Spoon the sauce over, garnish with the fennel fronds and serve.

Variation: Give the fennel sauce an intriguing extra strength by adding 1 or 2 tablespoons of pernod with the cream.

Tuna in Red Butter Sauce

When you are lucky enough to find fresh tuna, try cooking it with this unusual red butter sauce.

Serves 4
Preparation: 15 minutes
Cooking: 30 minutes

4 tuna steaks or fillets, together about 1½lb (700g)
14 fl oz (400ml) water
6 bay leaves, crumbled
1 lemon, sliced
1 teaspoon sea salt
12 black peppercorns

The sauce:
2 tomatoes, skinned
1 teaspoon tomato purée
a pinch of dried thyme
2 tablespoons red wine
5oz (150g) unsalted butter
a squeeze of lemon juice
salt and freshly ground black pepper

Rinse the fish under cold running water and pat dry.

☐ Put the water, bay leaves, lemon, salt and peppercorns into a steamer. Bring it to the boil, then let it simmer for 5 minutes.

☐ Place the fish in a steamer basket and set it over the cooking liquid. Cover the pan tightly and steam the fish for about 12 minutes or until the fish is opaque and flakes easily. Remove the pan from the heat and leave the fish in it to keep hot.

☐ Halve the tomatoes, scoop out the seeds and squeeze out the juice. Chop the flesh and put it into a small saucepan with the tomato purée, thyme, and wine. Bring to the boil then simmer for 5 minutes, stirring constantly.

☐ Purée the tomatoes and liquid in a liquidizer or food processor. Beat the butter until it is soft then gradually mix in the tomatoes.

☐ In a small saucepan, heat the sauce until hot, but not boiling, and season to taste with lemon juice, salt and pepper. Arrange the tuna on a warmed serving dish and serve the sauce separately.

Try using slices or wedges of orange, instead of lemon, as a garnish for fish. Not only does it make an interesting change and look more exciting, but the flavour of the juice goes well with most sauces – particularly those containing peppers or tomatoes.

Enriching sauces with butter

Add the butter to the sauce a piece at a time and beat to incorporate.

Tuna in Red Butter Sauce
Red vermouth in place of the wine gives an interesting spicy flavour.
This recipe works equally well with salmon or salmon trout.

Cod with Fennel and Seafish Sticks

Be very careful with the cooking time, as over-cooking cod makes it break up. Seafish sticks are an attractive and economical garnish. However, for a touch of luxury, use shellfish such as shrimp, prawns, or crab.

For an even quicker and easier dressing for the dish use a flavoured butter. Try making the classic French 'beurre maître d'hôtel' by beating 1 tablespoon of chopped parsley, the juice of $\frac{1}{2}$ a lemon and salt and pepper into 2oz (50g) butter.

Cod with Fennel and Seafish Sticks.

Cod with Fennel and Seafish Sticks

Enhance the flavour of cod by serving it on a bed of fennel, covered in rich sauce. Accompany with a creamy potato and celeriac purée and a tomato salad.

Serves 4 ☆☆☆
Preparation: 15 minutes
Cooking: 20 minutes

---

4 cod fillets, together about 1¼lb (575g)
3 small fennel bulbs, together about 1lb (500g)
7 fl oz (200ml) dry white wine
7 fl oz (200ml) Fish Stock
1 teaspoon sea salt
6 black peppercorns
4oz (100g) seafish sticks, sliced

The Quick 'Hollandaise' sauce:
3oz (75g) butter, softened
1 egg
1 egg yolk
1 teaspoon lemon juice
salt and freshly ground black pepper
1 teaspoon finely chopped fennel

Rinse the fillets under cold running water and pat dry with kitchen paper.

☐ Trim the fennel, reserving the tender fronds. Cut off and discard the base of each bulb then thinly slice the fennel.

☐ Put the fennel, wine, stock, salt and peppercorns into a steamer. Cover and simmer for about 5 minutes or until the sliced fennel is just tender, then remove it with a slotted spoon and keep hot.

☐ Put the cod and the seafish sticks into a steamer basket and set over the cooking liquid. Cover the pan tightly and steam for 5-7 minutes, or until the cod is opaque and firm.

☐ Remove any skin and arrange the fish over the fennel. Garnish the cod fillets with the seafish sticks as shown.

☐ Meanwhile, make a Quick 'Hollandaise' with the sauce ingredients, stirring in the finely chopped fennel at the end. Spoon the sauce over the fish and serve immediately.

Whiting with Quick Tomato Sauce

Serve with steamed new potatoes and broccoli.

Serves 4
Preparation: 15 minutes
Cooking: 15 minutes

4 whiting, together about 1½lb (700g), cleaned
6 bay leaves, crumbled
1 onion, chopped
1 teaspoon sea salt
6 black peppercorns

The sauce:
2 tablespoons flour
¼ pint (150ml) milk
about ¼ pint (150ml) tomato juice
salt and freshly ground black pepper
1oz (25g) butter
lemon or orange wedges, to garnish

Rinse the fish under cold running water and pat dry with kitchen paper.
☐ Put the bay leaves, onion, salt and peppercorns into a steamer in about 1 inch (2cm) of water.

☐ Bring it to the boil, then let it simmer gently, covered, for 5 minutes.
☐ Put the fish in a steamer basket and set it over the water. Cover the pan tightly and steam the fish for 5-7 minutes, until the flesh is opaque but firm.
☐ Meanwhile, make the sauce. Mix the flour to a smooth paste with a little of the cold milk. Heat the remaining milk in a saucepan, then stir a little into the flour 'paste'.
☐ Return it to the pan and cook gently, stirring constantly, until it has thickened. Gradually whisk in the tomato juice, until the sauce is thick enough to coat the back of a spoon. Whisk in butter.
☐ Season to taste, then serve the whiting with the sauce and a garnish of lemon or orange.

Whiting with Quick Tomato Sauce
Whiting also breaks apart as cod does, even if only slightly over-cooked, so watch it very carefully.
Add about ½ teaspoon paprika to the sauce to give it extra piquancy.

Fish cooked on the bone is often more juicy and flavoursome than filleted fish.

Carefully place the whiting on a little of the Quick Tomato Sauce for a more professional look.

Scallops will open more easily if first warmed through gently in a very low oven, rounded shell down.
Keep the rounded side of the shell and use, well scrubbed, for an individual serving.

Preparing scallops

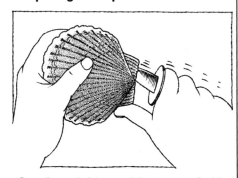

Cut through hinge with a strong knife.

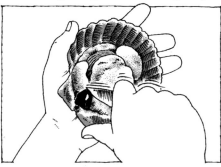

Remove membrane and black intestine.

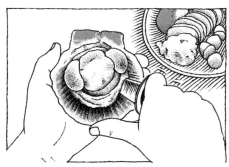

Prise scallop out of the shell.

Scallops in White Wine

Serve with Duchesse potatoes and crisp French beans.

Serves 4 ☆☆☆
Preparation: 35 minutes
Cooking: about 10 minutes

---

2 leeks, trimmed and washed
7 fl oz (200ml) Fish Stock
¼ pint (150ml) dry white wine
6 parsley stalks, roughly chopped
8 large scallops with their corals
salt and freshly ground white pepper
2oz (50g) butter
2 egg yolks
6 tablespoons double cream
chopped parsley to garnish

Chop the green part of the leeks roughly and put in the base of a steamer. Slice the white part of the leeks and set aside.

☐ Add the stock, wine and parsley to the pan. Bring to the boil and simmer while preparing the scallops.

☐ Wash the scallops. Pull off and discard any membrane and the black intestinal line. Slice the white part horizontally into three and prick the coral with a fork, to prevent its bursting during cooking.

☐ Place the sliced scallops with their corals into the steamer basket, set in place over the liquid and cover the pan tightly. Steam for 3-4 minutes, taking care to avoid overcooking. Remove the steaming basket as soon as the scallops and their corals become opaque.

☐ Put the reserved leeks into a saucepan and strain the cooking liquid over them. Add a little seasoning and the butter. Simmer over a gentle heat for 3-4 minutes until the leeks are just tender. Strain them off with a perforated spoon and place on a warmed serving dish. Arrange the scallops and corals on top and keep warm.

☐ Boil the cooking liquid over a vigorous heat to reduce it by about half. Meanwhile whisk the egg yolks and cream together in a small basin.

Stir in a little of the reduced liquid. Return to the saucepan, off the heat, and stir until the egg has cooked and the sauce thickened.

☐ Adjust the seasoning and pour over the scallops. Garnish with chopped parsley and serve.

Scallops with Peppercorn Sauce

Serve on a bed of lightly braised, finely shredded lettuce as an impressive dinner-party starter.

Serves 4 ☆
Preparation and cooking: 25 minutes

---

8 large scallops with their corals
7 fl oz (200ml) Fish Stock or water
¼ pint (150ml) dry white wine
½ a lemon, sliced
6 black peppercorns
1 tablespoon finely chopped tarragon
a sprig of fresh tarragon, to garnish
2 tomatoes, skinned, deseeded and finely diced, to garnish

The Six-minute Sauce:
2 tablespoons flour or cornflour
1oz (25g) butter
2 teaspoons green or pink peppercorns
grated rind and juice of ½ a lemon
salt and freshly ground white pepper

Prepare and cook the scallops as for Scallops in White Wine, putting the stock, wine, lemon slices and peppercorns in the base of the steamer.

☐ Transfer the scallops to a serving dish and keep hot while making a Six-minute Sauce, using the strained steaming liquid in place of the stock and adding the peppercorns, lemon rind and juice and salt and pepper to taste.

☐ Pour the sauce over the scallops, garnish with the tarragon and chopped tomato, and serve.

Tip: Green peppercorns are unripe versions of black peppercorns, while pink peppercorns are actually small berries of a different family and much milder in flavour. Both are sold pickled in brine or vinegar. Drain well before use.

Lobster with Butter Sauce

Serves 4 ☆☆☆
Preparation and cooking: 35 minutes

2 bunches of fresh dill, roughly chopped,
    or 2 teaspoons dill seeds
1 lemon, sliced
1 teaspoon sea salt
6 black peppercorns
2 fresh lobsters, each about 2lb (1kg)

The Old-fashioned Butter Sauce:
5oz (150g) chilled butter
3 tablespoons flour
salt and freshly ground white pepper
lemon wedges and dill to garnish

In a steamer put about 1 inch (2cm) water. Add the dill, lemon, salt and peppercorns. Bring to the boil and simmer for 5 minutes.

☐ Put the lobsters in a steaming basket and set over liquid. Cover tightly and steam for 18-20 minutes. The shell should be bright red when fully cooked. To check, twist off a little leg close to the body and break open. The flesh should be opaque and easy to detach.

☐ Remove lobsters from pan. Break off claws and crack them. Cut each lobster in half down the back, discard intestinal sacs and stomachs and keep lobsters hot.

☐ Make Old-fashioned Butter Sauce using the steaming liquid. Serve in a sauceboat and garnish lobsters with lemon and dill.

Lobster with Butter Sauce
For thorough and even cooking arrange the lobsters only one layer deep.
Hollandaise and other butter emulsion sauces also go well with steamed lobster.
Crayfish, crab, and king prawns can be steamed in the same way as lobster.
Allow   6-7 minutes for king prawns
        10-12 minutes for crab
        15-20 minutes for crayfish

Buying lobster
Try to buy lobster live on the day you intend to cook them. Ask the fishmonger to kill them for you quickly and humanely.

Lobster with Butter Sauce makes a magnificent dish for a special occasion, accompanied, quite simply, by boiled rice and a green salad.

Sweetbreads in Lettuce with Quick 'Hollandaise' Sauce

Serve with steamed rice and fresh garden peas.

Serves 4 ☆☆☆
Preparation: 30 minutes plus soaking
Cooking: about 30 minutes

2 pairs of calves' sweetbreads, together about 1lb (500g)
1 large crinkly-leaved lettuce
salt and freshly ground black pepper
¾ pint (450ml) dry white wine
7 fl oz (200ml) water
12 parsley sprigs, roughly chopped
1 canned truffle, thinly sliced, to garnish, (optional)

The Quick 'Hollandaise' Sauce:
2 egg yolks
1 egg
3½oz (100g) unsalted butter, softened
juice of ½ a lemon
salt and freshly ground black pepper

Soak the sweetbreads for at least 1 hour in several changes of lightly salted water until the water is clear.
☐ Rinse and put in a pan with water to cover and bring to the boil. Boil for 1-2 minutes then drain and rinse again under cold running water. Pat dry with kitchen paper.
☐ Trim off all traces of fat and gristle.
☐ Wash the lettuce and blanch 10 of the largest leaves for no more than 20 seconds in boiling water. Plunge them immediately into cold water, drain and pat dry with kitchen paper.
☐ Rub the sweetbreads with a little salt and freshly ground pepper. Wrap them in the lettuce leaves and then in pieces of muslin and secure with fine string.
☐ Bring the wine and water to the boil in the base of a steamer, add the parsley sprigs and 1 teaspoon of salt.
☐ Place the wrapped sweetbreads in a steaming basket, set over the liquid, cover the pan tightly and steam for 25-30 minutes.
☐ Remove the sweetbreads from the pan and unwrap them carefully. Slice thickly and arrange on warm individual plates and keep hot.
☐ Make a Quick 'Hollandaise' Sauce, using 4 tablespoons of the steaming liquid in place of the wine. Spoon some of the sauce around the sliced sweetbreads and serve the rest separately. Garnish each slice of sweetbread with a wafer thin slice of truffle, if using, and serve.

Bacon Roll with Cranberry Sauce

Serves 4 ☆☆
Preparation: 10 minutes
Cooking: 50 minutes

1 pint (600ml) water
a sprig of parsley
2 bay leaves
8 black peppercorns
1 onion, stuck with 4 cloves
1 celery stick, sliced
1 carrot, sliced
1lb (500g) joint of bacon for boiling

The sauce:
2 tablespoons cornflour
1 tablespoon cold water
3oz (75g) cranberry jelly
salt and freshly ground black pepper

Put the water, herbs and vegetables into the base of a steamer and bring to the boil.
☐ Put the bacon in a steaming basket and set over the liquid. Cover the pan tightly and steam for 45 minutes, or until the meat feels tender right through when pierced.
☐ Remove the cooked bacon and keep hot while you make the sauce.
☐ Strain off the cooking liquid and bring it to the boil in a saucepan. Mix the cornflour with the cold water until smooth, then stir in a little of the hot liquid. Return this to the pan and cook over a moderate heat, stirring constantly, for 2-3 minutes until thickened.
☐ Add the jelly and stir until melted and heated through. Season to taste. Slice the bacon thickly and serve the sauce separately.

Sweetbreads in Lettuce with Quick 'Hollandaise' Sauce
Lambs' sweetbreads can be prepared in the same way. Pack 2 or 3 sweetbreads in 1 lettuce leaf and tie up together. The sweetbreads can also be wrapped in endive, spinach or sorrel leaves. You can garnish with chives or mushroom caps or slices if not using the truffle.

Preparing the sweetbreads

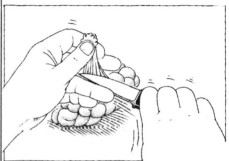

Trim all membrane, fat and gristle from the blanched sweetbreads.

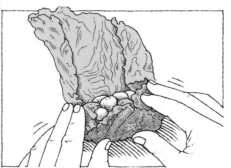

Roll each in a well-dried blanched lettuce leaf.

Wrap this in a piece of muslin and secure in place with fine string.

Guinea Fowl with Parma Ham

It is important to put the joints into the basket in a single layer to ensure even cooking. When the bird is fully cooked, the breast flesh at the ends of the parcels will be seen to be white and opaque. Check the leg pieces by slashing through on the underside along the bone: the flesh should be opaque but more like the dark meat of chicken.

With large guinea fowl, the breasts can be removed as one piece. With the more usual size of about 2lb (1kg), they come off separately as 2 fillets.

To prepare the guinea fowl portions

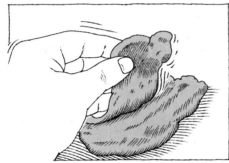

Separate the fillets, if necessary.

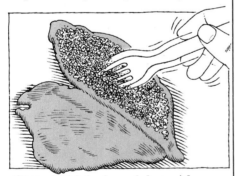

Spread with herbs and dust with pepper.

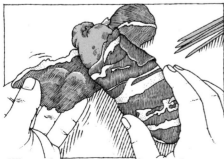

Wrap closely in Parma ham and secure.

Guinea Fowl with Parma Ham

Serve with potato and celeriac purée and crisp steamed French beans.

Serves 4   ☆☆☆
Preparation: 20 minutes
Cooking: about 45 minutes

---

1 guinea fowl, about 2lb (1kg)
2 tablespoons finely chopped parsley
1 tablespoon finely chopped celery
1 tablespoon chopped fresh thyme or
    1 teaspoon dried thyme
salt and freshly ground black pepper
4 large slices Parma ham
1 pint (600ml) Chicken Stock
¼ pint (150ml) dry white wine
6oz (175g) unsalted butter, softened
tomatoes and parsley for garnish

Cut away from the bird the breast fillets and the legs with their thighs attached.

☐ Spread one side of each piece with the herbs and sprinkle well with pepper. Carefully wrap each

Guinea Fowl with Parma Ham, garnished with tomato roses and parsley, makes an attractive and filling party dish.

piece with a slice of ham and secure with wooden cocktail sticks. Place the leg joints in a steaming basket.

☐ Put the stock and wine into the base of a steamer and bring them to the boil. Set the basket in place over the liquid and cover tightly.

☐ Steam for 10 minutes. Remove lid, add the breast pieces, cover again and steam for a further 20-25 minutes. Transfer to a serving dish, remove the cocktail sticks and keep hot.

☐ If necessary, boil the remaining stock vigorously to reduce to about 4 fl oz (125ml). Pour this into a basin and gradually whisk in the butter, about 1 rounded teaspoonful at a time. Season to taste and pour into a warm sauceboat.

☐ Garnish the guinea fowl rolls with tomato flowers and parsley.

Poussins with Sherry Sauce

Serve with buttery potato and parsnip purée and steamed courgettes.

Serves 4   ☆☆☆
Preparation: 10 minutes
Cooking: about 40 minutes

4 medium leeks, trimmed
18 fl oz (500ml) Chicken Stock
¼ pint (150ml) dry sherry
2 celery sticks, chopped
6 parsley sprigs, roughly chopped
1 bay leaf
2 cloves
4 oven-ready poussins, each about 12oz (350g)
8 shallots or pickling onions
2oz (50g) cold butter, cubed
salt and freshly ground black pepper

Wash the leeks and slice the green tops. Put tops in the base of a steamer with the stock, sherry, celery, parsley, bay and cloves and bring to the boil.

☐ Wipe the poussins inside and out with kitchen paper. Peel the shallots and place 2 inside each poussin. Place the birds in a steaming basket, or on a trivet, and set in place over the liquid.

☐ Cover tightly and steam for 20-25 minutes until the juices from the poussins run clear when pierced with a skewer. Transfer to a serving dish and keep hot while you make the sherry sauce.

☐ Strain the stock into a saucepan. Slice the white part of the leeks and add this to the stock. Bring to the boil, cover and simmer gently for 3-4 minutes or until tender. Remove leeks with draining spoon and arrange on serving dish around poussins.

☐ Boil the remaining stock vigorously until reduced to about ¼ pint (150ml). Add the butter one piece at a time, whisking each into the stock. Remove from the heat for the final addition. Adjust the seasoning to taste, spoon a little sauce over each poussin and serve the rest separately.

Chicken Livers in Wine

Serve with buttered rice and a green salad for a simple supper. Alternatively, these make an impressive starter, served on individual fried bread croûtes.

Serves 4   ☆☆
Preparation: 10 minutes, plus soaking
Cooking: about 25 minutes

1lb (500g) chicken livers
about ½ pint (300ml) milk
1½ teaspoons dried thyme
1½ teaspoons dried basil
salt and freshly ground black pepper
9 fl oz (250ml) Chicken Stock
8 fl oz (225ml) red wine
1oz (25g) flour
1oz (25g) butter
2 tablespoons single cream

Wash the livers and cut them in half or into bite-sized pieces. Soak them in the milk for about 1 hour then drain them and pat dry.

☐ Dust the livers well with the herbs and black pepper and place in a single layer in steaming basket.

☐ Put the stock and all but 4 tablespoons of the wine in the base of a steamer and bring to the boil. Set the livers over the liquid and cover the pan tightly. Steam for 5-8 minutes.

☐ Transfer to a serving dish and set aside to keep hot.

☐ Boil the steaming liquid rapidly for about 5 minutes until reduced to about ½ pint (300ml).

☐ Make a Brown Roux with the flour and butter in a saucepan then gradually add the reduced stock. Cook, stirring constantly, until the sauce is thick and smooth. Cook for a further 3 minutes then stir in the cream and seasoning to taste.

☐ Add a little of the reserved wine to adjust the consistency, if necessary. Spoon the sauce over the livers and serve immediately.

Tip: Add 1-2 tablespoons of brandy to the sauce for extra richness.

Poussins with Sherry Sauce
The little onions make a nice flavour and texture surprise as well as contributing to the taste of the poussin itself.

In summer, use spring onions in place of leeks.

Steamed pigeons
Pigeons are very good prepared in the same way, but need to be steamed for about 45 minutes.

Chicken Livers in Wine
If you have used a large pan for steaming, the liquid will perhaps not need to be reduced much further.
Cooking time for the livers will depend on taste: at 5 minutes they will still be soft and a little moist; by 8 minutes they will be dry and set.

Steamed Couscous

Couscous is actually coarse semolina. In North Africa, where it is prepared in many different ways, it is cooked in a 'couscoussière'. The lower part is a large stewing pot in which the meat is placed. The couscous is then put into the perforated upper section, so the whole meal cooks at one time.

A lot of the couscous available now is partly pre-cooked. The instructions given here are for this type of couscous.

Steamed Rice

Steaming rice for the last part of the cooking makes it light and fluffy. The grains remain separate but tender. Steamed rice can be served hot, but is also excellent cold in salads because it does not congeal into a sticky mass. Specially designed rice steamers are available in shops trading in Oriental goods. Instead of a rice steamer you can use a large saucepan with a metal colander or sieve, covered with foil.

Serves 4 ◯
Preparation and cooking: about 20 minutes

6oz (175g) long-grain rice
1 teaspoon salt

Put the rice and salt into a large pan of boiling water. Place the lid on the pan and simmer for 8 minutes. Drain.

☐ Turn the rice into a colander or steamer basket. Set over a pan of boiling water and cover tightly.

☐ Steam for 12 minutes or until tender.

Tip: For extra flavour, try adding chopped fresh parsley or some sliced onion and a teaspoonful or two of ground turmeric to the steaming water.

● The same method works very well for both brown rice and cracked wheat which should be steamed for about 45-50 minutes and 20-25 minutes respectively.

Steamed Couscous

This classic Berber dish is normally a part of a lamb and pepper stew. Serve as an accompaniment to any meaty casserole.

Serves 4 ☆
Preparation: 10 minutes
Cooking: 20 minutes

8oz (225g) couscous
½ pint (300ml) Meat or Chicken Stock
1oz (25g) butter

Mix the couscous and the stock and leave for 10 minutes until the couscous is soft and moist.

☐ Line a colander or steaming basket with a piece of dampened muslin. Fill with the soaked couscous.

☐ Set over a pan of boiling water, cover tightly and steam for 20 minutes.

☐ Turn into a warmed serving dish, stir in the butter and serve.

Tip: Make couscous into an interesting snack or supper dish on its own by making a spicy sauce with a little of the cooking stock mixed with some tomato purée, a little cumin, ground coriander and chilli powder to taste.

Couscous being set to steam in a classically styled couscoussière.

Steamed Chicory

Serve to accompany roast chicken or veal dishes, or with mashed potatoes and a good cheese sauce for supper.

Serves 4 ○
Preparation: 5 minutes
Cooking: about 5 minutes

---

8 heads of chicory, weighing about 2lb (1kg)
½ pint (300ml) Chicken Stock or water
chopped chives to garnish (optional)

Remove any blemished outside leaves and hollow out the centre core from the base of chicory. Place in a steaming basket.

☐ Set over a pan of boiling stock or water and cover tightly. Steam for about 5 minutes until tender. Garnish with the chives, if using, and serve.

Cucumbers Stuffed with Peas

These make an excellent accompaniment to fine fish dishes.

Serves 4 ☆
Preparation: 10 minutes
Cooking: about 10 minutes

---

1 cucumber, weighing about 1lb (500g)
8oz (225g) frozen peas
a sprig of fresh mint
salt and freshly ground black pepper
2 tablespoons double cream
1 tablespoon chopped parsley

Trim the ends from the cucumber, then peel it thinly. Cut into 4 equal lengths then cut each piece in half lengthways. Scoop out the seeds with a pointed spoon or sharp knife and discard.

☐ Place in a single layer in a steaming basket. Set over a pan of boiling water, cover tightly and steam for 7 minutes. Remove from the basket and keep warm.

☐ Meanwhile, cook the peas with the mint in boiling salted water for about 4 minutes, or until tender.

☐ Drain, remove the mint and

purée the peas in a liquidizer or processor. Mix in the cream and season to taste.

☐ Spread the purée in the cooked cucumber, sprinkle with parsley and serve immediately.
Variation: Steamed cucumber can be stuffed with several other purées to great effect. Try substituting any of the following:
watercress and celery; spinach with a dash of nutmeg; carrot and fresh dill.

Asparagus with Cream and Butter Sauce

Serve on its own as a splendid first course, or to accompany roast poultry and grilled fish.

Serves 4 ☆☆☆
Preparation: 5 minutes
Cooking: about 30 minutes

1¼lb (700g) asparagus
16 fl oz (450ml) Chicken Stock
¼ pint (150ml) double cream
3oz (75g) ice-cold unsalted butter
salt and freshly ground black pepper

Wash the asparagus and trim off the woody stem bases.

☐ Lay the prepared asparagus flat on the bottom of a steaming basket. Put the stock in the base of a steamer and bring it to the boil.

☐ Set the basket in place over the liquid, cover tightly and steam for 12-15 minutes, until tender when tested with a fork. Transfer the asparagus to a serving plate and keep hot.

☐ Boil the stock in the pan vigorously to reduce to about ¼ pint (150ml). Stir in the cream and boil again for about 5 minutes to reduce by about a half.

☐ Cut the butter into 4 pieces and beat these into the sauce one at a time using a wooden spoon, removing the sauce from the heat for the final addition and beating in process.

☐ Adjust seasoning, pour the sauce over the asparagus and serve immediately.

Cucumbers Stuffed with Peas
Try fresh dill instead of mint for a more subtle flavour.

If you have a proper asparagus steamer, stand the stems with their heads up in the basket. Steam in the same way then make the sauce in the base of the pan.

Chicken-stuffed Peppers in Cream Sauce

The recipe can easily be adjusted in quantity, allowing one pepper per person and the appropriate proportions of the other ingredients. If serving fewer people, use an appropriately sized pan for steaming, so the liquid is deep enough and not spread too thinly.

Different coloured peppers make Chicken-stuffed Peppers in Cream Sauce into a spectacular buffet dish.

Chicken-stuffed Peppers in Cream Sauce

Serve as a first course for a special family supper or with noodles and a salad as a main course.

Serves 8   ☆ ☆ ☆
Preparation: 20 minutes
Cooking: about 25 minutes

---

8 large peppers
4oz (125g) long-grain rice, cooked
1lb (500g) cooked chicken meat, chopped
4 large spring onions, chopped
4 eggs
4 fl oz (125ml) single cream
salt and freshly ground black pepper
1¾ pints (1 litre) Chicken Stock
½ pint (300ml) double cream
7oz (200g) ice-cold butter

Cut a thin slice from the top of each pepper. Remove and discard the stems from these slices, chop rest of top and add to the rice.

☐ Add the chicken, onion, eggs, and single cream to the rice and season generously. Stir well to combine all the ingredients thoroughly.

☐ Remove all the seeds and pith from the peppers and pack each full with the rice mixture. Stand upright in a steaming basket.

☐ Put the stock in the base of a steamer and bring to the boil. Set the basket over and cover the pan tightly.

☐ Steam for about 15-20 minutes until the peppers are tender. Remove the peppers and keep hot while you make the sauce.

☐ Boil the stock vigorously for about 10 minutes until reduced to about 9 fl oz (250ml). Add the cream and boil again to reduce by about half.

☐ Cut the butter into 8 pieces. Using a wooden spoon, gradually beat the butter into the sauce one piece at a time. Remove from the heat for the final addition.

☐ Pour over the peppers and serve immediately.

Tip: This dish is a very good way of using up leftover cooked rice and chicken. Other leftovers work equally well: try cooked ham, beef or Continental sausage.

Variation: The stuffed peppers are just as good cold. Let the reduced stock cool and then mix with ½ pint (300ml) mayonnaise, instead of cream and butter, and some lemon juice for a perfect dressing.

Steamed Sweetcorn

This method brings out the best of the sweet juicy flavour of young fresh corn-on-the-cob.

Serves 4 ☆☆
Preparation: 5 minutes
Cooking: about 10 minutes

4 large sweetcorn cobs
¼ pint (150ml) water or Chicken Stock
2oz (50g) cold butter, cubed
salt and freshly ground black pepper

Pull away and discard the covering leaves and 'silk' tassel from the corn.

☐ Place the cobs in a single layer in a steaming basket. Set over a pan of the boiling water or stock and cover tightly.

☐ Steam for 6-7 minutes until the kernels become opaque but still release juices when pierced with a fork.

☐ Remove the corn and keep hot. Boil the cooking juices rapidly until reduced to about 4 tablespoons. Gradually beat in the butter one piece at a time, until thick and smooth.

☐ Season to taste, pour over the corn and serve.

Steamed Artichokes

Serves 4 ☆☆
Preparation and cooking: 35 minutes

4 globe artichokes, trimmed
2 onions, sliced
juice and pared rind of ½ a lemon
½ pint (300ml) Chicken Stock or water
salt and freshly ground black pepper
2oz (50g) cold butter, cubed

Cook the artichokes as for Steamed Sweetcorn, adding the onion and lemon to the stock. Steam for 20-30 minutes until outer leaves pull away.

☐ Make a butter sauce in the same way, using the reduced strained cooking liquid, and serve separately.

Corn on the cob is very tender and juicy when steamed. Take care not to over-cook, otherwise it quickly becomes tough, dry and mealy.

Steamed Artichokes
These lend themselves well to stuffing. Scoop out the hearts and the hairy choke. Discard the choke and either cook the hearts separately or use as part of the stuffing mixture. Try any of the following chopped-up combinations:
rice, Parmesan cheese and parsley;
breadcrumbs, anchovies and garlic;
spinach, mushroom and cooked bacon.

Coffee and Walnut Marbled Pudding

To cook in a microwave oven, make a mixture using only 4oz (100g) each of butter, sugar and flour and 2 eggs. Reduce the walnuts slightly and add an extra 1 tablespoon of milk or water. Put in a 2 pint (1.2 litre) well-greased plastic or ceramic pudding basin, and cover loosely with cling film. Cook on high for 4 minutes. Uncover carefully and let stand for 5 minutes before serving.

Lining a pudding basin

To leave space for suet crust pastry to rise, make a pleat across the centre of the top before folding foil round basin.

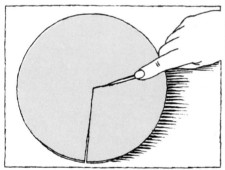

Cut a quarter from the pastry circle and reserve this for the top.

Press the cut edges together firmly.

Steak and Oyster Pudding

Serves 6
Preparation: 40 minutes
Cooking: 5 hours

The suet crust pastry:
12oz (350g) self-raising flour
½ teaspoon salt
5oz (150g) shredded suet
about 10 tablespoons cold water

The filling:
1¾lb (750g) topside of beef
4oz (100g) canned smoked oysters
2oz (50g) plain flour
a pinch of grated nutmeg
salt and freshly ground black pepper
3 tablespoons finely chopped parsley
4oz (100g) mushrooms, coarsely chopped
1 onion, coarsely chopped

Mix together the flour, salt and suet, and add enough water to make a dough. Knead lightly until the pastry is smooth, then roll out a circle about 14in (35cm) across.

☐ With a sharp knife pointed towards the centre, cut out quarter of the circle and reserve for the lid. Grease the inside of a 2 pint (1.2 litre) pudding basin, roll the pastry around the hand into a cone and fit neatly in basin. Press edges to seal.

☐ Cut the meat into 1in (2.5cm) cubes and put in a bowl. Rinse the oysters in cold water, drain well and add to the meat. Sieve the plain flour, nutmeg, salt and pepper over the meat and toss together. Stir in the parsley, mushrooms and onion.

☐ Half-fill the base of the steamer with water and bring to the boil.

☐ Fill the pastry-lined basin with the meat mixture. Roll out the reserved pastry to a circle the diameter of the basin and place it over the filling. Dampen the edges then roll the edge of the lining pastry up over lid and seal.

☐ Completely wrap the basin with foil, leaving space at top for pastry to rise. Steam for 5 hours, topping up with boiling water as necessary.

☐ Serve in the traditional way, with a napkin tucked around the basin.

Coffee and Walnut Marbled Pudding

Serves 6-8
Preparation: 15 minutes
Cooking: 1½-2 hours

6oz (175g) butter, at room temperature
6oz (175g) caster sugar
3 eggs, lightly beaten
6oz (175g) self-raising flour
a little milk
1oz (25g) walnuts, finely chopped
2 teaspoons instant coffee powder or granules
½ teaspoon vanilla essence

Half-fill the base of the steamer with water and put to boil. Butter a 1½ pint (900ml) pudding basin.

☐ Cream together the butter and sugar until light and fluffy.

☐ Add the eggs, a little at a time, beating well after each addition. Carefully fold in the flour, with a little milk, if necessary, until of a soft dropping consistency.

☐ Divide the mixture between two mixing bowls. Dissolve the coffee in 1 tablespoon of hot water and stir it into one bowl with the walnuts. Stir the vanilla into the other.

☐ Put alternate tablespoons of the two mixtures into the prepared basin. Cover tightly with foil and steam for 1½-2 hours. Serve with Butterscotch Sauce.

Rich Fig Pudding with Orange Mousseline Sauce

Serves 6-8
Preparation: 10 minutes
Cooking: 1½-2 hours

5oz (150g) self-raising flour
a pinch of salt
1oz (25g) ground almonds
3oz (75g) shredded suet
2oz (50g) muscovado sugar
4oz (125g) chopped dried figs
grated rind of 1 orange
2 eggs, lightly beaten
2 tablespoons milk

The sauce:
1 egg
1 egg yolk
3 tablespoons sugar
1 tablespoon orange juice
1 tablespoon orange liqueur
4 tablespoons cream

Half-fill the base of the steamer and put to boil. (If no steamer is available, boil enough water in a large pan to come halfway up basin.) Butter a 1½ pint (900ml) basin.

☐ Mix together the flour, salt, almonds, suet, sugar, figs and orange rind. Make a well in the centre and stir in the eggs and enough milk to produce a soft dropping consistency.

☐ Turn the mixture into the prepared basin and cover it tightly with foil, tied on with string. Steam for 1½-2 hours.

☐ About 10 minutes before serving, put all the sauce ingredients in a bowl over a pan of boiling water and whisk until mixture is thick and foamy. Serve immediately.

Almond Castle Puddings with Red Fruit Sauce

Serves 8   ☆☆
Preparation and cooking: 55 minutes

4oz (125g) self-raising flour
2oz (50g) fresh white breadcrumbs
2oz (50g) ground almonds
4oz (125g) butter
4oz (125g) caster sugar
2 eggs, lightly beaten
a few drops of almond essence
a little milk

The sauce:
1lb (500g) red fruit, such as raspberries or
    stoned dark cherries
¼ pint (300ml) red wine
4oz (125g) sugar
1 tablespoon redcurrant jelly
2 teaspoons arrowroot

Half-fill the base of steamer with water and boil. Butter 8 dariole moulds.

Rich Fig Pudding with Orange Mousseline Sauce and Almond Castle Puddings with Red Fruit Sauce.

☐ Mix together the flour, breadcrumbs and ground almonds.

☐ Cream the butter and sugar until pale and fluffy. Beat in the eggs gradually, with the almond essence.

☐ Fold in the flour mixture with just enough milk to give a soft dropping consistency.

☐ Spoon into the prepared moulds, cover tightly with foil and secure. Steam for 30-40 minutes.

☐ For the sauce, put the fruit, red wine, sugar and redcurrant jelly in a pan. Bring to the boil, reduce the heat and simmer very gently for 10 minutes. Blend the arrowroot with a little cold water and stir into the sauce, return to the boil and cook until thickened and clear. Serve hot, spooned over puddings.

COOKING IN HOT FAT OR OIL

Deep-frying • Shallow-frying
Sautéing • Stir-frying
Table-top cooking

Deep-frying

Deep-frying involves the total immersion of food in oil heated to a high temperature. The heat is imparted to the food more rapidly and uniformly than by any other cooking method.

Such a speedy process suits some foods better than others, fish for example, being fine for deep-frying as the flesh cooks in minutes, keeps its natural juices and texture – and makes a good contrast with the crisp outer coating. The exact temperature of the cooking medium is critical: too high a temperature and the outside of the food browns without the inside being cooked; too low and the food absorbs too much grease before it is cooked.

Foods that would not cook thoroughly at such speeds, such as poultry, need to be divided into bite-sized pieces or par-cooked first.

Most foods require some sort of protection from the high heat of the oil, or the outside of the food will burn. Batters and egg-and-crumb coatings are the most usual – the former for more moist food so that the moisture is sealed in and does not cause too much foaming on contact with the oil. Such coatings also help seal in flavour to prevent it leaking out into the oil and tainting it.

Most vegetables deep-fry very well and require no protection; French fried potatoes and potato crisps are good examples.

Deep-frying has an undeservedly commonplace association with greasy chips and smoke-filled kitchens, but care and imagination make it as simple and clean as any other method. Few processes can produce foods as delightful as, say, Chicken Kiev or cheese fritters, with their crunchy shells and melting liquid interiors.

Success with deep-frying

● Dry food as much as possible with kitchen paper to minimize foaming.
● Coat food thoroughly and pat crumbs on firmly, allowing any excess to drip or fall off. Slide batter-coated food immediately and carefully into the oil. Put crumb-coated food in a basket and then lower this into the oil.
● Always check that the oil is at the correct temperature before adding food to the pan.
● Never overload the deep-fryer. Temperature is critical and is quickly reduced by the addition of food. Adding too much at once lowers the temperature so that the food will cook too slowly and absorb oil.
● When frying uncoated foods such as vegetables, use a basket and lift it out two or three times as the fat foams up, until most surface moisture has been driven off.
● When cooked and golden-brown all over, drain the food thoroughly over the oil, place on crumpled kitchen paper and pat dry.
● If cooking in batches, keep cooked food warm in a preheated low oven with the door slightly ajar. Never cover or it will go soggy.

Frying fats and oils

Choice of frying medium is critical as many standard kitchen oils are quite unsuited to it. Oils for deep-frying must have two basic qualities: resistance to high temperatures and neutrality of taste. Lard, dripping and olive oil, for instance break down far too readily. Refined vegetable oils are by far the best choice as they are made to withstand the high temperatures involved.

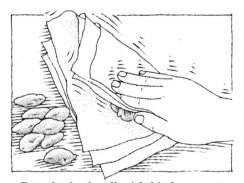
Dry the food well with kitchen paper.

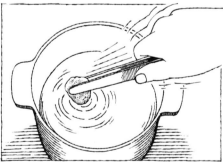
Dip in the batter to coat thoroughly.

Allow any excess batter to drain back.

Lower carefully into the oil.

Lift basket from oil to drain food.

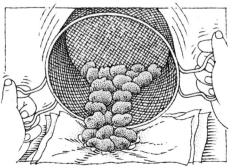
Turn out on kitchen paper to dry.

Deep-frying temperatures

These are generally in the region of 335-380F (180-194C). Foods that require a lot of cooking through, ie. larger pieces or densely fleshed foods, like potatoes, sometimes start at lower temperatures and are then finished off at a higher browning temperature.

Deep-frying equipment

If you have an automatic electric fryer, follow the manufacturers instructions closely. Some models have filters in the lids which remove much of the frying odour. In these pans, you heat the oil and do the frying with the lid in place. Control of temperature is automatic, but it is a good idea to check the actual temperature with a fat thermometer first.
If you fry in a pan on the cooker, be sure it is a heavy pan which sits level on the hotplate. Never either heat the oil or fry with the lid on.

Use and care of deep-frying oil

To get the best results from deep-frying and make your oil last as long as possible, use it carefully and care for it well. Over-heating, added moisture, cooked food particles and poor storage all make oil deteriorate more rapidly.

The rules for care are simple: Firstly, keep the temperature within the suggested temperature range at all times during the frying. Secondly, be sure that the food is as dry as possible and that, if coated, it is completely and thoroughly covered with little excess clinging to it. Thirdly, strain the cooled oil through a sieve lined with kitchen paper. Finally, store oil, used or fresh, in the fridge.

Previously used oil can be used repeatedly, but some fresh oil should be added each time. Some flavour is inevitably always picked up after each frying, so keep separate oils for frying strongly flavoured foods, such as fish, and for deep-frying sweet foods.

● The temperatures and times given with all the following recipes are based on testing in 3½pints (2 litres) oil in a fryer about 10in (25cm) in diameter. In a smaller fryer, given recipes will have to be cooked in a greater number of batches, so allow more total cooking time.

Temperature control

It isn't possible to maintain an absolute temperature when frying. It will obviously drop when food is added, and the temperature of the food and of the kitchen itself all play a part. For these reasons, only approximate temperatures and times are given.

● To control the oil temperature, it is best to use a fat thermometer, or an electric fryer with automatic control. That way, you will know when, and by how much, the temperatures rises and falls.

● Never guess the oil temperature by the old-fashioned method of looking for a blue haze. This is an indication that the oil has reached what is called 'smoke' point. With modern oils, the temperature would be so high it would just char the food. More importantly, the 'smoke points' of modern oils are dangerously near their 'flame points', ie the temperatures at which they spontaneously ignite!

● Fry only as much food at a time as can move freely in the oil. Overloading the pan reduces the temperature too much, and also causes uneven cooking.

Three rules for safety:

● Never fill a pan more than one-third full of oil, as it bubbles up.
● Never go away and leave a pan of oil on the heat, whether on the cooker or in an automatic fryer.
● To reduce the temperature, turn the heat down or off, and never move a pan filled with hot oil.

Classic Sole Colbert

Serves 4 ☆☆☆
Preparation: 15 minutes
Cooking: about 12 minutes

4 sole, each about 9oz (250g), skinned and
    heads removed
salt and pepper

The coating:
2 eggs
2 tablespoons cold water
5oz (150g) fresh breadcrumbs, sieved
oil for deep-frying

The garnish:
1 tomato, sliced
Maître d'Hôtel Butter (see sidelines)
a few sprigs of parsley to garnish

Rinse the fish and pat dry.

☐ On the thick side of each sole, cut
the flesh along the length of the
backbone. With scissors, snip
through the spine in 2 or 3 places.

☐ Use a small sharp knife to ease
the flesh back from the bones as
shown. Season well and roll the
fillets back into place.

☐ Beat the eggs and water together

lightly and place in a shallow dish.
Put some of the crumbs in another.

☐ Draw one sole through the egg.
Hold up by the tail to let any excess
egg drain off, then press the sole
into the crumbs to coat all over. Pat
the crumbs on firmly. Repeat the
egg-and-crumb coating a second
time.

☐ Coat the remaining sole in the
same way, adding fresh crumbs to
the dish as necessary. Lay the fish
flat on kitchen paper.

☐ Deep-fry in oil pre-heated to
355-360F (180-182C) for about 4
minutes until well browned. Fry
only as many fish at a time as your
pan will hold, and don't use the
basket if the pan is crowded.

☐ Remove the fried fish and drain
on crumpled kitchen paper. Keep
hot while the rest are being fried.

☐ With a sharp knife, fold back the
loosened fillets then lift out the
backbones. Garnish each sole with a
slice of tomato topped with a slice of
Maître d'Hôtel Butter, and with
sprigs of parsley.

Maître d'Hôtel butter

Whisk 3oz (75g) softened butter with 2
tablespoons finely chopped parsley, 1
tablespoon lemon juice and salt and freshly
ground pepper to taste. Shape into a cylinder
1in (2.5cm) in diameter. Wrap in foil and
store in the fridge. Cut in slices to serve.

Snipping the backbones of the fish makes
them easy to remove before serving.

Classic Sole Colbert

Even more traditionally, Sole Colbert are left
with their heads on and fried with the fillets
pressed back open, purse-like, between two
spatulas. This gives an even more decorative
effect and makes the cavity an effective
container for garnishes, notably Maître
d'Hôtel Butter.

*Preparing, cooking and serving
Classic Sole Colbert.*

Cod Beignets

Cod Beignets

Using a white sauce to coat fish produces the most delicious results. It is more complicated than just using egg to hold the crumbs but it gives a mouthwatering crisp outer crust with a melting layer just inside, around moist and tender fish.

You can prepare the fish ready for the crumb coating well in advance. Store in the fridge for up to 2 hours.

The various stages in preparing and cooking Cod Beignets.

Serves 3 ☆☆☆
Preparation and cooking: about 40 minutes

1lb (500g) thin cod fillets, skinned
salt and pepper
2 egg whites
about 2oz (50g) fresh breadcrumbs, sieved
oil for deep-frying

The coating sauce:
2oz (50g) butter
4 tablespoons flour
14 fl oz (400ml) Fish Stock
2 egg yolks
about 4 tablespoons single cream
2 tablespoons capers, chopped

Rinse the fish, pat dry and remove any bones. Cut into 6 equal-sized pieces.

☐ Make the sauce: Melt the butter in a 7in (18cm) saucepan over a moderate heat. Stir in the flour to make a thick paste. Gradually stir in the stock and simmer, stirring constantly, for 3 minutes.

☐ Beat the egg yolks together with 2 tablespoons of the cream. Mix in a little of the hot sauce and return the mixture to the saucepan. Stir over the heat for 1 minute.

☐ Remove from the heat and season.

☐ Sprinkle the fish with salt and pepper and coat each piece with sauce. Leave in a single layer on a plate, to cool and set, for about 20 minutes. Set the rest of the sauce aside.

☐ Whisk the egg whites lightly in a shallow dish. Put some of the crumbs in a second shallow dish.

☐ Dip each piece of coated fish first in crumbs, then in egg white, and again in crumbs. Pat the crumbs on well and place the coated fish on kitchen paper. Continue until all has been coated in this way, adding fresh crumbs as needed.

☐ Fry in oil pre-heated to 355-360F (180-182C) for about 4-5 minutes until crisp and golden brown. Fry only as many pieces at a time as the pan will hold in a single layer. Drain on crumpled kitchen paper.

☐ Put the fried fish on a warmed serving plate and keep hot. Place the sauce back on the heat and stir to warm through. Stir in the capers and about 2 tablespoons of cream to give the desired consistency.

☐ Pour into a warmed sauceboat to serve.

Fried Whitebait

Served with brown bread and butter and lemon wedges, these make a perfect starter to precede a salad main course.

Serves 4
Preparation and cooking: 20 minutes

2lb (900g) whitebait, thawed
4oz (125g) plain flour
salt and pepper
oil for deep-frying
Deep-fried Parsley to garnish

Rinse the fish in cold running water and pat dry.

☐ Put one-quarter of the flour, some salt and pepper and one quarter of the fish into a large plastic bag. Shake to coat with the flour.

☐ Turn the fish out into a sieve and shake to remove excess flour. Place in a single layer on kitchen paper.

☐ Coat the rest of the fish similarly in three more batches.

☐ Put one-quarter of the fish into the frying basket and lower into the oil pre-heated to 375F (190C). Fry for about 1 minute until lightly browned. Remove and drain on crumpled kitchen paper.

☐ Cook the other three batches of fish in the same way.

☐ When all of the whitebait has had an initial frying, re-heat the oil to 375 (190C). Put half the fish into the basket and fry for $2\frac{1}{2}$-3 minutes until they make a rustling sound when you shake the basket.

☐ Turn out on a warmed plate lined with a crumpled kitchen paper or a napkin. Repeat with remaining fish. Sprinkle with salt and pepper and garnish with fried parsley to serve.
Variation: Make Devilled Whitebait – mix $\frac{1}{2}$ teaspoon each of curry powder, ground ginger, and powdered mustard with the flour. Sprinkle with salt and cayenne to serve.

Deep-fried Parsley
Rinse the parsley thoroughly in cold running water. Drain well and pat very dry with kitchen paper or a tea towel. Put into the frying basket and plunge into oil pre-heated to 365-375F (186-190C) for a few seconds or until the sizzling stops. Remove immediately and drain on crumpled kitchen paper. Sprinkle with a little salt and cayenne and use to garnish fried fish dishes. Deep-fried parsley turns a particularly vivid green and makes a very attractive garnish.

Cook sprats in the same way as whitebait. They are larger, so cook them about twice as long on the first frying.

Fish croquettes

Croquettes can be made with other cooked fish or shellfish instead of the prawns. Firm fish, such as monkfish cut into small pieces, or queen scallops cut in quarters are especially suitable.

Preparing croquettes

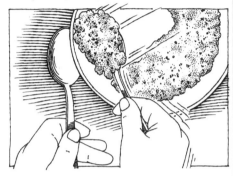

Scoop up a dessertspoonful of mixture.

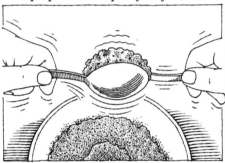

Mould carefully between two spoons.

Roll gently in breadcrumbs to coat.

Roll in the egg, then again in crumbs.

Monkfish Fritters

Serve hot – speared with cocktail sticks – to accompany drinks, or with a salad for lunch.

Serves 4   ☆☆☆
Preparation: 20 minutes
Cooking: 12-15 minutes

12oz (350g) monkfish fillets, skinned
2 streaky bacon rashers, rinded and finely chopped
1 small onion, finely chopped
4 tablespoons dry white wine
about 5 tablespoons milk
3oz (75g) plain flour
½ teaspoon baking powder
a pinch of salt
2 eggs, separated
oil for deep-frying

Rinse the monkfish and pat dry. Cut in ½in (1cm) cubes.

☐ Put the bacon and onion in a small frying-pan over a moderate heat. Stir for 4-5 minutes to soften the onion and lightly crisp the bacon.

☐ Put the monkfish into a small saucepan with the wine. Simmer for 3-4 minutes until the flesh is white and opaque.

☐ Strain off the wine and make it up to 4 fl oz (125ml) with milk.

☐ Mix together the flour, baking powder and salt in a large mixing bowl. Add the egg yolks and gradually stir in the liquid to make a stiff batter. Stir in the monkfish, bacon and onion.

☐ Stiffly whisk the egg whites and gently fold into the mixture.

☐ Drop teaspoonfuls of the mixture into oil pre-heated to 365-375F (186-190C). Fry for about 3 minutes until golden brown on the underside. Turn with a slotted spoon and fry the second side. Fry only as many at one time as the pan will hold without crowding.

☐ When cooked, remove with a slotted spoon and drain on crumpled kitchen paper.

Variation: Scallops may be cooked in the same way. The tiny 'queens' are best; they can be used whole.

Mussels in Beer Batter

Serves 4   ☆☆☆
Preparation: 30 minutes
Cooking: 20 minutes

4½lb (2kg) mussels in their shells
1 leek, coarsely chopped
1 large carrot, sliced
1 medium onion, coarsely chopped
2 garlic cloves, crushed
6 black peppercorns, crushed
¼ pint (150ml) light ale
oil for deep-frying
chopped chives for garnish

The batter:
4oz (125g) self-raising flour
½ teaspoon curry powder
½ teaspoon salt
¼ teaspoon cayenne

Scrub mussels in cold running water, remove beards. Put them in a pot with the leek, carrot, onion, garlic, peppercorns and the ale. Cover and bring slowly to the boil for about 3 minutes until all the shells open.

☐ Remove from the heat. Prising the shells open over the pot to save the liquid, scoop the mussels from their shells. Discard unopened ones. Lay in a single layer on kitchen paper.

☐ Strain off ¼ pint (150ml) of the cooking liquid. Put the flour, curry powder, salt and cayenne into a mixing bowl. Gradually beat in enough liquid to make a smooth creamy batter.

☐ With a slotted spoon, take up a scoop of mussels. Stir it through the batter to coat all the mussels well. Drain off, letting excess batter drop back into the bowl.

☐ Put the coated mussels immediately into oil pre-heated to 365-375F (186-190C). Fry for about 3 minutes until puffed, crisp and brown. Skim off with the spoon and drain.

☐ Arrange in single layers on oven trays lined with kitchen paper and keep hot in a low oven while you cook the rest of the mussels.

☐ Serve sprinkled with chives.

Prawn Croquettes

Step-by-step to Prawn Croquettes.

Makes 6   ☆☆☆
Preparation and cooking: about 20
minutes plus 2 hours chilling

8oz (225g) shelled prawns, thawed if frozen
2oz (50g) butter
3 tablespoons flour
¼ pint (150ml) milk
1 tablespoon dry sherry
1 tablespoon single cream
salt and pepper
a squeeze of lemon juice
1 tablespoon finely chopped parsley
oil for deep-frying

The coating:
1 egg
1 tablespoon water
5 tablespoons dry breadcrumbs, sieved

Rinse the prawns in cold running
water and pat dry.

☐ Melt the butter in a 6in (15cm)
saucepan over a moderate heat. Stir
in the flour to make a thick paste.
Gradually stir in the milk. Simmer,
stirring constantly, for 3 minutes.

☐ Stir in the sherry then the cream.
Flavour the sauce to taste with salt
and pepper, lemon juice and parsley.
Remove from the heat and cool
slightly. Stir in the prawns.

☐ Spoon the mixture on to a deep
plate. Smooth out level with a wet
knife. Cool, cover and chill for 2
hours until set firm.

☐ Cut the mixture into 6-8 equal
portions and shape as shown.

☐ Beat together the egg and water
in a shallow dish. Put some of the
crumbs in a second dish.

☐ Roll each croquette first in
crumbs, then in egg and then again
in crumbs. Press the crumbs on
firmly. Add fresh crumbs to the
plate for each croquette.

☐ Put the croquettes into the frying
basket. Lower into the oil pre-
heated to 355-360F (180-182C) and
fry for about 2 minutes until crisp
and golden brown. Remove and
drain on crumpled kitchen paper.
Tip: Create delicious cocktail snacks
by making smaller croquettes.

Deep-frying offal

Most offal deep-fries well because it requires such a short cooking time. A crisp coating keeps the meat succulent and makes an interesting contrast in texture.

Preparing brains

Sheeps' brains are very small and are sold complete. They require a much shorter blanching time than calves' brains.
Handle both kinds of brains carefully. When blanched, and cooked, they become very tender and fragile. For this reason, they are best given a protective coating of an ample amount of egg white rather than batter or sauce. Crumbs on the outside also give a firm crust to hold them together.

Preparing sweetbreads

Sweetbreads may be sold either complete in a whole piece, or divided into small segments. If whole, soak for the full time. Blanch, then trim off any hard pipes and remove the skin before slicing.
The sweetbread segments are usually already trimmed and skinned so they need only to be soaked and blanched for a short period.

The delicate flavour and texture of deep-fried brains and sweetbreads are best brought out by serving them with a sharp lemon mayonnaise, or a Tartare or Rémoulade Sauce.

Brain Beignets

Serves 4 ☆☆☆
Preparation: 30 minutes plus 1½ hours soaking
Cooking: about 10 minutes

---

2 whole calves' brains (or about 1lb (500g) sheep's brains)
a squeeze of lemon juice
salt and pepper
oil for deep-frying

The coating:
4 egg whites
4oz (125g) dry breadcrumbs, sieved

Rinse the brains in cold running water. Remove the covering membrane from calf brains, if necessary. Soak in cold water for about 1½ hours to remove any blood, changing the water as necessary.

☐ Drain and gently rub away any clotted blood. Cut out the arteries with a sharp knife and discard. Rinse brains well in fresh water, then put into a saucepan with cold water to cover. Add a squeeze of lemon juice and bring slowly to the boil.

☐ Simmer for about 5 minutes for small sheep brains, 15 minutes for calf brains. Turn during the process to ensure uniform cooking. Cook until white and set.

☐ Drain and pat dry with kitchen paper. Slice the calves' brains, but leave sheep's brains whole.

☐ Lightly beat the egg whites in a shallow dish. Put a little of the crumbs in another.

☐ Dip each piece of brain first in egg white, then in crumbs. Repeat the process, patting lightly to hold the crumbs in place. Slightly flatten each piece with a fish slice. Place on kitchen paper.

☐ Put one-third of the coated pieces in the frying basket. Lower into oil pre-heated to 355F (180C). Fry for about 3 minutes until golden.

☐ Drain and turn out on crumpled kitchen paper and pat dry. Fry the rest of the brains in the same way and serve as soon as all are cooked.

Sweetbread Fritters

Serves 4 ☆☆☆
Preparation and cooking: 40 minutes plus 1½ hours soaking

1lb (500g) calves' sweetbreads
a squeeze of lemon juice
salt and pepper
1oz (25g) butter
2 tablespoons flour
7 fl oz (200ml) Veal Stock
2 egg yolks
1 tablespoon single cream
oil for deep-frying

The coating:
2 egg whites
4-5oz (125g-150g) dry breadcrumbs, sieved

Soak the sweetbreads in cold water for about 1½ hours, changing the water until it is free of blood.

☐ Put into a large saucepan with cold water to cover. Add a squeeze of lemon juice. Bring slowly to the boil and simmer for 2-3 minutes.

☐ Remove immediately and plunge into cold water. Remove any skin or membrane. Slice, if whole. Pat dry and dust with salt and pepper.

☐ Melt the butter in a 6in (15cm) saucepan over a moderate heat. Stir in the flour to make a thick paste. Gradually stir in the stock and simmer, stirring, for 3 minutes.

☐ Beat the egg yolks and cream together. Whisk in a little hot sauce, return to the pan and stir over the heat for 1 minute. Remove, season and leave to cool and thicken.

☐ Coat each piece of sweetbread with sauce and leave for about 20 minutes to set.

☐ Whisk the egg whites lightly in a shallow dish. Put a little of the crumbs into another.

☐ Dip each piece first in crumbs, then in egg white and again in crumbs, patting the crumbs on well, and using fresh crumbs as required.

☐ Put one-third of the fritters in a frying basket, lower into oil pre-heated to 355F (180C) and fry for about 3 minutes until golden brown.

☐ Drain on crumpled kitchen paper. Keep warm while cooking the rest.

Liver Fritots

Serve for supper with Spicy Tomato Sauce and a green salad.

Serves 4 ☆☆☆
Preparation and cooking: 25 minutes

1lb (500g) calves' or lambs' liver
1oz (25g) flour
½ teaspoon paprika
salt and freshly ground black pepper
1 egg
1 tablespoon water
5oz (150g) dry breadcrumbs, sieved
oil for deep-frying

Rinse the liver and pat dry. Cut it into thumb-sized pieces.

☐ Mix together the flour and paprika and season well with salt and pepper. Roll the pieces of liver in the flour to coat them thoroughly.
☐ Mix the egg and water together in a shallow dish and put a little of the crumbs in another.
☐ Roll the pieces of liver first in the egg mixture then in the crumbs. Repeat, rolling them under the hand to press the crumbs on firmly.
☐ Put half the liver into a frying basket, lower into oil pre-heated to 355-360F (180-182C) and fry for 2½-3 minutes, until brown.
☐ Turn out on crumpled kitchen paper and pat dry. Cook the rest of the liver in the same way.

Preparing, cooking and serving Liver Fritots with Spicy Tomato Sauce.

Spicy Tomato Sauce
Put 14 fl oz (400ml) tomato juice in a 7in (18cm) saucepan over a moderate heat. Mix 4 teaspoons cornflour smoothly with 2 tablespoons red wine. Stir in a little of the hot juice, return to the saucepan and cook, stirring constantly, for 3 minutes. Season to taste with a pinch of sugar, a dash of cayenne, and a little Tabasco Sauce.

The denser flesh of poultry is best either cut in small pieces, like goujons, or partially cooked before being deep-fried.

Redcurrant Sauce
Put 4 teaspoons cornflour into a small saucepan. Gradually stir in 12 fl oz (350ml) Chicken Stock. Put over a moderate heat and bring to the boil, stirring constantly. Stir in 2 tablespoons port and 2 tablespoons redcurrant jelly. When the jelly has melted, remove from the heat and season to taste with salt and a little cayenne.

Chicken Fillets with Pineapple, served with fluffy boiled rice and Redcurrant Sauce, makes a special main course.

Chicken Fillets with Pineapple

Serves 6 ☆☆☆
Preparation and cooking: 40 minutes

about 1¼lb (575g) chicken breast fillets
salt and pepper
2oz (50g) butter
6 slices fresh pineapple
oil for deep-frying

The batter:
4oz (125g) plain flour
a pinch of salt
about ¼ pint (150ml) water
1 tablespoon melted butter
2 egg whites

Cut chicken into horizontal slices ¼in (5mm) thick. Pat dry and dust well with salt and pepper.
☐ Put the butter into a 8½in (21cm) frying-pan over a moderate heat. When it begins to brown, add half the chicken. Fry for 2-3 minutes on each side until set. Remove with a slotted spoon and repeat with remaining chicken.
☐ Pat the chicken dry again and leave to cool while you make the batter.
☐ Put flour and salt into a mixing bowl. Gradually stir in enough water to make a thick batter. Stir in the melted butter. Whisk egg whites to soft peaks and then mix into batter.
☐ Dip the chicken pieces in the batter. Hold up over the bowl to let excess drip off. Slide carefully into oil pre-heated to 365-375F (186-190C). Fry only as many as there is room for in the pan without overlapping. Fry for about 3 minutes until browned on one side. Turn and brown the second side for 2-3 minutes.
☐ Arrange the fried fillets in a single layer on trays lined with crumpled kitchen paper and keep warm in a low oven. Cook remaining chicken in the same way.
☐ Coat and fry the pineapple in the same way.
☐ Arrange alternate slices of chicken and pineapple on a warmed serving plate.

Southern-fried Chicken Drumsticks

Serve with Hot Pepper Sauce.

Makes 8 ☆☆☆
Preparation and cooking: 45 minutes

8 chicken drumsticks, each about 4oz (125g)
1 small carrot, chopped
1 small onion, chopped
1 bay leaf
4 black peppercorns
a sprig of fresh parsley
a sprig of fresh thyme
½ teaspoon salt
oil for deep-frying

The batter:
5oz (150g) plain flour
a pinch of salt
1 egg
about ¼ pint (150ml) milk

Put the drumsticks into a large saucepan with the vegetables, herbs, salt and water to cover. Cover and simmer for 20-25 minutes, until tender. Remove drumsticks. Cool.

☐ Meanwhile, make the batter: Sift the flour and salt into a tall jug. Break in the egg, and gradually stir in enough milk to make a smooth batter with the consistency of softly whipped cream.

☐ Pat the drumsticks dry and dip each in turn into the batter to coat.

☐ Place 4 of the drumsticks immediately into oil pre-heated to 355-360F (180-182C). Fry for 6-7 minutes until crisp and brown.

☐ Lift out with tongs and drain on crumpled kitchen paper. Fry the rest in the same way.

Chicken Fingers

Makes about 30 ☆☆
Preparation: 20 minutes
Cooking: about 6 minutes

8oz (225g) chicken breast fillets
1 egg, size 2
1 tablespoon water
1oz (25g) grated Parmesan cheese
3oz (75g) white breadcrumbs, sieved
oil for deep-frying

Pat the chicken dry and cut it into finger-sized pieces.

☐ Beat the egg and water together in a shallow dish. Mix the cheese and crumbs together and put a little in another dish.

☐ Coat each piece of chicken first in egg then in crumbs. Roll under the hand to press the crumbs on well. Add fresh crumbs as necessary.

☐ Put half the chicken into the frying basket, lower into oil pre-heated to 355-360F (180-182C) and fry for 3 minutes, or until browned.

☐ Drain and turn out on crumpled kitchen paper.

☐ Fry the rest in the same way.

Chicken Croquettes

Makes 8 croquettes ☆☆☆
Preparation and cooking: 20 minutes plus 2 hours chilling

10oz (275g) cooked chicken, finely chopped
2oz (50g) butter
3 tablespoons flour
¼ pint (150ml) Chicken Stock
2 tablespoons double cream
1 tablespoon finely chopped chives
1 tablespoon finely chopped parsley
salt and freshly ground black pepper
a dash of ground mace
oil for deep-frying

The coating:
1 egg, size 2
1 tablespoon water
5 tablespoons dry breadcrumbs, sieved

Melt the butter in a 6in (15cm) saucepan over a moderate heat. Stir in the flour to make a thick paste then gradually stir in the stock. Simmer, stirring for 3 minutes.

☐ Add the cream, herbs and chicken, mix well together and season with salt, pepper and mace.

☐ Spoon the mixture into a deep plate, smooth out level and cool.

☐ Cover and chill for 2 hours.

☐ Cut the mixture into 8 portions and roll each into a ball.

☐ Beat the egg and water together in a shallow dish. Put some of the crumbs into a second shallow dish.

☐ Fry as for Chicken Fingers.

Southern-fried Chicken Drumsticks
Use the chicken cooking liquid for soup or a sauce – or use it in place of half the milk to give a very flavourful batter.

Hot Pepper Sauce
Finely chop 1 onion and 2 garlic cloves and simmer in 1 tablespoon of butter in a small saucepan over a moderate heat for 5 minutes. Add 14oz (397g) canned pimientos with 2 tablespoons of their liquid, a little freshly ground black pepper, ½ teaspoon chilli paste and ½ teaspoon made mustard. Simmer for another 10 minutes until thick. Purée in a blender or sieve into a warmed sauceboat and serve.

Chicken Fingers
Serve hot or cold as a cocktail snack or as picnic finger food – with Curry Mayonnaise as a dip.

Chicken Croquettes
Serve these with a salad for supper, or make into smaller balls and serve – hot or cold – as cocktail snacks.

Frying potatoes

Potatoes are particularly versatile candidates for deep-frying. They are also handy for the cook as you can prepare them in advance and finish them just before serving. You can use them to make the good old stand-in chips—crisp and golden outside and tender inside—or crunchy straw potatoes, potato crisps and all sorts of croquettes, rissoles and more.

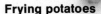

For best results fry no more than about 1lb (500g) potatoes at a time in 4 pints (2.25 litres) of oil. Too large a frying load reduces the temperature too much.

Buying potatoes for deep-frying

By far the best results are obtained using floury, maincrop varieties of potato, like the Desirée or King Edward.

French-fried Potatoes

Pommes Frites to the French, this American term for the British chip has spread with the rise of 'fast-food' hamburger restaurants.

Serves 4   ☆ ☆
Preparation and cooking: 25 minutes

1½lb (700g) potatoes
oil for deep-frying
salt

Wash the potatoes in cold water and peel them thinly. Cut into ⅜in (8mm) thick slices and cut into strips as wide as they are thick.
☐ Put into cold water and wash well twice to remove as much starch as possible. Drain and dry thoroughly.
☐ Put into a frying basket, lower into oil pre-heated to 370-375F (188-190C) and fry for about 3 minutes until brown at the edges.
☐ Lift out and drain. Put the chips on crumpled kitchen paper and pat dry. Set aside for up to an hour, or re-fry as soon as the oil reaches the correct temperature.
☐ Put the chips into the frying basket, lower into the oil heated to 390F (200C) and fry for about 1 minute until crisp and brown.
☐ Pat dry and sprinkle with salt.

Straw or Match-stick Potatoes

Cut the potatoes into thin slices then into matchstick-sized strips. Prepare in the same way as French-fried Potatoes and fry only once in oil pre-heated to 390F (200C) for about 2 minutes, until crisp and brown. Serve hot or cold, sprinkled lightly with salt.

Potato Crisps

Cut the potatoes into slices the thickness of the back of the knife you use to cut them, or slice them on a flat single-blade grater. Prepare in the same way as French-fried Potatoes and fry only once in oil pre-heated to 390F (200C) for 2-3 minutes, until crisp and brown. Serve hot or cold, sprinkled lightly with salt or paprika.

Fried Potato Skins

With a brush, scrub 1lb (500g) old potatoes well under cold running water. Pare very thinly and rinse the parings in cold water. Drain and pat very dry with a clean cloth. Put into the frying basket and lower into oil pre-heated to 390F (200C). Fry for about 1 minute until browned and crisp. Pat dry, sprinkle with salt and a little cayenne and serve.

Potato Beignets

Serves 4 ☆☆☆
Preparation: 15 minutes
Cooking: 3-4 minutes

10oz (275g) mashed potatoes, sieved
2oz (50g) grated Cheddar cheese
salt and pepper
a pinch of grated nutmeg
1 egg yolk
oil for deep-frying

The coating:
1 egg white
2 tablespoons grated Parmesan cheese
1oz (25g) dry breadcrumbs, sieved

Mix together the potatoes, Cheddar, salt, pepper and nutmeg. Stir in the egg yolk well to bind.

☐ Shape spoonfuls into 20 even-sized balls by rolling between the hands, then flatten them slightly.

☐ Whisk the egg white lightly in a shallow dish. Mix the Parmesan and the crumbs together. Put a little of this into a second shallow dish.

☐ Dip the balls first in the egg then in the crumbs, patting on well.

☐ Put one-third of the balls into the frying basket, lower into oil pre-heated to 375F (190C) and fry for about 1 minute until golden brown.

☐ Turn out on kitchen paper and fry the rest in the same way.

Potato and Ham Nuggets

Makes 36 ☆☆
Preparation: 30 minutes
Cooking: 4-6 minutes

10oz (275g) mashed potatoes, sieved
2oz (50g) butter, softened
4oz (100g) plain flour
2 eggs, size 2
1 tablespoon finely chopped parsley
1oz (25g) finely chopped ham
salt and pepper
a little flour to coat
oil for deep-frying

Put the potatoes, butter, and flour in a saucepan over a moderate heat and stir until the mixture is hot.

☐ Whisk the eggs lightly and stir them into the potato mixture. Cook, stirring constantly, for 4-5 minutes, or until it thickens.

☐ Stir in the parsley, ham and salt and pepper to taste.

☐ With 2 teaspoons, shape into 36 balls. Roll each in a little flour.

☐ Put half the balls in the frying basket, lower into oil pre-heated to 365-375F (186-190C) and fry for 2-3 minutes until golden brown.

☐ Drain and turn out on crumpled kitchen paper. Fry the rest of the balls in the same way and serve when all are cooked.

The versatility of the deep-fried potato, from left to right: French-fried Potatoes, Straw or Match-stick Potatoes, Potato Crisps, Potato Beignets and Potato and Ham Nuggets.

Potato Beignets
These are a perfect accompaniment to roast or grilled meat and poultry.

Potato and Ham Nuggets
Serve these speared with cocktail sticks to accompany drinks, or use—hot or cold—to make mixed salads into substantial main courses.

Deep-fried vegetables

Deep-fried mushrooms, and many other types of vegetable, make delicious snacks, interesting first courses, or accompaniments to main courses. Coat in batter and deep-fry until crisp and golden. Mushrooms should be dipped while raw, while other, less tender, vegetables are better peeled and par-boiled first. Particularly delicious deep-fried are asparagus, broccoli, cauliflower, Jerusalem artichokes and parsnips. Cubes or 'chips' of celeriac can be fried without any coating and they make an unusual alternative to fried potatoes.

Courgettes and aubergines make good fritters. To draw off the juices, first sprinkle with salt and leave for a while, then wipe very thoroughly before coating with batter.

A medley of Vegetable Fritters—made with young asparagus tips, broccoli and cauliflower florets—makes a memorable taste and texture treat for any occasion.

Vegetable Fritters

Serve these as accompaniments to roast meats and poultry, or with a savoury dip, spicy sauce or tangy mayonnaise as an unusual first course or hors d'oeuvre.

Serves 4   ☆☆
Preparation: 20 minutes
Cooking: about 4 minutes

1¼lb (575g) lightly par-boiled
   vegetables (see sidelines)
oil for deep-frying
salt for serving

The batter:
5oz (150g) plain flour
a pinch of salt
1 egg
about ¼ pint (150ml) light ale or
   vegetable cooking water

Use only small pieces of vegetables: florets of broccoli or cauliflower, heads of asparagus, fingers of parsnips, or small whole Jerusalem artichokes. Drain well and place on crumpled kitchen paper to pat dry.
☐ Sift the flour and salt into a bowl.

Make a well in the centre and break the egg into it. Gradually stir in the ale or vegetable water to make a thick batter with the consistency of lightly whipped cream.
☐ Dip each piece of vegetable into the batter in turn. Drain and carefully put into the oil pre-heated to 365-375F (186-190C). Fry for 1½-2 minutes until crisp and golden brown.
☐ Lift out with a slotted spoon and drain on crumpled kitchen paper. Keep hot in a low oven while frying the rest of the vegetables in the same way.
☐ Serve as soon as possible sprinkled with salt.
Tips: Prepare a mixture of vegetables in this way and serve Italian-style as 'fritto misto' with a tomato sauce or tomato dip as an antipasti. Sprinkle generously with grated Parmesan cheese or Cheddar cheese.
● You can par-boil the vegetables, and make the batter two or three hours in advance. Then quickly dip and fry just before serving.

Apple Beignets

Serves 4   ☆☆
Preparation and cooking: 20 minutes

4 dessert apples, each about 6oz (175g)
2oz (50g) caster sugar
1 teaspoon ground cinnamon
oil for deep-frying
sugar for dusting

The batter:
5oz (150g) self-raising flour
1 teaspoon caster sugar
1 egg
¼ pint (150ml) dry white wine

First make the batter: Sieve the flour and sugar into a basin. Beat together the egg and wine until well mixed. Gradually beat into the flour to make a thick batter with the consistency of lightly whipped cream.

☐ Peel and core the apples. Cut each across into 4. Mix the sugar and cinnamon in a shallow dish.

☐ Dip each slice of apple in the sugar to coat either side. Arrange in a single layer on kitchen paper.

☐ Dip each slice in the batter, draining off any excess. Carefully put into oil pre-heated to 365-375F (186-190C) and fry for about 2½ minutes until golden brown, turning as necessary.

☐ Lift out with a slotted spoon and drain. Keep hot while you fry the rest.

☐ Serve, sprinkled with sugar, as soon as all are cooked.

Crunchy Pineapple Slices

Serves 4   ☆☆
Preparation: 20 minutes
Cooking: 4 minutes

8 slices fresh pineapple
4oz (125g) boudoir biscuits
2 egg yolks
2 tablespoons milk
oil for deep-frying

The sauce:
2 teaspoons arrowroot
7 fl oz (200ml) pineapple juice
2 tablespoons kirsch

First make the sauce: Put the arrowroot in a small saucepan and slowly stir in the pineapple juice until mixed smoothly.

☐ Place over a moderate heat, gradually bring to the boil and simmer for 2 minutes. Stir in the kirsch, pour into a warmed sauceboat and keep hot.

☐ Remove the centres from the pineapple slices with an apple corer, trim out any 'eyes' and pat the fruit dry.

☐ Put the biscuits in a large plastic bag and crush with a rolling pin.

☐ Sieve and put a little of the crumbs in a shallow dish.

☐ Beat the egg yolks and milk together in a second shallow dish.

☐ Dip the pineapple slices, one at a time, first in the egg, letting any excess drain off, then in the crumbs,

Making and serving Apple Beignets. Serve piled with vanilla ice cream.

patting the crumbs on firmly all over and into all the notches. Place in a single layer on kitchen paper.

☐ Put as many pieces into the bottom of the frying basket as will fit comfortably. Lower into oil pre-heated to 365-375F (186-190C) and fry for 1½-2 minutes until crusty and browned.

☐ Lift out, drain and keep hot while you fry the remaining pineapple.

☐ Serve as soon as possible with the sauce passed separately.

Frying Cheese

Many cheeses deep-fry successfully. You can grate the very hard ones to add to crumb coatings. Medium hard cheeses can be grated or diced to mix into batters. Many—from firm hard-pressed Cheddar to the very soft Brie—are delicious deep-fried in slices or thinly coated in egg and crumbs, or even made into sandwiches.

Coating cheese

Whether it is being fried on its own or inside a sandwich, it is important to ensure that the cheese is well coated in egg and crumbs. If the coating is not thorough, the melted cheese runs out into the hot oil.

Dry, finely grated cheese mixed with breadcrumbs used to coat either cheese sandwiches or cheese cubes gives an even better flavour—Parmesan is a perfect candidate.

Cheddar Cubes

Serve as hot snacks with drinks. Try them with a dip of sweet pickle or even a sharp preserve such as gooseberry.

Deep-fried Cheese Sandwiches

Serve as a snack lunch or supper, garnished with gherkins, pickled onions and lemon wedges.

Deep-frying in batches

Put the drained, fried food on a tray lined with crumpled kitchen paper. Place into the oven pre-heated to 300F (150C) gas 2 to keep them hot while you fry the remaining batches.

Crumb-coated foods can be prepared up to an hour in advance, but coating with batter must be done immediately before frying.

Mozzarella Fritters

Serve with Spicy Tomato Sauce as a first course.

Makes 18
Preparation: 10 minutes
Cooking: 10-12 minutes

7oz (200g) Mozzarella cheese
3 eggs, size 2, separated
2oz (50g) plain flour
salt and freshly ground black pepper

Coarsely grate the cheese. Beat together with the egg yolks to mix well. Stir in the flour and season generously with salt and pepper.
☐ Whisk the egg whites to soft peaks. Fold gently into the cheese.
☐ Using large teaspoons to shape the fritters, scoop up a rounded spoon of the batter. With the second spoon scrape off into the oil pre-heated to 365-375F (186-190C).
☐ Fry for 2-3 minutes until browned, turning as necessary.
☐ Lift out with a draining spoon and pat dry with kitchen paper. Fry only as many at a time as the pan will hold with space for turning.
☐ Serve as soon as all are cooked.

Cheddar Cubes

Makes 36
Preparation: 20 minutes
Cooking: about 5 minutes

1¼lb (575g) Cheddar cheese
2 eggs, size 2
1 tablespoon water
5oz (150g) dry breadcrumbs
cayenne

Cut cheese into 1in (2.5cm) cubes.
☐ Beat the eggs together with the water in a shallow dish. Put some crumbs with a sprinkling of cayenne into a second.
☐ Working with 2 or 3 cubes at a time roll the cheese in the egg, lift out with a fork to drain off the excess egg and roll in the crumbs to coat. Pat on firmly.
☐ Repeat the entire process and set

on kitchen paper. Coat the rest of the cheese in the same way.
☐ Place one-third of the pieces of cheese in a frying basket. Lower into oil pre-heated to 365-375F (186-190C) and fry for about 1 minute until browned.
☐ Drain and turn out on crumpled kitchen paper and keep hot while frying the rest in the same way.

Deep-fried Cheese Sandwiches

Makes 4 small rounds
Preparation: 15 minutes
Cooking: about 5 minutes

---

about ⅓ small brown square loaf
5oz (150g) Edam, Cheddar, or Mozzarella
**   cheese**
2oz (50g) butter, softened
3 eggs, size 2
1 tablespoon water
3oz (75g) dry breadcrumbs, sieved

Cut off 8 very thin slices of the bread. Butter one side of each.
☐ Slice the cheese thinly. Lay on half the slices of bread leaving the crusts clear. Press a second slice of bread on top of each round, buttered-side down.
☐ Beat the eggs and water lightly in a shallow dish. Put a little of the crumbs into another.
☐ Quickly dip one sandwich into the egg mixture, turning to coat all round, and let excess drain off. Dip into crumbs, turn and press the other side into the crumbs. Pat the crumbs on well.
☐ Repeat the dipping in egg and crumbs a second time. Place on kitchen paper and coat the rest.
☐ Using a fish slice, lower two sandwiches into oil pre-heated to 365-375F (186-190C). Fry for about 1 minute to brown. Turn and fry the second side for 1 minute.
☐ Lift out, drain and pat dry on kitchen paper. Keep hot in a low oven while frying the remaining sandwiches in the same way.
☐ Cut in half to serve.

Shallow-frying

Frying is one of the most important and popular of the cooking techniques—and for good reason. The food is quickly cooked, its juices and flavour are sealed in, and the fat or oil we use, if wisely chosen, can contribute much to the flavour of the finished dish. Deep-frying is an art in itself, but more commonly we shallow-fry in a variety of ways. So first invest in the best quality heavy-based pan you can afford and learn the basic technique, then you can go on to finishing the dish in a sauce of its own and making a classic sauté. Shallow-frying suits a wide range of tempting foods and offers ample scope for the creative cook.

Selecting fats for flavour
Drippings, lards and olive oil all have their own distinctive tastes. Vegetable oils such as corn oil and seed oils, such as sunflower, tend to have least effect on the flavour of foods.

Not suitable for frying
Low-calorie spreads produced for slimmers should not be used for frying as their high water content makes them unsuitable and possibly hazardous. If in doubt, check the instructions on the package.

Frying chops or cutlets.

Frying fish fillets.

Frying poultry fillets.

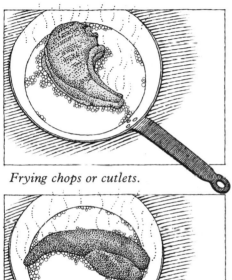
Frying game joints.

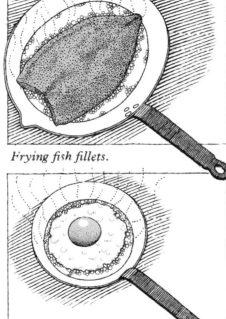
Frying an egg.

Frying batter mixtures.

Shallow-frying is quick, easy and successful if you bear one or two basics in mind. It cooks fast, over fierce heat, so choose suitable foods: chops, steaks, small whole fish, pieces of chicken, escalopes, eggs and batter mixtures all make good candidates.

When frying:
● choose even-sized pieces of food of an even thickness so they cook in the same time.
● don't overcrowd the pan.
● never use too much fat or oil.
● have the fat or oil sizzling hot or it seeps into the food instead of sealing it (butter should begin to brown; oil or

fat should 'tremble' in the pan).
● always drain fried food well to retain its crispness. Serve at once.
● wipe out the pan between batches to prevent foods from sticking.

Depth of fat:
Use little or none for foods with a high fat content, such as chops, cutlets, sausages or bacon.
Use as little as possible—just brush the pan—for lean meat.
Cover the bottom of the pan with a thin film when frying eggs or fish.
Brush the pan lightly at the beginning of cooking for crêpes, pancakes and scones. Don't add extra.

Fats for shallow-frying
Butter gives a good flavour—some say the best—but it contains solids of milk protein which burn at a fairly low temperature 120C (250F), well below that needed for a good fast fry. Remedy this by clarifying the butter first or by mixing it with an equal amount of oil to form a protective coating around these impurities and raise the burning point. Lards, drippings and other solid white fats can usually be heated to higher temperatures than margarine, butter or oils, although the smoke point is lower for fats containing emulsifiers.

Watchpoint
Older cookbooks often suggest that a 'blue haze' above the fat is an indication of the correct cooking temperature. Beware! Today's fats do not haze until they are dangerously near flame-point.

Fats for shallow-frying fish

Use clarified butter, white cooking fat, or a cooking oil for shallow frying fish. Lard, olive oil, and fresh butter burn easily if overheated and give a charred taste to the fish. Clarified butter is particularly good if using the lower temperature necessary for whole fish, fish steaks, or thick fillets. For thin fillets, a good oil or white cooking fat will stand the higher temperature much better.

Frying fish in batches

Unless you have a very large frying-pan it will usually be necessary to fry small fish in batches and large fish singly. Choose a pan that is large enough to hold the fish comfortably without leaving too much excess fat which might overheat. When adding more butter to fry each batch, don't forget to allow it to heat up and foam before putting in the fish.

Ensuring thorough cooking

To help penetrate round fish such as mullet, make diagonal slashes at intervals through the thickest part of the flesh, a technique that can also be adopted for thicker steaks.

Keeping fried fish crisp

Unless intending to serve fried fish with its own hot butter sauce, drain on crumpled paper towels after frying. The paper will soak up excess fat and the fish will be deliciously crisp.

Shallow-frying fish

Shallow-frying in oil or butter, or a mixture of the two, is an ideal cooking method for fish. The simple speedy process preserves the fragile texture of fish, seals in natural juices and delicately enhances the flavour.

Frying also gives fish an appetizing golden colour and a crisp outside which contrasts deliciously with the tender flesh. This can be enhanced—and the outside prevented from over-cooking before heat penetrates to the inside—by giving the surface of whole fish or fillets a coating of milk and seasoned flour. Alternatively, for a crunchier finish, the fish can be coated with egg and breadcrumbs, or even a coating of ground nuts.

By keeping in natural juices, such coatings also ensure that the cooked fish is moist, preserve the maximum flavour and, as a bonus, prevent the butter or oil spitting during the actual frying process.

Sole à la Meunière

Serve with plain boiled potatoes and a crisp green salad.

Serves 4   ☆☆☆
Preparation: 12-15 minutes
Cooking: 15-20 minutes

---

2 Dover soles, each weighing about 1lb (500g), skinned
3 tablespoons milk
4 tablespoons flour seasoned with salt and freshly ground black pepper
3-4oz (75-100g) clarified butter
juice of ½ a large lemon
1 tablespoon chopped parsley
sprigs of parsley and tomatoes, to garnish

Dip the fish in the milk, then turn it in the seasoned flour; shake off excess flour.

☐ Heat oven to 225F (110C) gas ¼.

☐ Heat half the butter in a frying pan until it foams.

☐ Lower the fish into the butter, skinned side uppermost; cook until golden brown—about 5 minutes. Turn and cook the second side for 3-4 minutes until brown. Transfer to a warmed serving dish and keep hot in the oven.

☐ Add remaining butter and cook the second fish.

☐ Stir lemon juice into the pan; let it bubble vigorously for a moment.

☐ Sprinkle the parsley over the fish and pour over the butter.

☐ Garnish with sprigs of parsley and tomato roses and serve.

Fried Turbot with Capers

Serves 4 ☆☆
Preparation: 5 minutes
Cooking: 8 minutes

---

3 tablespoons flour
salt and freshly ground black pepper
4 turbot steaks, each weighing about
    6oz (175g)
3 tablespoons milk
3oz (75g) clarified butter
2 tablespoons capers
2 tablespoons wine vinegar
1 tablespoon chopped parsley

Mix the flour with salt and pepper.

☐ Dip each piece of fish in the milk, then turn the pieces in the seasoned flour to coat them on either side. Shake off any excess flour.

☐ Heat the butter in a frying-pan until it foams. Lower the fish into the hot butter and fry for about 4 minutes until browned. Turn and fry the second side for a further 3 minutes–do not overcook.

☐ Transfer to a warmed serving dish and keep hot.

☐ Add the capers and vinegar to the pan. Allow to bubble vigorously for a moment then pour over the fish. Sprinkle with parsley and serve.

Breaded Sole Fillets

These are delicious served with fried potatoes, a mixed salad and, perhaps, a Tartare Sauce, or mayonnaise, curd cheese or plain yogurt mixed with chopped fresh parsley or chives.

Serves 4 ☆☆
Preparation: 10 minutes
Cooking: 10-12 minutes

---

3 tablespoons flour
3oz (75g) dry breadcrumbs
salt and freshly ground black pepper
1 egg, beaten
2 tablespoons milk
8 fillets lemon sole, weighing about 1½lb
    (700g)
3-4 tablespoons cooking oil

Mix the flour, breadcrumbs and salt and pepper to taste. Lightly beat together the egg and the milk.

☐ Dip the fillets in the egg then turn them in the breadcrumbs, patting on firmly with a palette knife.

☐ Heat the oil in a frying-pan over a medium heat.

☐ Place as many fillets, skinned side down, in the pan as it will hold.

☐ Cook for about 2 minutes, until browned on the underside. Turn and cook for a further 2 minutes to brown the other side. Transfer to a warmed serving dish and keep hot.

☐ Cook remaining fillets and serve.

Fried whole turbot

Occasionally small turbot weighing about 1½lb (700g) are available. These are best cooked whole. Remove the head, trim off the fins and clean the fish. Dip in seasoned flour and fry in the same way as the steaks, but allow about 5 minutes each side.
To serve, cut through the skin down the spine and slide the knife under each of the two fillets to lift away from the bones. Turn, and repeat on the second side. Lift off the skins before serving.

Skate wings

As a cheaper alternative, try wings of skate following the method given for turbot. Finish with the pan sauce of vinegar and capers.

Sole à la Meunière, fried whole Dover sole finished with its own sauce of hot butter and lemon juice.

Red mullet, dipped in milk and flour then crisply fried, make an attractive meal, especially if served with lemon wedges and a simple salad.

Fried Plaice with Cucumber

Serves 4 ☆☆
Preparation: 15 minutes
Cooking: 10 minutes

---

2 plaice, each weighing about 1½lb (700g) cleaned, trimmed, rinsed and dried
3 tablespoons milk
3 tablespoons flour seasoned with salt and freshly ground black pepper
3oz (75g) clarified butter
1 small cucumber, peeled and diced

Heat the oven to 225F (110C) gas ¼.
☐ Dip the fish first in the milk, then in the seasoned flour. Fry in the butter as for Sole à la Meunière, for 3 minutes on the first side and 2 minutes on the second. Keep hot on a warmed serving dish.
☐ Add the cucumber dice to the pan and stir over a moderate heat for about 3 minutes. Spoon the butter and cucumber over the fish and serve.

Fried Mullet or Gurnard

Serves 4 ☆☆☆
Preparation: 5-10 minutes
Cooking: 10 minutes

---

4 mullet or gurnard, each weighing about 10-12oz (275-350g), cleaned
salt and freshly ground black pepper
4 tablespoons flour
3 tablespoons milk
6-7 tablespoons oil

Rinse the fish, scraping away any scales with the back of a knife, then blot dry with kitchen paper.
☐ Season the flour, then dip each fish first in milk then in the flour.
☐ Heat the oil in a frying-pan over a moderate heat until it is hot enough to tremble.
☐ Add the fish and cook, turning, for about 10 minutes, until browned all over.
☐ Serve immediately with a crisp salad.

Scaling red mullet
Red mullet have large scales which must be removed before cooking. Scrape the fish well with the back of a knife or use a stiff brush then rinse thoroughly. If removing the heads, take great care not to discard the livers which are a great delicacy. Red mullet are also known as 'Sea Woodcock' because they are considered better and tastier cooked ungutted.

A Quick Tomato Sauce
A homemade tomato sauce makes a delicious accompaniment to any fried fish. Wash and cut up 1½lb (700g) ripe tomatoes. Simmer with a chopped onion, salt, pepper, a bay leaf and ¼ pint (150ml) red wine, for 20 minutes. Strain the sauce, rubbing as much of the flesh through as possible. Season to taste adding a little sugar if necessary. To give the sauce a glossy finish, beat in 1oz (25g) of cold butter, a little piece at a time.

Sautéed Potatoes

A good accompaniment to most grills, these are also excellent with roasts and creamy stews.

Serves 3 ☆☆
Preparation: 10-12 minutes
Cooking: 20 minutes

1½lb (700g) medium potatoes
2oz (50g) butter, clarified

Scrub the potatoes and trim to an even size. Par-boil in boiling salted water for 7-8 minutes until tender but still firm. Drain, leave until cool enough to handle, then remove the skins. Cut into ¼in (5mm) slices.
☐ Put the butter into a 9in (23cm) frying-pan over a moderate heat until it foams well. Stir in the potatoes a few at a time, to coat them all over with the butter.
☐ Continue to cook, stirring and turning frequently, for about 20 minutes until light golden and crisp on the outside and soft inside.
☐ Serve immediately.

Pommes Parisienne

These elegant accompaniments to roasts and grills are often also used for a garnish.

Serves 4 ☆☆
Preparation: 20 minutes
Cooking: 15-20 minutes

2lb (900g) large potatoes, peeled
4 tablespoons vegetable oil
1 tablespoon finely chopped parsley

Scoop out the potatoes with a melon baller. Rinse well, then par-boil for 5 minutes in boiling salted water. Drain, then dry off over a low heat.
☐ Heat oil in a 9in (23cm) frying-pan over moderate heat. Gradually add the potatoes. Fry, stirring and turning frequently, for 15-20 minutes until lightly browned.
☐ Serve immediately, sprinkled with chopped parsley.

Potato Pancakes

Serve with a breakfast fry-up.

Makes 16 ☆
Preparation: 3 minutes
Cooking: 20 minutes

14oz (400g) mashed potato
4 tablespoons plain flour
½ teaspoon dried thyme
salt and freshly ground black pepper
two eggs, size 2
about 6 tablespoons milk
3-4 tablespoons dripping or cooking fat

Mix together the potato, flour and thyme, and season generously.
☐ Beat in the eggs one at a time. Stir in enough milk to give the mixture a soft consistency.
☐ Heat 1 tablespoon of the dripping or fat in a 9in (23cm) frying-pan over a moderate heat until hot. Using a serving spoon, drop in 3 separate spoonfuls of mixture.
☐ Cook for 1-1½ minutes until brown on the underside. Turn and brown the second side.
☐ Keep hot while cooking the rest, adding more dripping as necessary.

Bubble and Squeak

Serves 1 ☆☆
Preparation: 2 minutes
Cooking: 12-15 minutes

3oz (75g) mashed potatoes
3oz (75g) cooked cabbage, finely chopped
½ teaspoon caraway seeds
salt and freshly ground black pepper
1 tablespoon dripping or cooking fat

Mix together the potatoes, cabbage, caraway and a little seasoning.
☐ Heat the dripping or cooking fat in a 7in (18cm) omelette pan over a moderate heat until it is very hot. Press potato mixture firmly into pan.
☐ Fry for about 10 minutes, until the cake is crusty around the edges and browned underneath. With a fish slice, turn it in one piece and brown for 5 minutes on the second side. Serve immediately.

Sautéed potatoes
For best results use potatoes with waxy flesh such as new potatoes, Maris Piper or Cyprus. When cooked they will have a golden and crumbly exterior and a soft or 'fondant' inside. Skilled cooks can toss potatoes or make them 'jump', the origin of the word 'sauter'. At home it's usually better just to stir and turn them with a spatula.

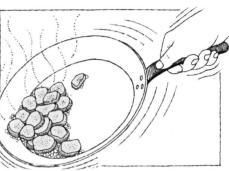
Carefully slide the potatoes to one side of the pan.

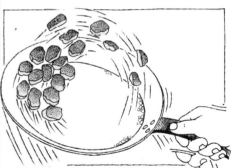
Quickly toss the potatoes in the pan to turn them.

Pommes Parisienne
The potato shell left after scooping out the ball shapes can be boiled and used for mashed potatoes–in Potato Pancakes, for example–or chopped and used to thicken soups and stews.

Potato Pancakes
These make an unusual and interesting way of using up leftover cooked potatoes. You can add any flavouring you like–various chopped herbs, spring onions or garlic.

Bubble and Squeak
Try substituting mashed cooked parsnips or swedes for the cabbage. Alternatively, make the Bubble and Squeak into a filling supper dish in its own right by adding 3oz (75g) chopped salt beef, corned beef, bacon or any leftover meat.

Cooking times for steaks

The time required depends on:–
the thickness of the steak,
how well done the steak is to be,
the density and fat content of the cut of meat
(close-textured rump, for instance, takes
about a third longer to cook than open
sirloin).

A rare steak is still quite red inside, with
freely flowing red juices, while a well-done
steak has a beige interior but is still quite
moist with clear juices. An overcooked steak
quickly becomes dry and leathery.

As a rough guide:
Sirloin steaks about ¾in (1.75cm) thick:
rare   2½ minutes per side
well-done   4 minutes per side

Fillet steaks about 1¼in (3cm) thick:
rare   2½-3 minutes per side
well done   4-5 minutes per side

You do not have to cut or pierce the meat to
gauge degree of doneness. Press the steak
with the back of the fork or spoon: a rare
steak is still quite soft and gives a great deal,
while a well-done steak is quite firm.

Turn the meat with spoons or tongs, as any
piercing encourages loss of juices.

If you like steak that is very brown on the
outside, have the pan initially very hot. If you
like the steak very rare (or 'blue') warm it
very gently first in the pan for a minute or
two and then remove briefly while heating
the pan to searing temperature.

Steak gravy

You can give the steak gravy a velvety
texture by beating in 1oz (25g) chilled butter
just before serving.

Fillet Steak with Stilton

Grated Cheddar goes well with sirloin or
rump steak–beat it in with the butter in the
same way as the Stilton. Try beer or cider in
place of the port.

Frying meat

Wipe meat dry with kitchen paper so
the proteins on the surface set quickly
(to seal in juices) and the meat browns
well. For those who prefer to season
before cooking, rub it on either side
with salt and pepper to season only
just before cooking, otherwise the salt
draws more moisture to the surface.
Normally, only the most tender of
steaks are shallow-fried. Nowadays,
however, you can buy thin tenderized
steaks which are best 'flash-fried' at
high temperatures in very little butter
or oil. An economical alternative to
sirloin and fillet steak is the thin end of
the eye of silverside. Slashed as shown
opposite, it can be used very successfully, particularly if sautéed and
served with a sauce.

Fried Steak

Serves 4   ☆☆
Cooking: 5-10 minutes

**4 pieces fillet or sirloin steak, each about
   6oz (175g)**
salt and freshly ground black pepper
2oz (50g) butter, clarified

Pat the meat dry with kitchen paper.
Rub both sides of the steaks with
salt and pepper.
☐ Heat the butter in an 8-9in (20-
23cm) frying-pan over a moderate
heat until it is foaming and
beginning to brown. Then fry the
meat, turning once, until browned
on both sides and cooked to the
required degree. Remove from the
pan with a slotted spoon, pat dry
with kitchen paper and keep hot.
☐ Pour off most of the fat and add a
dash of water to the pan. Boil for a
minute, stirring to scrape up the
sediment. Pour pan juices over the
steaks and serve immediately.
Variation: For richer and more
flavoursome gravies to accompany
fried steaks, deglaze the pan with 2
or 3 tablespoons of good meat stock
or red wine instead of water.

Fillet Steak with Stilton

Serve with baked potatoes and a crisp
green salad.

Serves 4   ☆☆☆
Preparation: 5 minutes
Cooking: 5-10 minutes

2oz (50g) butter, softened
2oz (50g) blue Stilton cheese
4 pieces fillet steak, each about 6oz (175g)
salt and freshly ground black pepper
2oz (50g) butter, clarified
3 tablespoons port
bunch of watercress, to garnish

Beat the butter and cheese together.
☐ Dry the meat well with kitchen
paper and rub with salt and pepper.
☐ Heat the butter in an 8-9in (20-
23cm) frying-pan over a moderate
heat until foaming and beginning to
brown. Fry the meat, turning once,
until browned on both sides and
cooked to the required degree.
Remove from the pan with a slotted
spoon, blot dry with kitchen paper
and keep hot.
☐ Pour off most of the fat. Add the
port and boil for 1 minute, stirring
to scrape up the sediment in the
pan, then spoon the pan juices over
the steaks. Top each steak with a
spoonful of the Stilton butter.
☐ Garnish with watercress and
serve immediately.

Steak Butters

A pat of any one of a wide range of
savoury butters on a steak makes a
delicious alternative to a sauce:
garlic–with a crushed garlic clove.
curry–with 1 teaspoon curry paste
and a few drops lemon juice.
herb–with 1 tablespoon finely chopped herbs such as parsley, chives, dill,
or tarragon.
    Beat 2oz (50g) butter until soft and
creamy. Beat in the flavourings then
chill until just firm. Place on a piece of
greaseproof paper and roll up the
paper to shape it into a log. Chill until
firm, remove paper and cut into discs.

Budapest Steak

This elegant dish makes an impressive main course for supper.

Serves 2 ☆☆☆

Preparation: 5 minutes
Cooking: 12-15 minutes

2 pieces rump steak each about 6oz (175g)
salt and freshly ground black pepper
1oz (25g) butter
1 medium onion, chopped
a pinch of paprika
2 teaspoons tarragon vinegar
3 tablespoons dry white wine
6 tablespoons single cream
2 gherkins, cut into julienne strips

Pat the steaks dry with kitchen paper and season well.

☐ Put the butter into a 9in (23cm) frying-pan on a moderate heat until it begins to brown. Fry the steaks, turning once, until they are brown and cooked to taste. Transfer to a warmed serving dish and keep hot.

☐ Add the onion to the pan. Cook, stirring, for about 5 minutes to glaze but not brown.

☐ Add the paprika, vinegar and wine. Boil for a minute or two. Stir in the cream and just allow it to heat through. Spoon sauce over steaks, garnish with the gherkins and serve.

Cut as shown, dressed with a paprika, wine and cream sauce and garnished with sliced gherkin, Budapest Steak has great appeal.

Steak with Red Wine Sauce

Serves 2 ☆☆☆

Preparation: 5 minutes
Cooking: about 30 minutes

¾ pint (450ml) red wine
¾ pint (450ml) Basic Brown Stock
1 onion, coarsely chopped
1 garlic clove, finely chopped
2 entrecôte steaks, each about 6oz (175g)
salt and freshly ground black pepper
3oz (75g) butter, clarified

Put wine, stock, onion and garlic, in a saucepan over a high heat. Boil rapidly to reduce to half the original volume. Strain and keep warm.

☐ Cook the steaks as Fried Steak using 2oz (50g) of the butter.

☐ Remove steaks from the pan and keep hot. Pour off frying butter, then add wine sauce. Boil briefly, stirring to scrape up meat sediment.

☐ Beat remaining butter into sauce, pour over steaks and serve.

Veal Olives

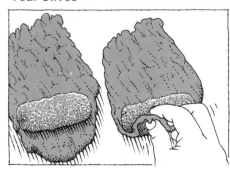

Place the rolls of stuffing across the escalopes and roll up firmly.

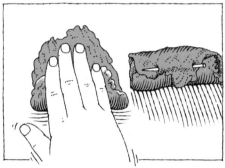

Secure with wooden cocktail sticks.

Veal Olives

To flatten veal escalopes, first rinse them in cold running water then place them inside a plastic bag. Pound with a rolling pin or a meat bat. These are cooked when the juices run clear if a sharp knife is inserted into the thickest part.

Frying Pork

When pork is cooked through it will be rigid to the touch if pressed with the flat part of a fork.

To prevent pork chops or steaks curling up during frying, cut notches in the fat around the edges.

Shallow-frying veal and pork

Shallow-frying and sautéing are both excellent quick ways of cooking veal and pork, either as escalopes, chops or steaks. Try escalopes plainly cooked or wrapped around a savoury stuffing, and chops or steaks with a sauce made from the pan juices.

Veal Olives

Serve with hot buttered noodles and a mixed salad.

Serves 4 ☆☆
Preparation: 15 minutes
Cooking: 25 minutes

---

4 veal escalopes, each about 4oz (125g)
2 tablespoons fresh breadcrumbs
2 tablespoons milk
1 tablespoon finely chopped parsley
5oz (150g) minced veal
1 tablespoon finely chopped onion
a pinch of dried rosemary
grated rind and juice of $\frac{1}{2}$ lemon
salt and freshly ground black pepper
2oz (50g) butter
4 tablespoons white wine

Flatten escalopes as thinly as possible and dry with kitchen paper.
☐ In a large bowl, mix together the breadcrumbs, milk, parsley, minced veal, onion, rosemary and lemon rind and season lightly. Shape into rolls to fit the escalopes.
☐ Place a roll of filling on each escalope, roll up firmly and secure with wooden cocktail sticks.
☐ Heat the butter in a 9in (23cm) frying-pan over a moderate heat until it begins to brown.
☐ Add the veal rolls, turn the heat down and cook them gently for about 20 minutes, turning frequently to brown them all over. Remove the sticks, place rolls on a warmed serving dish and keep hot.
☐ Add the lemon juice and wine to the pan. Let it bubble for a minute, stirring to scrape up any sediment. Season to taste, pour over the veal olives and serve immediately.

Pork Chops with Rosemary

Serves 3 ☆☆☆
Preparation: 3 minutes
Cooking: 12 minutes

---

3 pork chops, each about 6oz (175g)
salt and freshly ground black pepper
a pinch of dried rosemary
about 1oz (25g) lard
4 tablespoons water

Pat the chops dry with kitchen paper. Rub both sides with a little salt, pepper and rosemary.
☐ Put a 9in (23cm) frying-pan over a moderate heat. Rub the bottom of the pan well with the lard and heat until the fat is very hot.
☐ Fry the chops in the pan about 3 minutes on each side to brown them. Add the water, cover the pan, and reduce the heat. Cook for about 12 minutes, or until the juices run clear when the chops are pierced with a sharp knife.
☐ With a slotted spoon, transfer the chops to a warmed serving dish. If all the juices in the pan have evaporated, add another 2-3 tablespoons of water and stir to scrape up the sediment. When the juices boil again, pour them over the chops and serve immediately.

Pork Steaks with Creamy Tomato Sauce

Serve with boiled fresh pasta and sautéed courgettes.

Serves 4 ☆☆☆
Preparation: 5 minutes
Cooking: 30 minutes

---

4 pork steaks, each about 4oz (125g)
salt and freshly ground black pepper
a pinch of dried thyme
2oz (50g) butter
2 tablespoons finely chopped onion
1lb (500g) tomatoes, diced
$\frac{1}{4}$ pint (150ml) double cream
a pinch of sugar
1 tablespoon finely chopped olives

Pat the steaks dry with kitchen paper. Rub them on both sides with a little salt, pepper and thyme.

☐ Heat the butter in a 9in (23cm) frying-pan over a moderate heat until the foam begins to subside and the butter begins to brown.

☐ Fry the steaks for about 3 minutes on each side to brown. Cover the pan, reduce the heat and cook for about 6-10 minutes until cooked through (the juices run clear when it is pierced with a sharp knife). Remove the steaks to a warmed serving dish and keep hot.

☐ Add the onion to the pan and stir for a minute to glaze. Add the tomatoes and simmer for 10 minutes until pulpy. Rub the sauce through a sieve and then return it to the rinsed-out pan.

☐ Stir in the cream and boil for 2 minutes. Adjust the seasoning with sugar and a little salt and pepper. Pour the sauce over the steaks, garnish with the chives and serve immediately.

Variation: Instead of the thyme use dried sweet basil, or 1 teaspoon finely chopped fresh basil leaves.

● Try soured cream or crème fraîche in place of double cream.

Pork steaks with Creamy Tomato Sauce have a garnish of chopped chives.

Pork Steaks with Creamy Tomato Sauce
Omit the sugar and sweeten the sauce with 2 tablespoons sweet vermouth, for an interesting, subtle flavour.

Pork Bolognese Sauce

Minced lamb, available in some large supermarkets, is equally good in this dish. To gauge when the pan is hot enough to fry the meat, test-fry a small pinch of the mince.

✳Freezing

You can freeze the Pork Bolognese Sauce for up to 3 months. Leave to cool. Turn into a suitable container lined with foil or cling film. Cover, label and freeze. To use, allow to thaw in the refrigerator for 24 hours. Boil gently over a moderate heat for 5 minutes to serve.

The professional way to dice meat

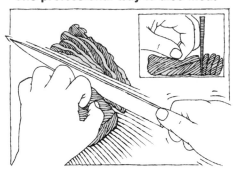

Hold the knife safely against the fingers like this, then slice the meat.

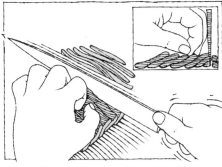

Cut slices into strips like this.

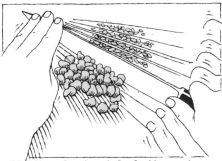

Holding the tip of the knife as pivot, dice the meat.

Honey-glazed Pork Chops

Serves 2   ☆☆☆
Preparation: 3 minutes
Cooking: 12 minutes

---

2 pork chops, each about 6oz (175g)
salt and freshly ground black pepper
a pinch of dried rosemary
1oz (25g) lard
4 tablespoons dry white wine
1 tablespoon clear honey

Cook chops as for Pork Chops with Rosemary, using the wine in place of the water. Keep hot.

☐ If all the juices have evaporated add another 2-3 tablespoons wine. Stir in the honey. Boil for a minute or two to thicken, spoon over the chops and serve immediately.

Normandy Pork Steaks

Serves 4   ☆☆☆
Preparation: 5 minutes
Cooking: 20 minutes

---

4 pork steaks, each about 4oz (125g)
salt and freshly ground black pepper
2oz (50g) butter
¼ pint (150ml) cider
1 large cooking apple, peeled and diced
¼ pint (150ml) double cream

Pat the steaks dry with kitchen paper. Rub with salt and pepper.

☐ Heat the butter in a 9in (23cm) frying-pan over a moderate heat until the foam begins to subside and the butter begins to brown.

☐ Fry the steaks for about 3 minutes on each side to brown. Pour the cider over and cover the pan. Simmer for about 6 minutes until the meat is tender. Transfer the steaks to a warmed serving dish and keep hot.

☐ Add the apple to the pan. Cook briskly, stirring frequently, for about 7 minutes until tender. Stir in the cream and boil for 2 minutes. Adjust the seasoning. Pour over the steaks and serve immediately.

Pork Bolognese Sauce

Serve over boiled fresh pasta.

Serves 4   ☆☆☆
Preparation: 5 minutes
Cooking: 4-5 minutes

---

3 tablespoons oil
1 large garlic clove, finely chopped
2oz (50g) onion, finely chopped
2oz (50g) minced pork
1 teaspoon dried sage
9 fl oz (275ml) dry white wine
salt and freshly ground black pepper
2 tablespoons tomato purée

Heat oil gently. Add the garlic and onion and cook gently, stirring occasionally, for 15 minutes–do not allow to brown! Remove to keep warm and raise heat to moderate.

☐ Add the pork and stir for 10-12 minutes to brown lightly.

☐ Return the onions and garlic to the pan and add the remaining ingredients. Simmer for 20 minutes.

☐ Adjust the seasoning and serve.

Beefburgers with Onions

Serves 4   ☆☆
Preparation: 15 minutes
Cooking: 12-15 minutes

1¼lb (575g) minced lean beef
1 egg yolk
5oz (125g) onion, finely choppped
2 garlic cloves, finely chopped
3-4 tablespoons water
salt and freshly ground black pepper
2oz (50g) butter

Thoroughly mix together the meat, egg yolk, 1 tablespoon of the onion, the garlic and 1 tablespoon of the water and season well.

☐ Shape the mixture into 4 cakes about 3½in (8.5cm) in diameter.

☐ Heat the butter in a 9in (23cm) frying-pan over a moderate heat.

☐ Fry the beefburgers for about 7 minutes on each side, or until well browned. Remove and keep hot. Pour off all but about 1 tablespoon

Beefburgers with Onions served with a lightly dressed salad of radicchio and cress or Fricadelles with Caper Sauce served with a tangy beetroot salad each make an interesting and unusual supper or lunch.

fat. Add remaining onion and fry, stirring for 4-5 minutes to brown.

☐ Add 2-3 tablespoons of water and boil. Spoon over beefburgers and serve.

Fricadelles with Caper Sauce

Serves 4   ☆☆☆
Preparation: 15 minutes
Cooking: 17-20 minutes

The fricadelles:
2 tablespoons white breadcrumbs
2 tablespoons canned consommé
1¼lb (575g) lean minced beef
1 egg yolk
1 tablespoon finely chopped onion
1 tablespoon finely chopped leek
salt and freshly ground black pepper
1oz (25g) butter

The sauce:
4 tablespoons canned consommé
1 tablespoon lemon juice
4oz (100g) unsalted butter, cubed
2 tablespoons capers

In a large bowl, mix together the breadcrumbs and consommé. Add all remaining fricadelles ingredients except the butter and mix thoroughly.

☐ Dampen the hands with cold water and shape the mixture into 8 cakes about 2½in (6cm) diameter.

☐ Heat the butter in a 9in (23cm) frying-pan over a moderate heat until it begins to brown. Add the fricadelles and cook for 5-6 minutes on each side, or until browned. Remove and keep hot in a warmed serving dish.

☐ To make the sauce; pour off all but about 1 tablespoon of the fat. Add the consommé and the lemon juice and boil vigorously for about 5 minutes to reduce to about 1 tablespoon.

☐ Stir in the butter cubes, one by one, to make a slightly thickened sauce. Add the capers and heat through for a minute or so. Pour over the fricadelles to serve.

Beefburgers with Onions
To give extra flavour to the beefburger gravy use red vermouth or port to deglaze the pan. Some butchers sell minced lamb which also makes very good 'burgers'.

Fricadelles with Caper Sauce
'Fricadelles' is the Belgian term for small meat patties. You can make them with beef, or a mixture of pork and beef, which is more traditional. Canned consommé is an excellent store cupboard source of stock. Don't add seasoning until the sauce is finished because canned consommé is well seasoned.

Italian Chops

To make this dish for 4 people, use half the number of butterfly lamb chops and 8oz (225g) canned tomatoes.

Gammon Steaks with Onion Sauce

If in a hurry, the onion sauce is just as good without being puréed or sieved. Just chop the onions finely.

Italian Chops for 8 people, with mangetout peas and sautéed potatoes.

Italian Chops

Serves 8 ☆☆☆
Preparation: 3 minutes
Cooking: 15-20 minutes

---

8 double or 'butterfly' lamb chops
a pinch of garlic salt
salt and freshly ground black pepper
1oz (25g) dripping or cooking fat
14oz (400g) canned tomatoes
½ teaspoon dried basil
dash of Worcestershire sauce
a pinch of sugar
mustard and cress, to garnish

Pat the chops dry with kitchen paper, slash fat around edges and rub with garlic salt and black pepper.
☐ Heat dripping in a 9in (23cm) frying-pan over moderate heat.
☐ Add half the chops, cover the pan and cook for about 5 minutes until browned. Turn the chops, then cover and cook for a further 4-5 minutes to brown the second side. Keep hot while cooking the rest.
☐ Add the tomatoes, basil, and sauce. Simmer uncovered for 7-8 minutes. Adjust the seasoning with sugar, salt and pepper. Strain the sauce and serve separately.
☐ Garnish the chops and serve.

Gammon Steaks with Onion Sauce

Serves 3 ☆☆
Preparation: 10 minutes
Cooking: 25 minutes

---

3 gammon steaks, each 4-5oz (100-125g)
freshly ground black pepper
1oz (25g) butter
8oz (225g) onion, coarsely chopped
½ teaspoon paprika
1 tablespoon plain flour
8 fl oz (250ml) stock
1 tablespoon finely chopped parsley

Pat the steaks dry with kitchen paper and slash them around the edges. Sprinkle with pepper.
☐ Heat the butter in a 9in (23cm) frying-pan over a moderate heat until it begins to brown.
☐ Add the steaks, cover the pan and cook for 4-5 minutes, then turn, cover and cook for about 5 minutes to brown the second side. Transfer to a serving dish and keep hot.
☐ Add the onion to the pan and cook, stirring frequently, for 10 minutes. Sprinkle with paprika and flour and stir in. Gradually stir in stock and simmer for 5 minutes.
☐ Rub the sauce through a sieve and return to the pan to heat through. Adjust the seasoning, and serve separately.

Shallow-frying offal

Shallow-frying and sautéing are among the best methods to cook liver, kidneys, sweetbreads, and brains. The short cooking brings out the flavour of such delicate meats and keeps them tender.

Sautéed Sweetbreads

Serve with buttered noodles and crisply cooked broccoli.

Serves 4   ☆☆☆
Preparation: 1 hour soaking, plus 20 minutes
Cooking: about 12 minutes

---

about 1¼lb (575g) sweetbreads
salt and freshly ground black pepper
2 tablespoons flour
1 egg, beaten
4 tablespoons white breadcrumbs
2oz (50g) butter
1 tablespoon finely chopped parsley

Soak the sweetbreads for 1 hour in lightly salted cold water, then rinse under cold running water.
☐ Put them in a saucepan with enough cold water to cover and add 1 tablespoon salt.
☐ Bring quickly to the boil, reduce the heat and simmer for 4 minutes. Drain and rinse again under cold running water.
☐ Remove all the membrane and any hard sections. Cut the sweetbreads into slices about ½in (1cm) thick and pat dry.
☐ Sprinkle with salt and pepper and dip both sides of each slice in flour, then in egg and finally in the crumbs. Pat the crumbs on firmly with a palette knife.
☐ Melt the butter in a 9in (23cm) frying-pan over a moderate heat until just beginning to brown. Add the sweetbreads in a single layer and brown for 2-3 minutes on each side.
☐ Sprinkle the sweetbreads with chopped parsley and place on a warmed serving dish. Pour the pan juices over and serve immediately.

Sautéed Kidneys with Red Wine

Serves 4   ☆☆
Preparation: 10 minutes
Cooking: 10 minutes

---

8 lambs' kidneys
salt and freshly ground black pepper
1oz (25g) butter
1 tablespoon oil
6 tablespoons Basic Brown Stock
6 tablespoons red wine

Remove fat, membrane and cores from kidneys. Pat dry and season.
☐ Heat the butter and oil in an 8in (20cm) frying-pan until browning.
☐ Fry kidneys for 2 minutes on each side. Remove and slice in half.
☐ Return to the pan cut-side down. Cook for 1 minute then transfer to a warmed serving dish and keep hot.
☐ Pour off all excess fat. Add the stock and wine and boil to reduce by about half. Spoon over kidneys.

Sage-Fried Liver

Serves 4   ☆☆☆
Preparation: 5 minutes
Cooking: about 12 minutes

---

about 1¼lb (575g) calves' or lambs' liver,
    very thinly sliced
2oz (50g) butter
2 tablespoons oil
2oz (50g) flour
salt and freshly ground black pepper
2 teaspoons finely chopped sage leaves

Pat liver dry with kitchen paper.
☐ Heat half the butter and oil in a 9in (23cm) frying-pan over a moderate heat until browning.
☐ Season the flour with salt, pepper and sage, and dust liver with it.
☐ Add as much liver to the pan as possible without crowding. Fry for about 4 minutes, turning once.
☐ Transfer to a serving dish and keep hot while cooking rest.
☐ Add 3-4 tablespoons water to pan and boil, stirring. Pour over liver to serve.

Don't overcrowd the sweetbreads when frying, or they will not cook quickly enough. If necessary, cook them in two batches.
To make a quick sauce, stir ¼ pint (150ml) double cream into the butter remaining in the pan. Boil briskly for about 2 minutes and pour over the sautéed sweetbread slices.

Blanching sweetbreads

Put the soaked sweetbreads in a pan of cold salted water and bring to the boil.

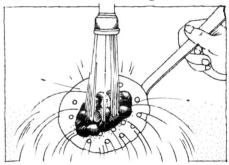

After 4 minutes' blanching, drain and quickly cool by refreshing under cold running water.

Frying kidneys
Perfectly fried kidneys will be brown on the outside, but tender and slightly pink inside. If you prefer kidneys well done, slice them before frying. Sauté only a few slices at a time, otherwise they lose their juices and don't brown properly.

Frying liver
Test the liver with a skewer to be sure it's cooked to your taste. The juices will be a rosy colour if it's slightly pink inside, or clear when it's well done. Overcooking makes liver solid, tough and dense.
Give the gravy extra piquancy by stirring in 2 teaspoons made mustard or by substituting marsala for the water.

If you buy a whole saddle of venison, the butcher will cut off chops for you. You can then freeze the remainder for roasting. Double chops cut across the saddle should be as thin as possible. For single chops, ask to have them cut about 1in (2.5cm) thick.

Marinades for venison:

Pour ¼ pint (150ml) red wine over venison chops. Add a few crushed black peppercorns, a bay leaf, and a sprig of rosemary. Store in the refrigerator for several hours, turning the meat occasionally. Alternatively, use gin, 2 or 3 crushed garlic cloves and some crushed juniper berries.

Frying venison

Pat the meat dry with kitchen paper before frying. Use any marinade to make the sauce, adding some port and redcurrant jelly.

Venison and hare are the most common furred game animals. The flavour of both is improved by hanging before cooking. This allows the full flavour to develop and makes the meat more tender. The butcher will do this for you, but if doing it yourself, allow 1-2 weeks for venison, and 7-10 days for hare—longer if the weather is cool.

Shallow-frying furred game

Only small cuts of young game are tender enough for frying. If you're unsure of their tenderness either marinate them or finish the cooking by stewing with a little liquid in a covered pan. Cooked in this way, pieces of hare or venison chops have a good flavour and should be tender. Those used to eating game may prefer it rare as it remains juicier. For those unused to game, it's better to cook it until well done.

Pork in the Manner of Wild Boar

Give ordinary pork steaks a pleasantly powerful gamey flavour by means of a traditional game marinade.

Serves 4   ☆☆
Preparation: 10 minutes, plus at least 6 hours marinating
Cooking: 25 minutes

---

4 pork steaks, each about 6oz (175g)
salt and freshly ground black pepper
¼ pint (150ml) red wine
1 tablespoon vinegar
1 onion, finely chopped
1 carrot, sliced
1 large garlic clove, pressed
1 bay leaf
a sprig of parsley
a large sprig of fresh sage or ½ teaspoon dried sage
4 juniper berries, crushed
1oz (25g) butter
2 teaspoons cornflour
about 3 fl oz (100ml) Game or Basic Brown Stock

Rub the pork well with salt and pepper. Place in a deep dish.

☐ Boil together the wine, vinegar, onion, carrot, garlic and herbs for 5 minutes. Leave to cool and then pour over the pork. Cover and chill for 6-8 hours.

☐ Remove the pork steaks from the marinade and pat dry.

☐ Melt butter in a 9in (23cm) frying-pan over a moderate heat until it begins to brown. Fry steaks for 5-6 minutes on each side to brown.

☐ Strain the marinade into the pan. Reduce the heat. Cover the pan and simmer for 5-6 minutes until the pork is cooked through. Remove the steaks, pat them dry with kitchen paper and keep hot.

☐ Blend the cornflour smoothly with a little of the stock. Mix in 2 tablespoons of the hot liquid and add the mixture to the pan.

☐ Bring to the boil, stirring constantly for about 3 minutes, until thickened. Gradually stir in more stock until sauce is of the desired consistency. Season to taste.

☐ Spoon sauce over pork and serve.

Venison Chops in White Wine

Serves 6   ☆☆
Preparation: 3 minutes
Cooking: about 40 minutes

---

6 single venison chops, from the saddle, about 1in (2.5cm) thick
salt and freshly ground black pepper
1oz (25g) butter
8 fl oz (250ml) white wine
a sprig of fresh rosemary
3 rounded tablespoons lemon jelly marmalade

Pat the chops dry with kitchen paper. Rub well with salt and pepper.

☐ Melt the butter in a 9in (23cm) frying-pan over a moderate heat until it begins to brown.

☐ Fry the chops for about 6 minutes on each side to brown.

☐ Add the wine and rosemary. Reduce heat, cover pan and simmer for 6-7 minutes until cooked. Transfer to a warmed serving dish and keep hot.

☐ Increase the heat and boil sauce for 12-15 minutes until it begins to thicken. Stir in the marmalade and simmer for 2-3 minutes until it dissolves and the sauce becomes syrupy. Remove the rosemary.

☐ Spoon the sauce over the chops and serve immediately.

Venison Chops with Juniper Sauce

Serve with a purée of potato and celeriac and fried chicory or cour-gettes.

Serves 4   ☆☆
Marinating: 1 hour
Cooking: 45 minutes

8 juniper berries
3 tablespoons gin
4 double venison chops, from the saddle, each about 8oz (225g)
salt and freshly ground black pepper
about 1oz (25g) butter for frying
8 fl oz (250ml) Game or Basic Brown Stock
1oz (25g) cold butter, cubed

Crush the juniper berries in a small basin. Pour over the gin and leave for an hour.

 Pat the chops dry with kitchen paper. Rub well on both sides with salt and pepper.

☐ Melt the butter in a 9in (23cm) frying-pan over a moderate heat until the foaming subsides and the butter begins to brown.

☐ Add as many chops to the pan as it will hold. Fry 6-7 minutes on each side to brown. Transfer to a warmed serving dish and keep hot. Cook the remaining chops in the same way, adding extra butter if necessary.

☐ Return the chops to the pan and strain the gin over them. Cover the pan and simmer for about 5 minutes or until the chops are cooked through. Transfer to a warmed serving dish and keep hot.

☐ Add the stock to the pan and boil for 12-15 minutes until the sauce begins to thicken. Gradually mix in the cold butter, then adjust the seasoning. Spoon over the chops and serve immediately.

Tip: Give the sauce the flavour of the forest by adding a blanched sprig of fir or pine to the stock.

Venison chops with Juniper Sauce.

Venison Chops with Juniper Sauce
Add a blanched sprig of fir to the stock to give added flavour. If available, use Dutch gin or 'old genever' for more flavour.
Test the chops with the tip of a sharp knife to tell when they're cooked to taste. If rare, the juices will run pink.

Remove the rind from the bacon and place each rasher on a flat surface. Stretch the rashers with the back of a large knife, then roll each up.

Chicken Maryland

Serve with buttered peas and Corn Fritters.

Serves 4
Preparation: 15 minutes
Cooking: 35 minutes

1 chicken, about 2½lb (1.25kg), quartered
3 tablespoons flour
salt and freshly ground black pepper
1 egg, size 2
1 teaspoon water
3oz (75g) white breadcrumbs
2oz (50g) butter

The garnish:
8 streaky bacon rashers, rinds removed
1oz (25g) butter
4 small bananas

Cut the drumsticks from the thighs and the wings from the breasts. Pat chicken dry with kitchen paper.

☐ Put the pieces of chicken in a large plastic bag together with the flour and salt and pepper to taste. Close the bag and shake well to coat the chicken thoroughly.

☐ Lightly beat the egg and the water together. Dip each piece of chicken first in the egg mixture then in the crumbs. Pat the crumbs on firmly with a palette knife.

☐ Melt the butter in a 9in (23cm) frying-pan over a moderate heat until it begins to brown.

☐ Fry the chicken pieces for about 5 minutes on each side to brown them lightly all over. Reduce the heat and fry gently for about 20 minutes, turning once, to cook through. Transfer to a warmed serving dish and keep hot.

☐ Prepare the garnish. Pre-heat the grill to moderate, roll up the bacon rashers and thread on skewers. Brown the bacon rolls under the grill for 2-3 minutes.

☐ Melt the butter in the frying-pan, until it is just beginning to brown. Fry the bananas for 2-3 minutes, turning once, to brown.

☐ Garnish the chicken with the bacon rolls and bananas and serve immediately.

Breaded Chicken Breasts

Serve with creamed potatoes and buttered leaf spinach. These are also delicious served cold with a green or mixed salad and make perfect buffet or picnic snacks.

Serves 4
Preparation: 5 minutes
Cooking: 15-20 minutes

4 chicken breasts, each about 4oz (125g)
2oz (50g) flour
salt and freshly ground black pepper
1 egg
2 teaspoons water
2-3oz (50-75g) white dried breadcrumbs
2oz (50g) butter

Flatten the chicken breasts, then pat them dry with kitchen paper. Season the flour with salt and pepper, then use to coat chicken.

☐ Lightly beat together the egg and the water. Dip each breast in the egg mixture then in the crumbs. Pat the crumbs on firmly with a palette knife.

☐ Melt the butter in a 9in (23cm) frying-pan over a moderate heat until it begins to brown.

☐ Fry the chicken for 3-4 minutes on each side to brown lightly. Reduce the heat and cook for a further 10 minutes, turning once, to cook through. Serve the chicken breasts immediately.

Tips: To ensure even and thorough cooking of chicken or turkey breasts it is better to flatten them first. Rinse them in cold water then place them one at a time flat inside a plastic bag. Pound flat with a rolling pin or meat bat.

For successful egg-and-crumb coating: first dip the breast into the egg and shake off the excess. To coat evenly in the crumbs, measure out only a small amount of crumbs at a time in a dish. This keeps the crumbs clean and dry and makes them go further. For best results, coat the breasts twice, pressing each side firmly into the crumbs.

To coat chicken breasts

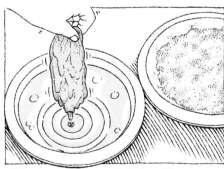

Dip in egg mix and shake off excess.

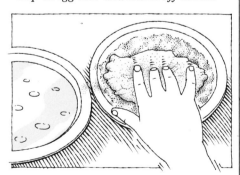

Next, press each side of the egg-coated breast into the breadcrumbs.

Italian-Style Turkey Escalopes

Serve with rice or potato croquettes and grilled tomatoes.

Serves 4   ☆☆
Preparation: 5 minutes
Cooking: 20 minutes

4 turkey escalopes, each about 4oz (125g)
2oz (50g) flour
salt and freshly ground black pepper
2oz (50g) butter
about 2oz (50g) Parma ham
2oz (50g) grated Parmesan cheese

Flatten the escalopes, coat them in seasoned flour and fry as for Breaded Chicken Breasts.

☐ Reduce the heat and place a slice of ham on top of each escalope. Sprinkle the cheese over the ham, cover the pan and cook very gently for about 10 minutes, or until the cheese is melted. Serve immediately.
Variation: Try adding 1 teaspoon of finely chopped sage leaves, or ½ teaspoon dried, to seasoned flour.

Chicken Indienne

Serve with boiled rice and sweetcorn.

Serves 4   ☆☆☆
Preparation: 3 minutes
Cooking: 30 minutes

8 chicken legs
2 tablespoons flour
¼ teaspoon mild curry powder
salt and freshly ground black pepper
3oz (75g) butter
7 fl oz (200ml) water

Put 4 of the chicken legs in a large plastic bag, together with the flour, curry powder and salt and pepper to taste.

☐ Close the bag and shake it well to coat the chicken thoroughly. Remove the coated chicken and repeat with the 4 remaining legs.

☐ Melt the butter in a 9in (23cm) frying-pan over a moderate heat until it begins to brown.

☐ Fry the chicken legs for 3-4 minutes on each side to brown. Sprinkle over any remaining flour.

☐ Add the water, lower the heat, cover the pan and simmer for about 20 minutes, stirring occasionally, until the chicken is tender. Transfer chicken to a warmed serving plate, garnish with chopped chives and keep hot. Boil the pan juices rapidly until thick and smooth, pour into a warmed sauceboat and serve.

❊ *To freeze:* cool the chicken with the sauce and put into a covered container. Label and freeze for up to 3 months. To serve, thaw in the refrigerator for 24 hours and re-heat in the oven at 350F (180C) gas 4 for about 20 minutes. Add a little more water to the sauce, if necessary.

Italian-Style Turkey Escalopes
These cuts from the breast come in different sizes and thicknesses. You can slice them and then pound them to make them as thin as you require.
Parma ham is sold in large, very thin slices. Cut the slices to fit the turkey escalopes.

Chicken Indienne, chicken legs fried in a lightly curried coating and served with a curry-flavoured sauce.

Frying batter

Delicate foods such as fish, cheeses and fruit are often cooked in a protective coating of batter before being fried. Fried batter itself, however, can make delicious and satisfying pancakes, crêpes and scones. Suitable for main courses, desserts and afternoon teas, such treats are also often a clever means of dressing up leftover food.

● Do not whisk batters too much or the results will be tough.

● If batter doesn't mix smoothly at first, leave it to stand for a few minutes, then whisk in the flour particles as they rise to the surface.

● 'Resting' the batter for 1-2 hours allows the gluten in the flour to relax and expand, and the batter thickens slightly. Although not strictly necessary, this does give a final product that is less doughy.

● Batter can be kept, covered, for up to 24 hours in the refrigerator.

Making pancakes and crêpes

If making these regularly, invest in a good pancake pan. However an omelette pan or any suitably sized heavy-based frying-pan serves just as well. To fry pancakes successfully it is very important to heat the pan over a moderate heat until hot enough to set the batter almost immediately, but not hot enough to burn it. It should bubble on top and brown underneath almost immediately. If the pan is not hot enough, the batter will stick.

● Do not use too much fat or oil as this gives heavy, greasy results. Merely coat the pan lightly with clarified butter or oil and pour off any excess for re-use.

● Stir the batter after making each pancake to prevent the flour settling on the bottom.

● Pancakes made with thicker batter take longer to cook than those made with thin batter, but as the thicker batter absorbs more heat the pan should still be as hot.

● Find a ladle or small cup that holds exactly the right quantity of batter just to cover the base of the pan. Once you discover the correct quantity of batter for your pan you will be able to make fine lacy crêpes, or more substantial pancakes, with great success.

❄ **To store the crêpes,** layer them with pieces of greaseproof paper. Wrap in foil or cling film and store in the refrigerator for 3-4 days, or in the freezer for up to 2 months. To serve, thaw and peel off crêpes. Roll or fold. Wrap in foil and heat in the oven for about 10 minutes at 350F (180C) gas 4.

Crêpes

Fold or roll these lacy crêpes and serve with sugar and lemon juice or a liqueur, or jam.

Makes 12
Preparation: 15 minutes plus resting
Cooking: 35 minutes

4oz (125g) flour
a pinch of salt
1oz (25g) caster sugar
2 eggs, size 2
½ pint (300ml) milk
clarified butter or oil, for greasing

Sift the flour, salt and sugar into bowl and make a well in the centre.

□ Drop the eggs into the well. Stir flour into the eggs then gradually whisk in milk until the mixture is the consistency of single cream.

□ Make sure the batter is smooth, then let it rest, covered, in the refrigerator for at least 30 minutes.

□ Lightly grease the base of a 7in (18cm) pan with butter. Put the pan over a moderate heat. When hot, spoon in 2-3 tablespoons of the batter, quickly turning and twisting the pan to make a thin even film over the base.

□ Cook for 1-1½ minutes or until brown at the underside, then turn and cook the second side. Continue in the same way until all the batter has been used and the crêpes cooked.

Soufflé Pancakes

Serve with honey, jam, or syrup.

Makes 8
Preparation: 15 minutes plus resting
Cooking: 25-30 minutes

4oz (100g) flour
a pinch of salt
a pinch of caster sugar
2 eggs, size 2
about 8 fl oz (250ml) milk
clarified butter or oil, for greasing

Sift flour, salt and sugar into a bowl and make a well in the centre. Drop 1 whole egg and 1 egg yolk in it.

□ Mix the flour into the eggs, then gradually whisk in enough milk to give the batter the consistency of single cream. Cover the bowl and let it stand for at least 30 minutes.

□ Whisk 1 egg white until it forms soft peaks and fold into batter.

□ Lightly grease a 5in(13cm) pan with clarified butter or oil and place over a moderate heat.

□ When the pan is hot, spoon in 2-3 tablespoons of batter, turning and twisting the pan to coat the base evenly. Cook for 1½-2 minutes or until brown on the underside, then turn and repeat on the other side. Continue until batter has been used.

Corn Fritters

Serve with fried bacon, sausages, or Chicken Maryland.

Makes 8 ☆
Preparation: 5 minutes
Cooking: 15 minutes

1oz (25g) fresh breadcrumbs
7oz (200g) canned sweetcorn, drained
2oz (50g) flour
1 teaspoon baking powder
½ teaspoon salt
1 egg, size 2
4 tablespoons milk
1oz (25g) butter

Put the breadcrumbs and sweetcorn in a bowl, then sift in the flour, baking powder and salt. Make a well in the centre and add the egg and milk. Mix the ingredients well, whisking until the batter is smooth.

☐ Cover and leave to rest in the refrigerator for 20 minutes.

☐ Melt half the butter in a 9in (23cm) frying-pan until it starts to brown.

☐ Drop 4 separate tablespoonfuls of batter into the pan and level with a knife. Cook for about 2 minutes on each side to brown. Melt the remaining butter and cook the rest of the batter.

Three-in-the-pan Cakes

Serve freshly made with lashings of butter, for afternoon tea.

Makes 12 ☆
Preparation: 10 minutes
Cooking: 15-20 minutes

9oz (250g) self-raising flour
a pinch of salt
1 egg, size 2
8 fl oz (250ml) milk
6oz (175g) mixed dried fruit
1oz (25g) butter

Sift the flour and salt into a bowl and make a well in the centre. Break the egg into the well and mix it with the flour. Gradually whisk in the milk to make a smooth thick batter. Stir in the fruit.

☐ Melt one-quarter of the butter in a 9in (23cm) frying-pan over a moderate heat until it begins to brown. Drop three separate tablespoonfuls of batter into the pan.

☐ Cook for about 2 minutes on each side to brown. Repeat this process, greasing the pan after each batch, until all the mixture has been used.

Corn Fritters
Use half wholemeal flour and half white flour to give the cakes a nice nutty taste.

Stuffed crêpes
For a quick and appetizing supper dish, omit sugar and fill crêpes with a mixture of cooked chicken, fish, or shellfish—or any suitable leftovers—in a thick creamy white sauce.

Three-in-the-pan Cakes
These are so called because 3 cakes are cooked in the pan at a time. Of course, there is no reason why you can't cook 4 at once if you have a large enough pan!

Keep cooked pancakes hot while frying the rest of the batter by stacking them on a plate, covered with foil, in a warm oven. Alternatively, put them in a deep dish over a pan of simmering water. For sweet pancakes, sprinkle each one with sugar to prevent them sticking to each other.

Mixing, frying and serving batter pancakes and scones.

Let the omelette flop gently out on the plate, angling the pan more steeply as it slips out to fold it. A perfect omelette should be creamy and soft inside, with a tender golden skin.

Hints for making a good omelette:
● use the right size of pan (see below)
● use butter both for flavour and as a good indicator of temperature
● agitate the surface of plain omelettes with a spatula during cooking
● serve the omelette immediately it's cooked

Pan size guide (measure the base):
6in (15cm)–2-egg omelette
7in (18cm)–3-egg omelette
9in (23cm)–4-egg omelette
A slightly larger size is better for soufflé omelettes.

Servings:
plain omelette: 2 eggs per person
sweet omelette: 2-3 eggs for 2 people

For leftovers
Omelettes make an excellent way of using up any leftover cooked meat and vegetables, and a way of trying out interesting and unusual combinations. Again, most items that do not melt, or cannot be grated or finely chopped, should first be warmed through gently.

Plain Omelette

Serves 2 ☆☆
Preparation: 2 minutes
Cooking: 2-3 minutes

4 eggs
3 tablespoons water
salt and freshly ground black pepper
1oz (25g) butter

Lightly beat together the eggs and water with salt and pepper to taste.
☐ Put the butter in a 9in (23cm) frying-pan or omelette pan over a medium heat until it is just beginning to brown. Tilt the pan and rotate it so the butter coats the sides.
☐ Pour the eggs into the pan. As soon as the mixture begins to set underneath, draw the edges away from the pan with a palette knife. Tilt the pan around to let the liquid egg flow under. Continue until most of the omelette has set but the top is still creamy.
☐ Finally loosen all round the edge of the omelette with the palette knife, then shake the pan sharply to make sure the omelette is not sticking before turning out onto a warmed plate as shown. Serve immediately.
Variation: Sprinkle with 1-2 tablespoons chopped fresh herbs before folding.

To fill a Plain Omelette: try spreading 4oz (100g) of any of the following over the omelette before folding and turning out:

Grated Cheddar or Parmesan cheese.
Mozzarella cheese, cut into thin slices.
Canned sweetcorn and tuna, the tuna flaked and both heated in a small saucepan and then well drained.
Cooked shelled prawns, heated through gently in a little butter, then mixed together with 2 tablespoons cream.

Ham Omelette with Herbs

Serves 1 ☆☆☆
Preparation: 8 minutes
Cooking: 2-3 minutes

2 eggs
2 teaspoons finely chopped parsley
1 tablespoon water
salt and freshly ground black pepper
1oz (25g) butter
2oz (50g) ham, chopped
2 teaspoons finely chopped chives

Lightly beat together the eggs, parsley, water and salt and pepper.
☐ Heat the butter in a 6in (15cm) omelette or frying-pan over a medium heat until it is just beginning to brown.
☐ Add the ham then pour the egg mixture over. Fry as for the Plain Omelette.
☐ Carefully slide the omelette on a hot dish, folding it as you turn it out, as shown. Serve immediately sprinkled with the chives.

Italian Frittata

Serves 2 ☆☆☆
Preparation: 2 minutes
Cooking: about 16 minutes

4 eggs
3 tablespoons water
2oz (50g) grated Parmesan cheese
salt and freshly ground black pepper
1oz (25g) butter

Lightly beat together the eggs, water, cheese and salt and pepper.
☐ Melt the butter in an 8in (20cm) omelette or frying-pan on a medium heat until it foams. Add the egg mixture and reduce to as low a heat as possible. Leave to cook for about 15 minutes until set but still runny on surface. Pre-heat grill to high.
☐ Flash frittata under grill for 30-60 seconds, to set but not brown.
☐ Loosen around the edges with a palette knife and slide, right way up, on to a warmed serving plate.

Apple Omelette

☆☆☆

Serves 2
Preparation: 5 minutes
Cooking: about 10 minutes

2oz (50g) butter
1 dessert apple, peeled, cored and diced
2 eggs
1 tablespoon water
2 tablespoons caster sugar

Put the butter and apple into a 5in (12.5cm) frying-pan or omelette pan. Place over a medium heat and cook, stirring occasionally, for 10 minutes, or until the apples soften.

☐ Meanwhile, lightly beat together the eggs and water. Pour into the pan and fry as for the Plain Omelette, but sprinkling with most of the sugar as it cooks.

☐ Carefully slide the omelette onto a hot dish, folding it as it is turned out. Serve immediately sprinkled with the remaining sugar.

Soufflé Omelette

☆☆

Serves 2
Preparation: 5 minutes
Cooking: 5-7 minutes

---

2 eggs, size 2, separated
3 tablespoons sugar
½oz (15g) butter
a little icing sugar

Pre-heat the grill to medium.

☐ Whisk egg whites to soft peaks, gradually adding sugar. Whisk yolks, then fold gently into whites.

☐ Heat the butter in an 8in (20cm) frying-pan over a moderate heat until just beginning to brown.

☐ Turn down the heat to low. Pour the mixture into the pan and cover. Cook for 3-5 minutes until the underside can be drawn away from the pan and is lightly brown.

☐ Place omelette under grill for about 2 minutes, just to set.

☐ Turn out, dust with icing sugar and serve with fresh fruit.

The different stages in making a soufflé omelette.

Apple Omelette

Use a tart dessert apple for best flavour and texture. Cooking apples very quickly turn to a pulp.

Party apple omelette

When entertaining, give it a dramatic and extravagant touch by flambéing it. Heat 2 tablespoons Calvados or brandy in a small saucepan until steaming. Set it alight and pour over the omelette just as it is served.

Jam Omelette

For a delicious last-minute dessert, heat 4 tablespoons of red jam in a small saucepan. Spoon the heated jam over one half of a plain omelette just before turning out. Dust the folded omelette well with icing sugar.

Fried bacon, egg, tomatoes and mushrooms make a hearty breakfast.

Fried eggs

Everyone likes their eggs fried in a different way. However, the perfect fried egg should have a clear upright yolk surrounded by a white which is just set and still tender. The two basic rules are: have enough fat to cover the base of the frying-pan, and use low heat so the eggs cook gently.

The 'Breakfast' Fry-up

Cooking a variety of foods in one pan to have them ready at the same time means careful timing. Some foods (sausages and eggs) cook more quickly in a covered pan, but this traps steam so the food cooks in that rather than frying crisply. Try cooking the items separately then transferring them to a large warmed serving platter in a warm oven.

Eggs that stick

Eggs stick to the pan and break when served because of burnt sediment from the cooking of other foods. For perfect fried eggs therefore, either use a separate clean pan or tip out and strain the fat and wipe out the pan before cooking the eggs.

Fried Eggs

Fry eggs in bacon fat, lard or cooking fat, oil or butter. For the whites to stay white, cook them in white fat, but remember that butter and bacon fat give better flavour.

Serves 4   ☆☆
Preparation and cooking:
2-3 minutes

---

about 2oz (50g) butter
4 eggs
salt and freshly ground black pepper

Heat the butter in a large frying-pan over a low heat. When the foam begins to clear, gently break the eggs into the pan one at a time and fry gently until the eggs are set.

☐ Sprinkle with salt and pepper and separate the egg whites with a knife. Using a large fish slice, carefully lift out each egg.

☐ Serve immediately on or with toast, or to accompany fried bacon, sausages, or kippers.

A Breakfast Fry-Up

The great British breakfast is a justly celebrated institution. The traditional fry-up is usually followed by mounds of hot buttered toast and marmalade, and a pot of tea or coffee.

The Fry-up also makes an excellent light supper, especially with the addition of a lamb's kidney or a cutlet.

Serves 1   ☆☆☆
Preparation: 5 minutes
Cooking: about 15 minutes

2oz (50g) button mushrooms
3 rashers bacon
1 tomato
salt and freshly ground black pepper
1oz (25g) lard or bacon fat
2 large sausages
1 egg

Wipe the mushrooms clean with kitchen paper and trim the stems level with the caps. Remove the rinds from the bacon, if liked. Cut the tomato across in half and season well.

☐ Heat the fat in an 8in (20cm) frying-pan over medium heat until sizzling, then reduce the heat slightly. Add the sausages and roll to coat in the fat. Cover the pan and fry for about 5 minutes until browned on one side.

☐ Remove the lid. Turn the sausages and fry for 2-3 minutes until browned, then add the bacon and mushrooms.

☐ After 1-2 minutes, turn the bacon, stir the mushrooms and add the tomato. Cook for a further 2 minutes. Lower the heat and move the well-browned foods back in the pan to leave room for the egg. Break it into the cleared spot and cook for 1-2 minutes until set to taste.

Tip: All of the foods included in the recipe are best cooked on a moderate heat with the exception of the egg which needs a low heat. Frying-pans made of different materials respond with varying speed to heat changes. Do not let the pan get too hot.

Sautés

Like shallow-frying, sautéing involves the rapid frying of food, stirring and tossing, to brown it quickly for taste and colour. Dishes referred to as sautés, however, can often then continue to cook with gentle stewing of the browned meat, fish or poultry, either in its own juices, or in a sauce with vegetables and other flavouring ingredients. The quantity of sauce is usually small, so cooking continues more by a process of steaming than stewing.

The classic French 'Poulet Sauté à la Normande', for instance, browns pieces of sliced apple after the chicken portions and both are then gently simmered in a mixture of chicken stock and Calvados.

Sautés give the creative cook great scope to combine unusual ingredients, use up leftovers in imaginative ways and create splendid one-pan meals at short notice.

Suitable foods for sautés
In general, the foods that lend themselves best to this sort of dish are the more tender cuts of meat and poultry. Chops and cutlets of beef, pork, lamb, veal and game can all be used to great effect as can small pieces of poultry and feathered game – and most foods chopped small. It is also a good way of preserving the flavour and texture of firm-fleshed fish and some types of offal.

Suitable fats for sautés
The usual range of cooking oils can all be used but, as the cooking medium plays a great part in the flavour of the finished dish, taste must play an equal part in the choice. For this reason, butter is much favoured in sautés and as the browning process is brief it doesn't usually have time to burn. Equal parts of butter and oil are popular when large quantities are involved and browning is likely to be lengthier.

Sautéed Pork Chops with Mushrooms

Serves 4   ☆☆☆
Preparation and cooking: 40 minutes

4 pork chops, each about 6oz (175g)
salt and freshly ground black pepper
6oz (175g) mushrooms, wiped and trimmed
4oz (125g) butter
1 tablespoon shallot or onion, finely chopped
1 tablespoon leek, finely chopped
1 tablespoon finely chopped parsley
1 tablespoon finely chopped celery leaves
1 tablespoon finely chopped coriander leaves
4 tablespoons water
3oz (75g) grated Cheddar cheese

Trim excess fat off the chops and pat dry with kitchen paper. Rub them well with salt and pepper. Slice the mushrooms as shown.

☐ Put 1oz (25g) of the butter into a 9in (23cm) frying-pan over a moderate heat until it begins to brown. Sauté half the mushrooms for about 2 minutes until the butter is absorbed and the mushrooms are just lightly browned. Remove and keep warm. Cook the remaining mushrooms, using another 1oz (25g) butter.

☐ Add 1oz (25g) butter to the pan with the shallot or onion, leek and herbs. Stir to coat and sauté lightly for a minute. Return all the mushrooms to the pan. Stir for 2 minutes. Season, transfer to a warmed shallow dish and keep hot.

☐ Add the remaining 1oz (25g) butter to the pan. When just browning, add the chops. Cook for about 3 minutes on each side. Add the water, cover and simmer for 5 minutes.

☐ Pre-heat a moderate grill. Remove the chops and arrange over the mushrooms. Stir up any sediment and pour pan juices over. (If the pan has cooked dry, add a little water.)

☐ Sprinkle the chops with cheese and brown under the grill for about 3 minutes before serving.

Suitable pans for sautés
The true sauté pan differs from the ordinary frying-pan in that it has slightly deeper, less flared sides to allow for ready access with the spatula – for rapid turning and stirring – while also providing a reservoir for any sauce. However, any fairly robust frying-pan will suffice as the quantities of liquid involved are never great. The size of the pan is critical as the browning cannot be satisfactorily effected if the pan is too crowded. If necessary, brown the food in batches. If the pan is too large, the juices will be too thinly spread and will evaporate too readily.

Preparing mushrooms
Fresh mushrooms only need wiping with paper towels. Only cut off the very base of the stem, which may be a little soft and brown. Leaving the stems on helps keep the mushrooms from shrinking. For less fresh mushrooms, pull off the very thin skin covering the cap and trim the stem level with the base of the head. The trimmings may be used to give added flavour to stocks and soups.

Finishing the sauces:
After browning and stewing, the pan juices are normally made into a sauce. If the food is cooked only in its own juices, the pan is usually deglazed with a little water, stock or wine. Flavoured liquids which have been used for the simmering stage – again basically stocks and wines – are mostly thickened either by rapid reduction or by the addition of any number of classic thickeners: cornflour, egg-and-cream liaisons; thick vegetable purées or plain butter or cream.

Slicing the mushrooms

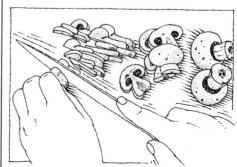

Cut the mushrooms into slices lengthways and cut these slices into strips.

Beef with peppers

For an alternative sauce, mix 2 teaspoons cornflour with the vermouth. Add the stock, herbs and tomato purée and stir in the mixed cornflour with the browned steak and peppers. Cook, stirring constantly, for 1 minute.

Quick Steak with Orange Sauce

Steak from one of the less tender cuts of beef is more economical, but if sold as 'flash-fry' or 'quick-fry' it has been pounded first with a special meat hammer which breaks up the fibres. This steak cooks very quickly and can make an attractive dish.

Beef with Peppers and Liver and Apple Sauté both make good, quick supper dishes to serve with boiled potatoes and a salad.

Beef with Peppers

Serves 3   ☆☆☆
Preparation and cooking: 15 minutes

**6 slices fillet steak, each about ¼in (5mm)
   thick weighing ¾lb (350g) in total
salt and freshly ground black pepper
1 large red pepper, deseeded
1 large green pepper, deseeded
3oz (75g) butter
¼ pint (150ml) Basic Brown Stock
3 tablespoons red vermouth
2 teaspoons tomato purée
½ teaspoon dried marjoram**

Pat the meat dry, season and cut into 2in (5cm) squares. Cut the peppers into julienne strips.

☐ Heat half the butter in a 9in (23cm) frying-pan over a moderate heat, until it begins to brown. Sauté peppers for about 3 minutes. Remove and keep hot.

☐ Add remaining butter to the pan. When browning lightly, add the meat in a single layer. Fry for 2 minutes, turning once, to brown. Remove and keep hot.

☐ Add remaining ingredients. Boil vigorously for about 5 minutes until syrupy. Return everything to the pan, stir together lightly and serve.

Quick Steak with Orange Sauce

Serves 3   ☆☆
Preparation and cooking: 15 minutes

**¾lb (350g) flash-fry steak
salt and freshly ground black pepper
2oz (50g) butter
juice of 1 large orange
about ¼ pint (150ml) Meat Stock
½ teaspoon dried oregano
6 black olives, halved and stoned
1 teaspoon grated orange rind**

Pat the meat dry. Rub with salt and pepper and cut into 2in (5cm) squares.

☐ Heat the butter in a 9in (23cm) frying-pan over a moderate heat until it starts to brown. Add the meat in a single layer. Fry for about a minute. Turn and cook a further 1-1½ minutes to brown. Transfer to a serving dish and keep hot.

☐ Make orange juice up to 7 fl oz (200ml) with stock. Add to the pan with the oregano. Boil vigorously for about 5 minutes until syrupy.

☐ Add the olives and the orange rind and mix thoroughly. Spoon over the steak and serve.

Liver and Apple Sauté

Two inexpensive ingredients sautéed together make an unusual light supper. Serve with fingers of toast.

Serves 4	☆☆

Preparation and cooking: 20 minutes

1¼lb (575g) lambs' or calves' liver
3 dessert apples, about 10oz (275g), peeled, quartered and cored
2oz (50g) butter
salt and freshly ground black pepper
chopped parsley to garnish

Pat the liver dry with kitchen paper. Cut into pieces about 1¼in (3cm) long and pat dry again. Cut the apple into thick slices.

☐ Heat one-third of the butter in a 9in (23cm) frying-pan over a moderate heat until lightly browning. Sauté half the liver for 2-3 minutes to brown lightly and 'set'. Transfer to a serving dish and keep hot.

☐ Sauté the remaining liver, using another third of the butter. Pour pan juices over the liver in the serving dish.

☐ Add the last of the butter to the pan. When browning lightly, add the apples and sauté for 2-3 minutes to soften. Season to taste and garnish with the parsley to serve.

Kidneys in Sherry

Serve for lunch on hot buttered toast or fried bread croûtes.

Serves 2	☆☆

Preparation and cooking: 25 minutes

---

4 lambs' kidneys
1oz (25g) butter
1 tablespoon olive oil
2oz (50g) shallots, finely chopped
2 garlic cloves
4 tablespoons dry sherry
salt and freshly ground black pepper

Remove all fat and the thin membrane surrounding each kidney. Cut out the core from the indentation in the short side of the kidney. Cut each kidney in half across and pat dry.

☐ Put the butter and oil together with the shallots and garlic in an 8in (20cm) frying-pan, set over a low heat. Sauté for about 10 minutes.

☐ Turn up the heat and sauté kidneys for about 5 minutes.

☐ Add sherry and season. Cook, stirring, for 2 minutes and serve.

Liver and Apple Sauté

Buy the liver in a piece so you can cut it into even slices about ¾in (1.5cm) thick.
Cook the liver to the degree your prefer. Thick pieces take longer than thin ones, but ¾in (1.5cm) slices will be cooked to medium-done by the time given.
Variation: Make this into a classic sauté by deglazing the pan with some Chicken Stock, cider, Calvados or red wine, and thicken with a little cornflour.

Liver cooked this way browns very little, and exudes juices which should be poured over the liver when serving.

Kidneys in Sherry

This is also a very quick dish to make. The kidneys don't brown, but stay pink and succulent and their natural juices provide a sauce which requires no thickening.

When cut into small pieces, chicken breast fillet cooks very quickly. Don't overcook it as it soon loses its succulence.

Chicken Taj Mahal
✳ To freeze:
Cool the dish. Put into a covered foil container. Label and freeze for up to 1 month.
To serve: thaw and re-heat in the covered container in an oven pre-heated to 350F (180C) gas 4 for about ½ hour. Stir well and add a little stock if necessary. Transfer to a warmed serving dish and stir in the grapes.

The various steps in preparing and cooking Chicken in Mustard Sauce – a basic sauté dish.

Chicken in Mustard Sauce

Serves 4 ☆☆☆
Preparation: 5 minutes
Cooking: 15 minutes

1lb (500g) chicken breast fillets
salt and freshly ground black pepper
2oz (50g) butter
3 tablespoons dry sherry
¼ pint (150ml) double cream
2 teaspoons French mustard
2 tablespoons Chicken Stock

Pat the chicken dry, cut into 1½in (3.5cm) squares and season well.

☐ Melt the butter in a 9in (23cm) frying-pan over a moderate heat. When it starts to brown, lay the pieces of chicken in the pan one at a time. Fry for 5-6 minutes, turning once to brown both sides. Remove and keep warm.

☐ Add the sherry to the pan. Boil for 2-3 minutes until almost evaporated.

☐ Add the cream and the mustard and boil for 3-4 minutes, stirring, until the sauce is thick. Stir in the stock and adjust the seasoning.

☐ Return the chicken to the pan, stir until heated through, and serve.

Chicken Taj Mahal

An exquisite and subtle curry flavour makes this a dish to remember and an easy one with which to impress when entertaining. Serve on a bed of fluffy white rice with a green salad.

Serves 4 ☆☆☆
Preparation: 25 minutes
Cooking: 35-40 minutes

1¼lb (575g) chicken breast fillets
4 tablespoons flour
salt and freshly ground black pepper
3oz (75g) butter
3oz (75g) onion, finely chopped
2 large garlic cloves, finely chopped
2oz (50g) celery, finely chopped
1 tablespoon curry paste
14 fl oz (400ml) Chicken Stock
¼ pint (150ml) single cream
a squeeze of lemon juice
3oz (75g) green grapes, deseeded and
    halved

Pat the chicken dry with kitchen paper and cut it into 1½in (3.5cm) squares. Shake in a plastic bag along with the flour and salt and pepper.

☐ Melt one third of the butter in 9in (23cm) frying-pan over a moderate heat until it is beginning to brown. Sauté half the chicken for 4-5 minutes until lightly browned. Remove and keep warm. Sauté the rest of the chicken using another third of the butter.

□ Reduce the heat. Add the last of the butter, the onion, garlic, celery and curry paste. Cook, stirring frequently, for 10 minutes. Do not brown!

□ Add any flour remaining in the bag. Mix in well. Gradually stir in the stock. Simmer for 10 minutes, stirring frequently. Stir in the cream and adjust the seasoning with salt, pepper and lemon juice.

□ Sieve the sauce and return it to the rinsed-out pan with the chicken. Cover and simmer for 5 minutes.

□ Stir the grapes into the chicken mixture and serve immediately.

Sautéed Walnut Chicken

Serves 4 ☆☆☆
Preparation: 5 minutes
Cooking: 25 minutes

4 chicken breast fillets, each about
    5oz (150g)
salt and freshly ground black pepper
3 tablespoons flour
3oz (75g) butter
2oz (50g) shelled walnuts, quartered
3 shallots, finely chopped
a sprig of fresh tarragon or a pinch of dried
    tarragon
¼ pint (150ml) dry white wine
7 fl oz (200ml) Chicken Stock

Pat the chicken dry with kitchen paper. Shake in a plastic bag with salt and pepper and 2 tablespoons of flour.

□ Put 2oz (50g) of the butter into a 9in (23cm) frying-pan over a moderate heat, until it begins to brown. Sauté walnuts to brown lightly. Remove and set aside in a warm place.

□ Lay the chicken in the pan and fry for about 3 minutes on each side to brown lightly. Remove; keep warm.

□ Stir the shallots and tarragon into the butter remaining in the pan and add any flour left in the bag.

□ Gradually stir in the wine and stock and cook for a minute. Adjust to a smooth coating consistency by stirring in a few pieces of beurre manié, made by kneading together the remaining flour and butter.

□ Return the chicken to the pan. Cover and simmer for 12-15 minutes until tender.

□ Transfer chicken to a warmed serving dish. Stir walnuts into sauce and pour it over chicken to serve.

Kneaded butter (beurre manié)
Beat together 4oz (100g) each of softened butter and flour. Stored in the refrigerator in a covered container, it provides a very convenient means of adjusting the consistency of sauces. Add the beurre manié to the hot dish by the teaspoonful and cook it in well, for at least 1 minute. This ensures that any floury taste is cooked out.

Sautéed Walnut Chicken
❋ To freeze:
Omit the walnuts. Put the chicken fillets one layer deep in their sauce in a shallow foil container. Cool, cover, label and freeze for up to 2 months.
To serve: thaw and re-heat the chicken in its container in an oven set to 350F (180C) gas 4 for at least ½ hour. Stir well and add a little stock or wine, if necessary. Meanwhile, fry the walnuts in a little butter and stir into the sauce just before serving.

Sweet potatoes

Choose smaller sweet potatoes for easier and more even cooking. If they are too long to fit into the available saucepan, cut them in half. Add 1 teaspoon lemon juice to the cooking water to prevent discoloration. Cook until the centres are still firm. If over-cooked, sweet potatoes break up during sautéing.

Beetroot (Beets)

Choose small ones for serving as a hot vegetable. Buy them uncooked so you can cook them to your taste. Beets which come at about 12 to the lb (500g) will cook in about 20 minutes in the summer, 25 minutes in winter. To test if they are cooked, rub the boiling beetroot with the back of a fork. When cooked, the skins rub off easily. Beetroot may be boiled in advance and stored in a covered container for a day or two in the refrigerator. Sauté them and make the sauce just before serving.

Sautéed Courgettes

An excellent accompaniment to grilled meats and poultry.

Serves 4 ☆☆

Preparation: 5 minutes

Cooking: 10 minutes

1¼lb (575g) courgettes
2oz (50g) butter
2 large garlic cloves, finely chopped
grated rind and juice of 1 lime
½ teaspoon ground cinnamon
salt and freshly ground black pepper
4 tablespoons natural yogurt

Trim off and discard the ends of the courgettes and cut them each into 2in (5cm) lengths.

☐ Melt the butter in a 9in (23cm) frying-pan over a moderate heat, until it begins to brown. Sauté the garlic and courgettes together for about 10 minutes until the courgettes are tender but still crisp.

☐ Add the lime rind and juice, cinnamon and salt and pepper to taste. Stir in the yogurt, warm through and serve.

Glazed Sweet Potatoes

This appetizing vegetable side dish goes particularly well with roast or boiled ham or game.

Serves 4 ☆☆

Preparation: 5 minutes

Cooking: about 15 minutes

1lb (500g) sweet potatoes
salt and freshly ground black pepper
2oz (50g) butter
1oz (25g) soft brown sugar
2 tablespoons orange juice
1 teaspoon grated orange rind
2 tablespoons dark rum

Wash the sweet potatoes under cold running water. Cook in a large pan of boiling salted water for about 10 minutes. Drain, strip off the skins and cut into slices about ¼in (5mm) thick.

☐ Melt the butter in an 8in (20cm) frying-pan over a moderate heat until lightly browned. Sauté the sweet potatoes with the sugar for 2 minutes until the sugar is melted and very slightly browned.

☐ Stir in the orange juice and rind, the rum and salt and pepper to taste. Simmer for 5 minutes, stirring occasionally and serve immediately.

Beets in Red Wine

Serve with roast meats and game dishes.

Serves 4 ☆☆

Preparation: 5 minutes

Cooking: 30-35 minutes

1lb (500g) small beetroot
2oz (50g) butter
coarsely ground black pepper
2 tablespoons raspberry vinegar
¼ pint (150ml) dry red wine
1 tablespoon sugar
2 teaspoons cornflour
1 tablespoon cold water
1 tablespoon finely chopped chives

Wash the beets under cold running water. Cook in a large pan of boiling salted water for 25-30 minutes until tender. Drain.

☐ Cut off the tops and tails, strip off the skins and cut the beets into slices about ¼in (5mm) thick.

☐ Melt the butter in a 9in (23cm) frying-pan over a moderate heat until beginning to brown. Stir in the cooked beets, sprinkle well with the black pepper and sauté for 3 minutes. Add the raspberry vinegar and the wine.

☐ Mix the sugar and cornflour smoothly with the water. Stir in a little of the hot liquid then stir the mixed cornflour back into the pan and cook, stirring constantly for 2-3 minutes until the red wine sauce is thickened and smooth.

☐ Sprinkle with the chopped chives before serving.

Stir-frying

This age-old Chinese method of cooking is enjoying a well-deserved vogue in the West. Food cut into small pieces is fried very quickly in a flavoured oil over a high heat. The natural textures and colours are well preserved, and the fullest flavour developed. Also, little of the nutritional value is lost as the cooking is so brief and no cooking medium is discarded. Stir-frying is also done in a minimum of oil or fat, making it a valuable method for the health-conscious.

Cut meat into equal-sized pieces.

The traditional vessel for stir-frying is the wok. The deep, rounded sides pool the oil at the bottom, distribute the heat and allow the food to be stirred and tossed vigorously for rapid and thorough cooking.

The cooking oil is generally flavoured at an early stage in the process by stir-frying ingredients such as garlic, spring onions and ginger in it to 'awaken' the wok. These may or may not be incorporated in the finished dish. The Chinese then pour a little rice wine around the wok which evaporates quickly but leaves an extra, subtle flavour.

The cooking itself is done at the highest of heats. The wok should be heated until it is smoking before the oil is added and then cooking proceeds when that oil is visibly hot and its surface trembling. The food is then 'surprised' by the wok and cooked so rapidly that any juices leaking from it quickly evaporate and form a surface seal. The food may or may not be browned. One of the joys of stir-frying is the ability to preserve natural coloration, like the white of cooked chicken flesh and the pale pinks and reds of seafood, and combine that with the vivid colours of leaf and root vegetables and vegetable fruits.

Food is cooked in successive batches normally starting with the meats, or any item requiring lengthier cooking, and finishing with any tender vegetable and fragile or volatile flavouring element. After all the batches are cooked, the ingredients are all returned to the wok and tossed to mix and re-heat.

Experienced wok-wielders can cook in this way without ever actually taking anything out of the pan – they merely push cooked batches up the sides. This is really only practicable at home when cooking small amounts. Otherwise keep a large, deep, covered serving dish warm in the oven to receive cooked food.

The process can also be continued with some gentle stewing in added stock or wine to ensure that the food is cooked through. This can then be thickened into a sauce.

Alternatively, tougher cuts of meat and denser vegetables may be par-cooked in advance.

Meats and poultry are often also prepared for stir-frying by marinating them in rice wine, soy sauce or even lemon juice.

Stir-frying is an excellent way of using up leftover food – both raw and cooked – and entire meals may be quickly cooked in the one pan.

However, the true satisfaction of stir-frying lies in bringing out the full flavours of fresh meat, poultry, fish, seafood and vegetables and marrying them together in arresting and unusual combinations of texture, type, colour and taste. Apart from being aesthetically satisfying, stir-frying can also be a lot of fun.

Finally stir-frying is a perfect method of cooking for entertaining. Most of the lengthy preparation can be done in advance and guests left only briefly for the few minutes it takes to toss up a memorable meal.

Foods for stir-frying

It is important to choose foods which are tender enough to cook quickly, but which have enough resilience to withstand constant stirring. White fish and some starchy vegetables tend to break up. Shellfish, monkfish, squid and carrots, for example, are all good.

Flavouring ingredients

Garlic and onions, particularly spring onions, make an important addition of flavour to stir-fried dishes. To extract as much flavour as possible, put them into the oil on a low heat at the beginning. Let them stew away for a few minutes then push aside before turning up the heat (they burn easily).
Fresh root ginger, sliced and then cut into fine strips gives an unusual, and distinctly oriental flavour to any stir-fry.

Monosodium glutamate, the 'taste catalyst', and soy sauce are the traditional seasonings in Chinese cuisine. Use salt very sparingly (and remember that soy sauce is very salty in itself) and freshly ground black pepper, of course. For variety, however, try a shake of cayenne, ground ginger, a little curry paste or chilli paste – sometimes even a little sugar or honey.

To use the wok

Place the wok straight over the heat source, and use a high heat. The wok can be supported on an accompanying 'converter' or stand. The cooking takes place at the very bottom of the bowl, so the fact that it doesn't sit flat on the cooker is not important. Stir-frying is not always easy on an electric cooker. Try using a sauté pan or high-sided, heavy-based frying-pan.

Lamb with Spring Vegetables

If you wish to add a more oriental flavour put in 2 or 3 slices of fresh root ginger, cut into fine strips, with the garlic. Alternatively, try marinating the lamb beforehand in equal parts soy sauce and rice wine – or leftover red wine. Season the finished dish with soy sauce rather than salt.

For an easier, quicker version, omit the baby onions and use about a dozen coarsely chopped spring onions.

Chicken with Crab and Broccoli

Use seafish sticks if crab sticks are not available, or try a small tin of crab meat, drained.

Step-by-step to Lamb with Spring Vegetables.

Lamb with Spring Vegetables

Serve on a bed of rice or noodles or with a buttery potato and celeriac purée.

Serves 4   ☆☆☆

Preparation: 30 minutes
Cooking: about 20 minutes

1¼lb (600g) boned leg of lamb
6oz (175g) mangetout peas, trimmed
6oz (175g) French beans, trimmed
6oz (175g) baby carrots, trimmed
12 small onions, about 6oz (175g)
salt and freshly ground black pepper
3 tablespoons oil
2 garlic cloves, finely sliced
3 spring onions, finely chopped
3 fl oz (100ml) Meat Stock

Cut the meat into slices about ½in (1cm) thick and pat dry with kitchen paper. Cut into cubes and spread them out on a plate.

☐ Cook the peas, beans, carrots and onions for 1 minute in boiling salted water, then rinse under cold running water. Drain them and peel the onions.

☐ Put 1 tablespoon of the oil in a wok set over a high heat until the oil is hot.

☐ Stir-fry the garlic for about 1 minute to flavour the oil, then remove and discard.

☐ Stir-fry the meat in 5 batches for about 3 minutes each, using more oil as necessary, removing each cooked batch with a slotted spoon and keeping warm. Let the oil re-heat between each addition until it stops sputtering.

☐ Add the peeled onions to the wok and cook for about 5 minutes until lightly browned.

☐ Return all the meat to the wok. Stir in the rest of the vegetables and the spring onions. Pour the stock over. Bring to the boil, lower the heat, cover and simmer for 5 minutes. Season to taste and serve immediately.

Chicken with Crab and Broccoli

Serves 4-6 ☆☆
Preparation: 20 minutes
Cooking: 10 minutes

8oz (225g) broccoli
salt and freshly ground black pepper
¾lb (350g) chicken breast fillet
8oz (225g) crab sticks, thawed if frozen
1oz (25g) butter
2 tablespoons oil
2 teaspoons cornflour
9 fl oz (275ml) Chicken Stock
soy sauce

Trim the florets from the broccoli, then cut the stems into ¼in (5mm) pieces. Discard any leaves. Wash the broccoli and drain.

☐ Cook the sliced stems for 3 minutes in boiling salted water. Drain and quickly rinse under running water. Drain again and pat dry.

☐ Pat the chicken and crab sticks dry and cut into thin fingers.

☐ Put the butter and oil in a wok set over a high heat. When the mixture browns slightly, stir-fry the chicken in 3 batches for 2-3 minutes each until lightly browned. Remove each batch when cooked and keep warm until all the chicken is cooked.

☐ Stir-fry the broccoli stems for 2 minutes. Remove and keep warm.

☐ Stir-fry the crab sticks in 3 batches for about 1 minute each. Remove each as it is cooked and keep warm.

☐ Put all the ingredients back in the wok together with the broccoli heads and cook for about 1 minute.

☐ Mix the cornflour with 1 tablespoon of the stock. Pour the rest of the stock into the wok. Bring to the boil, lower the heat, cover and simmer gently for 2 minutes.

☐ Add 2 tablespoons of hot stock to the cornflour mixture. Stir this mix well into the wok. Simmer gently for 2-3 minutes to thicken. Season with soy sauce and pepper, serve.

Chicken with Crab and Broccoli

Fats and oils for stir-frying

Any good cooking oil may be used for stir-frying. In addition to the more usual ones available in all supermarkets and the range of tasty olive oils, there are, for example, oils made from walnuts, almonds, soya beans, wheat germ, palm, coconut and sesame seeds which can all contribute a great deal to the flavour.

Drippings from roast poultry are also good. Be sure to strain them carefully while hot to remove any particles of meat. Store in a covered container in the fridge.

Lard is a good fat for pork cookery, as are the drippings from roast pork.

If butter is used, it should be mixed with equal parts of oil, or clarified to remove the solids which char when it is exposed to high heats.

Stir-fried chicken livers

The delicacy of chicken livers is fully preserved when they are stir-fried. They are particularly delicious in a sauce made with a purée of raw tomatoes flavoured with madeira. Cooking should be very brief, otherwise the livers quickly turn hard, then disintegrate.

Stir-fried chicken

Cooking chicken by stir-frying preserves more of its natural succulence and tenderness than any other method. The small pieces cook very quickly to an almost chalk white, with a faint hint of browning. Stir-fried chicken is good enough to eat on its own, but it also combines well with many other ingredients to make an amazing variety of stir-fried dishes. Try it with:
finely sliced fresh ginger;
shelled cashews;
grated lemon rind and juice;
shredded garlic and water chestnuts;
sliced black olives, tomatoes and Parmesan cheese.

Pineapple Chicken

Serves 4 ☆☆
Preparation and cooking: 35 minutes

1lb (500g) chicken breast fillets
3 tablespoons oil
½ medium onion, finely chopped
½ teaspoon ground ginger
freshly ground black pepper
15oz (425g) canned pineapple pieces
about ¼ pint (150ml) Chicken Stock
2 teaspoons cornflour
2 pieces of preserved ginger, finely chopped
2 teaspoons soy sauce

Pat the chicken dry with kitchen paper and slice into thin fingers.

☐ Put 1 tablespoon of the oil in a wok over a high heat until it is hot.

☐ Stir-fry the chicken in 5 batches for about 3 minutes each until lightly browned, adding more oil as necessary. Remove from the wok with a slotted spoon and keep warm. Let the oil reheat until it stops sputtering between each batch.

☐ When all the chicken is cooked, return the rest to the wok and stir in the onion. Stir-fry for 2 minutes. Sprinkle with ground ginger and pepper.

☐ Strain off the pineapple syrup and make up to 9 fl oz (275ml) with stock.

☐ Mix the cornflour with 1 tablespoon of stock mixture. Add the rest to the wok with the chopped ginger and pineapple pieces.

☐ Cover and simmer for 2 minutes. Stir in cornflour mixture and cook for 3 minutes, stirring constantly.

☐ Season with soy sauce and serve.

Chicken Livers in Madeira Sauce

Serve on toast as a first course.

Serves 4 ☆☆
Preparation and cooking: 30 minutes

1lb (500g) chicken livers
10oz (300g) tomatoes
1oz (25g) clarified butter
1 tablespoon finely chopped shallot
1 tablespoon finely chopped celery leaves
2 tablespoons madeira
½ teaspoon sugar
salt and freshly ground black pepper

Wash the livers well under cold running water then pat dry with kitchen paper. Cut off and discard any connective tissue or green-tinged flesh. Cut into equal-sized pieces.

☐ Halve the tomatoes, scoop out and discard the seeds and juice. Roughly chop the tomato flesh, then purée in a liquidizer or food processor. Press through a sieve.

☐ Melt the butter in a wok over a high heat until just beginning to brown. Stir-fry the livers and shallot together in three batches for 1-1½ minutes each, until the livers are firm and opaque. Remove with a slotted spoon and keep warm.

☐ When all are cooked, put them all back into the wok and add the celery leaves and tomato purée. Stir-fry for 2 minutes.

☐ Stir in the madeira, season with sugar, salt and pepper, and serve.
Tip: This dish also makes an interesting and unusual sauce for fresh pasta.

Devilled Turkey Livers

Serve on a bed of buttered rice as a main course with an accompanying salad, or with chunks of French bread as a starter.

Serves 4 as a main course ☆☆☆
or 6 as a first course
Preparation: 10 minutes
Cooking: 10-12 minutes

1lb (500g) frozen turkey livers, thawed
3 tablespoons oil
4 spring onions, sliced
juice and grated rind of ½ lemon
1 teaspoon capers
1 teaspoon curry paste
salt and freshly ground black pepper
3 fl oz (100ml) soured cream

Wash the livers well under cold running water. Pat dry with kitchen paper and cut across into finger-sized strips.

☐ Heat 1 tablespoon oil in a wok over a high heat until it is hot. Stir-fry the livers in three batches for 2-3 minutes each, until firm and lightly browned. Add more oil as necessary.

☐ Remove each batch of cooked livers with a slotted spoon and keep warm while frying the others.

☐ Add the spring onions. Stir-fry for 1 minute. Stir the livers back in with the onions. Add the lemon juice and rind, capers, and curry paste and season to taste with salt and pepper.

☐ Stir in the cream, cook for 1 minute just to heat through and serve immediately.

Turkey with Pineapple and Peppers

Serve on a bed of buttered noodles with an accompanying fresh mixed salad.

Serves 4   ☆☆
Preparation: 10 minutes
Cooking: 15 minutes

1lb (500g) turkey breast fillet
8oz (225g) green pepper, deseeded
8oz (225g) red pepper, deseeded
3 tablespoons oil or clarified butter
6oz (175g) canned pineapple chunks, drained
3 tablespoons dry white wine
salt and freshly ground black pepper
3 or 4 sprigs fresh thyme, leaves only

Pat the turkey dry with kitchen paper. Cut the fillet and the peppers into thin fingers or strips.

☐ Put 1 tablespoon of oil in a wok over a high heat until it is hot. Stir-fry the turkey in 3 batches for 3-4 minutes each until lightly browned. Set each cooked batch aside to keep warm. Add more oil as necessary.

☐ Add the peppers and stir-fry for 2 minutes. Return the cooked turkey to the wok. Add the pineapple, wine and a little salt and pepper. Bring to the boil, lower the heat, cover and cook gently for 3 minutes.

☐ Sprinkle with fresh thyme leaves and serve immediately.

Tip: Make a sauce by adding the syrup from the pineapple along with the wine. Mix 2 teaspoons of cornflour smoothly with 2 teaspoons of cold water and stir into the wok. Cook, stirring constantly, until thick and smooth.

Like chicken, stir-fried turkey marries well with many combinations of ingredients. Try it with:
cooked prawns and diced cucumber;
blanched broccoli and cauliflower florets and a sprinkling of sesame seeds;
button mushrooms and diced bacon;
chopped celery, baby onions, lemon rind and juice and some chopped fresh marjoram.

Turkey with Pineapple and Peppers needs only boiled rice and a green salad to make a hearty meal.

Wild Duck with Black Olives.

Wild duck with black olives

Cut the flesh from the bones with a sharp knife. Oven-ready duck may be used, and portions are sold in many supermarkets, but it will have a great deal less flavour. One large breast on the bone will produce one portion when filleted. Remove the fat and skin and use this and the bones to make stock.

Pick off the flesh from the rest of the bird to make into a pie and use the carcass and legs for stock.

Pigeon Breasts with apple

Pigeons are very economical birds and their very lean breasts are particularly suitable for stir-frying. Allow one pigeon per person. Use the rest of the carcass for making stock.

Wild Duck with Black Olives

Serve with riced potatoes and a green salad.

Serves 4 ☆☆
Preparation: 15 minutes
Cooking: 15 minutes

breast fillets from 3 wild ducks
salt and freshly ground black pepper
3 tablespoons oil
6oz (175g) black olives, halved and stoned
juice of 1 orange
grated rind of ½ orange
4 tablespoons brandy

Remove the skin from the fillets and cut the flesh into fingers. Pat dry and sprinkle with salt and pepper.

☐ Heat 1 tablespoon of oil in a wok over a high heat until hot. Stir-fry the duck in three batches for about 3 minutes each until lightly browned.

☐ Remove the cooked batches with a slotted spoon and keep warm. Add

more oil, as necessary, and reheat between batches until it stops sputtering.

☐ Return all the duck to the wok and add the olives, orange juice and rind, and stir together.

☐ Heat the brandy in a small pan. Set it alight and pour into the wok. Serve when the flames subside.

Pigeon Breasts with Apple

Serves 4 ☆☆
Preparation: 15 minutes
Cooking: about 15 minutes

breast fillets from 4 pigeons
salt and freshly ground black pepper
3 tablespoons oil
2 dessert apples, peeled, cored and sliced
4 tablespoons Calvados or brandy

Remove the skin and cut the pigeon breasts into fingers. Pat them dry with kitchen paper and sprinkle with salt and pepper.

☐ Put 1 tablespoon of the oil in a wok over a high heat until hot. Stir-fry the pigeon in three batches for 2-3 minutes each until lightly browned.

☐ Remove each cooked batch with a slotted spoon and keep warm. Add more oil as necessary, and re-heat between batches.

☐ Add the apples and stir-fry for 2 minutes, then stir and toss all the ingredients back together.

☐ Heat the Calvados in a small pan. Set it alight and pour it into the wok. Serve as soon as the flames subside.

Brussels Sprouts with Chestnuts and Mushrooms

Serve this crisp vegetable and nut mixture as a classic accompaniment to game and roast turkey.

Serves 4 ☆
Preparation and cooking: 1 hour

1lb (500g) Brussels sprouts, trimmed
salt
1oz (25g) clarified butter
1lb (500g) chestnuts, cooked and peeled
8oz (225g) small button mushrooms, wiped and trimmed
cayenne pepper

Cook the sprouts in a large pan of boiling salted water for 3 minutes. Drain well and quickly rinse them under cold running water. Drain well again and pat them dry.

☐ Put the butter in a wok over a high heat until it begins to brown. Add the cooked chestnuts and stir-fry them for 2-3 minutes to brown them lightly.

☐ Add the button mushrooms and stir-fry for about 2 minutes. Stir in the Brussels sprouts and stir-fry them for 1 more minute.

☐ Lower the heat, cover the pan and simmer gently for 2 minutes, until the sprouts are just tender.

☐ Season the mixture lightly with salt and cayenne pepper and serve.

Bean Sprout Medley

Serves 4 ☆☆
Preparation and cooking: 35 minutes

2oz (50g) poultry fat or clarified butter
4oz (125g) spring onions, chopped
4 large garlic cloves, finely chopped
2oz (50g) pine nuts
8oz (225g) mushrooms, wiped and sliced
1lb (500g) bean sprouts
salt and freshly ground black pepper

Put the fat in a wok over a low heat. Add onion and garlic and stir-fry for 10 minutes until tender – do not brown! Push up the sides of the pan.

☐ Turn heat to high. Stir-fry nuts for 1-2 minutes until lightly browned.

☐ Add mushrooms and stir to coat with fat. Mix in onion and garlic.

☐ Add bean sprouts and stir-fry everything together for 2-3 minutes.

☐ Season lightly and serve.

Crunchy Ham Stir-fry

Serves 4 ☆☆
Preparation and cooking: 35 minutes

1lb (500g) cooked ham in one piece
3 tablespoons oil
1 medium onion, sliced
2 large garlic cloves, finely chopped
3oz (75g) celery, trimmed and sliced
8oz (225g) button mushrooms, wiped
3 tablespoons Meat Stock
3 tablespoons dry sherry
salt and freshly ground black pepper
1 tablespoon finely chopped chives

Cut the ham into $\frac{1}{2}$in (1cm) strips.

☐ Put the oil in a wok over a low heat. Add onion and garlic and stir-fry for 10 minutes until tender – do not brown! Remove and keep warm.

☐ Turn the heat to high. Add the ham and stir-fry for about 5 minutes to brown. Remove and keep warm.

☐ Add the celery and stir-fry for 2 minutes, then stir in mushrooms.

☐ Return cooked ingredients to wok, stir in stock and sherry and boil. Simmer gently for 2 minutes.

☐ Season and sprinkle with chives.

Peeling chestnuts

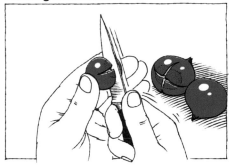

Cut a cross in base before cooking.

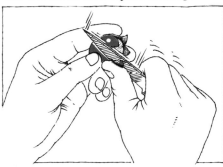

Pull off both shell and skin together.

Nuts make a particularly good texture contrast to stir-fried meats and vegetables. Almonds, pine nuts, and walnuts may be lightly browned in the oil before the other ingredients are cooked. Unlike meats, fish, and vegetables – other than garlic and onions – nuts do brown. In fact, they burn easily so need to be watched carefully.

Peeling and cooking chestnuts

The easiest way to cook chestnuts, and keep them whole, is to buy them a week or so in advance and leave them to sit and dry in a warm room. They then shrink slightly away from their skins, making it easier to remove the outer shells by piercing with a sharp knife and pulling them away. Cook the shelled chestnuts in boiling water for about 30 minutes until tender. One at a time, remove the nuts and use a small sharp knife to pull off the loose inner skin.

If you have to prepare the nuts without having time to let them dry out, cut them as shown. Cook them, then use a sharp knife to remove both shells and skins.

For a subtler but strong ginger flavour use thinly shredded fresh root ginger instead of ground and cook it with the garlic and onion.

Pork with Rice and Mushrooms

Turn this into a dinner-party dish by substituting Chinese rice wine for the stock and letting the pork marinate in it overnight before cooking. Garnish the dish with some cooked peeled prawns and a spoonful or two of cream mixed with chives.

To clarify butter

Melt the butter in a small pan over a low heat. When foam subsides remove from heat and skim off any remaining foam with kitchen paper. Then carefully pour off the liquid butter, leaving white solid residue in the pan.

Pork with Rice and Mushrooms

Serves 4 ☆☆
Preparation: 20 minutes
Cooking: 30 minutes

¾lb (350g) pork escalope or fillet, thinly
   sliced
½ teaspoon ground ginger
salt and freshly ground black pepper
1½oz (40g) butter, clarified
2 large garlic cloves, finely chopped
4oz (125g) spring onions, trimmed and sliced
4oz (125g) button mushrooms, wiped,
   trimmed and sliced
4oz (125g) cooked long-grain rice
6 tablespoons Chicken Stock
2 tablespoons finely chopped chives

Pat the meat dry with kitchen paper. Cut into 1½in (4cm) squares. Dust well with ginger, salt and pepper.

☐ Put the butter in a wok over a low heat along with the garlic and onion. Stir-fry for about 5 minutes to soften – but not brown! Remove with a slotted spoon and keep warm.

☐ Turn up the heat. When the butter is beginning to brown, stir-fry the meat in 3 batches for 3 minutes each until lightly browned. Remove each batch and keep warm. Re-heat the butter between each addition.

☐ Add the mushrooms. Stir for 1 minute to coat with butter. Add and stir in the cooked vegetables and pork.

☐ Stir in the rice and the stock and mix well. Bring to the boil then turn down the heat and cover the pan. Cook gently for about 25 minutes, stirring occasionally, until the pork is tender.

☐ Adjust the seasoning and serve, sprinkled with chopped chives.

Pork with Rice and Mushrooms makes a satisfying family 'one-pot' meal.

Table-top cooking

'Cooking at the table' is not just the province of showy restaurants. With the minimum of effort – and the most dramatic and impressive effect – many dishes can be heated, cooked or given a finishing touch on the table at home. Whether a fondue, a simple fry or scramble, or a last-minute flaming or flambéing, cooking at the table can also be one of the most relaxed (and spectacular) ways of combining cooking, eating and entertaining. And the host/hostess need never miss out on any of the fun.

Fondues

Fondues are perhaps the most familiar form of table-top cooking and informality is their key-note. Shopping, advance preparation and panics are minimal – and the guests do their own 'cooking'.

There are two basic types of fondue: those that need only to be kept warm, like the various cheese fondues, and those which actually *cook* food in hot oil or stock. Both are very simple to plan and prepare – bread and crisp vegetables and fruit for the cheese fondue, and good meat, tasty dips, baked potatoes or chips, and salads for the others.

An interesting variation is the Italian peasant *bagna cauda* (hot bath), a delicious sauce of anchovy and garlic, into which lengths of raw or blanched vegetables are dipped.

Oriental fondues demand slightly more planning and chopping, but with greater returns. The Japanese provide egg and cornflour dips to create a coating for meat, fish or vegetables – thus guests are both coating *and* cooking their own meal!

The Chinese 'fondue' uses hot stock instead of oil, in which prepared raw meat or fish is simmered briefly, and the resultant soup is served up separately at the end. This method is obviously far less calorie-laden: so at your next fondue party, supply one dish of hot oil and one of good stock – and please the health conscious as well as the gourmet!

Flaming

Most people are familiar with this technique, if only from setting the 'crown' on their annual Christmas pudding. Once you have proper table-top cooking equipment, however, you can fry steaks, stir-fry vegetables, scramble eggs or even sauté breakfast kidneys – but the most spectacular use must be that of flaming or flambéing. The blue flames that lick around the orangey sauce of Crêpes Suzette makes a magnificent finale to a meal.

And flambés are not solely the province of sweet dishes – Steak Diane is easy to serve at home (though best for 2 only); crushed juniper berries and flamed gin turn pork chops into something special; and the Burns' Night haggis would not taste the same without its whisky flames.

Various reasons are given for the need for flambéing – it can burn off excess fat, as well as take away the raw taste from the spirit used, leaving a subtler alcoholic flavour which adds considerably to the taste and richness of a dish. More importantly, perhaps, a last-minute flaming can dramatically heighten a sense of occasion.

Most of the basic food preparation can be done well in advance, then it can be heated in a suitable pan set over the lamp. Only spirits – say brandy or gin, and liqueurs – and certain fortified wines can be used, as they possess a sufficiently high alcohol content (ordinary wine, for instance, just will not flame).

Table-cooking Equipment

For either type of cooking, you will need a spirit lamp with a strong stand (camping gas equipment is not suitable as it is too top-heavy and liable to upset). Fondues need a flameproof pot and long forks. For flaming, you will need a shallow omelette or gratin pan (copper or aluminium is best, but hardened glass or ceramic can also be used).

Fondue Pots

For cooking, use deep pots with in-turned lips, to prevent splashing – for both stock- and oil-cooked fondues. Some come with lids with cleverly designed openings which serve to prevent splashing and also act as a support for the forks. For cheese fondues the pots are more broad-based and open and for sweet fondues, where gentle heat is necessary, earthenware pots set over candles are common.

Fondue Forks

These must be very long, to prevent burning, and each guest's should be easily identifiable to prevent confusion. Supply an ordinary fork as well, with which to eat the cubes of bread or meat. Two long forks per person prevents starvation when cooking meat fondues.

Fondue Faux-pas

Beware! If you drop your bread or meat in the fondue, you may be required to pay a forfeit – sing a song, kiss your neighbours or, less pleasurably perhaps, supply the next bottle of wine!

If you want to flame a dish, and it is proving difficult to ignite due to use of a liquid with a low alcohol content, add a large dash of vodka. This raises the alcohol content but does not substantially alter the taste of the dish.

Cheese fondue

To accompany a cheese fondue, serve lots of crisp salad and French-fried potatoes, or small baked potatoes.

Cubes of day old crusty white bread or French bread make excellent dipping agents or try:
- sesame seed bread sticks
- cubes or sticks of toast
- sticks of celery
- cauliflower or broccoli florets
- chunks of hard fruit like apple

Traditional Swiss Cheese Fondue

Serve with chunks of day-old bread.

Serves 6   ★★☆
Preparation: 20 minutes

1 large garlic clove, peeled
1¼lb (575g) Gruyère cheese, grated
12 fl oz (350ml) dry white wine
a squeeze of lemon juice
salt and freshly ground pepper
3 tablespoons kirsch

Cut the garlic in half, use it to rub the inside of a 3 pint (1.75 litre) flameproof pot and then discard.
☐ Add the cheese, wine and lemon juice to the prepared pot. Bring to the boil, stirring all the time. Cook, stirring, until all the cheese has melted.
☐ Season and stir in the kirsch.
☐ Set the pot over a lighted spirit lamp at the table.

Soft Cheese Fondue

Serve with chunks of unpeeled dessert apple, celery or fennel.

Serves 6   ★★☆
Preparation: 10 minutes

9 fl oz (275ml) dry cider
three 7oz (200g) packets full-fat cheese
1 teaspoon curry paste
salt to taste

Some different types of fondue set.

Put the cider into a 7in (18cm) saucepan over a moderate heat. When it begins to steam, gradually whisk in the cheese. Continue until all the cheese is mixed in, to give a soft creamy consistency. Add the curry paste then season with salt.

☐ Transfer to a suitable pot and place over a lighted spirit lamp at the table.

Farmhouse Cheese Fondue

Serve with boiled small new potatoes, blanched button onions and cauliflower or broccoli sprigs for dipping, to make a substantial supper dish.

Serves 6
Preparation: 30 minutes

---

1 tablespoon cornflour
about 9 fl oz (275ml) light ale,
    plus 2 extra tablespoons
1lb (500g) Cheddar cheese, grated
½ medium onion, grated
½ teaspoon dried thyme
½ teaspoon made mustard
3 tablespoons single cream
salt and freshly ground pepper

Mix the cornflour smoothly with 1 tablespoon of the ale. Put all but about 2 tablespoons of the rest of the ale in a heavy saucepan over a moderate heat. Bring to the boil slowly.

☐ Stir the hot ale into the mixed cornflour, return to the pan and cook, stirring constantly, for 2 minutes until thickened.

☐ Gradually stir the cheese into the ale until melted and well mixed.

☐ Stir in the onion, thyme, mustard and cream. Season to taste with salt and pepper.

☐ If necessary, stir in some of the reserved ale to give the required consistency. Transfer to a suitable pot and place over a lighted spirit lamp at the table.

Tip: Supply bowls of sweet pickle, made English mustard and thick tomato relish as accompanying sauces.

Meat and fish fondues

Small, bite-sized pieces of tender meats, poultry or fish are delicious cooked in hot oil at the table. It's a good idea to have two pots of oil – one for meats, the other for fish. Fill suitable pots about one-third full with good cooking oil. Heat on the stove top to about 375F (190C), then transfer to a lighted spirit lamp at the table. The guests then spear pieces of food on their forks and cook them in the hot oil. When the oil is hot enough, the food will cook in 1-2 minutes. When the oil cools below cooking temperature return to the kitchen for re-heating.

Suitable meats and fish for fondue cooking:
● fillet or sirloin steak
● leg of lamb
● pork and veal fillet
● chicken or turkey breast fillet
● monkfish, salmon, or halibut
● shelled mussels
● raw prawns, with heads and tails
● queen scallops

Fondue Bourguignonne

Another famous Swiss dish, Fondue Bourguignonne is entirely different from its cheese compatriot. It consists of small pieces of meat which guests cook for themselves in hot oil at the table.

Prepare the meat by cutting off and discarding all fat and connective tissue. Then cut into fingers or small cubes. Pile these on one large serving plate, or divide out on smaller individual plates. (Allow about 8oz (225g) per person.)

You can also make small meatballs from finely minced, very lean meat, mixed with a little salt and pepper and some dried herbs. Form the mix into small balls and roll them firmly under the hand. These may be used instead of, or in addition to, the cubes of meat.

Heat the oil to 375F (190C) on the stove top then present the meat and oil to the table with accompanying dips or sauces.

French Herb Dip
Whisk together 4oz (125g) cream cheese and 1 teaspoon soured cream with 1 tablespoon chopped chives, 1 tablespoon chopped parsley, and 1 finely chopped garlic clove. Season to taste.

Avocado Cheese
Whisk together 1 ripe avocado with 2oz (50g) full fat soft cheese, a squeeze of lemon juice, and salt and pepper to taste.

Tomato Butter
Whisk together 3oz (75g) softened butter with 2 teaspoons tomato purée and ¼ teaspoon hot chilli paste.

Green Pepper Mayonnaise
Into 4oz (125g) mayonnaise whisk 1 teaspoon crushed green peppercorns, and 2 tablespoons finely chopped green peppers.

Bagna Cauda

A delicious Italian speciality that is quick and easy to make.

Serves 6
Preparation: 30 minutes

1¾oz (49g) canned anchovies,
    finely chopped
6 garlic cloves, peeled
5oz (150g) butter, cubed small
¼ pint (150ml) olive oil

For dipping:
1 red pepper, deseeded and cubed
1 green pepper, deseeded and cubed
1 large fennel bulb, cut into 6
6 small carrots, peeled
4oz (125g) button mushrooms, wiped
small loaf crusty bread, cubed

Finely chop the anchovies. Put into a shallow saucepan suitable for the table. Crush the garlic into it.

☐ Add the butter to the pan. Heat gently on the stove top until the butter melts. Skim off the foam.

☐ Stir in the oil. Turn the heat to its lowest and leave for 20 minutes. Do not allow to brown.

☐ Transfer the pan to a lighted spirit lamp at the table.

Fondue Dinner Party

Fondue Dinner Party

Remember that simplicity is of the essence. Everything goes on the table at one time—there are no separate courses. Extra side courses of mixed salad and chips, and plenty of thickly sliced crusty bread keep the guests happy while you are re-heating the oil. Provide as many long-handled forks for cooking as you can—at least 2 per person, and don't forget lots of paper napkins!

If serving any accompanying sauce or dip hot, try to arrange to set it on a table-top warmer to *keep* it hot throughout the meal.

Serves 6   ☆☆☆
Preparation time: 30 minutes

2¼lb (1.25kg) trimmed meat, meatballs, poultry or fish, cut into bite-sized pieces (see the preceding pages)
1 small cauliflower, parboiled and broken into florets
4oz (125g) green beans trimmed and par-boiled

To accompany:
4 or 5 dips, sauces and butters (see preceding pages)
6 medium tomatoes
1 cucumber, thickly sliced
pickled gherkins
pickled onions
olives

Pat all the food to be cooked quite dry with kitchen paper.

☐ Try to have two fondue pots going at a time. One can be used for fish and the other one for meat, if necessary, or the two pots of oil will just help to speed the cooking and facilitate self-service at either end of the table.

☐ Just before eating, one-third fill each pot with oil and heat to 375F (190C) on the stove top. Bring to the table and place over two lighted spirit lamps at strategic points on the table.

☐ Each guest then spears one or two pieces of food on his or her own fork and places it into the hot oil. Cooking will take 1-2 minutes depending on the temperature of the oil and the size and type of the pieces of meat.

☐ The guests continue cooking, eating each batch as the next is cooking.

Oriental Fondues

These are much the same as Western fondues although the pieces for cooking are normally cut smaller and more emphasis is put on their presentation. There are, however, a few interesting regional variations.

Japanese-style fondues, for instance, although still cooked in a bath of hot oil, usually provide small dishes of beaten egg and cornflour. Delicious results are obtained by dipping the food to be cooked first in cornflour then in egg before frying it. Alternatively, the food may be dipped in soy sauce then in cornflour before frying. In either case, the outside turns an attractive golden brown and the crisp tasty batter sets off the fresh juiciness of the cooked food inside.

Chinese fondue, on the other hand, cooks in a pot of hot stock. When all the foods have been cooked, the stock is then served in cups or small bowls as a very flavourful soup.

In place of the French-fried potatoes or bread common with Western fondues, serve boiled noodles as a filling dish to accompany the tasty little morsels of food. Cook them in the kitchen until just tender, but still firm to the bite. Drain well and stir in a little oil to keep them from sticking together.

For real effect, try serving Eastern and Western fondues alongside one another. Then the guests who prefer slimming foods without fat can cook theirs in stock and those who like fried food also have a choice.

The next time you have a fondue party, try adding one exotic vegetable, like cardoon, or spice, such as five-spice powder, and soy or oyster sauce as a relish or dip. If you have a suitable miniature frying basket or infuser, try serving small batches of cooked Chinese noodles or beansprouts at the table.

For a really impressive effect – and even more fun – try serving Western and Oriental fondues side by side, using more or less the same basic ingredients with different accompaniments.

Flaming

Crêpes Suzette

Serves 6   ☆☆
Preparation: 30 minutes
Cooking: about 6 minutes

---

12 thin crêpes

The sauce:
6oz (175g) caster sugar
juice and grated rind of ½ orange
11oz (312g) canned mandarin oranges
6 tablespoons Grand Marnier

Make the crêpes. Fold each one in quarters, stack, wrap in foil and keep warm in a low oven.

☐ To make the sauce: Put the sugar, orange juice and rind, and the mandarin syrup in a 9in (23cm) omelette pan over moderate heat. Stir constantly until the sugar dissolves.

☐ Simmer for 12-15 minutes or until the mixture begins to thicken into a syrup. Set aside.

☐ At the table: Set one-third of the syrup in the pan over a lighted spirit lamp. Place 4 pancakes in the syrup as soon as it begins to bubble. Cook for 1 minute. Turn the pancakes carefully. Add one-third of the mandarins.

☐ Put 2 tablespoons of the liqueur into a metal ladle. Warm briefly over the spirit lamp. Set alight, then pour, flaming, over the pancakes.

☐ Serve as soon as the flames die down. Repeat with the rest.

Tip: The crêpes can be prepared some time in advance as they keep well in the fridge for 3 to 4 days, or in the freezer for up to 2 months. Heat through, still in their foil parcels, in an oven pre-heated to 350F (180C) gas 4 for 10-15 minutes for refrigerated crêpes or 20-25 minutes for frozen ones.

Crêpes Suzette is probably the best-known flambéed dish – and one of the most tasty.

Banana Flambé

Serves 6 ☆
Preparation and cooking: about 15 minutes

---

6 ripe bananas
¼ pint (150ml) dark rum
double cream for serving (optional)

The syrup:
juice of 2 oranges
grated rind of ½ orange
2oz (50g) caster sugar
2oz (50g) butter

First make the syrup: Put the orange juice, rind, sugar and butter into a 9in (23cm) omelette or sauté pan. Heat, stirring constantly, over a moderate heat until boiling.

☐ Simmer for 5 minutes. Remove and set aside.

☐ At the table: Set the pan of syrup over a lighted spirit lamp. Peel the bananas and carefully place them in the syrup. Simmer for 2 minutes. Turn and cook on the second side for 2 minutes. Set the pan aside on a heatproof mat.

☐ Pour the rum into a small saucepan. Warm briefly over the spirit lamp. Set alight and pour, flaming, over the bananas.

☐ Serve as soon as the flames die down, with the syrup spooned over. Pass cream separately, if using.

Flaming Alaska

Serves 4 ☆☆☆
Preparation and cooking: about 10 minutes

---

1 pint (600ml) vanilla ice cream
2oz (50g) flaked almonds, toasted
5 tablespoons brandy

The sauce:
3oz (75g) dark dessert chocolate
3 fl oz (100ml) double cream

Break the chocolate into small pieces and put, along with the cream, in a small heavy saucepan suitable for serving at the table.

☐ Stir over a moderate heat for 2-3 minutes to melt the chocolate. Mix together well. Remove from the heat and set aside.

☐ At the table: Divide the ice cream between 4 individual plates. Place the saucepan over a lighted spirit lamp and stir the sauce until hot.

☐ Pour sauces over the ice cream and sprinkle with the nuts.

☐ Pour the brandy into a large ladle or small pan. Warm briefly over the spirit lamp. Set alight and pour some, flaming, over each plate.

☐ Serve immediately.

Variations: Try this with all sorts of differently flavoured ice creams in exciting flavour combinations.

● strawberry ice cream flamed with kirsch

● coffee ice cream with a white chocolate sauce, flamed with Tia Maria

● butterscotch ice cream flamed with rum

● orange or lemon sorbets with a sauce of puréed raspberries, flamed with Grand Marnier.

Banana Flambé allows you to produce an impressive dessert for unexpected guests using only fruit-bowl and store-cupboard ingredients.

COOKING BY DIRECT HEAT

Grilling • Spit-roasting

Grilling

Grilling is one of the speediest and most exciting ways of cooking food. Literally before your eyes, the raw materials are turned into complete and satisfying dishes in a matter of minutes. Sealing in nutrients and using little or no fat, it's no wonder that it is one of the most increasingly popular ways of cooking. It is also very versatile: though the swift application of fierce direct heat can dry out the moistest foods, this is compensated by adding savoury butters, glazes and bastes.

In this section, there are new and delicious ways with fish, meat, poultry, game, vegetables and cheese.

In fact, although we tend to think of all grilling as the direct application of heat from above, there are several ways of grilling food. The conventional grill works from above and may have more than one position for the grill pan, allowing for heat control by lowering it.

The second form of grilling is really spit-roasting, where the joint revolves on a spit or skewer, then there's the barbecue or 'charcoal' grill, where the heat is less fierce and comes from below and finally the relatively recent invention of the ultra-hot infra-red 'contact' grill which cooks both sides simultaneously.

In conventional grilling there are only a few rules to learn.

Suitable food

Because the method is so quick, it is only suitable for the most tender and best-quality foods, fillet, rump and sirloin steaks, chicken joints, fish and some offal. Liver and kidneys, quickly grilled and served with a spicy mustard butter make a nourishing main dish. Even vegetables and cheeses – if you choose the right ones – will benefit from grilling. Herrings and kippers can actually be wrapped in foil then cooked under the grill. This semi-steaming makes fish very succulent, and reduces fish odours. Be sure to keep the foil out of contact with an electric grill!

Cooking quantities

Choose small pieces of food which fit comfortably on the grill pan, and which do not touch the element or flame as they cook. Only cook as much as is practicable–don't crowd the grill. If planning to cook for large numbers of people, have a serving dish ready in the oven or warming drawer to keep food hot until it is cooked and ready to serve. Plan to cook for small numbers when using a conventional grill–up to four is ideal, otherwise the essence of speed will be lost.

Choose pieces which are of an even thickness to ensure even browning and cooking. If several items are to be cooked at one time, it is perfectly easy to add smaller pieces later.

More or less fat?

Grilling cooks out the fat quickly, leaving juices in the pan below. As the heat is always high, brush the food with these juices, or a little oil or melted butter to compensate for its drying quality. Some meats and white fish benefit from basting with a savoury sauce as they cook.

How to grill

● Pre-heat the grill to the highest setting and wait until this is attained.
● Brush the food with any fat, oil or prepared glaze.
● Adjust grill position, if necessary.
● Slide the pan under the grill and brown the food on either side.
● Reduce the heat, if necessary, to finish cooking the food, or move the grill pan to a lower position.
● Brush with extra fat or pan juices during cooking.

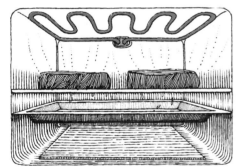

Conventional grill

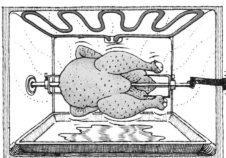

Spit-roast or rotisserie

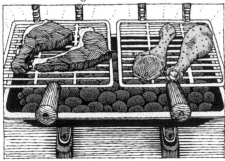

Barbecue

Contact grill

Grilling fish

Speedy grilling, is particularly suitable for fish. Steaks, fillets or small whole fish can all be cooked in this way. The most important thing to remember when you're grilling fish is to watch it closely. Fish over-cooks very quickly so it is best not to leave it while it cooks. Generally, turn it once during cooking, and remove it from the pan immediately it is done to prevent it over-cooking.

White fish such as sole and plaice:

Brush with oil or dot with butter when plain-grilling to help prevent the fish from drying out while cooking.
Season before and during cooking.

Medium-oily fish such as salmon and halibut:

Most often grilled as steaks, these benefit from being brushed with butter or oil. Serve with an emulsion sauce such as mayonnaise to counteract any dryness of texture.

Very oily fish such as herrings and mackerel:

Brush with oil just to coat the surface with a light film. Once the fish gets hot, it produces enough cooking oil of its own. These are good basted with a sharp-flavoured mixture during cooking.

How to tell when fish is cooked:

With whole fish, the eye will become opaque. With steaks and fillets a creamy, curd-like substance appears on the surface between the flakes of flesh.
Test with a skewer or the point of a knife by parting two flakes of flesh. If it is opaque, the fish is cooked.

Grilling Fish

Herrings with Hot Sauce

Serves 4
Preparation: 15 minutes
Cooking: about 5 minutes

---

4 herrings each about 12oz (350g), cleaned
salt and freshly ground black pepper
4 tablespoons olive oil
1 tablespoon white wine vinegar
½ teaspoon made mustard
1 garlic clove, crushed
½ teaspoon curry paste
2 medium tomatoes, sliced

Wash the herrings under cold running water and pat dry with kitchen paper. Remove the backbones. Season the inside of each fish with salt and pepper. Make 3 diagonal cuts on both sides of each fish.

☐ Pre-heat the grill to high and line the grill pan with foil.

☐ Mix the oil, vinegar, mustard, garlic and curry paste and brush a little over the herrings. Set the fish on the grill rack and cook for about 2 minutes or until well browned.

☐ Turn the fish. Arrange the tomato around them. Brush both the fish and tomatoes with more of the sauce. Grill for a further 3 minutes, or until the fish is well browned.

☐ Arrange the herrings on a heated serving dish with the tomatoes around them. Spoon the remaining sauce over and serve.

Tip: Oily fish such as herring and mackerel are delicious served with a Sweet and Sour Sauce. Or you can try glazing them before grilling with some tart redcurrant or cranberry jam – or even a bitter orange or lemon marmalade. Alternatively, make the jam or marmalade into a quick sauce by heating it with some stock or lemon juice.

Mackerel with Spinach and Savoury Butter

Serves 4
Preparation: 20 minutes
Cooking: 8-10 minutes

¾lb (350g) spinach, washed and trimmed
salt and freshly ground black pepper
a little grated nutmeg
1oz (25g) butter
1 large garlic clove, crushed
4 mackerel, each about 12oz (350g), cleaned
1 medium onion, thinly sliced
2 tablespoons mustard oil

The savoury butter:
3oz (75g) butter, softened
1 teaspoon made mustard
2 teaspoons grated horseradish
2 teaspoons lemon juice
salt

First make the savoury butter: beat together the butter, mustard, horseradish and lemon juice and season with salt. Shape it into a log about 1in (2.5cm) in diameter, wrap in foil and chill.

☐ Pre-heat the grill to high. Line the grill pan with foil.

☐ Chop the spinach coarsely and press it into the pan. Sprinkle with salt and pepper and a little grated nutmeg, and dot with the unflavoured butter and garlic. Press a piece of foil over the spinach.

☐ Wash the mackerel under cold running water. Pat dry inside and out with kitchen paper. Sprinkle the insides with salt and pepper and divide the onion slices between them.

☐ Slash the fleshiest part of the fish in 3 places on each side, then brush all over with the oil. Lay the fish on top of the foil covering the spinach, and grill for about 4 minutes each side, or until lightly browned. (It is cooked when the flesh is opaque and flakes easily when tested with the point of a knife.)

☐ Remove the fish to a hot serving dish, garnish with the spinach and top each with a slice of the savoury butter. Serve the rest separately.

Grilled Trout with Provençal Herbs

Fresh herbs are all you need to highlight the flavour of trout. Serve the fish with a tomato and basil salad and sliced boiled potatoes or French bread.

Serves 4   ☆☆☆
Preparation: 10 minutes
Cooking: about 10 minutes

4 trout, each about 12oz (350g), cleaned
salt and freshly ground black pepper
4 sprigs fresh thyme, or 2 teaspoons dried thyme
4 sprigs fresh parsley
2 tablespoons olive oil
lemon slices and parsley sprigs to garnish

The Provençal Herb Butter:
1 teaspoon chopped fresh thyme
1 teaspoon chopped fresh oregano
3oz (75g) softened butter
1 garlic clove, crushed with a little salt

First make the herb butter: beat the thyme and oregano into the softened butter. Beat in the garlic and mix well. Shape the butter into a 1in (2.5cm) diameter log, wrap it in foil and chill.

☐ Pre-heat the grill to high. Cover the grill rack with foil.

☐ Wash the trout well under cold running water, then pat dry with kitchen paper. Season the insides of each fish with salt and pepper and put in the thyme and parsley. Brush the fish all over with oil.

☐ Lay the trout on the grill rack and cook for 4-5 minutes on each side or until lightly browned, brushing with more oil as necessary during cooking.

☐ Garnish with slices of lemon and sprigs of parsley. Top each fish with a slice of Provençal Herb Butter and serve.

Tip: If the trout are not too large for the grill pan, whenever possible leave the heads on as this makes them much more attractive when served. Ask the fishmonger to clean and gut them for you, but leave them whole.

Line the grill pan with foil to save on washing up.... However, it is best not to cover the grill rack with foil if cooking very oily fish, or fish that has been coated liberally with oil. The oil cannot drain into the pan and will be quick to catch alight when placed under the heated grill.

Savoury butters
There are many succulent savoury butters in these recipes for grilling. Try them with other foods: the ones given with fish will suit beef, chicken or veal for example. And serve with pats of two or more flavours for an extra touch of sophistication .

Grilled Trout with Provençal Herbs. Garnish with lemon and parsley for serving.

Sole Colbert

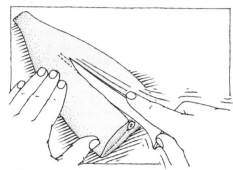

Remove head; slit along backbone.

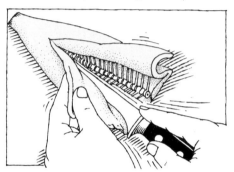

Keeping the knife flat against the bones, carefully slice away the flesh on either side. Open out to serve and place the pat of savoury butter in the opening.

The classic Sole Colbert is prepared as above, but coated with egg and crumbs and deep-fried. It is usually served with Maître d'Hôtel Butter.

Lemon-Parsley Butter

Beat 1 tablespoon of lemon juice, the grated rind of ½ lemon and 1 tablespoon chopped parsley into 3oz (75g) softened butter. Shape into a 1in (2.5cm) log, wrap in foil and chill until needed. This is good with grilled chicken portions as well as fish.

Grilled Sole 'Colbert'

Serve with a green salad, French beans, or mangetout peas.

Serves 2   ☆☆☆
Preparation: 15 minutes
Cooking: 12-14 minutes

2 Dover sole, each about 12oz (350g),
    cleaned and skinned
2 tablespoons oil
salt and freshly ground black pepper
2 small tomatoes, sliced

pats of Lemon-Parsley butter (see sidelines)

Pre-heat the grill to high. Line the rack with foil.

☐ Wash the fish under cold running water and pat dry with kitchen paper.

☐ Cut round the heads and remove them first if preferred. Otherwise, on the thicker side of each fish, cut around the head, down the backbone and across the fish just above the tail. Using a knife with a flexible blade, slice away the flesh along the backbone, close to the rib bones, first on one side, then the other. Cut slowly and bend the blade of the knife so it lies flat turning the fillets back as you cut. Leave the flesh attached at the outer edge of the fish (see sidelines).

☐ Snip through the spine in 2 or 3 places with kitchen scissors. When the fish is cooked, the backbone can then be removed easily.

☐ Place the sole, filleted side up, on the foil on the rack. Brush with oil. Grill for 6-7 minutes, or until the flesh flakes easily and is lightly browned.

☐ Carefully turn the fish, brush again with oil and grill for another 6 minutes.

☐ Transfer the fillets to heated plates and season. Carefully lift out the backbones from the fish. Arrange the tomatoes in the open 'pockets'. Top with pats of Lemon-Parsley Butter and serve.

Mediterranean-style Grilled Prawns

These make a delicious first course or a light snack. Serve the prawns on a bed of rice with a little soy sauce and lemon juice.

Serves 4   ☆
Preparation: 5 minutes
Cooking: 2-3 minutes

8 Dublin Bay prawns, cooked—or thawed, if
    frozen
2 tablespoons sesame oil
2 teaspoons sesame seeds
salt
a little white pepper (optional)
soy sauce, to serve
4 lemon wedges, to garnish

Remove the heads and legs from the prawns. Cut open along the back of the shell but leave the flesh intact on the underside. Remove the black veins. Wash the prawns under cold running water, then pat them dry with kitchen paper. Press the prawns flat and brush the flesh with oil.

☐ Pre-heat the grill to high and line the grill pan with foil. Lay the prawns, cut side up, on the grill rack. Cook for 1 minute.

☐ Brush with more oil and sprinkle over the sesame seeds and a little salt. Grill for about another 2 minutes. Season with pepper, if liked.

☐ Serve immediately with soy sauce and lemon wedges.

Tip: Most small pieces of seafood grill well. Try scallops with a sprinkling of Pernod, or oysters with garlic butter and a dash of Tabasco.

● Grilled seafood makes delicious last-course savouries, like the classic 'angels on horseback' – oysters wrapped in slices of bacon. The same treatment works just as well with prawns, mussels or scallops.

● Grilled savouries are possible with less expensive fare: substitute prunes for the oysters to make 'devils on horseback', for instance.

Fillet Steaks with Oven Chips, served with a crisp green salad.

Grilling Meat

Small pieces of tender cuts of meat are ideally suited to grilling. Choose pieces which are of the same thickness to ensure even cooking. Brush well with oil or melted butter before, and during, cooking to protect the meat from the fierce direct, dry heat of the grill, and use any juices which cook out of the meat into the pan for basting.

Slash any fat or skin around the outside edge of meats to prevent them curling up and cooking unevenly. If using, salt draws the juices from the meats and reduces the browning so it should only be added *just* before cooking, or used later as a condiment.

For a good brown exterior and a juicy red interior, cook the meat quickly on both sides. If you prefer meat well done, either reduce the heat of the grill, or move the meat further from the heat so it cooks for longer.

Beef steaks

There are several steaks which are good for grilling. Usually, the thicker the piece, the better. For large helpings, there is the outsize T-bone consisting of a portion of sirloin plus the entrecôte on one side of the bone, and the fillet on the other.

However, the sirloin is usually sold separately in slices about 1in (2.5cm) thick, but the fillet may be found in more than one guise. The slices may be taken at an angle to produce oval-shaped pieces, or sliced vertically into round cuts (used for classic 'tournedos' dishes). The slices can be almost paper-thin or as much as 1¼-1½in (3-4cm) thick.

Rump steak, too, may be grilled – provided the butcher deals in meat of top quality which has been adequately hung.

Fillet Steak with Oven Chips

Serves 4   ☆☆☆
Preparation: 10 minutes
Cooking: about 15 minutes

---

4 fillet steaks, each about 5oz (150g), and 1in (2.5cm) thick
2 tablespoons oil
1lb (500g) 'oven' chips
salt and freshly ground black pepper
sprigs of watercress to garnish

The Steak Butter:
1 tablespoon brandy
2 tablespoons chopped fresh herbs in season, such as parsley, chives, chervil or tarragon
2oz (50g) butter, softened

Pre-heat the grill to high. Line the grill pan with foil.

☐ Spread the 'oven' chips evenly over the foil. Slide under the grill and cook for 5-6 minutes, stirring occasionally. Season with salt and pepper.

☐ Meanwhile, make the steak butter. Gradually beat the brandy and herbs into the softened butter. Shape into a 1in (2.5cm) log and chill.

☐ Pat the steaks dry with kitchen paper. Brush on both sides with oil and place on the grill rack.

☐ Set the rack in the pan over the chips and cook the steaks for 2½-4 minutes on each side, depending on how brown and well done you like the steaks to be. Season with salt and pepper.

☐ Arrange them on a warmed serving dish and set a slice of Steak Butter on top of each. Garnish the plate with watercress and serve immediately with the chips.

Make sure meat that has been frozen is thoroughly thawed out and patted dry with kitchen paper before grilling, otherwise it will develop a grey, moist surface instead of a crisp brown one. The meat will partially steam-bake, rather than grill.

Tournedos
These are the most extravagant of all steak cuts but they make a good centrepiece for a very special occasion. Taken from the heart of the fillet, after slicing they are wrapped and then tied to help them hold their shape during cooking.

Beef Tournedos 'Marchand de Vins'
Serve with potato croquettes, carrots and grilled tomatoes. Or accompany with a purée of carrot – or parsnip – and potato, and Brussels sprouts.

Rump Steak and Mushrooms

Serve with sauté potatoes, or warm potato crisps and French beans.

Serves 4 ☆☆☆
Preparation: 10 minutes
Cooking: 8-10 minutes

12oz (350g) button or cup mushrooms
1oz (25g) butter, cut in tiny cubes
salt and freshly ground black pepper
4 pieces rump steak, each about 6oz (175g) and 1in (2.5cm) thick
1 tablespoon oil

Pre-heat the grill to high. Line the pan with foil.

☐ Wipe the mushrooms and trim the stems level with the caps. Arrange the mushrooms over the bottom of the pan, stem side up, and dot with the butter. Season well with salt and pepper and grill them for about 3 minutes.

☐ Pat the steaks dry with kitchen paper. Cut downwards at intervals of about 1in (2.5cm) through the fat along the outside edge to prevent the steaks from curling. Brush the steaks with oil on each side and set them ready on the grill rack.

☐ Set the rack with the steaks in position over the mushrooms and cook the steaks for 2-3 minutes on each side, to the required degree. Serve with the mushrooms arranged round them.

T-bone Steak with Mexican Sauce

Serve with a crisp green salad.

Serves 4 ☆☆☆
Preparation: 5 minutes
Cooking: 10-14 minutes

2 T-bone steaks, each about 1lb (500g), and 1¼-1½in (3-4cm) thick
1 tablespoon oil
2 tablespoons tomato purée
½ teaspoon chilli paste
½ teaspoon garlic paste
salt and freshly ground black pepper

Pre-heat the grill to high. Line the grill pan with foil.

☐ Pat the steaks dry with kitchen paper. Cut each steak at intervals of about 1in (2.5cm) through the fat along the outside edge to prevent curling. Brush the steaks with oil on both sides and set on the grill rack.

☐ Mix together the tomato purée, chilli paste, garlic paste and salt.

☐ Cook the steaks for 5-7 minutes on each side, to the required degree. Season with salt and pepper.

☐ Spread each steak with the tomato mixture. Return to the grill for 30 seconds. Serve immediately.

Beef Tournedos 'Marchand de Vins'

Serves 4 ☆☆
Preparation: 15 minutes
Cooking: 8-12 minutes

4 medium tomatoes, halved
1 tablespoon oil
salt and freshly ground black pepper
4 tournedos, barded with fat

The Wine Merchant's Butter:
3 fl oz (100ml) red wine
2 tablespoons port
small bay leaf, crumbled
1 shallot, finely chopped
2oz (50g) butter, softened

First, make the Wine Merchant's Butter: boil wine, port, bay leaf and shallot in a small pan over high heat until reduced to 2 tablespoons. Beat into softened butter and chill.

☐ Pre-heat the grill to hot. Line the grill pan with foil. Place the tomatoes in the pan, brush them with oil and season with pepper. Grill the tomatoes for 2 minutes.

☐ Pat the tournedos dry with kitchen paper. Place on the grill rack and brush with oil.

☐ Set the rack in position over the tomatoes and cook the steaks for 3-5 minutes on each side, depending on degree of cooking required.

☐ Season the steaks with salt and pepper and top each with a slice of Wine Merchant's Butter to serve.

Oriental Pork Chops

Serves 4 ☆☆☆
Preparation: 5 minutes
Cooking: about 10 minutes

---

4 pork chops, each about 8oz (225g)

The glaze:
3 tablespoons sesame seed oil
2 tablespoons clear honey
2 teaspoons sesame seeds, toasted

Pre-heat the grill to high. Line the grill pan with foil.

□ Pat the pork chops dry with kitchen paper. Make cuts at intervals of about 1in (2.5cm) through the fat around the outside edge.

□ Mix together the ingredients for the glaze. Set the chops on the grill rack and brush well with the glaze.

□ Cook for about 5 minutes until the first side is browned to the required degree, brushing once during cooking. Turn the chops, brush with glaze and cook for about 5 minutes, or until browned.

□ Spread any remaining glaze over the chops and serve.

Grilled Ham with Apricot Sauce

Serves 4 ☆☆☆
Preparation of sauce: 30 minutes
Cooking: 5-7 minutes

1¾lb (800g) cooked ham, in the piece
2 tablespoons oil
salt and freshly ground black pepper

The Apricot Sauce:
4oz (125g) dried apricots
9 fl oz (275ml) cold water
juice of 1 large orange
juice of 1 medium lemon
1oz (25g) soft brown sugar
4 whole cloves

To make the sauce: soak the apricots in the cold water for 2 hours, then bring to the boil and simmer for 20 minutes. Add orange and lemon juice, sugar and cloves. Simmer, stirring frequently, for 10 minutes or until the apricots are soft.

□ Sieve or mash the fruit to a thick purée and set aside.

□ Pre-heat the grill to high and line the grill pan with foil.

□ Cut the ham into slices about ½in (1cm) thick. Slash any fat around the edges and pat the slices dry. Brush on both sides with a little oil. Put the ham on the grill rack and grill for 3-4 minutes or until lightly browned. Turn, brush with oil and grill the other side for 2-3 minutes, or until cooked.

□ Serve immediately with hot or cold Apricot Sauce.

Grilling ham and bacon
The smaller cuts like steak or chops are good for grilling. You can grill slices cut from boiling bacon or gammon joints, or you can buy gammon already cut in thick slices. Some shops also sell 'bacon chops'.

Grilled Ham with Apricot Sauce

Grilling is a good way to re-heat boiled bacon or ham. Serve them with any one of a variety of fruit sauces.

Grilled Ham with Apricot Sauce
This sauce can be made in advance and kept in the fridge for up to 4 days.
Other dried fruits, such as apples or pears, may be substituted for apricots.

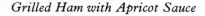

Gammon steaks with Grilled Apple

Serve with creamy mashed potatoes and broad beans.

You can substitute 4-6 canned pineapple rings for the apples in the recipe. Drain them well and pat dry before grilling, otherwise the glaze will run off the fruit.

Tomato-orange butter for lamb or fish

Beat 1 tablespoon orange juice and the grated rind of ½ a large orange into 3oz (75g) butter. Beat in 2 teaspoons tomato purée and season with pepper and a little salt. Shape and chill until required. This is good with lamb chops, or fish steaks.

Two-minute barbecue sauce for lamb chops

To 1 tablespoon of the juices from the grill pan, add a tablespoon of flour and stir and cook to a roux. Stir in ⅓ pint (200ml) hot water from cooking the potatoes, then flavour with a tablespoon of soy sauce, a dash of Worcestershire sauce, the chopped flesh of 2 skinned tomatoes and salt and pepper to taste. Stir until boiling, then simmer for about a minute.

Gammon Steaks with Grilled Apple

Serves 4   ☆☆
Preparation: 10 minutes
Cooking: about 10 minutes

---

4 pieces thickly sliced gammon, each about 5oz (150g), rind removed
2 large dessert apples, peeled and cored

The glaze:
1 teaspoon made mustard
3 tablespoons honey
2 tablespoons white rum
1 tablespoon oil

Pre-heat the grill to high and line the grill pan with foil. Cut each apple into 4 slices across and put them in the grill pan.

☐ Mix together the glaze ingredients. Brush some glaze over the apple slices and cook for about 3 minutes until lightly browned. Turn, and brush again with glaze.

☐ Meanwhile, cut down through any fat round the edges of the gammon slices at 1in (2.5cm) intervals. Pat them dry.

☐ Put the meat on the grill rack, brush one side with the glaze and cook over the apples for about 3 minutes. Turn, brush the other side with glaze and grill for about 3 minutes to cook the second side.

☐ Transfer the gammon to a heated dish and serve with the apples.

Spicy Lamb Cutlets

Serve with petits pois and small new potatoes cooked in their skins.

Makes 8   ☆☆
Preparation: 10 minutes
Cooking: about 10 minutes

---

8 single lamb cutlets, trimmed

The glaze:
½ teaspoon curry powder
2 tablespoons apricot jam, sieved and warmed
1 tablespoon oil

Pre-heat the grill to high. Line the grill pan with foil.

☐ Pat the meat dry with kitchen paper and set on the grill rack.

☐ Mix the curry powder into the warmed jam and add the oil to make the glaze.

☐ Liberally brush one side of the cutlets with glaze and cook for about 4 minutes until brown. Turn the cutlets, brush the other side with glaze, return to the grill and cook for a further 3 minutes to brown the second side.

☐ Put a cutlet frill on each and serve immediately.

Lamb Steaks with Whisky and Ginger

Serve with sweetcorn and warmed potato crisps.

Serves 4   ☆☆☆
Preparation: 5 minutes plus 1 hour marinating
Cooking: about 10 minutes

---

4 lamb leg steaks, each about 7oz (200g)

The marinade:
3 tablespoons whisky
2 tablespoons oil
1 tablespoon ginger marmalade
½ teaspoon ground ginger

Pat the meat dry with kitchen paper. Make cuts at intervals of about 1in (2.5cm) through any fatty skin around the outer edge.

☐ Mix together the marinade ingredients and pour into a shallow dish. Lay the steaks in the marinade, then turn them. Leave for about 1 hour, turning 2 or 3 times.

☐ Pre-heat the grill to high. Line the grill pan with foil. Set the rack in place and put the steaks on top.

☐ Cook for 4-5 minutes on each side, brushing the steaks with the marinade 2 or 3 times during cooking.

☐ Spoon any remaining marinade over the meat to serve.

Liver, Bacon and Tomato Grill

Serve with a crisp salad and French bread, or fluffy mashed potatoes.

Serves 4   ☆☆☆
Preparation: 10 minutes
Cooking: 12-15 minutes

---

4 medium tomatoes
2 teaspoons finely chopped fresh thyme or
   ½ teaspoon dried thyme
1 tablespoon finely chopped parsley
salt and freshly ground black pepper
1oz (25g) butter, cut into 8 cubes
1lb (500g) calves' or lambs' liver, cut in
   ½in (1cm) slices
3 tablespoons oil
¾lb (350g) back bacon rashers, rinds removed

Line the grill pan with foil. Pre-heat the grill to high.

☐ Trim the top and bottom from each tomato, then cut in half across. Place in the grill pan, cut-side up and sprinkle them with the thyme and parsley. Season with salt and pepper and dot with the butter.

☐ Rinse the liver under cold running water and pat dry with kitchen paper. Brush all over with oil and set on the grill rack.

☐ Put the grill rack over the tomatoes and cook the liver for 3-4 minutes to brown. Turn, brush the second side with oil and cook for another 2-3 minutes, or until browned.

☐ Transfer the liver to the pan below the rack, or to a heated serving dish. Arrange the bacon on the grill rack, overlapping the fat to cover the lean, and grill for 2-3 minutes to brown lightly. Turn and grill for another 2 minutes.

☐ Arrange the liver on the dish with the bacon around and the tomatoes on top to serve.

Variations: Try some chopped fresh sage, rosemary or basil instead of the thyme.

Liver, Bacon and Tomato Grill makes an appetizing supper dish.

A contact grill

Perfect for beefburgers, a contact grill cooks quickly on both sides of the food at once. Always brush the ridged contact plates with a little oil or fat when heated and before adding the food. This helps prevent sticking even on 'non-stick' grill plates.

Contact grills come in various sizes, from a single-sandwich 'toaster' type to a full, 4-portion meal size. They have a tendency to smoke during cooking if not kept scrupulously clean. To avoid this, wrap food portions in foil. Follow manufacturer's instructions with regard to the degree of heat required for different foods. Also remember that although the cooking process itself may be fast, they often take some time to get to the required temperature. Some grills have heat-control switches as well as an on-off mechanism. They are perfect for making toasted sandwich snacks!

Grilled Beefburgers

Serve for lunch with a crisp green salad, and tomatoes grilled alongside.

Serves 4
Preparation: 15-20 minutes
Cooking: 5-7 minutes

1¼-1½lb (600-700g) lean beef, minced
3 fl oz (100ml) cold water or Meat Stock
1 medium onion, finely chopped
1 large garlic clove, finely chopped
1-2 teaspoons chopped fresh sage or
   1 teaspoon dried sage
salt and freshly ground black pepper
8-12oz (225-350g) mushrooms, trimmed and
   thinly sliced
1oz (25g) butter, cut in small cubes, or
   2-4 rashers streaky bacon, rinds
   removed, diced
2 tablespoons oil for brushing

Pre-heat the grill to its hottest setting.

☐ Mix the meat with the water or stock, chopped onion, garlic and sage, then season with salt and pepper. Shape into 4 patties, each about 1in (2.5cm) thick.

☐ Sprinkle the mushrooms evenly over the grill, season with a little pepper and dot with the butter, or sprinkle the diced bacon over.

☐ Brush the patties all over with oil and set on the grill.

☐ Cook for 5-7 minutes; brush with oil during cooking.

☐ Transfer to a heated serving dish and garnish with the mushrooms and bacon, if using.

Stuffed hamburgers
Contact grilling allows you an unique and interesting way to ring the changes with the basic hamburger instead of the usual flavoured toppings. Make a small pocket in each patty with a knife or your finger – and pack this with a savoury butter or any of the following tasty stuffings:
● crumbled blue cheese and chopped cooked bacon;
● sweated finely chopped onion and mushroom;
● chopped gherkins and capers in a little mayonnaise.

Quick Pizza Grill

Serves 2 ☆☆☆
Preparation and cooking: about 20 minutes

---

2 pitta breads
a little olive oil or tomato purée for brushing
1 small onion, finely chopped
1 tablespoon chopped fresh marjoram or
   basil or 1 teaspoon dried
2oz (50g) button mushrooms, wiped and
   sliced
2 large tomatoes, thickly sliced
salt and freshly ground black pepper
4oz (125g) mozzarella cheese, sliced

Pre-heat grill to hottest setting.

☐ Brush each pitta bread lightly with olive oil or spread with a little tomato purée.

☐ Mix the onion and marjoram or basil and sprinkle over the breads. Arrange the mushrooms then the tomato slices over each and season well with salt and pepper.

☐ Finally, layer with cheese and season with black pepper.

☐ Place in the cooking tray and cook on the hottest setting for 5-10 minutes, depending on the type of grill.

☐ Serve immediately.

Variation: Use 4oz (125g) sliced salami instead of the tomatoes and mushrooms. Top with Cheddar cheese or mozzarella.

Toasted pitta bread sandwiches
For delicious and unusual snack meals, halve the pieces of pitta bread and prise each half open from the cut with a sharp knife to make cavities. Stuff with any of the following and cook for 3-4 minutes in a well-heated contact grill:
● leftover cooked lamb, tomato slices and sprigs of fresh mint;
● slices of salami and thickly cut wedges of mozzarella or camembert cheese;
● chopped cooked chicken, mayonnaise and a little curry powder;
● flaked canned tuna fish and sliced black olives with a little grated Parmesan cheese.

Grilling poultry

Small or medium chicken joints, turkey portions, whole small birds such as poussins and guinea fowl, and larger oven-ready chickens are all excellent for grilling. Pre-heat the grill to high, then turn it down to finish cooking once the outside is lightly browned.

There are two ways of controlling the heat, either by turning it down (gas) or by moving the grill pan to a lower position (electric) and then lowering the heat.

Always pat the flesh dry first and then keep brushing the surface with melted butter, oil, or a marinade during cooking. As a general rule, start cooking with the fleshy side up, then turn and finish cooking on the underside. For irregular-shaped pieces such as drumsticks, cook them farther from the heat source, reduce the heat and turn frequently, brushing often with oil or marinade.

It may help to brush the grill rack with oil to prevent sticking.

You need a fairly wide grill pan for whole chickens or guinea fowl—these are best dealt with by spatchcocking: split them down the middle on one side of the breastbone and open out flat (see next page). It is usual to remove the wishbone first, and skewers are useful to keep them flat. Otherwise, buy economical packs of similar portions.

Parmesan Chicken

Serves 4   ☆☆☆
Preparation and cooking: 10 minutes, not including sauce

---

4 double or 8 single chicken breast fillets, about 1½lb (700g) in total
3 tablespoons sunflower oil
salt and freshly ground black pepper
3oz (100g) grated Parmesan cheese
Simple Tomato Sauce (optional)

Pre-heat the grill to high. Pat the fillets dry with kitchen paper. Brush fillets and grid with oil, then grill the fillets for about 3 minutes, until lightly browned.

☐ Turn the fillets, brush again with oil and either lower the heat, or take grill pan to 3-4in (8-10cm) from heat source.

☐ Continue grilling fillets for about 5 minutes. Sprinkle with a little salt and pepper, then the cheese. Turn up the heat or return the grill pan to its original position and cook until the cheese is just lightly golden.

☐ Remove the fillets from the grill and serve immediately, with Simple Tomato Sauce, if liked.

Variations: Instead of cheese, use dry breadcrumbs, or a mixture of breadcrumbs and cheese, and serve with a dusting of paprika, or mix a pinch or two of curry powder with the breadcrumbs.

Parmesan Chicken

A clever way with sauces

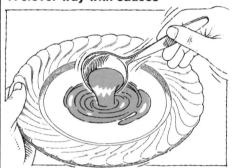

Tip sauce on to a wide-rimmed plate.

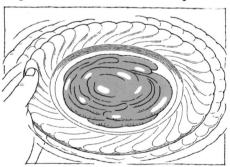

Move the plate in circles so the sauce runs smoothly to the edges.

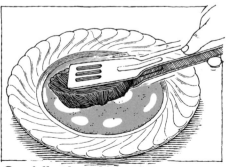

Carefully place chicken in centre.

When spit-roasting

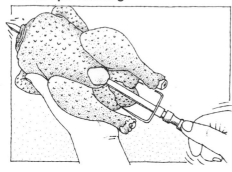

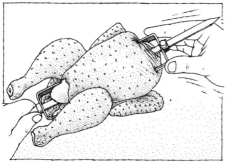

For spit-roasting, insert the spit through the body of the bird, and secure firmly with the holding forks.

Spatchcocked Sesame Chicken

Serves 2-3 ☆☆☆
Preparation: 10 minutes
Cooking: ¾-1 hour

1 oven-ready chicken, weighing about 2½-2¾lb (1.25kg)
salt and freshly ground black pepper

The Sesame Butter:
3 tablespoons sesame seeds
2oz (50g) butter

Pre-heat the grill to high. With a sharp cook's knife, split the chicken through down one side of the breastbone, leaving it intact on the underside. Open out chicken, press as flat as possible from the inside with the heel of your hand. Pat dry with kitchen paper.

☐ Cover the grill rack with foil, if liked, and brush it with oil. Season the chicken well and place it on the rack, cut-side down.

☐ To make the sesame butter: lightly toast the sesame seeds in a dry frying-pan over a moderate heat for 2-3 minutes. Place on a chopping board and crush with a rolling pin. Melt the butter and stir in the toasted seeds.

☐ Set the grill pan at the second grill position, or reduce the heat to medium.

☐ Cook the chicken for about 5 minutes, then turn the chicken over, pressing it as flat as possible with the back of a cook's knife. Grill for 10 minutes, then turn the chicken cut-side down again.

☐ Set the grill or grill pan to low. Spread with Sesame Butter and cook for another 30-40 minutes, until well browned. Turn the chicken frequently, to ensure even browning, brushing it each time with the butter.

☐ To serve, cut into portions with poultry shears and sprinkle with a little salt.

Spatchcocked Sesame Chicken

This recipe works well with spit-roast whole birds. There is no need to spatchcock them. Skewer them neatly as shown, then baste during cooking with the butter (or oil) and sesame seed mixture. You can also barbecue spatchcocked birds.

Note: when the grill rack is covered with foil, it should be placed in the lower position for grilling.

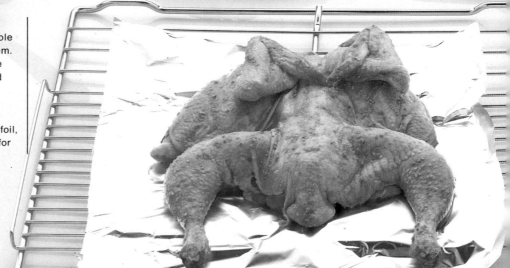

Spatchcocked Guinea Fowl

Serve hot with a mixture of green and white noodles and accompany with cranberry sauce.

Serves 2   ☆ ☆ ☆
Preparation: 5 minutes
Cooking: 35-45 minutes

1 oven-ready guinea fowl, about 1¾lb (800g)
2oz (50g) butter, melted
1 tablespoon mushroom ketchup

Pre-heat the grill to high. Prepare the guinea fowl in the same way as the chicken for Spatchcocked Sesame Chicken.

☐ Mix together the butter and ketchup, then brush this all over the bird.

☐ Cook as for the chicken, turning frequently, and brushing with the butter, for 35-45 minutes or until browned and cooked. Cut in half to serve.

Tandoori-style Chicken Joints

Makes 10   ☆ ☆
Preparation: 10-15 minutes plus at least 6 hours marinating
Cooking: 40 minutes

10 chicken joints, preferably the thighs

The marinade:
½ pint (300ml) natural yogurt
1 teaspoon each of onion purée, chilli purée, curry paste, tomato purée and garlic purée

Mix together all the marinade ingredients.

☐ Line the grill pan with foil. Place the chicken joints in the pan and coat them well with the marinade. Cover with foil and leave in a cool place for at least 6 hours, or overnight.

☐ Pre-heat the grill to high. Remove the foil covering the chicken. Place the chicken joints under the grill in the second grill position, if possible, then reduce the heat to moderate.

☐ Grill for about 15 minutes, or until the chicken is beginning to brown. Turn and baste the chicken with the marinade.

☐ Continue grilling, turning the chicken as necessary as it begins to brown. The cooking should take about 40 minutes altogether – test with a skewer. Serve hot.

Sesame Butter
Instead of the baste, toast 3 tablespoons sesame seeds in a dry frying-pan over a moderate heat for 2-3 minutes. Crush and beat into 2oz (50g) soft butter. Roll, wrap and chill.

Spatchcocked poussins
Cook small poussins like this. To keep them flat while cooking, a chef will split the bird as shown, turn it over and press the backbone hard with a closed fist or the heel of a hand to snap it. Two thin skewers are threaded, one through the wing pinions and body, the second through the thighs and body. Allow 12-14 minutes grilling time.

To tell when chicken is cooked
Insert a skewer or the point of a knife into the thickest part. The flesh should feel tender, the juices run clear.

Tandoori-style Chicken Joints
Serve these as a starter with natural yogurt, or with boiled rice, finely chopped raw onion and lemon wedges dipped in chopped parsley. They also make ideal party finger food.

Step-by-step to Spatchcocked Sesame Chicken, showing the technique of spatchcocking (flattening) the bird.

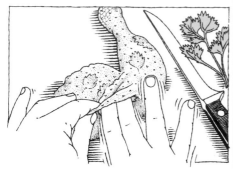

Carefully loosen the skin on the drumsticks and insert the herbs between skin and flesh as shown. The technique also works well with other chicken portions, such as breast.

Mustard Butter
Beat 2 teaspoons lemon juice and 1 teaspoon made mustard into 3oz (75g) softened butter. Shape into a 1in (2.5cm) roll and chill. This is particularly good with steaks or game fillets.

Serve mild-flavoured meats such as chicken, or even strong-flavoured meats such as game, topped with two flavours of savoury butter: garlic with tomato, or mustard with a steak butter.

Dijon-style Hare
The instructions will give meat which is nicely browned outside, and a bit pink inside. Cook for 2-3 minutes longer on each side at a reduced heat if you prefer the meat well done.

Grilled Chicken Drumsticks with Herbs

Use a variety of flavour combinations or make the drumsticks all the same flavour. Serve these as a hot snack for a party, or cool and pack to serve as picnic food.

Makes 10   ☆
Preparation: 15 minutes, plus 2-3 hours chilling
Cooking: 15-20 minutes

---

10 chicken drumsticks
a selection of small sprigs of fresh herbs, such as rosemary, thyme, dill, fennel, parsley and small bay leaves
orange, lemon, lime or grapefruit rind, as available, cut into small thin strips
3oz (75g) butter, melted

Loosen the skin at the fleshy end of the drumsticks by inserting a finger between skin and flesh.

☐ Slide the sprigs of herbs and strips of rind under the skin of each drumstick, then chill for 2-3 hours to let the flavours permeate the chicken.

☐ Pre-heat the grill to high. Line the grill pan with foil. Brush each drumstick with melted butter and place it on the rack. Set it at the second grill position, if possible, then reduce the heat.

☐ Cook, turning 2 or 3 times and basting frequently, for about 15 minutes or until the drumsticks are browned and cooked. Test one with a skewer.

☐ Cover tips with chicken frills to serve.
Variation: The recipe also works well with whole birds if you pull back the breast flap of skin, insert the fingers of one hand between flesh and skin as shown for the drumsticks then pack the space with the herbs and citrus rind or a layer of herb butter before roasting. Cover the breast of the bird with bacon rashers or foil to protect it during cooking.

Grilling game

Small tender cuts of furred game such as steaks or chops can be grilled. (Larger joints are better cooked by spit-roasting.) Add extra flavour and tenderness by soaking in a marinade, such as the one given in the sidelines on page 161.

Dijon-style Hare

Serves 4   ☆☆☆
Preparation: 10 minutes
Cooking: 13-15 minutes

---

4 joints of hare, each about 10oz (275g)

The glaze:
8 juniper berries, crushed
¼ teaspoon salt
freshly ground black pepper
½ teaspoon dried thyme
½ teaspoon dried rosemary
6 tablespoons olive oil
2 teaspoons Dijon mustard

The sauce:
2 tablespoons raspberry vinegar
2 tablespoons redcurrant jelly
¼ pint (150ml) soured cream
salt and freshly ground black pepper

Pre-heat the grill to high.

☐ Pat the hare joints dry and set them on the grill rack.

☐ Mix together all the glaze ingredients. Brush over the joints, then cook the hare, about 4in (10cm) away from the heat, for about 6 minutes, or until browned, brushing with more glaze 2 or 3 times during cooking.

☐ Turn, brush well with glaze and grill for a further 6 minutes. Use all the glaze and cook the joints to the required degree.

☐ Transfer the hare to a warmed serving dish and keep hot.

☐ Stir the vinegar, jelly, and cream into the juices in the grill pan. Heat for 2-3 minutes until bubbling, then strain into a basin. Whisk briefly to mix well and spoon over the meat to serve.

Sage-grilled Venison

Serve with straw potatoes tossed with sautéed onions, Brussels sprouts, and chicory sprinkled with a little grated nutmeg.

Serves 4 ☆☆
Preparation: 15 minutes
Cooking: 5-8 minutes

4 slices venison fillet, each about 5oz (150g) and 1in (2.5cm) thick
coarsely ground black pepper
2 tablespoons oil
1 tablespoon wine or cider vinegar
2 tablespoons sherry
1 tablespoon finely chopped fresh sage
2 tomatoes to garnish
sprigs of parsley to garnish

The Sage and Sherry Butter:
1 tablespoon sherry
2oz (50g) butter, softened
2 tablespoons finely chopped fresh sage

First make the butter: Gradually whisk the sherry into the softened butter, then beat in the chopped sage. Form into a log, about 1in (2.5cm) diameter, wrap in foil and chill.

☐ Pre-heat the grill to high. Line the grill pan with foil.

☐ Pat the meat dry with kitchen paper and sprinkle with pepper.

☐ Mix together the oil, vinegar, sherry and chopped sage. Place the steaks on the grill rack, brush with oil and vinegar mixture and cook the fillets for 2½-4 minutes on the first side, depending on your taste. Brush with oil and vinegar during cooking.

☐ Turn the steaks. Brush the second side with oil and vinegar, and grill for 2½-3 minutes until cooked to the required degree.

☐ Transfer the steaks to a heated serving dish. Top each one with a slice of Sage and Sherry Butter. Garnish with tomato lilies (see below) and sprigs of parsley.

Tip: To make tomato lilies, make a series of diagonal cuts, alternating to right and left, all round. Prise the halves apart.

Sage-grilled Venison served with braised chicory, Brussels sprouts and straw potatoes.

Grilling cheese

Cheese is easy to grill, whether it is grated or sliced. Most types may be used, but choose a cheese with a high fat content when you want it to brown.

Keep a supply of grated Cheddar, Parmesan, or Gruyère in the freezer in a plastic bag ready to sprinkle over chops, steaks, vegetables in cream sauce, or pasta. Brown quickly under the grill just before serving.

Slices of Cheddar or mozzarella also are good to store in the freezer. Remember to interleave the slices with greaseproof paper so they are easy to separate when required. Lay slices of the cheese on top of pizzas, burgers, or toast, and grill from frozen for a minute or two.

Grilled whole pieces of cheese about ¾-1in (1.5-2.5cm) thick make a good first course, or the base for a supper dish. Dutch cheese (Gouda or Edam), Cheddar, or mozzarella are all good served this way. Pre-heat the grill to high. Grill the slices of cheese just until they begin to melt. Turn and grill the second side. Top with a fried or poached egg to make a quick, savoury supper dish. Garnish with grilled tomatoes, or serve with a watercress salad.

Grilled Mozzarella with Sesame Seeds.

Grilling cheese on toast
Sprinkle with dried basil for an unusual warm and spicy flavour.

Grilled Mozzarella with Sesame Seeds
The truly adventurous should try substituting slices of chèvre (goat's cheese) for the mozzarella.

'au gratin'
This term is sometimes used for dishes sprinkled with a mixture of breadcrumbs and/or grated cheese and flashed under the grill to brown and crisp the top. It's a good way of finishing off fish pies, or anything coated with a thick white sauce. (Crushed corn flakes or potato crisps make a good emergency topping.)

Grilled Mozzarella with Sesame Seeds

Serve as a first course with chunks of wholemeal bread and butter, or as a lunch or supper dish with an endive, chicory or watercress salad.

Serves 4   ☆☆☆
Preparation: 5 minutes
Cooking: 5 minutes

---

4 tablespoons sesame seeds
4 slices mozzarella cheese, each about 3oz (75g) and ⅝in (1.5cm) thick
1oz (25g) butter, melted

Lightly brown the sesame seeds in a dry frying-pan over a moderate heat for 2-3 minutes. Spread out on a chopping board and lightly crush with a rolling pin.
☐ Pre-heat the grill to high.
☐ Lightly butter 4 shallow flameproof dishes. Put a slice of cheese into each and brush the tops with half of the melted butter.
☐ Sprinkle the cheese slices with half the seeds, pressing the seeds well into the cheese.
☐ Set the dishes on the grill rack and grill for 2-3 minutes until the cheese is beginning to melt.
☐ Turn the cheese, brush with melted butter and sprinkle with the rest of the sesame seeds, then press them into the cheese. Grill for a further 2 minutes.

Grilled Camembert

Serve with a crisp green salad and chunks of wholemeal bread, or thick slices of toast. It also makes a good dinner party first course.

Serves 4   ☆☆
Preparation: 5 minutes
Cooking: 5 minutes

---

2 tablespoons butter, melted
1 Camembert cheese, about 8oz (225g)
3-4 tablespoons dry breadcrumbs
1 teaspoon dried marjoram

Pre-heat the grill to high.
☐ Brush the inside of a shallow 5-5½in (13-14cm) flameproof flan tin with a little of the butter.
☐ Brush the top and bottom of the Camembert all over with the rest of the butter.
☐ Mix together the breadcrumbs and marjoram, then press the cheese firmly into the crumbs to coat both sides. Pat the crumbs on, if necessary, with the flat side of a cook's knife blade.
☐ Put the cheese in the flan tin. Set it on the grill rack and cook for 2-3 minutes until slightly browned and just beginning to melt. Turn the cheese and grill the second side in the same way.
☐ Remove from the flan tin and serve, cut into quarters.

Grilling vegetables and fruit

Certain vegetables and fruits can be cooked quickly and easily under the grill. Here are some savoury and sweet dishes to serve with grilled meat or fish, or on their own as first courses or desserts.

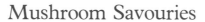

Aubergine and Egg Gratin

Serves 4   ☆☆

Preparation: 10 minutes, plus 30 minutes soaking

Cooking: 20 minutes

---

1 large aubergine, about 1¼lb (575g)
1 tablespoon salt
2 tablespoons olive oil
4 eggs, size 3
2oz (50g) grated Parmesan cheese

Wipe the aubergine, then trim off the top and bottom. Cut across into 4 pieces about 2½in (6cm) wide.

☐ Stir the salt into a large bowl of cold water, add the aubergine and leave for 30 minutes. Drain, rinse in cold water and pat dry.

☐ Pre-heat the grill to high and line the pan with foil.

☐ Carefully loosen the flesh from the skin around the sides of the aubergine with a sharp knife. Score the surface of the flesh into ½in (1cm) squares. Arrange aubergine slices on the rack and brush the cut surfaces with oil.

☐ Grill for about 5 minutes to brown lightly, then turn, brush again with oil and grill for about 5 minutes, until browned. Remove from the grill and reduce the heat.

☐ With the bowl of a tablespoon, make a deep well in the scored side of each piece of aubergine. Crack an egg into each and sprinkle with cheese.

☐ Grill for about 10 minutes to set the eggs and brown the cheese.

Mushroom Savouries

Serves 4   ☆☆☆

Preparation: 15 minutes

Cooking: 4-5 minutes

---

8 flat mushrooms, about 3in (8cm) diameter
4 tablespoons olive oil
3oz (75g) mozzarella or
    Cheddar cheese, cubed
3oz (75g) cooked ham, cubed
1 tablespoon chopped fresh marjoram or 2
    teaspoons dried marjoram
salt and freshly ground black pepper
2oz (50g) grated Cheddar cheese
2oz (50g) butter, cubed

Pre-heat the grill to high. Line the grill pan with foil.

☐ Wipe the mushrooms. Remove the stalks and slice them thinly.

☐ Brush the tops of the mushrooms with oil, set them gill-side down on the grill rack and cook for about 2 minutes to brown lightly.

☐ Mix the cheese and ham with the sliced mushroom stalks. Stir in the marjoram and season well with salt and pepper.

☐ Turn the mushrooms over, brush again with oil and spoon the cheese mixture into them. Sprinkle with the grated cheese and dot with butter.

☐ Return to the grill for about 2 minutes just to melt the cheese and colour the tops.

Top: Mushroom Savouries
Centre: Aubergine and Egg Gratin.

Angostura Grapefruit

A simple but delicious first course: the tang of the bitters goes well with fruit. It is a very good dish to precede rich meat dishes, or any fish dish.

Pineapple Flambé

The purpose of flambéing is to burn off the raw alcohol, and to caramelize the sugar.

Grilling other fruits

Other fruits, such as apricots, peaches and guavas can be grilled after peeling. Serve with the centres filled with raspberries, blackberries, or crushed macaroons, then sprinkle with desiccated coconut and serve with yogurt or soured cream.

Making brûlées

A brûlée top helps you make a very effective dessert very quickly. Put fruit, such as grapes, raspberries or ripe, peeled pears, in a shallow ovenproof dish and sprinkle with liqueur. Cover with a layer of stiffly whipped cream then with a thin layer of sugar. Flash under the grill just long enough to melt the sugar. Chill immediately for 30 minutes – 1 hour. The melted sugar will turn into a crunchy crackling top on the cream.

Angostura Grapefruit

Serves 4 ◯
Preparation: 10 minutes
Cooking: 2-3 minutes

---

2 large grapefruit
Angostura bitters
watercress to garnish

Pre-heat the grill to high and line the pan with foil.

☐ Cut the grapefruit across in half. Snip out the cores with kitchen scissors. Cut along either side of each segment with a sharp knife to loosen the flesh, then cut around the edges.

☐ Lift out the membranes, leaving the segments clear. Sprinkle each grapefruit half with a dash or two of Angostura.

☐ Grill for about 2 minutes to warm gently and lightly brown the surface.

☐ Garnish with watercress to serve.

Buttered Apples

Serves 4 ☆☆
Preparation: 5 minutes
Cooking: 10 minutes

---

4 large dessert apples, peeled and cored
2oz (50g) butter, melted
about 2oz (50g) caster or demerara sugar

Halve each apple and dip into the butter to coat all over.

☐ Pre-heat the grill to high.

☐ Set each apple half, cut-side down, on a square of foil. Turn up the edges to make little saucers and set on the grill rack.

☐ Grill at the second grill position, if possible, for about 5 minutes until the apples are beginning to brown. Turn, brush with any remaining butter and cook for about 4 minutes.

☐ Sprinkle with sugar and continue grilling for about half a minute until it melts. Serve immediately with cream, custard or ice cream.

Pineapple Flambé

Serves 4 ☆☆☆
Preparation: 10 minutes
Cooking: 3-4 minutes

---

8 slices of fresh pineapple, each about ½in (1cm) thick, cored and peeled
3oz (75g) butter, softened
3oz (75g) caster sugar
1 teaspoon ground cinnamon
4 tablespoons whisky
¼ pint (150ml) double cream

Pre-heat the grill to high. Line the grill rack with foil and roll the edges up to form a shallow rim. Set the pineapple on the foil.

☐ Mix together the butter, sugar and cinnamon. Spread over one side of the pineapple and cook for about 3 minutes.

☐ Spoon the whisky over the fruit. Return to the grill for a few seconds to set the spirit alight, and brown the tops of the fruit.

☐ Transfer the pineapple to warmed plates, spoon the juices over and serve with thick, cold cream.

Rum Bananas

Serves 4 ☆
Preparation and cooking: 10-15 minutes

2oz (50g) soft brown sugar
3 tablespoons dark rum
4 large under-ripe bananas
4 scoops vanilla ice cream
1oz (25g) chopped walnuts

Boil the sugar with the rum for a minute. Set aside.

☐ Pre-heat the grill to high.

☐ Wipe the bananas but do not peel them. Set on the grill rack and cook for 8-10 minutes. Turn frequently until the skin is dark brown all over and blistering slightly.

☐ Transfer to warmed plates, cut open lengthways with a sharp knife and pull back the skin. Spoon the sugar mixture over. Top with ice cream sprinkled with the nuts.

Spit-roasting

Probably the earliest of man's cooking methods practised by cavemen over open fires, most spit-roasting nowadays is done in conjunction with a domestic grill or grill element in the oven. The advantages of spit-roasting are obvious: the revolving motion ensures that the food is evenly cooked and the juices stay in the food rather than seeping out during the cooking

Spit-roast Chicken Kebabs

process, making the most of natural succulence – even of fairly dry and unfatty foods. Always start cooking on a high temperature, or with the grill pre-heated to high, then turn the heat down to a suitable temperature to finish. Bard lean meats such as veal or game birds. Many foods can be successfully cooked by this method, and the recipes on the following pages provide only a few examples for the creative cook. If you don't have a spit-grill or rotisserie, most of the dishes adapt well to ordinary oven roasting. One rule, however, is common to both: baste well and you will be rewarded . . .

Rules for spit-roasting
● Heat is conducted through the food by the metal skewer, so make sure it does not touch the bone or the distribution of heat will be uneven. Have joints boned and rolled wherever possible.
● The food – whether in one piece or several – must be evenly balanced on the spit to avoid uneven cooking.
● Awkward shapes such as poultry or game should be firmly tied to keep a neat shape, and to keep away from contact with the heat source.
● Always baste well with a flavoured butter or oil mixture. Use drip-tray juices for gravies or sauces.
● Follow the manufacturer's recommended temperatures for the type of appliance that you use.
● Always thaw frozen food thoroughly before cooking by spit-roasting.

Spit-roast Fillet of Beef

Serve with fried or sauté potatoes and a crisp green salad. If liked, serve cold with Ravigôte Sauce.

Serves 4-5 ☆☆
Preparation and cooking: 35-45 minutes

1½lb (700g) fillet of beef
2 garlic cloves
1oz (25g) butter, melted
½ teaspoon dried green peppercorns, crushed
salt and freshly ground black pepper
2 tablespoons water

Pre-heat the spit-grill to high.

☐ Pat the meat dry with kitchen paper.

☐ Slice 1 garlic clove, make small slits in surface of meat and push garlic into slits. Tie the fillet into a firm roll with string.

☐ Crush the second garlic clove and mix with butter and peppercorns.

☐ Insert the skewer from the spit through the meat and secure with the holding forks. Brush the meat well with the flavoured butter.

☐ Fix the skewer in the grill over the drip pan. Set the spit revolving, close the door and turn down the heat. Cook for about 30 minutes, brushing the meat frequently with the rest of the butter.

☐ Transfer the cooked beef from skewer to a hot serving dish. Season. Put the drip pan over a moderate heat, add the water and bring to the boil, stirring constantly to make a thin sauce.

☐ Slice the fillet and serve with the juices strained over.

Spit-roast Fillet of Beef served cold with Ravigôte Sauce.

Spit-roast Shoulder of Veal with Carrots

Serve with a rice pilaf or potatoes.

Serves 4-5

Preparation: 5 minutes
Cooking: about 50 minutes

1¾lb (800g) boned rolled shoulder of veal
several small rosemary sprigs
2 tablespoons good-quality orange
    marmalade
1 tablespoon orange juice
2oz (50g) butter
1lb (500g) carrots, par-boiled and drained
salt and freshly ground black pepper

Pre-heat the spit-grill to high.

☐ Pat the meat dry with kitchen paper. Carefully slide the tip of a sharp knife between the fat and the flesh in several places and tuck the rosemary in the slits.

☐ Insert the spit skewer lengthways through the meat and secure firmly with the holding forks.

☐ Warm the marmalade with the orange juice and butter in a small saucepan on a low heat. When melted and mixed, brush the glaze over the meat

☐ Place the skewered meat in position in the spit-grill. Lower the heat, start the spit and roast for 30 minutes, brushing the meat with the glaze several times during cooking.

☐ After 30 minutes, add the carrots to the drip pan under the meat, coating them well with the cooking juices. Continue cooking for 20-25 minutes, basting from time to time, until the meat is well browned and cooked.

☐ Transfer the meat from skewer to a hot serving dish. Season. Arrange carrots round meat to serve.

Tip: If you buy the veal in the piece, be sure to shape it into a firm, even, well-tied roll. Rolling the meat yourself gives you more opportunity for adding flavouring. Lay sprigs of rosemary, small thin slivers of orange rind, and thin slivers of garlic inside the meat before rolling.

Smoked Pork with Pineapple

Serves 6

Preparation and cooking: 55 minutes

1¾lb (800g) smoked cured pork loin
1 tablespoon lemon marmalade
1 tablespoon oil
1 teaspoon made mustard
2 teaspoons lemon juice
salt and freshly ground black pepper
6 slices fresh or canned pineapple

Pre-heat the spit-grill to high.

☐ Pat meat dry. Skewer lengthways and secure with the forks.

☐ In a small pan, melt the jam with oil, mustard and lemon juice. Mix well and brush over the pork.

☐ Put in the spit-grill, lower the heat and cook for 30-35 minutes, brushing frequently with glaze.

☐ Arrange pineapple in the pan below the pork and continue cooking for 10 minutes for fresh pineapple or about 5 minutes for canned, until pork is cooked. Season and serve thinly sliced.

Gammon with Herbs

Serves 4

Preparation: 15 minutes
Cooking: 45-50 minutes

1¾lb (800g) unsmoked gammon
1oz (25g) chopped fresh fennel or dill
2 tablespoons oil
salt and freshly ground black pepper

Pre-heat the spit-grill to high. Pat meat dry with kitchen paper.

☐ Make cuts between the skin and the meat with the tip of a sharp knife and insert most of the herbs.

☐ Tie the gammon into a firm roll at 1in (2.5cm) intervals.

☐ Mix remaining herbs with the oil, brush over the meat, skewer and secure.

☐ Lower the heat and cook for about 45 minutes, brushing 2 or 3 times with oil.

☐ Season and serve thinly sliced.

Spit-roast Fillet of Beef
If you have a large spit with large forks, you may not need to tie the meat. On smaller spits, it is advisable to tie the meat into a tight roll to keep it from hitting the pan as it revolves.

Spit-roast Shoulder of Veal with Carrots
As veal is a very dry meat, spit-roasting is an ideal way to cook it. The high dry heat sears the surface and keeps the juices sealed in.

Smoked Pork with Pineapple
This makes a good dinner-party dish, served with green beans and boiled potatoes sprinkled with parsley. Slice the meat very thinly for serving.

For an unusual accompaniment, simmer slices of kohlrabi in cream, then add a thinly sliced apple or two, and continue cooking until the kohlrabi is tender.

Gammon with Herbs
Cooked on the spit this way, gammon is very tender and succulent. Most gammon can be cooked without prior soaking. To test this, wet your index finger and rub it over the meat. If your finger tastes salty, soak the meat in cold water for 2-3 hours before cooking. Serve with braised red cabbage, boiled white cabbage, or with broccoli and fried potatoes.

Use a herb butter instead of the butter and oil: baste more often if you do so.

Seasoning
It is best to season meat after cooking as salt tends to draw the juices to the surface, thus reducing natural succulence.

Cooking potatoes with the meat
Potatoes cooked in the drip pan with the juices from the meat develop a delicious flavour. Use small even-sized potatoes, wash them well and prick them all over with a fork.

Spit-roasting whole birds

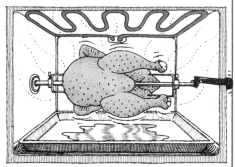

Be sure to skewer the bird lengthways through the middle so it turns evenly on the spit. Check that the legs or wing tips will not touch the flame or grill element as it revolves. If in doubt, tie the bird in 3 places with kitchen string to keep wing tips and legs in place.

Turkey Spit-roast
Serve with creamed potatoes and glazed turnips or parsnips, or with Brussels sprouts and glazed chestnuts.

Chicken-on-the-spit
Use rendered bacon fat instead of the flavoured butter for basting.
Serve with sautéed potatoes, carrots and the onion from the chicken, or with a warm potato and bacon salad dressed with vinaigrette, and crisp green beans.

Giblet Stock
While the chicken is cooking, put the giblets in a pan with 1 small carrot, 1 small onion, a coarsely chopped stick of celery and a sprig each of thyme and parsley. Bring to the boil in water to cover and then simmer with a few peppercorns and a pinch of salt for about 30 minutes. Add a little extra water as necessary. Strain before using.

Guinea Fowl with Leeks
Serve this with a mixture of green and white noodles (spinach and egg) and plenty of redcurrant or cranberry jelly.

Turkey Spit-Roast

Serves 4-5   ☆☆
Preparation: 5 minutes
Cooking: about 1 hour

1¾lb (800g) boneless turkey roast

The glaze:
1 teaspoon chopped fresh tarragon or
   ½ teaspoon dried
¼ pint (150ml) dry cider
1oz (25g) soft brown sugar
2oz (50g) butter

The gravy:
1 tablespoon flour
about ¼ pint (150ml) dry cider or Chicken
   Stock
salt and freshly ground black pepper

Pre-heat the spit-grill to high.
☐ Pat the turkey dry. Make sure the joint is firmly tied at about 1in (2.5cm) intervals.
☐ Insert the skewer lengthways through the roast and secure with the holding forks.
☐ For the glaze, boil the tarragon, cider and sugar together vigorously for 5 minutes. Remove from the heat and stir in the butter until melted.
☐ Brush the turkey all over with glaze. Reduce the heat, cook for about 1 hour, brushing frequently with glaze.
☐ Transfer the cooked roast to a serving dish and keep it hot while you make the gravy.
☐ Strain off fat and put drip pan over low heat. Stir in the flour, then the cider or stock and continue stirring until the gravy is thickened. Season with salt and pepper, strain and serve with the turkey.

Chicken-on-the-Spit

Serves 2-3   ☆☆☆
Preparation: 15 minutes
Cooking: 1 hour

---

1 oven-ready chicken, about 2¾lb (1.25kg)
   dressed weight
2 medium onions, quartered

1 tablespoon chopped fresh thyme or
   ½ teaspoon dried
salt and freshly ground black pepper
2oz (50g) butter, melted

The gravy:
1 tablespoon flour
Giblet Stock (see sidelines)
salt and freshly ground black pepper

Remove the giblets from the chicken and use for stock. Pre-heat the spit-grill to high.
☐ Pat the chicken dry with kitchen paper both inside and out. Put the onions and thyme inside the chicken and season with a little salt and pepper. Close the opening with skewers.
☐ Tie the legs together firmly and cut off the scaly part below the joints. Secure the wings and neck skin under the bird with small skewers.
☐ Insert the spit through the body of the chicken lengthways. Secure firmly with the holding forks and brush all over with melted butter.
☐ Reduce the heat and cook for about 1 hour, or until cooked, brushing occasionally with butter.
☐ Transfer the chicken to a serving dish and keep hot. Set the drip pan over a low heat. Stir in the flour. Gradually stir in stock and cook until thickened. Season to taste. Strain and serve with the chicken.

Guinea Fowl with Leeks

Serves 2-3   ☆☆☆
Preparation: 10 minutes
Cooking: about 50 minutes

---

1 guinea fowl, about 1¾lb (800g)
   dressed weight
2 medium leeks, sliced and well washed
a large sprig of fresh thyme
salt and freshly ground black pepper
2oz (50g) butter, melted
2 tablespoons brandy

Pat the fowl dry. Fill the cavity with the leeks, add the thyme and season with salt and pepper.

□ Close the opening with poultry pins or small skewers. Cut off the scaly part of the legs and tie the legs together firmly. Secure the wings and neck skin under the bird with poultry pins or small skewers.

□ Insert the skewer lengthways through the body and secure with the holding forks.

□ Stir together the butter and brandy and brush over the fowl.

□ Reduce the heat and cook the bird for about 50 minutes, or until browned and the juices run clear. Brush with more of the butter.

□ When cooked, remove the pins and strings, transfer the fowl to a hot serving dish and garnish with the leeks. Discard the thyme and spoon the pan juices over.

Honey-roast Duck

Honey-roast Duck

Serves 4 ☆☆☆
Preparation: 20 minutes
Cooking: about 1½ hours

---

1 duck, about 5lb (2.25kg) dressed weight

The stuffing:
6oz (175g) apples, peeled and finely chopped
3oz (75g) fresh brown breadcrumbs
2oz (50g) onion, finely chopped
1oz (25g) butter, melted
1oz (25g) clear honey
1 tablespoon finely chopped fresh rosemary
salt and freshly ground black pepper

The glaze:
1oz (25g) clear honey
1oz (25g) melted butter

Remove the giblets from the duck. Trim off all excess fat, and the skin from the neck. Cut off the scaly part of the legs.

□ Pre-heat the spit-grill to high.

□ Mix together all the stuffing ingredients and season well. Fill the body cavity of the duck and close with small skewers. Tie the duck in 3 places with string to hold the legs and wings close to the body. Prick the bird all over with the prongs of a fork to allow the fat to drain off during cooking.

□ Insert the skewer lengthways through the duck and secure with the holding forks. Reduce the heat and cook the duck for about 1½ hours, until the juices run clear.

□ Mix the honey and butter together and brush this glaze all over the duck. Continue cooking for a further 10 minutes, brushing with the glaze 2 or 3 times until it is all used and the duck is a rich brown.

Spit-roasting duck

Choose a duck which fits comfortably on to your spit. Secure it firmly and turn the heat to a setting lower than you would use for cooking smaller birds. This way the duck cooks through inside before it over-browns on the outside. Ducks cooked on the spit are good if left just a little rare. If you like them well done, cook until the juices run clear.

Honey-roast Duck

Serve with the stuffing, creamed potatoes and petits pois or a pilaff and mangetout peas.

Spit-roasting small birds

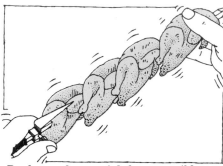

Pack together as tightly as possible.

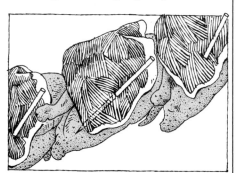

Secure the bacon over the breast of each, if necessary, with wooden cocktail sticks. Make sure they do not catch the flame or grill element as the skewer revolves during cooking.

To prevent charring, soak wooden cocktail sticks in cold water before use.

Pâté-stuffed Poussins
Serve these with green beans and game chips or 'shoestring' potatoes.

Spit-roast Quails
Serve with 'shoestring' potatoes or warmed potato crisps, pickled cherries and a green salad.

Stuffed Pigeons
Plain boiled rice – especially brown rice – mixed with sweetcorn, and carrots or parsnips go well with this dish.

Serve cranberry or elderberry jelly with roast pigeons.

Pâté-stuffed Poussins

Serves 4   ☆☆☆
Preparation: 20 minutes
Cooking: about 45 minutes

---

2 poussins, each about 14oz (400g) dressed
    weight
2oz (50g) smooth liver pâté
2 tablespoons madeira or medium sherry
4 tablespoons fresh breadcrumbs
2oz (50g) button mushrooms, finely chopped
2oz (50g) butter, melted
4oz (100g) oyster or flat mushrooms

Pat the poussins dry. Trim off the scaly ends of the legs and any excess neck skin.
☐ Pre-heat the spit-grill to high.
☐ Mix together the pâté, madeira, breadcrumbs and chopped mushrooms until well blended, then use to stuff the poussins. Close the poussins with small skewers. Tie with string to hold the wings and legs close to the bodies.
☐ Line the drip pan with foil. Insert the skewer lengthways through the birds and secure with the holding forks. Reduce heat and cook the birds for about 40 minutes, basting frequently with the butter.
☐ Arrange mushrooms in the pan and spoon over any remaining butter and the pan juices.
☐ Continue cooking for about 5 minutes. Remove strings and skewers. Halve the poussins down the breast. Arrange on a hot serving dish and garnish with mushrooms. Spoon over pan juices.

Spit-roast Quails

Serves 4   ☆☆
Preparation: 20 minutes
Cooking: 30-35 minutes

---

4 quails, each about 4oz (125g) dressed
    weight
4 small onions, par-boiled and peeled
4 sprigs fresh thyme
salt and freshly ground black pepper
4 rashers streaky bacon, rinds removed
1oz (25g) butter, melted

Rinse the quails thoroughly in cold water. Pat dry with kitchen paper.
☐ Put 1 onion and 1 sprig of thyme inside each bird. Sprinkle inside each with salt and pepper.
☐ Insert the skewer lengthways through the quails, packing them together very tightly. Secure with the holding forks and tie the legs firmly to the bodies.
☐ Wrap a rasher of bacon around each quail and secure with wooden cocktail sticks.
☐ Line the drip pan with foil. Reduce the heat and cook the birds for 30 minutes brushing frequently with butter.
☐ Take the birds from the oven. Discard the cocktail sticks, unwrap the bacon from the birds and put in the pan.
☐ Return the birds to the oven and cook for a further 10 minutes, brushing with the remaining butter.
☐ Transfer the quails to a hot serving dish discard the strings, garnish with the bacon and serve.

Stuffed Pigeons

Serves 2   ☆☆☆
Preparation and cooking: 55 minutes

---

2 pigeons, each about 8oz (225g) dressed
    weight
6 tablespoons fresh brown breadcrumbs
1 teaspoon finely chopped onion
1oz (25g) hazelnuts, finely chopped
2oz (50g) butter
½ teaspoon dried thyme
salt and freshly ground black pepper

Rinse the pigeons well, inside and out, in cold water. Pat dry.
☐ Pre-heat the spit-grill to high.
☐ Mix together the breadcrumbs, onion, nuts, half the butter, the thyme and a little salt and pepper. Pack the stuffing into the pigeons. Close with small skewers.
☐ Reduce the heat, and cook as for the quails, brushing frequently with the rest of the butter, for 40-45 minutes until browned.
☐ Serve with the pan juices.

Chicken Drumsticks on the Spit

Makes 10
Preparation and cooking: 35 minutes plus 2-3 hours chilling

---

10 chicken drumsticks
a selection of small sprigs of fresh herbs
orange, lemon, lime or grapefruit rind, as available, cut into small thin strips
3oz (75g) butter, melted

Prepare the drumsticks as for grilling (page 146).
☐ Thread a skewer through the length of each drumstick. Secure with string and brush with butter.
☐ Cook for about 20 minutes, brushing with butter 2 or 3 times.

Spit-roast Grouse

Serves 2 ⭐⭐⭐
Preparation: 5 minutes
Cooking: 45 minutes

---

2 grouse, each about ¾lb (375g) dressed weight
4 rashers, streaky bacon, rinds removed
1oz (25g) butter, melted

Pre-heat the spit-grill to high.
☐ Rinse the grouse thoroughly in cold water and pat dry with kitchen paper.
☐ Lay the bacon over the breasts of the birds. Tie the birds to secure legs and wings.
☐ Insert the spit-skewer lengthways through both grouse and secure with the holding forks.
☐ Line the drip pan with foil. Position the skewer, reduce heat and cook for 30 minutes, brushing with melted butter.
☐ After 30 minutes, remove grouse, cut and discard the strings; transfer the bacon to the pan.
☐ Return the grouse to the spit and cook for a further 15 minutes, brushing once or twice with the butter, until browned and the juices run clear.

☐ Transfer the grouse to a hot serving dish with the bacon. Strain the cooking juices over.

Spit-roast Stuffed Pheasant

Serve with the pan juices, fried fresh breadcrumbs, game chips and braised fennel. It is traditional to show pheasants with their feet on, but this is not practical with spit-roasted birds. The legs must be trimmed off short to ensure they clear the drip pan when turning. Spit-roasting is good for pheasant as it keeps the flesh moist.

Serves 3 ⭐⭐⭐
Preparation: 15 minutes
Cooking: 50-60 minutes

---

1 pheasant, about 2lb (1kg) dressed weight
sprigs of watercress to garnish

The stuffing:
2oz (50g) fresh breadcrumbs
2oz (50g) full-fat cream cheese
1oz (25g) walnuts, coarsely chopped
salt and freshly ground black pepper

The glaze:
2oz (50g) butter, melted
3 fl oz (100ml) Chicken or Game Stock

Pat the pheasant dry and cut off the scaly part of the legs.
☐ Mix together the stuffing ingredients and use to stuff the pheasant. Close with small skewers. Tie the legs together firmly. Secure the wings, and neck skin under the bird with poultry pins.
☐ Pre-heat the spit-grill to high.
☐ Insert the skewer through the body lengthways and secure with the holding forks. Mix together the butter and stock and brush over the pheasant.
☐ Reduce the heat and cook the pheasant for 50-60 minutes until browned and the juices run clear. Brush with the glaze during cooking until it is all used up.
☐ Remove the pins and strings, and transfer the pheasant to a hot serving dish. Garnish with watercress and serve.

To stuff poultry and game birds

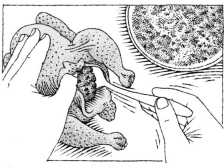

Leave room to fold skin flaps over.

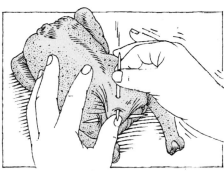

Tuck in 'parson's nose', then fold over skin as shown and secure with small skewers or poultry pins. For very small birds, large safety pins can be used, but do remove them before serving!

Game chips
To make game chips, peel and very thinly slice potatoes. Pat dry with kitchen paper and deep-fry in hot oil until golden brown.

For a really pretty accompaniment, slice the peeled potatoes on the ridged blade of a mandolin. Hold the potato against the blade, cut off the first slice and discard it. Give the potato a 90° turn and slice again: this will give a 'basketwork' effect. To complete the accompaniment, make a potato basket to serve the game chips in. Line the deep-frying basket with 'basketwork' potato slices, overlapping them so there are no gaps. Press a second deep-frying basket inside the first lined one and deep-fry in hot oil until golden. Turn out carefully and fill with game chips.

Wild Duck with Orange

Serve with game chips and oven-cooked celery. Wash and trim a large head of celery. Use the leaves for the stuffing and for garnish. Cut the celery into 1in (2.5cm) lengths. Par-boil for 5 minutes. Drain. Put into the drip pan under the duck for the last 20 minutes of cooking. Stir the juices through the celery.

Spit-roast Partridges with Cabbage

In place of the shredded cabbage, use finely shredded leeks.

Barbecues

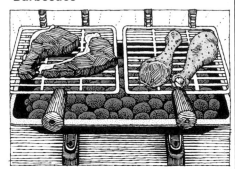

Many of the recipes for grills, spit-roasts or kebabs can be cooked equally successfully outdoors on a barbecue. Be prepared for longer cooking times as the coals settle to an even glow and the heat is not as fierce. Brush the grill grid with oil to help prevent the food sticking as it cooks, or wrap the chops, steaks or pieces of fish in foil with some of the basting liquid, or a savoury butter, to cook gently without smoking or charring. This does, however, remove the possibility of having that deliciously smoky 'charcoal-grilled' flavour.

● Have plenty of basting liquid on hand as much will drip into the coals.

● Flavour the coals (and the smoke) by sprinkling generously with herbs about 20 minutes before cooking.

● Use a long-handled thick pastry brush for basting and tongs for turning the food as it cooks.

● Never crowd the barbecue. Start with the foods that need longest cooking time and have plenty of salads and bread rolls on hand to fill the gaps.

● Cook with the 'presentation' side down first, then turn and finish cooking on the other side.

● Serve with a choice of relishes and spicy sauces.

Wild Duck with Orange

Serve with roast onions and a watercress or spinach salad.

Serves 2
Preparation: 20 minutes
Cooking: about 1 hour

---

1 wild duck, about 1½lb (700g) dressed weight
2 rashers streaky bacon, rinds removed
1oz (25g) butter, melted
1 large orange, segmented
celery leaves to garnish

The stuffing:
1oz (25g) brown rice, cooked and drained
1oz (25g) onion, chopped
2 tablespoons finely chopped celery leaves
1oz (25g) butter
salt and freshly ground black pepper
½ teaspoon dried thyme
1 tablespoon sunflower seeds

Rinse the duck thoroughly in cold water and pat dry.

☐ Mix together all the stuffing ingredients and spoon them into the duck. Close the vent securely with skewers. Pre-heat the spit-grill to high.

☐ Lay the bacon rashers over the duck breast, tie in 3 places, first to hold the bacon in place and then to secure the wings and legs against the body.

☐ Line the drip pan with foil. Insert the skewer lengthways through the duck and secure with the holding forks.

☐ Set the duck in the oven, reduce the heat and start the spit. Cook, basting frequently with the butter, for about 35 minutes.

☐ Take the duck from the oven, cut and discard the strings and remove the bacon.

☐ Return the duck to the spit-grill and cook for a further 20-30 minutes, until the juices run clear. Brush with the remaining butter and baste with the juices during cooking.

☐ Transfer to a hot serving dish. Remove skewers, garnish with orange segments and celery leaves and serve.

Spit-roast Partridges with Cabbage

Serve with roast potatoes and gooseberry jelly mixed with a little lemon or lime juice.

Serves 3
Preparation: 15 minutes
Cooking: about 50 minutes

---

2 partridges, each about 1lb (500g) dressed weight
4oz (100g) cabbage, finely shredded
1 tablespoon finely chopped onion
1 teaspoon caraway seeds
2oz (50g) butter, melted
salt and freshly ground black pepper
4 rashers streaky bacon, rinds removed

Rinse the partridges thoroughly with cold water and pat dry with kitchen paper.

☐ Mix together the cabbage, onion and caraway with half the butter. Season with salt and pepper.

☐ Pre-heat the spit-grill to high.

☐ Pack the cabbage mixture firmly into the partridges and close with poultry pins or small skewers. Lay 2 bacon rashers over the breast of each bird and tie. Also tie legs and wings in place.

☐ Insert the skewer lengthways through the partridges and secure with the holding forks.

☐ Line the drip pan with foil. Position the skewer, reduce the oven heat and cook for 30 minutes, brushing frequently with the remaining butter and the juices from the pan.

☐ Take the birds from the oven, cut away and discard the strings; transfer the bacon to the drip pan.

☐ Return the birds to the oven and continue cooking for about 20 minutes, brushing occasionally with the pan juices, until the birds are browned and the juices run clear.

☐ Arrange the partridges on a hot serving dish, remove the pins or skewers, and garnish with the stuffing.

☐ Chop the bacon and sprinkle over the birds, then strain the juices over for serving.

Spit-roast Rabbit with Marsala

Rabbits can be bought ready to cook, and they make a very economical meal. The almost complete lack of fat makes them attractive to those who wish to keep their fat intake low, and cooking on the spit keeps them more succulent than open roasting.

Serves 4
Preparation: 10 minutes
Cooking: 45 minutes

---

1 rabbit, about 1¾lb (800g),
    skinned and cleaned
2oz (50g) butter
1 large garlic clove, crushed
3 tablespoons marsala, medium sherry or
    madeira
1lb (500g) small onions, blanched and
    peeled

Pat the rabbit dry. Insert the skewer lengthways and secure with holding forks. Tie the rabbit around in 3 places to hold the legs close to the body.

☐ Pre-heat the spit-grill to high.

☐ Put the butter and garlic into a small saucepan and set on a low heat to melt the butter. Stir in the wine.

☐ Brush the rabbit well with the garlic butter. Reduce the heat and cook the rabbit for about 30 minutes, brushing frequently with the garlic butter.

☐ Put the onions in the drip pan and stir to coat them with the juices. Continue cooking for about 15 minutes, or until the juices from the rabbit run clear. Brush with the rest of the butter during cooking.

☐ Remove from skewer, discard the strings and cut the rabbit into portions. Transfer to a hot serving dish, garnish with the onions and pour the pan juices over.

Spit-roast Venison with Celery

Serve with croquette potatoes.

Serves 5-6
Preparation: 10 minutes
Cooking: about 50 minutes

2lb (1kg) boned haunch of venison
10-12 fresh sage leaves
4 tablespoons oil
1 teaspoon dried sage
large head of celery
salt and freshly ground black pepper

The Berry Butter:
1oz (25g) elderberry or cranberry jelly
4oz (100g) butter, softened

Make the Berry Butter: Beat the elderberry or cranberry jelly into the softened butter. Shape into a 1in (2.5cm) diameter log, wrap in foil and chill until required.

☐ Pat the venison dry. Tie firmly into a neat shape, if necessary. Tuck the sage leaves in wherever there is an opening in the meat.

☐ Insert the skewer lengthways through the meat. Secure firmly with the holding forks.

☐ Mix together the oil and dried sage and brush it over the meat.

☐ Pre-heat the spit-grill to high.

☐ Reduce the heat and cook the meat for 30 minutes, brushing with oil halfway through the cooking time.

☐ Wash and trim the celery. Cut into 1in (2.5cm) lengths. Boil for 5 minutes in salted water to cover. Drain.

☐ Add the celery to the drip pan. Stir to cover with the juices and cook for a further 20-25 minutes, brushing the venison with the oil 2 or 3 times during cooking.

☐ Season well and serve hot with the celery and Berry Butter.

Spit-roast Venison with Celery

Grilled Fish Kebabs

Kebabs are good to prepare ahead. Leave them soaking in the marinade and cook just before required. Served with chunky bread and a herb butter, they make an ideal first course, or a fine family supper accompanied by baked potatoes and a salad.

Serves 8 ☆
Preparation: 20 minutes plus marinating
Cooking: 7-8 minutes

1½lb (700g) firm-fleshed white fish fillets, such as monkfish, turbot, brill or cod
1 green pepper, de-seeded
8 small tomatoes
8 button onions, blanched and peeled
8 small cap mushrooms, wiped and trimmed

The marinade:
6 tablespoons olive oil
4 tablespoons lemon juice
1 teaspoon dried thyme
1½ teaspoons dried oregano
¾ teaspoon paprika
salt and freshly ground black pepper

Wash the fish under cold running water. Pat dry with kitchen paper. Remove the skin, and cut the fish into 32 even-sized chunks. Cut the pepper into 8 equal pieces.

☐ Thread 8 large skewers, alternating the fish cubes with the pepper, tomatoes, onions and mushrooms. Lay across a large plate or shallow dish.

☐ Mix together the marinade ingredients and pour over the kebabs. Leave for at least 1 hour, turning the skewers and brushing them with the marinade occasionally.

☐ Pre-heat the grill to high and cover the rack with foil. Set the skewers on the rack and grill for 7-8 minutes, turning occasionally and brushing with marinade. The kebabs are cooked when the fish is opaque and the vegetables are lightly browned.

Grilled Fish Kebabs

Fish kebabs
Any firm white fish can be used for making these kebabs. If grilling, do not cook the kebabs too close to the heat as some pieces may brown quickly but not be cooked through.

Spit-roast Chicken Kebabs

Serves 6   ☆☆

Preparation: 20 minutes
Cooking: 20-25 minutes

1½lb (700g) chicken breast fillet
8oz (225g) back bacon rashers,
    rinds removed
3oz (75g) butter, melted
1 tablespoon lemon juice
grated rind of ½ lemon
8oz (225g) button mushrooms, wiped
8oz (225g) small onions, blanched and
    peeled

Pre-heat the spit or grill to high and line the drip pan with foil.

☐ Pat the chicken dry and cut into thick, even-sized chunks.

☐ Cut each bacon rasher in half across. Fold each piece over to form a square.

☐ Mix together the butter, lemon juice and rind.

☐ Thread pieces of chicken on the kebab skewers, alternating with mushrooms, onions and bacon. Brush well with the butter mixture.

☐ Set the skewers on the supports, or over the grill pan.

☐ Reduce the grill or oven heat and cook the kebabs for 20-25 minutes until the meats are cooked. Brush with the butter several times during cooking.

Turkey Variety Kebabs

Serves 4   ☆☆

Preparation: 10 minutes plus at least 1 hour marinating
Cooking: 8-10 minutes

1lb (500g) turkey breast
8oz (225g) turkey livers, trimmed
8oz (225g) canned pineapple pieces in
    natural juice
2 tablespoons soy sauce
1 clove garlic, crushed
2 tablespoons oil
salt and freshly ground black pepper
1 teaspoon cornflour

Cut the breast meat and turkey livers into 1in (2.5cm) cubes.

☐ Mix together the juice from the pineapple, the soy sauce and garlic. Add the meat, stir, and leave to marinate for at least 1 hour, stirring occasionally.

☐ Drain the meat, reserving the marinade. Pat the meat dry with kitchen paper.

☐ Thread alternate pieces of turkey, liver and pineapple on 4 large skewers.

☐ Pre-heat the grill to high. Brush the kebabs with the oil and grill for 8-10 minutes, turning as necessary, until browned.

☐ Meanwhile, boil the marinade for 2 minutes to reduce it slightly. Season to taste. Blend the cornflour with 1 tablespoon water and stir into the liquid. Simmer for 1 minute.

☐ Serve the kebabs on a bed of rice, with the sauce spooned over.

Grilled Shish Kebabs

Serve on a bed of chopped green salad or in warm pitta bread with salad, accompanied by wedges of lemon.

Serves 4   ☆☆

Preparation: 15 minutes plus marinating
Cooking: 10-12 minutes

1½lb (700g) lean, boneless leg of lamb
¼ pint (150ml) natural yogurt
juice of 1 lemon
2 tablespoons sesame oil
salt and freshly ground black pepper
1 tablespoon chopped fresh mint

Trim the meat and cut into 1in (2.5cm) cubes. Put in a mixing bowl with the yogurt, lemon juice, oil and plenty of seasoning. Stir to coat the meat, cover and leave to marinate in the refrigerator for at least 5 hours, preferably overnight.

☐ Pre-heat the grill to high and thread the meat on 4 large skewers. Grill for 10-12 minutes, turning as necessary, and basting with any remaining marinade. Serve the kebabs sprinkled with the chopped fresh mint.

Making kebabs

Kebabs are simply made using almost any type of ingredient—fish, poultry or meat. They can be grilled, spit-roasted or cooked on a barbecue—the principles are the same.

● Have even-sized pieces of food so they all cook at the same rate.

● Pre-cook by boiling or blanching any of the 'tougher' ingredients before skewering. Small onions and pieces of red or green peppers benefit from this.

● Add softer ingredients such as tomatoes towards the end of cooking time. Small whole tomatoes are useful for threading on the ends of skewers to hold the other foods in place.

● Marinate meats for at least 2 hours or overnight—depending on the type of meat—in an oil- or yogurt-based marinade in order to tenderize the meat before cooking.

● Thread 'dry' meats such as veal or chicken between pieces of fatty pork or bacon to give added juiciness as well as flavour.

● Use flat skewers for preference as these hold the food better and ensure that it keeps turning with the skewer as it cooks.

● Always grease the skewers before threading them. This helps them to thread more easily.

● Never overcrowd the skewers.

● Have a good mix of complementary flavours and textures: scallops with bacon, beef with olives and onions, or chicken and turkey with ginger and pineapple.

● Try vegetable or fruit kebabs (peppers, onion, courgette, mushrooms, tomatoes and olives, or pineapple, apricot, apple and kumquats threaded with marshmallows).

● Always remember to baste regularly during cooking with flavoured oil or marinade.

A simple marinade

Mix together 4 tablespoons olive oil with an equal quantity of lemon juice. Add salt and pepper, 1 tablespoon chopped parsley, 1 tablespoon finely chopped onion, a finely chopped garlic clove (optional) and a couple of bay leaves or a sprinkling of thyme.

Browning meat kebabs on the spit

When thick chunks of meat are cooked on the spit, start the cooking on a reduced heat. When nearly cooked, increase the heat to maximum to brown the meat.

COOKING IN THE OVEN

Roasting

Roasting

The intense dry heat of the oven is perfect for the cooking of large cuts of meat and game, whole fish and birds. The dishes produced by oven-cooking not only make more spectacular presentations than individual portions, but the combination of crisp exterior and juicy interior makes them universal favourites. Once called 'baking', oven-cooking is now usually referred to as 'roasting', with the exception perhaps of gammon and fish. Roasting also provides an excellent way of coping with uneven or irregularly shaped pieces, and of feeding many people at once.

Joints of meat, game, whole poultry and fish are all well suited to oven-cooking, retaining most of their natural taste and a juicy texture. Fatty meats and poultry, such as duck, are set on racks to let the fat drain off, while lean 'dry' meats such as game are barded with strips of pork belly fat. Whole fish are usually given a coating of melted fat or butter to prevent drying out.

Degrees of roasting

Traditional cooking demanded that joints of meat be briefly fried on all sides on top of the stove, to brown the outside evenly and seal in the juices. For convenience, this has been replaced by initial 'searing' in the oven at a higher temperature for 5-10 minutes. However, everyone likes their meat cooked to different degrees of 'doneness'. Some like it brown outside and pink in the centre. Others prefer it less brown, but evenly cooked all the way through. Used correctly, the oven can give you meat just the way you want it.

Brown exterior

Start with a very high setting until the outside of the meat has browned. Reduce the setting and cook until as well-done inside as you like.

Less brown exterior

Cook the meat all the way at a moderate setting for as long as necessary to cook through as you like it—depending on the weight of the meat or game.

Today's ovens heat up so speedily, it is possible to put in the meat before heating to the required temperature. In this case, the meat heats up as the oven heats. This method is better if you want a less well-browned outside. Bear in mind that this is how it will cook if the oven is set to cook while you're out.

If you are cooking meat or poultry with a lot of fat in or around it, sprinkle well with salt near the end of the cooking time to add crispness to the outside.

Do not season meat before cooking, or the salt will draw juices out to the surface of the meat.

Roasting times

In an oven pre-heated to 350F (180C) Gas 4, rule-of-thumb cooking times to achieve the necessary internal temperatures are:

Beef (medium-done): 15 min per lb (450g) plus 15 min over
Beef (well-done): 20 min per lb (450g) plus 20 min over
Lamb: 25 min per lb (450g) plus 25 min over
Pork and poultry: 30 min per lb (450g) plus 30 min over

Why roasting?

First, it's a simple way of cooking anything that is suitable. Apart from the occasional basting, roast dishes require relatively little attention during cooking. If you have an oven with an automatic timer, it can be set to turn itself on in your absence, so roasts can be planned well in advance.

Second, it's more economical, for more than one dish can be cooked in the oven at the same time and at the same temperature. Vegetables, which benefit from cooking in the juices from the main roast dish, and baked sweet dishes—such as custards and fruits—can fill every corner of the oven while it is hot.

Today's entire meal and tomorrow's casserole can all be bubbling away in the oven while you work, or enjoy a Sunday lunchtime drink.

What to roast

Like grilling, roasting produces best results when used for the more tender cuts of meat, poultry and game. However, some tougher foods, like brisket, benefit from slower roasting at lower temperatures.

Whole birds are particularly suited to roasting as it ensures thorough cooking of all parts of their irregular form.

Roasting temperatures

Many factors are involved in the success of a roast: shape, thickness, and the presence or absence of bone all play a part. The best measure of 'doneness' is internal temperature. (Meat thermometers are invaluable kitchen aids, especially for larger joints.)

Beef is considered to be medium-done when it reaches an internal temperature of 160F (71C) and is well done at 174F (79C); lamb should reach an internal temperature of 180F (82C), and pork and poultry 190F (88C).

How to roast

Meats such as beef, which 'bleed' their juices, benefit from preliminary sealing by rapid browning on the hob, or from brief initial cooking at the oven's highest setting.

● Foods with a lot of natural fat like ducks and geese are pricked all over before cooking to allow the excess fat to run off. These and the fattier cuts of meat should be set on racks or trivets, or a bed of vegetables, to ensure that the bottom of the food doesn't simply fry.

● Drier meats, like veal and game birds, need to be given added fat by barding or larding. Most foods benefit from basting with their own cooking juices, or some added butter or oil. To preserve moisture, some foods such as fish or turkey are often wrapped in foil.

● Stuffings provide fish, poultry and rolled joints of meat with added flavour and extra fat for succulence. Seasoned or herbed coatings, or slivers of garlic and sprigs of herbs inserted into the flesh, also infuse roasts with flavours as they cook.

● Juices from the roasting pan make excellent sauces and gravies. Generally the pan is deglazed with a little stock or wine and thickened with flour, cornflour, cream, or vegetable purées.

Oven-baked fish

Round fish such as herring, mackerel, trout, cod, grey mullet and, of course, salmon are all particularly good for oven-cooking. Indeed, because they are round they benefit from the all-round heat of the oven, without any liquid cooking medium to leach out the flavour.

To cook even large fish is very simple: if you don't have a pan large enough, improvise with a sheet of foil to extend a baking tray or meat tin.

Cooking time is relatively short so whole fish can easily be prepared and served with little planning.

Baked fish looks and tastes excellent, and requires very little attention. It benefits from a favourite stuffing if you have time, but good fresh fish is almost better plain. Add a few herbs or a pat of a flavoured butter for a real treat.

Baked Herrings with Shallot Butter

Serves 8 ☆☆☆
Preparation and cooking: about 20 minutes

8 fresh herrings, cleaned
salt and freshly ground black pepper
2oz (50g) butter, melted
2 tablespoons finely chopped shallot
2 tablespoons finely chopped chives
1 tablespoon finely chopped parsley
2oz (50g) butter, softened

Set the oven to 400F (200C) gas 6.
☐ Rinse the herrings inside and out under cold running water. Pat dry with kitchen paper. Sprinkle the insides with salt and pepper. Brush the fish all over with melted butter and lay them flat in a large shallow roasting tin or deep baking tray.
☐ Cook for about 10 minutes, brushing with more melted butter.
☐ Meanwhile beat the shallot and herbs with the softened butter.
☐ Carefully transfer the herrings to a warmed serving dish. Dot with flavoured butter and serve.

Fennel-baked Trout

Serves 4 ☆☆☆
Preparation and cooking: about 15 minutes

2 teaspoons oil
3 tablespoons pumpkin seeds
salt
4 trout, each about 10oz (275g)
4 sprigs of fresh fennel leaves
1oz (25g) butter, melted
¼ pint (150ml) crème fraîche

Set the oven to 400F (200C) gas 6.
☐ Heat the oil in a small frying-pan over a moderate heat. Stir-fry the seeds for 2-3 minutes to brown lightly. Sprinkle lightly with salt and drain on kitchen paper.
☐ Rinse the trout and pat dry. Put a sprig of fennel inside each, and brush the outsides with butter.
☐ Arrange the fish flat on a shallow roasting tin, or deep baking tray. Bake for about 10 minutes, brushing with the rest of the butter.
☐ Carefully transfer to a warmed serving dish. Spoon the cream over and sprinkle with the seeds.

Herrings are rich in fat so therefore don't need much added during cooking – but butter does enhance their flavour.
Trout are much leaner fish. Add butter and cream for a better flavour and to add succulence. To lessen the calories, however, use only enough butter or oil to prevent sticking during baking and replace the cream with natural yogurt.

Crème Fraîche
To make crème fraîche, add 1 tablespoon soured cream to ½ pint (300ml) double cream. Heat to lukewarm, pour into a container and let it stand at room temperature for about 8 hours or until thickened. Stir, then cover and refrigerate until required.

Serve Baked Herrings with Shallot Butter accompanied by a sharply dressed onion, celeriac and beetroot salad topped with chopped gherkins.

Lemon baskets

With a sharp knife, slice across a lemon about half-way up, stopping just short of the centre. Turn the lemon and cut in from the other side in the same way. Cut down from one end to meet a crossways cut, and repeat with the second side. Lift out the thick wedges of lemon to leave the 'handle'. Cut carefully around the flesh of the half lemon, release and scoop it out. With scissors, cut free the flesh still attached to the 'handle'.

Lemon Butter

Beat 1 tablespoon lemon juice and the grated rind of ½ a lemon into 3oz (75g) softened butter. Beat in 2 tablespoons finely chopped chervil. Pipe into the baskets with a forcing bag fitted with a ½in (1cm) rose pipe. Alternatively just pile it in with a teaspoon and create decorative swirls with the tines of a fork.

Baked Salmon

Serves 6-8 ☆☆☆
Preparation and cooking: about 20 minutes

---

1 fresh salmon about 2lb (900g), cleaned and gutted
4oz (100g) butter, melted
salt and freshly ground black pepper
a few sprigs of fresh dill
lemon baskets (see sidelines)
Lemon Butter
a few sprigs of parsley for garnish

Rinse the salmon under cold running water and pat dry with kitchen paper. Brush the inside with butter, then sprinkle with salt and pepper. Place the dill in the cavity.
☐ Set oven to 400F (200C) gas 6.
☐ Line a roasting tin with foil and brush it with butter.
☐ Brush the salmon all over with butter and place in the lined tin.
☐ Cook in the pre-heated oven for 5 minutes, brush with butter then cook for a further 5 minutes.
☐ Turn the fish by lifting the foil and rolling it over. Brush with butter and cook for 5 minutes more.
☐ Pierce the fish at its thickest part with a thin sharp knife. When cooked the flesh will flake and look opaque.
☐ With two large fish slices, transfer salmon to a serving plate.
☐ Serve garnished with lemon baskets filled with lemon butter, and parsley.
To serve: With a sharp knife, cut the salmon lengthways along the spine. Slide the knife between the bones and the flesh on either side of the backbone. Cut the whole top fillet lengthways along the dividing ridge. Cut each of these pieces across into two.
Clip the spine across at top and tail with scissors. Lift it out. Cut the bottom fillet in the same way.

Spinach-stuffed Grey Mullet

Serve with warmed potato crisps and fresh garden peas.

Serves 6-8   ☆ ☆ ☆
Preparation: 20 minutes
Cooking: 35-40 minutes

2lb (1kg) grey mullet, after cleaning
Lemon Butter

The stuffing:
2oz (50g) fresh spinach, chopped
3oz (75g) onion, finely chopped
4oz (125g) fresh breadcrumbs
1 tablespoon lemon juice
salt and freshly ground black pepper
3oz (75g) butter, melted

Rinse the fish inside and out under cold running water. Pat dry. Scrape off any remaining loose scales with the back of a knife.
☐ Set oven to 400F (200C) gas 6.
☐ Mix together the stuffing ingredients, using only half the butter. Pack stuffing firmly into the cavity of the fish. Secure closed with wooden cocktail sticks.
☐ On either side, make 3 diagonal slashes along the fish at the thickest part. Brush the fish all over with the remaining melted butter.
☐ Line a baking tray or roasting tin with foil and set the fish in it.
☐ Cook in the oven for 30-35 minutes. Test with the tip of a sharp knife at the thickest part, pushing through into the stuffing. The knife will feel hot on the wrist when the fish is cooked through.
☐ With two large fish slices, transfer the fish to a warmed serving plate. Remove the cocktail sticks. Spoon the stuffing into a hot serving dish. Meanwhile, put the Lemon Butter into a sauceboat and place in the turned off oven, to melt.
To serve: Fillet the fish in the same way as the Baked Salmon. Accompany with the melted Lemon Butter and the stuffing.
Tip: Small whole cod, or large whiting may be cooked in the same way.

Baked Salmon surrounded by attractive Lemon baskets piped full of Lemon Butter makes a spectacular dinner-party main course served with sautéed whole new potatoes and baby carrots.

Cooking times for whole fish
Estimate the time by the thickness of the fish at the thickest part. Allow about 10 minutes per 1in (2.5cm). For stuffed fish, measure after stuffing.

Suitable pots for cooking large fish
If your roasting tin isn't quite long enough to take the whole fish and you don't have a fish kettle, place it diagonally across the tin. Or line a baking tray with foil and extend the foil beyond the end of the tray. But remember not to try to cook a fish which is too large for your oven as it will impede the air flow and the fish will not cook evenly.

Shapes and cooking times

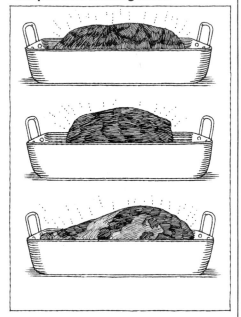

Joints of different shapes, and with different distributions of fat and meat, cook at different rates.

The accurate roasting time of large pieces will depend almost as much on the shape as on the actual weight. A long even roll like the one illustrated at the top will cook more quickly than one which is shorter but thicker, like the second one shown.

An irregularly shaped piece, like the third illustration (such as a leg of lamb) also takes longer – to ensure that the thickest part is also cooked through.

Roast forerib

This cut cooks nicely at a higher setting, to give a brown exterior and good gravy. This higher temperature is also good for cooking crisp Yorkshire pudding and roast potatoes.

Roasting meat on the bone is less easy to carve, but the price per lb (kg) is lower, they cook through more quickly and some find them more tasty.

Roasting meat

For home-cooking choose the joint of meat to suit the size of the family and the capacity of the oven. The average 'Sunday joint' will usually not be more than about 3lb (1.5kg) but it makes sense to buy a bigger piece of meat and eat 'cold roast' for at least the following day.

Cooking times for small pieces of meat seem long when compared to those for larger joints because the 'start-up time' is about the same for both. Cooking times are not as predictable as for large joints, so times are given for individual recipes.

The smaller the joint of meat, the better it is to choose one with a low fat content. However, fat does brown well and gives a better fuller 'roast' flavour. This is why it is usual to have some fat on roasting joints. If there is no natural fat, it should be added before or during the cooking by barding, larding or basting with oil or dripping.

Roasting beef

Some less tender cuts, and some of the very lean cuts, such as those listed below, are better cooked at a lower temperature.

Rolled topside is a very popular cut, with a barding layer of fat simply wrapped around and tied in place. Eye of silverside is sometimes sold as a long thin piece with almost no fat at all, and fillet, too, can be trimmed to give a very lean joint of a similar shape.

Sirloin and other rib cuts may be sold on or off the bone.

Leaner pieces of economical brisket make very good roasts if cooked slowly. This meat has a coarser texture, but the flavour is good and the higher fat content makes it brown well and gives a very good rich gravy.

The density, fat content and the shape all vary with the cut and need to be taken into account when calculating cooking times. Some cuts are better cooked until well-done, while others look and taste better when rare.

Roast Rib of Beef, Yorkshire Pudding, Roast Potatoes and Gravy

Serves 6-8 ☆☆☆
Preparation: 20 minutes
Cooking: about 1¼ hours

5½lb (2.5kg) (2-bone) forerib of beef
2lb (1kg) potatoes
½ pint (300ml) Meat Stock (optional)

The Yorkshire Pudding:
4oz (100g) plain flour
a pinch of salt
1 egg
¼ pint (150ml) milk
¼ pint (150ml) water
2oz (50g) dripping

Pat the meat dry with kitchen paper. Place in a roasting tin.

☐ Set oven to 425F (220C) gas 7.

☐ Sift the flour and salt into a mixing bowl. Make a well in the centre and add the egg. Beat into the flour, gradually adding the milk and water.

☐ Using a wire whisk, whisk to a smooth batter with the consistency of single cream. Set the batter aside.

☐ Divide the dripping among 12 small deep bun tins.

☐ Cook the potatoes in boiling salted water for 4 minutes, rinse under cold running water and drain.

☐ Put the meat in the oven and roast for 30 minutes, basting two or three times with the juices which collect in the pan.

☐ Add the potatoes to the pan. Turn in the juices to coat. Cook for 15 minutes, basting the meat once. Put the bun tins into the oven for 5 minutes to heat the fat.

☐ Whisk the batter well. Pour into the hot fat in the bun tins. Return to the oven. Cook for about 25 minutes until well puffed and crisp.

☐ Reduce the oven to its lowest setting. Transfer the meat, potatoes and Yorkshire puddings to hot serving dishes and keep warm in the oven while you make the gravy.

☐ Pour off any excess fat from the pan. Set over a moderate heat. Stir in the stock, or some of the water used to boil the potatoes. Boil briskly for 2-3 minutes, stirring to cook up all the meat residue.

☐ Strain the gravy into a warmed sauceboat. Serve immediately, with the meat, puddings and the roast potatoes.

Roast Sirloin with Soured Cream Sauce

Serve with creamed potatoes and crisp Brussels sprouts.

Serves 6-8 ☆☆☆
Preparation: 5 minutes
Cooking: 1¾-2 hours

3lb (1.5kg) rolled, boned sirloin
2 tomatoes, chopped
1 tablespoon flour
7 fl oz (200ml) Meat Stock
¼ pint (150ml) soured cream
2 small gherkins, chopped
1 tablespoon capers, chopped
1 tablespoon parsley, chopped
1 tablespoon chives, chopped
salt and freshly ground black pepper

Set the oven to 350F (180C) gas 4.
☐ Pat the meat dry with kitchen paper. Place in a roasting tin and put in the oven. Cook for about 1½ hours, to required degree, basting 3 or 4 times during cooking.

☐ Reduce the oven to its lowest setting. Transfer the meat to a serving plate and keep warm in the oven while making the sauce.

☐ Set the roasting tin over a moderate heat. Add the tomatoes and simmer for 5-7 minutes to soften, stirring frequently. Stir in the flour and gradually stir in the stock and cook for 2-3 minutes until thickened, stirring constantly.

☐ Sieve the sauce. Return to the rinsed-out pan. Stir in the soured cream, chopped gherkins, capers and herbs. Season to taste with salt and pepper and heat through.

☐ Pour into a warmed sauceboat. Serve with thick slices of the meat.
Tip: topside of beef can be cooked in the same way. To test rolled meats: pierce with the tip of a sharp thin knife right to the centre, and press meat to see if juices run clear.

Serve Rolled Sirloin with Soured Cream Sauce sliced thickly and garnished with extra chopped tomatoes, and gherkin fans.

Carving meat

The traditional wisdom dictates that joints of meat be allowed to 'rest' for a few minutes after they are removed from the oven before they are carved, to make carving easier. This allows time for the fibres to relax from the rigidity produced by the intense heat of the oven, and for the juices to distribute themselves more evenly through the meat. These effects, however, are barely noticeable in today's small-sized joints, and these will certainly be ready for carving in the few minutes taken to make gravy.

Roast boned and rolled meat

A lower setting causes less shrinkage of the meat. If cooked to the well-done stage, the outside of the meat will be browned. If you want the meat rare, the outside will obviously be a little less well-browned.

With boned, rolled joints, remember always to remove any string or elastic mesh before carving.

A lower oven setting is better suited to eye of silverside as the meat has very little fat to protect it from drying out. The soft, fine grain of this cut is very tender if cooked slowly and it is at its best cooked rare and served in thick slices.

Roast Silverside with Madeira Sauce

Serves 5-6 ☆☆
Preparation: 3 minutes
Cooking: about 50 minutes

2lb (1kg) trimmed eye of silverside
1oz (25g) dripping, melted
2 teaspoons flour
7 fl oz (200ml) water
3 tablespoons madeira
salt and freshly ground black pepper

Set the oven to 300F (150C) gas 2.
☐ Pat the meat dry with kitchen paper, brush all over with dripping and place in a shallow roasting tin. Roast for 20 minutes; turn the joint over, and brush with dripping.
☐ Cook for a further 20 minutes, then turn and brush again.
☐ Cook for 10-15 minutes, to the required degree. (For rare meat, the juices will be very pink if you pierce the joint with a fork, and the meat will 'give' when pressed.)
☐ Transfer to a carving board.

Cover with foil and leave for 5-10 minutes while you make the gravy.
☐ Put the roasting tin over a moderate heat. Stir in the flour. Gradually stir in the water until the gravy has thickened.
☐ Stir in the madeira and salt and pepper to taste. Cook, stirring constantly, for 2-3 minutes. Pour into a warmed sauceboat.
☐ Serve the meat cut in thick slices, garnished with vegetables as shown and serve the gravy separately.
Tip: garnish the beef with fresh vegetables *à la jardinière*: chopped turnips, tomato baskets filled with petits pois, mangetout peas, baby carrots, young green beans and broccoli tips. Cook each vegetable lightly, arrange in separate piles and alternate the colours for greater effect.

Roast Silverside with Madeira Sauce dressed with a striking jardinière of freshly cooked vegetables makes an impressive, but economical, dinner-party main course.

Roast Entrecôte with Oven Chips and Brandywine Sauce

Serves 4 ☆☆☆
Preparation: 3 minutes
Cooking: about 1¼ hours

1¾lb (800g) entrecôte in the piece
1oz (25g) butter, melted
salt and freshly ground black pepper
1lb (500g) frozen oven chips
¼ pint (150ml) Meat Stock
¼ pint (150ml) red wine
2 tablespoons brandy
tomato lilies and parsley sprigs to garnish

Set the oven to 350F (180C) gas 4.
☐ Pat the meat dry with kitchen paper. Brush all over with butter. Set on a rack in a roasting tin.
☐ Roast for 10 minutes. Turn the meat on the rack and brush again with butter.
☐ Roast for another 10 minutes. Turn, brush again and continue roasting for 20 minutes. Turn the oven up to 425F (220C) gas 7.
☐ After about 5 minutes, season the meat with salt and pepper. Put the chips in a single layer in a shallow pan and place in the oven on the shelf above the meat. Cook for about 15 minutes to brown the chips and the meat.
☐ Turn the oven to its lowest setting. Remove the meat to a warmed serving plate and the chips to a dish. Keep hot in the oven while you make the gravy.
☐ Put the roasting tin over a moderate heat and let the contents bubble until all the moisture evaporates and the fat stops sizzling. Gradually stir in the stock and the wine.

☐ Boil vigorously for about 5 minutes, stirring to cook up the sediment from the pan. Add the brandy and strain into a hot sauceboat.
☐ Garnish the meat with tomato lilies and parsley and serve the chips and gravy separately.
Tip: to serve the meat cold, remove to a carving board when cooked. Leave to cool. Carve thinly and wrap in cling film. Store in the refrigerator for up to 24 hours. Deglaze the pan juices with the wine and brandy only, let cool and then mix this into ¼ pint (150ml) mayonnaise to make a superb cold dressing.
✳ This meat also freezes very well. Wrap the slices singly, first in cling film then in foil. Store in the freezer for up to 2 months. Thaw in the wrapping in the refrigerator overnight, or for 2 hours at room temperature.

Roast entrecôte
Like all the most tender cuts of beef, entrecôte is at its best rare. If you prefer it well done, allow about 15 minutes longer at the lower oven temperature.

Roast Entrecôte with Oven Chips and Brandywine Sauce needs only a fresh green salad to make a superb family meal.

Roast brisket

Often considered only suitable for stewing or stock-making, brisket makes an excellent economical roasting joint if it is cooked slowly and thoroughly to ensure tenderness. It really benefits from being served with a sauce, such as those given on this page. Alternatively, try it with a Gourmet Mustard Sauce or Espagnole Sauce. When brisket is served cold, it benefits from a Rémoulade Sauce or alternatively a Gribiche Sauce would be good.

Like entrecôte, brisket can easily overcook and lose its natural succulence, so take care in the last stages of cooking.

Roast Brisket with Tomato Sauce

As a change from new potatoes, serve this with Lyonnaise potatoes baked in cream and cheese in the oven over the meat, along with some braised field mushrooms.

Roast Brisket with Mushroom Sauce

Try this with diced carrots and parsnips par-boiled, then sautéed with a little butter and lemon or lime juice. A julienne garnish of thinly pared lemon or lime rind turns it into a party dish.

Rolling and tying joints of meat

See the sidelines and diagrams on page 194.

Joints such as brisket make a marvellous pot-roast or braise. Use red or white wine, and a few quartered onions, carrots and broad beans. Add herbs to taste.

Roast Brisket with Tomato Sauce

Serve accompanied by boiled new potatoes dressed with a little fresh mint or parsley, and crisply cooked Brussels sprouts, French beans or courgettes.

Serves 4-5 ☆☆☆
Preparation: 3 minutes
Cooking: about 1¾ hours

2lb (1kg) lean rolled brisket
4 small bay leaves
1oz (25g) dripping, melted
8 medium tomatoes
salt and freshly ground black pepper
2 teaspoons flour
about ¼ pint (150ml) water
2 teaspoons tomato purée

Set the oven to 300F (150C) gas 2.
☐ Pat the meat dry with kitchen paper. Insert the bay leaves in any openings in the roll of meat. Brush the meat all over with the melted dripping.
☐ Put the brisket in a shallow roasting tin and cook in the oven for 20 minutes.
☐ Turn the meat over. Brush again with dripping. Cook for a further 1 hour, turning and brushing every 20 minutes or so.
☐ Place the tomatoes stalk-end down so that they sit steadily. Dust them with salt and pepper and place in the tin around the meat. Cook for about 20 minutes.
☐ This cut of meat is better if cooked right through, but take care not to over-cook it. When you add the tomatoes, start testing the meat, and continue testing until thoroughly cooked. (The juices will run clear when you pierce the centre of the meat with a large fork. It will also feel increasingly firm to the touch as it cooks.)
☐ Transfer to a carving board and cover with foil to keep hot while you make the gravy. Pour off excess fat from the roasting tin.
☐ Put the tin over a moderate heat and stir in the flour. Gradually stir in the water until the sauce has thickened. Add the tomato purée, and salt and pepper to taste. Cook for 2-3 minutes more, stirring constantly.
☐ If a thinner sauce is preferred, add a little more water. Pour into a warmed sauceboat.
☐ Serve the meat thinly sliced, garnished with the tomatoes and with a little of the sauce spooned over.
Tip: add a little chopped fresh basil, or ½ teaspoon dried basil to the roasting tin with the water.

Roast Brisket with Mushroom Sauce

Serves 4-5 ☆☆☆
Preparation: 10 minutes
Cooking: 1¾ hours

2lb (1kg) lean rolled brisket
1 garlic clove, thinly sliced
1oz (25g) dripping, melted
1 small onion, finely chopped
8oz (225g) flat mushrooms, sliced
2 teaspoons flour
about ¼ pint (150ml) Basic Brown Stock
2 tablespoons soured cream
salt and freshly ground black pepper

Pat the meat dry with kitchen paper. Make slits with the point of a knife into the meat and insert slivers of garlic. Brush all over with the dripping and cook as in Roast Brisket with Tomato Sauce.
☐ After 1 hour of roasting, add the onion and mushrooms to the tin, stir to coat with dripping and return to the oven.
☐ When the meat has cooked through and the mushrooms and onion are soft, transfer the meat to a carving board and keep warm. Pour off excess fat from the roasting tin.
☐ Set it over a moderate heat, stir in the flour then gradually add the stock. Simmer for 5 minutes, stirring constantly. Add the cream, season to taste and allow just to warm through. Pour into a warmed sauceboat and serve with the meat sliced thinly.

Roast Fillet of Beef

Roast Fillet of Beef

Serve with creamy mashed potatoes and buttered fresh garden peas.

Serves 6-8 ☆☆
Preparation and cooking: about 1 hour

4lb (1.8kg) fillet of beef in the piece
4 tablespoons olive oil
salt and freshly ground black pepper
2oz (50g) canned pimientos, chopped
2 teaspoons flour
7 fl oz (200ml) Meat or Basic Brown Stock
3 fl oz (100ml) port

Set the oven to 425F (220C) gas 7.
☐ Pat the meat dry with kitchen paper. Trim away any membrane, then form the meat into a neat roll. Tie around at intervals with string.
☐ Brush the meat all over with oil and dust with pepper. Set on a rack in a roasting tin.
☐ Roast for 10 minutes, then turn the meat and brush with oil.
☐ Roast for a further 40 minutes or so, turning and brushing two or three more times during cooking.
☐ When the meat is well browned, remove from the oven and turn the

oven to its lowest setting.
☐ Transfer the meat to a warmed serving plate and keep hot.
☐ Put the roasting tin over a moderate heat. Allow the juices to bubble until the moisture has almost all evaporated. Stir in the pimiento and cook for 1 or 2 minutes.
☐ Stir in the flour. Gradually stir in the stock and the port and cook, stirring constantly, for 3 minutes.
☐ Season to taste and strain into a warmed sauceboat.
☐ Slice the meat thinly, spoon a little sauce over to serve.

Spread even layer of stuffing to within ¾in (2cm) of edge.

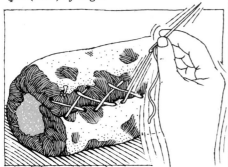

Fold meat around stuffing, overlap edges and sew together as shown using a strong needle and fine white cotton string or button thread. A larding needle also does the job well.

Stuffed veal

If you like a lot of stuffing with your veal, make extra and shape it into little balls. Cook in the juices around the meat for the last 20 minutes of the roasting time.

It is better not to use nylon thread or fibrous string for sewing up joints of meat. Nylon may be affected by the oven heat and coarse string fibres may stick to the meat.

Roasting veal

Veal can be cut into much the same types of joint as beef, since it is a younger version of the same animal. The pieces are, of course, smaller, so they often lend themselves to cooking methods which are unsuitable for beef cuts.

The flesh of veal is soft and fine in texture, and very delicate in flavour. Since there has not been time for fat to develop, it is also a very lean meat. If you haven't tried cooking it in the oven before, you'll find it is better if slightly under-cooked, otherwise it does dry out very quickly.

Veal is not available from all butchers but those who do have it – or will order it for you – will often cut pieces to suit your requirements. Order in advance to allow them time to prepare the exact piece you want or suggest a suitable alternative for the cooking method.

Stuffed Breast of Veal Marsala

Serve with roast potatoes and spinach purée.

Serves 4-5   ☆ ☆ ☆
Preparation: 20 minutes
Cooking: about 1 hour

2lb (1kg) boned breast of veal
2 tablespoons oil
salt and freshly ground black pepper
2 teaspoons flour
about ¼ pint (150ml) Veal Stock
3 tablespoons marsala

The stuffing:
2oz (50g) brown breadcrumbs
1oz (25g) butter, melted
1oz (25g) pine kernels, chopped
1oz (25g) onion, finely chopped
8oz (225g) minced veal
2oz (50g) mushrooms, finely chopped
½ teaspoon dried rosemary
salt and freshly ground pepper

Set the oven to 350F (180C) gas 4.
☐ Pat the meat dry with kitchen paper and place flat on a work surface.
☐ Mix together all the stuffing ingredients and season well with salt and pepper. Knead well with the hands to mix thoroughly.
☐ Spread the stuffing in an even layer over the meat to within ¾in (2cm) of the edge all round. Fold the meat lengthways over the stuffing, overlapping one long edge of meat over the other.
☐ Sew together as shown, pressing the stuffing back from the edge as you stitch. Press in firmly at the ends.
☐ Brush the roll of meat all over with oil. Set into a shallow roasting tin.
☐ Roast for about 20 minutes. Turn the roll over, and brush again with oil.
☐ Return to the oven for about 40 minutes, turning and brushing twice more. Cook until browned all over. Insert the tip of a sharp knife right into the centre of the roll. It should feel hot on the wrist when the meat and stuffing are both cooked through.
☐ Transfer the meat to a carving board. Cover with a piece of foil to keep hot while you make the gravy.
☐ Put the roasting tin over a moderate heat. Stir in the flour. Gradually stir in the stock until the sauce is thick and smooth. Stir in the marsala and season to taste. Add a little more stock for a thinner gravy, if preferred.
☐ Serve the meat cut in slices about ¼in (5mm) thick with the gravy spooned over.
Variations: rolled joints of veal lend themselves well to stuffing with rich mixtures which enhance their flavour and keep the meat moist. Try substituting dried fruit such as seedless raisins or chopped dried apricots for the pine kernels and mushrooms in the stuffing, and make an orange sauce using orange juice and grated rind in place of the marsala.
● Minced pork makes a good choice in place of the minced veal in the stuffing, providing extra taste and some fatty succulence.

Kidney-stuffed Pork with its fine sherry sauce makes an elegant and tasty main course.

Roasting pork

Although it takes longer to cook than some other meats, pork is an easy meat to roast. The relatively high fat content means that very little fat – if any – need be added and the meat is self-basting.

Pork must be well cooked all the way through to be palatable and the outside should be well browned. A temperature of 350F (180C) gas 4 achieves this combination without too much shrinkage or drying.

For large joints with a good outer covering of fat, set the meat on a rack in the roasting tin. Smaller joints, and those with less fat, can go straight into the roasting tin.

Loin and leg are the most usual cuts of pork used for roasting, but other more economical cuts are also worth trying. Cuts such as belly of pork, and blade bone are flavourful and economic, and perfect for smaller families.

Kidney-stuffed Pork

When cooking a small piece of pork like this, with kidneys inside, it is better to cook it in the roasting tin without a rack. This helps prevent the meat from over-browning before the kidney cooks.

To test: Pierce through to the stuffing with a skewer. If you like the kidney a little pink, remove from the oven when there is still a little pink showing in the juices. Otherwise, continue to cook and test every 10 minutes until the juices run quite clear.

If the piece of meat you are using is irregular in shape, sewing as well as tying with string will make it into a neater roll.

Kidney-stuffed Pork

Serve with sautéed potatoes and crisp boiled cabbage.

Serves 5   ★★☆
Preparation: 15 minutes
Cooking: about 1¾ hours

2¼-2¾lb (1-1.25kg) chump-end loin of pork
½lb (225g) pigs' or lambs' kidneys
salt and freshly ground black pepper
½ teaspoon dried sage

The sauce:
1oz (25g) onion, finely chopped
¼ pint (150ml) Basic Brown Stock
¼ pint (150ml) sherry

Set oven to 350F (180C) gas 4.

☐ Remove the bone from the meat: with a strong sharp knife, slice down the length and scrape the meat away from the bone. Pat the meat dry with kitchen paper and open it out flat on the work surface.

☐ Trim off any skin, membrane, and the cores from the kidneys. Place them along the width of the meat. Sprinkle with salt and pepper and the sage.

☐ Wrap the meat around the kidneys and sew the overlap together with string. Also tie around the joint at intervals with string to make a neat roll.

☐ Place in a small roasting tin and cook for about 1½ hours until well browned. Sprinkle with salt.

☐ Reduce the oven to its lowest setting. Transfer the meat to a warmed serving plate and place in the oven to keep hot.

☐ Set the roasting tin over a moderate heat. Add the onion and simmer, stirring, for about 5 minutes until the moisture has evaporated and the fat has stopped sizzling. Pour off any remaining fat.

☐ Stir in the stock and the sherry and boil vigorously for 5 minutes, stirring up the meat residue from the tin. Season to taste and strain into a warmed sauceboat.

☐ Serve the meat cut in slices about ¼in (5mm) thick with a little of the sauce spooned over and the rest served separately.

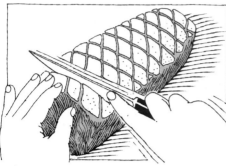

To ensure thorough cooking of the meat, cut through any skin and fat in a series of diagonal slashes to make a diamond pattern as shown.

Loin of Pork

If you ask the butcher to chop—not chine as for a rack—the joint, it will be easier to cut it into thin slices.

Loin is often sold with the skin and some of the fat removed. If you like to have crackling, buy a piece with the skin on.

To test pork

It is important to cook pork thoroughly. Pierce right through at the thickest part with a skewer or a sharp knife, when you think it will be ready. Ease the meat back so you can see that the meat inside is free of any hint of pink. Test again every 5 minutes or so until cooked through.

Roast Loin of Pork

Serve accompanied by apple sauce, roast potatoes and celeriac purée.

Cutting crackling

As this is often quite difficult, try using a sharp craft knife fitted with a razor-type blade instead of a kitchen knife. These are also safer when exerting a lot of pressure.

Roast Loin of Pork

Serves 4 ☆☆☆
Preparation and cooking: 1¾ hours

2¼lb (1.25kg) loin of pork, skin removed
1 tablespoon melted lard

Set the oven to 350F (180C) gas 4 and pat the meat dry.
☐ If there is a thick layer of fat on the outside curve of the meat, slash into a diamond pattern with a sharp knife as shown. Brush any uncovered part of the meat with lard.
☐ Place in a roasting tin, fat-side up and cook for about 1½-1¾ hours, or until well browned and cooked through, brushing with the pan juices two or three times.

Roast Pork with a Cheese Crust

Serves 4 ☆☆☆
Preparation and cooking: 1¾ hours

2¼lb (1.25kg) loin of pork, skin removed
1 tablespoon melted lard

The crust:
2 slices of crispbread, crushed
2 tablespoons grated Parmesan cheese
1oz (25g) butter, melted

Cook meat as Roast Loin of Pork.
☐ Mix together the ingredients for the crust. Pack this on the outer curve of the meat 15 minutes before the end of cooking and roast until crust is browned and crunchy.

Roast Leg of Pork

Serves 6 ☆☆☆
Preparation and cooking: 1¾ hours

3lb (1.5kg) leg of pork
1 tablespoon melted lard
2 teaspoons cornflour
¼ pint (150ml) Basic Brown Stock
¼ pint (150ml) dry cider
salt and freshly ground pepper

Set the oven to 350F (180C) gas 4 and pat the meat dry. Brush the cut sides with lard and place in a roasting tin, one cut side up.
☐ Cook for 1½-1¾ hours until browned and well cooked, brushing once or twice with lard or the cooking juices from the meat.
☐ Transfer meat to a carving board and cover with foil to keep hot.
☐ Pour off the excess fat. Set the roasting tin over a moderate heat. Mix the cornflour smoothly with 1 tablespoon of the stock.
☐ Add the rest of the stock and the cider to the pan and bring to the boil. Stir a little of the hot liquid into the cornflour mixture and return this to the pan.
☐ Cook, stirring constantly for 3 minutes to thicken. Season and strain into a warmed sauceboat.
☐ Serve the meat thinly sliced, with a little of the gravy spooned over.

Roast Belly Pork

Serves 4-5 ☆☆☆
Preparation: 2-3 minutes
Cooking: about 1½ hours

2¼lb (1.25kg) belly pork with the rind left on and well scored
1 tablespoon melted lard
salt

Set the oven to 350F (180C) gas 4.
☐ Place the meat rind-side up in a shallow roasting tin. Brush the rind with the lard and sprinkle liberally with salt.
☐ Roast without basting for about 1½ hours until well cooked through.
☐ If the rind is not sufficiently crisp, sprinkle with more salt and place under a pre-heated hot grill for 2-3 minutes.
☐ Alternatively, raise the oven setting to 400F (200C) gas 6 for the last 10-15 minutes.
Tip: If you have to score the pork yourself for crackling, make sure you cut right through the outer layer of skin into the fat, but not through into the flesh.

Roast Leg of Pork served with a 'bouquetière' of fresh spring vegetables.

Carving leg of lamb

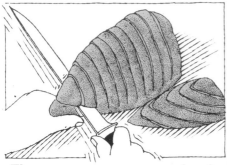

There are two ways to carve a leg of lamb. Take a slice off the bottom to allow it to sit steadily and then cut down at intervals as shown above. A single horizontal cut then releases the slices. (The process may be reversed and the first cut be horizontal.) Alternatively, start to cut from the middle making alternate cuts on either side, as shown in the photograph of Cumbrian Leg of Lamb.

Roasting lamb

Most cuts of lamb roast well. The layer of fat which covers many of the cuts, and the fact that lambs are young and have been exercised very little, means that the meat is almost always tender and succulent.

Joints with an outer coating of fat may be set on a rack in the roasting tin so that the fat can cook down through the meat. If the fat has been trimmed off, add a little stock to keep the more bony cuts from drying out.

Cumbrian Leg of Lamb

Serves 6　　　　　☆☆☆
Preparation: 10 minutes
Cooking: about 2½ hours

4-4½lb (1.8-2kg) leg of lamb
2 large cloves garlic, peeled
3 tablespoons redcurrant jelly
9 fl oz (275ml) red wine
juice of 1 orange
juice of ½ a lemon
salt and freshly ground black pepper

Set the oven to 350F (180C) gas 4 and pat the meat dry with kitchen paper. Make insertions over the surface with the tip of a sharp knife. Cut the garlic into slivers and press these into the cuts.

☐ Set the lamb on a rack in a roasting tin and cook for 1½ hours.

☐ Sprinkle with salt and then roast for about 30 minutes, until well browned and cooked to taste.

☐ Transfer the meat to a warmed serving plate and keep hot in the oven while you make the sauce.

☐ Set the roasting tin over a moderate heat until the fat stops sizzling. Pour off excess fat.

☐ Add the jelly to the pan and stir for 3-4 minutes until melted. Gradually stir in the wine and the fruit juices. Boil for 5 minutes.

☐ Season to taste and strain into a warmed sauceboat to serve.

Tip: If there isn't room in the meat tin to cook enough roast potatoes, par-boil them then cook in a separate tin with a little hot fat set on the shelf above the meat.

Cumbrian Leg of Lamb served with roast potatoes and glazed carrots.

Roast Rack of Lamb

Accompany with boiled small new potatoes and broccoli.

Serves 6 ☆ ☆ ☆
Preparation: 2 minutes
Cooking: 1½-1¾ hours

1 rack of lamb, about 3½lb (1.5kg)
7 fl oz (200ml) Basic Brown Stock
1oz (25g) butter, softened
salt and freshly ground black pepper

Set the oven to 350F (180C) gas 4 and pat the meat dry with kitchen paper.

☐ Place it in a roasting tin, bone-side down. Pour half the stock over. Roast for 30 minutes. Turn the meat with the ribs up, spread half the butter over the ribs and baste with juices. Cook for 30 minutes.

☐ Turn the meat again and spread the rest of the butter over the meat. Roast for about 30 minutes or until cooked to taste.

☐ To test the meat: Cut down beside the centre bone with a sharp knife and ease the meat back so you can see the degree of pink. Test every 5 minutes until cooked as you like it.

☐ Transfer the meat to a carving board. Cover with foil to keep it hot while you make the gravy.

☐ Pour off any excess fat from the tin. Set over a moderate heat and add the rest of the stock. Boil for 3-4 minutes, stirring to cook up the meat residue from the pan.

☐ Strain the gravy into a warmed sauceboat and serve with the lamb cut into chops.

Tip: It is easier to cook the whole rack in a piece in the oven when you have 6 people, than to cook the separate cutlets. They don't require very much attention when cooking in the oven. This cut of meat may also be referred to as a loin or 'carré' and consists of all the rib bones on one side with the meat on the upper part.

If you ask the butcher to trim off the fat at the bone ends, or do it yourself, you get the more characteristic 'rack' look which is so attractive when presented at the table – particularly with cutlet frills on each bone.

Meat thermometers

These really come into their own when roasting larger joints of meat – particularly lamb and pork – and large poultry, which all require a higher internal temperature to cook thoroughly and for which precise degrees of 'doneness' are more critical. Make sure the spike is inserted into the deepest part of the flesh and is not touching any bone, or it will give an erroneous reading.

Roast leg of lamb

If the meat is well covered with fat, it will require no basting so can be cooked on a rack. If it is very young 'spring' lamb, it may have very little fat. In such a case, set the lamb in the tin and keep basting it.

Step-by-step to Roast Rack of Lamb.

If you like lamb cooked slightly rare, remove it from the oven when it is browned to taste and the juices are still running pink.

Lamb 'El Chalil'

Serves 8 ☆☆☆
Preparation: 25 minutes plus 6 hours soaking
Cooking: about 2 hours

---

shoulder of lamb, about 4½lb (2kg) boned weight

The stuffing:
8 preserved dates
4 large prunes
8 large dried apricots
2 tablespoons sultanas
2 tablespoons currants
7 fl oz (200ml) orange juice
2oz (50g) blanched almonds, chopped
grated rind of ½ orange
grated rind of ½ lemon
1 teaspoon ground cloves
salt and freshly ground black pepper

Put all the fruit into a saucepan with the orange juice. Soak for 6 hours or overnight. Remove the stones from the dates and the prunes. Chop the dates, prunes, and apricots.

☐ If necessary, simmer for 5-7 minutes until all the juice is absorbed by the fruit, then leave to cool. Mix with the rest of the stuffing ingredients and season well.

☐ Set oven to 350F (180C) gas 4.

☐ Spread the meat out as flat as possible. Pack the stuffing into the cavity left by the bones. Roll up and sew together along the overlap. Tie around with string at intervals to form a neat roll.

☐ Place on a rack in a roasting tin and roast for about 2 hours, until cooked to taste.

☐ Transfer to a carving board and cover with foil to keep hot for 5-10 minutes and 'rest'. Carve in thick slices to serve.

Tip: If the meat shows signs of getting brown before it is cooked, turn the oven down slightly. To test, pierce through the thickest part in two or three places with a sharp knife, right through to the stuffing. When cooked, the juices from the meat should be clear, and the blade of the knife should feel hot on the wrist or the cheek.

Middle-eastern Lamb 'El Chalil' makes an unusual party dish to serve with steamed rice or couscous and a cucumber and black olive salad.

Roasting poultry

Roast domestic fowl with their well-browned skin and moist, juicy flesh are among the nation's most popular dishes. Roasting is the easiest way to cook poultry, makes the most of its natural taste and texture and is the best way to deal with birds which have a naturally irregular size and shape. It also gives the opportunity of varying the dish with a delicious array of different stuffings.

To tell when poultry is cooked: Pierce the thickest part of the flesh inside the leg. The juices should run clear. Another test is to move one of the legs: It should move easily in its socket. Most poultry should be well cooked but tender ducks are very good if slightly under done.

Cashew-stuffed Roast Chicken

Serve with potato croquettes and crisp broccoli florets.

Serves 5   ☆☆☆

Preparation: 25 minutes

Cooking: about 1½ hours

4lb (1.8g) oven-ready chicken
2oz (50g) clarified butter
2 teaspoons flour
9 fl oz (275ml) Chicken or Giblet Stock
salt and freshly ground black pepper

The stuffing:
3 tablespoons oil
1 large stick celery, sliced
1 medium onion, sliced
3oz (75g) fresh breadcrumbs
2oz (50g) salted cashew nuts, chopped
1 teaspoon dried thyme

Set the oven to 350F (180C) gas 4 and pat the chicken dry with kitchen paper.

☐ Put the oil in a 8in (20cm) frying-pan over a moderate heat. Add the celery and onion. Cook, stirring occasionally, for 5 minutes to soften the vegetables.

☐ Mix with breadcrumbs and nuts, then season to taste with thyme and salt and pepper.

☐ Spoon the stuffing into the body cavity of the chicken. Pin or sew the skin together to hold the stuffing in place. Truss the bird with string to hold the wings and legs close to the body.

☐ Place in a shallow oven dish or roasting tin. Brush all over with the clarified butter.

☐ Roast for 1¼-1½ hours until well browned and cooked, brushing every 15 minutes with butter or pan juices.

☐ Transfer the chicken to a warmed serving dish. Discard the pins or string and keep hot.

☐ Set the roasting tin over a moderate heat.

☐ Stir in the flour until well mixed in. Gradually stir in the stock. Cook for 3 minutes, stirring constantly until thick and smooth.

☐ Season the gravy to taste. Strain into a warmed sauceboat and serve with the chicken.

Variation: For another superb flavour, use butter instead of oil and substitute finely chopped fresh tarragon for the thyme.

Cashew-stuffed Roast Chicken looks good when garnished with a ring of freshly steamed broccoli florets.

To give a richer deeper colour and heightened flavour to the chicken skin, add 2 teaspoons soy sauce to the butter for brushing.

Giblet Stock

Cook the giblets in water to cover with a little chopped celery, onion and carrot. Add a sprig of parsley, thyme and a bay leaf, to make an excellent stock for the gravy. For an even richer flavour, add 2 tablespoons sherry to the stock at the end of cooking.

When using nuts in a stuffing mixture such as this one, do not prepare too far in advance of use, or the nuts will lose their crisp texture.

If cooking large frozen birds, such as turkeys, ensure that they are totally defrosted before roasting. Check that the legs move freely and feel for ice inside the cavity. It is inadvisable to stuff recently thawed frozen turkeys as the cooking of both stuffing and interior of the bird is retarded. Cook the stuffing separately.

Roasting turkey

As turkey flesh is drier than chicken, it is often best to start roasting with the bird breast-side down so that the juices collect in the breast. Turn the bird breast-side up for the last hour of cooking so that the breast will brown sufficiently.

Roast Turkey with Olives makes a perfect special occasion family meal. Serve it with baked potato croquettes, celery and cranberry sauce.

Roast Turkey with Olives

Serves 12 ☆☆
Preparation: 20 minutes
Cooking: about 3 hours

10lb (5kg) oven-ready turkey
salt and freshly ground black pepper
3oz (75g) clarified butter
2 tablespoons flour
18 fl oz (500ml) Chicken or Giblet Stock
3 tablespoons whisky
2oz (50g) stuffed olives, sliced

The stuffing:
3oz (75g) butter
2oz (50g) onion, chopped
7oz (200g) fresh breadcrumbs
2oz (50g) stuffed olives, sliced
2 teaspoons dried oregano

Set the oven to 350F (180C) gas 4 and pat turkey dry inside and out.
☐ Make the stuffing: Melt the butter in 8in (20cm) frying-pan over a moderate heat. Add the onion and cook, stirring for 5 minutes to soften but not brown.
☐ Mix the breadcrumbs, olives and oregano and season to taste.
☐ Spoon stuffing into the body cavity. Close with skewers or string.
☐ Set the turkey in a large roasting tin and brush with clarified butter.
☐ Roast for about 2¾ hours until well browned and cooked through. Brush with butter or pan juices several times during cooking.
☐ Transfer the turkey to a serving dish, discard the pins or string and keep the turkey hot.
☐ Pour off any excess fat from the tin. Set over a moderate heat and stir in the flour. Gradually stir in the stock and cook, stirring constantly, for 3-4 minutes until thick and smooth.
☐ Add the whisky. Strain the gravy then return to the tin. Stir in the olives, heat through and season.
☐ Cover the tips of the turkey legs with paper frills. Mask the plate with a little of the gravy and serve the rest separately.

Turkey Roast with Apples

Serve with Duchesse potatoes and buttered parsnips.

Serves 4 ☆☆☆
Preparation: 5 minutes
Cooking: about 1½ hours

1¾lb (800g) boneless turkey roast
several tiny sprigs of fresh rosemary
2oz (50g) butter, melted
3 dessert apples
3 fl oz (100ml) dry cider
3oz (75g) cranberry jelly

Set the oven to 350F (180C) gas 4 and pat the roast dry with kitchen paper. Tuck the sprigs of rosemary inside the containing strings evenly around the roast.

☐ Set the meat in a small roasting tin and spoon half the butter over it.

☐ Roast for 30 minutes, turn the joint over and pour over the rest of the butter. Roast for a further 30 minutes, basting occasionally during cooking.

☐ Peel and core the apples and cut into thick slices. Place in the tin around the turkey and pour the cider over the roast.

☐ Cook for another 30 minutes, basting two or three times with the juices. The meat should be a good rich brown, and the juices should run clear when pierced at the thickest point with a sharp knife or a skewer.

☐ Transfer the meat to a carving board and cover with foil. Arrange the apples on a warmed serving dish and keep both hot in the oven at its lowest setting.

☐ Set the roasting tin over a moderate heat. Stir in the cranberry jelly and simmer, stirring, for about 2 minutes.

☐ Carve the turkey into slices about ¼in (5mm) thick and arrange on the plate with the apples. Spoon the sauce over to serve.

Variation: Use cooking apples in conjunction with a sweeter fruit jelly, such as blackcurrant.

Roast Guinea Fowl

Serves 2-3 ☆☆☆
Preparation: 10 minutes
Cooking: about 1¼ hours

2lb (900g) oven-ready guinea fowl
2oz (50g) butter, melted
2 teaspoons flour
¼ pint (150ml) Chicken Stock
5 fl oz (142ml) carton soured cream
salt and freshly ground black pepper
3oz (75g) small green grapes, seeded
sprigs of watercress to garnish

Set the oven to 350F (180C) gas 4 and pat the bird dry.

☐ Brush well all over with butter and set breast-side up in a small shallow roasting tin.

☐ Roast for 1¼-1½ hours, brushing with butter every 15 minutes, until the bird is well browned and its legs can be moved easily in their sockets.

☐ Transfer the bird to warmed serving plate and keep hot.

☐ Set the roasting tin over a moderate heat. Stir in the flour, then gradually stir in the stock. Boil for 3 minutes, stirring constantly, until thick and smooth.

☐ Stir in the cream. Turn off the heat and season the gravy to taste. Stir in the grapes. Let stand for 2-3 minutes just to heat the fruit through.

☐ Spoon the sauce over the fowl and serve immediately, garnished with the sprigs of watercress.

Tip: Although actually commercially reared birds, guinea fowl are often hung in the way of wild game, to allow flavour to develop and the flesh to become more tender. Ask your poulterer or game merchant to recommend one in the right condition for you to roast. Like the wild birds, they are lean and the flesh is dry unless fat is added during cooking.

Guinea fowl can also be used to effect in most recipes for pheasant and in several simple turkey dishes.

Carving Large Turkeys

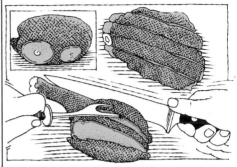

Cut the drumsticks from large turkeys at the ball joint, then carve as shown.

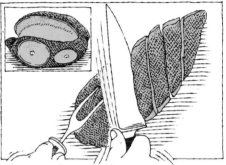

Remove the entire breasts as shown and slice across diagonally or cut lengthways into thin slices.

Carving turkey roast

It's best to leave the strings on the roast until after carving, to hold the slices together.

Carving goose

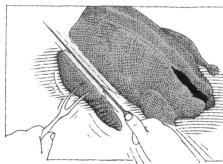

First cut off the wings.

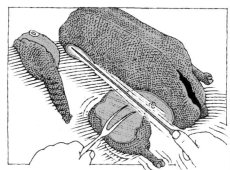

Remove the legs in the same way.

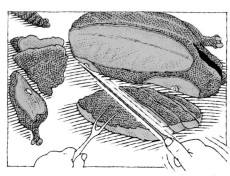

Cut off the entire breast in one piece and slice it across as shown. Separate the thigh from the lower leg at joint.

You can also carve the breast in thin slices along the length of the breast, if preferred.

Roasting ducks and geese

As both of these birds are much more fatty than other domestic fowls, they don't need fat in the stuffing as more than enough cooks out of the bird.

Stock for duck and goose gravy

Cook the giblets with water to cover, onion, carrot, celery, and leek and sprigs of fresh herbs as available.

Duck and goose fat

Strain off the fat which cooks from the birds through clean muslin. Cool, and store in a covered container in the refrigerator. Both will keep for several weeks and are very good for cooking, adding a fine rich flavour to stews and fried dishes.

Roasting Ducks and Geese

Commercially reared ducks and geese are much fattier than domestic poultry. They require no basting and cook to a good rich brown with little attention during cooking. Ducks can range in size, providing up to 5-6 generous portions: large geese will serve 12 or more.

Rice-stuffed Roast Duck

Serve with minted peas, sautéed cucumber and new potatoes.

Serves 4	☆☆☆
Preparation: 25 minutes	
Cooking: about 2 hours	

4½lb (2kg) oven-ready duck
2 tablespoons flour
9 fl oz (250ml) Giblet Stock
¼ pint (150ml) red wine

The stuffing:
2oz (50g) butter
1 medium onion, finely chopped
2 celery sticks, finely chopped
4oz (100g) cooked brown rice
1 small apple, peeled, cored and chopped
1 teaspoon dried rosemary
salt and freshly ground black pepper

Set the oven to 350F (180C) gas 4 and pat the duck dry with kitchen paper.

☐ Make the stuffing: melt the butter in an 8in (20cm) frying-pan over a moderate heat. Add the onion and celery and stir for 5 minutes until soft. Mix with the rice and the apple and season to taste with rosemary, salt and pepper.

☐ Stuff into the body of the duck and close with small skewers or poultry pins. Tie the legs together with strings and secure the wings and the neck skin with skewers or pins.

☐ Set the duck, breast-side up, on a rack in a roasting tin. Prick the skin all over with a sharp fork and sprinkle with a little salt.

☐ Roast for about 2 hours, until the skin is crisp and brown and the juices run clear when the flesh is pierced.

☐ Transfer the duck to a warmed serving dish and keep hot.

☐ Pour off the excess fat from the roasting tin and reserve (see sidelines). Set the tin over a moderate heat. Stir in the flour, then gradually stir in the stock and the wine. Cook for 2-3 minutes, stirring constantly, until thick and smooth. Season to taste and strain into a warmed sauceboat.

☐ Remove the pins and strings from the duck and serve with the gravy and stuffing.

Roast Goose with Gooseberry Stuffing

Serve with baked croquette potatoes, Brussels sprouts and red and white cabbage.

Serves 10-12	☆☆☆
Preparation: 15 minutes	
Cooking: 3-3¼ hours	

12lb (5.5kg) oven-ready goose
1lb (500g) gooseberries, thawed if frozen
8oz (225g) onions, coarsely chopped
8oz (225g) fresh breadcrumbs
1 teaspoon dried sage
salt and freshly ground black pepper
a few fresh sage leaves
3 tablespoons flour
1 pint (600ml) Chicken or Giblet Stock
3 tablespoons brandy

Set the oven to 350F (180C) gas 4 and pat the goose dry inside and out with kitchen paper. Cut away any excess pieces of fat.

☐ Finely chop the gooseberries, mix with the onion and breadcrumbs and season to taste with the dried sage, salt and pepper. Stir in the whole sage leaves.

☐ Pack into the body cavity of the goose and close the opening with small skewers or poultry pins.

☐ Tie the legs together with string. Wrap the wings and legs with crumpled foil to prevent charring.

☐ Set, breast-side up, on a rack in a roasting tin. Cover loosely with aluminium foil.

☐ Roast for 1¾ hours, remove the foil and roast for a further 1¾-2 hours, until the goose is well-browned all over and cooked through (the juices should run clear when the flesh is pierced at the thickest point).

☐ Transfer the bird to a carving board and cover with foil to keep hot.

☐ Pour off all but about 1 tablespoon of the fat and reserve (see sidelines). Set the roasting tin over a moderate heat. Stir in the flour and then gradually stir in the stock. Cook stirring constantly for 2-3 minutes. Season to taste and add the brandy. If a thinner gravy is preferred, add a little more stock. Strain into a warmed sauceboat.

☐ Transfer the stuffing to a serving dish and carve the goose as shown.

The various stages in preparing, cooking and serving a stuffed roast goose. Quartered apples, onion and sage or bay leaves make a splendid alternative stuffing to the gooseberry mixture.

Roasting game birds

Game birds are much smaller than domestic fowls, each usually serving from one to three people. They are generally much drier and require the addition of fat, and sometimes stock, during cooking to keep them moist and tender. They may be brushed with butter, or the breasts can be covered with bacon or strips of pork fat to protect them.

Lemon jelly glaze for roast duck, goose or game birds

Melt 2 tablespoons lemon jelly marmalade and spread over the cooked bird. Heat 3 tablespoons brandy or whisky in a small saucepan until it steams. Set alight and pour, flaming over the bird.

For an alternative glaze, use 2 tablespoons clear honey and 2 tablespoons orange juice (as in Chinese-style Wild Duck) per bird. Garnish with orange or grapefruit segments.

Chinese-style Wild Duck

Serve on a bed of egg-fried rice or pilaff, accompanied by sweetcorn kernels.

Roast Grouse

Serve with gaufrette potatoes, garden peas and carrots. Another excellent accompaniment to these is fried breadcrumbs: Melt 2oz (50g) butter in a 9in (23cm) frying-pan over a moderate heat. Stir in 4oz (100g) fresh white breadcrumbs. Cook, stirring constantly, until golden brown.

Roast Pheasant

Serve with game chips, Brussels sprouts and braised celery.

It is traditional to serve pheasants with the tail feathers on as a garnish.

Frothing

To give game birds a crisp brown skin, they are often 'frothed' at the end of roasting. First, they are sprinkled with flour or salt and then generously basted with stock, cider or wine.

Chinese-style Wild Duck

Serves 4 ☆☆☆
Preparation and cooking: 1¾ hours

---

2 wild ducks, each about 1½lb (700g) dressed weight
4 fl oz (100ml) clear honey
4 tablespoons orange juice

The stuffing:
1 large orange, segmented
3oz (75g) fresh breadcrumbs
1 medium onion, finely chopped
½ teaspoon salt
½ teaspoon dried thyme
3 celery sticks, chopped

Set the oven to 350F (180C) gas 4. Rinse and pat dry inside and out.

☐ Mix together all the stuffing ingredients and pack into the ducks. Secure closed with poultry pins.

☐ Put the ducks in a roasting tin. Mix together the honey and orange juice and spoon over the ducks.

☐ Cover the tin loosely with foil and roast for 20 minutes.

☐ Brush the ducks well with the pan juices, re-cover and cook for a further 20 minutes. Repeat process and cook for another 20 minutes.

☐ Remove the foil and continue roasting for 25-30 minutes, brushing 3 or 4 times with the pan juices, until browned and cooked through.

Roast Grouse

Serves 4 ☆☆
Preparation and cooking: 1 hour

---

2 grouse, each about 1lb (500g) dressed weight
6 rashers streaky bacon, rinds removed
¼ pint (150ml) Chicken Stock
2 tablespoons raspberry jelly
¼ pint (150ml) port
2oz (50g) raspberries

Set the oven to 375F (190C) gas 5. Rinse the grouse inside and out and pat dry. Trim off neck flap.

☐ Lay 3 rashers of bacon lengthways along the breast of each grouse. Secure the bacon in place by tying around with string in 2 places. Wrap each leg in crumpled foil.

☐ Place the grouse in a shallow roasting tin (large enough to leave about 1in (2.5cm) between them).

☐ Roast for 45-50 minutes, until the legs can be easily moved.

☐ Cut the strings and remove the bacon. Discard the foil. Cut the grouse lengthways with poultry shears. Keep hot on a serving plate.

☐ Set the roasting tin over a moderate heat. Add the stock and boil vigorously for 5 minutes. Add the jelly and the port and boil, stirring constantly, for 3 minutes.

☐ Strain the gravy into a warmed sauceboat and stir in raspberries.

Roast Pheasant

Serves 4 ☆☆☆
Preparation and cooking: 1¼ hours

---

2 pheasants, each about 2lb (900g) dressed weight
2oz (50g) butter, melted
juice of 1 lemon
½ pint (300ml) Chicken Stock

The stuffing:
6oz (175g) fresh breadcrumbs
1 medium onion, finely chopped
2 tablespoons finely chopped parsley
grated rind of 1 lemon
1 teaspoon dried basil
2oz (50g) butter, softened
salt and freshly ground black pepper

Set the oven to 375F (190C) gas 5. Rinse the pheasants and pat dry.

☐ Mix together all the stuffing ingredients, season well and use to stuff both pheasants. Tie the legs of each together with string.

☐ Place them in a roasting tin. Mix together the butter, lemon juice and stock and pour over birds.

☐ Roast for about 1 hour, basting several times with the juices, until tender when tested with a skewer on the inside of the legs.

☐ Transfer pheasants to a carving board and cover with foil.

☐ Place the roasting tin over a moderate heat and bring the juices to the boil. Season and serve.

Roast Hare
with Mushrooms

Serves 6   ☆ ☆ ☆
Preparation and cooking: 1¾ hours

1 hare, about 4½lb (2kg) dressed
    weight
4oz (125g) butter, melted
4 long thick rashers smoked streaky bacon
1lb (500g) button mushrooms, wiped
2 teaspoons dried oregano
½ teaspoon dried thyme
1 small bay leaf, crumbled
½ pint (300ml) Game Stock
3 fl oz (100ml) port
¼ pint (150ml) double cream
salt and freshly ground black pepper
1 tablespoon chopped chives for garnish

Set the oven to 325F (160C) gas 3.
☐ Rinse the hare both inside and
out and pat dry. Using a sharp knife
and poultry shears remove the 4 legs.
☐ Brush the pieces with butter and
place in a large roasting tin. Cut the
bacon to a suitable length and place
over saddle.
☐ Roast for 15 minutes, lift the
bacon, brush the meat well with
butter again and replace the bacon.
☐ Roast for about 1¼ hours,
brushing with the butter in the same
way every 15 minutes. Cook until
the juices run clear when pierced.
☐ Transfer to a warmed serving
plate. Cover with foil to keep hot.
☐ Set the roasting tin over a
moderate heat. Add the mushrooms,
herbs, stock and port and boil for 3
minutes, stirring constantly. Scrape
into a saucepan and return to heat.
☐ Warm cream in a separate pan.
☐ Arrange the pieces of hare in
their original shape on the serving
plate. Drain the mushrooms with a
perforated spoon and arrange
around the hare. Keep hot.
☐ Boil the stock vigorously for 3
minutes, stir in the heated cream
and bring to the boil again.
☐ Season to taste, spoon a little
over the hare and serve the rest
separately. Sprinkle over chives.

*Step-by-step to Roast Hare with
Mushrooms.*

COVERED COOKING

Pot roasting • Braising and baking
Casseroles and stews

Pot roasting

True 'dry' roasting in the oven is really only suitable for the prime cuts of meat with sufficient natural tenderness to require no added moisture. Pot roasting, braising and stewing, however, are all methods of cooking which introduce liquid into the basic process, and are therefore excellent ways of dealing with the less tender cuts of meat or game—be they large or small. A successful pot roast—done on top of the stove or in the oven—produces succulent, tasty meat and helps to prevent shrinkage during cooking. The juices can be used as the basis of a delicious sauce.

Pot roasting is a method used almost exclusively for cooking the larger cuts of meat—whole joints, in fact—which are often first browned in a little fat on top of the stove. They are then cooked in very little or no liquid, in a partially covered pan to reduce steaming, thus giving the meat a more 'roasted' result. Sometimes vegetables are put in with the liquid, and these give added flavour to the gravy or, if left whole, they can even be served on the platter around the meat.

Pot roasting is a 'combination' method of cooking involving two or more techniques. The initial shallow-frying seals in the meat's own natural juices, then the extra ingredients are added and the cooking continues over low heat on the stove top or in the oven.

Another way of flavouring and tenderizing meat before cooking is to marinate it. This is often done with beef and particularly game, which can be very 'dry', especially after it has been hung for the requisite length of time. The marinade can then form the liquid in which the meat is cooked.

Equipment

If you are planning to brown the meat first on top of the stove before transferring it to the oven, make sure that the pot you choose is flameproof rather than merely heatproof. Enamelled steel, cast iron, copper (tin-lined, of course) or aluminium pots are all suitable.

● If the pot is a metal one, make sure it has a thick base if you plan to pot roast on top of the stove. You can protect the base to some extent—and prevent burning—by investing in a metal heat-diffuser to fit over the heat source.

● If you have an earthenware or heatproof glass dish, use a frying-pan or—better still—a saucepan to brown the meat first. Transfer the meat to the casserole dish, and continue cooking in the pre-heated oven.

● Don't worry if you haven't a suitable lid. Foil makes an excellent lid for pot roasting, with the added advantage that it can be left slightly open at one side to allow steam to escape.

● Choose a pot of the right size and shape round, oval or rectangular—to hold the type and size of meat you usually intend to cook this way. (Pot roasting chicken is particularly effective.)

● Make sure the pots used for cooking this way on top of the stove are approximately the same size as the burner or hotplate. It saves fuel, prevents uneven cooking and is less likely to damage the hob.

● Turning large pieces of meat or whole poultry or game birds can be tricky—and you have to do this to brown them. Use two large wooden spoons or a pair of slotted spoons. It helps if the pan is deep rather than wide to prevent slipping.

Dutch oven

Earthenware casserole

Enamelled self-baster

Cast iron casserole

A wide range of pots are suitable for pot roasting and also for braising. A 'Dutch oven' is so-called because the Dutch do most of their roasting—and pot roasting—on the stove top. If you have a pottery casserole that can be taken from oven to table, brown the meat in a frying-pan first. The best pots are those of cast iron.

Vegetables are not pot roasted, but braised with a little added butter, fat or stock in a heavy pan with a close-fitting lid.

Fish cooked in the oven are more usually termed 'baked' and—unless whole—are generally almost completely immersed in poaching liquid or stock.

Why pot roast?

Pot roasting has several advantages: the moisture created inside the covered pot ensures that even the less expensive cuts of meat are juicy and tender. In addition, browning adds flavour and colour to both the meat and its juices to make it look and taste more like an expensive roast. Even very small joints can be cooked this way without drying out the meat.

Pot roasting is also a good way to save fuel. You can cook the meat in the oven along with other food, or on the hob when you do not want to heat up the oven.

One of the most important reasons for pot roasting is that extra richness it gives to meat. A limitless variety of flavours can be added with spices, herbs and wines to turn many cuts of meat into gourmet dishes.

What to pot roast

The slightly less tender brisket, silverside or topside of beef, and breast and shoulder of veal and lamb are the most common pot roasts, though fillet of beef is also delicious cooked in this way. Poultry and, in particular, game, are very suitable as these tend to be dry and lacking in natural fat.

How to pot roast

Heat the fat – butter, lard or oil – in a pan into which the meat fits snugly, or a frying-pan. Brown the meat in the fat over a moderate heat, turning so that the meat browns all over. If you are using vegetables, such as carrots, onions and celery, for added flavour, remove the meat from the pan and fry the vegetables until soft. Return the meat and add any flavourings and the liquid to the roasting pot. Cover and cook as directed. Small joints may be cooked either on the hob or in the oven, but large joints are best cooked in the oven. For large joints, remove the lid for the last 30 minutes of cooking to allow the meat to brown.

Herbs and spices

A bouquet garni, parsley, celery leaves, thyme, rosemary and bay are some of the most popular used for pot roasts. Peppercorns, juniper berries, cloves, caraway and dill seeds are also good.

Liquids

Use water or stock, or leftover wine to give your pot roast added flavour. Cider or beer is good for strong-flavoured meats. Try apple juice with pork, pineapple juice with chicken, or juice from canned raspberries with duck.

If pot roasting or braising in earthenware pots or other non-flameproof vessels, brown the meat, poultry or game first in a saucepan or frying-pan.

Cast iron or enamelled steel pans are best for pot roasting, but ensure that the lids have vents to allow the steam to escape. Otherwise, use foil to cover the pan and leave one side open. The liquid will evaporate and the contents brown.

Pot roasting on top of the stove

Suitable joints

Small joints of rolled topside are well suited to pot roasting on the hob. Choose a piece of meat which is uniform in size, and turn it regularly to ensure even cooking.

Dry the meat well and season it *just before* draining otherwise the salt draws the juices out, makes the surface moist, and prevents the quick searing so necessary to seal in juices.

Cooking small joints of meat in a pan on top of the cooker allows you to cook for a small family – even just yourself – the most delicious Sunday joint without the expense of heating the oven.

This technique also lends itself to the preparation of special one-pot dinners for two which can be left to cook slowly while you are out at the theatre or cinema.

When the meat is to be cooked entirely on top of the cooker, choose small regularly shaped pieces weighing about 1-1¼lb (500-575g). If the meat is irregularly shaped it will not cook uniformly and pieces which are too large will not cook through completely. It is important to match the size of the joint to the capacity of the pot: a 1lb (500g) joint of beef, for instance, will fit snugly into a 6in (15cm) casserole.

Frying each side in a little fat to brown the meat at the start gives it a better flavour and a more attractive appearance, akin to that of dry roast meat. Cooking in a partly closed pot with the addition of a little wine or stock makes a delicious 'roast' with very little effort, and makes a significant saving on fuel expense.

Always cook over a very low heat to avoid losing the cooking liquid by evaporation and any toughening of parts of the meat by overcooking.

Use only pots with very heavy-duty bases and try to set them on a burner of approximately the same size as the base. It is also a very good idea, whenever possible, to make use of a metal heat diffuser, or a heat-diffusing mat, between the pot and the burner as this will help avoid any overcooking of the parts of the meat in contact with the base.

Try to turn the meat and baste it regularly. If not, try to turn the meat over at least once in the middle of the cooking process. Avoid using any sharp instruments when doing so as these will only puncture the sealed outer layer and allow juices to escape.

Choose a suitable pan. Heat the fat over a moderate heat until hot.

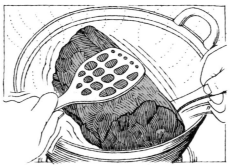

Add the meat and turn to brown all over. Use 2 spatulas to turn the meat.

If fat gets too hot before meat is browned, add a little cold butter to cool it.

Add herbs, spices and other flavourings with the liquid. Partly cover the pan.

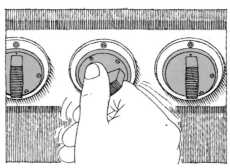

Turn the heat low so the meat will cook gently.

Baste occasionally, and turn the meat at least once during cooking.

Pot roasting beef in the oven

Larger pieces of meat are better cooked in the oven where they then require very little attention. Instead of browning the meat first, you can remove the lid towards the end of the cooking and let the joint brown at that stage.

Rump of beef is well suited to cooking in this way, but silverside is almost as good and much more economical. Ask the butcher to cut off the size of piece you want from what he calls a 'primal' cut.

The meat may then be left in its natural triangular shape for cooking, but many cuts are usually rolled to give them a less awkward shape to cook and to make them easier to carve. Joints of meat such as silverside, topside and sirloin of beef are prepared in this way. Usually the butcher removes all bones, excess fat and connective tissue before rolling.

Silverside with White Wine Sauce

Serve with roast potatoes and braised leeks.

Serves 4-6 ★★☆
Preparation: 5 minutes
Cooking: 1¼ hours

2-2¼lb (900g-1kg) rolled silverside
salt and freshly ground black pepper
1oz (25g) beef dripping or white vegetable fat
8 fl oz (250ml) dry white wine
a sprig of fresh rosemary

The sauce:
1 tablespoon flour
1 tablespoon cold water
salt and freshly ground black pepper

Pat the meat dry with kitchen paper. Rub all over with pepper and salt.
☐ Pre-heat the oven to 350F (180C) gas 4.
☐ Put the dripping in a casserole or roasting tin. Place over a moderate heat until a faint haze shows.
☐ Fry the meat for 15-20 minutes, turning frequently, until browned all over. Pour off the fat.
☐ Add the wine and rosemary to the pan. Cover and cook in the oven for about 1 hour.
☐ Remove the meat and cover with foil to keep warm while you make the sauce.
☐ Place the pan over a moderate heat. Mix the flour smoothly with the cold water and stir the mixture into the pan. Simmer, stirring constantly, for about 4 minutes until well thickened and smooth. Remove the rosemary and adjust the seasoning, if necessary.
☐ Carve the meat and arrange on a serving plate. Strain the sauce into a warmed sauceboat and serve.

Rolled Sirloin with Sour Cream Sauce

Serve with green beans and small boiled potatoes.

Serves 4-6 ★★☆
Preparation: 5 minutes
Cooking: 1¼ hours

2-2¼lb (900-1kg) rolled sirloin
salt and freshly ground black pepper
1oz (25g) dripping
4 tablespoons Basic Brown Stock

The sauce:
5 fl oz (142ml) carton soured cream
1 tablespoon chopped gherkins
1 tablespoon chopped parsley

Prepare and cook the meat in the same way as the Silverside with White Wine Sauce. Remove the meat and set aside, covered with foil to keep warm.
☐ Put the pan over a moderate heat and simmer, stirring, for one minute. Gradually stir in the soured cream and simmer for a further minute. Stir in the gherkins and parsley.
☐ Carve the meat and arrange on a warmed serving dish. Spoon the sauce around and serve immediately.

Testing for degree of doneness
Insert the tip of a sharp knife into the thickest part of the joint. Juices will run slightly pink and the knife will feel hot on the back of the hand when medium done. The time stated in the recipes produces medium-done results. For well done meat, cook until the juices run clear.

Carving
Before carving rolled joints always remove the string first in the kitchen.

Pot roasting hints
Only a moderate heat should be used for browning the meat. If the initial heat is too high, the outside will char before the inside can cook properly in the added juices.
● Always have a warmed serving dish ready at the end of cooking time and leave the meat to 'rest' in exactly the same way you would if roasting. Ten or fifteen minutes' resting time allows the fibres to relax, the juices to re-distribute throughout the meat, and it makes the meat easier to slice.
● Meat is always easier to pot roast and slice if cooked off the bone.

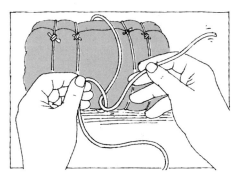

The professional way to tie a rolled joint of meat.

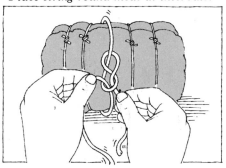

Place string round meat at intervals.

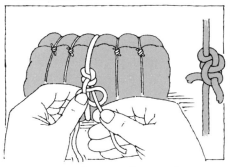

Thread short end round as shown.

Tighten; make extra loop and secure.

Beef with Mushrooms and Red Wine Sauce

Serve with sautéed potatoes and leaf spinach.

Serves 4-6 ☆☆☆
Preparation: 20 minutes
Cooking: 2 hours

2-2¼lb (900g-1kg) rolled topside
salt and freshly ground black pepper
1oz (25g) beef dripping or white
    vegetable fat
¼ pint (150ml) red wine
2oz (50g) butter
½lb (225g) button mushrooms, wiped and
    trimmed
½ pint (300ml) Basic Brown Stock
1 tablespoon chopped parsley

Pat the meat dry with kitchen paper, then rub it with pepper and salt.

☐ Put the dripping or fat into a flameproof casserole or a saucepan of about 4 pint (2.25 litres) capacity and set over a moderate heat until the fat shows a faint haze.

☐ Add the meat fat-side down. Fry, turning, for about 15 minutes until it is browned all over.

☐ Pour off all the fat, then add 4 tablespoons of wine to the pan. Partly cover the pan, turn down the heat and cook very gently for about 1½ hours, turning the meat occasionally. Remove the meat and set aside, covered with foil.

☐ Meanwhile, melt the butter in another saucepan over a moderate heat until it begins to brown. Fry the mushrooms for about 3 minutes until lightly browned, remove with a slotted spoon and set aside.

☐ Put the rest of the wine and the stock in the pan in which the mushrooms have been fried and boil vigorously for about 15 minutes to reduce to about half.

☐ Add the reduced stock to the meat pan. Boil for a minute or so to cook up the juices from the bottom of the pan. Add the mushrooms and simmer for one more minute.

☐ Slice the meat and arrange on a warmed serving dish. Spoon the mushrooms over and sprinkle with parsley. Serve the sauce separately.

Beef with Green Peppercorn Sauce

Serve with potato and celeriac purée and steamed broccoli.

Serves 4-6 ☆☆☆
Preparation: 20 minutes
Cooking: 2 hours

2-2¼lb (900g-1kg) rolled topside
salt and freshly ground black pepper
1oz (25g) beef dripping or white
    vegetable fat
½ pint (300ml) Basic Brown Stock
2 tablespoons brandy
6 fl oz (175ml) single cream
2 tablespoons green peppercorns
1 tomato, peeled and diced,
    for garnish

Prepare and cook the meat as for Beef with Mushrooms and Red Wine Sauce, using some of the stock in place of the wine.

☐ Transfer the cooked meat to a carving board and cover with foil to keep warm.

☐ In a saucepan, boil the reduced stock rapidly to reduce it by about half.

☐ Add the brandy and reduced stock to the pan juices and boil

rapidly for a minute or two, stirring constantly.

☐ Lower the heat and add the cream and peppercorns. Stir to heat through for a minute or so.

☐ Slice the meat and arrange on a warmed serving dish. Spoon the sauce around and garnish with the tomato.

Horseradish Beef

Serves 4-6   ☆ ☆ ☆
Preparation: 20 minutes
Cooking: 2¼ hours

2-2¼lb (900g-1kg) rolled topside
salt and freshly ground black pepper
1oz (25g) beef dripping
¼ pint (150ml) beer
½ pint (300ml) Chicken Stock
5oz (150g) fresh horseradish, grated
2oz (50g) fresh white breadcrumbs
1 teaspoon made mustard
8 fl oz (250ml) double cream

Prepare and cook the meat as for Beef with Mushrooms and Red Wine Sauce, using some beer in place of wine.

☐ Transfer the cooked meat to a carving board and cover with foil.

☐ Add the remaining beer, stock and horseradish to the pan and bring to the boil, stirring up the pan juices. Simmer for 15 minutes.

☐ Press the sauce through a sieve into a clean saucepan. Boil rapidly to reduce by about half.

☐ Stir in the breadcrumbs and boil for 2 or 3 minutes until thickened. Add the mustard and cream, adjust the seasoning and heat through.

☐ Slice the meat thickly and arrange on a warmed serving plate. Spoon some sauce over and serve the rest separately.

Step by step to making Beef with Mushrooms and Red Wine Sauce.

Pot roasting fillet of beef

Once in a while give yourself a real treat and pot roast a piece of fillet. Its natural tenderness is preserved and its juiciness enhanced. Ask the butcher to skin and trim the piece to a more regular shape. Not only does this make it more attractive but it helps ensure even cooking. Buy a piece of about 1lb (500g) for 2 or 3 people, or 1¾lb (800g) for 6.

Cooking times:
for 1lb (500g) – rare : 15 minutes browning
+15 minutes cooking
– medium : 15 minutes browning
+20 minutes cooking.
The more well done the meat becomes the firmer it is to the touch – test with the back of a fork.

The various steps in preparing, cooking and serving Pot Roast Fillet of Beef.

Pot Roast Fillet of Beef

Serve with French fries and a mixed salad.

Serves 2-3   ☆☆☆
Preparation: 5 minutes
Cooking: about 30 minutes

1lb (500g) fillet of beef
salt and freshly ground black pepper
a knob of butter
1 tablespoon oil

The sauce:
3 tablespoons Basic Brown Stock
1 tablespoon brandy
1oz (25g) cold butter, cubed

Pat the meat dry with kitchen paper. Rub the surface all over with salt and pepper.
☐ Put the butter and oil in a 6in (15cm) casserole over a moderate heat until it begins to brown. Fry the beef for 12-15 minutes, turning frequently, until brown all over.
☐ Pour off the fat. Add the stock and the brandy to the pan and partially cover it. Reduce the heat and cook very gently for 15-20 minutes. Remove the meat, cover with foil and set aside.
☐ Turn up the heat and boil the liquid vigorously for 2 minutes. Then lower the heat and add the butter one cube at a time.
☐ Carve the meat in thick slices and arrange them on a warmed serving plate. Spoon some of the sauce around and serve the rest separately.

Marinating meat for pot roasting

Overnight soaking in a marinade tenderizes tougher joints of meat and adds flavour. The marinade also supplies delicious juices in which to pot roast and subsequently use to make tasty sauces. Red wine is a traditional marinade base, but cider or beer make good alternatives.

Red Wine Marinated Beef

Serve this party dish hot with creamy mashed potatoes, glazed carrots and braised red cabbage. Alternatively, serve cold as part of a buffet meal accompanied by a salad with a mustardy dressing.

Serves 14   ☆☆☆
Preparation: 20 minutes
Marinating: 24 hours
Cooking: 2 hours

6lb (2.75kg) silverside of beef
salt and freshly ground black pepper
14 fl oz (400ml) red wine
½ pint (300ml) Basic Brown or Meat Stock
3 tablespoons brandy
4 sprigs parsley, coarsely chopped
2 sprigs celery leaves, chopped
½ teaspoon dried thyme
1 bay leaf
2 cloves garlic, pressed or chopped
1 small onion, sliced
6 black peppercorns, crushed
4oz (100g) cold butter, cubed

Wipe the meat dry with paper towel. Rub well all over with salt and pepper. If there is a thick layer of fat on top of the meat, score it across several times with a sharp knife.

☐ Put all the remaining ingredients, except the butter, in a deep meat tin just large enough to hold the meat. Set the piece of silverside in the tin, fat side up.

☐ Cover the tin and set it in a cool place for 24 hours. Baste the meat with the marinade from time to time.

☐ Heat oven to 350F (180C) gas 4.

☐ Uncover the tin and pat the top surface of the meat dry with kitchen paper. Re-cover the tin and cook in the oven for about 1¼ hours.

☐ Uncover and cook for about another 30 minutes to brown the fat. Remove the meat and set aside, covered with foil to keep it hot.

☐ Strain the pan juices into a saucepan and boil them vigorously for 10 minutes. Beat the butter into the pan, one cube at a time, then pour into a warmed sauceboat. Carve the beef thickly to serve.

Tip: If serving cold, boil the pan juices rapidly to reduce by half. Leave to cool and then beat them into an equal part of mayonnaise to make a delicious dressing for the sliced beef.

Alternative marinades

For a more economical marinade, use wine vinegar in place of the red wine – perhaps sweetened to taste with a spoonful or two of honey.

Alternatively, give beef a gamey flavour akin to that of venison by substituting 1 teaspoon of crushed juniper berries and two or three cloves for the thyme and bay leaf.

Beef set in a red wine marinade.

To carve a leg of lamb

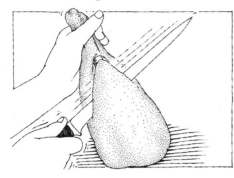

Cut a slice to form a base.

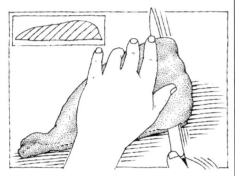

Loosen the meat by cutting right along the bone.

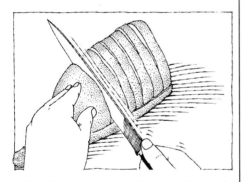

Cut the meat vertically into slices.

Pot roasting a leg of lamb
Allow about 35 minutes per 1lb (500g) at 350F (180C) gas 4 for medium-done meat. When you can pierce the meat easily with a fork, and there is no give in the flesh it is well done.

Breton Lamb with Haricot Beans
The cooked beans, cooled and then covered will keep in the fridge for up to 3 days.

Pot roasting lamb

Pot roasting a leg of lamb produces particularly succulent results: the slow cooking in a moist atmosphere gives the full flavour and breaks down connective tissue to give a tender, juicy texture.

You can brown the meat on top of the stove before pot roasting, but it is easier to brown it in the oven towards the end.

Continental Lamb Pot Roast

Serve with a medley of crisp boiled potatoes, carrots and leeks.
This is also delicious served cold with a fresh minty mixed salad.

Serves 6   ☆☆☆
Preparation: 10 minutes
Cooking: 2¾ hours

4lb (1.8kg) leg of lamb
salt and freshly ground black pepper
3 garlic cloves, peeled
2 sprigs of fresh thyme
¼ pint (150ml) dry white wine
¼ pint (150ml) Basic Brown Stock

Pat the meat dry with kitchen paper. Rub well with salt and pepper.

☐ Cut the garlic into slivers. Pierce the outside layer of lamb fat in several places with a sharp knife and insert the garlic slivers.

☐ Heat oven to 350F (180C) gas 4.

☐ Put the thyme and the wine into a meat tin just large enough to hold the joint and set in the meat.

☐ Cover the tin loosely with foil, leaving it slightly open at one side. Cook for 2 hours. Remove the foil and cook for 30 minutes more to brown the meat lightly.

☐ Transfer it to a carving board and cover with foil.

☐ Skim off as much fat as possible from the roasting tin, place it over a moderate heat to boil vigorously for 3 minutes, then strain it and serve separately. Carve the meat as shown and serve immediately.

Breton Lamb with Haricot Beans

Serves 6   ☆☆☆
Preparation: 10 minutes plus overnight soaking
Cooking: 2¾ hours

½lb (225g) haricot beans
salt and freshly ground black pepper
4lb (1.8kg) leg of lamb
3 garlic cloves
2 sprigs of fresh thyme
9 fl oz (275ml) Basic Brown or Lamb Stock
1oz (25g) butter
4oz (100g) onions, chopped
1 tablespoon flour
3 tablespoons tomato purée
3 tablespoons port
a pinch of sugar
2 tablespoons snipped chives

Soak the beans overnight in cold water. Drain and discard the water. Cover with fresh water and bring to the boil. Cover pan, remove from heat and leave for about ¾ hour.

☐ Drain and discard the water. Cover beans with fresh water, lightly salted to taste. Cover and simmer for 1–1½ hours until tender, then drain.

☐ Prepare and cook the lamb as in Continental Lamb Pot Roast, using stock in place of the wine. Remove cooked lamb to a carving board and cover with foil.

☐ Spoon off as much fat as possible from the pan juices. Add beans and boil over a moderate heat for 3 minutes.

☐ Strain the juices into a jug. Keep beans hot on a large serving dish.

☐ Melt the butter in a 2 pint (1.2 litre) saucepan over a moderate heat. Cook onion for 10 minutes, stirring

☐ Stir in the flour, then gradually stir in the tomato purée, port and enough of the meat juices to make a sauce of the desired consistency. Cook, stirring constantly, for 3 minutes. Adjust the seasoning with salt, pepper and sugar.

☐ Carve the lamb and arrange on the plate with the beans. Strain the sauce and serve separately. Sprinkle the chives over the beans and serve.

Serve Breton Lamb with Haricot Beans as a dinner-party main course, with a tossed green salad.

Stuffed Breast of Lamb

Serve with boiled new potatoes and braised onions or leeks.

Serves 4   ☆☆☆
Preparation: 15 minutes
Cooking: 1½ hours

1 large boned breast of lamb, about
   1½lb (700g)
salt and freshly ground black pepper
8oz (225g) minced lamb
4 tablespoons fresh breadcrumbs
1 egg, size 4
2 tablespoons chopped fresh herbs, such as
   parsley, celery leaves, or chervil
1 tablespoon finely chopped onion
1oz (25g) butter
¼ pint (150ml) dry white wine
¼ pint (150ml) dry white vermouth
1 tablespoon tomato purée
2 teaspoons cornflour
a pinch of sugar

Pat the meat dry with kitchen paper. Rub well with salt and pepper.

☐ Mix together thoroughly the minced lamb, breadcrumbs, egg, herbs and onion. Season well with salt and pepper. Shape into a cylinder about 1in (2.5cm) shorter than the widest part of the breast.

☐ Place the stuffing across the lamb. Roll up firmly and tie at intervals with string.

☐ Heat oven to 350F (180C) gas 4.

☐ Heat the butter in a flameproof casserole about 8in (20cm) diameter over a moderate heat, until it begins to brown. Fry the meat, turning occasionally, for 12-15 minutes until browned all round.

☐ Pour off most of the fat. Add the wine and vermouth and bring to the boil. Partly cover and cook in the oven for 1¼-1½ hours, until cooked through. Remove the meat and cover with foil.

☐ Boil the juices in the pan for 5 minutes. In a small mixing bowl or cup, mix the tomato purée and cornflour together smoothly. Stir in one tablespoon of the hot liquid, then return this to the pan and simmer, stirring constantly, for 3 minutes. Adjust the seasoning with salt, pepper and sugar.

☐ Slice meat and arrange on hot plates. Spoon a little sauce over and serve the rest separately.

Preparing, cooking and serving Stuffed Breast of Lamb. This recipe is excellent for a special Sunday lunch.

Is the stuffing cooked through?
To test: insert a sharp knife into the centre of the thickest part of the roll. If the tip then feels hot when touched to the back of the hand the stuffing is cooked.

Pork with Grape Sauce

Serve with fluffy boiled rice and a crisp mixed salad.

Serves 4   ☆☆☆
Preparation: 15 minutes
Cooking: about 40 minutes

2 pork fillets, each about ¾lb (350g)
salt and freshly ground white pepper
1oz (25g) butter
3 tablespoons dry white wine

The sauce:
7 fl oz (200ml) Meat Stock
7 fl oz (200ml) dry white wine
1 leek, sliced
2 tablespoons finely chopped celery leaves
1 tablespoon finely chopped parsley
1oz (25g) butter
2 tablespoons flour
3 tablespoons dry white vermouth
¼lb (100g) green grapes, halved and seeded

Pat the meat dry with kitchen paper and rub with salt and pepper.

☐ Melt the butter in a 8in (20cm) frying-pan over a moderate heat, until the butter begins to brown.

☐ Fry the meat for 5-7 minutes, turning, to brown all over. Add the 3 tablespoons wine, reduce the heat and cover the pan.

☐ Cook for 20-25 minutes, or until meat feels firm and juices run clear. Turn once or twice during cooking.

☐ Transfer meat to a carving board and cover with foil to keep hot.

☐ Make the sauce: place the stock, wine, leek, celery and parsley in another pan and cook over a moderate heat for 3 minutes. Add the juices from the meat and strain.

☐ Melt the butter in the frying-pan set over a moderate heat. Stir in the flour to make a smooth paste. Gradually stir in the strained liquid and cook for 5 minutes until thick.

☐ Add the vermouth and adjust the seasoning to taste. Just before serving, add grapes to the sauce and heat through gently for 1 minute.

☐ Carve meat as shown and serve with sauce spooned around.

Pork with Grape Sauce.

Tarragon Chicken with Garlic

There is no need to peel garlic when cooking it this way. Just crush the cloves flat with the blade of a large knife. Cooking garlic in butter gives a very subtle flavour to the chicken, and it is important to use *several* cloves to get the right taste.

Honey-glazed Poussin

Be sure to turn the bird frequently when cooking on the top of the stove, to ensure even cooking. Baste with the juices in the pan to help the poussin brown and give it a good flavour.

For more than one serving, just increase the ingredients by the number of guests you are feeding. Each poussin may be cooked separately or you can cook as many as will fit together into a larger casserole.

Bouquet garni

A classic flavouring for many soups, stocks and stews, the fragrant bundle is cooked in the liquid with the other ingredients and then discarded at the end of the cooking.

You can use other combinations of herbs, as available. Chervil is good in place of parsley, rosemary in place of thyme. Experiment with the herbs in your garden, but bay leaves and parsley are always a good foundation.

Make several bouquets garnis at a time to have them ready when you need them.

If you are going to strain a sauce at the end of cooking, you can put the herbs in loose.

Pot roasting poultry and game birds

Cooking in this way, with a little added butter and some seasoning herbs, makes poultry lusciously juicy, tender and flavoursome. The herbs flavour the flesh and also help make a delicious gravy.

Pot roasting is particularly effective for game birds which are less tender and lacking in fat and may be drier from lengthy hanging. Small birds can be cooked on top of the stove, but larger ones cook more evenly in the oven.

Tarragon Chicken with Garlic

Serves 3-4 ☆☆☆
Preparation: 5 minutes
Cooking: 1½ hours

2¼lb (1kg) oven-ready chicken
salt and freshly ground white pepper
3oz (75g) butter
8 large garlic cloves, crushed
a small spray of fresh tarragon or
 ¾ teaspoon dried tarragon
3 tablespoons brandy

Pre-heat oven to 350F (180C), gas 4.
☐ Pat chicken dry with kitchen paper and rub with salt and pepper.
☐ Heat the butter with unpeeled garlic in a 9in (23cm) oval flameproof dish over a low heat or until garlic is soft but not brown.

☐ Add the tarragon and place the chicken on top. Brush the bird all over with the buttery mixture. Loosely cover dish with foil, leaving open at one end.
☐ Cook in the oven for 1 hour, basting frequently.
☐ Remove the foil and cook for a further 30 minutes or until the chicken is well browned, basting occasionally. It is cooked when the juices run clear when a thigh is pierced with a skewer.
☐ Remove from the oven. Heat the brandy in a ladle and set alight. Pour, flaming, over the chicken.
☐ When the flames have died down transfer the chicken to a hot serving dish. Strain over the juices and serve.

Chicken Provençale

Serve with boiled small onions and potatoes. This dish is also excellent with ratatouille.

Serves 3-4 ☆☆☆
Preparation: 5 minutes
Cooking: 1½ hours

2¼lb (1kg) oven-ready chicken
salt and freshly ground black pepper
3oz (75g) butter
1 garlic clove, crushed
a sprig of fresh thyme
1 tablespoon chopped fennel leaves

The sauce:
¼ pint (150ml) dry white vermouth
2 egg yolks
1 tablespoon lemon juice

To make a bouquet garni: cut a 4in (10cm) square of clean muslin. Place 6 peppercorns, 1 bay leaf, a sprig of parsley and a sprig of thyme on it.

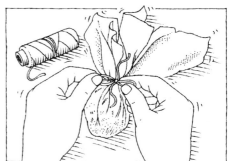

Draw up the four corners of the muslin square to enclose the contents securely. Hold firmly and tie into a bundle with cotton thread.

Prepare and cook the chicken with the butter, garlic and herbs as for Tarragon Chicken with Garlic. Transfer to a warmed serving dish and keep hot.

☐ To make the sauce: scrape all the juices from the casserole and pour into a small saucepan. Add the vermouth and boil for 3 minutes.

☐ In a small bowl, lightly beat together the egg yolks and lemon juice. Strain the hot liquid into the bowl, return to the saucepan and heat briefly until the sauce thickens. Adjust the seasoning, if necessary.

☐ Spoon the sauce over the chicken and serve.

Honey-glazed Poussin

Serve with sautéed potatoes and a green salad.

Serves 1   ☆☆☆
Preparation: 5 minutes
Cooking: 1½ hours

---

1 oven-ready poussin, about 1lb (500g)
salt and freshly ground black pepper
1oz (25g) butter
a sprig of fresh rosemary
a strip of lemon rind
1 teaspoon lemon juice
2 teaspoons clear honey
1 tablespoon Chicken Stock

Pat the chicken dry with kitchen paper and rub with salt and pepper.

☐ Melt the butter, in a 6in (15cm) flameproof casserole over a low heat. Add the rosemary and lemon rind and cook gently for 10 minutes.

☐ Remove lemon and rosemary from butter and place inside poussin. Put poussin in casserole, breast up.

☐ Mix together lemon juice, honey and stock. Spoon over poussin and cover.

☐ Cook for about 1½ hours, turning and basting frequently. When cooked, transfer to a warmed serving plate, cover and keep hot.

☐ Boil juices to reduce to 2 tablespoons. Strain over poussin and serve.

Preparing and cooking Honey-glazed Poussin.

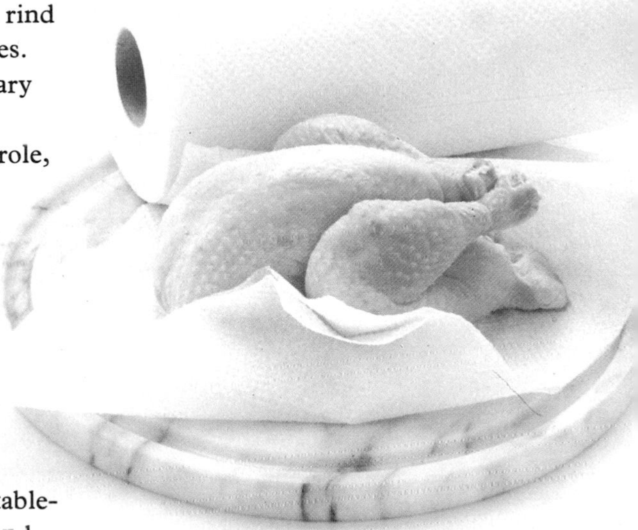

Pot Roast Pheasant

Pheasant is a rather dry bird, lacking fat, so it is better cooked in a basting liquid. This helps both to make it more tender and to give it a very good flavour. Serve the basting liquid as a sauce.

It is usual to cook a brace of pheasants at a time. Use a pan large enough to hold the two birds side by side and double the basting and sauce ingredients.

Pheasant carcasses make a superbly flavoured stock which can be used as a base for good game soups or stews.

Pot Roast Pheasant

Serve with creamed potatoes, Brussels sprouts and game chips.

Serves 3 ☆☆☆
Preparation: 10 minutes
Cooking: 1½ hours

1 oven-ready pheasant, about 2¼lb (1kg)
salt and freshly ground black pepper
a large sprig of thyme
2oz (50g) butter
2 streaky bacon rashers, rinds removed
    and chopped
1 small onion, chopped
3 tablespoons brandy
3 teaspoons tomato purée
¼ pint (150ml) Chicken Stock

The sauce:
2 tablespoons madeira
1oz (25g) cold butter, diced

Pre-heat the oven to 350F (180C), gas 4.

☐ Pat the pheasant with kitchen paper and rub with salt and pepper. Place the thyme inside the bird.

☐ Melt the butter in a 9in (23cm) oval flameproof dish over a low heat. Add bacon and onion and cook,

Pot Roast Pheasant in its madeira sauce.

stirring, for 10 minutes.

☐ Add the brandy, tomato purée and stock, increase heat to moderate and boil for 3 minutes.

☐ Place the pheasant in the pan and baste well with the juices. Loosely cover the pan with foil, leaving it open at one end.

☐ Cook in the oven for 1 hour, basting frequently.

☐ Remove the foil and cook for a further 25-30 minutes or until well browned, basting occasionally. Transfer the pheasant to a warmed serving dish and keep hot.

☐ Strain the juices into a small saucepan, add the madeira, and boil for 2 minutes. Beat or whisk the cold butter into the sauce, one piece at a time. Spoon over the pheasant and serve.

Braising and baking

Like pot roasting, braising is suitable for meat, fish, game and poultry. The food is often set on a bed of lightly cooked vegetables with a little added liquid, and cooked in a pot with a tightly fitting lid on gentle heat – either on top of the stove or in the oven. Food cooked this way is kept moist and succulent and gains added flavour from the vegetables and any other extras such as herbs, wine or stock. Suitable for large joints, smaller portions or chopped meat, the flavour can also be enhanced by marinating beforehand, or by previous browning.

The cooking in the oven of some savoury foods, mainly fish and vegetables, is commonly referred to as 'baking'. Such cooking often approximates closely to braising, as it is done in a closed container whenever the preservation of natural moisture is essential. Vegetables, however, are often cooked uncovered in order to drive off excess moisture and possibly brown them slightly.

Fish are frequently baked whole, often with a stuffing, but it is not uncommon to bake cutlets, steaks and fillets – also with the fillets wrapped around a stuffing. Vegetables can be chopped, shredded, or left whole, depending on the type.

Baking is one of the easiest ways of cooking as it requires little attention. The cooked food can also be served in the same dish that is used in the oven. Most important, several dishes can be baked at the same time, combining practicality with economy. Baking tenderizes food while keeping it succulent, and can impart an attractive, tasty, crisp brown surface. Longer slower cooking can also give flavours a chance to develop more fully, nor is the cooking liquid discarded, so it retains all the natural goodness and flavour.

Suitable utensils
Most casserole dishes and other oven-proof vessels lend themselves well to baking. Earthenware pots are best suited to long, slow cooking, while cast-iron and other metal utensils are better for cooking fish, which requires only a short cooking time. Toughened glassware has the right qualities for both and is commonly used for this type of cooking.

Choose a dish that is the right size for the food to be cooked. If the dish is too large, the amount of liquid cooks away more quickly. If you need a lid, but the dish doesn't have one, use foil.

Blanching
Most vegetables are better blanched before baking in the oven. Brief cooking in boiling water followed by 'refreshing', or thorough rinsing under cold running water, softens the tougher fibres and sets the colour. Blanching can also be done a little in advance.

Marinades
A mixture of spices and herbs in a small amount of liquid – usually stock, wine, lemon juice or vinegar – gives added piquancy to many baked vegetable and fish dishes. The foods can be left to soak up the flavour of the mixture before any actual baking and the juices are often also used later, thickened or reduced by rapid boiling, as a sauce.

✳ Freezing stocks and sauces
Whenever you make a stock or a sauce, freeze a little of it in a small container, such as a cream or cottage cheese carton. These thaw quickly and help you turn out baked dishes of distinction at short notice.

Vegetable water-content
Vegetable fruits such as tomatoes, aubergines and squashes have a high water content and produce a lot of their own liquid during cooking. When cooking these, remove lid or covering for at least the last 15 minutes of cooking time to allow some of the moisture to evaporate. Most other vegetables, however, require a little extra butter, oil or stock to prevent them drying out during cooking.

'Gratin' toppings
Toppings of breadcrumbs mixed with butter, grated cheese or perhaps a light sauté of garlic and breadcrumbs can be sprinkled over a baked dish and grilled just before serving to produce an attractive crispy golden gratin crust. Also try crushed potato crisps, cereal flakes or oatmeal. The gratin ingredients may also be sprinkled over the dish before it is put in the oven so it browns there. If you do this, turn up the oven heat for the last 5-10 minutes to brown the topping.

*Preparing Mousseline-stuffed
Baked Salmon.*

Mousseline-stuffed Baked Salmon

This exquisite dish makes an excellent dinner-party main course, served with baked potatoes and sautéed diced cucumber.

Serves 4
Preparation: 45 minutes
Cooking: about 30 minutes

---

4 pieces salmon fillet, each about 6oz (175g)
2 tablespoons lemon juice
6oz (175g) fillet of sole, haddock or whiting
1 egg white
4 tablespoons single cream
2 tablespoons chopped parsley
2 tablespoons chopped chives
2 tablespoons chopped onion
salt and freshly ground black pepper
about 1oz (25g) small spinach leaves
4oz (125g) unsalted, iced butter
5 tablespoons Fish Stock
3 tablespoons brandy

Skin the salmon fillets and slice into rectangular pieces about $\frac{1}{2}$ inch (1cm) thick, as shown.

☐ Rinse the fish in cold running water. Pat dry with kitchen paper, then brush with half the lemon juice.

☐ Set oven at 350F (180C), gas 4.

☐ Cut the white fish into small pieces. Process or liquidize to a fine, soft pulp. Add the egg white, cream, parsley, chives and onion and season generously with salt and pepper. Mix to a smooth cream.

☐ Wash and drain the spinach. Pat the salmon dry and rub with salt and pepper.

☐ Put a layer of spinach leaves over half of each slice of salmon. Spread the mousseline stuffing over the other half. Fold over and press the two halves together firmly and secure with wooden cocktail sticks.

☐ Grease a 9 inch (23cm) ovenproof dish with 1oz (25g) of the butter. Lay the stuffed salmon in the dish. Pour over the stock and the brandy and cover the dish.

☐ Cook in the oven for about 20 minutes. Transfer the salmon to a warmed serving dish and keep hot.

☐ Strain the cooking juices into a small saucepan. Add the remaining lemon juice. Boil vigorously for 5-7 minutes to reduce to about 3 tablespoons of liquid.

☐ Cut the remaining butter into 6 pieces. Beat in, one piece at a time, to make a lightly thickened sauce to serve separately.

Tip: For an extra touch of luxury fold 2oz (50g) cooked peeled prawns into the mousseline before stuffing the salmon.

Baked Whiting

Serve for an economical family supper, with mashed potatoes and garden peas.

Serves 4
Preparation: 20 minutes
Cooking: about 35 minutes

---

2 whiting, each about 1lb (500g), gutted
1 tablespoon lemon juice
1oz (25g) butter
6oz (175g) leeks, trimmed, washed and sliced
4oz (125g) mushrooms, wiped, trimmed and sliced
4oz (125g) green pepper, deseeded and sliced
salt and freshly ground black pepper
6 tablespoons dry white wine

Set the oven at 350F (180C), gas 4.

☐ Wash the fish in cold running water. Cut off the heads and tail fins. Pat dry with kitchen paper and brush the inside with lemon juice. Grease a 10 × 8in (25 × 20cm) ovenproof dish with some of the butter and scatter the vegetables over the bottom of the dish.

☐ Lay the fish on top of the vegetables. Season with salt and pepper, dot with the remaining butter and pour over the wine.

☐ Cover the dish and bake for about 30 minutes.

☐ To serve, cut off a side of a fish as a portion. Lift out the backbone and discard, then serve the two halves of the second fillet. Spoon some vegetables and juice over each fillet.

Mousseline-stuffed Baked Salmon
Centre cut of salmon makes the rectangular pieces illustrated, but a tail piece of salmon is more economical. Cut it into 4 fillets, then fill and fold these lengthways. Add any trimmings from the salmon to the mousseline.
Any mixture of available white fish may be used for this filling.

You will know when the salmon is properly cooked: the flesh becomes opaque, and oozes what is called 'cream'.

Baked Whiting
Whiting over-cooks very easily. Check it after about 25 minutes. When cooked, it will be opaque right through and the flesh will flake easily.

When stuffing thin fillets

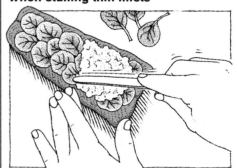

Spread spinach leaves across the whole piece and lay stuffing on top.

Carefully fold over and secure with wooden cocktail sticks.

Fennel Stuffed Baked Trout

If you're very careful in handling the stuffed fish, you may be able to do without any securing sticks. Just press the fish closely around the stuffing. If preferred, you can process or liquidize the garnishing red peppers with the cooking juices to make a thick sauce for the fish.

To tell when the fish is cooked: insert a skewer into the thickest part. When the fish is cooked through, the tip of the skewer will emerge hot to the back of the hand and the flesh will look white and opaque.

Stuffing the trout

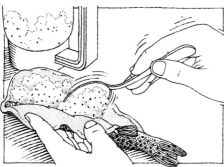

Spoon the stuffing into the cavities.

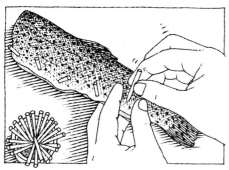

Secure the fish closed with wooden cocktail sticks.

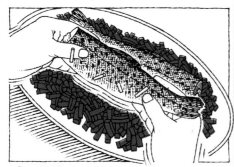

Carefully lay the stuffed fish on its bed of diced vegetables.

Fennel-stuffed Baked Trout

Serve with boiled new potatoes and braised chicory.

Serves 4 ☆☆

Preparation: 25 minutes

Cooking: about 50 minutes

---

4 whole trout, each about 9oz (250g), boned
1 tablespoon lemon juice
8oz (225g) whiting, haddock or lemon sole
1 egg white
6 tablespoons single cream
4 tablespoons finely chopped fresh fennel
2 tablespoons finely chopped onion
salt and freshly ground black pepper
2oz (50g) butter
2 large red peppers, deseeded and cut into strips
4 tablespoons Fish Stock

Wash the trout thoroughly in cold running water. Pat dry with kitchen paper.

☐ Remove the heads, if preferred, and brush the insides of the fish with lemon juice.

☐ Set oven at 350F (180C), gas 4.

☐ Cut the white fish into small pieces. Process or liquidize to a fine soft pulp. Add the egg white, cream, fennel, onion, and season well with salt and pepper. Mix well to a smooth cream.

☐ Stuff the prepared trout cavities with the fish mixture. Secure with wooden cocktail sticks.

☐ Line a 12 inch (30cm) square roasting tin with foil. Grease well with butter, put the peppers in the tin and spoon over the stock. Set the trout on top and dot with the remaining butter.

☐ Cover the tin with another piece of foil. Bake for 40 minutes. Uncover and cook for a further 5-10 minutes.

☐ Remove the cocktail sticks, set the fish carefully on a hot serving dish, garnish with the cooked strips of pepper and serve immediately.

Tip: For a memorable taste combination add 1 or 2 tablespoons of Pernod with the peppers and Fish Stock.

Scandinavian Stuffed Baked Mackerel

Serve with baked potatoes and a watercress salad.

Serves 4 ☆☆☆

Preparation: 20 minutes

Cooking: about 35 minutes

---

4 whole mackerel, each about 12oz (350g), boned
4oz (100g) fresh breadcrumbs
2oz (50g) butter
6 tablespoons finely chopped fresh dill
1oz (25g) finely chopped onion
6oz (175g) cucumber, peeled and diced
salt and freshly ground black pepper
vegetable oil, for greasing
5 fl oz (150ml) soured cream

Wash the mackerel thoroughly in cold running water and remove heads and tails.

☐ Set oven at 350F (180C), gas 4.

☐ Mix together the breadcrumbs, butter, 4 tablespoons of the dill, the onion and cucumber, and season well with salt and pepper. Divide this stuffing equally among the mackerel. Secure closed with wooden cocktail sticks.

☐ Cut 4 pieces of foil about 12 inches (30cm) square and brush well with oil.

☐ Lay a mackerel diagonally across each piece of foil and wrap it like a parcel. Set the foil parcels on a baking tray.

☐ Bake the fish for 25 minutes. Open up the foil and spoon the soured cream over the fish. Sprinkle with the remaining dill.

☐ Return the fish to the oven and cook for a further 10 minutes. Serve immediately, in the foil.

Variations: Oily fish like mackerel and red mullet lend themselves well to stuffing, particularly with items that help cut the oiliness. Try some of the following mixtures:
breadcrumbs, onion and puréed gooseberries;
chopped, blanched leaf spinach and mushrooms;
grated lemon rind, chopped onion and horseradish cream.

Lemon-baked Cod Tail

Serves 4   ☆☆

Preparation: 10 minutes
Cooking: 25-30 minutes

---

1 cod tail, about 2¼lb (1kg)
1 teaspoon salt
3oz (75g) butter
1oz (25g) dry breadcrumbs
2 tablespoons lemon juice
¼ pint (150ml) Fish Stock
a few sprigs of parsley, to garnish
1 lemon, sliced, to garnish

Set the oven at 400F (200C), gas 6.

☐ Wash the fish in cold running water and pat dry with kitchen paper. Trim off the tail so the fish fits into an oval ovenproof dish about 10 inches (25cm) long. Rub the fish well with salt.

☐ Put the butter in the dish and place in the oven to melt.

☐ Roll the piece of fish in the butter, then dip one side in the crumbs. Pat the crumbs on firmly with a palette knife. Lay the fish in the dish and sprinkle with any remaining crumbs.

☐ Pour the lemon juice and the stock into the dish around the cod.

☐ Bake for 25-30 minutes until well browned. Serve garnished with the parsley and slices of lemon.

☐ To serve, cut steaks by slicing downwards and cutting through backbone with strong scissors.

Lemon-baked Cod Tail, served straight from the dish, is delicious accompanied by potato and parsnip purée and braised beetroot.

Lemon-baked Cod Tail
Cod overcooks very quickly so test it after about 25 minutes, using the tip of a sharp knife. It should enter easily at the thickest part, and the flesh should be white and opaque.

To prepare decorative lemon slices as shown: use a cannelle knife to pare away strips of lemon skin at regular intervals, then cut the lemon in slices.

Beef Rolls

Serve with baked jacket potatoes and steamed baby carrots.

Serves 4 ☆☆☆
Preparation: 20 minutes
Cooking: 2-2¼ hours

1¾lb (800g) round steak
8 bacon rashers, rinds removed
1 tablespoon made mustard
salt and freshly ground black pepper
1oz (25g) butter
1 tablespoon oil
1 small onion, chopped
4 medium tomatoes, chopped
¼ pint (150ml) Meat Stock
¼ pint (150ml) red wine
a sprig of parsley, chopped, for garnish

Pre-heat the oven to 300F (150C) gas 2.
☐ Pat the meat dry with kitchen paper. Cut into 8 even-sized pieces and flatten each to about ⅛in (3mm).
☐ Stretch each rasher of bacon across with the back of a knife.
☐ Lay a strip of bacon on top of each piece of meat. Spread with mustard and season with salt and pepper. Roll up firmly and secure with wooden cocktail sticks.
☐ Melt the butter and oil in a medium frying-pan over a moderate heat. When the butter starts to brown, add half the meat rolls.
☐ Cook, turning frequently, for about 10 minutes or until browned all over. Transfer to a large ovenproof dish. Brown the remaining rolls and add to the dish.
☐ Add the onion and tomatoes to the frying-pan and cook gently, stirring, for 4-5 minutes until softened. Pour in the stock and wine and bring it to the boil. Spoon the mixture over the beef rolls. Tightly cover the pan and bake for 1¾-2 hours, or until the beef is tender.
☐ Lift out the rolls and discard the cocktail sticks. Arrange the rolls on warmed plates. Strain the sauce into a warmed sauceboat, pour a little over each plate and hand the rest separately. Sprinkle with the parsley and serve.

The various stages in preparing, cooking and serving Beef Rolls.

Braised Brisket of Beef

Serve this tasty, economical dish for family suppers, with potato croquettes and leeks sautéed with tomatoes. Alternatively, serve cold with a mixed salad. Use the gravy mixed with mayonnaise and horseradish as a dressing.

Serves 6-8 ☆☆☆
Preparation: 10 minutes
Cooking: 3½-4 hours

4lb (1.8kg) rolled brisket
salt and freshly ground black pepper
1oz (25g) dripping
1 large carrot, chopped
1 large leek, sliced
2 large garlic cloves, chopped
1 medium onion, chopped
1 stick celery, sliced
6 black peppercorns
6 whole cloves
1 teaspoon dried marjoram or thyme
1 bay leaf
¾ pint (450ml) red wine

Pat the meat dry with kitchen paper, and rub well all over with salt and pepper.

□ Heat the dripping in a deep flameproof casserole, about 6 pints (3.5 litres) capacity, until a faint haze shows. Cook the meat, turning, for 10-12 minutes until browned all over. Remove and set aside.

□ Add the vegetables and cook for 3-4 minutes, stirring, until lightly browned. Add the peppercorns, cloves and herbs. Set the meat on top and pour over the wine. Bring to the boil briefly then lower the heat to a minimum.

□ Cover the casserole and cook very gently for 3½-4 hours, or until tender.

□ Transfer the meat to a warmed serving dish. Skim off as much fat as possible from the pan juices, then strain them into a warmed sauceboat. Adjust the seasoning if necessary.

□ Serve the meat cut in thick slices.
Tip: For a more economical dish, substitute Meat or Basic Brown Stock for the wine.

Boeuf à la Mode

Serve this deliciously succulent classic French braised dish with Duchesse potatoes and glazed button onions.

Serves 6 ☆☆☆
Preparation: 15 minutes
Cooking: 2½ hours

2lb (1kg) clod or neck of beef
3 tablespoons flour
salt and freshly ground black pepper
2oz (50g) dripping
1 medium onion, sliced
1 large carrot, diced
6 black peppercorns
2 large sprigs of fresh thyme
2 sprigs of fresh savory
2 bay leaves
¾ pint (450ml) red wine
¼ pint (150ml) water

Pre-heat oven to 300F (150C) gas 2.
□ Cut the meat into 3in (7.5cm) squares. Pat dry with kitchen paper. Put the pieces into a plastic bag with the flour seasoned well with salt and pepper. Shake the bag to coat thoroughly.

□ Melt the dripping over a moderate heat in a deep flameproof casserole or roasting tin, about 8 × 12in (20 × 30cm) until a faint haze shows. Fry the slices of meat for 3-4 minutes on each side to brown them. Remove and set aside.

□ Add the onion and carrot and cook, stirring, for 3-4 minutes until lightly browned. Sprinkle over any remaining flour. Lay meat on top.

□ Sprinkle over the herbs, then pour in the wine and water. Cover and cook for about 2¼ hours, or until the meat is tender.

□ Arrange meat on a serving dish, strain pan juices, adjust seasoning and pour over meat.

❄ *To freeze:* place the meat and gravy in a shallow container, then cover, label and freeze.
To thaw, put the container into the refrigerator about 12 hours before required. Re-heat in an oven-proof dish, covered, for 20-25 minutes at 350F (180C) gas 4.

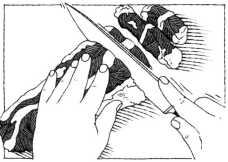

To cube beef: first cut into slices across the grain.

Then cut these pieces across into even-sized portions.

Braising meat
The tougher cuts of meat which lend themselves to braising generally require fairly long gentle cooking but little preparation or attention during cooking. Braising in the oven ensures more even cooking than on a hot plate and takes about the same time. Dishes which have flour thickening in them may need to be stirred occasionally if cooked on top of the stove. If sauces are thicker than you like, stir in a little wine or stock then re-heat just before serving.
Cooking time will vary depending on the thickness and cut of the meat. For example, neck of beef will take longer than chuck steak.

Braised Brisket of Beef
Brisket is a good meat to serve cold so it's worthwhile to cook more than you require to serve for the first meal.

Spare Ribs with Green Cabbage

Spare Ribs with Green Cabbage

When you're buying spare ribs for this dish, look for flat slabs of rib bones with a thin covering of meat. Some shops sell the ribs ready cut apart, if not the butcher will cut them for you.

Spare ribs really need to be picked up by the fingers for eating so be sure to provide finger bowls and napkins as well as a fork for the cabbage.

Spare Ribs with Green Cabbage

An economical and substantial supper dish, serve this with mashed potatoes and cauliflower cheese.

Serves 6   ☆☆☆
Preparation and cooking: 65 minutes

4lb (1.8kg) pork spare ribs
6 tablespoons oil
2 medium onions, chopped
1 garlic clove, finely chopped
1 small green cabbage, shredded
¼ pint (150ml) dry white wine
salt and freshly ground black pepper

Pat ribs dry with kitchen paper.
☐ Heat the oil in a deep 9in (23cm) frying-pan over moderate heat until a faint haze shows.
☐ Fry half the ribs, turning frequently, for about 7 minutes or until well browned. Remove and set aside.
☐ Repeat with the rest of the ribs.
☐ Lower the heat. Add the onions and garlic and cook, stirring, until softened but not brown. Stir in the cabbage and wine, then season well.
☐ Return the spare ribs to the pan and mix with the cabbage. Cover the pan and simmer for 30 minutes, or until the meat is tender. Adjust seasoning, and serve.

Pork Chops in Cider

Serve with rice, sliced kohlrabi and apple cooked in cream.

Serves 4   ☆☆☆
Preparation: 10 minutes
Cooking: 30 minutes

4 pork chops, each about 6oz (175g)
1oz (25g) lard
2 small onions, finely chopped
2 medium cooking apples, sliced
½ teaspoon dried sage
salt and freshly ground black pepper
9 fl oz (275ml) cider

Pat chops dry with kitchen paper.
☐ Melt the lard in a medium frying-pan over a moderate heat. When a faint haze shows fry the chops for about 5 minutes on each side until browned, then remove and set aside.
☐ Add the onion, apples and sage to the pan. Season to taste, then cook, stirring, for 2-3 minutes. Pour in the cider and bring it to the boil.
☐ Return the chops to the pan and reduce the heat. Simmer for about 15 minutes or until tender and season, if necessary. Transfer chops to a warm serving dish and strain sauce over.
Tip: Try adding 1 tablespoon Calvados or brandy with the cider for a richer flavour.

Veal Chops in Tomato Sauce

A rich casserole of succulent veal, braised in a tomato and wine sauce. Serve with some pasta and blanched spinach.

Serves 4

Preparation: 15 minutes
Cooking: 20 minutes

4 veal chops, each about
   6oz (175g)
2 tablespoons flour
salt and freshly ground black pepper
3 tablespoons olive oil
2 garlic cloves, crushed
1 bay leaf
1 teaspoon dried oregano
¼ pint (150ml) red wine
5 medium tomatoes, chopped
1 tablespoon tomato purée

The garnish:
2 tomatoes, skinned and diced
1 tablespoon chopped parsley

Pat the chops dry with kitchen paper. On a plate, season the flour with salt and pepper and coat the chops well with it.

☐ Heat the oil into a 9in (23cm) frying-pan over a moderate heat until a faint haze shows. Fry the chops for 3-4 minutes on each side until brown.

☐ Sprinkle any remaining flour over then add garlic, herbs, wine, tomatoes and season well with salt and pepper. Cover the pan and reduce the heat.

☐ Simmer for about 15 minutes, or until the meat is tender. Remove and keep hot.

☐ Stir in the tomato purée, bring the sauce to the boil and cook it for 5 minutes. Strain it, then return the sauce to the pan.

☐ Add the chops and the diced tomato garnish, cover and simmer for 5 minutes.

☐ Put the meat and sauce into a serving dish or serve from the casserole, garnished with parsley.

Tip: This dish is also excellent using pork steaks, but cook them for at least 30 minutes.

Veal or Pork Chops with Leeks

Serves 4 ☆☆☆

Preparation: 10 minutes
Cooking: 20 minutes

4 veal or pork chops, each about 6oz (175g)
1oz (25g) butter
2 large garlic cloves, crushed
3 small leeks, sliced
½ teaspoon dried rosemary
3 fl oz (100ml) dry white wine
salt and freshly ground black pepper

Pat chops dry with kitchen paper.

☐ Melt butter in a 9in (23cm) frying-pan over a low heat. Add garlic and fry for 10 minutes, without browning, then discard garlic.

☐ Increase the heat to moderate. When the butter begins to brown, add the chops. Fry for about 3 minutes on each side, until brown. Remove chops and reduce heat.

☐ Add the leeks, rosemary, and wine and season to taste. Put the chops on top, cover the pan and cook gently for about 15 minutes, for veal or 30 minutes for pork.

☐ Arrange chops on a bed of leeks on a hot serving dish. Boil the pan juices for 1 minute, then spoon over meat and serve.

Veal Chops in Tomato Sauce

There is no need to skin tomatoes if you're going to sieve them.

For a garnish: cut a cross on the bottom of the tomatoes then drop them into a pan of boiling water for about 15 seconds. Remove and run cold water over the tomatoes until they're cool. You will then be able to strip the skins back easily.

Veal Chops in Tomato Sauce

Serve Rabbit with Prunes accompanied by a buttery potato and parsnip purée and sautéed courgettes.

Rabbit with Prunes

Rabbit with Prunes

The flavour of prunes marries well with that of rabbit.

The sauce will vary in consistency depending on how juicy the fruit is. If you find your sauce a little too thick, add more wine at the end.

❄ **To freeze** Put the rabbit and the sauce in separate containers, cover, label and freeze. To thaw, place in the refrigerator 24 hours before required. Mix the sauce well until smooth. Put the rabbit into a casserole and pour the sauce over. Cover and re-heat for 20-25 minutes in an oven pre-heated to 350F (180C) gas 4.

Serves 4   ☆☆☆
Preparation: 5 minutes plus soaking
Cooking: 1¼ hours

½lb (225g) prunes
¾ pint (450ml) dry white wine
¼ pint (150ml) water
1 rabbit, about 2¼lb (1kg), cut into
    8 pieces
3 tablespoons flour
salt and freshly ground black pepper
2oz (50g) butter
1 small onion, chopped
1 bay leaf
2 sprigs of fresh thyme
¼ pint (150ml) single cream

Soak the prunes in the wine and water for at least 8 hours.
☐ Heat oven to 350F (180C) gas 4.
☐ Pat the rabbit pieces dry with kitchen paper, then place them in a large plastic bag along with the flour seasoned well with salt and pepper.

Shake to coat well.
☐ Melt the butter in a 9in (23cm) frying-pan over a moderate heat. When the butter begins to brown, fry the rabbit, turning, for about 10 minutes until evenly browned. Transfer to a deep ovenproof casserole.
☐ Fry the onion for 2-3 minutes until soft. Add the prunes, their liquid and the herbs. Simmer 10 minutes.
☐ Spoon the juices over the rabbit. Cover and cook in the oven for about 45 minutes, or until tender.
☐ Transfer rabbit and about half prunes to a serving dish, keep hot.
☐ Stone remaining prunes and liquidize with the strained cooking juices. Strain them into a saucepan, add the cream and heat through gently. Adjust seasoning, if necessary, spoon a little sauce over rabbit and serve rest separately.

Turkey in Sherry Sauce

Serve with croquette potatoes and sautéed courgettes.

Serves 4 ☆☆☆
Preparation: 15 minutes
Cooking: 30 minutes

---

4 boned turkey joints, each about 9oz (250g)
2 tablespoons flour
salt and freshly ground black pepper
2oz (50g) butter
1 medium onion, cut in half and sliced
3 medium tomatoes, chopped
1 large carrot, cut into julienne strips
1 medium leek, trimmed, halved and sliced
¼ pint (150ml) Chicken Stock
4 tablespoons sherry
2 tablespoons single cream
2 tablespoons tomato purée
1 tablespoon lemon juice
1 spring onion, finely chopped, for garnish

Pat the turkey pieces dry with kitchen paper. Put in a plastic bag with the flour, seasoned generously with salt and pepper. Shake to coat the turkey well.

☐ Melt the butter in a deep 9in (23cm) frying-pan over a moderate heat. As soon as the butter begins to brown, fry the turkey, turning, for about 5 minutes or until well browned. Remove the turkey and set aside. Add all the vegetables, sprinkle over any remaining flour, then stir in the stock and sherry.

☐ Return the turkey to the pan. Cover and cook gently for about 25 minutes, or until tender.

☐ Transfer the turkey to a warmed serving dish and keep hot.

☐ Add cream and tomato purée, stirring constantly until at boiling point. Adjust the flavour with lemon juice, salt and pepper. Slice the joints across as shown, spoon the sauce around them, sprinkle with the spring onion and serve.

Tip: Try adding 1 or 2 tablespoons of chestnut purée with the cream for a particularly rich sauce. If it is unsweetened you may also have to add a pinch of sugar.

❄ **Freezing** Put the sauce into a plastic container with a lid. Cool, then freeze. Wrap the cooled turkey joints in foil and freeze.

To thaw and re-heat, place the sauce and the parcel of turkey in the refrigerator at least 12 hours in advance. Put the sauce in an ovenproof dish, stir well and cover. Heat the turkey and the sauce in the oven at 350F (180C) gas 4 for about 20 minutes, until very hot.

Turkey in Sherry Sauce
This recipe works equally well with ordinary chicken joints.
Madeira and port sauces can be made in exactly the same way, substituting the respective fortified wines for the sherry. Both are excellent with poultry and game.

Preparing and serving Turkey in Sherry Sauce.

Step-by-step to Potato and Bacon Gratin.

Potato and Bacon Gratin

Serves 4   ★★☆

Preparation: 15 minutes

Cooking: 35 minutes

1¼lb (700g) potatoes, par-boiled

1oz (25g) butter

4 garlic cloves, crushed

6oz (175g) grated Cheddar or Gruyère
   cheese (optional)

salt and freshly ground black pepper

6oz (175g) belly pork or fat bacon, rind
   removed and cut into strips

½ pint (300ml) single cream

½ teaspoon paprika

Set the oven at 350F (180C), gas 4.

☐ Slice the potatoes and grease a 3
pint (1.75 litre) ovenproof dish with
the butter. Use half the potatoes to
make a layer of overlapping slices in
the bottom of the dish. Sprinkle

over half the garlic and cheese (if
using), and then season with salt and
pepper. Make another similar layer.

☐ In a frying-pan over a low heat,
cook the pork or bacon rind gently
to melt its fat. Discard the rind,
increase the heat to moderate and
fry the pork or bacon strips gently,
turning frequently, for 2-3 minutes,
without browning.

☐ Sprinkle the cooked pork or
bacon over the potatoes.

☐ Mix together the cream and
paprika and pour it over the potato
mixture. Cover and bake for 20
minutes, or until tender.

☐ Meanwhile, set the grill to high.

☐ Place the dish under the grill for
3-4 minutes to brown the top.

Stuffed Baked Potatoes

Serves 4   ☆

Preparation: 10 minutes

Cooking: 50 minutes

---

4 large potatoes, each about 8oz (225g)

3 fl oz (100ml) soured cream

1 teaspoon dried thyme

salt and freshly ground black pepper

2 tablespoons finely chopped chives

Set the oven at 350F (180C), gas 4.
□ Scrub the potatoes well. Pat them dry with kitchen paper and prick with a fork in 2 or 3 places.
□ Set them on a heated baking tray and bake in the oven for about 45 minutes, or until tender.
□ Cut the potatoes in half lengthways and scoop out the flesh. Mash this well and mix in the cream, thyme and salt and pepper to taste.
□ Spoon stuffing back into skins and sprinkle with the chives. Re-heat for 5 minutes, then serve.
Tip: This versatile side dish goes well with grilled or fried meat or fish and also makes a filling lunch or supper served with a mixed salad.

Baked Salsify

A refreshing accompaniment to roast or casseroled chicken or veal.

Serves 4
Preparation: 15 minutes
Cooking: 30 minutes

1¼lb (600g) salsify
salt and freshly ground black pepper
grated rind and juice of ½ a small lemon
2 tablespoons dry white wine
1oz (25g) cold butter, cubed
1 tablespoon chopped parsley
1 tablespoon chopped chives

Set the oven at 350F (180C), gas 4.
□ Scrub the salsify under cold running water to remove all traces of sand, then blanch it in boiling salted water for 3 minutes. Drain then rinse under cold running water.
□ Trim off the tops and tails, then scrape off the skin. Cut it into pieces approximately 2 inches (5cm) long and place in an ovenproof dish.
□ Sprinkle lightly with salt and pepper and the grated lemon rind. Spoon over the lemon juice and wine, then dot with the butter.
□ Cover the dish and bake for about 25 minutes or until the salsify is tender.
□ Sprinkle over the parsley and chives and serve.

Baked Beetroot

This dish is particularly suitable for serving with grilled or baked ham, and game dishes.

Serves 4 ☆
Preparation: 10 minutes
Cooking: 45 minutes

1½lb (700g) beetroot, boiled
1oz (25g) butter
salt and freshly ground black pepper
2 tablespoons Chicken or Veal Stock
4 tablespoons dry breadcrumbs
2oz (50g) grated Cheddar cheese

Set the oven at 350F (180C), gas 4.
□ Peel the beetroot and cut it into ¼ inch (5mm) slices. Grease a shallow ovenproof dish with a little of the butter and layer the beetroot in overlapping slices. Season lightly with salt but generously with pepper, then spoon over the stock.
□ Mix the breadcrumbs and cheese, then rub in remaining butter and sprinkle this over the beets.
□ Cover and bake for 30 minutes. Remove the lid and continue cooking for another 15 minutes, or until browned.

Curried Parsnips

Serves 4 ☆ ☆
Preparation: 10 minutes
Cooking: 20 minutes

2oz (50g) butter
1½lb (700g) parsnips, peeled and sliced
salt and freshly ground black pepper
½ teaspoon curry powder

Set the oven at 350F (180C), gas 4.
□ Melt the butter in a 1¾ pint (1 litre) shallow ovenproof dish.
□ Blanch the parsnips in boiling, salted water for 3 minutes, then drain and pat dry.
□ Put the parsnips in the dish and season with salt, pepper and curry powder. Turn to coat them in the butter. Bake in the oven for 5 minutes. Baste, then bake for a further 10 minutes, until tender.

Boiling beetroot
Scrub them well in cold running water. Cook in a large pan of boiling water for 45-50 minutes, or until the skins rub off easily when forked. Drain and allow to cool before pulling off the skins.
The cooking water makes an excellent soup base.
For convenience, cook, peel and slice the beets up to a day in advance of baking, and store, covered, in the refrigerator.
Small beetroot are more tender than large ones.

Baked Salsify
Add 2 tablespoons lemon juice to the blanching water to keep the salsify white.

Preparing salsify

Scrub the salsify well under cold running water to remove all sand.

Cook in a deep pan of boiling salted water for 3 minutes. Drain and rinse.

Scrape off the skins when cool.

Ratatouille

Serve it with grilled meats or sausages, or make it into an even more substantial supper dish by covering the top with a thick layer of grated cheese before baking.

To prepare runner beans

First wash in cold running water, top and tail and pull off side strings.

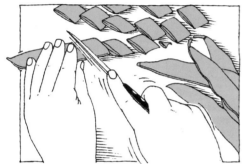

Cut diagonally for greater appeal.

There are several kinds of dried beans which are suitable for oven-baking. It is important to allow ample cooking time because it is almost impossible to tell how long different kinds will take to cook. Length of cooking time depends on type and age of beans, and on how long they have been stored prior to purchase.

Boston Baked Beans

This method of cooking dried beans avoids lengthy soaking and makes the beans less 'gassy'. If it is more convenient, however, simply soak them overnight and omit the first boiling and soaking.

Ratatouille

This classic dish, from Provence in the South of France, needs only French bread as an accompaniment to make an excellent first course or snack. Alternatively serve as a side-dish with roast chicken or lamb.

Serves 6   ☆☆
Preparation: 45 minutes
Cooking: about 1 hour

---

1 medium aubergine, about ¾lb (350g), trimmed
salt for dégorging (removing bitter juices)
3 fl oz (100ml) olive oil
3 medium onions, thinly sliced
6 large garlic cloves, crushed
4 small courgettes, trimmed and sliced
1 large green pepper, deseeded and sliced
1 large red pepper, deseeded and sliced
salt and freshly ground black pepper
2 tablespoons chopped parsley
3 tablespoons of fresh basil chopped, or
    3 teaspoons dried basil
4 medium tomatoes, skinned and sliced

Set the oven at 350F (180C), gas 4.
☐ Cut the aubergine into 1 inch (2.5cm) cubes and put them in a colander. Sprinkle with plenty of salt and leave to dégorge for 30 minutes. Rinse well under cold running water, drain and pat dry with kitchen paper.
☐ Meanwhile, heat the oil in a 9 inch (23cm) frying-pan over low heat. Add the onion and garlic and fry, stirring occasionally, for about 15 minutes or until soft but not brown.
☐ Place the aubergine, courgettes, onion, garlic and peppers in layers in a shallow 5 pint (2.75 litre) ovenproof dish, sprinkling each layer with salt, pepper, parsley and basil.
☐ Place the tomatoes over the top and pour over any remaining oil from the frying-pan.
☐ Cover the dish and bake for about 45 minutes or until the vegetables are just tender. Adjust the seasoning, and serve.
Tip: If the vegetables produce a lot of liquid, cook uncovered for the last 15 minutes.

Runner Beans with Tomatoes

Serve with baked fish or beef casserole.

Serves 4   ☆
Preparation: 10 minutes
Cooking: about 30 minutes

¾lb (350g) runner beans, trimmed
salt and freshly ground black pepper
2 tablespoons olive oil
1lb (500g) tomatoes, skinned and sliced
1 teaspoon dried oregano

Set the oven at 350F (180C), gas 4.
☐ Cook the beans in a large pan of boiling, salted water for 3 minutes. Drain and rinse thoroughly under cold running water.
☐ Brush the inside of an 8½ × 6in (21 × 15cm) ovenproof dish with oil. Put half of the tomatoes in the bottom of the dish. Cover with the beans then sprinkle with the oregano and a little salt and pepper. Finish with a layer of the remaining tomatoes and pour over the rest of the oil.
☐ Cover the dish and cook in the oven for about 25 minutes or until the beans are tender.

Boston Baked Beans

This substantial dish is traditionally served with dark brown bread but it is also delicious with baked potatoes or tomatoes, and a salad.

Serves 4   ☆☆☆
Preparation: 10 minutes plus soaking time
Cooking: 3½ hours

1lb (500g) dried haricot beans
1lb (500g) salt belly pork or streaky bacon,
    rind removed and cut into cubes
8oz (225g) onions, chopped
2 teaspoons mustard powder
3oz (75g) molasses or soft brown sugar
½ pint (300ml) water
freshly ground black pepper

Put the beans in a large saucepan and cover with cold water. Cover the pan and bring it to the boil.

Turn off the heat and leave for 1 hour, then drain and rinse the beans under cold running water.

☐ Return the beans to the saucepan with enough cold water to cover. Bring it to the boil, skimming off any foam, then cover. Simmer for 1½-2 hours until all the water is absorbed, or the skins begin to burst.

☐ Twenty minutes before the beans are done, heat the oven to 325F (160C), gas 3.

☐ Rinse the pork or bacon under cold running water, drain and pat dry with kitchen paper. Put half the beans in a casserole dish followed by half the onion and half the pork or bacon. Repeat the layers.

☐ Mix together the mustard, molasses or sugar and water and season well with pepper. Pour over the beans. Cover the dish and bake in the oven for about 1½ hours or until the beans are tender. Add a little more water towards the end of cooking, if necessary.

☐ Adjust the seasoning and serve.

Gratin of Lettuce

An unusual and surprisingly tasty vegetable accompaniment.

Serves 4   ☆☆☆
Preparation: 15 minutes
Cooking: about 25 minutes

---

1 large head of round lettuce
4oz (100g) butter
3 onions, thinly sliced
a sprig of fresh thyme, crushed
salt and freshly ground black pepper
4 tablespoons fresh breadcrumbs

Set the oven at 400F (200C) gas 6.

☐ Remove any brown or damaged leaves from the lettuce. Wash it well under cold running water, then drain. Cut into 1 inch (2.5cm) slices.

☐ Blanch the lettuce in a large pan of boiling salted water for 1 minute. Drain, then rinse well under cold running water. Drain thoroughly.

☐ Melt half the butter in an 8 inch (20cm) frying-pan over a moderate heat until it begins to brown. Add the onions and fry, stirring frequently, for 3-4 minutes, or until soft and lightly browned.

☐ Put half the cooked onions in a ¾ pint (450ml) ovenproof dish. Sprinkle over the thyme then layer the lettuce on top, cover with the remaining onions and season lightly.

☐ Sprinkle the breadcrumbs over and dot with the remaining butter. Bake in the oven for 20 minutes until lightly browned.

Stuffed Chicory

This goes well with gammon, chicken or turkey.

Serves 4   ☆☆
Preparation: 15 minutes
Cooking: about 30 minutes

---

4 large heads chicory, about ¾lb (350g) in total
2 tablespoons chopped parsley
1 tablespoon chopped capers
2 garlic cloves, finely chopped
4oz (100g) grated Cheddar cheese
2oz (50g) soft cheese
salt and freshly ground black pepper
4 teaspoons olive oil
4 teaspoons lemon juice

Set the oven at 350F (180C), gas 4.

☐ Wash the chicory, cut off base and carefully ease out leaves to open up.

☐ Mix together the parsley, capers, garlic and cheeses and season with salt and pepper. Form them into 4 equal-sized rolls. Press one roll into the centre of each head of chicory then re-shape the leaves around it and secure with string.

☐ Place the stuffed chicory in an ovenproof dish, season lightly with salt and pepper and spoon over the oil and lemon juice.

☐ Tightly cover the dish and bake in the oven for 25-30 minutes.

Step-by-step to Gratin of Lettuce.

Freezing cream sauce

You can make the cream sauce in advance and store it in the refrigerator for a day, or in the freezer for up to 2 months. Thaw by immersing the container in warm water for 30 minutes. Stir the sauce before use.

Baked Celery in Cream

This rich dish goes well with simple omelettes, steamed fish and grilled ham steaks. Serve straight from the dish or transfer to a warmed serving dish before adding the sauce.

Remember: When serving from cooking dishes, wipe around the sides with a clean damp cloth for neater presentation.

Marinated Fennel

Serve hot with roast lamb or baked fish. Alternatively, let the fennel cool in the marinade and serve cold as an hors d'oeuvre. For extra flavour, let the cut bulbs of fennel sit in the simmered marinade for an hour or two before baking.

Baked Celery in Cream

Baked Celery in Cream

Serves 4

Preparation and cooking: 45 minutes

---

1 large head of celery, trimmed
salt
1oz (25g) butter
1oz (25g) onion, finely chopped
2 tablespoons flour
9 fl oz (250ml) single cream
5 fl oz (150ml) milk
¼ teaspoon ground mace
2 tomatoes, skinned and diced, for garnish

Set the oven at 350F (180C), gas 4.
☐ Blanch the celery in boiling, salted water for 3 minutes. Drain, then rinse well under cold running water.
☐ Put the celery in a 2 pint (1 litre) ovenproof dish, cover and bake for about 20 minutes until tender.
☐ Meanwhile, melt the butter in a saucepan and cook the onion gently until soft but not brown. Stir in the flour and cook for 1-2 minutes. Gradually stir in the cream and milk. Bring to the boil, whisking constantly. Reduce heat and season with mace and salt.
☐ Spoon over celery, garnish and serve.

Marinated Fennel

Serves 4

Preparation: 10 minutes
Cooking: about 35 minutes

---

2 tablespoons olive oil
4 tablespoons Chicken Stock
1 tablespoon lemon juice
½ teaspoon salt
¼ teaspoon coriander seeds, crushed
¼ teaspoon green peppercorns
1 tablespoon chopped parsley
4 fennel bulbs, about 1¼lb (600g), trimmed

Set the oven at 350F (180C), gas 4.
☐ Put all the ingredients except the fennel in a saucepan and simmer gently for 3 minutes.
☐ Cut fennel bulbs vertically and place cut-side down in an ovenproof dish. Pour over marinade, cover and bake for about 35 minutes.

Casseroles and stews

Slow stewing in the oven can be among the most rewarding of techniques for the creative cook. Like braising, it is better for tougher cuts of meat, poultry and game, and some fish and vegetables also benefit from prolonged cooking at a fairly low temperature. However, more liquid is used and the principal ingredients are often almost totally immersed. This allows the cook to add secondary flavouring ingredients such as vegetables, herbs, spices – or even fruit. The cooking medium itself plays a part in the final flavour and stock, wine, cider, beer, milk or cream can all be used. In some recipes the food may be browned first for added colour and taste and most stews can also be cooked entirely on top of the stove, though the oven does provide the best means of ensuring the steady low temperatures required.

Many regard 'stews' as humble cooking, and the term for the French oven dish, 'casserole', has increasingly been adopted in its stead to give greater respectability. Whether a 'stew' or a 'casserole', such dishes provide an unequalled means of blending different foods and flavours in an economical way, to produce results that are not just elegant but impressive. They are also perfect for entertaining, as most of the cooking proceeds unattended in the oven. Similarly, a casserole or stew makes the perfect one-pot meal for the busy household.

Stewing: the composite technique.

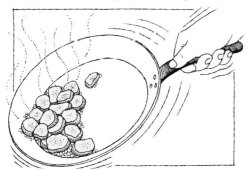

First, coat any meat or poultry in seasoned flour and sauté lightly.

Put in ingredients that take longer to cook. Add liquid. Cover closely.

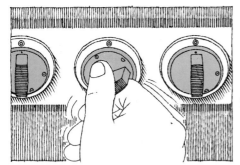

Long, slow cooking at low temperatures is always best.

Cook fish in a shallow roasting tin. Cover with foil.

Stewing step by step:
● Choose a deep ovenproof dish large enough to take all the ingredients comfortably. Too large, and the food may dry out; too small and the food will not cook evenly.
● Choose a deep flameproof dish if you are browning any ingredient first on top of the stove, or cooking the whole stew on top of the stove.
● Put out the ingredients in cooking order: those that take the longest, first.
● For meat or poultry stews, there will be time to prepare vegetables while the meat is cooking. For fish stews, prepare and almost cook the vegetables before adding the fish.
● If necessary, brown the principal ingredients by sautéing them briefly first. Coating them in seasoned flour helps to thicken the finished dish.
● Place the main ingredients in the dish. Pour over cooking liquid to cover. Add herbs and seasonings and cover tightly.
● Later, when the tougher ingredients are partially cooked, add any vegetables and adjust seasoning.
● 15 minutes before the end of cooking, add any ingredients, such as mushrooms or spinach, which would lose texture if slightly overcooked.
● At this stage, check if any fat needs to be skimmed off, then add any thickening agent required, such as cornflour mixed with water, beurre manié (kneaded butter) or an egg and cream liaison.

Choosing the dish
Most deep ovenproof dishes will do, but the traditional casserole, made of cast iron or earthenware, takes up and distributes the heat to its contents in the most effective way. It is also better if the dish has a close-fitting lid to seal in all moisture and encourage the circulation of condensed cooking juices back into the dish.

Re-heating casseroles and stews
Many stews, particularly those containing alcohol of some kind, are even better if allowed to cool and then re-heated. Stewing is a perfect means of 'réchauffage', that is the French term for making the most of leftovers or pre-cooked meats. A turkey fricassee made from cold roast turkey is a perfect example.

Haddock Chowder

Cut a small French bread stick into thick slices. Spread these with butter, then with a little garlic purée and top with grated Cheddar cheese. Bake with the chowder for the last 10 minutes. Serve each portion topped with slices of the hot bread.

Corn on the cob

Fresh corn has the best flavour and the starch in it absorbs a little of the sauce. When fresh corn is not available, use about ¾lb (350g) frozen kernels.

✳ Freezing fish dishes

Arrange these in shallow containers so they can be re-heated evenly without breaking up the fish. Choose firm fish which will hold its shape – sole, turbot and monkfish are good examples. Fish which flakes easily, like haddock and cod, is better frozen cooked and flaked in a sauce.
This may need thickening with a little arrowroot after freezing. Add egg and cream liaisons when re-heating the dish, and not before freezing.

Fish stews

These are quick to cook and delicious when re-heated from frozen (see sidelines). Use firm-fleshed white fish, a mixture of white and oily, or smoked fish. Fish 'stews' vary from chowders (see below) to baked dishes with whole fillets or steaks, served with a sauce made from the cooking juices.

Haddock Chowder

A chowder is a North American thick soup – a cross between a soup and a stew. This makes a good supper dish served with crisp rolls.

Serves 4   ☆
Preparation: 20 minutes
Cooking: 1½ hours

---

2 medium potatoes, peeled and diced
1 small carrot, sliced
1 celery stick, sliced
1 medium onion, coarsely chopped
½ pint (300ml) boiling water
1 teaspoon salt
1 bay leaf
a handful of parsley sprigs
1 teaspoon dill seeds
6 black peppercorns
6 whole cloves
1lb (500g) haddock fillets, skinned
2 corn-on-the-cob, fresh or frozen
½ pint (300ml) milk
2 tablespoons chopped chives

Set the oven to 300F (150C) gas 2.
☐ Put the potato, carrot, celery and onion into a 3½ pint (2 litre) casserole. Add the water and salt.
☐ Gather the bay, parsley, dill seeds, peppercorns and cloves into a small bundle in a piece of clean muslin. Tie securely with thread. Add to the casserole and cook for about 45 minutes, until the vegetables are soft.
☐ Meanwhile, rinse the fish in cold running water and cut into squares. Slice the kernels from the corn.
☐ Add the milk, fish and corn to the casserole. Re-cover and cook for 45 minutes.
☐ Serve sprinkled with chives.

Matelote Bourguignonne

These classic French fish stews vary from region to region. This version from Burgundy makes clear that fish and red wine can make a good marriage. Serve with croûtons.

Serves 4   ☆ ☆
Preparation: 10 minutes plus 1 hour marinating
Cooking: 45-50 minutes

2¼lb (1kg) freshwater fish fillets such as perch, carp, bream, pike, trout or eel, skinned
salt and freshly ground black pepper
3 tablespoons brandy
¾ pint (450ml) red wine
1 large onion, sliced
1 carrot, sliced
2 garlic cloves, finely chopped
2 or 3 sprigs of parsley
1 bay leaf
a sprig of fresh thyme or ½ teaspoon dried thyme
16 button onions, blanched and peeled
8oz (225g) button mushrooms, wiped and trimmed
2oz (50g) butter
2 tablespoons flour

Rinse the fish under cold running water and pat dry. Cut into bite-sized pieces, place in a shallow bowl, season and pour over the brandy. Marinate in the refrigerator for at least 1 hour.
☐ Set oven to 350F (180C) gas 4.
☐ Put the wine with the onion, carrot, garlic, parsley, bay leaf and thyme in a deep oven dish. Cover and cook in the oven for 30 minutes until vegetables are tender.
☐ Add the fish with the brandy and return to the oven for another 10-15 minutes until the flesh is beginning to flake.
☐ Add the blanched onions and all but one or two of the button mushrooms and beurre manié made by kneading the flour and butter together. Stir gently and return to the oven for 5 minutes until the sauce is thick and smooth.
☐ Slice the reserved button mushrooms very thinly and use to garnish the finished dish.

Cod with Mushrooms in Lemon Sauce

Serves 4   ☆☆
Preparation: 15 minutes
Cooking: 25 minutes

1¼lb (700g) cod fillet in thick pieces, skinned
salt and freshly ground pepper
2 tablespoons flour
2oz (50g) butter
1 large garlic clove, peeled and crushed or
    finely chopped
½ pint (300ml) milk
8oz (225g) button mushrooms, wiped and
    trimmed
2 egg yolks
1 teaspoon grated lemon rind
a squeeze of lemon juice, or to taste
1 hard-boiled egg, sliced

Set the oven to 350F (180C) gas 4. Rinse the fish and pat dry with kitchen paper. Dust both sides with salt, pepper and a little of the flour.

☐ Grease the inside of a shallow oval ovenproof dish with some of the butter. Sprinkle the garlic in the dish and arrange the fish on top.

☐ Pour the milk over the fish. Cover the dish with foil and cook for 15-20 minutes, until the flesh flakes easily.

☐ Drain off and reserve as much of the cooking liquid as possible. Keep the fish hot in its dish.

☐ While the fish is cooking, melt the remaining butter in a small saucepan over a moderate heat. Add the mushrooms and sauté for about 3 minutes, or until lightly browned. Lift out with a slotted spoon and set aside.

☐ Add the remaining flour to the butter remaining in the pan and mix well. Gradually stir in the cooking liquid from the fish. Boil for 2 minutes, stirring constantly.

☐ Mix the egg yolks in a bowl. Stir in a little of the hot sauce. Return it to the pan and stir in lemon rind and juice to taste.

☐ Pour the sauce over the fish, return it to the oven for 5 minutes just to 'set'. Spoon the mushrooms over the fish and garnish with the egg slices. Leave to heat for 2-3 minutes in the oven before serving.

Variation: For a party version, replace ¼ pint (150ml) milk with ¼ pint (150ml) single or double cream.

Cod with Mushrooms in Lemon sauce makes a good family supper dish, served with fluffy white rice and a green salad.

Cod with Mushrooms in Lemon Sauce
In this delicate-tasting fish dish the 'stewing' juices are used to make the sauce.

Cooking cod in the oven
If the fillets are thick, they will take about 20 minutes to 'stew' in a covered dish. Thinner fillets should be checked earlier to ensure they don't over-cook. Always serve cooked fish at once, unless freezing the dish.

Rich Beef Stew with Dumplings

Serve with chunky bread and butter and boiled cabbage.

Serves 8-10 ☆☆☆
Preparation: 30 minutes
Cooking: about 2¼ hours

3lb (1.5kg) chuck steak
3oz (75g) flour
salt and freshly ground black pepper
3oz (75g) beef dripping
3 medium onions, sliced
2 large celery sticks, sliced
1½ pints (900ml) water
½ pint (300ml) dry cider
juice and grated rind of 2 large oranges
8 black peppercorns, crushed
2 bay leaves
large sprig of parsley
1½lb (700g) carrots
a knob of butter
2oz (50g) walnut halves

The dumplings:
1oz (25g) lard
4oz (100g) self-raising flour
about 4 tablespoons milk

Set the oven to 300F (150C) gas 2.
☐ Pat the meat dry with kitchen paper and cut it into 1in (2.5cm) cubes, discarding any fat and connective tissue.
☐ Season the flour generously with salt and pepper and put it in a large plastic bag. Add one-third of the meat at a time to the bag and shake well to coat with the flour.
☐ Put one-third of the dripping into an 8in (20cm) frying-pan over a moderate heat. When a faint haze shows, add the onion. Stir-fry for about 3 minutes to glaze. Transfer to a 6-pint (3.5 litre) ovenproof casserole.
☐ Add more dripping, heat and fry the celery for about 3 minutes. Transfer to the casserole.
☐ Brown the meat in three batches, adding more dripping as required.
☐ Pour the water, cider and orange juice over the meat and vegetables. Stir in the orange rind, peppercorns, bay leaves and parsley.
☐ Cover the casserole and cook in the oven for 1 hour.
☐ Meanwhile, peel the carrots and cut them into finger-sized sticks. Stir into the stew. Remove the bay leaves, and cook for a further hour.
☐ To make the dumplings: Rub the lard into the flour. Gradually stir in the milk to make a firm dough. Cut into 10 equal-sized pieces and roll into balls.
☐ About 20 minutes before the end of cooking time, place the dumplings on top of the stew. Cover and return to the oven until they are well risen.
☐ Meanwhile, heat the butter in a small frying-pan over a moderate heat. Brown the walnuts for a minute or so, sprinkle with a little salt and dot over the finished stew.
✳ Put into shallow foil containers. Cool, cover, label and freeze for up to 2 months.

To re-heat: Put the covered containers into the oven pre-heated to 350F (180C) gas 4 for about 40 minutes, or until very hot. Turn out into a casserole dish. If dumplings are being included, add them at this stage and return casserole to the oven for about 15 minutes.

Belgian Waes Stew

Serves 4   ☆ ☆ ☆
Preparation: 30 minutes
Cooking: 2-2¼ hours

1¼-1½lb (575-700g) chuck steak
2oz (50g) beef dripping
3 medium onions, coarsely chopped
1 large carrot, coarsely chopped
salt and freshly ground black pepper
¼ pint (150ml) Meat Stock
7 fl oz (200ml) dark beer or stout
1 tablespoon tomato purée
1 tablespoon herb vinegar
1 tablespoon crushed coriander seeds
1oz (25g) breadcrumbs

The topping:
6 tablespoons dry brown breadcrumbs
2 tablespoons grated Parmesan cheese
1oz (25g) butter

Set the oven to 300F (150C) gas 2.

☐ Pat the meat dry with kitchen paper and cut into 1¼in (3cm) cubes.

☐ Put half the dripping into a frying-pan or wok over a high heat. Stir-fry the meat in three batches for about 3 minutes each until lightly browned. Remove each batch with a slotted spoon and set aside.

☐ Cook the onion and carrot in the same way with the rest of the dripping.

☐ Return all the meat and vegetables to the pan or wok. Season well and stir-fry together for a minute or so.

☐ Transfer to a shallow 4-pint (2.25 litre) ovenproof dish.

☐ To make the sauce: Mix the rest of the ingredients together in a 7in (18cm) saucepan. Bring to the boil, then simmer for 3 minutes, stirring.

☐ Pour the sauce over the meat and vegetables, cover the dish and cook in the oven for about 2¼ hours, until the meat is tender. Turn up the heat to 400F (200C) gas 6.

☐ To make the topping: Mix together the crumbs and cheese, then rub in the butter. Sprinkle over the centre of the cooked casserole dish.

☐ Return to the hotter oven for about 10 minutes to brown.

Belgian Waes Stew

This is just one of many delicious casserole dishes which incorporate beer – Carbonnade of Beef being perhaps the best known.

❋ To freeze

Turn the cooked mixture into shallow foil dishes. Cool. Cover, label and freeze for up to 2 months.

To thaw and re-heat: Put the covered dishes into the oven pre-heated to 350F (180C) gas 4 for about 50 minutes. Turn out into a shallow ovenproof dish, cover with the crumb mixture and brown under the grill or in the oven as above.

The crumb topping can be made 2-3 weeks in advance and stored in the fridge.

The various stages in preparing, cooking and serving Belgian Waes Stew. Accompany with buttered noodles and braised chicory.

Pork Chops Provençale

Spare-rib chops are an economical cut of meat. Cooked slowly in a well-flavoured sauce they make a delicious supper dish. If loin chops are used instead, cook the dish for only 30-40 minutes.

Pork Chops Provençale

Serve with boiled pasta and a crisp green salad.

Serves 4   ☆☆☆
Preparation: 45 minutes
Cooking: 1 hour

4 pork spare-rib chops, each about
     8oz (225g)
salt and freshly ground black pepper
3 tablespoons olive oil
1 large onion, chopped
2 large garlic cloves, crushed
a large sprig of fresh thyme
1lb (500g) tomatoes, peeled and diced
2 tablespoons flour
about 8 fl oz (250ml) rosé wine
2oz (50g) black olives, stoned
1 tablespoon chopped chives

Set the oven to 325F (160C) gas 3.
☐ Pat the meat dry and season.
☐ Put the oil in an 8in (20cm) frying-pan over a moderate heat. When hot, add 2 of the chops and brown for 5 minutes on each side.

☐ Transfer the chops to a 7½in-10½in (19-26cm) ovenproof dish. Brown the other 2 chops in the same way and add to the casserole.
☐ Add the onion and garlic to the frying-pan. Stir-fry for 4-5 minutes until tender but not brown.
☐ Add the thyme and tomatoes and simmer for 5 minutes.
☐ Sprinkle the flour over, mix it in and gradually stir in the wine. Simmer for 10 minutes, stirring.
☐ Strain the sauce over the meat. Add the olives and stir into the sauce.
☐ Cover the dish and cook in the oven for about 1 hour, until the meat is tender. Sprinkle with chopped chives to serve.
Tip: You can make this dish in advance, cool it, and store it in the fridge for up to 24 hours. Re-heat in the oven, pre-heated to 350F (180C) gas 4 for about 30 minutes.
This dish does not freeze well.

Navarin of Lamb

Serve with new potatoes and garden peas.

Serves 4
Preparation: 30 minutes
Cooking: about 2½ hours

2lb (1kg) middle neck of lamb
salt and freshly ground black pepper
2oz (50g) beef dripping
2 medium carrots, diced
1 large onion, coarsely chopped
2 teaspoons sugar
4 tablespoons flour
1 tablespoon tomato purée
1 large garlic clove, crushed
18 fl oz (500ml) Lamb Stock
a sprig of rosemary
a sprig of parsley
1 bay leaf

Set the oven to 300F (150C) gas 2.
☐ Cut the lamb into single-rib pieces, discard excess fat and pat ribs dry. Season all over.
☐ Put half the dripping in an 8in (20cm) frying-pan over a moderate heat. When a faint haze shows, stir-fry half the ribs for 6-7 minutes to brown lightly.
☐ Transfer the meat to a 4-pint (2.25 litre) ovenproof casserole and brown the rest of the ribs in the same way.
☐ Add remaining dripping to the pan. When melted, add the carrot and onion and sprinkle over the sugar. Stir-fry for 4-5 minutes to glaze.
☐ Pour off all excess fat. Sprinkle the flour over the vegetables. Stir in the tomato purée and garlic, followed by the stock and herbs and simmer for 5 minutes. Season well.
☐ Strain the sauce into the casserole. Cover and cook in the oven for about 2½ hours, until the meat comes away easily from the bones.
Tip: This dish may be made in advance and re-heated when required. Cool, cover and store in the fridge for up to 24 hours. To re-heat, place the casserole in the oven, pre-heated to 350F (180C) gas 4, for 30-40 minutes.

Blanquette de Veau

Serves 6
Preparation: 30 minutes
Cooking: about 1¼ hours

2lb (1kg) stewing veal
½ pint (300ml) dry white wine
6 white peppercorns
½ teaspoon salt
a bouquet garni, consisting of
    1 bay leaf, a sprig of parsley, a sprig of
    fresh tarragon and strip of lemon peel
½lb (225g) button onions, blanched
    and peeled
½lb (225g) button mushrooms, wiped
a pinch of paprika

The sauce:
2 oz (50g) butter
3 tablespoons flour
about ¼ pint (150ml) milk
salt and freshly ground black pepper
2 tablespoons lemon juice

Set the oven to 325F (160C) gas 3.
☐ Pat meat dry with kitchen paper, remove any fat and connective tissue and cut into 1in (2.5cm) cubes.
☐ Put into a 2½ pint (1.4 litre) ovenproof casserole with the wine, peppercorns and salt. Tie the bouquet garni in a small piece of clean muslin and add to the dish. Cover and cook for 30 minutes.
☐ Add the onions and cook for a further 10 minutes.
☐ Meanwhile, melt the butter in a 7in (18cm) saucepan over a moderate heat. Stir in the flour then gradually stir in the milk. Simmer for 2 minutes, stirring constantly.
☐ Season to taste with salt and pepper and the lemon juice. Pour into the casserole, add the mushrooms, cover and continue cooking for about 30 minutes.
☐ Discard the bouquet garni and sprinkle with paprika to serve.
❋ Put into shallow foil containers. Cool, cover, label and freeze for up to 6 weeks.
To thaw: Put the covered containers into the oven pre-heated to 350F (180C) gas 4 for about 30 minutes. Put into a casserole and mix lightly with a fork. Cover and heat for a further 20 minutes.

Navarin of Lamb
This turns into the classic French dish Navarin d'Agneau Printanière by garnishing it with glazed button onions, tiny carrots, small turnips, peas and green beans.

Blanquette de Veau
Serve with buttered noodles and glazed carrots.

In a blanquette, as with a fricassée, the meat is usually cooked from the start in the liquid without any previous browning.

Timing
The exact timing depends on the depth of the casserole and the material from which it is made. Shallow dishes heat through more quickly than deep ones; metal heats more quickly than earthenware, though earthenware retains its heat for longer.

❋**Freezer note:** It is most important, when re-heating any casserole or stew that has been frozen, to bring it to the boil, then simmer gently until thoroughly hot. It is not wise to eat stews that are only lukewarm after freezing.

Poultry casseroles and stews

There are many recipes for cooking chicken, turkey and duck 'en casserole'. Generally depending on the size of the joints, poultry casseroles take longer to cook than meat. They are a good choice for entertaining as the flesh blends well with many other flavours, from a creamy sauce to a piquant curry. Uncooked pieces may be gently stewed in wine or stock, and used to make more elegant dishes, and cooked joints make a quick last minute 'casserole'. Most re-heat well and can be frozen.

Poulet Normande

Serve with baked tomatoes and mangetout peas.

Serves 4 ☆ ☆ ☆
Preparation: 30 minutes
Cooking: 30 minutes

---

4 chicken pieces, about 2¼lb (1kg) total weight
2oz (50g) butter
2 tablespoons oil
3 tablespoons Calvados
1 tablespoon finely chopped onion
2 celery sticks, finely chopped
leaves from a large sprig of fresh thyme
¼ pint (150ml) Chicken Stock
3 fl oz (100ml) dry cider
6oz (175g) cooking apples, peeled, cored and chopped
¼ pint (150ml) double cream
salt and freshly ground pepper
1 tablespoon chopped parsley

Set the oven to 325F (160C) gas 3.
☐ Remove the skin from the chicken, and pat dry with kitchen paper.
☐ Put the butter and oil in a 9in (23cm) frying-pan over a moderate heat. When the mixture has stopped foaming add the chicken. Fry for about 5 minutes on each side to brown lightly.
☐ Put the Calvados into a small saucepan or large ladle. Warm on a hotplate or over a burner until it begins to steam. Set alight and immediately pour over the chicken.

☐ When the flames have died down, transfer the chicken to a 3 pint (1.75 litre) casserole.
☐ Add the onion and celery to the frying pan. Reduce the heat. Cook, stirring, for 5 minutes to soften.
☐ Add the thyme, stock, cider, and apples. Simmer for about 7 minutes to soften the apples.
☐ Stir in the cream, and season to taste with salt and pepper. Spoon over the chicken and cover the dish. Cook in the oven for about 30 minutes or until the chicken is tender. Sprinkle with parsley to serve.

Simple Chicken Casserole

Serve accompanied by boiled small potatoes.

Serves 6 ☆ ☆
Preparation: 10 minutes
Cooking: 45-50 minutes

3½lb (1.5kg) chicken, jointed into 6 pieces
1 medium onion, sliced
1 large carrot, diced
1 celery stick, sliced
a large sprig of fresh thyme
a strip of thinly pared lemon rind
1 teaspoon salt
6 black peppercorns
¾ pint (450ml) Chicken Stock
¼ pint (150ml) dry white wine
1 tablespoon finely chopped parsley
1 tablespoon finely chopped chives

Set the oven to 325F (160C) gas 3.
☐ Put the chicken into a 4 pint (2.25 litre) casserole with the vegetables.
☐ Put the thyme, lemon rind, salt, peppercorns, stock and wine into a saucepan. Bring to the boil and simmer for 3 minutes. Pour over the chicken.
☐ Cover and cook in oven for 45-50 minutes, until chicken is tender.
☐ Remove the thyme and sprinkle with the chopped herbs to serve.
Tip: In a hurry, substitute a large can of condensed chicken broth for all the ingredients but the fresh herbs and wine.

Ragoût of Turkey with Red Pepper

Serves 6-8   ☆ ☆

Preparation and cooking: about
1 hour

2¾lb (1.25kg) boneless turkey joint
2oz (50g) flour
1 tablespoon paprika
salt and freshly ground black pepper
2oz (50g) butter
2-3 tablespoons oil
1 medium onion, chopped
1 tablespoon tomato purée
14.6 fl oz (415ml) canned tomato juice
¼ pint (150ml) dry white wine
1 teaspoon dried marjoram
1 teaspoon caraway seeds
1 tablespoon chopped parsley
1 tablespoon chopped chives
1 large red pepper, deseeded and coarsely
   chopped
8oz (225g) tomatoes, skinned, deseeded
   and coarsely chopped

Set the oven to 300F (150C) gas 2.
Pat the meat dry with kitchen paper
and cut into 1in (2.5cm) cubes.

☐ Season the flour with paprika,
salt and pepper and put in a large
plastic bag. Add the turkey meat
and shake well to coat.

☐ Put one-third of the butter and
oil into a deep 8in (20cm) frying-
pan over a moderate heat. When
foaming stops, add one-third of the
meat.

☐ Stir-fry for about 8 minutes to
brown lightly. Transfer to a 4-pint
(2.25 litre) ovenproof casserole.
Repeat the process with the
remaining butter, oil and meat until
browned.

☐ Add the onion to the pan with a
little more oil, if necessary. Stir-fry
for 3-5 minutes to soften but not
brown. Add to the casserole.

☐ Stir into the frying-pan any flour
left in the bag along with the tomato
purée. Gradually stir in the tomato
juice, then bring to the boil. Add the
rest of the ingredients and boil for 3
minutes.

☐ Pour the sauce over the meat in
the casserole and cook in the oven
for about 30 minutes until the meat
is tender. Adjust seasoning to serve.

✳ Turn the cooked mixture into
shallow foil containers. Cool, cover,
label and freeze for up to 2 months.
To thaw: Put the covered containers
into the oven pre-heated to 350F
(180C) gas 4 for about 50 minutes,
until thoroughly hot.

*Serve Ragoût of Turkey with Red
Peppers with jacket-baked potatoes or
rice and a fresh green salad.*

Partridge Casserole

As an alternative to the elderberry jelly sauce, flame the casserole contents with 2 tablespoons of brandy at the end of cooking and add about 24 seedless grapes. Allow just to warm through before serving.

Pigeons with Raisins and Apples

Nowadays pigeon breasts are sometimes available ready boned and make the preparation of this dish that much easier. Try adding a tablespoon or two of Calvados to the sauce for extra flavour. Serve with rice and Creamy Cabbage.

With both partridges and pigeons remember to examine the birds carefully for damage, and remove any shot that might be left in the flesh.

Partridge Casserole

Serve with a mixture of brown and wild rice and a carrot purée.

Serves 2 ☆
Preparation: 15 minutes
Cooking: about 1 hour

---

1 partridge, about 12oz (350g) dressed
    weight
1 large leek, sliced
1 medium celeriac root, diced
1 celery stick, sliced
1 tablespoon chopped celery leaves
¼ teaspoon celery seeds
4 whole cloves
salt and freshly ground black pepper
¼ pint (150ml) dry cider

The sauce:
1 tablespoon softened butter
2 teaspoons flour
1 tablespoon elderberry jelly
½ teaspoon vinegar

Set the oven to 300F (150C) gas 2.
☐ Wash the partridge and pat dry. Cut in half with poultry shears.
☐ Put the leek, celeriac, celery, celery leaves and seeds, and the cloves into a 1¾ pint (1 litre) casserole. Season well and stir.
☐ Set the partridge on the vegetables and pour the cider over.
☐ Cover the casserole, cook in the oven for about 50 minutes or until the partridge is tender.
☐ Transfer the bird to a serving plate, spoon vegetables around, cover with foil and keep hot.
☐ Melt the butter in a small saucepan over a moderate heat. Stir in the flour. Gradually stir in the strained stock from the casserole.
☐ Bring to the boil and simmer for 2-3 minutes, stirring constantly, to thicken. Stir in the jelly and vinegar. Simmer for 1 minute to melt jelly.
☐ Season to taste and spoon the sauce over the partridge to serve.
Tip: You can make the casserole in advance and just make the sauce at the last minute. Put the cooked partridge and the vegetables on an ovenproof plate and cover with foil. Re-heat in the oven set to 350F (180C) gas 4 for about 20 minutes.

Pigeons with Raisins and Apples

Serves 4 ☆☆☆
Preparation and cooking: about 2¼ hours

---

4 pigeons, dressed
2 tablespoons flour
salt and freshly ground black pepper
2oz (50g) butter
4 rashers streaky bacon, rinds removed
    and coarsely chopped
½ pint (300ml) Basic Brown or Game Stock
¼ pint (150ml) dry cider
½ teaspoon ground allspice
16 button onions, blanched and peeled
a pinch of caster sugar
2 large dessert apples
3oz (75g) seedless raisins, soaked in warm
    water to cover

Set the oven to 325F (160C) gas 3.
☐ Split the pigeons in two with poultry shears and trim away the flesh from the carcass with scissors. Season the flour with salt and pepper and place in a large plastic bag with the pigeon pieces. Shake to coat.
☐ Melt some of the butter in a small frying-pan set over a moderate heat. When the foaming subsides, fry the bacon, stirring frequently, until lightly browned.
☐ Remove with a slotted spoon and transfer to a 4 pint (2.25 litre) casserole. Brown the pigeons in the same way and add to the casserole.
☐ Pour over the stock and cider, add the allspice and any flour left in the bag, cover tightly and cook in the oven for 30 minutes.
☐ Meanwhile, dust the onions lightly with caster sugar and brown them in the remaining butter in the frying-pan. Remove with a slotted spoon, add to the casserole and return to the oven for a further 30 minutes.
☐ Peel, core and thickly slice the apples and add to the frying-pan. Stir-fry for about 5 minutes until beginning to soften, add to the casserole with the drained raisins and return to the oven for a further 15 minutes.

3-Bean Casserole

Serves 4-6 ☆☆☆
Preparation: 10 minutes plus soaking
Cooking: 2¾-3 hours

4oz (100g) dried green beans
4oz (100g) dried red beans
4oz (100g) dried white beans
1¼lb (575g) belly pork
2 medium onions, sliced
3 sprigs of fresh sage
2 tablespoons mustard oil or 1 teaspoon
     made mustard mixed with 2 tablespoons
     oil
1½ teaspoons salt
18 fl oz (500ml) Meat Stock

Soak all the beans in cold water overnight. Discard water.

☐ Set oven to 300F (150C) gas 2. Remove the skin from the pork. Cut the meat into 1in (2.5cm) cubes, removing as much meat as possible from the bones.

☐ Put alternate layers of beans, onion, pork, including the bones, and sage into a deep 4-pint (2.25-litre) casserole. Stir in the mustard oil, salt and stock.

☐ Cover the casserole and cook in the oven for 2¾-3 hours.

Lentil Stew

Serves 4 ☆
Preparation: 30 minutes plus soaking
Cooking: about 1¾ hours

8oz (225g) red lentils
1 large carrot, sliced
a large garlic clove, pressed
1 large onion, sliced
½ teaspoon curry paste
about 14 fl oz (400ml) Meat Stock
1 medium parsnip, sliced
1 celery stick, sliced
1 large leek, sliced
1 tablespoon chopped parsley
2oz (50g) salted cashew nuts
3 tablespoons natural yogurt
salt and freshly ground black pepper
1 tablespoon chopped chives

Soak the lentils in cold water to cover overnight. Discard the water.

☐ Set oven to 300F (150C) gas 2.

Put the lentils in a 4-pint (2.25-litre) casserole.

☐ Stir in the carrot, garlic, onion, curry paste, and 8 fl oz (250 ml) stock.

☐ Cover the casserole and cook in the oven for 45 minutes.

☐ Stir, add ¼ pint (150ml) more stock and cook for a further 20 minutes.

☐ Stir in the parsnip, celery, leek, parsley and nuts. If the lentils appear dry, add 1-2 tablespoons more stock.

☐ Cook for about 45 minutes or until the lentils are fully cooked. Stir in yogurt and salt and pepper to taste and sprinkle with chopped chives.

Creamy Cabbage

Serves 4 ☆☆
Preparation and cooking: 1-1¼ hours

1½lb (700g) cabbage
2oz (50g) butter
1 small onion, finely chopped
2 tablespoons flour
14 fl oz (400ml) milk
½ teaspoon celery seeds
salt and pepper
1½ teaspoons caraway seeds

Set the oven to 300F (150C) gas 2.

☐ Trim the cabbage, discard the outer leaves and the core and cut into thin slices as shown. Wash in cold water and drain thoroughly.

☐ Put the butter in a 7in (18cm) saucepan over a moderate heat. Add the onion and cook, stirring, for 5 minutes to soften but not brown.

☐ Add the flour and mix well. Gradually stir in the milk and simmer for 2 minutes. Season to taste with celery seeds, salt and pepper.

☐ Put a layer of cabbage into a 3½-pint (2-litre) shallow casserole. Sprinkle with some caraway seeds and spoon over half the sauce.

☐ Finish with another layer of the cabbage, caraway and sauce. Cover tightly and cook for about 50 minutes until just tender.

Preparing cabbage

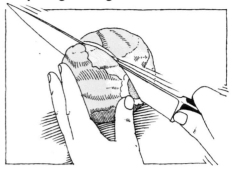

Cut across in half.

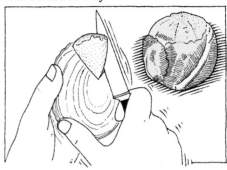

Trim out the hard base core.

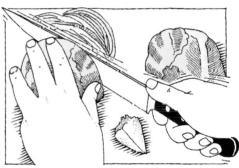

Slice or shred as shown.

To test lentils

The instructions given are for lentils which hold their shape and feel slightly crisp when bitten. If you prefer them to be mushy, add 2-3 more tablespoons of stock and cook for about 30 minutes longer. In that case, add the parsnips, etc, after 1½ hours.

To test beans

The instructions given will produce beans which will be tender but still hold their shape. For softer beans cook longer, testing every 15 minutes until cooked as required.

The best accompaniment to sauerkraut dishes is chunky bread with cold butter.

Cooking sauerkraut
Beer and Riesling wines are traditionally used in Alsace and Germany for cooking sauerkraut. Other white wines and cider are also suitable.

Sauerkraut with Chicken Livers

Serves 4
Preparation: 20 minutes
Cooking: 25-30 minutes

18oz (500g) packet sauerkraut
8oz (225g) smoked bacon, in the piece
8oz (225g) chicken livers
1 small onion, finely chopped
8oz (225g) mushrooms, wiped and sliced
2oz (50g) butter
7 fl oz (200ml) Riesling wine
salt and freshly ground black pepper

Set oven to 375F (190C) gas 5.
☐ Drain the sauerkraut well and cut the bacon into ½in (1cm) cubes. Wash the chicken livers in cold water, pat dry and trim off any membrane. If large, cut in half.
☐ Melt half the butter in a 9-in (21-cm) frying-pan over a moderate heat. Add the onion and stir-fry for 2-3 minutes to glaze. Transfer to a 3-pint (1.75-litre) casserole.
☐ Add the rest of the butter to the frying-pan. When beginning to brown, add the mushrooms and stir-fry for 2-3 minutes. Remove with a slotted spoon and add to casserole.
☐ Add the bacon to the frying-pan. Stir-fry for about 5 minutes to brown lightly. Spread over the mushrooms and onion in the casserole.
☐ Add the chicken livers to the frying-pan and stir-fry lightly for about 3 minutes just to set the livers. Remove and set aside.
☐ Pour the wine into the frying-pan. Bring to the boil and pour over the contents of the casserole.
☐ Spoon the sauerkraut on top of the other ingredients. Season with salt and pepper. With two forks, mix in lightly but thoroughly.
☐ Cover the dish tightly and cook in the oven for 25 minutes.
☐ Stir again with the forks and place the chicken livers on top. Cover and cook in the oven for a further 5 minutes. Serve immediately.

Sauerkraut with Beer

Serves 4
Preparation: 15 minutes
Cooking: about 1 hour

18oz (500g) packet sauerkraut
1lb (500g) belly pork
2oz (50g) butter
2 large onions, coarsely chopped
1 garlic clove, pressed or crushed
1 tablespoon finely chopped celery leaves
1 teaspoon fennel seeds
7 fl oz (200ml) Pilsner lager
salt and freshly ground black pepper

Set the oven to 325F (160C) gas 3.
☐ Drain the sauerkraut well. Cut the pork into 1-in (2.5-cm) cubes.
☐ Put half the butter in a 9-in (21-cm) frying-pan over a moderate heat. Add the pork and stir-fry for about 5 minutes to brown.
☐ Transfer to a shallow 3-pint (1.75-litre) ovenproof dish. Reduce the heat, add the rest of the butter to the frying-pan. Stir in the onion and garlic and cook, stirring frequently, for 3 minutes.
☐ Add the celery leaves, fennel, lager, and salt and pepper. Bring to the boil.
☐ With two forks, mix the sauerkraut into the casserole. Pour in the contents of the frying-pan and stir again.
☐ Cover the dish and cook for 50-60 minutes until the meat is tender. Serve immediately.

Other ways with sauerkraut
1 Cut 1lb (500g) large pork sausages into 1in (2.5cm) lengths. Brown in a little fat. Substitute for the bacon and ham in Sauerkraut with Ham.
2 Use Chicken Stock for wine in Sauerkraut with Chicken Livers.
3 Use packet sauerkraut to make easy store-cupboard stews with stand-bys like canned cocktail sausages, peas, pimientos and sweetcorn.
4 Sauerkraut makes an excellent salad if you toss it with a chopped spring onion, a little chopped fresh pineapple and parsley. Stir together with mustard vinaigrette.

Sauerkraut with Ham in White Wine

Serves 4 ☆☆☆
Preparation: 15 minutes
Cooking: 25-30 minutes

18oz (500g) packet sauerkraut
8oz (225g) smoked bacon, in the piece
10oz (275g) cooked ham, in the piece
2oz (50g) butter
4oz (125g) onion, finely chopped
1 garlic clove, pressed or crushed
½ teaspoon dried thyme
salt and pepper
1 bay leaf
7 fl oz (200ml) dry white wine

Set the oven to 375F (190C) gas 5.
☐ Drain the sauerkraut well and cut the bacon and ham into ½in (1cm) cubes.
☐ Put half the butter in a 9-in (21-cm) frying-pan over a moderate heat. When the butter begins to brown, add the meats.
☐ Stir-fry for 7-8 minutes to brown lightly. Transfer to a 3-pint (1.75-litre) shallow ovenproof dish.
☐ Reduce the heat and add the rest of the butter. When melted, stir in the onion and garlic. Cook, stirring constantly, for 3 minutes.
☐ Stir in the thyme, salt and pepper, bay leaf and wine. Bring to the boil.
☐ With two forks, mix the sauerkraut into the meat in the casserole. Pour the contents of the frying-pan over and stir again.
☐ Cover the dish and cook in the oven for about 25 minutes until the bacon is tender.
☐ Remove the bay leaf and serve immediately.

Sauerkraut–cabbage pickled with juniper berries–is now readily available, canned or in packets, from most good supermarkets and continental delicatessens. Some will even sell it fresh from the barrel. Drain well before use, to avoid making the dish too salty.

Sauerkraut with Ham in White Wine
Cooked ham and smoked bacon give this dish a distinctive flavour when cooked with white wine. The dish is quickly made and provides a good substantial meal.

Three ways with sauerkraut – with ham and white wine, with chicken livers and with beer.

STOCK, SOUP AND SAUCE-MAKING

Stocks and soups • Making sauces

Stocks and soups

Every good cook enjoys making a soup and the techniques you can use are many and varied. You can choose to blend a rich, smooth and creamy soup with a delicate flavour, skim off a clear bouillon or broth to add sparkle to a dinner party, or put together a hearty meat or fish soup that's a meal in itself. Soup-making gives the creative cook great scope and it's the thriftiest way of using left-overs. Vegetables, meat, pasta, rice, bones and gravies—all can be pressed into service to suit the occasion. But it cannot be too strongly stressed that the basis of most good soups is a well-flavoured stock of the appropriate type. Make up a quantity at a time, freeze it in portion sizes and you'll never be at a loss when unexpected visitors arrive.

You can master the art of making a good stock if you bear three basic rules in mind: don't add flavourings that fight with the basic ingredient (juniper berries to a fish stock, for example); make sure the stock has been simmering away for long enough to draw out all the various flavourings fully; and if at all possible when using the stock for making soup, allow time to reduce the bubbling stock to about half its original quantity to concentrate the flavour.

Almost anything can go into your stock as long as you have some idea of the soup you intend to make from it. Bones of meat and poultry can be mixed—beef and veal or beef and turkey or chicken—but it is better to keep game carcasses to themselves: the flavour would otherwise overwhelm and spoil a more delicate taste.

A very good stock can be made from vegetables alone as long as you don't add too much cabbage. The brassicas (cabbage, cauliflower, broccoli) are very powerful agents and will quickly drown out other flavours. Root vegetables tend to cloud a stock, so use them when you need a creamy soup made, perhaps from a base of vegetable purée and thinned down with stock before serving. Onions not only add flavour, but can give colour to a pallid stock if they are browned first.

Of the recipes that follow, the Basic Stock on page 236 makes an excellent sauce base or alternatively a soup for two.

Other stock recipes given here make equally good soups, for instance the Meat Stock on page 238, the Homemade Stock on page 262 and the Chicken Stock on page 239.

For a truly professional clear soup, use any meat stock and learn to clarify it.

To clarify stock the classic way: Lightly whip 2 egg whites and add them to the cold stock. Pour into a large saucepan. Whisk the stock over moderate heat until it comes to the boil.

☐ Stop whisking and allow the stock to boil up to the top of the pan, then remove from the heat and leave to settle for a few minutes.

☐ Repeat the boiling-up process twice, being careful not to break the solidified egg white crust. Line a sieve with a clean kitchen cloth which has been rinsed in boiling water and pour the stock through it, into a bowl, holding back the egg white with a spoon. Tip the egg white into the sieve so that it forms a filter, rinse out the pan and pour the stock through the cloth again, back into the pan. The stock should now be perfectly clear. Cool and store in a fridge for up to 3 days.

Clear and thickened soups

Broths and most soups are usually served as starters rather than as a main course meal. A clear soup is the best choice if the other courses are substantial. A thick soup is more suitable when you need a light lunch, or when the meal consists of two or three light courses. A thick soup also makes an informal supper snack.

Making stock

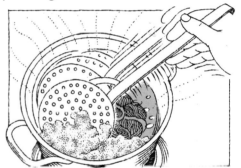
First skim the boiling stock.

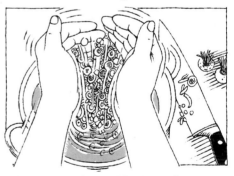
Add vegetables and herbs to flavour.

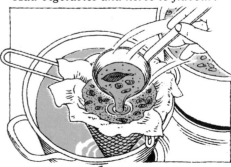
Strain well through a lined sieve.

Meat glaze

When stock is boiled down enough, almost all the liquid evaporates—this may take as long as 2½ hours. The residue is a rich syrup which sets into a jelly when cold. Store it in a covered container in the refrigerator where it will keep for at least two weeks. The glaze (also known as **glace de viande**) is a highly concentrated flavouring: about 4 pints (2.5 litres) stock will reduce down to ½ pint (300ml). Use a teaspoon of the jelly to give an excellent flavour to sauces or soups, or dissolve a spoonful in hot water and use as a stock.

Ingredients for stock-making.

Basic Stock

Make this everyday stock with bits of vegetables, meat scraps or bones which have collected in the refrigerator over a few days. Either freeze them and make the stock later or cook them up and have the stock ready. Use this stock for soups, stews and gravy.

Preparation: about 1 hour ☆
Makes about 1 pint (600ml)

---

about 1lb (450g) of bones and pieces of meat
    from chicken, turkey or other roast joints
3 tablespoons oil or dripping
1 large onion, roughly chopped
1-2 cloves of garlic, chopped
1 stick of celery, sliced
2 carrots, sliced
1½ pints (900ml) water, or water mixed with
    wine or cider
1 bay leaf, crumbled
4 juniper berries, crushed
4 black peppercorns
large sprig of parsley
pinch of dried thyme or rosemary
salt and pepper to taste

Chop the bones and any scraps of meat into pieces to fit into the available pan.

☐ Heat the oil or dripping in the pan and brown the bones and meat. Set aside.

☐ Now brown the onion, garlic, celery and carrot in the same fat. Return the bones and meat to the pan along with the remaining ingredients. Cover and simmer gently for about 30 minutes.

☐ Strain the stock into a bowl, discard the solid ingredients. Taste the stock and add seasoning.

Basic Brown Stock

Makes 3 pints (1.75 litres)
1¾ pints (1 litre) if concentrated
Preparation and cooking: 3½ hours,
plus chilling

2lb (1kg) beef and veal bones
1lb (500g) carrots, sliced
8oz (250g) tomatoes, quartered
1 clove garlic
1 large onion, coarsely chopped
1lb (500g) shin of beef, cut into 2in
    (5cm) pieces
1 bay leaf
small piece of mace, or small pinch of
    ground mace
4 pints (2.25 litres) water
salt and pepper

Preheat the oven to 425F, 220C,
Gas 7.

☐ Put the bones, carrots, tomatoes,
garlic and onion into a large roasting
pan. Bake for 15 minutes, or until
well browned.

☐ Transfer the contents of the
roasting pan to a large saucepan.
Add the beef, bay leaf, mace and
water. Bring to the boil and remove
the scum which rises to the surface.

☐ Lower the heat, cover the pan
and simmer gently for about 3
hours.

☐ Strain through a sieve lined with
dampened muslin or kitchen paper.
Season to taste, then allow the stock
to cool.

☐ Refrigerate overnight if possible,
then remove the solidified fat.

Tip: To concentrate the stock, do
not season with salt and pepper.
Bring to the boil, and boil rapidly
until reduced to about 1¾ pints (1
litre). Now add salt and pepper. If
clarified stock is specified, follow the
instructions for clarifying given on
page 235.

Vegetable Stock

Makes 3 pints (1.75 litres)
Preparation and cooking: 2½ hours
plus cooling

½oz (15g) butter
8oz (250g) onions, roughly chopped
8oz (250g) leeks, cleaned and sliced
8oz (250g) carrots, sliced
3 sticks celery, sliced
4oz (125g) mushrooms or mushroom
    trimmings
asparagus trimmings, if available
outside leaves of lettuce, if available
1 strip of lemon rind
bouquet garni
4 pints (2.25 litres) water
a little yeast extract to taste
salt and pepper

Melt butter in a large, heavy-based
pan, add all the vegetables and cook
over low heat until browned.

☐ Add the lemon rind, bouquet
garni and water, bring to the boil,
cover and simmer for 2 hours.

☐ Add yeast extract, and season to
taste. Strain through a sieve lined
with dampened muslin or kitchen
paper.

☐ Cool, then remove any solidified
butter from the surface.

☐ Measure the quantity and, if
necessary, boil rapidly to reduce to 3
pints (1.75 litres).

Bouillon with Fresh Herbs

Serves 4
Preparation and cooking: about
20 minutes

1¾ pints (1 litre) clarified Basic Brown stock
2 tablespoons finely chopped parsley
1 tablespoon finely chopped chervil
salt and pepper
1 tablespoon finely chopped chives
juice of ½ lemon

Bring the beef stock to the boil. Stir
in the parsley and chervil.

☐ Season to taste with salt and
pepper and serve, garnished with
the chopped chives and sprinkled
with a few drops of lemon juice.

Basic Brown Stock

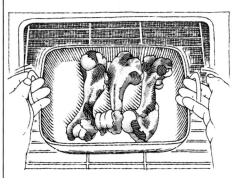

If large beef and veal bones are used it is
easier to brown the stock ingredients in the
oven. However, if the bones are small or cut
into pieces they can be browned on top of
the stove in a frying-pan in a little fat, if
preferred.

❋**Freezing stock:** collect ingredients for
stock over a period of several weeks and
store them in the freezer, then have one big
stock-making session to make basic stocks
for sauces, gravies and soups. Reduce the
finished stock to about ¼ of its original
volume, so that it takes up less freezer
space, and pack it in small quantities. Freeze
it in ice cube trays and heat up from frozen if
required. Most brown and vegetable stocks
keep for up to 6 months.

Vegetable Stock
A well-flavoured vegetable stock can be used
to replace meat stock in many dishes. It can
be used in the following recipes in this
section:
Thick Tomato Soup, Thick Pepper Soup,
Thick Curry Soup and Thick Onion Soup.

Meat Stock

This is a richer, more substantial stock for which you will need a large piece of meat with bones, and fresh vegetables. Use the stock for meat sauces, as a braising liquid for meat, vegetables and stews or, in fact, for any savoury cooking which requires a well-flavoured liquid. You can boil this stock down to make a rich concentrate and it will keep in this form in the refrigerator for at least 3 weeks. For longer storage, freeze it.

Vegetable stocks

Use the cooking water from the vegetables to add colour and flavour to soups and sauces; the water contains nutrients as well. For maximum flavour when preparing a vegetable stock, sweat a selection of chopped vegetables in butter, add water and simmer until tender. Strain the stock before use.

Other ways of making stock

Long slow simmering does give the best flavour to stock, but a pressure cooker will make a pot of stock very quickly. A slow cooker will take longest of all but as there is no danger of the contents boiling over or boiling dry, you can leave it to cook while you're elsewhere.

In a pressure cooker

To allow the liquid sufficient room to boil, never fill the cooker more than half full. Remove the trivet. Add the water and any bones being used—well broken or chopped. With the lid off, bring to the boil and skim. Add the rest of the ingredients, and cook under pressure for 35-40 minutes. Add extra liquid after cooking to make up to the required amount.
For brown stock, brown the meat, bones and vegetables in the uncovered pan first.

In a slow cooker

Put all the stock ingredients into the pot. Since the stock doesn't actually boil, you can fill the pot to within 1in (2.5cm) of the rim. As with other methods, make sure the bones and vegetables are covered by the liquid at the start of cooking. Cover and cook for about 12 hours. For brown stock, brown the meat, bones and vegetables in a separate pan first then transfer to the slow cooker.

Meat Stock

Preparation and cooking: 4 hours
Makes: 3½-4 pints (2-2.25 litres)

5lb (2.25kg) shin of beef with bones
6 pints (3.5 litres) water
8oz (225g) carrots
1 small parsnip
2 leeks, white parts only
2 sticks of celery
12oz (350g) onions
bouquet garni of 6 whole cloves, 1 bay leaf, large sprig of parsley, large sprig of thyme, 6 peppercorns
2 teaspoons salt

Ask the butcher to cut the meat into thick slices so that each piece of meat has some bone. The meat could be cooked in one piece but cut pieces fit more easily into pans.

☐ Put the meat into a very large pan with the water and place over a low heat. Bring to the boil very slowly, spooning off any scum which comes to the surface. When boiling point is reached, add a little cold water—about half a teacupful—to arrest the boiling and bring more scum to the surface for skimming off. Bring to the boil, add cold water and skim once more. This helps to make a clearer stock with a better flavour.

☐ While the meat and bones are coming to the boil, prepare the other ingredients: peel and slice the carrots and parsnip, thoroughly wash and slice the leeks and celery, and coarsely chop the onions. Make a bouquet garni by tying the cloves, herbs and peppercorns in a small piece of clean muslin.

☐ When the liquid is simmering, add the salt, vegetables, and the bouquet garni. Bring back to the boil and skim once more. Cover, and simmer for 3-3½ hours. Keep the heat very low so the water barely bubbles. You can cook the stock on top of the stove or in an oven pre-heated to 300F (150C) gas 2.
To use: Remove the pieces of meat and discard the bones. Serve the meat with freshly cooked vegetables. Strain off the liquid for use as stock.

Cool as quickly as possible, then chill in the refrigerator. The fat will solidify on the surface and you can spoon it off easily. To freeze the stock, put it into containers of various sizes so it will be available quickly in the quantity you require. For example, 4oz (100g) cottage cheese cartons, or 8oz (225g) cottage cheese or margarine tubs are particularly useful. Store in the freezer for up to 3 months.

Lamb Stock

Lamb stock is rather pronounced in flavour. However, it is useful for soups such as Scotch Broth, and for various lamb-based dishes.

Makes 1¾ pints (1 litre)
Preparation: 10 minutes
Cooking: 2½ hours plus about an hour's chilling and reducing

12oz (350g) stewing lamb, coarsely chopped
½lb (250g) lamb bones
1 large onion, sliced
1 leek, sliced
2 sticks of celery, sliced
bouquet garni
3 pints (1.75 litres) water

Put all the ingredients into a large pan and bring to the boil, removing the scum as it rises.

☐ Reduce the heat, cover the pan and simmer for about 2½ hours.

☐ Strain the stock through a sieve lined with damp muslin or kitchen paper, allow to cool, then chill.

☐ Remove the solidified fat from the surface and measure the stock. Bring it to a rapid boil and reduce it to 1¾ pints (1 litre).

Brown Stock

Make with the same ingredients as Meat Stock, but start the cooking differently. Put a little dripping into a pan and brown the pieces of meat and bones. Remove them to a plate and brown the vegetables. Put all the ingredients into the pan (including the meat and bones) and cook as for Meat Stock. Use for brown sauces, soups and stews.

White Stock
Chicken or Veal

White stock is the professional cook's term for a stock made from chicken or veal. It has a much milder flavour than a meaty beef stock, and is used as a basis for the more subtly flavoured soups such as those made from asparagus, celery and other similar vegetables, as well as mushroom and chicken soups. The aim is to make a stock which is well flavoured enough without overwhelming the main soup ingredients. Chicken or veal can be used, with the addition of a pig's trotter or calf's foot, if available, to give extra body and setting properties, if a jellied stock is required.

Chicken Stock

Makes 1¾ pints (1 litre)
Preparation and cooking:
2½-3 hours, plus chilling

the carcasses of 2 uncooked jointed
    chickens plus 1 large chicken joint, or 1
    boiling fowl
1 pig's trotter or calf's foot, if available,
    scrubbed
4oz (100g) button mushrooms
1 medium onion, roughly chopped
1 stick of celery, roughly chopped
bouquet garni
3 pints (1.75 litres) water

Cut up the carcasses, then put them into a large saucepan with the rest of the ingredients.
☐ Bring to the boil, removing the scum as it rises to the surface. Lower the heat, cover the pan and simmer for 2-2½ hours.
☐ Strain the stock through a sieve lined with damp muslin or kitchen paper. Rinse the pan.
☐ Measure the stock, and if necessary, return it to the rinsed-out pan and boil rapidly to reduce to about 1¾ pints (1 litre).
☐ Cool, refrigerate, then remove the solidified fat from the surface of the stock.

Game Stock

An excellent well-flavoured stock can be made from the bones and trimmings of all types of game. The best stock is made from raw meat; stocks made from cooked bones are better used in thick soups. The cooking time varies with the type of game: allow 1½ hours for stock made from pigeon and other small birds, 2½ hours for stock made from venison, hare or larger birds. If a limited number of game bones are available, supplement them with raw beef or chicken. The stock will not have such a full flavour but will still make a good soup.

Makes 1¾ pints (1 litre)
Preparation and cooking:
1½-2½ hours depending on type

about 2lb (1kg) bones and trimmings of raw
    game
4oz (100g) mushrooms
1 large onion, roughly chopped
1 clove garlic
2 carrots, sliced
6 juniper berries
6 black peppercorns
1 bay leaf
a sprig of thyme
3 pints (1.75 litres) water

Preheat oven to 425F (220C) gas 7.
☐ Put the bones and trimmings into a roasting pan and bake for 10-15 minutes or until browned.
☐ Transfer them to a large saucepan and add the remaining ingredients.
Bring to the boil and remove the scum as it rises to the surface.
☐ Reduce the heat, cover the pan and simmer for about 2½ hours (1½ hours for stock made from pigeon or other small birds).
☐ Strain the stock through a sieve lined with damp muslin or kitchen paper. Rinse the pan.
☐ Measure the stock and, if necessary, return it to the rinsed-out pan and boil rapidly to reduce it to 1¾ pints (1 litre).
☐ Cool, refrigerate. Lift off the solidified fat when cold.

Reducing stock
While simmering, the stock needs to be covered to lessen evaporation; once strained, it is reduced and evaporated to concentrate the flavour. This is done most quickly in a wide, shallow pan by boiling the stock very rapidly without a lid.

White stock
Both chicken and veal can be used in the same stock. Add a trotter or calf's foot to give the stock extra flavour and greater setting qualities. It means that the stock will set as a clear jelly when cooked. Use white wine or cider to replace part of the water in the recipe, and add extra flavour.
If a boiling fowl is used for chicken stock, the meat can be cut up and served with fresh vegetables, or shredded and used in one of the chicken soups which follow.
Turkey stock—the carcass, leftovers and giblets (without the liver) of a turkey can be used instead of chicken to make a turkey soup. If using cooked turkey, boil the stock for 1½ hours only.

Veal stock
Use the recipe for Chicken Stock, but substitute 2lb (1kg) veal bones plus 1lb (500g) pie or stewing veal. Put the bones into a large pan with water to cover, bring to the boil, drain and rinse, then continue as for Chicken Stock.

Fish stock with fresh herbs

By adding fresh herbs such as parsley to your stock, you will get a spicier, stronger taste that will enhance the flavour of the fish. Fish stock made with fresh herbs will be even tastier if you double the quantity of parsley and add a coarsely chopped piece of the parsley root while the stock is cooking.

Keeping to the cooking time

Do not cook fish, or indeed any other stock for too long. The ingredients will have released all their flavours in the time given and longer cooking will only make the stock taste bitter.

Fish Soup with Crab

When you add the rice, stir 2 or 3 tablespoons of tomato purée into the soup to give it a good colour and flavour. You can add 3 tablespoons of port as well to enrich the soup.

Break large fish carcasses into pieces so they fit into the pan.

Fish Stock

Made from bones and trimmings with wine and herbs, this simple fish stock, when strained, makes a delicious basic broth as well as a poaching liquid. If you double the quantity of fish given below, the flavour will be more concentrated.

Makes about 1½ pints (900ml) ○
Preparation and cooking: 25 minutes

12oz (350g) fish bones and trimmings
1 tablespoon chopped parsley
3 white peppercorns, crushed
2 lemon slices
¾ pint (450ml) dry white wine
about 1 pint (600ml) water
½ bay leaf
1 teaspoon salt

Put the fish into a pan with the rest of the ingredients and bring to the boil. Remove the scum that rises to the surface.

☐ Lower the heat and simmer the stock gently for 15-20 minutes, skimming from time to time, if necessary.

☐ Strain through a sieve lined with muslin or kitchen paper.

Tip: Dampen the muslin, if used, so the fibres swell and help to trap tiny particles.

Fish Soup with Crab

Serves 4 ☆
Preparation and cooking:
15-20 minutes

5-7oz (150-200g) cooked crabmeat
1½ pints (900ml) fish stock
2 tablespoons finely chopped parsley
4 tablespoons boiled rice
4-6 tablespoons cooked peas
salt and white pepper
a few drops of Tabasco sauce
a few drops of lemon juice

Cut the crabmeat into small pieces, removing any pieces of shell.

☐ Bring the fish stock to the boil. Add the parsley and rice and bring it back to the boil.

☐ Add the peas, simmer for about a minute, then add the crabmeat and remove from the heat at once.

☐ Season the soup with salt, pepper and a few drops of Tabasco and lemon juice.

Fish Soup with Prawns and Tomatoes

Serves 4 ○
Preparation and cooking: 15 minutes

1½ pints (900ml) fish stock
salt and white pepper
3-4 large tomatoes, peeled
4-5oz (125-150g) peeled prawns, chopped if large
2 tablespoons finely chopped parsley
1 tablespoon finely chopped chives
a few drops of lemon juice

Bring the stock to the boil, reduce the heat to a simmer, then season with salt and pepper. Halve the tomatoes, remove the seeds and juice, then chop the flesh. Add to the fish stock and cook gently for 2 minutes.

☐ Stir in the prawns and the chopped parsley, remove the pan from the heat and ladle the soup into warmed bowls or plates. Sprinkle with chives. Sharpen the taste with lemon juice for serving.

Fish Soup with Herbs

Serves 4 ○
Preparation and cooking:
10-15 minutes

1½ pints (900ml) fish stock made with double the quantity of fish
salt and white pepper
1½ tablespoons finely chopped parsley
1½ tablespoons finely chopped chervil
1 tablespoon finely chopped chives
a few drops of lemon juice

Bring the strained stock to the boil. Season to taste.

☐ Stir in the parsley and chervil and sprinkle with chives to serve. Sharpen the taste with lemon juice.

Cream of Fish Soup with Tomatoes

Serves 4 ☆
Preparation and cooking: 50 minutes

1½lb (700g) ripe tomatoes, skinned
    and chopped
4 tablespoons chopped parsley
1 bay leaf
1¼ pints (750ml) fish stock
1½oz (40g) butter
1½oz (40g) flour
salt and white pepper
pinch of sugar (optional)
1 tablespoon chopped chives
3-4 tablespoons boiled rice (optional)

Put the tomatoes into a pan. Add 3 tablespoons parsley with the bay leaf. Pour in ¼ pint (150ml) stock and bring to the boil, then cover the pan and simmer for 15-20 minutes.
☐ Make a roux with the butter and flour and slowly stir in the rest of the stock. Cook over a low heat for a few minutes, stirring continuously.
☐ Rub the cooked tomato mixture through a sieve to remove the seeds, then stir the purée into the soup. Bring it to the boil.
☐ Season to taste with salt, pepper and sugar, then stir in the remaining tablespoon of chopped parsley, the chives and the rice, if using.
☐ Simmer for a minute just to heat through the cooked rice, and serve immediately.

Cream of Fish Soup with Tomatoes.

Paprika Fish Soup

Serves 4 ☆
Preparation and cooking: 15 minutes

1oz (25g) butter
1oz (25g) flour
½ teaspoon paprika
4 tablespoons tomato purée
1¼ pints (750ml) fish stock
salt and white pepper
pinch of sugar (optional)
2 tablespoons finely chopped parsley
4 tablespoons single cream

Make a roux with the butter and flour. Blend in the paprika, stir in the tomato purée, then gradually add the stock, stirring continuously.
☐ Cook the soup, stirring until it thickens, then simmer for 3 minutes to cook the flour thoroughly.
☐ Season and add sugar, if using. Stir in the parsley and serve with a swirl of cream on each portion.

Cream of Fish Soup with Tomatoes
Add small cubes of fish to this soup—about 6oz (175g). First cut the fish fillets into small cubes, then add to the soup after you have stirred in the strained tomatoes. Let the soup simmer over a low heat for 4-6 minutes or until the fish is cooked.

Paprika Fish Soup.

Consommé

This classic type of soup is made from really good stock which has been clarified. It can be served hot or cold (when it forms a lightly set jelly), and lends itself to a variety of garnishes. Cans of consommé may be used to make a quick jellied soup. Garnish with chopped parsley or lemon slices.

'Royale'

A traditional French garnish for consommé which is made from a custard mixture which is cooked until set and then cut into shapes.

Making a royale garnish

Steam the custard mixture, covered, until it is set.

Turn it out and leave to cool.

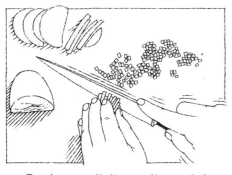

Cut into small dice or diamond shapes.

Consommé

To make a successful consommé the stock must be of a good flavour, perfectly clear and have a good rich colour. A white stock (chicken or veal) can be used in the following recipes if preferred as long as you clarify it as described on page 235.

Consommé Royale

Serves 4 ☆
Preparation and cooking: 45 minutes

1¾ pints (1 litre) Meat Stock, clarified
salt and freshly ground pepper
dry sherry to taste
2 tablespoons finely chopped parsley

The royale garnish:
a little butter
2 eggs
2 tablespoons cream
a few drops Worcestershire sauce

Make the garnish: use the butter to grease a small dariole mould or heatproof cup. Beat the eggs, cream and Worcestershire sauce together and strain the mixture into the mould. Leave to stand until air bubbles have stopped rising. Cover with foil, put into a pan and pour in enough boiling water to come two-thirds of the way up sides of the mould. Simmer very gently for 20 minutes or until the custard is set.

☐ Turn the custard out on to a board, cool, and cut into diamond shapes or tiny cubes as shown.

☐ Pour the stock into a pan and bring it to the boil. Season to taste then add the sherry.

☐ Serve garnished with the custard shapes and a sprinkling of parsley.

Consommé Julienne

Serves 4 ○
Preparation and cooking: 25 minutes

---

1 small leek, cleaned and trimmed
2 small carrots, peeled
a few French beans
1¾ pints (1 litre) Meat Stock, clarified
salt and freshly ground pepper
dry sherry to taste
2 tablespoons finely chopped parsley
a sprig of basil (optional), chopped

Cut the vegetables into thin strips.

☐ Bring the stock to the boil, add the vegetables and simmer for 4-5 minutes.

☐ Add salt, pepper and sherry. Just before serving stir in parsley and basil.

Cream of Spinach Soup

Serves 4 ☆☆
Preparation and cooking: 25 minutes

1lb (500g) spinach
1oz (25g) butter
1oz (25g) flour
1¾ pints (1 litre) White or Vegetable Stock
5 fl oz (150ml) cream
salt and freshly ground pepper
freshly grated nutmeg
2 tablespoons finely chopped parsley
2 hard-boiled eggs, sliced

Pick over the spinach and wash it thoroughly. Remove the tough stalks and chop the leaves roughly.

☐ Melt the butter in a large pan and add the spinach. Cover the pan and cook for about 5 minutes, stirring frequently or shaking the pan to ensure even cooking.

☐ Remove from heat, sprinkle the flour over the spinach and stir it in.

☐ Return to a moderate heat and gradually add the stock, stirring constantly until the soup begins to thicken. Simmer for 3 minutes.

☐ Blend or process until smooth, or pass it through a food mill.

☐ Add the cream and reheat. Do not allow it to boil. Season with salt, pepper and nutmeg and serve garnished with parsley and egg slices.

Cream of Broccoli Soup

Serves 4 ☆☆
Preparation and cooking: 25 minutes

12oz (350g) broccoli, washed
1¾ pints (1 litre) White or Vegetable Stock
1oz (25g) butter
1oz (25g) flour
5 fl oz (150ml) cream
salt and freshly ground pepper

Cut the florets off the stalks and divide them into small pieces. Chop the stalks roughly.

☐ Bring the stock to the boil and cook the broccoli stalks for 10 minutes, or until tender. Purée in a blender or food processor or pass through a food mill and set aside.

☐ Make a roux with the butter and flour in the rinsed-out pan, then gradually add the stock, stirring constantly. Bring to the boil, season to taste and add the broccoli florets. Simmer for 3-5 minutes, until the broccoli is cooked.

☐ Remove from the heat, stir in the cream and, if necessary, reheat gently before serving. Do not allow to re-boil.

Spinach Soup variation

Replace a quarter of the spinach with sorrel. This leafy plant, which has a distinctive acidic flavour, is becoming more available, and is easily homegrown.

Other vegetable soups

Use the same method as for Spinach and Broccoli Soups to make other vegetable soups—try carrot with orange, celery, or mushroom.

From left to right: Consommé Royale, Consommé Julienne, Cream of Spinach Soup, Cream of Broccoli Soup.

Clear Vegetable Soup.

French Onion Soup
The flavour can be enhanced by replacing a
little of the stock with wine or beer.

Clear Vegetable Soup

A perfect soup for slimmers, which
can be made more substantial by
adding cooked rice or small pasta
shapes to the soup with the vegetables.

Serves 4 ○
Preparation and cooking: 20 minutes

1¾ pints (1 litre) White or Vegetable Stock
8oz (225g) carrots, sliced
1 head of fennel, sliced
3 sprigs of thyme
8oz (225g) French beans, trimmed and cut
    into short lengths
4 sticks of celery, sliced
1 leek, sliced
4oz (100g) mangetout, topped and tailed
salt and pepper

Bring the stock to the boil in a large
pan. Add the carrots, fennel and
thyme and cook for 5 minutes before
adding the remaining vegetables.
☐ Simmer for about 3 more
minutes, or until the vegetables are
cooked but still crisp.
☐ Remove the sprigs of thyme,
season and serve with grated cheese.

French Onion Soup

Serves 4 ☆☆
Preparation and cooking: 40 minutes

1oz (25g) butter
1 tablespoon oil
1lb (500g) onions, finely sliced
1¾ pints (1 litre) Meat or Basic Brown Stock
salt and freshly ground black pepper
8 slices crusty French bread
4oz (100g) Gruyère cheese, grated

Melt the butter and oil in a large,
heavy-based pan. Fry the onions
gently for about 20 minutes, or until
they are golden and very soft.
☐ Add the stock and bring to the
boil. Reduce the heat, cover the pan
and simmer for 10 minutes. Season
to taste.
☐ Toast the bread on both sides,
divide the cheese between the slices
and grill until browned.
☐ Serve the soup with the slices of
toast floating on top, cheese-side
uppermost.

Vichyssoise

Serves 4   ☆☆☆

Preparation and cooking: 45 minutes
Cooling and chilling: 1½-2 hours

1oz (25g) butter
white part of 2lb (1kg) leeks, finely sliced
3 medium potatoes, diced
1¾ pints (1 litre) Chicken Stock
salt and freshly ground pepper
freshly grated nutmeg
½ pint (300ml) cream
1 tablespoon finely chopped chives

Melt the butter in a large pan, add the leeks and cook them very gently for about 15 minutes.

☐ Add the potatoes, stock, salt, pepper and nutmeg and simmer for 20 minutes.

☐ Purée the soup in a blender or processor or rub through a sieve with a wooden spoon.

☐ Cool, then chill the soup. When ice cold stir in the cream and sprinkle with the chives.

Cauliflower Cheese Soup

Serves 4   ☆☆☆

Preparation and cooking: 30 minutes

1 small cauliflower
scant pint (500ml) Chicken Stock
2oz (50g) butter
2oz (50g) flour
1 pint (600ml) milk
4oz (100g) Cheddar cheese
salt and freshly ground black pepper
a sprinkling of grated nutmeg

Divide the cauliflower into florets and rinse well. Bring the stock to the boil and cook the cauliflower until tender.

☐ Purée the cauliflower with some of the stock, using a blender or food mill.

☐ In a second pan mix together the butter and flour to make a roux. Gradually add the milk, stirring constantly until it comes to the boil and thickens. Cook for 5 minutes,

then remove from the heat and beat in the cheese.

☐ Gradually whisk in the cauliflower purée and the remaining stock and bring the soup to the boil.

☐ Season to taste, sprinkle with nutmeg and serve.

Variation: Replace the Cheddar cheese with 3oz (75g) of Stilton to give a distinctive flavour.

Variation: Instead of cauliflower cook 1lb (500g) courgettes in the stock and continue as above.

Chicken and Sweetcorn Chowder

Originating from Newfoundland and in the north-eastern coast of the United States, creamy, thick chowders can form a complete meal.

Serves 4   ☆☆☆

Preparation and cooking: 20 minutes

1¾ pints (1 litre) Chicken Stock
1 onion, finely diced
1 large potato, finely diced
1lb (500g) sweetcorn kernels
1lb (500g) cooked chicken, diced
2 hard-boiled eggs, finely chopped
salt and freshly ground black pepper
1 tablespoon finely chopped parsley
5 fl oz (150ml) double cream

Bring the stock to the boil, add the diced onion, potato and the sweetcorn and simmer for 5 minutes.

☐ Add the chicken and the egg, and season to taste. Stir in the parsley.

☐ Lightly whip the cream until it forms soft peaks.

☐ Serve the soup in individual bowls, topped with a spoonful of cream.

Variation: Replace the chicken stock and chicken with fish stock and shellfish such as prawns, mussels or scallops, or chunks of white fish. If raw, cook the shellfish or fish in the stock with the onion, potato and sweetcorn, together with some fried diced unsmoked bacon for a classic New England chowder.

Canned consommé

If there is no time to make stock use canned ready-made consommé as a basis for soups. The simplest way to present it is with a vegetable garnish such as finely diced leeks, which can be cooked very quickly in the soup as it is heated.

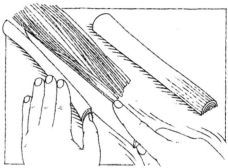

Clean the leeks and trim away the green part. Slice lengthways.

Cut across the strips to make very small dice.

Cream of Chicken Soup

Serves 4-6   ☆☆☆
Preparation and cooking:
15-20 minutes

1¾ pints (1 litre) Chicken Stock
5 fl oz (150ml) dry white wine
1oz (25g) butter
1oz (25g) flour
2 cooked chicken joints, or meat from a
    boiling fowl if used to make the stock, cut
    into bite-size pieces
salt and freshly ground pepper
2 egg yolks
5 fl oz (150ml) cream
2 tablespoons finely chopped mixed herbs

Bring the stock to the boil with the wine.

☐ Make a roux with the butter and flour in a separate pan, remove from the heat and gradually stir in the hot stock. Return to the heat and bring to the boil, stirring constantly.

☐ Add the chicken and season to taste with salt and pepper. Reduce the heat and simmer gently for 5 minutes.

☐ Beat the egg yolks and cream together. Take the soup from the heat and stir in the egg and cream liaison. Add the herbs and serve.

Chicken Liver and Tomato Soup

Serves 4   ☆☆
Preparation and cooking: 40 minutes

4oz (100g) chicken livers
2oz (50g) butter
2 tablespoons brandy
1oz (25g) flour
14oz (396g) can of tomatoes
1¾ pints (1 litre) Chicken Stock
salt and freshly ground pepper
1 tablespoon finely chopped chives

Rinse the chicken livers in cold water and pat dry with kitchen paper. Trim off any skin, fat or greenish parts.

☐ Melt half of the butter in a large saucepan and cook the livers gently, without browning.

☐ Remove the livers, slice them and sprinkle with the brandy. Leave to absorb the flavour while making the soup.

☐ Wipe out the pan with kitchen paper, then make a roux with the remaining butter and the flour.

☐ Press tomatoes through a sieve with juice, then stir the purée into the roux. Simmer for 10-15 minutes until thick, then add the stock.

☐ Bring to the boil and season to taste.

☐ Serve garnished with the chicken livers and the chives.

Clear Chicken Soup with Cucumber

Based on a well-flavoured chicken stock, which complements the subtle flavour of the cucumber, this clear soup would make a perfect first course to precede a substantial meal.

Serves 4   ○
Preparation and cooking: 15 minutes

---

1 small cucumber
1¾ pints (1 litre) Chicken Stock
4 tablespoons Madeira or dry sherry
salt and freshly ground pepper
1 tablespoon finely chopped parsley
1 tablespoon finely chopped chives

Peel the cucumber, if preferred. Otherwise cut it in half lengthways. Scoop out the seeds and slice as shown.

☐ Pour the stock into a pan and bring it to the boil. Add the cucumber and simmer for 5 minutes. Stir in the Madeira or sherry and season to taste.

☐ Just before serving, stir in the parsley and chives.

Preparing cucumber

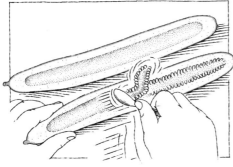

Halve the cucumber lengthways and scoop out the seeds with a teaspoon.

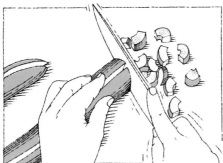

Cut into quarters and slice across into chunks.

Clockwise from the top: Cream of Chicken Soup, Chicken Liver and Tomato Soup and Clear Chicken Soup with Cucumber.

Huntsman's Soup

Huntsman's Soup

Try adding some roughly chopped, cooked chestnuts to the soup for extra flavour and a contrast in texture.

Huntsman's Soup

Serves 4   ☆☆
Preparation and cooking: 45 minutes

2oz (50g) butter
4 sticks of celery, finely sliced
1 onion, finely chopped
2oz (50g) streaky bacon, diced
2 cloves of garlic, crushed
8oz (250g) mushrooms, finely sliced
4 tomatoes, skinned and deseeded
2oz (50g) flour
1¾ pints (1 litre) Game or Basic
    Brown Stock
4 fl oz (125ml) red wine
about 4oz (100g) of the meat from the stock
    bones
1 tablespoon finely chopped mixed herbs

Melt the butter in a large pan and add the celery, onion, bacon and garlic. Cook gently until soft and beginning to colour.

☐ Add the mushrooms and tomatoes and cook for three more minutes.

☐ Sprinkle the flour over the vegetables and stir to blend.

☐ Bring the stock to the boil and stir it into the vegetable mixture. Add the red wine and return to the boil, stirring until the soup thickens. Simmer for 10 minutes.

☐ Stir in the meat and the herbs, and adjust the seasoning before serving.

Variation: To add a Scottish flavour to this soup replace the meat with the cooked flesh of a mature grouse. Thicken the soup with coarse oatmeal rather than flour and finally, at the end of the cooking time, add 2 tablespoons of whisky.

Variation: To make a satisfying puréed soup add cooked lentils rather than thickening it with the flour and butter roux, and purée with a blender or food mill.

Rossolnick

Turkey and beef soup

Serves 4

Preparation and cooking: 2 hours

1oz (25g) lard or dripping
1 set of turkey giblets, without the liver
8oz (225g) shin of beef, chopped roughly
1 turkey carcass, raw or cooked, cut up
1 large onion, sliced
bouquet garni
½ teaspoon salt
6 black peppercorns
2 pints (1.2 litres) water
1oz (25g) butter
1oz (25g) flour
2 rashers streaky bacon, diced
4-6oz (125-175g) cooked turkey, diced
1 small dill cucumber, finely chopped
salt and freshly ground pepper
1 carton (5 fl oz/142ml) soured cream
lemon juice to taste

Melt the lard or dripping in a large pan and use to brown the giblets and beef.

☐ Add the turkey carcass, onion, bouquet garni, ½ teaspoon salt and peppercorns, and the water.

☐ Bring to the boil, removing the scum as it rises, then reduce the heat, cover the pan and simmer for 1½-2 hours.

☐ Strain the stock through a sieve lined with damp muslin or kitchen paper.

☐ Make a roux with the butter and flour, and gradually add the hot stock. Stir until the soup thickens slightly, then simmer for 5 minutes. Remove from the heat.

☐ Meanwhile, fry the bacon pieces until brown and crisp.

☐ Add the turkey meat and dill cucumber to the soup and season with salt and pepper. Stir in the soured cream, add lemon juice to taste, and serve sprinkled with the bacon.

Variation: Make a clear soup with the same ingredients as above, but omitting the butter and flour roux and the soured cream. Clarify the stock after straining it, and serve garnished with the bacon, turkey and dill cucumber.

Scotch Broth

Serves 4

Preparation: 10 minutes

Cooking: 1¼ hours

1¾ pints (1 litre) Lamb Stock
2 tablespoons pearl barley
1 large leek, sliced
2 carrots, diced
2 turnips, diced
2 sticks celery, sliced
1 onion, finely chopped
salt and freshly ground pepper
cooked meat picked off the lamb
    used for making stock
1 tablespoon finely chopped parsley

Bring the stock to the boil in a large pan, and add the barley. Cover the pan and simmer for 45 minutes.

☐ Add the vegetables and season to taste. Simmer for 30 minutes.

☐ Cut the meat into small pieces and add it to the soup.

☐ Serve sprinkled with parsley.

Ham and Pea Soup

If you have boiled a gammon or ham joint, the cooking water and any left-over meat can be used as the basis of a very simple, protein-packed soup. For an easy quick-to-make version, use frozen or canned peas in this thick, rich mixture, (though cooked dried peas are more traditional).

Serves 4

Preparation and cooking: 10 minutes

1lb (500g) frozen peas
1¾ pints (1 litre) Ham Stock
2-3oz (50-70g) cooked ham, diced
freshly ground pepper

Cook the peas in stock to cover, then purée them in a blender or food mill.

☐ Add to the rest of the stock and bring to the boil.

☐ Stir in the ham, season with pepper and serve.

Garnishes for soups

A garnish is added to a soup to improve its appearance, and usually to complement it in flavour or texture. Choose something which is a contrasting colour and suited to the soup –garnishes suitable for a chunky, thickened soup might look very out of place with an elegant consommé. Many can be made in quantity and frozen. Reheat before using.

Some suggested garnishes

Croûtons–small cubes of bread fried in butter, served sizzling hot. Or you can bake them in a moderate oven and serve lightly browned and crisp.

Croûtes–small slices of toasted or fried bread, often cut into a decorative shape, and spread with anchovy paste, mustard or with cheese toasted on top.

Fleurons–scraps of puff pastry, cut into small oval or crescent shapes, and baked or deep fried.

Dumplings–small balls of dough flavoured with herbs poached in the soup or stock.

Herbs–usually finely chopped parsley, but others such as chives or fennel are suitable. Leaves such as chervil and dill are attractive left whole to float on top of the soup.

Hard-boiled egg–thin slices will float on top of the soup.

Quails' eggs–whole or halved make an elegant garnish for consommé.

Orange or lemon slices–floated on the soup.

Cream–try a spoonful of cream or yogurt swirled into each bowl of soup.

Profiteroles–tiny balls of choux pastry, baked or deep fried, filled with paté.

Lumpfish roe–black or red.

Bacon–fried or grilled until crisp, then crumbled or diced.

Meatballs–poached in the soup or stock.

For thicker soups

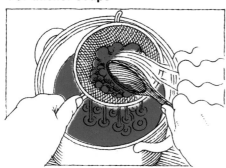

Rub vegetables through a sieve.

To thicken a base of chopped, cooked vegetables, sift in the flour to avoid lumps, then stir it in well.

Clear Tomato Soup

Stir 3-4 tablespoons of sherry or port into a clear soup. This will greatly enhance the flavour.

To make this soup very quickly use canned beef consommé instead of clarified beef stock.

Main course soups

For main course soups, add cooked pasta shapes or rice or 3-4 coarsely grated potatoes to make them more filling.

Clear Tomato Soup

Serves 4 ○
Preparation and cooking: 50 minutes

2lb (900g) ripe tomatoes
4oz (125g) chopped mixed vegetables, such as carrot, leek and celery
1 bay leaf
1¾ pints (1 litre) clarified Basic Brown Stock
salt and pepper
a pinch of sugar
a few drops of Tabasco (optional)

Wash the tomatoes, reserving 3 of the firmest ones for garnish. Roughly chop the rest and put them in a large pan with the other mixed vegetables and the bay leaf.
☐ Pour on ¼ pint (150ml) stock, cover and simmer very gently over a low heat for about 20 minutes.
☐ Strain the contents through a sieve lined with dampened muslin or kitchen paper–do not press the tomatoes and vegetables through or the soup will be cloudy.
☐ Transfer this flavoured base to the rinsed pan, add the remaining stock and bring to the boil.
☐ Season with salt, pepper and a pinch of sugar. Add a few drops of Tabasco, if using.
☐ Skin the reserved tomatoes, cut each in half horizontally, squeeze out the seeds and chop the flesh into neat small dice. Add to the soup just before serving.

Thick Tomato Soup

Serves 4 ☆
Preparation and cooking: 50 minutes

1¼lb (700g) ripe tomatoes
8oz (225g) chopped mixed vegetables, such as carrot, leek, and celery
1 bay leaf
1½ pints (900ml) Basic Brown or Vegetable Stock
1oz (25g) butter
1oz (25g) flour
salt and pepper
a pinch of sugar

Wipe and roughly chop the tomatoes. Put them into a large saucepan with the other vegetables and the bay leaf. Add ¼ pint (150ml) stock and bring to the boil.
☐ Lower the heat, cover and simmer gently for 20 minutes.
☐ Strain the tomato mixture through a sieve, rubbing as much of the vegetable through as possible.
☐ Make a roux with the butter and flour and add the stock gradually, stirring constantly. Continue stirring until the soup begins to thicken, then add the tomato purée.
☐ Simmer for 3 minutes longer, then season with salt, pepper and sugar to serve.

Thick Pepper Soup

Serves 6 ☆☆
Preparation and cooking: about 40 minutes

3 large red peppers
3oz (75g) butter
1 onion, sliced
1 clove garlic, finely chopped
3 tablespoons tomato purée
1 tablespoon finely chopped celery
2oz (50g) flour
2¾ pints (1.5 litres) Basic Brown or Vegetable Stock
salt and pepper
4oz (125g) cooked rice or small cooked pasta shells
2 tablespoons finely chopped parsley

Wipe the peppers, cut them in half and remove the stalks, cores and seeds. Finely chop the flesh.
☐ Heat the butter and fry the onion and peppers until the onion begins to colour. Add the garlic, stir well, then add the tomato purée and celery.
☐ Sift the flour over the fried vegetables, and stir until well mixed. Pour in the stock, and bring to the boil, stirring constantly.
☐ Season to taste, and stir in the cooked rice or pasta.
☐ Reheat the soup and just before serving, sprinkle in the chopped parsley.

Thick Curry Soup

Serves 6 ☆☆
Preparation and cooking: 40 minutes

1 large red pepper
2oz (50g) butter
1 large onion, sliced
1½ tablespoons curry powder
2oz (50g) flour
2¾ pints (1.5 litres) Basic Brown or Vegetable Stock
1 small leek, washed and finely chopped
salt and pepper
2 hard-boiled eggs, finely chopped
3 tablespoons double cream

Wash the pepper, cut it in half and remove the stalk, core and seeds. Chop finely.
☐ Melt the butter in a pan and fry the onion with the curry powder until the onion is beginning to colour. Add the chopped pepper and cook gently for a few minutes more.
☐ Sift the flour over the vegetables and stir to mix it in well. Gradually add the stock, stirring continuously, until the soup begins to thicken.
☐ Cook, stirring, for 2 or 3 minutes, then add the leek. Simmer the soup over a low heat for about 5 minutes, then season with salt and pepper.
☐ Just before serving, stir in the chopped eggs and the cream.
Tip: For a hearty main course soup, serve with a garnish of cubes of some of the meat used to make the stock and a loaf of crisp French bread. Alternatively add 4oz (125g) cooked rice.

Thick Onion Soup

Serves 4 ☆
Preparation and cooking: 25 minutes

1½oz (40g) butter
2 large onions, coarsely chopped
1oz (25g) flour
1½ pints (900ml) Basic Brown or Vegetable Stock
3 tablespoons red wine
salt
a pinch of cayenne pepper
1 tablespoon finely chopped chives

Melt the butter and fry the onion, stirring until it begins to colour.
☐ Sift the flour over the onion and cook, stirring, until it browns slightly. Gradually add the stock, stirring constantly until the soup thickens.
☐ Pour in the red wine and let the soup simmer gently for at least 10 minutes.
☐ Strain the soup to remove the onion or serve it as it is, whichever you prefer. Season with salt and a pinch of cayenne and sprinkle with chopped chives for serving.

Thick Curry Soup
Instead of leek and pepper you can add 7oz (200g) of thinly sliced button mushrooms.

Thick Onion Soup
To heighten the flavour, add 1 or 2 cloves of finely chopped garlic to the onions before stirring in the flour.

Left: Thick Curry Soup.
Below: Thick Onion Soup.

Oxtail Soup

It is economical to make two dishes from one oxtail. Either make an oxtail stew with the tail, then add extra stock and vegetables to the leftover stew to make a thick soup, or make clear soup from the fresh oxtail and use the meat as a basis for an oxtail stew.

Rich Oxtail Soup

Stock made from oxtail is an excellent basis for soup. It has a rich beefy taste and combines well with fresh vegetables and herbs. Reduce the stock, clarify it if you like, and garnish with parsley and peas for a clear soup, or transform it into a thick soup by whisking it into a butter and flour roux. The stock can also be used as the base for a Madeira Sauce. If possible, make the stock the day before and chill it so that the fat solidifies and can be lifted off easily.

Serves 4
Preparation and cooking: 3½ hours, plus overnight chilling if possible

---

3 tablespoons oil
2oz (50g) lean smoked bacon, cut into strips
1 oxtail, weighing about 1½lb (700g), roughly chopped
1 onion, sliced
3 pints (1.75 litres) boiling water
2 carrots, sliced
2 tablespoons coarsely chopped parsley
2 sticks of celery, coarsely chopped
1 bay leaf
1 sprig fresh thyme or a pinch of dried thyme
6 peppercorns, crushed
salt
2 tablespoons Madeira (optional)
2 tablespoons finely chopped parsley
2 tablespoons cooked peas

Heat the oil in a large, heavy-based saucepan and fry the bacon, oxtail and onion until well browned all over.

☐ Pour in the boiling water and return to the boil, removing the scum as it rises to the surface.

☐ Add the carrots, parsley, celery, bay leaf, thyme and peppercorns. When the liquid returns to the boil, lower the heat and simmer for 2½-3 hours.

☐ Strain the stock into a bowl through a sieve lined with dampened muslin or kitchen paper, then allow to cool. Refrigerate, then remove the solidified surface fat.

☐ Remove the meat from the bones, then either press as described or cut into small pieces and reserve.

☐ Measure the stock, and if necessary boil it in a clean pan to reduce it to about 1¾ pints (1 litre). Adjust the seasoning.

☐ Just before serving, add the Madeira, parsley, peas and the reserved meat.

Variations: To make a thicker soup, whisk the stock into a roux made from 1½oz (40g) butter and 1½oz (40g) flour and simmer for 5 minutes.

To make Mulligatawny Soup, add 1 tablespoon of curry powder, more chopped onions and 2 tablespoons red lentils. Cook until both onions and lentils are soft and serve with crisply fried onion rings.

Tip: To give Oxtail Soup a really professional touch, press the meat from the bones so that it can be cut into neat strips or cubes to garnish the soup. Put the pieces of meat into a small, shallow bowl and put a plate over it to fit snugly inside the bowl. Place a heavy weight on top and leave to stand for a few hours. Just before serving, dice the meat neatly and add it to the hot soup.

Rich Oxtail Soup made from a flavourful base of oxtail stock.

Making sauces

There's something special about a sauce, whether it's a light, flavoursome vinaigrette or a thick and glossy mayonnaise. Both add life and texture to crisp salad ingredients. A creamy sauce with a sprinkling of fresh herbs or a dash of liqueur gives a touch of luxury to a chicken joint. A quick brown sauce—with onions, tomatoes and cloves—will lift a chop into the gourmet class, while the merest hint of a whipped butter sauce transforms a poached fish into something spectacular.

Learning to make beautiful sauces is the best, most effective way of giving your whole style of cooking a new and immediate appeal. Even if you're a complete novice at sauce-making, there's no quicker way of transforming the familiar ingredients into exciting and satisfying dishes.

Start with something simple—a salad dressing made with yogurt or soft cheese, a five-minute sherry sauce for a thin-cut steak, or a foamy fruit sauce to pour over ice cream.

And when you've discovered just how easy it can be, go on and try something new. Experiment with different tastes and flavours, different textures and techniques. Soon, you'll be able to make the most of whatever is to hand and start creating sauces of your own.

All you need at the beginning are a few simple tools, so don't think that to make a good sauce you have to spend hours and hours in simmering and stirring. Today's electric whisks, blenders and non-stick pans all make light work of blending sauces.

Follow the few basic rules and you'll discover the secrets of the great classics, many of which have been modified in keeping with to-day's tastes and trends in cooking. Even if you are already an expert sauce-maker, there are new flavour combinations for you to try.

The galaxy of sauces

Salad dressings
White sauces
Velouté sauces
Brown sauces—simple and advanced
Mayonnaises
Hollandaise-based sauces
Sweet sauces of many kinds

The rôle of a sauce

A sauce should add piquancy, heighten flavour and give a good contrast of colour and texture. It should enhance rather than dominate the food it accompanies.

Many satisfying dishes include elements of the four basic tastes—sweet, sour, salty and bitter—as well as appealing aromatically to the sense of smell. It is the cook's skill in balancing these elements which often makes a dish and its sauce seem right and complete. So when you are next test-tasting a sauce as you make it, ask yourself which of the four elements needs adding to or balancing up.

Types of sauces

A sauce can be as simple or as complex as you like to make it. At its very simplest, a sauce is unthickened—a dab of melted butter on vegetables, or a warmed syrup poured over a steamed pudding. The easiest of the thickened sauces is made by adding just one thickening agent (eg. flour) to one type of liquid (eg. milk). As they grow more complex, however, two or more thickeners (flour and egg yolks) may be added to two or more liquids (stock, wine and cream) to add texture and flavour to the basic sauce.

From these three elements then— **thickener + liquid + flavouring** —a whole host of exciting sauces, hot and cold, savoury and sweet, can be created. Here are five basic categories into which the sauces can be divided.

Unthickened sauces

Some of the easiest and most popular sauces require no thickening at all: think of Bread Sauce, Mint Sauce, jam, syrup or apple sauces. Other unthickened sauces—those made with a base of whipping cream or yogurt— are either thick enough in themselves, or can be quickly whipped or whisked to the required consistency before flavouring.

Creamed sauces

These are simply made by adding one starch thickener (flour, cornflour) to a little cold liquid (milk, stock) and mixing, or creaming, them together. The rest of the liquid is then heated and the creamed mixture stirred or whisked in and cooked until the required consistency is achieved. A simple white sauce or pouring custard is made in this way.

Roux-based sauces

This is one in which the thickener consists of two elements: melted fat (butter) is combined with a starch (flour) to form a paste known as a roux. The chosen liquid (stock, milk) is added carefully and slowly and the sauce is stirred or whisked until cooked and thick. A lovely onion sauce can be made this way, or an old fashioned butter sauce.

Emulsion sauces

These are the mayonnaise-type of sauces, made by whisking oil or liquid fat into eggs or egg yolks until buttery and thick. The consistency of the sauce depends on the amount of oil the egg yolks will absorb, and the flavourings can be many and various—from fresh herbs, through spices to orange, lemon and spirits.

Liquids for sauce-making : Wine, milk and stock

Left : Whipped cream makes an unthickened sauce to flavour with fruit juice, purée or wine.
Right : Oil and butter for a Hot Vinaigrette

Egg sauces

These are all the ones which use eggs as a thickener, cooked gently into a liquid—such as milk, cream, or wine. Some of the creamier custards are made this way, also the tangy Italian classic Zabaglione. These sauces tend to be sweet rather than savoury, and are served both hot and cold. For special occasions, they can be flavoured with coffee or liqueurs.

Some basic principles

Remember that a starch cannot thicken a sauce until it is moistened with liquid, then cooked.

The thickening power of starch may be affected by certain other ingredients: fat will soften the thickening effect and give a richer, creamier result (a roux); acids such as vinegar or lemon juice will slow down the thickening process and should therefore be added at the end of cooking.

Lemon juice is a very useful flavour-heightener. Just a touch added when the sauce is ready for serving will make a world of difference to the taste. Salt and sugar are two other magic ingredients which work in this way.

When making sauces

Use a small saucepan when making cooked sauces so that none of the sauce is wasted by being cooked on to the pan.

Use a small mixing bowl when making uncooked sauces—it's easier to gather the finished sauce together and save waste in this way.

Sauce quantity guide
The richer the sauce, the less you need.

Vinaigrette: allow about 1 tablespoon per person

Mayonnaise: allow a sauce made with $\frac{1}{2}$ pint (250-300ml) oil to serve 8

White sauces: allow $\frac{1}{4}$ pint (150ml) per person

Brown sauces (and gravies): allow $\frac{1}{2}$-$\frac{3}{4}$ pint (300-450ml) to serve 4

Hollandaise: allow a sauce made with 4oz (100g) butter to serve 4

Hard butter sauces (eg. Brandy Butter): allow 6-8oz (175-225g) made-up sauce to serve 4

Hot custard-type sauces: allow $\frac{1}{4}$ pint (150ml) per person

Rich chocolate sauce: allow $\frac{1}{2}$ pint (300ml) to serve 4

Fruit sauces: allow about $\frac{1}{2}$ pint (300ml) to serve 4

The classic Mayonnaise

A foamy raspberry sauce is served hot or cold

Pouring custard can be thickened with eggs or custard powder

Butter and flour form a roux base

Salad dressings

A salad dressing is, quite simply, what makes a 'salad' out of lettuce. Leafy green vegetables, apples and grapes, peppers, onions and cold cooked vegetables—these are just some of the ingredients that are given a new lease of life when tossed, stirred or marinated in a well-flavoured dressing.

Vinaigrette

The chief of the cold dressings is the one called 'French' or 'Vinaigrette'. Made with **one part vinegar to three or four parts oil**, it can be flavoured, as you wish, with herbs, herb-flavoured vinegars, or the finely grated rind of lemon, orange or lime. Lemon juice or dry white wine can be used instead of vinegar—especially for salads using fruits as well as vegetables, though the dressing may not keep so long if stored.
Vinaigrette dressing is simple to make, and is based on the principle that shaking or stirring the oil into the vinegar mixes them together into a temporary emulsion, which soon re-separates if left to itself.

Hot Vinaigrette

Heat 2 tablespoons vinegar and ½ teaspoon made mustard in a small saucepan. Gradually whisk in 1½oz (40g) butter and 2-3 tablespoons oil. Season to taste and serve with avocado halves sprinkled with lemon juice.

Vinaigrette

It's a good idea to keep a small screw-top jar of this in the fridge ready to use. It will keep for several days. Store it in an 'instant coffee' jar with a plastic top which won't be corroded by the salt in the dressing.

Try different oils and vinegars until you find your favourite flavour combinations in different foods.

---

2 tablespoons vinegar   ☆☆
salt
white pepper
½ teaspoon made English or French mustard
pinch of white sugar
6 tablespoons oil

Put the vinegar, a good pinch of salt, a dash of pepper, the mustard, and the sugar into a basin. Stir until the salt and sugar have dissolved. Gradually beat in the oil until the mixture turns cloudy.
☐ Taste the dressing before using and adjust the flavouring: add more oil if it's too acidic; more vinegar or salt if it lacks flavour.
Tip: You can also make this sauce in the screw-top jar. Just make sure the top is on tight, then shake all the ingredients together.

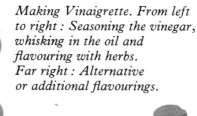

Making Vinaigrette. From left to right : Seasoning the vinegar, whisking in the oil and flavouring with herbs. Far right : Alternative or additional flavourings.

Vinaigrette with Garlic and Herbs

Try this as an alternative to a plain Vinaigrette. Finely chopped spring onion may be used instead of garlic.

Vinaigrette as recipe   ☆☆
1 tablespoon finely chopped parsley
1 tablespoon finely chopped chives
1 teaspoon very finely chopped celery
   leaves
1 clove garlic

Shake or stir the herbs and celery leaves into the dressing along with the garlic.
Tip: If you're storing the dressing for a time, leave the garlic whole, but if you want to serve it immediately, put the garlic through a garlic press or chop it finely.

Mint Sauce

So easy to make, this popular sweet-sour dressing is excellent with salads as well as the traditional roast lamb. The sauce itself is made just like tea—by steeping leaves in boiling water.

---

a handful of fresh mint leaves   ☆
4 teaspoons sugar
3 tablespoons boiling water
3 tablespoons vinegar

Finely chop the mint and put into a small heatproof dish or sauceboat with the sugar. Pour on the boiling water and stir until the sugar dissolves. Leave to cool to allow the flavour to develop.
☐ Stir in the vinegar just before serving.

Honey-Yogurt Dressing

For a very simple sweet-sour dressing, there's nothing better than yogurt and honey. Be sure to mix it just before serving because yogurt quickly separates once stirred.

5oz (142ml) carton natural yogurt ☆
1 tablespoon strained lemon juice
1 tablespoon clear honey
salt and white pepper

Stir all the ingredients together in a small basin. Spoon immediately over the salad of your choice.

Soured Cream Dressing

Soured cream is another excellent foundation for salad dressings as an alternative to yogurt. Use whatever fresh leafy herbs are available—particularly dill, parsley, basil or chives.

2 tablespoons chopped, mixed fresh ☆
    herbs
5oz (142ml) carton soured cream
salt and pepper to taste

Stir the herbs into the soured cream, season, then serve immediately.

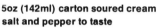

Roquefort Dressing

Of course, this dressing is named after the famous French blue cheese but other blue cheeses are also good: try Bleu de Bresse, Bleu d'Auvergne, Danish Blue, or Stilton. Taste the dressing before adding salt—all blue cheeses are fairly salty.

5oz (142ml) carton soured cream ☆☆
1 teaspoon strained lemon juice
2oz (50g) Roquefort or other blue cheese

Stir together the cream and lemon juice. Rub the cheese through a sieve into the cream and mix until smooth. Adjust the flavour with more lemon juice if liked.

Tip : A little coarsely grated dessert apple makes a good addition to this dressing, especially if you've overdone the salt after all.

Fresh Cream Dressing

A lovely dressing for fruits and other mild-flavoured foods; store up to 3 days in the fridge. Use finely grated orange or lime rind instead of lemon.

5oz (142ml) carton double cream ☆☆
1 egg yolk
1 tablespoon lemon juice
salt
a few drops liquor from bottled green
    peppercorns
a little finely grated lemon rind

Put all the ingredients into a small bowl and whisk until the mixture just holds its shape. Taste and adjust the seasoning if necessary.

Creamy dressings

Other marvellous dressings are quickly and simply made with plain yogurt, soured cream, soft cheeses or double cream as the base. They can be as tangy or as rich as you like; you can also experiment with the non-fat soft cheeses eg. the German quark and the French fromage blanc—now much more widely available. Quicker to whip up than either a mayonnaise or a salad cream, they can be flavoured with any of the suggestions already given for Vinaigrette, or try a light sprinkling of curry powder or spice.

Honey-Yogurt Dressing

Particularly good with iceberg lettuce, orange slices and salted peanuts; or with chicory, grapefruit and bananas.

Soured Cream Dressing

To make your own lightly soured cream, stir 1 tablespoon lemon juice or a few drops of vinegar into $\frac{1}{4}$ pint (150ml) double cream. This dressing is good with cucumbers, or with any variety of canned beans: use a mixture of red, green, yellow, and white as available. Always drain the beans thoroughly first.

Roquefort Dressing

Serve with a salad of sliced oranges, onions, and black olives for a delicious first course; try it with unskinned diced dessert apple, roughly chopped walnuts and sliced celery, or serve with grilled steak or rare roast beef.

Fresh Cream Dressing

Serve with grapefruit segments on a bed of crisp lettuce, or with cold poached white fish.

White Sauces

The family of white sauces, once mastered, will be your friends for life. There are three basic ones—white, béchamel and velouté—from which a host of others can be made. They enhance many a dish from eggs and vegetables to poultry, meat and fish, and can be flavoured in many different ways.

TEN GUIDELINES FOR SUCCESSFUL SAUCES

1 Use a wooden spoon for stirring and a small, heavy-based pan to help with heat control.

2 Use a wire balloon whisk. This helps disperse the flour particles more quickly and makes for a smoother sauce.

3 Keep the heat low and the sauce gently simmering.

4 Simmering also helps to cook out the taste of raw flour. It's surprising how all-pervading uncooked flour can be over other, stronger flavourings...

5 Add liquid gradually and let the sauce cook well between each addition to avoid lumps.

6 The longer you cook the sauce, the thicker it becomes. Sauces made with stock are thinner than those made with milk. From thinnest to thickest, the liquids are:
stock/skimmed milk/full-fat milk/cream.

7 Acids, such as lemon juice or vinegar, inhibit thickening. Add them *after* the sauce has reached the consistency you require.

8 Freezing usually thickens a sauce. Be prepared to add more liquid once a sauce is thawed.

9 Egg yolk or cheese stirred in at the end of cooking will thicken a sauce, as will Beurre Manié.

10 If, despite all precautions, the sauce does turn lumpy, whisk vigorously with the pan off the heat. If this doesn't work, strain the sauce through a fine-meshed sieve, pressing it through with the back of a wooden spoon. Return the sauce to the pan and carefully re-heat, adjusting the consistency with a little extra liquid if required.

The simplest of all white sauces—and the answer in a crisis—is a blended sauce (see the next page), made with flour or cornflour on the same principle you use for thickening gravy. It is cooked in a matter of minutes, can be varied to suit the occasion, and is particularly good with vegetables.

The trio of classic white sauces are all thickened with a roux base (see page 260) made of a mixture of fat—usually butter for best flavour and texture—and flour or cornflour, They all require the same simple techniques of blending and whisking. The difference is in the liquids used.

● A Basic White Sauce is usually made with milk, or milk and stock mixed.

● A Béchamel is made with flavoured milk.

● A Velouté (its name, velvety, describes its rich texture) is made with chicken, veal or fish stock and enriched with egg yolk and cream at the end of the cooking time.

You'll have success in making white sauces if you remember that more haste really does mean less speed! Keep the heat well controlled at every stage of cooking. Too high a heat at the start scorches the fat and prevents the flour from thickening properly. Too high a heat when the liquid is added—and lumps will form. Excess heat during cooking causes the sauce to stick to the pan and, if it boils vigorously, the sauce won't necessarily cook more quickly but you'll lose a great deal due to evaporation.

Heat the liquid—milk or stock—to lukewarm before adding it gradually to the sauce. This makes it easier to mix into the fat-flour roux and speeds up the cooking. Take the pan off the heat each time before adding the liquid, and stir continuously and carefully as you cook. This keeps the flour mixed into the milk or stock and helps prevent it dropping out into lumps.

A Béchamel sauce,
made with flavoured milk,
is perfect for
a classic Cannelloni.

Six-minute Sauce

Serves 2-4, depending on
 what it is served with. ☆☆
Preparation: 1 minute
Cooking time: 3-5 minutes

---

2 tablespoons flour or cornflour
½ pint (300ml) cold milk, or white or fish stock
salt and pepper
1oz (25g) butter or margarine, optional

In a small basin mix the flour or
cornflour smoothly with a little of
the cold liquid. Put the rest of the
liquid into a small saucepan over a
moderate heat.

☐ Stir a little of the hot liquid into
the mixed flour (or cornflour) then
stir this back into the saucepan.
Cook for 3-5 minutes, stirring
constantly until thickened.

☐ Add a little more liquid to adjust
the consistency to your taste. Season
with salt and pepper, add the butter
and flavour as follows:

For a Herb Sauce: Stir in
2 tablespoons chopped chives and
parsley. Serve with fried fish.

For a Cheese Sauce: Add 2-3oz
(50-75g) grated cheese and stir until
melted. Serve with boiled cauliflower
or macaroni.

For a quick Mustard Sauce: Mix in
2 teaspoons made English or French
mustard. Serve with grilled herrings.

Variations

● For carrots, use flour and half
milk, half single cream. Add butter.
Flavour to taste with lime juice or
lemon juice, grated lime or lemon rind
and chopped tarragon.

● For spinach, a slimmer's sauce. Use
cornflour and skimmed milk. Omit
butter. Stir in 2oz (50g) skimmed milk
quark. Flavour to taste with nutmeg
and lemon, or lime juice and rind.

● For broad beans or celery, use
cornflour and milk. Add butter. Stir
in single cream to taste. Flavour with
chopped parsley, or stir in 1 clove
garlic pressed through a garlic press
(or crushed with flat side of knife
blade), and 1¾oz (49g) can anchovies,
drained and finely chopped. Dilute, if
necessary.

BLENDED WHITE SAUCES

The easiest and surest way to make a smooth
white sauce is by the blended (slaked, or
creamed) method. All these names mean
that you first mix flour or cornflour with a
little cold liquid, and cook in a hot liquid.
You can make the sauce with milk or stock
and have it ready in a very few minutes.
Adjust the consistency by adding a little
extra liquid, and add flavourings as
available. One of the good things about this
sauce is that you can make it without fat.
One rule to remember: Mix the flour or
cornflour with cold liquid first, before stirring
in some hot liquid. This way you heat it up
gradually (too sudden an application of heat
cooks the flour or cornflour into lumps).

The second rule: Stir the sauce constantly
while it cooks. And it is as simple as that.
This is not one of the great sauces of classic
cuisine, but it is a good sauce for a busy
day. You can make it while the potatoes are
boiling, or while the chops are grilling.
You can use a little more liquid with
cornflour than with flour. Cornflour makes a
sauce which is slightly more translucent and
it is easier to mix than flour.

Variations

● Use dry white wine as part of the liquid.
● To make a richer sauce, stir in a little
cream instead of milk or stock when
adjusting the consistency. Cream makes a
thicker sauce; skimmed milk makes a
thinner sauce.
● Add tomato purée, curry paste, anchovy
essence, chopped capers or chopped
prawns.
● For hot or spicy flavours, start with 1
teaspoon and add more to taste.

*Three different ways: Carrots with a
lemon sauce, spinach with a skimmed
milk sauce and broad beans with an
anchovy and herb sauce.*

A ROUX (pronounced 'roo')

A roux is a kind of paste made by cooking together almost equal quantities of fat and flour. The sauce is usually easier to make if a little more fat than flour is used. The paste it forms is the foundation of a large family of sauces—usually savoury—which can be served with meat, fish, poultry and vegetables.

Roux-based white sauces

Different liquids and flavourings are added to the roux base to give a marvellous variety of sauces, like those on the following pages.

For a white sauce Add the liquid as soon as the paste is formed and before it colours. Continue cooking for a few minutes, stirring constantly. The resulting sauce is a pale creamy colour. This roux is used for most of the basic white sauces, including béchamel.

For a blond sauce Cook the roux for slightly longer, until it turns a light straw colour. A crust of bubbles will form over the surface as the liquid from the butter evaporates. When you add the liquid—milk or stock—continue cooking, stirring constantly. The resulting sauce is slightly darker in colour. This roux is used for the family of velouté (velvety) sauces.

Basic White Sauce

To serve with boiled or steamed vegetables.

Serves 4

Preparation and cooking time:
    15 minutes

¾ pint (450ml) milk
2oz (50g) butter
3 tablespoons flour
salt and pepper

Heat the milk to lukewarm in a small saucepan set over low heat.

☐ Meanwhile, melt the butter slowly in a medium-size heavy-based saucepan. When the foam begins to subside, add the flour. Mix well with a wooden spoon.

☐ Continue to cook, stirring constantly, for a minute or two.

☐ Remove the pan from the heat and stir a little of the warm milk into the roux.

☐ Return to the heat and cook, stirring constantly, until the mixture thickens. Continue to add the milk gradually, taking the pan off the heat each time and still stirring, until all the milk has been added.

☐ Continue simmering and stirring the mixture for about 5 minutes to make sure all the flour is cooked into the sauce. By now, it should be well thickened and smooth.

☐ Season to taste with salt and pepper and serve, or allow to cool, then pack and freeze.

Variations: Add 2 tablespoons chopped fresh herbs or 2 tablespoons lightly sautéed mushrooms.

Cheese Sauce

Serve with cauliflower, leeks, onions, eggs, macaroni, or poached fish.

Serves 4

Preparation and cooking time:
    15-20 minutes

---

1 recipe Basic White Sauce
2oz (50g) grated Cheddar cheese
a generous pinch of grated nutmeg

Make the Basic White Sauce, then beat in the cheese. Adjust seasoning, then add the grated nutmeg.

Tip: Use half milk and half cooking water from the vegetable.

Mornay Sauce

This is an enriched version of Cheese Sauce. The egg and cream mixture is called a liaison and is added at the end. Serve with eggs or poached fish.

Serves 4

Preparation and cooking time:
    20 minutes

1oz (25g) butter
1oz (25g) flour
12 floz (350ml) lukewarm milk
5oz (150g) grated Cheddar or Gruyère cheese
1 egg yolk
4 tablespoons single cream
salt and pepper
a few drops of Worcestershire Sauce

Make the sauce in the same way as for Basic White Sauce.

☐ Mix in the cheese thoroughly, whisking or beating until the sauce is smooth and glossy. Do not allow to overheat otherwise the cheese will turn stringy and tough.

Making a roux

Sift the flour into the butter.

Beat until it holds together in a ball.

Slowly add warm milk, stirring well.

In a small basin, mix together the egg yolk and cream and stir 4-5 spoonfuls of the hot liquid into it. Return this mixture to the saucepan and stir in well.

☐ Remove the pan from the heat and continue whisking to mix well and just cook the egg. Do not allow the mixture to boil or the egg yolk will cook too well and 'curdle' (scramble) in the sauce.

☐ Season to taste with salt, pepper and Worcestershire sauce.

Béchamel Sauce

This is made in exactly the same way as the Basic White Sauce, but the milk is first flavoured with vegetables and herbs. It takes a little longer to make. Serve with either boiled or poached vegetables.

Serves 4 ☆☆

Preparation and cooking time:
    20 minutes

1 small bay leaf
1 blade of mace
4-5 peppercorns
1 small onion, stuck with 4-5 whole cloves
1 small carrot, peeled and cut in chunks
¾ pint (450ml) milk
2oz (50g) butter
3 tablespoons flour
salt and pepper

Put the flavourings into the milk. Set the milk over low heat and leave to heat up very slowly for about 10 minutes. It should *not* be allowed to boil.

☐ Take the pan off the heat, strain off the vegetables and flavourings and proceed as for Basic White Sauce.

Gourmet Mustard Sauce

This is another variation of either the Basic White or Béchamel Sauce. Serve with grilled herrings or poached white fish.

Serves 4 ☆☆

Preparation and cooking time:
    20 minutes

Basic White or Béchamel Sauce as recipe
1 tablespoon French mustard
a squeeze of lemon juice

Make the Basic White, or Béchamel, Sauce.

☐ Beat in the mustard and season to taste with a little extra salt and pepper. Add a little lemon juice.

Tip: Don't cook the sauce for long after the mustard is added as it will make the sauce bitter. If serving with poached fish, replace some of the milk with poaching liquid.

Adding a liaison

A liaison is a mixture of egg yolk and cream—single or double—which is added to a white or a velouté sauce towards the end of the cooking time to enrich the basic sauce and make it creamy in texture. It has a thickening effect and also makes a good addition to cream soups.

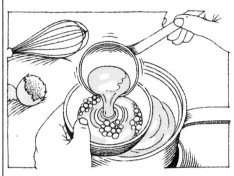

Put the egg yolk in a small basin with the cream. Add a little hot sauce.

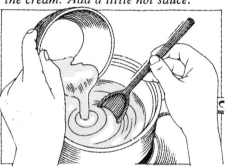

Pour the egg-and-cream liaison back into the hot sauce in the pan, stirring well. Then remove the pan from the heat and continue stirring or whisking. If the heat is too high, the egg yolk will curdle and spoil the sauce.

Mornay Sauce

As a topping for fish, or chicken casseroles, brown the sauce until bubbling under a hot grill just before serving.

Top: Mornay Sauce.
Bottom: Gourmet Mustard Sauce.

VELOUTÉ SAUCE

A Velouté sauce is made in exactly the same way as the Basic White Sauce, but with stock. If there's not enough time to make stock from the recipe given, here are some quick alternatives:

Quick stocks

Stock cubes with a chicken flavour are one of the most useful standbys in the store cupboard. They keep well, take very little space, and they're so easy to use. Remember that they are made mainly of fat and flavouring salts so don't add any seasoning without tasting the stock first. Stocks made from cubes are not suitable for reducing, or for clarifying.

Canned chicken consommé is sometimes available, but it is expensive. It is made in the same way as homemade stock, so it is an excellent substitute to use in sauces. However it, too, is rather highly flavoured so you may need to dilute it with water or dry white wine. Again, always taste before adding any seasoning.

White wine and cider are not technically stocks but they are valuable to use in dishes with poultry or any of the light meats. A can of cider or the wine left over from parties can give a lift to the most ordinary dish. With wine, use about one-third to one-half wine to water, fruit juice, or stock. Use cider undiluted.

Fruit juices are also a good alternative to stocks. Pineapple juice in a sauce to serve with chicken, apricot juice with duck, or apple juice with pork all make delicious sauces. Thickened with cornflour, they have a semi-clear appearance (see page 259).
Use them undiluted or half-and-half with stock. Fruit juice sauces are enhanced by the addition of spices and herbs: try cloves with apple juice, or rosemary with pineapple juice.

Homemade Stock

Stock is needed for many classic sauces, so a basic stock recipe is given here for easy reference. Other good stock recipes may be found on pages 236-240.

Homemade Stock

The carcass from the Sunday chicken, duck, or turkey need never be wasted. If you haven't time to make stock with it immediately, freeze it until needed.

Makes about 2 pints ◯
Preparation time: 30 minutes
Cooking time: 30 minutes

---

the bones and carcass from cooked chicken, duck, or turkey
1 medium onion, chopped
1 medium carrot, sliced
1 stick celery, sliced
½ small parsnip, sliced
½ small leek, sliced
1 small bay leaf
4 white peppercorns
1 teaspoon salt
sprig of parsley
sprig of thyme or 1 teaspoon dried thyme
cold water to cover

Break or chop the carcass so it will fit into a large saucepan. Add all the other ingredients and the water. Bring slowly to the boil and skim off the foam. Cover and simmer for 30 minutes. Strain off the stock and cool quickly before storing in the fridge, or use immediately.

Velouté Sauce

Serve with chicken or veal cooked in stock, or poached fish.

Serves 4 ☆☆
Preparation and cooking time:
    15 minutes

2oz (50g) butter
3 tablespoons flour
¾ pint (450ml) fat-free chicken stock
salt and pepper

Heat the stock gently to lukewarm. Melt the butter in a pan, add the flour and cook, stirring, to a blond roux. Gradually add the stock and, stirring, cook without boiling, until the sauce thickens.
☐ Season with salt and pepper.
Tips: For a richer sauce, beat in a knob of butter with the seasoning. For a finer, more delicate sauce, add an egg and cream liaison (see page 261).

Parsley Sauce

Serve with poached fish, or chicken.

Serves 4
Preparation and cooking time:
    20 minutes

Velouté Sauce as recipe
3 tablespoons finely chopped parsley
a squeeze of lemon juice

Make the Velouté Sauce.
☐ Add the parsley and lemon to taste. Remove from the heat immediately to keep the parsley green and fresh.
Variation: Chopped tarragon, dill, or chives may be used in place of parsley, or use a mixture of herbs.

White Wine Sauce

Serve with poached fish.

Serves 4 ☆
Preparation and cooking time:
    20 minutes

1oz (25g) butter
1oz (25g) flour
7fl oz (200ml) fat-free stock
5fl oz (150ml) dry white wine
1 egg yolk
3 tablespoons single cream
salt and pepper

Make the sauce in the same way as the Velouté Sauce.
☐ Add an egg and cream liaison (see page 261).

Tarragon Sauce

Serve with chicken, turkey or veal.

Serves 4
Preparation: 8-10 minutes
Cooking time: 15 minutes

---

1 teaspoon fresh tarragon or ¼ teaspoon dried tarragon
White Wine Sauce as recipe

Steep the tarragon in the wine over a low heat for about 10 minutes to extract the flavour. Strain off the tarragon before using the liquid.
☐ Make the White Wine Sauce.

Old-fashioned Butter Sauce

Serve with asparagus, celery or spinach.

Serves 4   ☆ ☆ ☆

Preparation and cooking time:
   20 minutes

Velouté Sauce as recipe
3½oz (100g) ice-cold butter, cut into small pieces

Make the Velouté Sauce.

☐ Remove the sauce from the heat and gradually beat in the butter.

Tip: Do not re-heat this sauce as the butter will separate out. The sauce should be served warm, not boiling. If it does separate from over-heating, drop in an ice cube and beat again until the sauce is smooth. It is most important that the butter is chilled, otherwise it will not do its work of thickening properly.

1 *Tarragon Sauce*
2 *White Wine Sauce*
3 *Parsley Sauce*
4 *Old-fashioned*
  Butter Sauce
5 *Velouté Sauce*

WHEN FREEZING SAUCES

Make double quantity and freeze half.

Use cornflour rather than flour for best results when the sauce is thawed.

Remember that small quantities thaw more quickly than large chunks.

Cool completely before packing in rigid containers for labelling and freezing.

As soon as the sauce is solid, remove from container and re-wrap in freezer foil for longer-term storage.

Choose containers with straight or outward-sloping sides for easy removal of the frozen sauce.

For the best flavour, use within 2 months.

Caper Sauce

Serve with poached fish or roast lamb. It also goes well with cold roast meat such as lamb or turkey.

Serves 4

Preparation and cooking time:
20 minutes

1 recipe Old-fashioned Butter Sauce
2 tablespoons capers
a little liquid from the capers, to taste
1 tablespoon chopped chives, optional

Make the Butter Sauce, then beat in the capers, a little of the liquid and sprinkle with chopped chives.

Left: Making Caper Sauce
Below: The finished Caper Sauce
Right: French Onion Sauce

French Onion Sauce

Serve with roast lamb or egg dishes.

Serves 4

Preparation and cooking time:
30-40 minutes

1oz (25g) butter
2 tablespoons olive oil
8oz (225g) onions, finely chopped
3 tablespoons flour
½ pint (300ml) chicken stock or vegetable water
7fl oz (200ml) single cream
salt and cayenne pepper
a squeeze of lemon juice

Heat the butter and oil in a large saucepan over a low heat just to melt the butter. Add the onions and cook very slowly and gently for 10-15 minutes. The onions should be soft but not browned. Sprinkle over the flour and stir in well.

☐ Heat the stock and cream together until lukewarm. Gradually stir into the onions, cooking gently and stirring constantly to make a thick sauce. Cook over low heat for about 10 minutes. Liquidize or purée, then rub through a sieve. Return to the heat and season with salt, cayenne, and lemon juice.

Tip: Replace part of the stock with white wine and add a sprig of thyme. Remove the thyme before making into a purée. Delicious with roast chicken.

Ingredients for Espagnole Sauce.

Espagnole Sauce

This is the most elaborate of the brown sauces, and forms the base for other rich sauces. Make it when you have time in hand, and remember that it freezes well until needed. Serve with grilled steaks, cutlets, or with game.

Preparation: enriched stock   ☆ ☆
    about 1 hour
Cooking time: 45 minutes
Makes about ¾ pint (450ml)

The enriched stock:
1¾ pints (1 litre) brown stock
6 black peppercorns
sprig of fresh thyme
1 bay leaf, crumbled
1 shallot or small onion studded with 4 whole
   cloves

The sauce:
2oz (50g) butter
2oz (50g) streaky bacon, chopped
1oz (25g) onion, chopped
1 large carrot, sliced
3 tablespoons flour
4 large ripe tomatoes
1 teaspoon vinegar
1 teaspoon sugar
salt and freshly ground black pepper
2 tablespoons ruby port (optional)

First make a rich-flavoured stock by simmering together all the stock ingredients until reduced to about half the original volume. When the enriched stock is sufficiently concentrated, strain off and use to make the sauce.

☐ To make the sauce, melt the butter in a medium-sized saucepan and cook the bacon to extract the fat and slightly brown the bacon. Add the onion and carrot before the bacon is too dark, and continue to stir over a low heat until the onion has begun to brown. Sprinkle the flour over and stir in well, cooking until it is lightly browned.

☐ Remove from the heat and gradually stir in the reduced stock. Return to the heat and cook, stirring constantly, until the sauce boils and thickens. Reduce the heat and leave to simmer.

☐ Chop the tomatoes, add them to the sauce, and cook very gently for a further 20 minutes, stirring occasionally to prevent sticking. Strain the sauce and adjust the flavour with vinegar, sugar, and salt and pepper. Add a little ruby port to make this one of the finest sauces of all.

✳ It is worth making this sauce in quantity when you have enough stock, as it can be frozen in portions.
Tip: Add Madeira instead of port. Serve with boiled ham or tongue.

Mushroom Sauce

Preparation: enriched stock about
    1 hour
Cooking time: 50 minutes   ☆ ☆
Makes about 1 pint (600ml)

Espagnole Sauce as recipe
dash of cayenne pepper
4oz (100g) mushrooms, finely chopped
2 tablespoons finely chopped chives

Prepare the Espagnole Sauce but season it with cayenne instead of black pepper and omit the vinegar. Add the mushrooms to the sauce. Cook for 5 minutes, stirring constantly.

☐ Add the chives just before serving.

Creamed brown sauces

The creamed or blended method of thickening sauces works as well for brown sauces as it does for white. Cornflour is quick and easy to use and is particularly well suited to these two sauces for serving with barbecued food or Chinese-style dishes.

Barbecue Sauce

This is particularly good with grilled pork chops or spare ribs. Use it to baste the meat while it is grilling or roasting and then serve more sauce as an accompaniment. The sauce can also be enjoyed as a dip.

Sweet and Sour Sauce

Serve this one with crisp-coated fried chicken, deep-fried pork, or prawns in batter.

Stirring in flour to thicken the sauce.

Barbecue Sauce

Preparation: 5 minutes
Cooking time: 25 minutes
Makes ¾ pint (450ml)

3 tablespoons oil
2 cloves garlic, crushed or finely chopped
1 medium onion, finely chopped
½ small red pepper, finely chopped
¼ pint (150ml) wine vinegar
¼ pint (150ml) brown stock or dry sherry
2oz (50g) brown sugar
1 teaspoon salt
¼ teaspoon chilli powder
2 tablespoons cornflour
½ teaspoon dry mustard
2 tablespoons cold water
dash of Tabasco sauce
juice of ½ lemon

Heat the oil in a medium saucepan until it looks very thin, add the vegetables and cook for about 10 minutes over a moderate heat, stirring constantly, until they are lightly browned.

☐ Add the vinegar, stock or sherry, sugar, salt and chilli powder and simmer for 10 minutes, stirring from time to time.

☐ Mix the cornflour and mustard smoothly with the cold water. Add a little of the hot liquid, then return it to the pan. Cook for about 3 minutes, stirring constantly, until thickened. Add Tabasco sauce and lemon juice, and serve.

Sweet and Sour Sauce

Preparation: 8 minutes
Cooking time: 15 minutes
Makes ¾ pint (450ml)

2 tablespoons oil
2 cloves garlic, crushed or finely chopped
1 small carrot, peeled and cut into shreds
1 shallot or small onion, finely diced
¼ red pepper, finely diced
green parts of 2 spring onions, chopped, or a few snipped chives
½ pint (300ml) chicken stock or pineapple juice
1 tablespoon honey
1 tablespoon cornflour
1 tablespoon soy sauce
½-canned pineapple ring, drained and shredded (optional)
2 tablespoons wine vinegar
salt and pepper

Heat the oil in a medium saucepan until it looks very thin, then add the vegetables and cook, stirring continuously, for about 5 minutes. Lower the heat, if necessary, so that the vegetables do not brown. Add the stock or juice and simmer for a further 5 minutes. Add the honey.

☐ Stir the cornflour into the soy sauce, blend until smooth, then stir in a little of the hot liquid. Return it to the pan. Add the pineapple, if using, and cook, stirring constantly, for about 3 minutes, or until the sauce is thickened. Stir in the vinegar and season to taste.

Sweet and Sour Sauce.

Making mayonnaise

Mayonnaise is one of the loveliest of all sauces. Light in texture and delicate in flavour, it suggests buffet suppers, summer lunches and elegant entertaining. It can transform everyday dishes into something quite special and it complements many different foods. Moreover, once you have mastered the technique of making your own mayonnaise, you will find that it serves as the basis for a whole range of other sauces. These are simply achieved by adding different flavourings, or adapting the method.

A cold buffet displays some of the many tempting dishes that are enhanced by homemade mayonnaise: poached salmon, lobster, potato and cucumber salads. A sauceboat of vinaigrette for seasoning asparagus and Salade Niçoise stands by the mayonnaise.

Mayonnaise is a basic emulsion sauce, made by whisking together eggs and oil. There's no cooking involved and you need no special equipment. When the oil is added slowly and carefully to the egg yolks, a stable emulsion is formed with the oil suspended and held in tiny droplets throughout the whisked egg. The result is a thick, sumptuous and delicate yellow cream for serving with salads, cold meats, shellfish and egg dishes.

Although the sauce appears to thicken miraculously when whisked, making mayonnaise is no mystery if you start with the right technique. The egg yolks should be large (size 1 or 2) and fresh—the fresher they are the more oil they will absorb. One egg yolk can absorb up to 6 fl oz (175ml) of oil but you can stop adding oil well before this point if the sauce is thick enough.

It is best to start with the ingredients at room temperature and some cooks like to warm the mixing bowl before using it. (Dip the bowl in hot water, then dry it.) Use a wire balloon (sauce) whisk or a small wooden spoon to beat the mixture. Add the oil drop by drop—vital at first if the emulsion is to form properly. You can add it either from a teaspoon or from a small jug. Best of all, pour it from a bottle with a plastic top with only a small aperture so you can control the rate of the flow. Add the oil to the centre (vortex) of the mixture. Beat continuously, and make sure you incorporate every drop of oil before adding more.

Basic Mayonnaise

Serves 6-8 ☆☆☆
Preparation: about 30 minutes

2 egg yolks
a little salt
dash of white pepper
pinch of dry or made mustard
about 2 tablespoons vinegar or lemon juice
½ pint (300ml) oil

Put the egg yolks into a clean bowl with the seasonings and a tablespoon of the vinegar or lemon juice. Whisk the mixture until creamy and smooth.

☐ Start adding the oil, drop by drop, as you continue whisking, until the sauce begins to form and thicken. You will feel this happening as you whisk.

☐ Once the sauce begins to thicken, start adding the oil more quickly in a series of thin trickles. Add each new trickle of oil *only* after the previous one has been fully absorbed into the sauce. The consistency of the mayonnaise should be like thick cream which has been whipped until it just holds its shape.

☐ If the sauce is too thick, whisk in a few extra drops of vinegar, *or* a few drops of warm water.

Tip: Adjust seasoning to taste with a few drops of Worcestershire sauce, a little lemon juice or a pinch of sugar, depending on the strength of flavour of the oil you have used.

Note: If substituting lemon juice for vinegar, it is wiser to use the mayonnaise on the day it is made. If stored, the lemon juice can make the mayonnaise clot.

Right: Three stages in the making of mayonnaise: the egg yolks are put in a clean bowl with vinegar or lemon juice, then whisked lightly. Lastly, the emulsion forms and the sauce thickens as oil is added.

Blender Mayonnaise

Preparation: 10-15 minutes

You can make mayonnaise quickly and successfully in a blender or food processor. Follow the basic recipe, but if you are using a blender you can use one whole egg instead of the two egg yolks. Mayonnaise made with a whole egg is lighter in texture and paler in colour and saves you having to use up leftover egg whites. Put all the ingredients except the oil into the goblet or bowl and start the machine. Pour in the oil in a thin, steady trickle, which can turn into a stream as the eggs begin to absorb the oil and thicken. Stop when the required volume has been reached.

Herb Mayonnaise

Use lemon juice instead of vinegar when making the Basic Mayonnaise for this recipe; it gives a pleasantly fresh taste.

Serves 6-8 ☆☆☆
Preparation: 40 minutes,
    plus 30 minutes chilling

Basic Mayonnaise as recipe
2 tablespoons finely chopped parsley
2 tablespoons finely chopped chives
1 teaspoon very finely chopped celery
½ teaspoon finely chopped tarragon or dill

Prepare the mayonnaise.

☐ Stir the chopped herbs into the mayonnaise. Leave in a cool place (not the refrigerator) for 30 minutes so the flavours can develop.

☐ Stir again before serving.

Tomato Mayonnaise

Serve with poached or fried white fish, shellfish or hard-boiled eggs. A tablespoon of finely chopped chives makes a good addition.

Serves 6-8   ★☆☆
Preparation: 30 minutes

Basic Mayonnaise as recipe
3 tablespoons tomato purée
pinch of sugar

Prepare the mayonnaise.

☐ Mix the tomato purée with the sugar, then gradually stir into the mayonnaise. Add just enough to suit your taste.

Variations: Just before serving, whip $\frac{1}{4}$ pint (150ml) whipping or double cream to the same consistency as the mayonnaise. Stir lightly into the mayonnaise and adjust the seasoning with salt and pepper. This also works well with leftover mayonnaise if you adjust the quantity of cream: use in the ratio of 1 part cream to 2 parts mayonnaise.

You can also add 1 or 2 tablespoons of chopped fresh tomato to the mayonnaise and 2-3 tablespoons of ruby port.

Storing mayonnaise

Mayonnaise is at its very best when completely fresh, but it can be stored in a covered container in the refrigerator for a few days. If a deeper yellow skin forms on the surface, just whisk it in before serving.
The timings are based on making the mayonnaise and its variations by hand. It will be much quicker to prepare in a blender or processor.

Rescuing mayonnaise

Even if you know the way, accidents can sometimes happen. If you find you have added too much oil too quickly in the early stages and the mixture has separated or 'curdled', do not despair. There are two ways of rescuing the sauce at this point:

● Put a fresh egg yolk in a bowl and gradually stir in the curdled mayonnaise drop by drop until a true, smooth emulsion forms again. Then continue to add oil to the mayonnaise, following the basic recipe.

● Put a teaspoon of made mustard and a tablespoon of the curdled sauce into a warmed bowl and whisk the two together. Add the curdled sauce a teaspoon at a time and the mayonnaise will thicken again. This is also a useful way to 'bring back' mayonnaise that has separated or thinned out while stored in the refrigerator.

1. Basic Mayonnaise 2. Tartare Sauce 3. Tomato Mayonnaise 4. Herb Mayonnaise.

Curry Mayonnaise

This sauce makes a delicious accompaniment to fruit-and-rice, hard-boiled eggs, or cooked chicken or fish. If serving with chicken or white fish, add about 4 tablespoons peeled, chopped prawns, or cooked crab meat.

Green Mayonnaise

For a really special treat, add a few drops of dry vermouth at the end.

Slimmers' Mayonnaise

Mix some of the Basic Mayonnaise with an equal quantity of natural yogurt, or low-fat cheese. This reduces the fat content (and the number of calories) and gives the mayonnaise added bite. It also makes it go further! For splashes of colour, stir in finely chopped red peppers and chives.

Mixing it

When folding together two mixtures—such as whipped cream and mayonnaise—you will find that they blend all the better if they're the same consistency to start with. Cream which is whipped too stiffly tends to stay in little chunks when folded into a softer mixture.

Whipping up cream

Double and whipping cream are both easier to whip when they have been stored in the refrigerator for a day or two before use.

Right: 1. Curry Mayonnaise
2. Green Mayonnaise 3. Chantilly
Sauce 4. Gribiche Sauce
5. Slimmers' Mayonnaise
6. Ravigôte Sauce.

Curry Mayonnaise

Serves 6-8
Preparation: 30 minutes,
    plus 10-15 minutes

Basic Mayonnaise as recipe
1 tablespoon oil
3 tablespoons finely chopped onion
1 tablespoon curry powder or paste
2 tablespoons dry sherry
1 tablespoon finely chopped chives (optional)

Prepare the mayonnaise.
☐ Heat the oil in a small saucepan. Add the onion and curry powder and cook over a low heat, stirring frequently, until the onion is transparent. Cool. Pass the mixture through a sieve.
☐ Stir the onion purée into the mayonnaise and add the sherry. Stir in the chives if liked.

Green Mayonnaise

The colour of this sauce enhances white fish, chicken, or salmon.

Serves 6-8
Preparation: 30 minutes,
    plus 10-15 minutes

Basic Mayonnaise as recipe
1oz (25g) spinach leaves, chopped
1oz (25g) chervil or parsley
1oz (25g) watercress
sprig of tarragon
salt and white pepper
a few drops of lemon juice
3 floz (100ml) double or whipping cream

Prepare the mayonnaise.
☐ Place the spinach, chervil or parsley, and watercress in a colander over the sink. *Slowly* pour 3½ pints (2 litres) boiling water over the leaves to part-cook them.
☐ Add the tarragon to the colander and pour about 3½ pints (2 litres) ice-cold water over. Drain well.
☐ Rub the green pulp through a sieve to make a purée, or use a food processor or blender.
☐ Whisk the purée into the mayonnaise until completely mixed. Adjust the seasoning with salt, pepper and lemon juice. Whip the cream to the same consistency as the mayonnaise, then lightly fold it in.

Chantilly Sauce

This deliciously light French sauce is superb with asparagus, seafood or cold chicken.

Serves 6-8
Preparation: 30 minutes,
    plus 15 minutes

Basic Mayonnaise as recipe
1 tablespoon lemon juice, strained
¼ pint (150ml) double cream
salt and white pepper

Prepare the mayonnaise.
☐ Stir in the lemon juice. Whip the cream to the same consistency as the mayonnaise and stir in a little salt and pepper to taste. Lightly fold into the mayonnaise.

Gribiche Sauce

Since it is made with cooked egg yolk, this is not a true mayonnaise, but it is of the same family. The texture of finely chopped egg white plus gherkins and capers makes this a good sauce to serve with cold poached fish.

Serves 6-8
Preparation: about 30 minutes

4 hard-boiled eggs
salt and pepper
1 teaspoon made English or French mustard
½ pint (300ml) oil
2 tablespoons vinegar
2 tablespoons finely chopped parsley
2 tablespoons finely chopped gherkins
1 tablespoon chopped capers

Shell the eggs, cut them in half, and remove the yolks. Finely chop or shred the whites and set aside. Rub the yolks through a sieve into a bowl; add salt, pepper and mustard (you may find you need more mustard but this can be added at the end). Mix well together.
☐ Add the oil and vinegar alternately, drop by drop to begin with, then more quickly as for Basic Mayonnaise, whisking all the time.
☐ When the mixture has thickened, stir in the parsley, gherkins and capers; add the chopped egg whites; then adjust the seasoning if necessary.

Ravigôte Sauce

Mayonnaise with soured cream and herbs is delicious with a plate of cold meats. Served with a green salad and game chips, this makes a lovely summer supper.

Rémoulade Sauce

This colourful version of mayonnaise is made with several herbs, capers, pickled onions and gherkins. Use whichever green herbs are available and vary the quantitites to suit your taste. Remember that since the sauce is flavoured with mustard, it is particularly good with grilled fish, pork and beef.

Tartare Sauce

The best possible accompaniment to fried, grilled or baked fish, especially if the sauce is home-made. If you are serving a dry white wine with the fish, omit the hard-boiled eggs. They give a metallic tang to the wine.

Rub cooked egg yolks through a fine-meshed sieve for Tartare Sauce.

Use a cradle knife (a double-handled herb chopper) with a rocking motion to chop egg whites finely for sauces such as Gribiche and Tartare.

Ravigôte Sauce

Serves 6-8
Preparation: 35 minutes,
    plus 30 minutes' standing

Basic Mayonnaise as recipe
5fl oz (142ml) carton soured cream
2 tablespoons finely chopped parsley
2 tablespoons finely chopped stuffed olives
1 tablespoon finely chopped chervil,
    tarragon, or celery leaves
1 tablespoon onion or shallot, cut into fine
    strips
salt and white pepper

Prepare the mayonnaise.

☐ Gradually stir in the soured cream, then add the herbs and onions. Stir lightly just to mix. Adjust the seasoning. Leave in a cool place (not the refrigerator) for 30 minutes for the flavour to develop fully.

☐ Stir again before serving.

Rémoulade Sauce

Serves 6-8
Preparation: 40 minutes,
    plus 30 minutes' standing

Basic Mayonnaise as recipe
1 teaspoon made English or French mustard
3 tablespoons finely chopped gherkins
3 tablespoons finely chopped cocktail onions
2 tablespoons finely chopped parsley or
    chervil
1 tablespoon finely chopped celery leaves,
    tarragon or dill
2 tablespoons capers, drained and chopped
a little juice from the capers
a little anchovy paste

Mix the mayonnaise with the other ingredients and leave in a cool place (not the refrigerator) to stand for 30 minutes for the flavours to develop.

☐ Stir again before serving.

Right: Rémoulade Sauce.

Tartare Sauce

Serves 6-8
Preparation: 45 minutes,
    plus 30 minutes' standing

Basic Mayonnaise as recipe
1 teaspoon made mustard
2 hard-boiled eggs
3 tablespoons finely chopped gherkins
1 tablespoon finely chopped parsley
1 tablespoon finely chopped chives
1 tablespoon finely chopped onion
1 tablespoon capers, drained and chopped
salt and white pepper

Mix together the mayonnaise and the mustard. Shell the eggs, cut them in half and remove the yolks. Rub the yolks through a sieve and finely chop the whites.

☐ Mix the egg yolks thoroughly into the sauce, then lightly stir in the remaining ingredients, including the chopped egg whites. Adjust the seasoning to taste.

☐ If the sauce is too thick, thin it down with a little juice from the capers, or a little cream if it is already sufficiently well-flavoured. Leave to stand in a cool place (not the refrigerator) for 30 minutes for the flavours to develop.

☐ Stir again before serving.

Cocktail Sauce with Whisky

This goes especially well with chicken or shellfish.

Serves 8   ★★☆
Preparation: 35 minutes

Basic Mayonnaise as recipe
2-3 tablespoons tomato purée
2 tablespoons whisky
salt
pinch of cayenne pepper
¼ pint (150ml) double or whipping cream

Prepare the mayonnaise, then stir in the tomato purée followed by the whisky, salt, and a very little cayenne (but remember it is *hot*).

☐ Just before serving, lightly whip the cream to the same consistency as the mayonnaise and fold it in lightly.

Cocktail Sauce with Brandy and Port:

Substitute 1 tablespoon brandy and 2 tablespoons ruby port for the whisky. Season with salt and pepper and you have a delicious sauce for prawns, crab or lobster.

Green Cocktail Sauce with Vermouth

This sauce is excellent with mussels, or with any poached fish.

Serves 6-8   ★★☆
Preparation: 1 hour

Tartare Sauce as recipe
3 fl oz (100ml) double cream
2 tablespoons dry vermouth

Prepare the Tartare Sauce.

☐ Whip the cream and the vermouth together until they have reached the same consistency as the sauce. Lightly fold into the sauce.

Anchovy Cocktail Sauce

Serve with hard-boiled eggs.

Serves 6-8   ★☆☆
Preparation: 35 minutes

Basic Mayonnaise as recipe
6 anchovy fillets, finely chopped
grated rind of ½ lemon
squeeze of lemon juice

Prepare the mayonnaise.
☐ Add anchovies and lemon rind. Adjust the flavour with lemon juice.

COCKTAIL SAUCES

Mayonnaise makes the perfect base on which to create a cocktail sauce to serve with shrimps, prawns, mussels, crab and other types of seafood. These cocktail sauces also complement canned fish and, with a sprinkling of parsley or a fine chopping of egg white to garnish, you have a quickly made and popular first course. A little alcohol lifts a sauce like this into the 'special' class.

Cocktail sauces need not be limited to serving with seafood. Hand one of these round with cold roast chicken, turkey or poached or fried white fish.

Remember not to overwhelm the food with the sauce, or the sauce with the flavouring.

Serving tips

● Pieces of leftover cooked poultry mix well with prawns, shrimps or other seafood.
● You can 'stretch' crab and lobster by mixing it with pieces of cooked white fish such as plaice, whiting or monkfish, or even cooked diced vegetables such as celery, carrot or fennel.

Left to right:
Cocktail Sauce with
Whisky, Green Cocktail
Sauce with Vermouth,
Cocktail Sauce with
Brandy and Port.

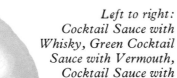

DIPS

These come halfway between a sauce (they're richer in flavour) and a spread (they're thinner in texture). As they are well-flavoured, they go with raw vegetables and cocktail snacks such as crisps and savoury biscuits. Don't limit them to party occasions. Make a dip or two when there's a casserole in the oven or cold food for later, and the family are all going to arrive at different times.

Remember that texture is important—nothing is sadder than a runny dip—and try some of the following:

Foundations cottage cheese, cream cheese or low/medium-fat soft cheese

Fillers (mash, mince or finely grate) hard cheese, hard-boiled egg, cooked poultry or cold meats

Thinners soured cream, double or whipping cream (whipped), mayonnaise, plain yogurt

For colour and texture (chopped or minced) capers, gherkins, onions, cocktail onions, spring onions, garlic, chives, celery, cucumber, olives, peppers and nuts, raw dessert apple, pineapple, leafy green herbs

Seasonings (to suit the main ingredient) barbecue sauce, mushroom or tomato ketchup, Worcestershire sauce, Tabasco, soy sauce, horseradish sauce, made mustard, curry paste, lemon juice, cayenne, chilli pepper, spices

Left to right: Tomato Dip, Curry Dip with Onion, Salmon Dip.

Tomato Dip

Serves 4 ☆☆☆
Preparation: 35-40 minutes

4 tablespoons Basic Mayonnaise as recipe
3oz (75g) low or medium-fat soft cheese
3 tablespoons soured cream
2 tablespoons tomato purée
1 teaspoon tomato ketchup
pinch of sugar
salt and pepper

Prepare the mayonnaise.

☐ Beat together the cheese and cream, mix in the mayonnaise and flavour to taste with the remaining ingredients. The consistency should be like softly whipped cream.

Curry Dip with Onion

Serve this with poppadums.

Serves 4 ☆☆☆
Preparation: 40 minutes

2 tablespoons Basic Mayonnaise as recipe
3oz (75g) cream cheese
2 tablespoons finely chopped onion
1 tablespoon curry paste
1oz (25g) finely grated apple
1 tablespoon raisins or sultanas, chopped
salt and a dash of cayenne pepper

Prepare the mayonnaise.

☐ Beat together the cheese, onion and curry paste. Stir in enough mayonnaise to give the consistency of softly whipped cream. Add the apple and raisins and season.

Salmon or Tuna Dip

Serves 6 ☆☆☆
Preparation: 45 minutes

2-3 tablespoons Basic Mayonnaise as recipe
8oz (225g) can of salmon or tuna
2oz (50g) low- or medium-fat soft cheese
2 teaspoons tomato ketchup
salt and pepper
squeeze of lemon juice
1 tablespoon finely chopped dill, parsley or chives

Prepare the mayonnaise.

☐ Drain the fish well and remove any skin. Mash in a bowl, then add the soft cheese. Mix well.

☐ Add enough mayonnaise to give the consistency of softly whipped cream, then flavour to taste with the remaining ingredients.

Variation: Use sardines instead of salmon or tuna, and add a little French mustard.

Hollandaise sauces

Like mayonnaise, Hollandaise is an emulsion sauce and the mother of a whole family of variations. Unlike mayonnaise however, it is a cooked sauce for serving warm (with vegetables, eggs, fish and meat) and the emulsion is formed from egg yolks with butter rather than oil. Hollandaise is flavoured with lemon juice, vinegar and herbs. Though rich, it has a delicate flavour which has earned it a place as one of the great classic sauces. On the following pages you will find easy instructions for making Hollandaise and for varying it by the addition of whipped cream, fresh tomato purée or orange juice. When flavoured with tarragon, it becomes a Béarnaise, or you can add concentrated fish stock to make a Hollandaise to serve with fish dishes. Also included in this section are quick recipes for a 'mock' Hollandaise and for a lovely homemade salad cream.

Golden rules for successful Hollandaise

● Start with good fresh ingredients at room temperature and with unsalted, softened butter.

● Take care not to overheat the egg yolks at any stage. This means applying heat slowly and gradually so the eggs do not scramble.

● Add the butter a little at a time and make sure one batch has been thoroughly absorbed into the sauce before adding more. If you add the butter too quickly the sauce may separate. One egg yolk can hold up to 4oz (100g) butter but there is no need to use the maximum amount and, if you are a beginner, it is safer to use only 2oz (50g) butter per egg yolk.

● If at any time you think the sauce is getting too hot, stand the pan in a bowl of cold water to arrest the cooking.

● Keep Hollandaise warm, or re-heat it, over very gentle heat, such as that provided by a pilot light on top of the stove, or by standing the bowl in a pan of warm water. It is best not to keep Hollandaise warm for longer than about an hour before serving. Any sudden fluctuation in temperature will make it curdle.

● It is really best to make the Hollandaise directly before serving. With practice, this doesn't take long.

Left: Broccoli served with a classic Hollandaise Sauce.

Unsalted butter

It is best to use unsalted butter for the Hollandaise family of sauces as it gives a better flavour. Seasoning—including salt—is added at the end of cooking.

Rescuing Hollandaise

If you are unlucky and do slightly overheat the sauce so that it separates, here is a simple remedy. Drop in an ice cube; you will find you can then beat the sauce back to smoothness again.

Peeling tomatoes for Tomato Hollandaise

Pour boiling water into a bowl. Nick the skins of the tomatoes to be peeled by cutting a small cross on the base opposite the stalk end, then immerse them in the boiling water. After 1-2 minutes, lift out with a slotted spoon, or drain the tomatoes. Their skins should now peel off easily using a knife or your fingers. (If peeling them by hand, let them cool a little first, or keep them under running cold water for a minute or two.)

Hollandaise Sauce

Serve with asparagus, broccoli or salmon.

Preparation and ☆☆☆
  cooking time: about 45 minutes
Makes ¾ pint (450ml) to serve 6-8

The stock:
3 tablespoons white wine vinegar
2 tablespoons water
4 coarsely ground black peppercorns
1oz (25g) finely chopped shallot
    or onion
small bay leaf
sprig of parsley, roughly chopped

The sauce:
3 egg yolks, size 2
5-7oz (150-200g) unsalted butter,
    softened
salt and white pepper
few drops lemon juice

Put the ingredients for the stock into a small saucepan over a low heat. Simmer gently, stirring occasionally, until the liquid has been reduced by at least half. The more slowly the stock cooks and the longer it takes to reduce, the better will be the flavour.

☐ Strain the liquid through a piece of muslin (as shown) or cheesecloth, or through a coffee filter paper.

☐ Put the egg yolks into a small pan or basin (or in the top compartment of a double-boiler) over a pan of water on a low heat. Gradually stir in the strained liquid and cook until it is just beginning to thicken. Keep the water below boiling point to prevent the sauce curdling.

☐ Gradually whisk in 2 rounded teaspoons of the butter. Remove from the heat and continue to whisk in the rest of the butter, a little at a time. The finished sauce will be smooth and glossy and fairly stiff.

☐ Season to taste with salt, pepper and lemon juice. Serve in an unheated sauceboat.

Tip: This sauce is always served lukewarm because if over-heated it separates; hence the unheated sauceboat.

Right: Ingredients and equipment for making the perfect Hollandaise. Straining the reduced stock through muslin or cheesecloth and cooking the sauce in a double saucepan.

Tomato Hollandaise Sauce

This rich, apricot-coloured sauce is one of the loveliest of the Hollandaise family. Making the tomato stock takes a little patience but it gives the sauce the most subtle, delicate flavour. Serve with poached white fish.

Preparation and   ☆ ☆ ☆
   cooking time: about 1 hour
Makes ¾ pint (450ml) to serve 6-8

The stock:
6oz (175g) ripe tomatoes
1 tablespoon unsalted butter
pinch of sugar
few drops Worcestershire sauce
salt and white pepper

The sauce:
3 egg yolks, size 2
5-7oz (150-200g) unsalted butter,
   softened
a few drops lemon juice
salt and white pepper

Peel the tomatoes (see the sidelines on the opposite page), cut them in half and scoop out the seeds. With your hand, press the tomatoes flat on kitchen paper to remove as much liquid as possible. Liquidize or process the tomatoes to a purée.

☐ Melt the butter in a small saucepan over a low heat. Add the tomato purée and simmer for 2 minutes, stirring all the time. Season with sugar, Worcestershire sauce, salt and pepper.

☐ Use this stock to make a sauce with the egg yolks and butter in the same way as for the basic Hollandaise Sauce.

☐ Adjust the flavour with lemon juice and seasoning.

Tip: Ready-made concentrated tomato purée is too strong in flavour for this sauce.

Variation: Add some chopped chives to the sauce before serving.

Whisking egg yolks in a bowl at the start of making Hollandaise.

Adding the stock to the egg yolks over gently simmering water.

Below: Adding concentrated orange juice to make Maltese Sauce, and a sauceboat of Mousseline Sauce (Hollandaise with whipped cream added). Both these recipes are on the next page.

Mousseline Sauce

Serve with poached trout, grilled sole, broccoli, seakale and asparagus. Serve as soon as possible as it is very light and delicate.

Preparation and ☆☆☆
   cooking time: about 1 hour
Makes ¾ pint (450ml) to serve 6-8

Hollandaise Sauce as recipe
4 tablespoons double cream
salt and white pepper

Prepare the Hollandaise Sauce and leave to cool.
☐ Whip the cream to soft peaks. Whisk the Hollandaise until it is completely cool.
☐ Fold in the whipped cream and season to taste.

Maltese Sauce

The juice of blood oranges is used as a 'stock' (or flavouring liquid) and a little orange peel is added as a garnish. Serve with salmon, trout, asparagus or calabrese.

Preparation and ☆☆☆
   cooking time: about 45 minutes
Makes ¾ pint (450ml) to serve 6-8

3 egg yolks, size 2
3 tablespoons blood orange juice
5-7oz (150-200g) unsalted butter, softened
salt to taste
squeeze of lemon juice
a few strips of orange peel, to garnish

Heat the egg yolks with the orange juice and whisk in the butter in the same way as for Hollandaise Sauce. Add salt and lemon juice to taste.
☐ To prepare the orange peel garnish, thinly pare an orange, taking care not to remove any white pith with the peel. Cut the peel into thin strips and blanch in boiling water for 2-3 minutes. Drain and rinse in cold water. Sprinkle the strips over the sauce.
Tip: When blood oranges are not available, any type of orange may be used.

Béarnaise Sauce

Tarragon is the characteristic flavour of this great sauce so it is best to make it with the fresh herb. Serve with steak and other grilled meats.

Preparation and ☆☆☆
   cooking time: about 45 minutes
Makes ¾ pint (450ml) to serve 6-8

The stock:
4 tablespoons white wine vinegar
4 white peppercorns
1 tablespoon finely chopped shallot
   or onion
1 tablespoon finely chopped leek,
   white part only
small bay leaf, crumbled
sprig of parsley, roughly chopped
sprig of fresh tarragon

The sauce:
3 egg yolks, size 2
5-7oz (150-200g) softened butter
2 teaspoons finely chopped fresh
   tarragon
salt
squeeze of lemon juice

Combine the stock ingredients, cook to reduce by half and use to make the sauce as for Hollandaise Sauce.

Salad Cream

Preparation and ☆☆☆
   cooking time: 20 minutes
Makes ¾ pint (450ml) to serve 6-8

3 egg yolks, size 2
1 teaspoon made mustard
4 tablespoons oil
4 tablespoons double cream
2 tablespoons white wine vinegar
salt and white pepper
dash of Worcestershire sauce
1 teaspoon sugar (optional)

Put the egg yolks, mustard, oil, cream and vinegar into a large basin and set over a pan of water on a low heat. Keep the water just below boiling point, and whisk at intervals until the sauce begins to thicken. Continue whisking until it resembles a thick, smooth custard.
☐ Remove from the heat and add salt, pepper and Worcestershire sauce. Add the sugar, if liked.

Mousseline Sauce

Whisk double cream to soft peaks with an electric whisk.

Stir the whipped cream into the Hollandaise sauce.

Salad Cream
We have become so accustomed to having salad cream from a bottle that we forget how good—or how easy it is to make at home.
It can be served hot with poached fish dishes but is best if left to get cold. Serve with cold cooked vegetables, salads, cold chicken and fish. If serving with shellfish, add a little tomato purée.

The following are all easy to make.

Parsley Sauce: Add 2 tablespoons of finely chopped parsley just before serving.

Chive Sauce: Add 2 tablespoons of finely chopped chives.

Dill Sauce: Add 1 tablespoon of finely chopped dill.

Horseradish Sauce: Add 1 tablespoon of grated horseradish and a pinch of sugar.

Lemon Sauce: Add a little grated lemon rind and substitute more lemon juice for some of the wine. This sauce is particularly good with French beans.

Caper Sauce: Replace the lemon juice with liquid from the capers and add 1 tablespoon of drained capers.

Tarragon Sauce: Replace the lemon juice with white wine vinegar and add 1 teaspoon of finely chopped fresh tarragon.

Quick 'Hollandaise'

This sauce, with its variations, is a cross between a savoury egg custard and a true emulsion. It is much quicker and easier to make than the preceding sauces. Although less subtle, it is a very good sauce for when you have little time to cook as you can use an electric whisk. All are very good served cold. Serve with freshly cooked vegetables, asparagus, artichokes, celery or spinach.

Preparation and ☆☆☆
   cooking time: 10-15 minutes
Makes ¾ pint (450ml) to serve 6-8

2 egg yolks, size 2
1 whole egg, size 2
2 teaspoons lemon juice
4 tablespoons white wine
3½oz (100g) unsalted butter,
   softened
salt and white pepper

Whisking the ingredients for Quick 'Hollandaise' Sauce. There is no need to have the pan over heat, especially if an electric whisk is used. If the speed is not easy to regulate, try using one of the beaters instead of both.

Put all the ingredients into a 2 pint (1.2 litre) basin and whisk just to mix; the butter will separate into small pieces.

☐ Set the basin over a pan of hot, but not boiling, water on a low heat and whisk until beginning to thicken. During the cooking–about 5 minutes–scrape down the sides of the basin 2 or 3 times so that no sauce is wasted. (A plastic spatula is very useful for this purpose.)

☐ As soon as the sauce is thickened, remove from the heat. It will have the consistency of thick custard and will be very smooth. Do not re-heat but serve as soon as possible in an unheated sauceboat.

❋ Freezing and thawing Hollandaise sauces

The following sauces freeze well and as they all take time to make, it is good to have a supply in the freezer: Hollandaise, Tomato Hollandaise, Mousseline Sauce, Maltese Sauce, Béarnaise Sauce, Quick 'Hollandaise,' White Wine Hollandaise.

To thaw: Turn out into a basin, cover with foil and leave in a warm place–but not near direct heat. The airing cupboard is a good place. Allow about 1 hour to thaw ½ pint (300ml) sauce.

To re-heat (except Quick 'Hollandaise'): Set the covered basin over a pan of warm water on a very low heat. Remember that this type of sauce should never be more than tepid. If the butter shows signs of separating out, apply the ice cube treatment (see Rescuing Hollandaise). Allow the sauce at least 30 minutes to re-heat, stirring occasionally.

Re-heat the Quick 'Hollandaise' in a saucepan over direct heat but keep the flame low, and stir constantly.

Above: Poached fillets of plaice with White Wine Hollandaise.

Fish fumet
A fishmonger will usually give you fish bones and heads for a very modest sum when you buy fish. If bones are not available, use a mixture of small, whole fish such as whiting, halibut and plaice. The bones of Dover sole are excellent, but avoid lemon sole which makes stock cloudy.

Fish Fumet

Fish stock takes only a short time to cook. It is used in its concentrated form (fumet) in the White Wine Hollandaise to serve with fish.

Preparation: 45 minutes
Makes about ¾ pint (450ml)

2-3 fish carcasses or a mixture of fish heads and bones
1 onion, chopped
1 carrot, chopped
bouquet garni of 1 bay leaf, a sprig of parsley, a few peppercorns, ½ teaspoon fennel seeds and a blade of mace
1 teaspoon salt
2 pints (1.2 litres) water and white wine mixed

Put all ingredients in a pan. Cover and simmer gently for 30 minutes.
□ Strain and cool. This gives you the basic fish stock.
To make fumet: reduce the stock to a syrup by boiling vigorously. This fumet can become the basis of a sauce (as right) or can be made into an aspic with which to serve cold fish.

White Wine Hollandaise

Serve with poached fish, fish fillets or fish soufflés.

Preparation and
  cooking time: 2½ hours   ☆☆☆
Makes ¾ pint (450ml) to serve 6-8

The stock:
2-3 tablespoons fish fumet as recipe

The sauce:
3 egg yolks, size 2
5-7oz (150-200g) unsalted butter, softened
salt and white pepper
few drops lemon juice

Prepare fish fumet and let it cool.
□ Make the sauce as for Hollandaise, using the fish fumet instead of the vinegar stock. Take care when seasoning as the fumet already contains salt.
□ Add a little lemon juice and serve the sauce lukewarm in an unheated sauceboat.
Variation: Add a little grated orange rind to the finished sauce.

Sweet sauces

Sweet sauces add the finishing touch to the chapters on sauce-making. They are simple, quick and practise the principles already covered. With this set of basic sauces you can create a host of others to complement the puddings and desserts you most enjoy. Learn to whip up a speedy Butterscotch Sauce or a Celebration Strawberry Sauce, and you'll never be at a loss when unexpected guests arrive. Some, like the Sabayon and the Chocolate Sauce, can be turned into desserts on their own. Most can be served hot or cold, and keep well for several days in the fridge, ready to transform a winter pudding, summer ice or creamy rice pudding into something special.

Sweet sauces, such as the basic Vanilla Sauce, are usually thickened with cornflour (or arrowroot) and often eggs as well, because these give a finer, more glossy finish to a sauce. However, the hard butter sauces, many of the fruit purée sauces, and those based on jam or syrup need no thickening.

Master the basic technique, then experiment as you like with essences and spices, or a subtle drop of spirit or liqueur, to create your own variations of flavour and texture.

Vanilla Sauce

Serves 4 ☆☆
Preparation and cooking time:
10-15 minutes

½ vanilla pod (split lengthways)
18 fl oz (500ml) milk
2 teaspoons cornflour
2 tablespoons caster sugar
3 egg yolks, size 2

Place the vanilla pod in a heavy-based saucepan with the milk. Set the pan over a low heat and bring very slowly to just below boiling point. Take the pan off the heat and remove the vanilla pod.

☐ In a small basin, mix together the cornflour, sugar and egg yolks until smooth. Stir in a little of the hot milk, then pour this mixture back into the milk in the pan.

☐ Return the pan to the heat and cook gently, stirring all the time, until thickened and smooth. For a slightly thinner sauce, stir in a little extra milk.

Tip: It is natural for a skin to form as the sauce cools. Either skim it off before serving or, if keeping the sauce hot, cut out a piece of greaseproof paper or foil and press it lightly over the surface. This should prevent a skin from forming.

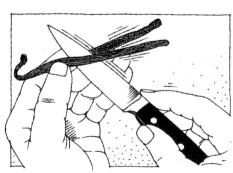

Split the vanilla pod lengthways for maximum flavour.

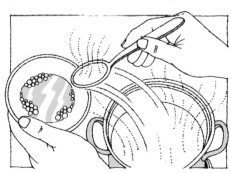

Add a little hot milk to the yolks before stirring them in.

Rules for sweet sauces

1 When making milk-based sauces such as Vanilla Sauce, always keep the heat moderate to avoid the milk 'catching' on the base of the pan.
2 Stir constantly when making milk-based sauces, to avoid scorching and uneven thickening.
3 With egg-based sauces, keep to a moderate heat, otherwise the egg will separate out before the sauce is cooked.
4 Sauces made with cornflour can be cooked quickly in a saucepan, but they're even better if you cook them more slowly in a double boiler. This way you should only need to stir them occasionally.
5 Arrowroot is often used in sauces instead of cornflour. It gives a softer 'set' and a greater translucency. It is most commonly used as a glaze for fruit tarts and cakes.
6 Richer sauces can be made by replacing part of the milk with single cream.
7 When flavouring sauces, always start with a little, then gradually add the chosen flavouring until it's the depth you need.

To tell when a pouring custard is cooked. Dip a metal tablespoon into the sauce, then invert it over the pan. The custard should form a rim around the edge of the spoon when it's ready.

Vanilla Sauce

Hot vanilla sauce is good with steamed puddings, light fruit sponges and hot fruit pies. Cold, it makes a delicious accompaniment to fresh fruit salad, compotes, and jellies.

Variations

Mix instant coffee, ground cinnamon, ginger or nutmeg into the cornflour when making the sauce. Try 1 level teaspoon first, until you decide the strength of flavour.
● Coffee goes well with steamed puddings.
● Cinnamon goes well with poached apples.
● Ginger goes well with poached pears.
● Nutmeg goes well with prunes.
For a rich Vanilla Sauce, if cold, fold in 3 fl oz (100ml) whipped cream just before serving.

Instead of using a vanilla pod, use vanilla sugar, made by storing a split vanilla pod in a jar of sugar.
You can use a vanilla pod over and over again until the flavour gradually goes. Just wipe it dry after use and store it in its jar until the next time it's needed.

Fluffy Vanilla Sauce

This sauce is made in the same way as the basic Vanilla Sauce but egg whites are whisked and folded in at the end. You can vary the flavour as you wish, but the sauce should be served while still hot because the egg whites tend to separate out if the sauce is left to cool. It goes well with light sponges or fruit pies.

Making Caramel Sauce

First pour the sugar into a heavy-based saucepan. Stir all the time.

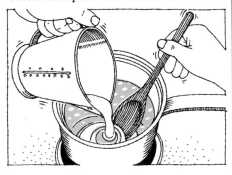

When the sugar is light brown, pour in the milk, still stirring.

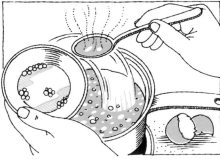

With a metal spoon, add some of the hot sauce to the egg yolks.

Fluffy Vanilla Sauce

Serves 4
Preparation and cooking time:
   15 minutes

½ vanilla pod (split lengthways)
18 fl oz (500ml) milk
2 teaspoons cornflour
2 tablespoons sugar
3 eggs, size 2, separated

Place the vanilla pod in a heavy-based saucepan with the milk. Set the pan over a very low heat and bring very slowly to just below boiling point. Take the pan off the heat and remove the vanilla pod.

☐ In a small basin, mix together the cornflour, sugar and egg yolks until smooth. Stir in a little of the hot milk, then pour this mixture back into the milk in the pan.

☐ Return the pan to the heat and cook gently, stirring all the time, until the sauce is thickened and smooth. If you like a slightly thinner sauce, stir in a little extra milk.

☐ Whisk the egg whites until they form peaks and gradually whisk in the cooked sauce. Serve at once.
Variation: If you add spices or coffee flavour, use soft brown sugar for added colour and flavour.

Coffee Custard Sauce

You can make a very simple, very good cold sauce from a packet of custard powder or a sachet of 'instant' custard. Serve with fresh raspberries or poached pears.

Serves 4
Preparation and cooking time:
   10 minutes (plus cooling)

---

1 sachet (or 2 tablespoons) custard
   powder
2 tablespoons sugar
2 teaspoons instant coffee granules
½ pint (300ml) milk
5 fl oz (142ml) carton double cream and
   5 fl oz (142ml) carton single cream

Mix together the custard powder, sugar and coffee in a little of the cold milk until smooth.

☐ Heat the rest of the milk in a small saucepan until almost boiling. Stir into the custard mixture, then return to the saucepan. Cook, stirring constantly, over a gentle heat for 2-3 minutes until thickened.

☐ Remove from the heat and pour into a basin. Cover with a piece of buttered greaseproof paper and leave to get cold–about an hour.

☐ Mix together the two creams and whip to a soft dropping consistency, then whisk into the cold custard.

Caramel Sauce

This takes a little care; the flavour comes from caramelizing the sugar which can burn so quickly if you look away for an instant.
Caramel makes one of the best of all sauce flavours while burnt sugar tastes bitter.

   It is good served hot but is even better cold with ice cream, blancmange or other moulded desserts. Whisk before serving.

Serves 4
Preparation and cooking time:
   12-15 minutes

5oz (150g) caster sugar
9 fl oz (250ml) milk
7 fl oz (200ml) single cream
2 teaspoons cornflour
2 eggs, size 2, whisked

Put the sugar into a heavy-based saucepan and place over a moderate heat. Watch it until it begins to melt and turn colour, then stir with a wooden spoon to ensure that the sugar browns evenly.

☐ As soon as the sugar is a rich brown, remove the pan from the heat and immediately pour in the milk. Stir until the caramel dissolves into the milk then stir in the cream. Heat until steam begins to rise.

☐ Whisk the cornflour with the eggs in a bowl until light and fluffy, then quickly stir or whisk the hot milk into this mixture. Return it to the saucepan and stir over a low heat until thickened. Do not allow to boil before serving.

Butterscotch Sauce

Serves 4 ☆☆
Cooking time: 5 minutes

8oz (225g) golden syrup
2oz (50g) butter
½ teaspoon vanilla essence

Heat all the ingredients together in a saucepan until well melted. Remove from the heat, stir, and serve hot or cold.

Quick Chocolate Sauce

Serves 4 ☆☆
Cooking time: 5 minutes

8oz (225g) golden syrup
2oz (50g) butter
2 tablespoons cocoa
½ teaspoon vanilla essence

Make in the same way as for the Butterscotch Sauce.

Syrup sauces
Golden syrup makes an excellent quick butterscotch or chocolate sauce to serve with hot puddings or with ice cream. Either stores for 2-3 weeks in the fridge in a screw-top jar. If they get too thick when cold, just set the container in a pan of hot water.

Instant Custard Sauce
For a really last-minute sauce, keep a packet of instant custard in the cupboard. Make up with slightly less water than indicated then stir in single cream to taste.

1 Caramelizing the sugar.
2 Stir until the caramel dissolves in the milk.
3 Return the egg yolk and cornflour mixture to the pan.
4 The finished Caramel Sauce.

Making Fluffy Vanilla Sauce.

A Soft Fruit Sauce goes well with blancmange.

Chocolate Sauce

One of the simplest of all the sweet sauces is thickened just with cornflour. To this basic sauce, you can add whatever flavour you like. This chocolate sauce is just one example; another is the Raspberry Sauce.

You'll notice there are no eggs to act as additional thickeners, so the amount of cornflour has to be increased. Some recipes tell you to mix the sugar with the cornflour and cocoa; if you stir it in at the end there is less chance of the mixture sticking to the pan.

Chocolate Dessert

Leave the Chocolate Sauce to get cold, then quickly turn it into a light dessert. Remove any skin from the top and fold in 3 fl oz (100ml) lightly whipped double cream.

Sabayon Sauce

If you have no madeira or marsala, use sherry instead (dry or sweet according to taste). If serving on its own as a dessert, serve with small, crisp biscuits such as langues de chat.

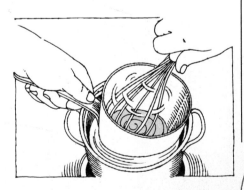

A Sabayon pan: deep for immersing in water, rounded for whisking.

Chocolate Sauce

Serve hot with chocolate sponge pudding, steamed lemon pudding, vanilla blancmange, or hot or cold with ice cream or ice cream desserts.

Serves 4 ☆
Preparation and cooking time:
  5 minutes

18 fl oz (500ml) milk
2 tablespoons cornflour
2 tablespoons cocoa
a few drops vanilla essence
2oz (50g) sugar

Mix a little of the cold milk in a basin with the cornflour and cocoa to form a smooth paste. Put the rest of the milk on to heat until nearly bubbling, then stir it into the cornflour mixture.

☐ Return the flavoured milk to the saucepan and cook, stirring constantly, over a moderate heat until the sauce is thickened and smooth. Stirring in a little vanilla essence helps to heighten the chocolate flavour. Add the sugar.

Tip: For a thinner sauce, stir in more milk before serving.

Note: This sauce can be boiled (because it contains no egg), but cooking it more slowly improves the flavour and less is wasted by being cooked on to the pan.

Sabayon Sauce

Although this is similar to one of the most famous of Italian desserts (Zabaglione), it can also be made as a sauce. Try it with poached pears, ice cream, or a light sponge pudding. It should be served warm because it separates out as it cools.

Serves 4 as a dessert, 8 as a sauce ☆
Preparation and cooking time:
  15 minutes

5 eggs, size 2, separated
2oz (50g) sugar
5 tablespoons madeira or marsala
grated rind of ½ lemon

Place all the ingredients except the egg whites into a basin, or the top of a double boiler, and set this over a pan of hot water on a low heat. Whisk until very thick and foamy, then remove from the heat.

☐ Whisk the egg whites until they form soft peaks, then fold into the cooked mixture. Serve immediately.

Sweet White Wine Sauce

Serves 4 ☆
Preparation and cooking time:
  10-15 minutes

2 eggs, size 2, separated
2oz (50g) sugar
7 fl oz (200ml) sweet white wine
2-3 tablespoons orange juice

Put the egg yolks, sugar, and wine into a basin and set it over a pan of hot water on a low heat. Whisk occasionally until the mixture cooks to a light custard.
☐ Stir in orange juice to taste.
☐ Whisk the egg whites until they form soft peaks and fold them into the custard. Serve immediately.
Variation: Substitute the juice of 1 lemon for the orange juice, adding extra sugar if necessary.

From left to right: Chocolate Sauce, Sabayon Sauce, Sweet White Wine Sauce and Cumberland Rum Butter.

Cumberland Rum Butter

Serves 4 ☆☆☆
Preparation: 8-10 minutes

4oz (100g) unsalted butter, softened
4oz (100g) soft brown sugar
grated rind of ½ orange or ½ lemon
about 3 fl oz (100ml) light or dark rum

Beat the butter and sugar together until very soft, pale and fluffy.
☐ Beat in the grated orange or lemon rind, then gradually beat in the rum, until the sauce is the consistency of thickly whipped cream.
Variation: If you prefer a smoother texture, use icing sugar instead of the soft brown sugar. The sauce will be paler, but still delicious.

Sweet White Wine Sauce
This delicious sauce is perfect with any of the fresh berried fruits, or with Summer Pudding. Serve it within half an hour of making or, like other sauces into which whisked egg whites are folded, the egg whites will separate out. Cook the sauce over hot water to moderate the heat and prevent separation.

If serving the sauce cold, allow to cool, then fold in the whisked egg whites just before serving.

Cumberland Rum Butter
Christmas pudding just isn't complete without this traditional sauce. It can be made a few days in advance and stored in a cool place. If stored in the fridge it will keep at least a week, but the chilling makes it hard again.

Brandy Butter
Use brandy instead of rum.

Sauces with liqueurs
Most sweet sauces benefit from a little spirit or liqueur. Add a drop or two, taste it, then add more until the necessary depth of flavour is reached. Remember that the aim is to improve the flavour, not overwhelm it.
As a guide, use about 3 tablespoons spirit or liqueur for any of these recipes:
● Try crème de cacao in chocolate sauce to serve with chocolate or lemon ices.
● Try orange-flavoured liqueurs in vanilla sauces (omit the vanilla). Serve with chocolate mousse or poached pears.
● Amaretto is delicious in either chocolate or vanilla sauce. Serve with poached or baked apples, or with pancakes or waffles.
● Try maraschino or kirsch with raspberry, pineapple, or cherry sauce. Serve with mousses, ices or rice puddings.

Soft Fruit Sauce

Canned fruits are particularly good for making sauces because they are already cooked and therefore easy to purée. Use your blender or processor to do this for you, or rub the fruit with its juice through a mouli-mill or a sieve using the back of a wooden spoon. With fresh fruit, cook it with a little water and sugar to taste then use in the same way.

Fruit sauces are extra-good with the addition of a little liqueur:

● Amaretto with apricots.
● Kirsch with pineapple.
● Port with plums.

Celebration Strawberry Sauce

Some of the best fruit sauces are made without either cooking or thickening. This one is for special occasions and superb to serve with ice cream, sorbets and mousses.

Try it, too, with one of the low-fat soft cheeses (such as quark), or with Petit Suisse cheeses.

Soft Fruit Sauce

Serve hot with a light sponge pudding, ice cream, or cold with cream-filled meringue shells.

Serves 4
Preparation and cooking time:
  10 minutes

15½oz (430g) can of fruit—peaches,
  pineapples, apricots, gooseberries or
  plums
1 tablespoon cornflour
sugar to taste
a few drops of lemon juice

Purée the fruit with its juice.

☐ Mix a little of the cold purée with the cornflour in a large basin and put the rest in a pan to heat.

☐ Stir the hot purée into the cornflour mixture, return this to the saucepan and continue cooking over a moderate heat. Stir frequently until thickened.

☐ Add sugar to taste, then add a little lemon juice to heighten the flavour.

Celebration Strawberry Sauce

Serves 4-5
Preparation: 10 minutes

12oz (350g) fresh strawberries
3 tablespoons port
2-3oz (50-75g) caster sugar

Hull the strawberries, then cut them into small pieces. Rub through a sieve or mouli-mill, or blend or process to a purée. Stir in the port and sugar to taste. Serve immediately.

☐ When serving, set a jug of the chilled sauce in a dish of crushed ice and garnish with whole fresh strawberries.

Tip: If making this ahead, whisk lightly before serving, as some of the juice separates out on standing.

Note: You can also use frozen strawberries, or thawed strawberry purée for this sauce.

From left to right: Soft Fruit Sauce made with canned peaches, Celebration Strawberry Sauce, Orange Sauce and Foamy Raspberry Sauce.

Orange Sauce

Serve hot with puddings, or cold with sorbets and water ices such as lemon, orange, or apricot.

Serves 4-6
Preparation and cooking time:
  5-10 minutes

---

grated rind of ½ orange
14 fl oz (400ml) orange juice
3 tablespoons cold water
1 tablespoon cornflour
squeeze of lemon juice
about 1 tablespoon sugar

Heat the orange rind and juice in a saucepan until just beginning to bubble.

☐ Mix the water and cornflour to a smooth paste in a large bowl, then stir in the hot liquid. Return this to the saucepan and cook, stirring constantly, for 2-3 minutes until lightly thickened.

☐ Add lemon juice and sugar to taste. If served cold, stir before serving.

Foamy Raspberry Sauce

Serves 4-6   ☆
Preparation and cooking time:
  15 minutes

---

4 eggs, size 2
½ pint (300ml) raspberry juice
caster sugar to taste

Whisk the eggs in a basin. Heat the juice in a saucepan, then gradually whisk the juice into the eggs. Pour the juice back into the saucepan or into the top of a double boiler. Set the pan over another filled with hot water, over a low heat.

☐ Cook, whisking frequently, until the sauce begins to cling to the whisk and only falls from it if the whisk is shaken lightly. Remove from the heat and stir in a little sugar if liked. Serve hot or cold.
Tip: If the sauce is to be served cold, lightly whisk it again just before serving.

Orange Sauce

Many fruit juices are now available in cans or cartons, or sometimes in bottles, and these are very good to use for sauces like this. Serve it with hot desserts such as chocolate or ginger sponge, or warm a plain madeira or almond sponge cake in foil in the oven, and serve it with a sauce like this.

As with many of the sauces, this one can be made special with the addition of a liqueur such as curaçao, Grand Marnier, or even whisky.

Foamy Raspberry Sauce

In this sauce, whole eggs are used for the thickening. In fact, this is really a raspberry-flavoured egg custard, and it's just the right texture with desserts such as upside-down peach pudding, hot waffles, ice cream or a cool, creamy rice pudding.

CAKE, PASTRY
AND BREAD-MAKING

Cake-making • Biscuit-making
Pastry-making • Yeast cookery

Cake-making

Baking cakes is the perfect opportunity to direct your creative skills towards cooking for compliments. Imaginative cake-making not only provides delicious tea-time treats but can create decorative desserts to impress dinner-party guests.

Methods of making cakes

One of the main objectives when preparing cakes for baking is to make the finished product as light as possible. The three techniques commonly used are: 'rubbing-in' which relies mainly on raising agents, 'creaming' where eggs are included and air is beaten in and, finally, 'whisking' where the mixture relies almost entirely on whisked-in air for its light texture.

Rubbing-in The fat is rubbed into the flour with the fingertips to form a breadcrumb-like consistency. Sugar and eggs are added and perhaps a little liquid. This type of cake is quick and easy to make and is at its best fresh.

Creaming With 'creamed' cakes, the fat and sugar are beaten together until very light. The secret lies in very thorough beating at this stage to incorporate a lot of air. This process is made easier if you start with softened (*not* melted) fat. The eggs are then beaten in and flour folded in lightly.

Whisking Eggs and sugar are whisked until the mixture is very thick, airy and pale. The flour is lightly folded in and, sometimes, melted fat is added at the end to enrich.

Cake Ingredients

Flour is available in several forms and it is important to use the one called for in the recipe. Plain flour is used when it is necessary to adjust the amount of raising agent used. Self-raising flour is very convenient, but it contains a fixed quantity of raising agent. 'Sponge flour' should only be used with recipes provided by the manufacturer as it requires a special balance of ingredients.

● **Fats** used in baking are mainly butter or margarine. Butter gives the best flavour in cakes, but many people prefer to use margarine. When substituting margarine for butter, be sure to use the brands sold in block form. The soft types need specially devised recipes.

● **Sugars** differ widely but, among the white sugars, caster sugar gives the best results. Cakes can be made with icing sugar if a denser consistency is required. Larger-grained sugars do not beat in quite so well and can produce coarse cake. Soft brown sugar should only be used in specially devised recipes. It is not only very fine but it also has a degree of acidity which can affect the cake's structure.

Cake tins

If you are baking a large cake, it will bake a little more quickly in aluminium or tin than in ovenglass containers.

● A cake baked in an 8-in (20-cm) round tin will take approximately the same time as one baked in a 10-in (25cm) loaf pan.

Turning out cakes

For best results, use non-stick pans or tins with loose bottoms. There are also tins available which are made with a spring-form or a moving scraper which loosens the cake.

● When using ordinary tins or pans, after greasing the pan, line the centre bottom with a small square of greaseproof paper.

● If you have difficulty in releasing a baked cake from its tin, loosen round the edges with a palette knife then invert the tin on to a cooling rack. If the cake is domed on top, quickly reverse it on to a second rack.

Apart from the heavier fruit cakes, most cakes taste better when they are eaten within a day of baking. If you need to store a cake for longer, wrap it in foil or place it in an airtight tin. Keep cakes in a cool, dry place but not in the refrigerator as low temperatures make them rather solid.

❄ Freezing

Cakes which have a high fat content will generally freeze well while plainer cakes are better served when fresh. It is better to freeze cakes before decorating or filling. You can freeze either a whole cake, well wrapped in foil or freezerwrap, or individual slices wrapped separately. These individual portions are very convenient and any appropriate number can be thawed quickly. To retain the best flavour, do not store a cake in the freezer for more than about 2 months. To thaw, leave the cake in its wrappings to defrost at room temperature. A whole 4-egg cake will need about 5 hours to thaw while you only need to allow about 1½ hours to defrost individual slices.

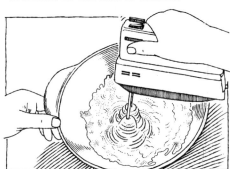

For 'creamed' cakes, beat the butter and sugar until very soft and light.

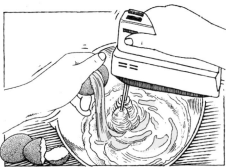

Add one egg at a time and beat each in well.

Add the flour in two or three batches and mix in lightly with a spatula.

Creamed Method

For this type of cake the butter and sugar must be very well beaten together to incorporate air which lightens the cake. Add eggs only after the mixture is very light and creamy.

If there is a slight separation when you beat in the last egg, shake a little flour over the surface and stir it in lightly.

When you add the flour, be sure it is well mixed in but don't beat the mixture at this stage. Otherwise, beaten-in air will be lost and the flour will form gluten which toughens the cake. Just fold and turn with a spoon or rubber spatula.

Basic Rich Cake

Makes 16-18 thin slices ☆ ☆
Preparation: 15 minutes
Cooking: 1-1¼ hours plus cooling

8oz (225g) butter, softened
8oz (225g) caster sugar
grated rind of 1 lemon
4 eggs, size 2
8oz (225g) self-raising flour
4 tablespoons milk
butter or oil for greasing

Set the oven to 300F (150C) gas 2 and grease a 10-in (25-cm) loaf tin.
☐ Beat the butter until very soft. Add the sugar and lemon rind and beat thoroughly for 5-7 minutes until very soft and creamy.
☐ Add the eggs one at a time, beating in well after each addition.
☐ Put the flour into a sieve, and shake about one-third into the creamed mixture. Add 1 tablespoon of milk and fold in lightly.
☐ Add the rest of the flour and milk and fold in only until smoothly and evenly mixed.
☐ Turn the mixture into the prepared tin and bake in the oven for 1-1¼ hours.

The various stages in preparing, making and serving a Basic Rich Cake.

☐ When baked, the cake will be well-browned and a skewer inserted into the centre will come out clean. As a final check, listen to the cake – it should not sizzle.

☐ Leave in the tin to cool for 10 minutes then loosen around the sides with a knife and turn out and leave to cool on a wire rack.

Tip: Use only 1 tablespoon of milk if using a round 8-in (20-cm) tin.

Feather-iced Chocolate Cake

Makes 8 slices ☆☆
Preparation and finishing: 30 minutes
Cooking: about 25 minutes plus cooling and setting

4oz (100g) butter, softened
3oz (75g) soft brown sugar
3oz (75g) golden syrup
½ teaspoon vanilla essence
2 eggs, size 2
5oz (125g) plain flour
1½ teaspoons baking powder
3 tablespoons cocoa
1 tablespoon warm water
4oz (100g) apricot jam, warmed
1oz (25g) walnuts, finely chopped
butter or oil for greasing

The icing:
5oz (125g) icing sugar
about 4 teaspoons cold water
1 teaspoon cocoa
2 teaspoons hot water

Set the oven to 350F (180C) gas 4 and grease two 7-in (18-cm) sandwich tins.

☐ Beat the butter until very soft. Add the sugar, syrup and vanilla and beat until very light and creamy.

☐ Add the eggs one at a time, beating thoroughly after each.

☐ Put the flour, baking powder, and cocoa into a sieve. Sift about half into the mixture. Fold in lightly. Repeat with remaining flour. Add water.

☐ Turn into the prepared tins and bake for about 25 minutes until well risen, and springy to the touch.

☐ Turn out on to a rack to cool.

☐ Sandwich the cakes with some of the jam and spread the rest around the sides. Press the nuts firmly on the sides and wrap with a band of greaseproof paper.

☐ Mix the icing sugar with enough water to give a stiff spreading consistency. Transfer a generous tablespoon to a separate bowl.

☐ Mix the cocoa smoothly with hot water then mix that with the 1 tablespoon of white icing. Put into a small paper forcing bag.

☐ Ice the top of the cake with white icing. Feather with the chocolate icing (see sidelines) and leave to set.

☐ Serve fresh, cut into wedges.

Streusel-topped Spice Cake

Makes 24 pieces ☆
Preparation and cooking: 1 hour

10oz (275g) plain flour
6oz (175g) caster sugar
6oz (175g) butter, cubed
2 teaspoons baking powder
2 teaspoons mixed spice
4oz (100g) raisins
2 eggs, size 2
5 tablespoons milk
butter or oil for greasing

Set the oven to 350F (180C) gas 4.

☐ Grease a 6½ × 10½in (16 × 26cm) shallow tin. Lay a strip of foil 3in (7.5cm) wide and 14in (35cm) long across the bottom and up the sides.

☐ Sift the flour and sugar into a bowl. Add the butter and rub in well to make fine crumbs.

☐ Set aside 5oz (125g) of mixture.

☐ Sift the baking powder and spice into the rest and stir to mix well. Stir in the raisins, eggs and milk.

☐ Spread the cake mixture evenly into tin. Sprinkle with crumb mixture.

☐ Bake in the oven for about 40 minutes until a skewer inserted into the centre comes out clean.

☐ Leave to cool in the tin for 15 minutes. Loosen along the sides and corners with a palette knife. Use the foil strip to lift it out carefully. Cool.

☐ Serve fresh, cut in squares.

Coating a cake with chopped nuts
Put the nuts in a line across the centre of a piece of greaseproof paper. With one hand underneath and the other one on top, lift the cake. Roll the sides of the jam-coated cake in the nuts then press them on firmly with a palette knife.

Converting recipes for cakes from loaf to round, and vice versa, is a tricky business because of the complexities of varying heat transference due to differing pan and cake surface areas. In general, more liquid is used in loaf type cakes to keep the surface from 'doming' too much and splitting. Wherever possible, stick to instructions – we give alternatives in some recipes.

To feather-ice a cake
Wrap a double thickness of greaseproof paper, as broad as the depth of the cake, around the sides like a bandage. Secure with 2 or 3 pins. Spread the top of the cake with icing.

While still wet, draw parallel lines across the cake with the chocolate icing, at about 1in (2.5cm) intervals.

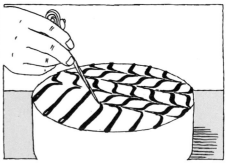

Immediately, draw the tip of a skewer at right angles across the chocolate lines at regular intervals in alternating directions.
When set, remove the pins and carefully pull away the paper collar.

Tiger Cake makes an attractive tea-time treat.

In this variation of a classic marbled cake all you have to do is put alternating layers of white and chocolate cake mixtures into a loaf tin. During baking, the two colours bubble up and mix together to give each slice the tiger-like markings that endow the cake with its name.

Tiger Cake

Makes 16-18 thin slices   ☆☆
Preparation: 20 minutes
Cooking: about 1¼ hours

---

3 tablespoons cocoa
3 tablespoons milk
8oz (225g) butter, softened
8oz (225g) caster sugar
1 teaspoon vanilla essence
4 eggs, size 2
8oz (225g) self-raising flour
butter or oil for greasing

Set oven to 300F (150C) gas 2 and grease a 10-in (25-cm) loaf tin.
☐ Warm the cocoa and milk in a small saucepan over a low heat. Stir until well mixed, then leave to cool.
☐ Beat the butter until very soft. Add the sugar and vanilla and beat thoroughly until soft and creamy.
☐ Add the eggs one at a time, beating well after each addition.
☐ Put the flour into a sieve. Shake about half into the creamed mixture and fold in lightly.
☐ Add the rest of the flour. Fold in only until smoothly and evenly mixed. Put half into a separate bowl.
☐ Lightly and evenly stir the melted cocoa into one bowl.
☐ Spread half the white mixture into the prepared tin. Cover with half the chocolate mixture. Repeat the layers of batter.
☐ Bake for about 1¼ hours.
☐ Leave to cool in the tin for 15-20 minutes. Loosen with a palette knife. Turn out on a wire rack and leave to cool.
☐ Serve fresh cut in thin slices.
Tip: The addition of the grated rind of 1 orange to the white mixture makes a good flavour combination with the chocolate.

Amaretto Layer Cake

Makes 10-12 thick slices ☆☆☆
Preparation: 15 minutes plus
20 minutes decoration
Cooking: 1¼ hours plus cooling

1 Basic Rich Cake

The filling:
4oz (125g) white chocolate
2oz (50g) butter, softened
3 fl oz (100ml) double cream
2 tablespoons Amaretto liqueur

The decoration:
¼ pint (150ml) double cream
3-4 oz (100g-125g) flaked almonds

Cut the cake lengthways into 3 slices.

☐ Break the chocolate into small pieces and put in a bowl set over a pan of hot water on a low heat. Stir until it melts but doesn't become warm. Remove from the heat.

☐ Beat the butter until well softened, then gradually beat in the melted chocolate. Whip the cream and liqueur together until it forms soft peaks. Fold this into the chocolate mixture and chill until it is of a firm spreading consistency.

☐ Make the decoration: Whip the cream to soft peaks. Brown the almonds under grill (spread in a single layer), or in a dry frying-pan over a moderate heat, stirring frequently. Leave to cool.

☐ To assemble the cake: Sandwich the 3 layers with the chocolate filling. Spread the whipped cream all over the outside and press the nuts on with a palette knife.

☐ Leave the cake to stand in a cool place-but *not* in the fridge—for about 1 hour before serving, to allow the full flavour to develop.

☐ Serve while fresh, cut into slices.

Amaretto Layer Cake is delicious with coffee, but can also serve as a dinner-party dessert.

Step-by-step to filling, assembling and decorating Mocha Buttercream Layer Cake.

Storing buttercream cakes
Cakes filled and iced with buttercream should be kept in a cool place but *not* the refrigerator or freezer as such a low temperature solidifies the butter and the cream loses all of its light fluffiness.

Mocha Buttercream Layer Cake

Makes 10-12 thick slices ☆☆☆
Preparation and cooking: 2 hours

8oz (225g) butter, softened
8oz (225g) caster sugar
4 eggs, size 2
8oz (225g) self-raising flour
4 tablespoons white rum
butter or oil for greasing
1oz (25g) chocolate coffee beans

The Mocha Buttercream:
2 tablespoons instant coffee
2 tablespoons boiling water
5 tablespoons Tia Maria
10oz (275g) butter, softened
12oz (350g) icing sugar

Make and bake the cake in the same way as the Basic Rich Cake, using the rum in place of the milk. Allow to cool.

☐ Make the Mocha Buttercream: Mix the coffee in sufficient boiling water to dissolve, and add the Tia Maria.

☐ Beat the butter until very soft. Gradually whisk in the icing sugar, then whisk in the coffee liquid.

☐ Cut the cake lengthways into 3. Sandwich with some buttercream and spread outside with more.

☐ Put the remaining buttercream into a forcing bag fitted with a small rose pipe. Shape rosettes along the top as shown. Top with beans.

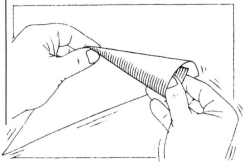

Cut a piece of greaseproof paper to form a rectangle 16 × 11in (40 x 28cm). Holding a point on the bottom edge 2½in (6.5cm) in from one short side, fold the opposite bottom corner up to bring the lower edge parallel with the short edge. Cut or tear along the fold line.

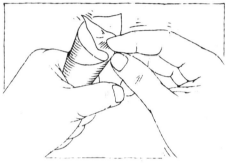

Hold one piece by its right-angle corner and roll the 'blunt' corner in and around to meet that right angle. Then wrap the 'sharp' corner over around and up the outside, so that all three corners are roughly together and a cone shape is formed. Adjust so that the paper layers are flat against one another and a neat tight cone is obtained. Fold the projecting corners over into the cone, make a small tear down through these layers of paper and fold one side over firmly to hold cone shape securely.

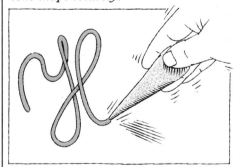

With scissors, cut off a snippet of paper from the tip to allow a flow of icing. Put in place any nozzle being used. Fill the paper cone two-thirds full with icing and fold the top in to close.

To decorate the Mocha Buttercream Cake

Buttercream is easy to spread if you beat it well. Use a flexible palette knife to smooth it over the sides of the cake. Set the cake on a serving plate and spread the top.

Fit a small rose pipe into a forcing bag and fill with the remaining buttercream. To make this easier, stand the bag in a large jug and turn the top of the bag down over the edges. The bag will then be held in place securely.

To pipe, first just twist the bag gently above the level of the cream to force out any air bubbles then try 1 or 2 practice rosettes on a piece of paper. Hold the bag vertically and with a short 'round-and-round' action, rotating nozzle as well as bag, form a little rosette in position. Or, if you find it easier, just press out a star. Then make rosettes or stars along the length of each side.

Chocolate coffee beans make a simple, attractive and appropriate decoration – tasting good on a mocha cake. They can be found in most good confectioners and some large supermarkets.

Another attractive and very easy way to decorate a cake covered with buttercream is with the back of a fork. After coating the cake smoothly, draw wavy lines all over and then sprinkle with a little grated chocolate.

Fruit cakes

Most fruit cakes are made by the creaming method, but the recipe here is much easier. The butter is simply rubbed into the dry ingredients before stirring in the fruit and eggs.

All traditional fruit cakes are better left to mature for a few days and many keep for a long time. However, this version of the ever-popular Dundee Cake is best served within 4 to 6 weeks. To store, wrap in foil and keep in a cool dry place.

Lining cake tins

Fruit cakes bake better in tins which have been lined with a double thickness of greaseproof paper. Butter the paper between the thicknesses and on the side which is placed next to the tin, to hold it in place.

Splitting almonds

Bring the whole skinned almonds to the boil. Strain off the water. Insert the tip of a sharp knife into the tip of the almond and prise apart at the dividing mark.

Dundee Cake

Dundee Cake

Makes 12-14 slices
Preparation: 20 minutes
Cooking: about 1½ hours

5oz (150g) raisins, cleaned
5oz (150g) currants, cleaned
3 fl oz (100ml) dark rum
8oz (225g) self-raising flour
5oz (150g) soft brown sugar
grated rind of ½ orange
5oz (150g) cold butter
2oz (50g) glacé cherries, quartered
2oz (50g) candied peel, chopped
2oz (50g) blanched almonds, chopped
3 eggs, size 2
butter for greasing

To decorate:
2oz (50g) blanched almonds, split

Set the oven to 300F (150C) gas 2 and grease and line an 8in (20cm) round cake tin.

☐ Put the raisins and currants into a bowl, pour the rum over and leave to soak.

☐ Sieve the flour and sugar into a bowl. Add the orange rind and butter. With the fingertips, rub the butter in, to form a mixture with a crumb-like consistency.

☐ Add fruit, cherries, peel, chopped almonds and 1 egg and mix together. Add the 2 remaining eggs and stir together well.

☐ Turn into prepared tin. Arrange the split almonds over the top and bake in the oven for about 1½ hours until a warmed skewer inserted into the centre comes out clean.

Variation: If you like a darker cake, add 2 teaspoons of mixed spice to the flour, and use dark brown sugar.

Tip: If the top of your baked fruit cake is a little too crusty for your taste, put a layer of sliced raw apple over it just before you wrap the cake in foil. In a day the cake will become soft and moist.

Whisked sponges

The lightest and most delicate types of cake are those made by whisking the eggs and sugar together until they are light and creamy and then gently folding in the flour. Plain flour or flour with only a small amount of raising agent is used.

These sponges are tender and moist but have a slight elasticity which makes them less crumbly and therefore easier to ice.

Genoese sponges

If a richer sponge cake is required, melted butter is lightly stirred into the mixture. This type is called 'genoese' and, although as tender and moist as those made without fat, they tend to be firmer.

Baking tins

The easiest way to bake both basic whisked sponges and the genoese type is to use sandwich tins. If you are making a cake with several layers and have insufficient sandwich tins, use large, round, loose-bottomed or springform tins.

If the cake is to be rolled or sandwiched in strips, use a shallow Swiss Roll tin. If you want to serve a sponge cake whole, it is a good idea to use a tin which has a centre tube so that the cake cooks evenly. Loaf tins are unsatisfactory for baking sponges because the cake cooks unevenly with the outer edges cooking quicker than the centre.

Testing for thorough baking

The cakes should be well-risen with a good golden-brown colour. They should feel springy and there should be no sound of sizzling.

Removing baked cakes from tins

Sponge cakes baked in sandwich, or other shallow tins, can be turned out immediately after baking. Loosen each cake around the sides with a warmed knife. Invert on to a wire rack, then flip over on to a second rack.

Rules for success:

● Whisk the egg-and-sugar mixture very thoroughly. This is to ensure that the sugar is dissolved and the mixture is as elastic as possible. Setting the bowl over warm water helps to make the whisking time shorter but do not let the water get hot enough to cook the egg. Continue whisking until the mixture has increased in volume about threefold. It should appear to have the consistency of soft whipped cream.

● A wide mixing bowl rather than a deep one makes it easier to fold in the flour without breaking down too much of the foam.

● Sprinkle the flour over the whole surface. Continue to cut and turn gently to ensure that all the flour is evenly mixed in. Be certain that there are no lumps or pockets of flour left in the mixture.

Basic Whisked Sponge

Serves 6-8
Preparation: 20 minutes
Cooking: 20-25 minutes

---

3 eggs, size 2
2 egg yolks from size 2 eggs
6oz (175g) caster sugar
6oz (175g) plain flour
butter or oil for greasing

Set the oven to 375F (190C) gas 5 and grease two 9in (23cm) sandwich tins.

☐ Put the eggs, yolks and sugar into a bowl and set over a pan of hot water on a low heat.

☐ Whisk the mixture for about 10 minutes until it is very thick and the whisk leaves a trail on the surface. Remove from the heat.

☐ Sift half the flour over the surface and fold it in lightly. Repeat with the rest of the flour.

☐ Turn into prepared sandwich tins and bake for 20-25 minutes.

☐ Turn out on a wire rack and cool. Use while fresh, or freeze.

Variation: Alternatively, put the mixture into a greased 9in (23cm) deep springform or loose-bottomed cake tin and bake at 350F (180C) gas 4 for about 40 minutes.

Don't try making sponge cakes in non-stick pans—the mixture can't grip the sides during cooking, so the cakes don't rise properly and cave in on themselves.

Making Genoese Sponge

Like Basic Whisked Sponge but with melted butter stirred in.

Whisk the eggs and sugar until very thick and fluffy.

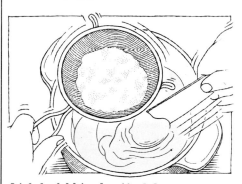

Lightly fold in the sifted flour.

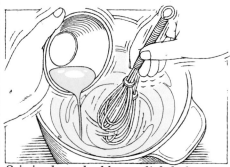

Stir in the melted butter lightly but thoroughly.

Banana and Kiwi Cake

It is better not to refrigerate a cake with bananas as they tend to darken when very cold.

It is a good idea to make a quantity of praline in advance and store it in an airtight jar in a cool dry place. It will keep well for 3 to 4 weeks.

Praline Cream Cake

This method of making a whisked sponge is preferred by some to that given for the Basic Whisked Sponge, as it is a little quicker.

Slices of Banana and Kiwi Cake make a refreshing and unusual dessert.

Grated chocolate

Hold a block of chocolate with a piece of paper wrapped around to prevent it melting due to the warmth of the hand. Use the coarse side of a grater and grate on to a sheet of greaseproof paper. You can store the grated chocolate in an airtight jar in the fridge for several weeks.

As an alternative to the praline, fold coarsely-grated chocolate into the cream. Also try flavouring the cream with rum, brandy or an orange liqueur.

Banana and Kiwi Cake

Serves 8 ☆☆
Preparation: 45-50 minutes

Basic Whisked Sponge baked in a
   9in (23cm) round cake tin

The filling and topping:
12 fl oz (350ml) sweet white wine
2 tablespoons brandy
2 teaspoons powdered gelatine
3 large bananas
2 large kiwi fruit

To decorate:
3 fl oz (100ml) double cream
3oz (75g) flaked or chopped almonds

Put the wine, brandy and gelatine into a small saucepan. Set over a low heat and stir until the gelatine is dissolved and the liquid is clear.

☐ Remove from the heat and set the pan into cold water until cool. Chill for a few minutes in the fridge until it is beginning to set.

☐ Cut the cake across into 3 equal layers. Peel and slice the fruit. Arrange banana slices over two pieces of cake, and a mixture of kiwi and banana on the third piece.

☐ Carefully spoon about one-third of the jelly over each of the banana layers and stack them one on top of the other.

☐ Set the top layer in place and spoon remaining glaze over. Leave in a cool place for a few minutes.

☐ Whip the cream to spreading consistency. Put the nuts into the bottom of the grill pan and place under a pre-heated moderate grill for 2-3 minutes, stirring until lightly browned, then allow to cool.

☐ Spread the sides of the cake with the whipped cream. With a palette knife, press the nuts on to the cream to make a neat finish. Cool but do not refrigerate.

☐ Serve within 2 or 3 hours.
Variations: Raspberries, strawberries or fresh peaches are equally good for this cake.

● In place of nuts, try grated chocolate or coconut for decoration.

Praline Cream Cake

Serves 6 ☆☆☆
Preparation: about 25 minutes
Cooking: about 45 minutes

---

3 eggs, size 2, separated
4oz (125g) caster sugar
3oz (100g) plain flour
¼ teaspoon baking powder
butter or oil for greasing

The Praline:
2oz (50g) caster sugar
2oz (50g) chopped almonds

To finish:
¼ pint (150ml) double cream

Set the oven to 350F (180C) gas 4 and grease a 8½in (21cm) fluted ring mould.

☐ Put the egg whites into a large bowl and whisk to soft peaks.

☐ Whisk in half the sugar until the mixture resembles soft meringue.

☐ Put yolks and remaining sugar into a bowl. Whisk until pale and fluffy, then fold lightly into whisked whites.

☐ Put the flour and baking powder into a sieve. Sift about half over the surface of the whisked eggs and fold it in lightly. Repeat with remainder.

☐ Turn into the prepared mould and bake for about 45 minutes.

☐ Invert on a wire rack and leave to cool. Release from the tin by easing it out with the tip of a sharp knife. Use fresh, or freeze.

☐ To make the Praline: put the sugar into a heavy frying-pan set over a moderate heat. Keep turning the pan to heat evenly – but do not stir – until sugar melts. Add almonds.

☐ As soon as sugar is golden brown, turn out on a piece of greased greaseproof paper.

☐ Tap with a rolling pin to break into pieces then put in a plastic bag and crush with the rolling pin to the size of coarse breadcrumbs.

☐ Whip the cream to spreading consistency and lightly fold in praline.

☐ Spread all over the top and sides of the cake and serve within 2 hours.

Swiss Roll

Makes 12 slices ☆
Preparation: 10 minutes
Cooking: 15 minutes

---

3 eggs, size 2, separated
4oz (125g) caster sugar
3oz (100g) plain flour
¼ teaspoon baking powder
butter for greasing
caster sugar for sprinkling

The filling:
¼ pint (150ml) double cream
about 3oz (75g) plum (or other red) jam

Set the oven to 350F (180C) gas 4 and generously grease a 9 × 13in (23 × 33cm) Swiss Roll tin with butter.

☐ Make the sponge mixture in the same way as for Praline Cream Cake.

☐ Spread into the prepared tin and bake in the oven for 12-15 minutes until golden and coming away from the sides of the tin.

☐ Turn out on greaseproof paper lightly sprinkled with caster sugar. Trim and roll (see sidelines). Allow cake to cool still rolled around the paper.

☐ Whip the cream to spreading consistency and warm the jam in a small saucepan until it will spread easily.

☐ Unroll the cake, spread it well with jam, then cream – keeping the cream to within about a thumb's width of the edges. Re-roll.

☐ Serve while fresh, cut in slices, for tea.

Sponge Slices

Make and bake the sponge mixture in the same way as for Swiss Roll. Turn out and leave flat until cool.

☐ Cut into strips about 4 × 3in (10 × 7cm). Sandwich together in pairs with jam. Spread the tops with whipped cream and dust with grated chocolate, praline or chopped nuts and mixed glacé fruits. Serve fresh, cut into slices.

Chocolate Roulade

Serves 6 ☆☆☆
Preparation: 20 minutes, plus 8-10 hours setting
Cooking: about 15 minutes

---

about 1½oz (40g) plain chocolate
2 tablespoons cocoa
2 tablespoons warm water
3 eggs, size 2, separated
4oz (100g) caster sugar
a little oil for greasing

The filling:
2oz (50g) plain chocolate
1 tablespoon water
¼ pint (150ml) double cream

To serve:
¼ pint (150ml) double cream
3 tablespoons brandy

Set the oven to 350F (180C) gas 4. Liberally oil a 12 × 8in (30 × 20cm) Swiss Roll tin, line it with greaseproof paper and oil again.

☐ Put the chocolate, cocoa and water in a bowl set over a pan of hot water on a low heat. Stir until melted but not hot. Remove.

☐ Whisk the egg yolks and sugar until very pale and thick. Add the chocolate. Whisk until well mixed.

☐ Whisk the egg whites until they form soft peaks. Fold lightly but thoroughly into the chocolate.

☐ Turn into the prepared tin and bake for about 15 minutes until a firm crust forms on the surface.

☐ Remove and immediately wrap the cake and tin together in foil. Leave for 8-10 hours then unwrap.

☐ Invert on to a piece of greaseproof paper dusted with caster sugar. Carefully scrape the lining paper away and trim off the sides.

☐ To make filling: Melt chocolate in a bowl with the water as before.

☐ Whip the cream to soft peaks. Add the melted chocolate and whip to a thick spreading consistency.

☐ Spread over the chocolate to within a thumb's width of the edges. Roll up like Swiss Roll. Slice.

☐ Whip the cream and brandy to soft peaks and top slices.

Rolling a Swiss Roll
If a Swiss Roll is to be filled with jam only, you can spread it on before its first rolling. For other fillings, it is important to cool the cake before filling it.

Turn the baked cake out on a piece of greaseproof paper lightly sprinkled with caster sugar. Trim off the crisp edges and straighten the sides. About 1in (2.5cm) in from the nearer short end, slice a groove across the sponge about halfway through its depth. To facilitate folding, fold this grooved end over to start the rolling.

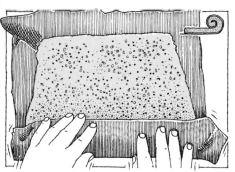

Roll the cake up with the paper and leave to cool on a wire rack.

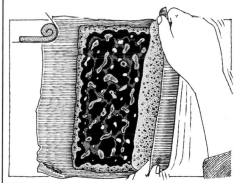

Unroll the cooled cake and spread with filling. Re-roll.

Chocolate Roulade
A roulade is not a true cake, but it is made by the same method of whisking eggs and sugar. It makes a rich and delicious dessert. During the 'setting' inside the foil covering, the crust softens so the roulade can be rolled. If cracks form, smooth them together using the paper and dust over with sugar.

Chocolate Log Cake

To make rolling the cake easier, place a clean, damp tea towel underneath the sheet of paper as this keeps in moisture and prevents the cake from becoming too brittle. When cake is complete, store for up to 12 hours in a cool place—but not in the fridge!

Preparing and decorating a Chocolate Log Cake. Serve as a special occasion dessert or as a rich coffee or party cake.

Chocolate Log Cake

Makes about 12 slices ☆☆☆
Preparation: 25 minutes
Cooking: 15 minutes

3 eggs, separated
4oz (125g) caster sugar
3oz (100g) plain flour
½ teaspoon baking powder
butter or oil for greasing

The Chocolate Ganache:
8oz (225g) plain chocolate
4oz (125g) butter, softened
7 fl oz (200ml) double cream
4 tablespoons coffee liqueur (optional)

To decorate:
a few chocolate coffee beans
a few walnut halves

Make a Swiss Roll as on the previous page. Trim, roll and cool.
☐ To make the Chocolate Ganache: Break the chocolate into small pieces and put into a bowl set over a pan of hot water on a low heat. Stir until melted but not hot. Remove.

☐ Beat the butter until well softened. Gradually beat in chocolate.
☐ Whip the cream and liqueur, if using, to soft peaks then fold this into the chocolate mixture. Chill until of a spreading consistency.
☐ Carefully unroll the cake. Spread thinly with ganache. Re-roll. Cut a slice at an angle from each end.
☐ Spread a little ganache on the underside of each slice and press on top of the roll to represent branch stumps.
☐ Put a ½in (1cm) rose pipe into a large forcing bag. Fill the bag with the rest of the ganache mixture.
☐ Pipe lines lengthways along the roll to represent the bark of the log, leaving the 'stumps' clear. Decorate with beans and walnuts.
☐ Serve cut in slices.

Raspberry Cheesecake

Serves 10   ☆ ☆ ☆
Preparation: 40 minutes plus
chilling
Cooking: 15 minutes

---

3 eggs, size 2, separated
5oz (125g) caster sugar
5oz (125g) plain flour
butter or oil for greasing

The filling:
¼ pint (150ml) sweet white wine
2 sachets of powdered gelatine
¼ pint (150ml) canned orange juice
2 eggs, size 2
3oz (75g) caster sugar
1½lb (675g) cream cheese
¼ pint (150ml) double cream

To decorate:
¾lb (350g) fresh raspberries
icing sugar for dusting

Set the oven to 400F (200C) gas 6
and mark a 9in (23cm) circle on a
piece of greaseproof paper. Place
marked-side down on a greased
baking tray. Grease a 9in (23cm)
springform or loose-bottomed tin.

☐ Whisk the egg whites until
beginning to form soft peaks. Add
half the sugar. Whisk until
resembling soft meringue.

☐ Add remaining sugar to the egg
yolks. Whisk until very pale and
light, then fold gently into whites.

☐ Sift about one-third of the flour
into the bowl and fold in lightly.
Add the rest of the flour similarly.

☐ Turn two-thirds of the mixture
into the tin and spread the rest over
the marked circle.

☐ Bake both in the oven: about 8
minutes for the top piece and about
15 minutes for the cake in the tin.

☐ Leave the base in the tin to cool.
Remove the top from the paper and
cool on a wire rack.

☐ To make the filling: Put the wine
and the gelatine into a small
saucepan over a low heat. Stir until
clear, but do not allow it to get hot!
Remove from heat and add juice.

☐ Whisk together the eggs and
sugar until very thick and pale. In a
separate bowl, whisk together the

cheese and cream. Add the egg
mixture, followed by the gelatine.
Spoon over the cake base and chill
for at least 6 hours.

☐ To serve: Run a warm knife
around the inside of the tin to
release the cake. Transfer to a
plate and spread the fruit over.

☐ Cut the top into 12 wedges. Dust
heavily with icing sugar and set
on top. Serve within an hour.

Sponge Petits Fours

Makes about 36   ☆
Preparation: 20 minutes
plus cooling
Cooking: about 5-7 minutes

---

1 egg, size 2, separated
1oz (25g) caster sugar
1oz (25g) plain flour
a pinch of baking powder
butter for greasing

The icing:
3-4 teaspoons water
about 7 tablespoons icing sugar
a few drops of food colouring

To decorate:
coloured dragees; crystallized petals; tiny
pieces of nut and angelica

Set the oven to 400F (200C) gas 6
and grease large petits fours moulds.

☐ Make the sponge mixture in the
same way as for Praline Cream
Cake, and pour into prepared
moulds set on baking trays.

☐ Bake for about 5-7 minutes, until
well risen and golden brown.

☐ Use the tip of a small sharp knife
to ease the cakes from their moulds.
Turn out and cool on wire racks.

☐ Make up a little glacé icing of
spreading consistency. Add food
colouring to produce a pastel colour.

☐ Set a rack of the cooled cakes on
a clean baking tray. Spoon a little
icing on each cake and let it run
down the sides. Decorate variously.

☐ If the icing which runs on to the
tray is free of crumbs re-use.

☐ Leave the cakes in a cool place –
not in the refrigerator – for ½ hour to
set. Serve fresh.

Raspberry Cheesecake
For a more straightforward cheesecake, omit
the sponge top and glaze the raspberries
with some raspberry jelly melted with a dash
of kirsch.

Sponge Petits Fours
Serve these tasty and attractive small cakes
as an accompaniment to after-dinner coffee.

Making Strawberry Gâteau

It is more convenient if you make both the cake and the Crème Pâtissière the day before required. Finishing the gâteau is then very easy. The cake also tastes better if left to mature for a day.

Crème Pâtissière

If the cream is too thick to spread easily, whisk again until creamy. Use immediately, or store in a covered container in a cool place – not in the fridge – for up to 24 hours.

Jelly glaze

Gelatine mixtures in small quantities set very quickly so it is better not to chill the glaze. But if you are in a hurry, put one or two ice cubes into the pan of cold water to make the glaze set more quickly.

Strawberry Gâteau

Serves 8   ☆☆☆
Preparation: 1 hour, plus chilling
Cooking: 30-35 minutes

The Genoese Sponge:
4 eggs, size 2
4oz (125g) caster sugar
4oz (125g) less 1 tablespoon, plain flour
2oz (50g) butter, melted and cooled

The Crème Pâtissière:
2 tablespoons flour
2oz (50g) caster sugar
1 egg yolk from a size 2 egg
4 fl oz (125ml plus 1 tablespoon) milk
4 tablespoons kirsch
6oz (175g) unsalted butter, cubed small

To decorate:
3-4oz (75-125g) flaked almonds
3 fl oz (100ml) sweet white wine
½ teaspoon powdered gelatine
¾lb (350g) small strawberries

Set the oven to 350F (180C) gas 4 and grease and flour a 9in (23cm) springform or loose-bottomed cake tin.

☐ Put the eggs and sugar into a large bowl. Set over a pan of hot water on a moderate heat.

☐ Whisk for about 10 minutes, scraping the mixture down the sides of the bowl during whisking, until the centre of the mixture feels tepid, and the mixture has increased to about three times its original volume.

☐ Sieve one-third of the flour over the mixture. Add one-third of the butter at the side of the bowl. With a balloon whisk or rubber spatula, mix very lightly but thoroughly.

☐ Repeat with remaining flour and butter.

☐ Turn into the prepared cake tin and bake for 30-35 minutes.

☐ Invert on a wire rack. Cool, then

remove from the tin. Use immediately, or wrap and store in a cool place for not more than a day, or freeze for up to 2 months.

☐ To make the Crème Pâtissière: Mix the flour, sugar, and egg yolk smoothly with a little of the cold milk. Put the rest of the milk into a small saucepan over a moderate heat.

☐ When the milk bubbles around the edge, stir it into the flour mixture. Return this to the saucepan and cook, stirring constantly, for 3-4 minutes until thick and smooth.

☐ Remove from the heat and stir in the liqueur. Gradually whisk in the cubes of butter until it has the look of a rich mayonnaise. Cool.

☐ To decorate: Put the almonds into a dry frying-pan over a moderate heat and stir for a few minutes to brown lightly.

☐ Put the wine and the gelatine into a small measuring jug. Set in a saucepan of hot water over a low heat. Stir until the liquid is clear.

☐ Remove the jug and set in a pan of cold water.

☐ Cut the cake across into 3 equal slices. Sandwich with Crème Pâtissière and spread a little around the sides of the cake.

☐ Press the nuts on the sides and spread remaining Crème Pâtissière on top.

☐ Arrange the berries on top. When the jelly begins to thicken, spoon it carefully over the fruit.

☐ Chill for $\frac{1}{2}$ hour before serving.

It is important to have the butter melted so it will mix into the cake, but it must not be hot or it may set some of the egg.

Whisking the cake
Whisking over hot water helps shorten the process. Do not let the bowl become warmer than is comfortable to hold against the hand. Otherwise, if the bottom of the bowl becomes hot it will begin to cook the cake mixture.

The various stages in making, assembling and decorating a Strawberry Gâteau made with Genoese sponge.

Coffee Caramel Crystal Gâteau

Makes 8-10 slices
Preparation: 30 minutes
Cooking: 30-35 minutes

4 eggs, size 2
4oz (125g) caster sugar
4oz (125g) minus 1 tablespoon plain flour
2oz (50g) butter, melted and cooled
oil or butter for greasing

The filling and coating:
10oz (275g) butter, softened
12oz (350g) icing sugar
2 tablespoons instant coffee
2-3 tablespoons boiling water
5 tablespoons Tia Maria

The Caramel Crystal:
5oz (150g) caster sugar
4 tablespoons water
oil for greasing

To decorate:
1-2oz (25-50g) chocolate coffee beans

Coffee Caramel Crystal Gâteau.

Make, bake and cool the cake as for Strawberry Gâteau. Cut across into 3 layers.

☐ Make the filling as for Mocha Buttercream Layer Cake.

☐ Make the Caramel Crystal: Put the sugar and water into a small saucepan. Place over a low heat and stir until the sugar dissolves. Do not boil until the syrup is quite clear. Wash any sugar down the sides of the pan with a wet pastry brush.

☐ Boil the syrup rapidly until it turns a light brown. Immediately pour into a greased shallow cake tin.

☐ Leave until the caramel has set and cooled. Invert the tin over a sheet of greaseproof paper on a flat surface and tap the tin to release the caramel. Break it into large pieces.

☐ Put the pieces into a large plastic bag and pound or roll with a rolling pin to break into pea-sized pieces.

☐ Put into a sieve and shake to remove the fine 'dust'. Reserve this for use in other cakes. Put the caramel pieces in a line along the centre of the piece of greaseproof paper.

☐ To finish the gâteau: Sandwich the layers and coat the sides with the Mocha Buttercream. Roll the sides in the Caramel Crystal to coat well and press on the shards with a palette knife.

☐ Set the gâteau on a serving plate and spread the top lightly with more buttercream. Put the rest of the buttercream into a forcing bag fitted with a ½in (1cm) rose pipe. Decorate the top of the cake as shown.

Tips: Make the cake, the filling and the crystal in advance. The last-minute finishing will then only take a few minutes.

● Make the cake and store in the freezer for up to 2 months.

● The buttercream should not be made more than about a day ahead, and it must be stored in a cool place – not in the refrigerator!

● Before you let the syrup for the caramel come to the boil, rub a little between the fingers. It should feel completely smooth if the sugar is properly dissolved.

● The size of tin on which you pour the cooked caramel is not important.

● Caramel Crystal is a useful ingredient to make and store for use when required. As long as it is kept completely dry, it will last for several weeks.

Peach and Kiwi Gâteau

Makes 8-10 slices ☆☆☆
Preparation: 30 minutes
Cooking: 30-35 minutes

4 eggs, size 2
4oz (125g) caster sugar
4oz (125g) minus 1 tablespoon plain flour
2oz (50g) butter, melted and cooled
oil or butter for greasing

To fill and decorate:
4oz (125g) peach jam
juice of ½ an orange
2 tablespoons orange liqueur
about 9 fl oz (250ml) double cream
2 large kiwi fruit
4 peaches

Make, bake and cool the cake as for Strawberry Gâteau. Cut across into 3 layers.

☐ Put the jam into a small saucepan with orange juice and liqueur. Place over a moderate heat until jam melts. Simmer briefly until it develops a spreading consistency. Remove and let cool.

☐ Whip the cream until it just holds soft peaks. (Don't over-whip as it may separate during piping, as the action works the cream even more). Put into a forcing bag fitted with a ½in (1cm) rose pipe.

☐ Sandwich the 3 layers of cake with some of the jam.

☐ Set the cake on an icing turntable. Hold the forcing bag nearly upright so the pipe is almost parallel to the sides. Pipe fingers of cream all the way around the sides of the gâteau. Carefully transfer to a serving plate.

☐ Peel and slice the kiwi fruit. Peel the peaches and cut inwards towards the stones to shape wedges.

☐ Sieve the remaining jam. Arrange the peaches and kiwis over top of the gâteau as shown. Carefully spoon the jam glaze over the fruit. Finish off with a whirl of cream if liked.

☐ Serve fresh, cut into wedges.

Tip: When peaches are not in season, use a good brand of canned ones.

Variation: Fresh oranges are also good in this recipe. Either peach jam or orange marmalade can be used as the filling and glaze.

Peach and Kiwi Gâteau makes an elegant dessert to follow a rich meal.

Peach and Kiwi Gâteau

To remove the skins from peaches more easily and neatly, first blanch them in hot water. Dip one peach at a time into a pan of boiling water. Take them out as soon as you can rub the skin off with the back of a fork. Immediately refresh under cold running water to prevent the fruit going soft.
If you want to prepare the peaches a little in advance, put them into a basin with a little lemon juice after you have cut them into slices, to prevent discoloration.

To make it easier to move the cake on and off the icing turntable, leave it on its base when cooling.

Do-it-yourself Gâteau:

The basic cakes

Bake either a Basic Whisked Sponge or Genoese Sponge mixture in whatever baking tin you have available. The quantities given fit the following:

    two 9in (23cm) sandwich tins *or*
    one 9in (23cm) springform or
    loose-bottomed cake tin *or*
    one 8½in (21cm) fluted ring mould *or*
    one 9 × 13in (23 × 33cm) Swiss Roll tin

Fillings and toppings

- Whipped cream flavoured with brandy, rum or a suitable liqueur
- Chocolate Ganache
- Crème Pâtissière
- various jams and marmalades
- glacé icing
- jelly glaze
- buttercream

Decorations

- chocolate coffee beans
- grated chocolate
- Caramel Crystal
- praline
- chopped and/or flaked and/or whole nuts: almonds, walnuts, hazelnuts, pistachios
- glacé fruits
- crystallized flowers: violets, roses and mimosa
- coloured dragees; gold, silver, and other assorted colours
- whole or sliced fresh fruit as available
- canned pineapple, apricots, peaches or cherries

Icing turntable

If you want to make decorated cakes and gâteaux it is useful to have an icing turntable. If you don't have one, set your cake on a thin cake board and place it on top of an inverted bowl. This will keep the edges free so icing can run off neatly.

Creating your own gâteau

Once you know how to make the two different types of whisked sponge, there is no limit to the beautiful gâteaux you can create for yourself.

Pineapple Cream Gâteau

Makes 6-8 slices
Preparation: 20 minutes

9in (23cm) cake – Basic Whisked Sponge or Genoese Sponge as for Strawberry Gâteau
8oz (225g) canned pineapple slices

The filling:
Crème Pâtissière using pineapple syrup in place of milk, and 2-3 tablespoons kirsch
½ pint (300ml) double cream
3-4oz (75-100g) flaked almonds, browned

Layer, top and decorate as shown.

Pineapple Cream Gâteau.

Coffee and Chocolate Gâteau

Makes 6-8 slices
Preparation: 10 minutes

Basic Whisked Sponge (with 3 teaspoons liquid coffee essence added to the egg yolks before whisking) baked in a 9 × 13in (23 × 33cm) Swiss Roll tin
¾ pint (450ml) double cream, whipped
3 tablespoons brandy (optional)
3oz (75g) grated chocolate
6oz (175g) sifted icing sugar
1 or 2 tablespoons water
walnut halves to decorate

Cut the slab of cake across into 3. Sandwich with whipped cream, flavoured with brandy if using, to make a 3-tier cake. Spread the sides with whipped cream and coat with grated chocolate.

☐ Mix the icing sugar with enough water to give a glacé icing with a stiff coating consistency and ice the top with it. Decorate with walnuts.

Biscuit-making

Baking is one of the most satisfying of cooking techniques to master, and the baking of biscuits must be its easiest and most pleasurable application. Who doesn't look forward to the unmistakable smell wafting from the kitchen, or to eating biscuits warm from the oven?

Biscuits come in all shapes, sizes, colours and flavours, with a multitude of textures—crisp and chewy, soft and moist, or buttery, rich and sweet. Basically they are an amalgam of flour, sugar and butter: and the addition of any other ingredients dictates the nature of the finished biscuit; self-raising flour gives a crisper result than plain; brown sugar gives colour and a molasses taste; eggs give a richer texture and taste; cocoa alters the colour as well as giving a chocolate flavour; and citrus peel or nuts lend tang or crunch. Home-made biscuits can be stored in airtight tins or in the freezer (before *and* after baking), and can contribute to every meal and occasion, whether lunch-time snack or champagne picnic.

Lemon Crisps

This recipe is very versatile and can be adapted in several different ways. The dough can be frozen either in one piece or already shaped, and the baked biscuits also freeze well.

Makes 72   ☆
Preparation: 30 minutes
Cooking: 10-20 minutes

4oz (100g) butter, softened
grated rind of 1 lemon
4oz (100g) caster sugar
1 egg, size 3
8oz (200g) plain flour
1 teaspoon baking powder

Beat the butter, lemon rind, and sugar until very light and creamy.
☐ Put the egg into a small screw-top jar. Shake well to mix. If you are using metric measurements, discard 1 teaspoonful of the egg. Gradually beat the egg into the butter-sugar mixture.
☐ Sift the flour and baking powder into the bowl. Gradually stir in the egg mixture with a wooden spoon. Work with the hand to mix to a smooth dough.
☐ Set oven to 350F (180C) gas 4.

☐ Shape and bake in any of the three ways given below then transfer to cooling racks until completely cool. Store in an airtight container in a cool place for up to 3 days, or in the freezer for up to 2 months.
☐ For sliced biscuits: Divide the mixture into 4 equal parts. Roll on a work surface under the hands to make 4 logs about 1⅓in (3.5cm) in diameter. Wrap each in a piece of foil and chill in the freezer for ½-¾ hour until hard. Cut into thin slices using a sharp knife. Place on greased baking trays and bake for about 5 minutes until lightly browned.
☐ For forked biscuits: Roll the dough into balls the size of large marbles. Place on greased baking trays. Press flat with the back of a fork dipped into flour. Bake for 8-10 minutes until lightly browned.
☐ For rolled biscuits: Working with about one-third of the dough at a time, roll it wafer thin with a rolling pin on a lightly floured work surface. Stamp out with shaped biscuit cutters and transfer to greased baking trays with a palette knife. Sprinkle with coloured sugar and bake for about 6 minutes until lightly browned.

Rolling biscuit dough

Different types of mixtures are best rolled in different ways. For instance, rich shortbread doughs can be rolled between two sheets of greaseproof paper so that you don't roll extra flour into the dough.
Other doughs containing egg or milk are better rolled on a work surface lightly dusted with a little flour.

Shaping rolled biscuits

Nowadays there is a wealth of attractive, differently shaped ornamental biscuit cutters available from most kitchen shops. (For easier and neater cutting, dip metal cutters in some flour first!) If you don't have any ornamental cutters to hand, improvise with handy kitchen items, like tumblers and apple corers:

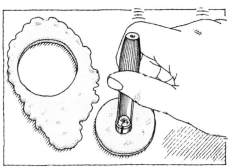

With an inverted tumbler, cut plain circles of dough. Remove centres with an apple corer.

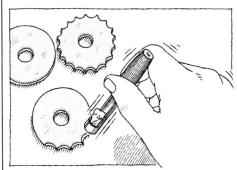

To make a scalloped edge: work around the outside with the edge of the corer.

The various stages in making Simple Shortbread Squares.

Flavoured shortbread

You can easily make biscuits of different flavours with the same dough. Use a little sachet of vanilla sugar in place of some of the sugar. Grated orange or lemon rind is easy to work into the dough, or you can add a few drops of any good flavouring essence, such as almond or cinnamon.

❄ Freezing biscuits

Biscuits store well in the freezer, baked or unbaked.

Baked and cold, they should be packed into plastic bags, closed tightly and frozen; if laid out on a serving plate, they will thaw in half an hour at room temperature.

Unbaked biscuit dough can be shaped into blocks of not more than 1in (2.5cm) thickness, open frozen then overwrapped. Thaw at room temperature for an hour, then shape and bake. Or the dough can first be shaped on trays, open frozen, and then decanted into plastic bags; to bake, remove from bag, lay out on trays, and bake immediately (allow 4-5 minutes longer than for fresh dough).

Shortbread biscuits

The simplest of all biscuits to make are those using the shortbread formula with no liquid ingredients: commonly one part sugar, two parts butter, three parts plain flour – although the not-so-frugal Scots use equal parts in their classic recipes. You simply rub all the ingredients together and quickly work to a dough.

For this rich mixture, there is no need to grease the baking tins, as the biscuits come off cleanly. Instead of rolling and cutting the dough, then placing it on trays, you can simply smooth it out into a shallow tin. Cut into squares and bake in the same way. Just make sure the dough is not thicker than a digestive biscuit.

Simple Shortbread Squares

Makes 36 ☆
Preparation and cooking: 20 minutes

6oz (150g) plain flour
2oz (50g) caster sugar
4oz (100g) firm butter

Set the oven to 325F (160C) gas 3.
☐ Sieve the flour and sugar into a bowl. Add the butter.
☐ Cut the butter into cubes with two knives and then rub it in well with the tips of the fingers until the mixture resembles fine crumbs.
☐ Work the crumbs together with the hand to form a smooth dough.
☐ Place the dough between 2 sheets of greaseproof paper on a work surface. Roll into a rectangle the thickness of a digestive biscuit.
☐ Peel off the top sheet of paper and with a long knife, mark the dough into 1½in (3.5cm) squares. Carefully lift each with a palette knife and place in rows 1in (2.5cm) apart on two baking trays.
☐ Re-roll and cut the trimmings.
☐ Bake for about 15 minutes until lightly browned.
☐ Transfer to a cooling rack.

Sugar Almond Wreaths

Makes 24 ☆☆
Preparation and cooking: 30 minutes

3oz (75g) caster sugar
6oz (150g) plain flour
grated rind of ½ lemon
5oz (125g) cold butter, cubed small
1 egg, beaten
2 tablespoons nibbed sugar
about 1oz (25g) flaked almonds

Set the oven to 350F (180C) gas 4.
☐ Mix the sugar, flour and lemon rind together in a mixing bowl.
☐ Add the butter to the dry ingredients and rub in with the tips of the fingers to form coarse crumbs.
☐ Dribble 1 tablespoon of egg over the mixture, stir together and work with the hand to a soft dough.
☐ Working with a small amount of the dough at one time, and keeping the rest chilled, roll out on a lightly floured work surface to the thickness of a digestive biscuit.
☐ Stamp out into 2½-in (6-cm) rounds. Cut out the centres.
☐ Sprinkle with the sugar nibs. Crush the almonds in your hand, sprinkle on top and press.
☐ Bake for about 8 minutes until lightly browned. Transfer to a wire rack to cool.

Spicy Buttons

Makes 30 ☆
Preparation: 10 minutes
Cooking: 12-14 minutes

2oz (50g) butter, softened
2oz (50g) soft brown sugar
2 teaspoons mixed spice
4oz (100g) self-raising flour
2 tablespoons beaten egg

Set the oven to 350F (180C) gas 4.
☐ Beat together the butter, sugar and spice.
☐ With a wooden spoon, gradually stir in the flour and egg. Work with the hands to make a smooth dough.
☐ Roll the dough in the hands to form it into balls the size of large marbles. Place on large greased baking trays.
☐ Bake for 12-14 minutes until set. Transfer to a wire rack to cool. Store in an airtight container in a cool place for up to 3 days or for up to 2 months in the freezer.
Tip: You can flatten the biscuits slightly before baking, if preferred: dip a palette knife into flour and press each ball of dough. The baked biscuits will then be more crisp.

From left to right; Sugar Almond Wreaths, Spicy Buttons and Dutch Butter Biscuits.

Dutch Butter Biscuits

Makes 18 ☆☆☆
Preparation: 15 minutes
Cooking: 10-12 minutes

5oz (125g) butter, softened
2oz (50g) icing sugar
¼ teaspoon vanilla essence
6oz (150g) self-raising flour
1-2 tablespoons double cream

Set the oven to 325F (160C) gas 3.
☐ Beat together the butter, sugar and vanilla essence until light and creamy.
☐ With a wooden spoon, gradually stir in the flour. Finally, mix in the cream.
☐ Fit a ½in (1cm) rose pipe into a forcing bag. Fill with the mixture.
☐ On baking trays, pipe 'N' shapes about 1½in (4cm) long with the 3 bars just touching.
☐ Bake for 10-12 minutes until lightly browned.
☐ Transfer to a wire rack to cool. Store in an airtight container in a cool place for up to 3 days, or in the freezer for up to 2 months.
Tip: For biscuits with a crisply defined outline, add only 1 tablespoon of cream to the dough. The extra cream makes the mixture easier to pipe, but it does then spread more as it bakes.

Spice cookies

The colour and flavour of these biscuits will vary depending on the darkness of the sugar used. Demerara sugar is not suitable for this recipe but all of the moist brown sugars produce good results.

To blanch almonds

Put the almonds in their skins into a saucepan of cold water. Bring to the boil, drain the almonds and squeeze each between the fingers to release the skin.

To skin hazelnuts

Put the nuts in a single layer on a tray in an oven pre-heated to 350F (180C) gas 4. Leave for only 5-10 minutes to loosen the skins without browning the nuts. Put the hot nuts on a clean cloth, gather up the edges like a sack and shake the contents. The skins then come off on the cloth.

Coloured sugar

You can buy coloured sugar from good grocers, confectioners and larger supermarkets, or make your own: put a little caster sugar into a small screw-top jar, add a few drops of food colouring and shake the jar to mix the colour through. If any colour remains unmixed, rub it into the sugar with a small spoon.

Almond Squares

Makes about 48 ☆☆
Preparation and cooking: 30 minutes

6oz (150g) plain flour
3oz (75g) ground almonds
3oz (75g) caster sugar
4oz (100g) cold butter, cubed small
1 egg, size 2, lightly beaten or shaken
1oz (25g) blanched almonds

Set the oven to 325F (160C) gas 3.
☐ Mix together the flour, ground almonds and sugar.
☐ Add the butter and rub in with the fingertips to fine crumbs.
☐ Gradually stir in 1 tablespoon egg.
☐ Work with the hand to bind into a smooth, evenly mixed dough.
☐ Place between two sheets of greaseproof paper on a work surface. Roll and smooth into a rectangle the thickness of a digestive biscuit.
☐ Peel off the top paper. Mark the dough into 1-in (2.5-cm) squares.
☐ Split the almonds in half. Press a piece into each square and brush with egg.
☐ Carefully place in rows 1in (2.5cm) apart on two baking trays. Re-roll and cut trimmings.
☐ Bake for 12-15 minutes until lightly browned.
☐ Transfer to a wire rack to cool.

Spice Cookies

Makes about 48 ☆☆
Preparation and cooking: about 45 minutes

6oz (150g) plain flour
2 teaspoons mixed spice
4oz (100g) soft brown sugar
4oz (100g) cold butter, cubed small
1 tablespoon egg, lightly beaten or shaken
2oz (50g) flaked almonds

Set the oven to 350F (180C) gas 4.
☐ Mix together the flour, spice and sugar.
☐ With the tips of the fingers, rub the butter into the dry ingredients to form crumb-like mixture.
☐ Sprinkle the egg over the crumbs and stir it in. Work with the hand to make a smooth dough.
☐ Divide the mixture into 48 equal-sized pieces. Roll between the palms to form balls and place on greased baking trays. Flatten each with a dampened knife.
☐ Sprinkle the nuts over and press them on the surface.
☐ Bake for 7-8 minutes until lightly browned.
☐ Transfer to a wire rack to cool.
Variation: Make Ginger Cookies by substituting ground ginger for the mixed spice.

Hazelnut Crescents

Makes 36 ☆☆
Preparation: 20 minutes
Cooking: about 8 minutes

3oz (75g) butter, softened
3oz (75g) caster sugar
5oz (125g) plain flour
3oz (75g) finely chopped hazelnuts
1 egg, lightly beaten or shaken

Set the oven to 350F (180C) gas 4.

☐ Beat the butter and sugar together until light and creamy.

☐ With a wooden spoon, gradually mix in the flour. Add the nuts and mix in well.

☐ Stir 1 tablespoon of the egg into the biscuit mixture.

☐ Work well with the hand to bind together into a dough.

☐ Roll the dough on a lightly floured board to the thickness of a digestive biscuit.

☐ Stamp out 2½in (6cm) rounds with a fluted cutter. Cut out an oval from each biscuit to leave crescent shapes.

☐ With a palette knife, transfer to baking trays and brush with some of the remaining egg.

☐ Bake for about 8 minutes until lightly browned.

☐ Transfer to a wire rack to cool. Store in an airtight container in a cool place for up to 3 days.

Sugar Crisps

Makes 24 ☆☆
Preparation: 10 minutes
Cooking: about 15–17 minutes

4oz (100g) butter, softened
2oz (50g) caster sugar
grated rind of ½ an orange
5oz (125g) self-raising flour
milk for brushing
1oz (25g) flaked almonds
2 tablespoons nibbed sugar

Set the oven to 325F (160C) gas 3.

☐ Beat the butter, sugar and orange rind until light and creamy.

☐ With a wooden spoon, gradually mix in the flour. Then work with the hand to form a smooth dough.

☐ Roll the dough between 2 sheets of greaseproof paper to a rectangle about 9½ × 7½in (24 × 19cm). Strip off the top sheet of paper.

☐ Slide the paper with the dough on a baking tray. Brush the dough all over with milk. Sprinkle with the almonds and the nibbed sugar and press these into the surface with the hand.

☐ Bake for 15–17 minutes until lightly browned.

☐ Remove from the oven. With a large knife, cut across into halves and then cut each half into 12 fingers. Place them on a wire rack to cool. Store in an airtight container in a cool place for up to 3 days or up to 2 months in the freezer.

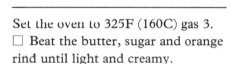

From left to right: Almond Squares, Spice Cookies, Hazelnut Crescents, Sugar Crisps, Cinnamon Crunches, Orange Shells and different types of Zebra Biscuit.

Sugar Crisps

You can easily double this recipe if you have tins of suitable size. Just smooth the dough out to the thickness of ⅛in (3mm).

Sugar nibs are sold by grocers, confectioners and better large supermarkets. Your local baker might also sell you some. If unavailable, crush some sugar cubes in a plastic bag using a rolling pin.

Zebra Biscuits

Leftover trimmings of dough can be rolled together into a log. When sliced, the biscuits will have a nice random marbled effect.

Shaped Biscuits

Other petits fours tins may be used in the same way as the shell-shaped moulds to make flower, cushion or oval shapes.

When biscuit doughs are too soft to shape easily, wrap in foil or film and chill for a few minutes in the fridge.

Baking of biscuits

Baking times can vary a great deal depending on the thickness of the biscuits. Watch them carefully—even an extra minute can be too long!

Cinnamon Crunches

Makes 48
Preparation and cooking: 40 minutes

4oz (100g) butter, softened
4oz (100g) caster sugar
2 teaspoons ground cinnamon
1 egg, size 3
8oz (200g) plain flour

Set the oven to 350F (180C) gas 4.
☐ Beat the butter, sugar and cinnamon together until light and creamy. Beat in the egg.
☐ With a wooden spoon, gradually mix the flour in. Work the mixture with the hand to a smooth dough.
☐ Roll small pieces of the dough between the hands into balls the size of large marbles and place them on greased baking trays.
☐ Press the little balls of dough flat with the back of a floured fork.
☐ Bake for 8-10 minutes until lightly browned.
☐ Transfer to a wire rack to cool.

Orange Shells

Makes 24 ☆☆
Preparation and cooking: 20 minutes

6oz (150g) self-raising flour
2oz (50g) caster sugar
4oz (100g) cold butter, cubed small
about 2 tablespoons orange liqueur

Set the oven to 350F (180C) gas 4.
☐ Mix the flour and sugar together in a bowl.
☐ Add the butter to the dry ingredients and rub in with the fingertips to make light crumbs.
☐ Press the crumbs firmly into small shell-shaped moulds and set them on baking trays.
☐ Bake for 9-10 minutes until lightly browned.
☐ Remove from oven and sprinkle about $\frac{1}{4}$ teaspoon liqueur over each.
☐ Leave in the tins for 5 minutes then, with the tip of a sharp knife, prise out of moulds and cool.
☐ Serve fresh, within 2-3 hours.

Zebra Biscuits

Makes about 72 ☆
Preparation: 30 minutes plus
30 minutes chilling
Cooking: 7-10 minutes

The white dough:
4oz (100g) butter, softened
4oz (100g) caster sugar
1 teaspoon vanilla essence
1 egg, size 3
8oz (225g) plain flour
$\frac{1}{4}$ teaspoon baking powder

The cocoa dough:
4oz (100g) butter, softened
4oz (100g) caster sugar
1 teaspoon vanilla essence
1 egg, size 3
7oz (200g) plain flour
3 tablespoons cocoa
$\frac{1}{4}$ teaspoon baking powder

Set the oven to 350F (180C) gas 4.
☐ Make the doughs separately:
☐ Beat the butter, sugar and essence together until light and creamy, then beat in the egg.
☐ Sift in the dry ingredients and mix to form a smooth soft dough.
☐ To make pinwheels: Place each piece of dough between 2 sheets of greaseproof paper. Roll each to a rectangle about 15 × 8in (38 × 20cm).
☐ Chill for $\frac{1}{2}$ hour until firm.
☐ Peel off the top papers. Turn chocolate layer over on top of white. Remove papers and trim edges neatly.
☐ Roll up like a Swiss roll then cut across into thin slices. Place on greased trays, 1in (2.5cm) apart.
☐ To make chequer boards: Roll each dough to about $\frac{1}{4}$in (5mm) thick, and cut into 5 fairly equal-sized rectangular pieces. Make two stacks of alternating layers of dough 5 thicknesses each—one with the outer layers white, the other with both outer layers coloured. Cut each across in $\frac{1}{4}$in (5mm) slices. Lay alternating slices from each stack one on top of another, so that the white stripes fall on top of coloured, then slice across to make boards.
☐ Bake for 7-10 minutes.
☐ Transfer to a wire rack to cool.

Pastry-making

The skills of pastry-making can soon be mastered with practice. Once you can confidently turn out good shortcrust, plain and sweet flan pastry, choux pastry and the various types of flaky pastry, a range of impressive dishes will be at your command.

Shortcrust pastry

The traditional method of making this pastry is to rub the fat finely into plain flour and then bind it together using as little water as is necessary to form a dough. Too much will result in a pastry that is tough. During cooking the water evaporates and the pastry's texture is created by the fat and flour binding together. Usually the fat ingredient used is a mixture of butter and lard but there are many recipes which require a single fat. For a less rich pastry, margarine can be used instead. Butter and margarine both contain a certain amount of water, so if using one or other on their own you will require more fat. White fats like lard have no water content and will produce a shorter pastry, so less is needed if it is used alone.

Baking times and temperatures

These vary depending on the recipe. As a rough guide, 400F (200C) gas 6 is the usual setting.

Baking blind

To prepare a flan case or tart for a liquid, or ready-cooked filling, it is 'baked blind'.

This is done by placing a piece of aluminium foil or greaseproof paper in the uncooked tart or flan case. (It is sometimes weighted by filling it with dried beans, uncooked pasta shapes or rice kept especially for the purpose.) This prevents the pastry from rising and supports the sides. The base of the pastry is usually also pricked well with a fork.

Cook the pastry for between 10-20 minutes.

Secrets of success

● Use chilled fats and cold water and try to make pastry in a cool kitchen.
● Handle pastry as little as possible.
● Rub the fat in thoroughly so that all the flour particles are well coated with fat. Shake the bowl occasionally to bring unmixed fat to the surface.
● Add the water a little at a time. Too much generally results in tough and unevenly baked pastry.
● When cooking in glass or ceramic dishes, put them on pre-heated baking trays.
● Roll the pastry thinly on a lightly floured surface, taking care not to include too much added flour.
● Roll pastry lightly in 2 directions. This prevents it from becoming over-stretched and shrinking when baked.

English Shortcrust Pastry

Makes about 1½lb (700g) ☆☆☆

1lb (400g) plain flour
4oz (100g) firm butter, cubed
4oz (100g) firm lard, cubed
4-5 tablespoons cold water

Put the flour into a large bowl and add the fats. With the tips of the fingers, rub the fat into the flour until mixture resembles fine crumbs.
☐ Dribble the water over the surface, one tablespoon at a time, mixing in with a palette knife. Continue adding water, carefully, until you form a firm ball of dough.
☐ Turn out on a lightly floured surface and knead lightly until the dough is smooth and evenly mixed.
☐ Use at once or wrap and freeze.

Storing shortcrust pastry

Shortcrust pastry stores well in several forms. A jar of the flour-fat mixture will keep in the fridge for up to 2 weeks or in the freezer for up to 2 months. Made-up pastry, uncooked, can be stored, well wrapped, in the freezer for up to 2 months – but, if kept in the fridge, it must be used within 2 days. If you have space in your freezer, you may find it convenient to line plates or tins with pastry ready for baking. Many baked dishes made with shortcrust, such as small pastries, tarts with fairly dry fillings, or top-crust-only pies also store well in the freezer.

Making shortcrust pastry

Rub the fat into the flour until it resembles fine dry crumbs.

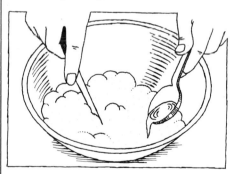

Stir the water in a little at a time until you can form a firm ball of dough.

Pear Dumplings

Makes 6 ☆☆☆
Preparation: 20 minutes
Cooking: 30-35 minutes

---

about 1½lb (700g) English Shortcrust Pastry
6 large firm pears, each about 7oz (200g)
3oz (75g) golden syrup
2oz (50g) butter
single cream to serve

Set oven to 400F (200C) gas 6. Butter a shallow baking dish. On a lightly floured surface roll out the pastry to a thickness of ⅛in (3mm). Cut into ¾in (1.75cm) wide strips.

☐ Peel and core a pear from the base, leaving stalk intact. Starting at the bottom, wind a strip of pastry around in a spiral. If necessary, join on a second strip, dampening the ends of the pastry.

☐ Repeat with the other pears and place in the baking dish.

☐ Melt the syrup and butter in a small saucepan. Brush well over the dumplings.

☐ Bake in the oven for 30-35 minutes until the pastry is well browned, and the pears are tender when pierced with a skewer.

☐ Serve hot or warm with cream.

Tips: Work with only one pear at a time because they discolour very quickly.

● Try to leave the stalks on when peeling the pears as this gives the finished dumplings an extra decorative touch.

● To make it easier to core the pears, first cut a small slice from the base.

Variations: Try filling the cavity of the pears with any of the following before wrapping with pastry:

● chopped nuts
● glacé cherries
● syrup and dried fruit.

Some of the diverse uses of English Shortcrust Pastry.
Clockwise from the top: Koulibiac, Pear Dumplings, Tricorns, Steak and Stuffing Pie and Country Meat Pasties.

Koulibiac

Serves 6 ☆☆☆
Preparation: 30 minutes
Cooking: 35-40 minutes

---

about 1½lb (700g) English Shortcrust Pastry
beaten egg to glaze

The filling:
4oz (100g) onion, peeled and chopped
4oz (100g) mushrooms, sliced
2oz (50g) butter
3 tablespoons flour
8 fl oz (250ml) milk
12oz (350g) cooked white fish, flaked
a squeeze of lemon juice
salt and pepper
2 tablespoons finely chopped fresh dill

Set the oven at 400F (200C) gas 6.

☐ Put the onion, mushrooms, and butter into a saucepan over a moderate heat. Cook for about 5 minutes, stirring frequently, until soft but not browned.

☐ Sprinkle in the flour. Gradually stir in the milk. Cook for 3-4 minutes, stirring, until thick.

☐ Lightly fold in the fish. Season to taste with lemon juice, salt and pepper and dill. Cool.

☐ On a lightly floured surface, roll out the pastry to a thickness of ⅛in (3mm). Cut out a 12in (30cm) square. Roll around the rolling pin then unroll on a baking tray. Brush the edges with egg.

☐ Spoon the filling into the centre of the pastry. Bring the four corners of the pastry up to the centre, overlapping a little along the edges. Pinch together to close the seams, but leave a tiny hole in the centre as a steam vent.

☐ Brush the pie with beaten egg. Re-roll the pastry trimmings. Use to make decorative shapes. Decorate the top of the pie as shown. Brush again with egg.

☐ Bake the koulibiac in the oven for 35-40 minutes, until well browned.

☐ Serve hot.

Tip: A mixture of fish, such as salmon with cod or haddock, works well in this dish.

Country Meat Pasties

Served hot, with some freshly cooked vegetables, these make a filling lunch or supper. Cold with a salad they are ideal picnic or packed lunch fare.

Makes 8 ☆☆☆
Preparation: 30 minutes
Cooking: 40 minutes

---

about 1½lb (700g) English Shortcrust Pastry
beaten egg to glaze

The filling:
1½lb (700g) lean minced pork, veal or beef
7oz (200g) onion, peeled and finely chopped
7oz (200g) potato, peeled and coarsely grated
6oz (175g) carrot, peeled and coarsely grated
1 teaspoon dried thyme or rosemary
3 tablespoons mushroom ketchup or Worcestershire Sauce
salt and pepper

Set the oven to 400F (200C) gas 6. On a lightly-floured surface roll out the pastry to a thickness of ⅛in (3mm). Cut out eight 6½in (16cm) circles of pastry.

☐ Mix together the minced meat, onion, potato, carrot, dried herbs and ketchup, and season to taste. Divide between the pastry circles spooning in a line down the centre of each. Brush the pastry edges with the egg. Draw up the pastry on either side to cover the meat. Pinch to seal.

☐ Place on the baking tray and brush with the egg. Bake in the oven for about 40 minutes until brown.

☐ Serve hot or cold.

Tips: Use the lid of a small saucepan or a saucer as a guide for cutting circles of pastry.

Variations: Pasties are a good way of using up any leftover meat and cooked vegetables. Try including:

● mashed potato flavoured with curry powder
● diced gammon and sweet pickle
● smoked fish and chopped hard-boiled egg.

Decorating pie edges

The simplest way to finish off the edge is to squeeze the pastry gently between the thumb and finger of one hand and, using the forefinger of the other, push the pastry in between the other two fingers. Repeat all round.

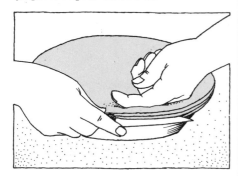

A more professional way to finish off your pie is to 'knock up' the pastry by pressing gently with one finger and lightly cutting the edge with a knife to create a raised edge.

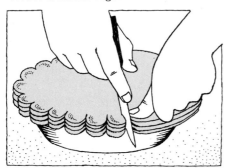

Then 'scallop' the knocked-up edge by pressing down with the thumb and drawing the pastry back to one side with the knife.

Using leftover shortcrust pastry
Gather together into a ball and roll thinly. Make barquettes (tiny boats) or tartlet cases. Store in plastic bags in the freezer ready to fill with a quiche mixture, pizza filling, jam or fruit.

Tricorns
Cut out 3in (7.5cm) rounds of pastry. Place a rounded teaspoon of mincemeat, jam or other filling in the centre. Brush the edges of the circle with water. Draw up the pastry from 3 equidistant points around the edge. Press together in the centre to seal. Bake in the oven pre-heated to 400F (200C) gas 6 for 10-12 minutes.

Steak and Stuffing Pie

Serves 4-5
Preparation and cooking: 1¾ hours

---

about 1lb (450g) English Shortcrust Pastry

The filling:
12 pitted prunes, soaked overnight in
    ¼ pint (150ml) port or sweet sherry
1½lb (675g) chuck steak, trimmed and cubed
1oz (25g) butter
2 tablespoons oil
1 medium onion, chopped
2 celery sticks, sliced
2 teaspoons dried mixed herbs
2 tablespoons flour
¼ pint (150ml) Basic Brown Stock
salt and pepper

The forcemeat stuffing:
4oz (125g) fresh white breadcrumbs
2oz (50g) shredded suet
1 tablespoon chopped parsley
1 teaspoon dried mixed herbs
grated rind of ½ lemon
2oz (50g) bacon, rinded and chopped
1 size 2 egg, beaten

Heat the butter with 1 tablespoon of oil in a large saucepan over a moderate heat and add one-third of the meat. Fry for 5 minutes, stirring frequently, to brown lightly. Remove the meat and cook the remainder in the same way in 2 batches, adding extra oil.

☐ Add the onions and the celery and cook for 5 minutes to soften without colouring. Return all the meat to the pan and add the herbs and the flour. Drain the prunes and add the port to the pan, stirring constantly. Gradually add the stock and cook for 2-3 minutes until thick. Cover and simmer gently for 45 minutes.

☐ Season the meat to taste and transfer to a 1½ pint (900ml) pie dish and allow to cool slightly.

☐ Make the forcemeat stuffing balls: In a large bowl mix the breadcrumbs, suet, parsley, dried mixed herbs, lemon rind, bacon and nearly all the beaten egg, reserving some for brushing the top of the pastry. Season the mixture with salt and pepper and divide into 12 small balls.

☐ Set oven to 400F (200C) gas 6. On a lightly floured surface roll the pastry out to a thickness of ⅛in (3mm). Cut a piece of pastry to fit the top of the dish and re-roll the trimmings. Cut a strip about ½in (1cm) wide and long enough to go round the edge of the dish.

☐ Add the drained prunes and the forcemeat balls to the meat in the dish and mix in. Brush the edge of the dish with water and place the pastry strip around. Brush the strip with water and cover with the pastry top. Seal the edges and decorate the top with pastry trimmings. Make a small steam hole in the centre.

☐ Place dish on a baking tray and bake for 30-40 minutes. Serve hot.

Fruit Lace Tart

Serves 4
Preparation and cooking: 55 minutes

12oz (350g) English Shortcrust Pastry
¼ pint (142ml) carton double cream, whipped
8oz (225g) raspberries or redcurrants
2 tablespoons redcurrant jelly
1 tablespoon water
icing sugar to dust

Set the oven to 400F (200C) gas 6.

☐ To make the top: roll one-third of the pastry on greaseproof paper to a thickness of ⅛in (3mm). Use an inverted 7in (18cm) fluted flan tin to cut out a circle of pastry. Use aspic cutters to punch out a lace pattern over the pastry. Slide paper on to a baking tray. Bake for 12-15 minutes until lightly browned. Cool.

☐ Roll out remaining pastry and use to line flan tin. Bake blind for 15-20 minutes. Cool.

☐ Spread cream over pastry and cover with the fruit.

☐ Heat jelly and water in a small pan until syrupy. Cool and spoon over fruit.

☐ Slide pastry top on to fruit. Dust with icing sugar and serve at once.

Honey Crumb Pie

Serves 6 ☆☆
Preparation and cooking: 1¼ hours

8oz (225g) English Shortcrust Pastry

The filling:
12oz (350g) cooking apples
1 tablespoon lemon juice
grated rind of ½ lemon
6oz (175g) clear honey
3oz (75g) fresh breadcrumbs
1oz (25g) butter, cubed

Set the oven to 350F (180C) gas 4.
Roll out pastry to a thickness of ⅛in
(3mm). Use to line an 8in (20cm)
pie plate and trim.
☐ Cut out triangles of the pastry all
the way round the rim of the plate
to give a saw-toothed effect.
☐ Peel, core and finely chop apples
and mix with remaining ingredients.
☐ Spread over the pastry base. Fold
pastry 'teeth' in over filling.
☐ Bake for about 50 minutes until a
golden brown. Serve hot.

Mincemeat Meringue Tart

Serves 6 ☆☆
Preparation: 20 minutes
Cooking: 25-30 minutes

8oz (225g) English Shortcrust Pastry

The filling:
10oz (275g) mincemeat
8oz (225g) canned pineapple pieces, drained

The meringue:
2 egg whites
4oz (100g) caster sugar

Set the oven to 375F (190C) gas 5.
On a lightly floured surface, roll the
pastry to a thickness of about ⅛in
(3mm). Use to line a 10in (25cm)
ovenproof plate, trim the edges and
prick the bottom with a fork.
☐ Re-roll the trimmings of pastry
very thinly. Using aspic cutters,
stamp out pastry shapes. Brush the

edges of the pastry with water. Press
the shapes around the edge. Secure
by piercing with a skewer through
to plate edge.
☐ Bake blind for 15 minutes. Mix
the mincemeat with the pineapple
and spread the mixture over the
pastry base.
☐ Whisk the egg whites to soft
peaks. Gradually whisk in half the
sugar to make a very stiff meringue.
Fold in the rest of the sugar gently
with a metal spoon.
☐ Put the meringue into a forcing
bag fitted with a ½in (1cm) rose pipe
and decorate the edge of the tart as
shown in the photograph above, or
spoon meringue over.
☐ Bake in the oven for 10-15
minutes to brown the meringue
lightly.
☐ Serve immediately with pouring
cream or vanilla ice cream.
Tip: If you bake tarts with fillings in
ovenproof glass you can see when
the underside of the pastry is baked.
However, because glass is a slower
conductor of heat than metal, place
pie dish on a baking tray to speed up
the cooking and ensure a well-baked
pastry base.

*Mincemeat Meringue Tart makes an
unusual dinner-party dessert, served
with pouring cream.*

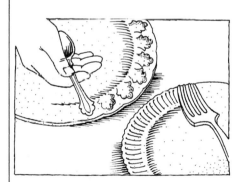

*Make a quick decorative border by
pressing with the prongs of a fork, or
the handle of a spoon, at intervals
along the edge of the pastry.*

Vegetarian Pie

Serves 6   ☆☆☆
Preparation and cooking: 1¼ hours

The filling:
1¼-1½lb (575-675g) mixed vegetables: such as
    leeks, celery, onions, peppers, green
    beans, garlic and tomatoes, washed,
    trimmed and sliced
3-4 tablespoons oil
salt and pepper

The sauce:
1oz (25g) soft margarine
3 tablespoons flour
about 7 fl oz (200ml) milk or Vegetable Stock
3-4oz (75-100g) low fat soft cheese
salt and pepper

The pastry:
5oz (150g) soft margarine
2 tablespoons water
10oz (300g) plain flour
beaten egg, for glazing

Sauté the vegetables lightly in oil, in several batches. Drain each batch and transfer to a 10in (25cm) oval oven dish, reserving the cooking juices. Season to taste.

☐ Make the sauce: Put margarine, flour, and milk or stock into a saucepan. Whisk over a moderate heat for 4-5 minutes to thicken. Stir in reserved juices and cheese. Season to taste. Add more liquid, if necessary, to make a thick pouring sauce. Stir into vegetables.

☐ Set oven to 375F (190C) gas 5.

☐ Make the pastry: Put the margarine, water and one-third of the flour into a bowl. Beat together well. Add remaining flour and fold in. Mix well to a smooth ball.

☐ On a lightly floured surface, roll dough to a thickness of ⅛in (3mm).

☐ To assemble the pie: Moisten edges of dish with water. Cover with pastry. Trim and seal edges. Make decorative shapes from trimmings.

☐ Brush pie top with beaten egg. Decorate and brush with egg.

☐ Bake for 35-40 minutes.

Step-by-step to Vegetarian Pie. Serve with a lentil or carrot and celeriac purée for a delicious meatless meal.

Bakewell Tart

Serves 6 ☆☆☆
Preparation: 20 minutes
Cooking: 50 minutes

10oz (300g) English Shortcrust Pastry
3oz (75g) butter
3oz (75g) caster sugar
3 eggs, size 2
4oz (125g) ground almonds
2oz (50g) self-raising flour
8oz (225g) raspberry jam
icing sugar to dust

Set oven to 375F (190C) gas 5 and grease a 1¾ pint (1 litre) flan dish.
☐ Roll the pastry out to a thickness of ⅛in (3mm) and use to line the dish. Bake blind for 10 minutes.
☐ Beat the butter and sugar together until very light and creamy. Beat in the eggs one at a time. Add the ground almonds and the flour. Fold them in lightly.
☐ Spread the jam in the bottom of the pastry case. Spoon the filling on top of the jam and spread level.
☐ Bake in the oven for 25 minutes. Reduce the heat to 300F (150C) gas 2 and bake for about 15 minutes until set in the centre.
☐ Dust with icing sugar and serve hot or cold.

Apple Custard Tart

Serve, heaped with ice cream, for a special family dessert.

Serves 4-6 ☆☆☆
Preparation: 15 minutes
Cooking: about 1¼ hours

12oz (350g) English Shortcrust Pastry
8oz (225g) cooking apples
1 teaspoon ground cinnamon
2 eggs, size 2
½ pint (284ml) carton soured cream
2oz (50g) caster, or soft brown, sugar
1 tablespoon demerara sugar

Set the oven to 350F (180C) gas 4 and grease a deep 7½in (19cm) loose-bottomed flan tin. Roll the pastry

out to a thickness of ⅛in (3mm) and use to line the tin. Bake blind for 10 minutes.
☐ Peel, core and thinly slice the apples and spread into the baked pastry case. Bake in the oven for 15 minutes. Remove from the oven and sprinkle with the cinnamon.
☐ Mix together the eggs and soured cream. Strain and stir in the caster, or soft brown, sugar. Carefully spoon the mixture over the apples.
☐ Bake for about ¾ hour until the custard is set. Sprinkle with the demerara sugar and bake for a further 5 minutes.
☐ Serve warm.

Lemon Chiffon Pie

Serves 4-6 ☆☆☆
Preparation: 20 minutes
Cooking: 30 minutes

10oz (300g) English Shortcrust Pastry
3 eggs, size 2, separated
6oz (175g) caster sugar
grated rind and juice of 1 large lemon
3 tablespoons water

Set the oven to 325F (160C) gas 3. Grease a 1¾ pint (1 litre) flan dish.
☐ Roll the pastry to a thickness of ⅛in (3mm) and use to line the dish. Bake blind for 10 minutes.
☐ Put the egg yolks and 4oz (100g) of the sugar into a bowl with the lemon juice and rind and the water. Set over a pan of hot water on a low heat.
☐ Whisk until the mixture is very thick and pale and a trail is left after the whisk is removed. Remove from the heat.
☐ Whisk the egg whites to soft peaks. Gradually whisk in the remaining sugar to form a meringue which holds stiff peaks.
☐ Lightly fold the meringue into the lemon mixture. Turn into the baked pastry case. Bake in the oven for about 20 minutes until well risen and golden brown.
☐ Serve immediately.

The traditional Bakewell Tart, which the locals insist must be called 'Bakewell Pudding' did not contain ground almonds, and was more like the custardy 'mirlitons' of France than the rich moist tarts nowadays so popular.

Pineapple Tartlets
Line 18 small tartlet tins with pastry. Bake blind and cool. Drain a 8½oz (250g) can of crushed pineapple and put the juice in a small pan with 2 tablespoons of pineapple jam. Simmer for 4-5 minutes until syrupy. Sieve and cool. Brush tartlets with a little syrup. Spoon drained fruit on top. Whip ¼ pint (142ml) carton of double cream with 1 tablespoon of kirsch. Spoon on top and drizzle over the remaining syrup.

Pastry tartlet cases

It is easier to line a tin with pastry if you have a little extra. Use the trimmings to make little individual flan cases. Store them in the freezer ready to fill with savoury mixtures for hors d'oeuvres, first courses or to make decorative containers for vegetable accompaniments.

Flavouring pastry for savoury flans

Try adding a dash of cayenne, a pinch of celery seeds, or a teaspoon of dried herbs to the flour before you rub in the butter.

Adding the water

Sprinkle 1 tablespoon of water over the surface and mix in. Then add more water, just 1 teaspoon at a time, mixing continually until you can form the dough into a ball. Even a teaspoon too much water can make your pastry less tender.

Making Plain Flan Pastry.

If you are making a large batch of dough, you can measure out the water and dribble it in gradually. For the given recipe, it is better to use a spoon so you add only a very little at a time.

Savoury Flans

There are many mixtures of savoury foods which make delicious and economical lunch or supper dishes when baked in a flan.

Cooked meats, poultry, fish, seafood and vegetables with a cheese sauce or a savoury custard can be used, and the pastry may be cooked in advance or made fresh – or even bought from the supermarket freezer. For savoury flans, the pastry is made with only flour and butter – and just enough water to mix. It is quick to make, but if you make a large batch at a time you can store it for later use. Freeze the dough in the piece or as shaped unbaked cases of various sizes – or even as baked cases.

When making pastry for savoury flans, remember that the more you rub the butter into the flour, the less water you will need for mixing – and the more tender your pastry will be. It will also hold its shape better in baking.

If you don't have a spring-form tin, use a cake tin with a loose bottom or a deep flan ring set on a greased baking tray.

Plain Flan Pastry

Makes about 12oz (350g)
Preparation: 15 minutes

7oz (200g) plain flour
4oz (125g) cold butter
1-2 tablespoons cold water

Put the flour and butter into a mixing bowl. Cut the butter into as small pieces as possible. With the fingertips, rub in the butter thoroughly to make a mixture with the consistency of coarse moist crumbs.

☐ Gradually stir in cold water until you can form the mixture into a ball of dough.

☐ Turn out on a floured surface and work lightly into a smooth dough. Sprinkle the dough with a little flour to prevent sticking.

☐ Roll the dough out to about ¾-in (1.5-cm) thickness. Fold over one-third of it, then fold the remaining third over the top of that.

☐ Wrap the dough in film or foil and chill for half an hour before rolling. Or, freeze for up to 2 months.

With two knives, cut butter into flour, then rub in with the fingertips.

Stir in enough water to bind, mixing constantly.

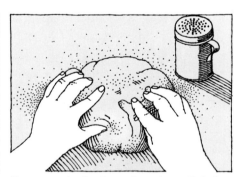

On a sparingly floured surface, lightly work to a smooth dough.

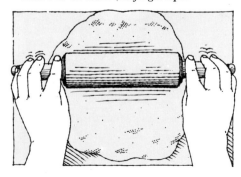

Roll out to an even rectangle.

Fold the pastry in three as shown.

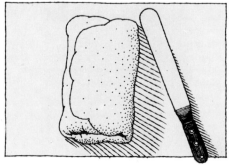

Wrap in foil or film and chill.

Leek and Ham Flan

Serves 6 ☆☆☆
Preparation: 20 minutes
Cooking: 40 minutes

about 12oz (350g) Plain Flan Pastry
1oz (25g) butter
8oz (225g) leeks, trimmed and sliced
4oz (125g) sliced cooked ham

The sauce:
1oz (25g) butter
2 tablespoons flour
9fl oz (250ml) milk
4oz (125g) grated cheese
1 egg, size 2
salt and freshly ground black pepper
½ teaspoon dried thyme

Set the oven to 425F (220C) gas 7.
☐ On a lightly floured board, roll the pastry into a circle about 12-in (30-cm) across. Fold in half then in half again into a fan shape.
☐ Lift into a 9½-in (24-cm) diameter spring-form tin and place the tip of the fan in the centre. Unfold the pastry and smooth carefully back across the bottom and up the sides of the tin. Press gently but firmly against the tin.
☐ With a knife, trim the pastry to a depth of about 1¼-in (3-cm) around the sides. Prick the base with a fork. Line the pastry with foil 12-in (30-cm) square, pressing the foil into the pastry.
☐ Bake 'blind' for 10 minutes in the oven. Lift away the foil and bake for about another 10 minutes until the bottom of the pastry is set.
☐ While the pastry is baking, prepare the filling: Put the butter into a medium frying-pan over a moderate heat. Cook the leeks gently, turning frequently, for about 10 minutes to soften without browning.
☐ To make the sauce: Melt the butter in a medium saucepan over a moderate heat. Stir in the flour then gradually stir in the milk until the mixture is thick and smooth. Mix in the cheese and egg and season to taste with salt, pepper and thyme.
☐ Arrange the ham over the bottom of the baked pastry. Spread the leeks over the ham and cover with the sauce.
☐ Bake for about 20 minutes to brown the top of the filling.
☐ Serve hot or cold, cut into wedges.

The various stages in preparing and cooking Leek and Ham Flan.

Cream cheese and low fat soft cheese

These two cheeses are quite different, although they look similar. Cream cheese is made of rich cream, and it has the colour of the cream, as well as being very thick. Low fat soft cheese is made from partly-skimmed milk. It is much softer and much whiter. It is, of course, also much lower in calories.

Mushroom Tartlets

These make a delicious and unusual first course. No extra thickening is needed for this recipe. The rich cream thickens when cooked with the butter in the mushrooms to make a delicious – and very easy – sauce.

Serving savoury flans

These flans all make delicious family lunch or supper dishes, accompanied only by a good fresh salad or a crisp green vegetable.

Bacon and Egg Flan

Serves 4-6   ★★☆

Preparation and cooking: 55 minutes

about 12oz (350g) Plain Flan Pastry
1oz (25g) butter
4oz (100g) onions, finely chopped
7oz (200g) low fat soft cheese
2 eggs, size 2
½ teaspoon made mustard
3 fl oz (100ml) milk
salt and pepper
4-5 rashers streaky bacon, rinded

Set the oven to 425F (220C) gas 7.
☐ Make a pastry case 8-in (20-cm) across and 1¼-in (3-cm) deep as for Leek and Ham Flan. Line with foil 12in (30cm) square.
☐ Bake 'blind' for 10 minutes, remove foil and bake for about 10 minutes more, until the bottom is set. Reduce the heat to 375F (190C) gas 5.
☐ Meanwhile melt the butter in a medium-sized frying-pan over a moderate heat. Cook onion gently, without browning, for 10 minutes.
☐ Mix together smoothly the cheese, eggs, mustard and milk. Stir in onion, season and spread in case.
☐ Cut the bacon into neat strips and lay in parallel lines across top.
☐ Bake for 30-35 minutes until the filling is set. Serve hot or cold.

Unbaked Supper Flan

Serves 4-6   ★☆☆

Preparation and chilling: 45 minutes

12oz (350g) Plain Flan Pastry
4oz (125g) cooked chicken, diced
1 red pepper, deseeded and chopped
1 green pepper, deseeded and chopped
2-3 spring onions, sliced
7oz (200g) cream cheese
salt and pepper
½ small cucumber, sliced

Make and bake the flan case as for Bacon and Egg Flan and cool.
☐ Mix together the chicken, peppers, onion and cheese and season.
☐ Spread the filling in the pastry case and top with cucumber.
☐ Chill for ½ hour and serve cold.

Prawn and Mushroom Tart

Serves 4-6   ★★☆

Preparation and cooking: 55 minutes

about 12oz (350g) Plain Flan Pastry
1oz (25g) butter
1 small onion, finely chopped
4oz (125g) mushrooms, sliced
8oz (225g) peeled cooked prawns
2 egg yolks
1 egg, size 2
¼ pint (150ml) milk
salt and pepper

Set the oven to 375F (190C) gas 5.
☐ Make and bake a 7in (18cm) pastry case as Bacon and Egg Flan.
☐ Melt the butter in a frying-pan over a moderate heat. Cook onion, without browning, for 10 minutes.
☐ Stir-fry mushrooms for 3-4 minutes. Spoon into case over prawns.
☐ Mix together the egg yolks, egg, and milk. Season strain over prawns.
☐ Bake for about 35 minutes until lightly browned. Serve hot or cold.

Mushroom Tartlets

Serves 8   ☆★☆

Preparation and cooking: 15 minutes

eight 4-in (10-cm) pastry tartlet cases
3oz (75g) butter
2 large cloves garlic, finely chopped
1 teaspoon dried oregano
1 tablespoon chives, finely chopped
1 tablespoon parsley, finely chopped
12oz (350g) small mushrooms, sliced
½ pint (284ml) carton double cream
salt and pepper
ground mace
squeeze of lemon juice

Melt the butter with the garlic cloves and the herbs in a large frying-pan over a moderate heat. Stir-fry the mushrooms for about 5 minutes.
☐ Stir in the cream and simmer, stirring, for 3-5 minutes.
☐ Season to taste with salt and pepper, mace and lemon juice. Spoon into the cases and serve immediately.

Broccoli and Ham Quiche

Serves 6   ☆☆☆

Preparation: 10 minutes
Baking: 30-35 minutes

9½-in (24-cm) baked flan case
6oz (175g) broccoli heads
4oz (125g) sliced ham
7oz (200g) grated Cheddar cheese
3 eggs, size 2
10 fl oz (284ml) carton of single cream
salt and pepper
grated nutmeg

Make and bake a pastry case as for Leek and Ham Flan. If you like, you can freeze the case and fill it without thawing it.

☐ Cook the broccoli for 5 minutes in a large pan of boiling salted water. Drain and quickly refresh in cold running water. Drain well.

☐ Set oven to 425F (220C) gas 7.

☐ Arrange the ham over the bottom of the pastry case. Cover with half the cheese, lay the broccoli over that, then sprinkle with the rest of the cheese.

☐ Beat together the eggs and cream. Season with salt and pepper and nutmeg and strain into the flan.

☐ Bake in the oven for about 30 minutes, or 35 if using frozen pastry, until the filling is set and browned all over.

☐ Serve while still hot.

Variations: Try any of the following filling ingredients in place of the broccoli and ham:

● Sliced cooked pork sausages and drained, canned sweetcorn kernels.

● Smoked salmon trimmings, juice of a lemon and sliced tomatoes.

● Thawed frozen spinach and chopped cooked bacon.

● Fresh cooked or drained canned asparagus, and grated Parmesan cheese.

Broccoli and Ham Quiche makes a substantial main course served only with a simple mixed salad.

Broccoli and Ham Quiche

It is best to serve this flan while fresh, otherwise moisture seeps out of the broccoli and makes the filling watery.

Pastry for deep flans

Remember that the thicker your pastry, the longer it will take to bake. But to make a deep flan, it is easier to shape the pastry by moulding with the hands than by rolling it.

The pastry mixtures for the little savoury balls and for the shortbread are very rich in butter. It is easier to cut the butter in well to such a mixture with a pastry blender.

Chopping hazelnuts
Put the nuts in a plastic bag. Hold the end closed, then crush the nuts with a rolling pin. Transfer to a chopping board and chop with a sharp knife (otherwise, without initial flattening, the nuts roll around and are difficult to chop).

Cheese Snacks, Cheese Shortbread and Savoury Nut Balls all make excellent cocktail snacks.

Cheese Snacks

Makes about 48   ☆☆
Preparation and cooking: about 25 minutes

4oz (100g) plain flour
5oz (125g) finely grated Cheddar cheese
cayenne
3oz (75g) cold butter, cubed small

Set the oven to 400F (200C) gas 6.
☐ Mix the flour and cheese in a bowl and add cayenne to taste.
☐ Add the butter to the dry ingredients and rub in finely with the fingertips. Knead together into a dough.
☐ Pinch off pieces of dough about the size of a small walnut. Roll under the hand on a work surface to form smooth little balls.
☐ Place on greased baking trays and bake in the oven for about 10 minutes until lightly browned.
☐ Transfer to a wire rack to cool. Store in an airtight container in a cool place for not more than a day, or in the freezer for up to 1 month.
☐ To serve hot: Re-heat in the oven pre-heated to 325F (160C) gas 3 for 5-7 minutes.

Cheese Shortbread

Serves 8-10   ☆☆☆
Preparation and cooking: 1 hour

11oz (300g) plain flour
4oz (125g) Dutch cheese, finely grated
10oz (275g) cold butter, cubed small
1 tablespoon finely chopped parsley
1 tablespoon finely chopped celery leaves
2-3 tablespoons milk for glazing

Set the oven to 350F (180C) gas 4.
☐ Mix the flour and cheese together in a bowl and add the butter.
☐ With 2 knives or a pastry blender, cut the butter up until it is about the size of small peas.
☐ Stir in the herbs. Knead into a dough. Put in a 9½-in (24-cm) loose-bottomed flan tin. Press it firmly and evenly into the tin.
☐ Brush the top of the shortbread with milk and bake for 30 minutes. Re-glaze then bake for a further 5-10 minutes until a good brown.
☐ Press flat then cool in the tin.

Savoury Nut Balls

Makes about 24   ☆☆
Preparation and cooking: 40 minutes

4oz (100g) self-raising flour
2oz (50g) hazelnuts, skinned and finely chopped
3oz (75g) cold butter, cubed small

Set the oven to 350F (180C) gas 4.
☐ Put the flour and nuts in a mixing bowl and add the butter. With 2 knives or a pastry blender, cut the butter in until the mixture resembles coarse dry crumbs.
☐ Work the mixture well with the hand to form it into a ball of dough. Pinch off walnut-sized pieces and roll to make little balls.
☐ Place on baking trays with about 1in (2.5cm) between them. Bake for 20-25 minutes, until lightly browned.
☐ Serve while hot, or cool on a wire rack and store in an airtight tin in a cool place for up to 2 days.

Basic sweet pastry

Sweet pastry is made in the same way as many biscuits, but usually with less sugar. Cold butter is finely rubbed into the flour and sugar, then the crumbs are bound with beaten egg.

Sweet Flan Case

☆☆

Preparation and cooking: 35 minutes

8oz (225g) plain flour
3oz (75g) caster sugar
4oz (125g) cold butter
grated rind of ½ an orange or lemon
    (optional)
1 egg, size 2, lightly beaten

Set the oven to 350F (180C) gas 4.
☐ Sieve the flour and sugar into a bowl. Add butter and rind, if using.
☐ With 2 knives cut the butter into the dry ingredients as finely as possible, then rub it in with the fingertips to make fine crumbs.
☐ Gradually stir in the egg. Turn out on a lightly floured surface and knead to a smooth dough.
☐ Place in a 9½-in (24-cm) buttered flan tin. Press with knuckles to fit.
☐ Trim off the spare pastry, then prick the pastry case with a fork.
☐ Press a 12-in (30-cm) square of foil into the pastry-lined tin.
☐ Bake 'blind' for 10 minutes. Lift out the foil then bake for about 10 minutes until lightly browned.
☐ Cool on a rack. Remove from tin.

Step-by-step to a Sweet Flan Case. You can roll this type of sweet pastry very thinly to make all sizes of flan case, or simply shape it into the tin as shown with your hands. If using sandwich tins, such as these, butter them well beforehand so that the baked cases can be removed easily.

From left to right: unglazed and glazed versions of Strawberry Flan, Blackcurrant Tart, Tarte à l'Orange and Kiwi and Banana Flan.

Making fruit flans

Sweet pastry flans are all made in much the same way except for the type of glaze used to cover the filling. With a baked pastry case in the freezer, you can very quickly produce a beautiful and delicious dessert using seasonal or frozen fruits.

The glazes given with the different recipes are interchangeable. Just vary the flavour to suit the fruit.

You can bake sweet pastry cases in flan dishes then serve from the dish. Or you can use loose-bottomed or spring-form tins, or flan rings set on baking trays. Use the trimmings from large flans to make individual tart cases. Store them in the freezer for later use.

Rolling sweet pastry

For a thinner, crisper pastry, roll it with a rolling pin on a lightly floured surface to an ⅛in (3mm) thickness. Loosen from the surface with a palette knife. Roll around the rolling pin then unroll over the tin. Press neatly into place with the fingers. Trim off excess dough.

Fruit-filled flans should be served soon after making, otherwise moisture from the fruit makes the pastry soggy. A thin layer of jam or whipped cream between the two helps but does add calories! The flans should not be frozen after filling!

Strawberry Flan

Serves 6   ☆☆
Preparation: 10-15 minutes
plus chilling

9½-in (24-cm) baked Sweet Flan Case
2 tablespoons strawberry jelly or jam
12oz (350g) fresh strawberries

The glaze:
2 teaspoons arrowroot
¼ pint (150ml) dry white wine
2 tablespoons strawberry jelly or
    sieved strawberry jam
a few drops of red colouring

Spread the 2 tablespoons jelly or jam over the bottom of the flan case and arrange the fruit on top.

☐ To make the glaze: Mix the arrowroot smoothly with 1 tablespoon of the wine. Put the rest of the wine in a small saucepan over a low heat with jelly or sieved jam.

☐ Stir this into the mixed arrowroot and return it to the saucepan. Simmer, stirring constantly, for 2-3 minutes until thick and smooth.

☐ Remove from the heat. Stir in a few drops of red colouring and cool.

☐ Spoon the glaze over and chill to set – but serve within 2 hours!

☐ Alternatively, omit the glaze and decorate the flan with whipped cream.

Blackcurrant Tart

Serves 6   ☆☆
Preparation: 10-15 minutes
plus chilling

9½-in (24-cm) baked Sweet Flan Case
12oz (350g) frozen blackcurrants
3oz (75g) caster sugar
about 4 tablespoons red wine
2 teaspoons arrowroot
whipped cream to decorate (optional)

Put the currants, sugar and 3 tablespoons of wine into a saucepan over a moderate heat and bring to the boil.

☐ With a slotted spoon, lift out and drain the blackcurrants and set aside to cool.

☐ Mix the arrowroot with 1 tablespoon of red wine. Stir in the hot liquid and return it to the saucepan. Cook, stirring constantly, for 2-3 minutes until thick and smooth. Add a little more wine if a thinner glaze is desired.

☐ Remove from the heat and cool.

☐ Arrange the blackcurrants in the pastry case and spread the glaze over. Chill to set, but serve within 2 hours. If liked, decorate with piped whipped cream, or serve with a bowl of lightly whipped cream.

Tarte à l'Orange

Serves 6 ☆☆

Preparation: 20 minutes
plus 30 minutes chilling

9½-in (24-cm) baked Sweet Flan Case
4 large oranges

The glaze:
¼ pint (150ml) sweet white wine
2 tablespoons orange liqueur
1 teaspoon powdered gelatine

Peel the oranges and remove all the
white pith. Cut neatly into segments
and pat dry.

☐ Put the wine and liqueur into a
small saucepan. Sprinkle the
gelatine over the surface.

☐ Place on a low heat and stir until
the gelatine is dissolved and the
mixture is completely clear.

☐ Remove from the heat and set the
saucepan in a large pan of cold
water. Stir occasionally, until the
mixture begins to thicken.

☐ Arrange the orange in the case
and spoon the jelly over.

☐ Chill for about 30 minutes.

Variation: Use dessert apple slices.
Poach in a little water and sugar and
use cooking liquid in place of wine,
and brandy instead of liqueur.

Kiwi and Banana Flan

Serves 6 ☆☆

Preparation: 10 minutes

9½-in (24-cm) baked Sweet Flan Case
2 large bananas
2 large kiwi fruit

The glaze:
5 teaspoons liquid glucose
4 teaspoons banana liqueur or white rum

Peel and slice the bananas and kiwi
fruit. Arrange in the baked pastry
case.

☐ Heat the measuring spoon under
hot running water then use to
measure out the liquid glucose into a
small saucepan. Add the liqueur or
rum.

☐ Place over a low heat and stir
until well mixed and of a good
pouring consistency.

☐ Remove from the heat, cool and
spoon over the fruit. Serve
immediately.

Tip: Liquid glucose is available in
jars from chemists and makes a
good instant glaze. It is like a very
thick syrup and is crystal clear. It is
easier to measure accurately if you
use a hot spoon, so that it doesn't
stick to it.

Raspberry Tartlets

Makes 9 ☆☆☆

Preparation: 20 minutes

---

9 baked deep sweet pastry tartlets
about 3-in (7.5-cm) diameter

The glaze:
2 tablespoons raspberry or redcurrant jelly
1-2 tablespoons water

The filling:
¼ pint (150ml) double cream
2 tablespoons kirsch
8oz (225g) raspberries

First make the glaze: Put the jelly
and 1 tablespoon water into a small
saucepan over a low heat. Stir
occasionally until melted to a thick
syrup. If required to give a pouring
consistency, add a little more water.
Cool.

☐ Make the filling: Whip the cream
and liqueur together until stiff. Pile,
or pipe, into the baked cases.

☐ Arrange the fruit over the cream
then carefully spoon the glaze over.

☐ Serve within an hour or so.

Tip: It is easy to make these
delicious little tartlets – with any
fresh fruits – if, whenever you make
a flan, you use the pastry trimmings
to make cases and freeze them.

Deep Apple Lattice Tart

Deep Apple Lattice Tart

If you don't have ground almonds, finely chopped almonds are good instead.

It is better to use dessert apples for this dish as cooking apples are a bit too juicy and this spoils the pastry.

Small cubes of butter dotted over the surface of the apples before covering gives an even more delicious flavour.

Serves 6   ☆☆☆
Preparation: 20 minutes
Cooking: 40-50 minutes

The pastry:
9oz (250g) plain flour
4oz (125g) caster sugar
5oz (150g) cold butter
1 egg, size 2, lightly beaten

The filling:
2¼lb (1kg) dessert apples
4oz (125g) ground almonds
4oz (125g) caster sugar
a little beaten egg to glaze

Make the Sweet Flan Pastry as directed on page 329. Roll thinly on a lightly floured surface and fold into 4 to form a fan-shape.

☐ Place the pastry in a 9½-in (24-cm) spring-form tin or loose-bottomed cake tin with the tip of the fan in the centre. Unfold the pastry.

☐ Press firmly and neatly across the bottom and up the sides. Trim off the top with the back of a knife.

☐ Set oven to 350F (180C) gas 4.

☐ Make the filling: Peel and core the apples. Cut into cubes and mix with the ground almonds and sugar. Place in the pastry-lined tin.

☐ Roll the pastry trimmings into thin ropes. Moisten the edges of the pastry with water, and arrange the ropes across in a lattice.

☐ Trim and press the edges firmly. If there is enough dough left, shape it into another rope to press around the edge to finish neatly.

☐ Brush the lattice all over with a little beaten egg.

☐ Bake in the centre of the oven for 35-40 minutes, or until well browned.

☐ Move the tin to the floor of the oven and bake for a further 5-8 minutes to ensure that the underside of the pastry is cooked.

☐ Set the tin on a wire rack and leave to cool. Remove the sides of the tin and transfer the tart to a serving plate.

☐ Serve immediately, cut in wedges.

The various stages in making, decorating and cooking Deep Apple Lattice Tart.

Tarte Pensée

Serves 8 ☆☆☆
Preparation and cooking: 55 minutes

The pastry:
8oz (225g) plain flour
3oz (75g) caster sugar
4oz (125g) cold butter
1 egg, size 2, beaten

The filling:
5oz (150g) ground almonds
5oz (150g) icing sugar
1 egg white
about 3 tablespoons single cream

The topping:
4 tablespoons apricot jam
6 tablespoons icing sugar
about 3 tablespoons Maraschino liqueur

Make the Sweet Flan Pastry as directed on page 329. Roll about two-thirds of it very thinly on a lightly floured surface, and line a 9½in (24cm) loose-bottomed shallow flan tin.

☐ Set oven to 350F (180C) gas 4.

☐ Then make the filling: Mix together the ground almonds, sugar, and egg white. Work in enough cream to give a spreading consistency.

☐ Smooth the almond paste evenly over the base of the pastry thinly. It will just about half fill the tin.

☐ Roll the rest of the pastry thinly. Wrap around the rolling pin, then unroll over the top of the tart.

☐ Press firmly on the filling and around the sides. Trim the edges.

☐ Bake in the centre of the oven for 30 minutes. If the top crust bubbles or rises, gently press flat. Put the tart on the floor of the oven and bake for a further 5-8 minutes to ensure that the underside of the pastry is well cooked.

☐ Remove from the oven and make the topping: Warm the jam gently in a small saucepan and spread over the hot tart. Leave to cool. Remove from the tin before icing.

☐ Mix the icing sugar smoothly with the liqueur. With a wetted palette knife, spread over the top.

☐ Serve in thin wedges at tea time.

Variations: Try other ways with this traditional tart – substitute 1 tablespoon of lemon juice for 1 tablespoon of cream and add 1 teaspoon grated lemon rind.

Or, use raspberry jam instead of the apricot, and kirsch in place of Maraschino.

Tarte Pensée
This is a very rich and delicious tart. It is best served on its own with coffee or tea – cut in very small slices.

The tart should be made the day before it is served, to allow the full flavours to develop.

A miniature bottle of Maraschino will provide about the desired quantity.

Easing thinly rolled pastry into cases
To avoid tearing the pastry, use a small ball of excess pastry, instead of the fingertips, to press into corner.

Dealing with cracks and tears in pastry cases
Brush over the crack or tear with a little lightly beaten egg before baking blind.

Making and layering a Tarte Pensée.

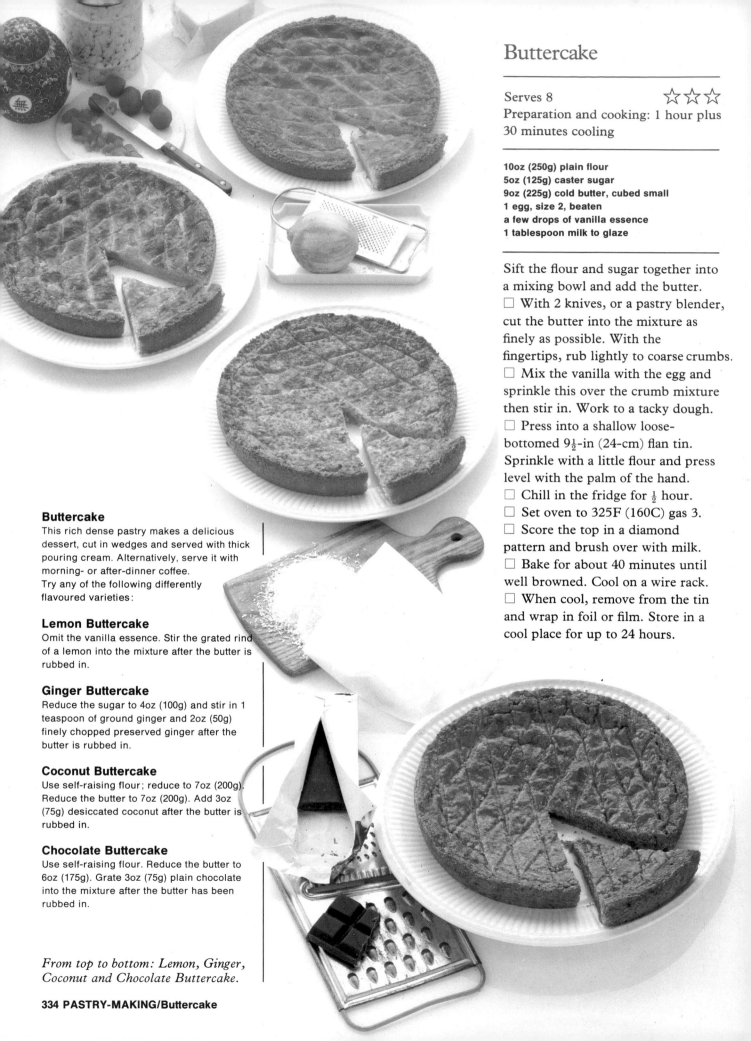

Buttercake

Serves 8   ☆☆☆
Preparation and cooking: 1 hour plus
30 minutes cooling

10oz (250g) plain flour
5oz (125g) caster sugar
9oz (225g) cold butter, cubed small
1 egg, size 2, beaten
a few drops of vanilla essence
1 tablespoon milk to glaze

Sift the flour and sugar together into
a mixing bowl and add the butter.
☐ With 2 knives, or a pastry blender,
cut the butter into the mixture as
finely as possible. With the
fingertips, rub lightly to coarse crumbs.
☐ Mix the vanilla with the egg and
sprinkle this over the crumb mixture
then stir in. Work to a tacky dough.
☐ Press into a shallow loose-
bottomed 9½-in (24-cm) flan tin.
Sprinkle with a little flour and press
level with the palm of the hand.
☐ Chill in the fridge for ½ hour.
☐ Set oven to 325F (160C) gas 3.
☐ Score the top in a diamond
pattern and brush over with milk.
☐ Bake for about 40 minutes until
well browned. Cool on a wire rack.
☐ When cool, remove from the tin
and wrap in foil or film. Store in a
cool place for up to 24 hours.

Buttercake

This rich dense pastry makes a delicious
dessert, cut in wedges and served with thick
pouring cream. Alternatively, serve it with
morning- or after-dinner coffee.
Try any of the following differently
flavoured varieties:

Lemon Buttercake

Omit the vanilla essence. Stir the grated rind
of a lemon into the mixture after the butter is
rubbed in.

Ginger Buttercake

Reduce the sugar to 4oz (100g) and stir in 1
teaspoon of ground ginger and 2oz (50g)
finely chopped preserved ginger after the
butter is rubbed in.

Coconut Buttercake

Use self-raising flour; reduce to 7oz (200g).
Reduce the butter to 7oz (200g). Add 3oz
(75g) desiccated coconut after the butter is
rubbed in.

Chocolate Buttercake

Use self-raising flour. Reduce the butter to
6oz (175g). Grate 3oz (75g) plain chocolate
into the mixture after the butter has been
rubbed in.

From top to bottom: Lemon, Ginger,
Coconut and Chocolate Buttercake.

Flaky pastries

Flaky pastries are very different from all the other kinds of pastry. They are enriched with a much higher proportion of fat and this is incorporated into the pastry in an entirely different manner.

The first type is puff pastry with its many crisp layers and light texture. It is considered to be one of the highest achievements in the whole of the cookery repertoire. In this pastry, the fat, usually butter, is left in a block and a dough is wrapped around it. Repeated foldings, turnings and rollings create the many layers. At each stage the pastry must be wrapped and chilled to prevent it becoming difficult to handle.

The second type, rough puff, is a much more easily-made pastry. It is crisp and flaky but does not rise into the many layers of puff. The fat is coarsely cut into the flour and left in small pieces before adding the water. The rolling is quicker too, with less chilling.

The ingredients

● White bread flour is very good for flaky pastries. It contains a higher percentage of gluten which helps to hold the greater proportion of butter used and give good distinct firm layers.

● For making puff pastry, butter is best – giving a rich colour, excellent flavour and good crisp layers. For rough puff, use either all butter or equal parts of butter and lard. It is important that the fat is cold but not too hard when making both pastries or hard edges of pieces of fat will cause the pastry to tear during rolling. In the case of rough puff it should be firm enough for the cubes to retain their shape as they are being mixed in.

More liquid is added to bind than in shortcrust pastry because the flour particles are not so well coated with fat. Cold water must be used to help prevent the fat becoming oily.

Storage

Both types of pastry store well. If you wrap them closely in foil or cling film you can keep them in the fridge for 2-3 days or freeze for up to 2 months or longer. Roll the pastry to a thickness of $\frac{1}{2}$-$\frac{3}{4}$in (1-1.75cm) before wrapping. Thaw in the wrapping for about 2 hours at room temperature but away from direct heat. Puff pastry can be shaped into vol-au-vents, bouchées and slices, before they are frozen.

Hints for success with flaky pastries

● Use the fat at the stage where, when pressed lightly, it is firm enough to take the imprint of the finger. If too hard, the dough will tear during rolling; if too soft, the fat will roll into the layers of pastry and make it greasy.

● Put a few ice cubes in the water to ensure that it is well chilled.

● Keep the dough cool all the time you are working with it. As soon as there is a hint of the fat becoming soft and sticky wrap the dough in foil or cling film and chill.

● Chill the dough for only 15 minutes to the stage where it rolls easily. If it becomes too hard, leave it out of the fridge for a few minutes.

Puff pastry is the most dramatic and impressive of the flaky pastries – its richness lightened by the many crisp airy layers.

Ways to perfect puff pastry

● It is easier if you work with a small amount of pastry. Too large a piece of dough is difficult to roll easily and neatly.

● Temperature control is very important. Wrap the dough and chill as often as necessary. The fridge is just as important as the oven in the making of puff pastry.

● Rolling butter between 2 sheets of greaseproof paper prevents it sticking to either the board or the pin. You can also use the paper to lift the butter on to the dough.

● Roll the dough large enough to completely encase the butter. No butter should come through the edges of the envelope at any stage. Allow a thumb's width between butter and the edge of the dough.

● It isn't necessary to continue with all the stages at one session. If necessary, you can spread the rolling and folding out over 24 hours. Be sure to wrap the dough well before putting in the refrigerator and allow it to 'come to', after refrigeration, before working with it.

● To keep the dough edges straight, bat them into line with a ruler held perpendicular to the board.

Rolling flaky pastries

Work on a lightly floured board and add as little flour as possible when it is needed to prevent the dough sticking as this causes distortion and produces uneven layers. Use a rolling pin which is at least as long as the width you want the pastry to be. It is difficult to roll pastry evenly with a pin which is too short.
Roll with short strokes and a firm action rather than stretching or pulling the pastry. For puff pastry, it is important to roll the dough to the same thickness each time to ensure good, even rising when cooked.

Glazing and baking puff pastry

Egg gives a rich, deep colour to puff pastry, but it's important not to let it run down the edges—it makes the edges stick together and sticks the pastry to the tray.
When the pastry is baked on the underside, it will move easily on the tray.

Puff Pastry

Makes about 1lb (450g)

8oz (225g) strong white flour
8oz (225g) butter
7-8 tablespoons iced water
1 teaspoon lemon juice

Sift the flour into a large bowl. Cut off a small piece of the butter and add it to the flour. Rub it in finely with the fingertips.

☐ Mix together the water and lemon juice. Gradually stir in enough to bind to a dough.

☐ Turn on to a lightly floured board and knead gently to a smooth elastic ball.

☐ Shake a little flour into a plastic bag. Add the ball of dough, seal the bag and put in a cool place for half an hour.

☐ Place the block of butter between 2 sheets of greaseproof paper. Tap and roll with a rolling pin to a square about ¾in (1.75cm) thick.

☐ On a lightly floured surface roll the dough to a rectangle about ½in (1cm) thick. Set the flattened butter in the centre of it.

☐ Fold the long ends of the dough in over the butter, overlapping them to form a sealed 'envelope'. Tap the seams closed.

☐ Give the dough parcel a quarter turn so that the folded ends are at the sides. With a short firm action roll to a rectangle three times as long as it is wide, keeping the edges straight. Fold over in three again as before. Chill for 15 minutes.

☐ Repeat the rolling, folding, and chilling 6 times in all, giving the dough a quarter turn in the same direction each time and always rolling to the same thickness.

☐ Use the pastry while fresh or wrap and store in the fridge for up to 3 days. You can freeze puff pastry for up to 2 months. Thaw it in its wrapping in the fridge overnight or for 2 hours at room temperature.
Tip: If you make a great deal of pastry, a marble slab will help as it keeps the dough cool.

Folding and rolling Puff Pastry

Roll to a rectangle ½in (1cm) thick and place butter in centre.

Fold the bottom third up and top third down to form an envelope.

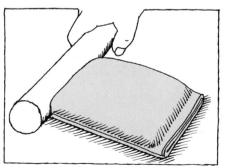

Press the pastry edges closed with the rolling pin.

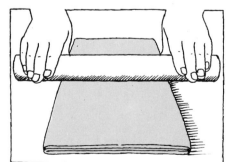

Give a quarter turn so that folds are at the sides. Roll as before.

Steak and Kidney Pie

Serves 6   ☆☆☆
Preparation and cooking: 1¾ hours

1lb (450g) Puff Pastry
beaten egg for glazing

The filling:
1½lb (675g) chuck steak, trimmed and cubed
8oz (225g) ox kidney
1oz (25g) butter
1-2 tablespoons oil
1 onion, thinly sliced
3 tablespoons flour
2 teaspoons mixed herbs
about 14 fl oz (400ml) Meat Stock
salt and pepper

Make the filling: Cut the lobes of kidney away from the central core. Cut each in half. Pat them, and beef, dry.

☐ Melt the butter with 1 tablespoon of oil in a large frying-pan over a moderate heat. Sauté one-third of the meat for about 5 minutes to brown. Remove and set aside. Cook the rest in two batches, adding an extra tablespoon of oil if necessary.

☐ Add the onions to the pan. Fry gently for 5 minutes to soften. Return all the meat to the pan.

☐ Sprinkle over flour and herbs.

☐ Gradually stir in the stock and cook, stirring constantly, for 2-3 minutes until thick. Cover and simmer gently for 45 minutes. Add a little more stock if you prefer a thinner gravy.

☐ Season to taste with salt and pepper and spoon into a 2 pint (1 litre) pie dish. Cool.

☐ Set oven to 400F (200C) gas 6.

☐ On a lightly floured board roll the pastry to a thickness of ⅛in (3mm).

☐ Cut a piece of pastry to cover the pie dish generously. From the remaining pastry, cut a strip about ½in (1cm) wide.

☐ Brush the edge of the pie dish with water, place the strip of pastry around it. Press firmly and then brush it with water. Place the top over the pie.

☐ 'Knock-up' the edges. Make a small steam vent in the centre. Cut leaves for decoration from the trimmings.

☐ Brush the top of the pie with egg. Decorate, and brush again. Place dish on a baking tray.

☐ Bake for 35-40 minutes until well risen and browned. Serve hot.

Steak and Kidney Pie with a crisp golden puff pastry top.

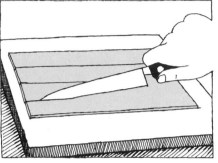

Pastry leaves

Roll trimmings and cut into 1in (2.5cm) strips. Cut diagonally to form diamonds.

With the back of a knife, lightly score the surface of each to make veins.

Baking puff pastry pies
Puff pastry is usually baked at a higher temperature when used for small items. For a large pie the temperature is kept a little lower to prevent the pastry burning before the filling is cooked through.

Pie dishes
The best dish in which to make a pie with puff pastry is one with a flanged rim to support the pastry edge. These are normally made of hardened glass, earthenware or ovenproof porcelain.

Variations on the theme
For those for whom kidneys hold no magic, many other combinations of ingredients work equally well in such fillings. Make a steak and oyster pie by substituting a small can of unsmoked oysters for the kidneys—adding them just before filling the pie dish. Alternatively, use uncooked gammon in place of the beef, Chicken Stock instead of Meat Stock, rosemary rather than mixed herbs, and add some sliced mushrooms and drained canned sweetcorn kernels to cook with the onion for a delicious Ham and Sweetcorn Pie.

Flaky Pastry

Simple traditional English flaky pastry is made by a combination of processes. The same proportions of flour and fat are used, but half of the butter is first mixed into the flour to make a typical 'short' dough. This is rolled out to a rectangle and half of the remaining butter is dotted over the bottom two-thirds. The pastry is rolled and folded as for puff pastry for two 'turns'. The pastry is then dotted with the remaining butter as before and the balance of the foldings, rollings and turnings are executed. It is used rolled thinly for sausage rolls, jam puffs and other small pies and pastries.

When you are more experienced and can work quickly, you can mix the pastry with the fingertips. Squash the cubes of fat into flat flakes and coat well with flour.

Rough Puff Pastry

Makes about 1¼lb (575g) ☆☆☆

10oz (275g) strong white flour
8oz (225g) butter, cubed
6-7 tablespoons cold water

Sift the flour into a shallow dish and add the butter.

☐ With 2 knives or a pastry blender, cut the butter into the flour coarsely until the pieces are about the size of large peas.

☐ Gradually stir in sufficient water to bind to a rough dough.

☐ Turn out on a lightly floured board and sift a little flour over the top. Roll with a short, firm action to a strip ½in (1cm) thick and three times as long as it is wide. Fold the bottom third up and the top third down to form an envelope, give the pastry a quarter turn and seal the edges with a rolling pin.

☐ Repeat the rolling and folding process three more times.

☐ Wrap in foil or cling film and chill for 30 minutes before using. Store in the fridge for up to 4 days, or freeze for up to 2 months.

Tip: In case you are distracted and forget how many times you have rolled out and folded the pastry, mark it lightly with the fingers to indicate.

Making Rough Puff Pastry

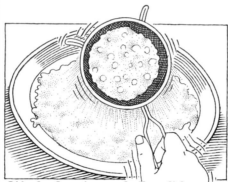

Sift the flour into a shallow dish.

Cut the fat in with 2 knives.

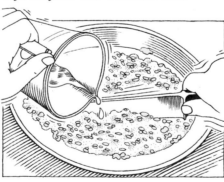

Add the water gradually.

Form into a ball of dough.

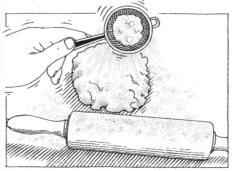

Put on a floured board and sprinkle with a little flour.

Roll with short firm strokes to an even thickness.

Chicken and Mushroom Pie

Serves 6   ☆☆☆
Preparation: 30 minutes
Cooking: about 25 minutes

about ¾lb (350g) Rough Puff Pastry

The filling:
2oz (50g) butter
1 onion, thinly sliced
4oz (100g) button mushrooms, sliced
1 small red pepper, seeded and sliced
3 tablespoons flour
7 fl oz (200ml) Chicken Stock
¼ pint (142ml) carton single cream
salt and pepper
a pinch of ground mace
1lb (450g) cooked boneless chicken, cubed
beaten egg to glaze

Set the oven to 425F (220C) gas 7.
☐ Make the filling: In a saucepan, over a moderate heat, melt the butter and cook the onions, stirring, for 5 minutes until softened but not brown.
☐ Add the mushrooms and cook for 3-4 minutes until soft. Add the peppers and sprinkle the flour over. Gradually stir in the stock. Cook for 2-3 minutes, stirring constantly, until thick and smooth.
☐ Stir in the cream. Remove pan from the heat and season to taste with salt, pepper and mace. Stir in the chicken.
☐ Put a pie funnel in the centre of a 2½-3 pint (1.5-1.75 litre) oven dish and spoon the filling around it. Cool.
☐ On a lightly floured board, roll the pastry ⅛in (3mm) thick. Cut out a piece the size of the top of the dish. Re-roll the rest of the pastry. Cut a strip about ½in (1cm) wide and long enough to go around the top of the dish.
☐ Brush the edge of the dish with water. Lay the strip of pastry around, press firmly and brush with water. Lay the top pastry in place and seal well.
☐ Mark a diamond pattern over the top of the pie with the back of a knife and 'knock-up' the edges, then decorate as shown. Make a steam vent in the centre with a skewer. Brush the top of the pastry with beaten egg and place the dish on a baking tray.
☐ Bake the pie in the oven for about 25 minutes until well browned.
☐ Serve hot with freshly cooked vegetables as a lunch or supper dish, or cold with salad.

Chicken Mushroom Pie is just as good with a puff or rough puff pastry top.

Chicken and Mushroom Pie
Mark the diamond effect with the back of a knife and press lightly so you don't cut right through the pastry. Glaze the top carefully so the egg doesn't dribble down the edges. This makes the layers stick together and prevents rising at that point.

Cooked turkey is also good in this pie.

An assortment of delicious cocktail tit-bits that make the most of flaky pastry's rich flavour and fine texture.

Puff Pastry Party Food

Trimmings from Rough Puff Pastry need never be wasted. Roll thinly and use in one of the following ways to serve hot with drinks.

Sesame Biscuits

Cut small rounds of pastry. Brush with egg. Sprinkle with salt then with sesame seeds. Press the seeds into the pastry.

☐ Place on baking trays. Bake in the oven pre-heated to 425F (220C) gas 7 for about 10 minutes, until crisp and brown.

Anchovy Twists

Cut narrow strips of pastry the length of canned anchovy fillets. Cut the anchovies into very narrow ribbons and press into the pastry. Twist the ends of the pastry ribbons around several times. Bake as Sesame Biscuits.

Cheese Bows

Cut 1in (2.5cm) wide pastry strips, brush with beaten egg and sprinkle with finely grated cheese and cayenne pepper. Cut the strips into finger lengths and dip the underside of each in egg then in grated cheese. Twist once. Bake as Sesame Biscuits.

Cocktail Bouchées

Cut small rounds of pastry, then cut small circles out of the centres of half of them. Brush with water one side of the rings thus formed and press on to rounds. 'Knock-up' edges and prick bases.

☐ Brush rims and small cut-outs with beaten egg. Bake cases and 'lids' in oven pre-heated to 425F (220C) gas 7 until well risen.

☐ Fill with taramasalata, smoked fish pâté or cream cheese.

Cocktail Sausage Rolls

Makes 32 ☆☆
Preparation and cooking: 35-40 minutes

about ¾lb (350g) Rough Puff Pastry
a little made English mustard
1lb (450g) pork chipolata sausages
beaten egg to glaze

Set the oven to 425F (220C) gas 7.
☐ On a lightly floured surface, roll out the pastry to ⅛in (3mm) thick. Cut into strips about 3in (7cm) wide.
☐ Spread the mustard along the centre of each strip and place the sausages on top, end to end.
☐ Brush along one edge of the pastry with water. Fold over the other edge to enclose the sausages. Press along the edges firmly to seal. 'Knock up' the pastry edges and cut the roll into 1½in (3.5cm) lengths. Brush the tops with beaten egg and cut across through the top of the pastry in one or two places.
☐ Place on baking trays and bake for 20-25 minutes until well browned.
☐ Serve hot.

Steps to making sausage rolls

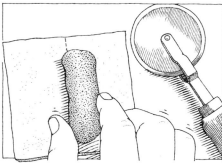

Cut a 4in (10cm) square of pastry. Place a sausage in the centre.

Dampen edges with water. Fold over and press edges firmly with a fork to seal.

Vanilla Slice

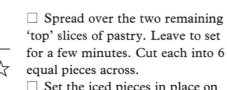

Makes 12 slices
Preparation: 20 minutes
Cooking: 10-15 minutes

☆☆☆

1¼lb (575g) Rough Puff Pastry

The filling:
Crème Pâtissière
½ pint (284ml) carton double cream
8oz (225g) icing sugar
a little water to mix

Set oven to 425F (220C) gas 7. Divide the pastry into two equal pieces. On two separate sheets of greaseproof paper roll each piece into a rectangle about 12 × 8in (30 × 20cm).

☐ Slide each piece of pastry on its paper on to baking trays. Prick the pastry all over.

☐ Bake for 10-15 minutes until well-browned and crisp.

☐ Transfer the papers to wire racks. When the pastry is cool, cut each in half lengthways.

☐ Spoon the Crème Pâtissière into a forcing bag fitted with a ½in (1cm) plain pipe. Whip the cream to soft peaks. Spoon into a second forcing bag fitted with ½in (1cm) rose pipe.

☐ Trim the edges of the pastry slices so they are exactly the same size. Pipe the Crème Pâtissière along the length of two slices. Pipe cream on top of each.

☐ Mix the icing sugar with cold water, 1 teaspoon at a time, to a consistency which will just run off the back of a spoon.

Step-by-step to Vanilla Slice.

☐ Spread over the two remaining 'top' slices of pastry. Leave to set for a few minutes. Cut each into 6 equal pieces across.

☐ Set the iced pieces in place on top of the filled bases. Cut through with a sharp knife.

☐ Serve fresh.

Tip: You can prepare the pastry slices in advance then just fill and ice them when required. Store, well wrapped in freezerwrap or foil, in a cool place for a day, or freeze for up to a month. The slices of pastry must be supported by pieces of stiff card underneath and care must be taken not to set anything heavy on top of them in the freezer as they break easily.

You can fill and ice the pastry without thawing it. It will thaw almost completely during the time it takes to finish the vanilla slices.

You can use jam and cream as a filling if you don't have time to make a Crème Pâtissière.

Savoury slices
Fill the pastry slices with cooked chicken or fish in a thick sauce, or cream cheese beaten with mayonnaise and herbs. Leave the top slices plain or sprinkle with grated cheese and place under the grill for a minute or two to melt it.

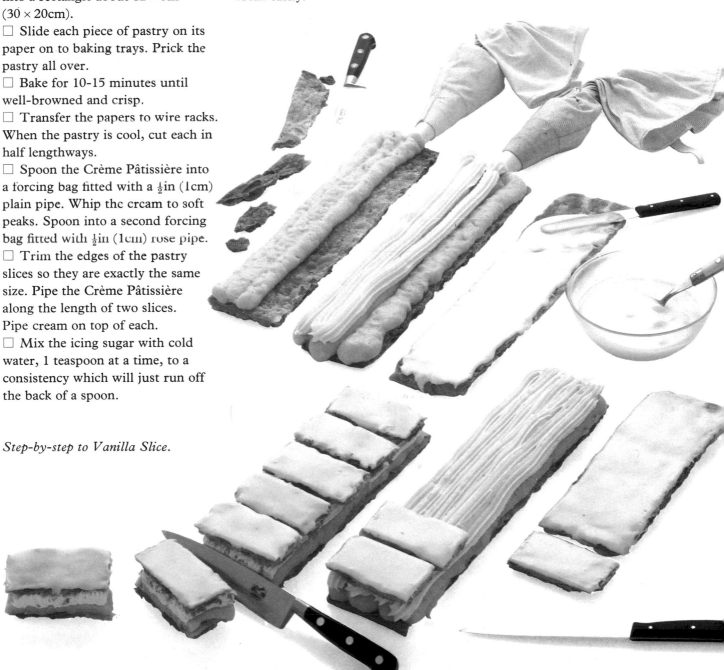

Tarte Tatin

This delicious French recipe is one of the best of all apple pies. Unlike others, it is turned out of its dish and served upside down. Cooking the apples with butter and sugar gives them a rich caramel flavour which goes particularly well with puff pastry.

Little puff pastries

Use puff pastry trimmings for crisp, caramelized tea-time treats, or accompaniments for iced and fruit desserts. Bake them at 425F (220C) gas 7.
Conques: Cut small circles of pastry and roll them out over teaspoons full of caster sugar placed on the work surface, into oval shapes. Lay sugar side up on baking trays. Bake for 7 minutes.
Palmiers: Roll pastry on a sugar dusted surface and cut into 6in (15cm) strips. Sprinkle with more sugar and fold the two long sides to the centre. Fold sides in again to make 8 layers in all. Slice across the strip at ⅜in (1.75cm) intervals and place on baking trays. Sprinkle with more sugar and pinch ends together. Bake for 12 minutes before turning pastries over and cooking for a further 2-3 minutes.

A Fruit Millefeuille quickly makes a spectacular dinner-party dessert.

Fruit Millefeuille

Serves 8   ☆☆☆
Preparation and cooking: 35 minutes

**1-1¼lb (450-575g) Puff Pastry
beaten egg to glaze**

The filling:
**¾ pint (450ml) double cream
about 1lb (450g) fresh or canned fruit such
    as black grapes, canned mandarins,
    pineapple or peaches
icing sugar to dust**

Set oven to 425F (220C) gas 7.
☐ On a lightly floured sheet of greaseproof paper roll the pastry to a rectangle 15 × 12in (38 × 30cm). Divide into three 12 × 5in (30 × 13cm) slices, cutting right through the paper.
☐ Slide the pastry and paper on to 3 baking trays. 'Knock up' the edges (page 320) and prick all over. Brush with egg.
☐ Bake for 10-15 minutes until well risen and golden brown. Cool.
☐ To fill: Whip the cream to soft peaks. Prepare the fruit if fresh or drain if canned. Cut into bite-sized pieces.

☐ Reserving the best piece for the top, place one piece of pastry on a serving plate. Spread with half the cream and top with half the fruit.
☐ Repeat with a second layer of pastry, cream and fruit. Set the last piece of pastry on top. Dust well with sugar and serve promptly.

Tarte Tatin

Serves 8   ☆☆☆
Preparation and cooking: 1¼ hours plus chilling

**about 1lb (450g) Puff Pastry
2oz (50g) soft brown sugar**

The filling:
**3oz (75g) butter
2lb (1kg) cooking apples, peeled
    cored and thinly sliced
4oz (100g) caster sugar**

Set oven to 400F (200C) gas 6.
☐ Make the filling: Spread all of the butter over the inside of a 2 pint (1 litre) oven dish. Pack alternating layers of apples followed by caster sugar into the dish, pressing down well.
☐ Place dish on a baking tray and bake for 20-25 minutes until the apples are tender but still hold their shape.
☐ Raise oven temperature to 425F (220C) gas 7. Roll pastry on a lightly floured board to a ⅛in (3mm) thickness. Wrap around rolling pin, then unroll it over cooked apples.
☐ Trim off the excess pastry and 'knock up' the edges.
Wrap the pie in foil and chill for at least 15 minutes or for up to 8 hours.
☐ Cook for 35-40 minutes until well risen and browned.
☐ Pre-heat a grill to high.
☐ Place a large plate over the pastry. Quickly invert dish and plate. Shake to free apples from the dish. Sprinkle with the brown sugar. Put under the grill for 3-4 minutes to glaze fruit.
☐ Serve hot with cream.

Choux Pastry

Choux pastry is one of the most delightful and versatile pastries, and surprisingly easy to make. It is produced by simply cooking water, butter and flour together to create a paste. When a firm ball of dough forms as the mixture is stirred in the saucepan, eggs are then beaten in.

Unlike other pastries, choux is not rolled with a rolling pin. You can shape it by dropping from a spoon, or with a forcing pipe. It can be made into small buns or fingers, into bases for large gâteaux or as shells and toppings for large savoury pies.

During baking, the pastry puffs up to about three times its original size.

The baked pastry is light and tender with a crisp shell surrounding a pocket of air. The cavity within baked choux pastry can be filled with sweet or savoury mixtures.

Flavoured whipped cream, ice cream, Crème Pâtissière and fruit quickly transform choux pastry into delicious desserts and traditional favourites such as profiteroles and éclairs. Or you can fill choux buns with shellfish, cooked chicken or vegetables in a cream sauce. For more substantial dishes, a piped ring of choux pastry can be filled with a hot savoury mixture and served as a main course. Serve choux pastry hot or cold, but serve it immediately it is filled or it will lose its delicious crispness.

✳ To freeze choux pastry
After the pastry has been shaped and baked, cool and set on trays to freeze. Transfer to plastic bags and store in the freezer for up to two months. To thaw: Remove from the bags and place on baking trays. Crisp and re-heat for a few minutes in an oven pre-heated to 350F (180C) gas 4. Use as fresh pastry.

Some of the many ways in which choux pastry may be shaped and filled to make a wide variety of sweet and savoury treats.

Basic Choux Pastry

Makes about 18oz (500g) ☆☆
Preparation: 10 minutes

3oz (75 g) butter
¼ pint (150ml) water
4oz (125g) plain flour, sifted
3 eggs, size 2

Put the butter and water in a saucepan over a moderate heat until the butter melts. Increase the heat to bring to a rolling boil.

☐ Remove from the heat. Add all of the flour and beat the mixture well until it forms into a ball and comes away cleanly from the sides of the pan.

☐ Turn the dough into a bowl and add one egg at a time, beating vigorously after each addition, to make a stiff glossy paste.

Choux Buns

Makes 12 ☆☆☆
Preparation: 10 minutes
Cooking: 15-18 minutes

Basic Choux Pastry (as left)
½ pint (300ml) double cream
a few drops of vanilla essence
oil for greasing
icing sugar for dusting

Set the oven to 425F (220C) gas 7 and grease two large baking trays.

☐ Put a ½in (1cm) plain pipe into a forcing bag and fill with pastry.

☐ Squeeze to shape into 12 mounds on the baking trays. Bake for 15-18 minutes until crisp and firm.

☐ With the tip of a sharp knife, immediately cut a small slit in the side of each bun to allow excess moisture to escape. Leave the buns to cool on a wire rack.

☐ Whip the cream with the vanilla to soft peaks. Slice the buns across horizontally, sandwich back together with the cream and dust with icing sugar. Serve fresh.

Variation: You can simply drop the choux mixture on to greased trays using a spoon instead of piping it.

Step-by-step to Choux Buns.

Chocolate Profiteroles

Serves 6-8 ☆☆☆
Preparation and cooking: 25 minutes

---

12 choux buns (as left)
½ pint (300ml) double cream
2 tablespoons rum or brandy

The chocolate sauce:
7oz (200g) golden syrup
3-4 oz (75-100g) plain chocolate

Cut the buns open at one side. Whip the cream and spirit to soft peaks and spoon into the buns. Pile in a pyramid on a serving dish.

☐ Put the syrup into a small saucepan over a low heat. Break the chocolate into small pieces and add it to the syrup. Heat gently to melt, stirring well to mix.

☐ Serve the sauce in a warmed sauceboat to accompany the buns.

Variation: Make the buns half the size. Bake in the same way, cool, and fill with the whipped cream. Divide among 6 or 8 serving glasses and serve with the sauce dribbled over.

Fish Gougère

Serves 4-6
Preparation: 45 minutes
Cooking: 25 minutes

Basic Choux Pastry (opposite)
melted butter for greasing

The filling:
8oz (225g) salmon steaks
8oz (225g) thick haddock fillets
4 large scallops, deveined
½ pint (300ml) milk
a sprig of fresh tarragon
1 small onion, chopped
a few green peppercorns
4oz (100g) button mushrooms, sliced
4oz (100g) peeled cooked prawns

The sauce:
2oz (50g) butter
3 tablespoons flour
3 tablespoons double cream
5 tablespoons dry white wine
2oz (50g) grated Gruyère cheese
a squeeze of lemon juice
salt and pepper

Set oven to 350F (180C) gas 4.
☐ Rinse the fish and scallops and pat dry. Place in a shallow oven dish about 7in (18cm) square.
☐ Add the milk, tarragon, onion and peppercorns. Cover and cook in the oven for about 15 minutes until all the fish is just firm and opaque.
☐ Strain the cooking liquid from the fish and reserve.
☐ Remove any skin and bones from the fish and flake the flesh into bite-sized chunks. Cut the scallops to about the same size.
☐ Return the cooked fish to the rinsed oven dish with the mushrooms and prawns.
☐ Make the sauce: Put the butter into a medium saucepan over a moderate heat. When melted, stir in the flour. Gradually add the strained fish cooking liquid and cook, stirring constantly, for about 5 minutes until thick and smooth.
☐ Add the cream, wine, cheese and lemon juice. Season to taste and pour sauce over the filling.
☐ Cover with a piece of foil the exact size of the dish and, with a brush, grease the top with butter.

☐ Set oven to 425F (220C) gas 7.
☐ Make the choux pastry as directed (opposite). Fit a forcing bag with a rose pipe about ¾in (1.75cm) and fill the bag with the choux pastry. Pipe around the edges of the dish.
☐ Bake in the oven for about 25 minutes until well risen and browned then carefully remove the foil by pulling from the centre.
☐ Serve immediately.

Savoury Bouchées

Makes about 48

Make the Basic Choux Pastry. Put small teaspoonfuls of the mixture on greased baking trays. Bake at 425F (220C) gas 7 for about 15 minutes until crisp and brown. Pierce tops with a skewer.

Cocktail Éclairs

Makes about 24

Put the Basic Choux Pastry mixture into a forcing bag fitted with a ½in (1cm) plain pipe. Shape into fingers or crescents about 4in (10cm) long on greased trays. Bake as above.

Shrimp Filling

Fills 48 bouchées or 24 éclairs

1oz (25g) butter
2 tablespoons flour
¼ pint (150ml) single cream
salt and pepper
a pinch of grated nutmeg
1 tablespoon brandy or sherry
4oz (125g) peeled or cooked shrimps

☐ Melt the butter with the flour in a saucepan on a low heat. Gradually stir in the cream. Cook, stirring constantly, for 4-5 minutes until thick and smooth.
☐ Season to taste with salt and pepper, nutmeg and the brandy or sherry. Stir in the shrimps.
☐ Use hot or cold.

Tips to success with choux
● Be sure to use plain flour. Choux pastry made with self-raising flour collapses when baked.
● It is important to form a ball of dough before the eggs are added. If necessary, return the pan to the heat for a minute or so, mixing continuously.
● Use a strong whisk or a wooden spoon for beating in the eggs, or put the mixture into a food processor.

Choux pastry is very good with savoury fillings, as well as sweet, and can be made into small buns or finger shapes for use as hot savouries to serve with drinks. It also makes an excellent top for fish or chicken pies. Keep a supply of baked choux pastries in the freezer for use when required.

Choux pastry pies
You can make the choux mixture and keep it in a forcing bag in the fridge for an hour or two. About half an hour before required, pipe it on top of your favourite savoury filling. Chicken or turkey, or cheese and hard-boiled egg, mixed with the sauce used for Gougère all make delicious pies.

Small choux-topped pies
Put a suitable filling into individual shell dishes and pipe the choux pastry around the edges. Or, if you prefer, spoon a small mound of pastry in the centre.

Savoury choux buns
Fill Choux Buns with a suitable savoury mixture and serve with a hot cheese sauce poured over them.

Fish Gougère
The greased aluminium foil prevents the choux mixture from becoming soggy on contact with the filling.

Other fillings for Savoury Bouchées and Éclairs
● Substitute diced cooked chicken for the seafood. Cook in the sauce for a minute or two and flavour with a little curry paste in place of nutmeg.
● Or stir 2oz (50g) grated cheese into the basic hot sauce and season with a little paprika.

Chocolate Icing

Use a small heavy pan and keep the heat very low. For extra flavour, use Crème de Cacao in place of water.

Coating buns with icing

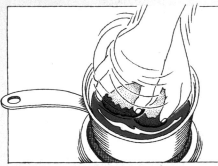

Using a twisting action, dip the bun into the warm icing.

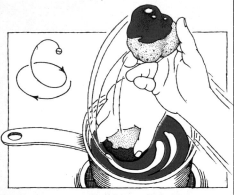

Lift out the bun and quickly turn it upright; this will hold the icing in place and prevent dribbling down the sides.

Peach Cream Buns

Makes 12
Preparation: 30 minutes

12 Choux Buns
7 fl oz (200ml) milk
3 tablespoons flour
2 egg yolks from size 2 eggs
2oz (50g) sugar
3 tablespoons brandy
8oz (225g) cold butter, diced
4 fresh peaches
icing sugar for dusting

Mix a little of the cold milk with the flour, egg yolks and sugar to make a smooth paste. Put the rest of the milk in a small saucepan over a low heat.

☐ When the milk begins to bubble around the edges, stir it into the flour mixture. Return this to the saucepan and cook, stirring constantly, for 3-4 minutes until very thick and smooth.

☐ Remove from the heat and stir in the brandy. Gradually whisk in the cubes of butter then let the sauce cool.

☐ Peel the peaches and cut them into thin slices.

☐ Cut the buns across in half. Place a spoonful of filling on each base. Put some peach slices on top.

☐ Cover with the rest of the filling. Set the tops of the buns in place, dust with icing sugar and serve immediately.

Mandarin Whirls

Makes 12
Preparation: 30 minutes plus 30 minutes setting

12 Choux Buns

The chocolate icing:
3oz (75g) plain chocolate
2 tablespoons water
about 8oz (225g) icing sugar

To fill and decorate:
¾ pint (450ml) double cream
11oz (300g) canned mandarin oranges, drained

Cut the Choux Buns across in half.

☐ Make the icing: Break the chocolate into small pieces and put with the water in a small saucepan set over a low heat. Stir until the chocolate melts.

☐ Gradually stir in sufficient icing sugar to give the consistency of thick cream.

☐ Dip the tops of the buns into the chocolate icing as shown. Set upright on a wire rack and leave to cool for about half an hour until set.

☐ Whip the cream to soft peaks. Put a ½in (1cm) rose pipe into a forcing bag.

☐ Pipe a whirl of cream into each bun. Setting aside 12 mandarin segments for decoration, divide the remaining fruit between the buns. Set the iced bun tops in place.

☐ Pipe the rest of the cream on top and decorate with the reserved mandarin segments.

Coffee Cream Puffs

Makes 12   ☆☆☆
Preparation: 20 minutes

12 Choux Buns
1 tablespoon instant coffee
2 teaspoons boiling water
3 tablespoons coffee liqueur
¾ pint (450ml) double cream
2oz (50g) chocolate coffee beans
a little finely grated chocolate

Dissolve the instant coffee in the water. Mix in the liqueur.

☐ Whip the cream until it begins to thicken. Add the liqueur mixture and whip to soft peaks.

☐ Put a ½in (1cm) rose pipe into a forcing bag. Fill the bag with the whipped cream.

☐ Cut half-way through the buns horizontally. Pipe some of the cream into the centre of each bun and set them on a serving plate.

☐ Pipe the rest of the cream on top. Decorate with the chocolate coffee beans and a little grated chocolate.

Tip: To dust with icing sugar or grated chocolate, put the sugar or chocolate into a tea strainer and stir with a small spoon over the top of the buns. Alternatively, use empty herb jars or parmesan cheese tubs with pierced tops—these make very good 'casters'.

Strawberry Swirls

Makes 12   ☆☆☆
Preparation: 20 minutes

12 Choux Buns
½lb (225g) small strawberries, trimmed
¾ pint (450ml) double cream
3 tablespoons kirsch
icing sugar for dusting

Whip the cream until beginning to thicken, add the kirsch and continue whipping until soft peaks form.

☐ Put a ½in (1cm) rose pipe into a forcing bag and fill it with the whipped cream.

☐ Cut a slice from the top of each bun. Pipe a swirl of cream on the base, cover with strawberries and pipe with more cream. Set the tops in place.

☐ Dust with icing sugar and serve immediately.

Choirboys

The Italians make similar small buns. Slice the tops in the same way, fill them with cream only and replace the top, upside down, to give the effect of a choir boy's frill. The little 'choirboys' are then dusted with sugar.

Peach Melbas

Fill Choux Buns with ice cream and fresh peaches. Purée 8oz (225g) fresh or thawed frozen raspberries with 2 tablespoons kirsch as a sauce to pour over the buns.

Banana Nut Sundaes

Fill Choux Buns with ice cream and sliced bananas. Serve them with Chocolate Sauce and sprinkle with some finely-chopped walnuts.

Scissors are very useful for cutting through the 'springy' texture of choux pastry.

From left to right: Peach Cream Buns, Mandarin Whirls, Coffee Cream Puffs and Strawberry Swirls.

Petit 'Paris-Brest'

Makes 9
Preparation and cooking: about 45 minutes

Basic Choux Pastry
oil for greasing
flour for dusting
Crème Pâtissière
2oz (50g) flaked almonds
icing sugar to dust

Set the oven to 425F (220C) gas 7. Grease and flour 3 baking trays.
☐ Put a ½in (1cm) plain pipe into a large forcing bag. Fill with pastry.
☐ With the handle of a wooden spoon, mark three 3½in (9cm) rings on each tray.
☐ Pipe the pastry on the marked rings. Sprinkle with the almonds.
☐ Bake for 15-18 minutes until crisp. Pierce with a skewer. Cool.
☐ Slice and sandwich each ring with Crème Pâtissière. Dust with icing sugar.

Banana Éclairs

Serves 8
Preparation: 10 minutes

8 éclairs (see Cocktail Éclairs page 345)
4 small or 2 large bananas
Crème Pâtissière
¼ pint (150ml) double cream, whipped to soft peaks
icing sugar for dusting

Cut the éclairs in half lengthways. Spread the bottom half of each with Crème Pâtissière.
☐ Trim the bananas to fit. Lay one piece of banana on each éclair base and pipe cream over each.
☐ Set the tops of the éclairs in place. Dust with icing sugar and serve immediately as a dessert.
Tips: Pipe with a rose pipe to give a ribbed effect. For icing with chocolate, use a plain pipe.

Chocolate Éclairs

Pipe 8 éclairs in the same way as Cocktail Éclairs. Cut as for Banana Éclairs, fill with whipped cream and coat the tops with chocolate icing.

Serve Petit 'Paris-Brest' or Banana Éclairs as desserts or to accompany coffee.

Peach Puff

Serves 8
Preparation and cooking:
1¼ hours plus 20 minutes assembly

The pastry base:
3oz (75g) plain flour
1oz (25g) ground hazelnuts
1oz (25g) caster sugar
1oz (25g) butter, diced
1 egg yolk
oil for greasing

Basic Choux Pastry

The filling:
3-4 peaches, peeled and sliced
2oz (50g) peach jam
¼ pint (150ml) double cream
1 tablespoon water

Set the oven to 350F (180C) gas 4 and grease 3 baking trays. Mark 8in (20cm) circles on 2 sheets of greaseproof paper. Place marked-side down on 2 trays and grease.
☐ To make the pastry: Mix together the flour, nuts and sugar. Add the butter and rub it in. Stir in yolk to make a firm dough.
☐ Place the dough in the centre of one of the circles. Roll or press to fit. Prick all over with a fork.
☐ Bake for 10-12 minutes until set and lightly browned. Cool.
☐ Raise oven to 425F (220C) gas 7.
☐ Put the choux pastry into a large forcing bag fitted with a ¾in (1.75cm) rose pipe. Pipe in a fluted ring just inside the second circle.
☐ On the third tray, pipe the remaining mixture as small buns.
☐ Bake for about 15 minutes for the buns and 25 for the large ring, until browned and crisp.
☐ Pierce around the bottom edges of the pastries and cool on a rack.
☐ To serve: Spread the pastry base with some of the jam. Whip the cream to soft peaks. Spread it over the jam and set the ring on top.
☐ Pile the peaches in the centre.
☐ Simmer the remaining jam with the water in a small pan until syrupy. Sieve over the choux ring.

Yeast cookery

Homemade bread is quite a treat and surprisingly simple to make. The basic ingredients are flour, salt, yeast and water. The spongy elasticity of the dough enables a wide range of shapes and sizes to be created. By adapting the basic recipe and using different flours, you will be able to produce a variety of bread and rolls.

Flour

The gluten in flour forms the actual structure of the dough. When it is baked the moisture and gases present will expand and cause the dough to blow up like a balloon. To ensure a good elastic dough choose strong flour made from hard wheat which contains the most gluten. There are several types of wheat flour to choose from.

White flour: Ground from wheat grains that have had the outer bran layer and inner wheatgerm removed. Usually called bread flour or strong flour. Ordinary household flour can be used but the dough is less starchy and the finished result considerably heavier.

Wholemeal or wholewheat flour: As its name suggests, nothing has been removed. It is highly nutritious and makes a heavier bread with a thicker crust and a nutty flavour. It is more absorbent and will require more liquid added to the the dough.

Brown or wheatmeal flour: Part of the bran and wheatgerm have been removed. It will have a lighter texture than wholemeal bread.

These flours may be used on their own or mixed with one another. A proportion of white flour in a recipe will contribute a superior quality and higher quantity of gluten to the dough.

Yeast

This is a minute plant that feeds on the starch and sugar present in flour. With the right conditions—food, moisture and warmth—it will produce carbon dioxide gas which causes the dough to rise up. The more elastic the dough the higher it will rise. You can choose between fresh or dried yeast—there is no evidence to prove that one type is any better than the other for breadmaking. However, check that the yeast you use is fresh as the results will be very disappointing if it is not.

Fresh: May be difficult to buy but it is usually available from health food shops and bakers baking on the premises. It will keep for up to 2 weeks in the fridge if well wrapped. It may also be frozen for 6 weeks and is best packed in suitable quantities for recipes. It may be used straight from the freezer. To use fresh yeast simply dissolve it in hand-hot liquid.

Dried: In a sealed container it will keep for 1 year. Once opened it should be used within 4 months. It does have a short storage life and therefore it is advisable to buy small sachets of dried yeast unless you plan to use it frequently. To use dried yeast simply stir it into hand-hot liquid with a little sugar and leave for about 10 minutes. By this time it will have developed a head of foam on top of the liquid.

Liquid

Water is usually used in plain bread and it is important to add the correct quantity. Too much will weaken the gluten and the risen dough will collapse. Not enough will make a dough that is too tight to rise well.

Milk may also be added on its own or mixed with water. It improves the keeping qualities of the bread and gives a better coloured crust and softer crumb texture. Whichever liquid is used, it should be heated to a

How much?

Fresh or dried yeast is equally good. Their equivalents are:
1oz (25g) fresh yeast = $\frac{1}{2}$oz (15g) or 1 tablespoon dried yeast

Instant dried yeast

This is available in packets from supermarkets and should be used as directed by the manufacturers.

Good flavour

The best flavour and the most spongy crumb is made with the smallest amount of yeast and the longest rising time. For faster rising more yeast may be used but the crumb will be coarser and more crumbly and the bread will stale more quickly.

Rising times

This is partly controlled by the quantity of yeast and partly by the temperature.
Quick rise: 2 teaspoons yeast to 1lb (450g) flour requires $1\frac{1}{2}$-2 hours in a warm place.
Medium rise: $1\frac{1}{2}$ teaspoons yeast to 1lb (450g) flour requires $2\frac{1}{4}$-$2\frac{1}{2}$ hours in a warm place.
Slow rise: 1 teaspoon yeast to 19oz (550g) flour requires 12 hours in a warm place. Allow 30 minutes longer if rising at room temperature.

temperature of 100F (38C). This can be obtained by mixing $\frac{2}{3}$ cold and $\frac{1}{3}$ boiling liquid.

Salt
Salt gives flavour to the finished dough but should be added with care. Too much will prevent the dough from working and may even kill the yeast.

Sugar
Yeast can convert the starch in the flour to sugar but usually a little is added to start the process.

Fat
A small quantity will improve the colour and texture of the dough as well as extend the keeping qualities. Butter and lard give the best flavour although oil may be used.

The stages in making bread dough

There are several distinct stages and they are all interspersed with fairly long rising times before the dough is ready to bake.

Mixing and kneading
The yeast liquid is added to the flour and salt and mixed to form a dough. It will be quite sticky at this stage.
To knead: Turn the dough out on to a lightly floured surface. Fold the dough in half towards you and then push down and away from you (see sidelines). Give the dough a quarter turn and repeat the folding and pushing action vigorously. You should aim to build up a rhythm and use the heel of the hand as a means of pushing the dough. Do not add too much flour at this stage as you will find that the dough loses its stickiness and becomes smooth and elastic. It will take about 10 minutes for white dough and 4 minutes for wholemeal or brown dough to reach this stage.

Rising
The dough is left to rise and double its original size. Traditionally it should be risen twice for the best flavour and texture although quicker methods, which only require one rising of the dough, can be used when time is short. The dough must be kept covered at this stage to prevent a skin forming on the surface and prevent it from drying out.

This is easily done by using a large, clean polythene bag and placing $\frac{1}{2}$ teaspoon of oil inside. By screwing up the bag and rubbing it between the hands you can coat the inside lightly with oil. Alternatively the dough can be placed in a bowl and covered tightly with cling film. Depending on the temperature the dough will take anything from $1\frac{1}{2}$ hours to 12 hours to rise. Choose the method and length of time to suit you.

Knocking back
Before the dough is shaped it must be 'knocked back'. This removes the air bubbles to ensure a better rise and an even texture to the finished loaf. The dough is punched enough to deflate it and then kneaded until a firm dough is obtained. It is then ready to shape and place in tins or on baking sheets.

Proving (second rise)
The dough is covered again with a greased polythene bag or cling wrap and allowed to prove. The time will vary depending on the temperature but it will have doubled in size and be light and puffy. It is then baked.

Basic White Bread 1
(*Quick rise*)

Makes: about $1\frac{3}{4}$lb (800g) dough ☆
Preparation: 30 minutes
Rising: $1\frac{1}{2}$ hours
Baking: about 50 minutes

$\frac{1}{2}$ pint (250ml) hand hot water
$\frac{1}{2}$ teaspoon sugar
2 teaspoons dried yeast
1lb (450g) strong white flour
$1\frac{1}{2}$ teaspoons salt
1oz (25g) lard
oil for greasing

Measure the water into a jug and stir in the sugar to dissolve. Sprinkle the yeast on top and leave for about 10 minutes until there is a good head of foam.
☐ Sift the flour and salt into a large mixing bowl. Rub in lard.
☐ Add the yeast liquid all at once and stir with a wooden spoon or your hand. Mix to a ball of dough.
☐ Turn out on to work surface and knead until silky, smooth, and elastic.
☐ Shape and place in loaf tins or on baking trays. Lightly oil a large polythene bag and place the tin or tray inside. Put in a warm place to prove for about $1\frac{1}{2}$ hours.
☐ Remove the bag and brush the top of the dough with lukewarm water. Bake at 400F (200C) gas 6 for 20-25 minutes. Reduce the oven setting to 350F (180C) gas 4 and bake for a further 20-25 minutes.
☐ Remove from the tin and cool on a wire rack.

Basic White Bread 2
(*Medium rise*)

Makes: about $1\frac{3}{4}$lb (800g) dough ☆
Preparation: 30 minutes
Rising: $2\frac{1}{4}$-$2\frac{1}{2}$ hours
Baking: about 50 minutes

Ingredients as for Basic White Bread 1 but only use $1\frac{1}{2}$ teaspoons dried yeast

Make and knead the dough as above. Shape into a ball and place in a large oiled polythene bag. Fasten at the end, leaving as much room as possible for the dough to rise. Leave in a warm place for about $1\frac{1}{2}$ hours.
☐ Turn out on to the work surface and punch down to remove the large air bubbles. Shape as liked and place in tins or on trays.
☐ Place in large oiled polythene bags and prove in a warm place for about 50 minutes.
☐ Bake as for Basic White Bread 1. Remove from the tin and cool on a wire rack.

A traditional Cottage Loaf.

Basic White Bread 3

(slow rise)

Makes: about 2lb (900g) dough ◯
Preparation: about 50 minutes
Rising: 13 hours
Baking: about 50 minutes

The yeast batter:
¼ teaspoon sugar
½ teaspoon dried yeast
2 tablespoons hand hot water
5oz (125g) strong white flour
¼ pint (150ml) tepid water

The dough:
¼ teaspoon sugar
½ teaspoon dried yeast
3 tablespoons hand hot water
14oz (375g) strong white flour
2 teaspoons salt
¼ pint (150ml) tepid water

To make the yeast batter: Dissolve the sugar then the yeast in 2 tablespoons of water. Allow to stand for 10 minutes.

☐ Sieve the flour into a bowl. Add the dissolved yeast and the remaining water. Beat well to make a thick batter. Scrape down the mixture from the sides. Cover bowl with foil or cling film.

☐ Store in the fridge for about 8 hours. Remove bowl and place over a pan of hot water away from the heat. Leave for 30 minutes.

☐ To make the dough: Dissolve the sugar followed by the yeast in the 3 tablespoons of water. Allow to stand for 10 minutes. Sift the flour and salt into a large bowl. Add the yeast liquid, the yeast batter and the remaining water.

☐ Mix and knead as usual. Put the bowl into a lightly greased polythene bag. Fasten at the end and let rise in a warm place for about 3 hours.

☐ Turn out the risen dough and shape. Prove in a warm place for about 1½ hours.

☐ Bake as for Basic White Bread 1. Remove from the tin and cool on a wire rack.

Adding the liquid
Add the liquid all at once so that odd spots of the flour do not become over-wet while some are left dry. This will prevent uneven mixing and rising. In time you will become more experienced at adding the exact amount of liquid that should be used with the various flours.

Quality control
The many factors which affect the quality of the bread make it difficult to give exact recipes. A very small amount, more or less, liquid, a different brand of flour, can easily have an effect on the finished loaf. With practice you will quickly learn to tell what changes to make to your recipe.

Make space
Make sure your greased polythene bag is large enough to allow plenty of space for the dough to rise without sticking.

Kneading the dough

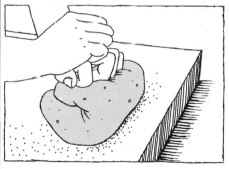

Fold the dough in half towards you and then push down and away from you. Give the dough a quarter turn and repeat the folding and pushing action.

Tough stuff
Bread dough will stand a great deal of shaping and re-shaping without coming to harm so even if you are inexperienced you will be able to produce a good-to-eat loaf.

NOTE
In the metrication of the recipes some of the quantities have been altered to make the weighing and measuring easier. This accounts for any discrepancies between the recipes. It is important to follow EITHER imperial OR metric weights in the recipes. If working in metric the quantities will yield slightly less dough than imperial.

Dusting with flour

If you wish to dust the loaf with flour instead of glazing it, this should be done just before baking.

Razor sharp

For slashing bread dough, be sure to use a very sharp, thin-bladed knife. If the knife is dull or the blade too thick it will leave a torn effect. Some bakers use a razor for this job.

Tin sizes

The Basic Recipe for quick and medium time bread makes about 1¾lb (800g). This can be baked in a 2lb (900g) loaf tin, but you will achieve a better result if you bake about 1¼lb (575g) of the dough in a 1lb (450g) tin. Shape the rest of the dough into rolls.

Other containers

A 5½in (14cm) cake tin or soufflé dish will take a 1lb (450g) quantity of dough. Brush the inside of all containers well with melted lard. There is no need to line or flour them.

Shaping breads

Moulding or shaping the dough into different loaves is an important skill in breadmaking. After knocking back, the dough is kneaded again to prepare it for neat shaping. Use knocked back and kneaded dough for each of the following round loaves:

● Coburg: Use about 1¼lb (575g) dough. Shape into a round ball by bringing the outside edges to the centre. Turn, seam-side down, on to a greased baking tray and smooth the top and sides down to the base. After proving and just before baking cut a cross on the top with a sharp knife.

● Cob: Made as above with no cuts.

● Cottage: Use about 1¼lb (575g) dough. Cut into two pieces of one-third and two-thirds respectively. Form each into a neat ball. Leave to stand for 10 minutes. Place the larger piece on to a greased baking tray and smooth neatly. Set the smaller piece on top and press down through the centre with the handle of a wooden spoon to force the dough from the top well down into the lower dough.

● Crown: Cut 6 2oz (50g) each pieces of dough. Shape into neat balls. Arrange 5 around the edge of a 6in (15cm) greased sandwich tin. Set the 6th ball of dough in the centre.

● For long loaves: Make a cylinder of dough first. Flatten this to form an oval and fold the ends towards the centre. Roll up like a Swiss Roll. Make the length of the roll a little shorter than you need because you can always smooth it out once shaped in order to make it longer.

● Bloomer: Use 1¼lb (575g) dough, rolling out the ends with the hands to taper slightly. Place on a greased baking tray and prove. Just before baking, make diagonal cuts in the top with a very sharp knife.

● Farmhouse: Use 1¼lb (575g) dough. Make in the same way as the bloomer but just before baking cut lengthways with a sharp knife along the top of the loaf.

● Scissor loaf: Use 1¼lb (575g) dough.

Flatten slightly into a large oval and leave to prove for only 10 minutes. Slash with scissors in a walking action along the length. If liked, the dough may be sprinkled with flour before slashing.

● Epi (French for 'ear of corn'): Use 1¼lb (575g) dough. Stretch out a little at the ends to lengthen. Slash with a knife inwards from either side at intervals of about 1½in (4cm) along the length.

● Plait: Use the full recipe of 1¾lb (800g) dough without rolling into a roll. Divide equally into three. Stretch each piece into a long sausage by gently rolling the dough under your hands, starting at the centre and working outwards. Work firmly but gently so you don't break the dough. Roll each piece to about 1in (2.5cm) thickness and taper at the ends. To get an evenly-shaped loaf, plait from the centre to one end, turn the plait and repeat. Use the simple plaiting action of right over left then left over right for a 3-strand plait. Tuck the ends under and lay the plait cornerways on a greased baking tray.

Other shapes you may like to try:

● Crescent: Shape a cylinder and taper at the ends. Bend into a crescent on a greased baking tray. Slash at intervals along the top just before baking.

● Mob cap: Make a cottage loaf then just before baking slash downwards around the edge of the bottom layer with a sharp knife.

The loaves in the crock clockwise from front left: Bloomer, Farmhouse, Scissor Loaf, Epi.
Foreground, clockwise from the front right: 3-Strand Plait. Coburg, Crown, Tin, Cottage, 2 uncut Cylinders.

A selection of savoury breads:
*Quick Cheese Bumpy and Cheese
Rolls, Herb and Onion Plait.*

Quick Cheese Bumpy

Makes 2lb (1kg) loaf ☆
Preparation: 20 minutes
Rising: 1½ hours
Baking: 40-50 minutes

¼ teaspoon sugar
2 teaspoons dried yeast
½ pint (250ml) hand hot water
1lb (450g) strong white flour
1½ teaspoons salt
¼ teaspoon dry mustard
1 tablespoon soft margarine
4oz (100g) Cheddar cheese, grated
1 small onion, grated
lard for greasing
beaten egg and milk to glaze

To finish:
about 1oz (25g) Cheddar cheese, grated

Grease a 2lb (900g) loaf tin.
☐ Dissolve the sugar then the yeast
in the water. Sift the flour, salt and
mustard into a large bowl. Rub in
the margarine. Stir in the cheese and
the onions.
☐ Make and knead the bread as for
Basic White Bread 1.
☐ Divide the dough into 4 equal
pieces. Shape each into a ball then
press to an oblong to fit across the
width of the tin.
☐ Press the dough pieces side by
side along the length of the tin. Put
the tin into a large oiled polythene
bag and leave in a warm place to
prove for about 1½ hours.
☐ Set oven to 400F (200C) gas 6.
☐ Remove tin from the bag and
brush the top of the dough with
glaze. Bake for 20-25 minutes to set
the dough. Reduce the oven setting
to 350F (180C) gas 4. Sprinkle the
loaf with the grated cheese and
return to the oven for a further 20-
25 minutes until brown.
☐ Cool on a wire rack.
Variation: For Cheese Rolls, divide
the dough into 6-8 pieces of equal
weight. Shape each piece into a ball
then press flat to about ½in (1cm)

thickness under the palm of the
hand. Make a depression in the
centre of each roll with the knuckles.
Place on greased baking trays and
then into oiled polythene bags.
Prove for about 1 hour. Glaze and
bake as for the loaf, sprinkling with
cheese after 10 minutes and cooking
for a further 10 minutes at the same
temperature. Cool on a wire rack
and serve while hot.

Herb and Onion Plait

Makes about 1¾lb (800g) loaf ○
Preparation: 30 minutes
Rising: 2¼-2½ hours
Baking: 40-50 minutes

¼ teaspoon sugar
1½ teaspoons dried yeast
½ pint (250ml) hand hot water
1lb (450g) strong white flour
1½ teaspoons salt
1 small onion, finely chopped
1 tablespoon dried mixed herbs

To finish:
beaten egg and milk to glaze
poppy seeds

Dissolve the sugar then the yeast in
the water. Mix the flour, salt, onions
and herbs together in a large bowl.
Make, knead and rise the dough as
for Basic White Bread 2 (see page
350).
☐ Knock back and knead the
dough. Divide into 5 equal pieces.
Roll each piece into a 15in (38cm)
strand.
☐ Place side by side vertically on
the work surface and squeeze
strands together at the top. Lift the
left outside strand over the next two
strands. Turn the outside right
strand in over the middle three
strands.
☐ Continue until you reach the end.
☐ Tuck the ends under and place
cornerways on a greased baking
tray. Put into a greased polythene
bag and leave to prove for 50-60

minutes.
- ☐ Set oven to 400F (200C) gas 6.
- ☐ Bake for 20-25 minutes. Reduce the oven to 350F (180C) gas 4. Brush with egg glaze and sprinkle with seeds. Bake for 20-25 minutes. Cool on a wire rack.

Salmon Roll

Makes 10 slices ☆
Preparation: 10 minutes
Rising: 50-60 minutes
Baking: about 30 minutes

1lb (450g) risen Bread Dough

For the filling:
6oz (175g) flaked cooked salmon
3 tablespoons double cream
2 tablespoons chopped fresh dill
1 tablespoon chopped chives
salt and freshly ground black pepper
a squeeze of lemon juice
lard for greasing
beaten egg and milk to glaze

Knock back and knead the dough. Roll out on a lightly floured work surface to a 14in × 7in (35cm × 18cm) rectangle.
- ☐ Mix the salmon with the cream, herbs, salt, pepper and lemon juice to taste. Beat together to make a paste.
- ☐ Spread the filling over the rolled dough, leaving a thumb's width free along the two long sides. Roll up firmly like a Swiss Roll to a 14in (35cm) length.
- ☐ Place on to a greased baking tray in the shape of a horseshoe. With a sharp knife slash through the outside edge at intervals of about 1in (2.5cm). Leave a connecting spine of uncut dough around the inside of the curve.
- ☐ Put the tray inside a polythene bag and leave to prove in a warm place for 50-60 minutes.
- ☐ Set oven to 400F (200C) gas 6.
- ☐ Remove tray from the bag and brush dough with the glaze. Bake for about 30 minutes until brown.
- ☐ Serve hot or cold, sliced and spread with butter.

Small breads and rolls

It is much easier to work with small pieces of dough when you are beginning to learn about shaping. You can use either brown or white dough but for the more complicated shapes white is softer and therefore more adaptable. Use whichever bread recipe you prefer and proceed as for large shapes to the 'knocked back' and kneaded stage. Divide the dough into pieces weighing 1½-2oz (40-50g) and shape as follows:
- ●Dinner roll: Roll dough into a smooth ball using the palm of the hand. Slash across the top for a small Coburg.
- ●Small cottage: Cut off one-third of the dough and roll each piece into a smooth ball. Place smaller ball on top of larger and, using a floured forefinger, push through the centre of both pieces.
- ●Clover leaves: Divide each piece into three. Roll into small balls and place three together in a greased bun tin.
- ●Winkle: Roll into 10in (25cm) ropes and coil into an upward spiral.
- ●Knot: Roll into a 6in (15cm) rope and tie loosely into a knot.
- ●Cauliflower: Make a dinner roll shape and cut three slashes evenly across the top, turn and cut three more slashes at right angles.
- ●Fan: Roll dough to a 6in (15cm) circle. Fold in half and in half again. Press lightly to make the layers hold together.
- ●Twist: Roll to a 10in (25cm) rope and loop over one finger. Twist the two ends loosely.

Baking rolls

As you shape each piece of dough place on a greased baking tray. Leave a roll's width between each one to allow for spreading during proving. Prove for 25 minutes until doubled in size. Glaze and decorate rolls as you would for bread and bake in the same way but for 15-20 minutes less.

Plaited bread
It is better to have a tighter dough for making a plait. The water is therefore reduced a little for this recipe.

❋ Freezing rolls
These do not 'shell' in the same way as bread and keep successfully for up to 3 weeks. Cool and pack into polythene bags and freeze immediately.
To thaw: Place in a single layer on baking trays. Cover loosely with foil and place in a pre-heated oven, 400F (200C) gas 6 for 10-15 minutes. Rolls usually benefit from refreshing in the oven, but if you prefer, allow them to thaw in the sealed bag at room temperature for 1½ hours.

Flower Pot Loaf

Makes 1 × 1¾lb (800g) loaf or 18 individual rolls ○
Preparation: 20 minutes
Rising: 50-60 minutes
Baking: about 50 minutes for loaf 20 minutes for rolls plus cooling

---

about 1¾lb (800g) risen Bread Dough
lard for greasing
milk for brushing

Set oven to 375F (190C) gas 5. Thoroughly wash and dry 1 × 6in (15cm) flower pot or 18 small ones. Grease thoroughly inside and out with lard and place on baking trays in the oven. Bake the empty pot(s) for about 10 minutes until all the

A selection of Flower Pot Loaves and Bagels.

lard has been absorbed. Repeat this process several times before using pot(s) for the first time. Subsequent use will require a thorough grease only.
☐ Knock back and knead the dough. Shape into a neat round ball. Drop seam side down into the large flower pot or, if making rolls, divide the dough into 18 pieces of equal weight, and place after shaping into small pots.
☐ Place pots on baking trays and place inside polythene bags. Leave to prove in warm place for 50-60 minutes.
☐ Set oven to 375F (190C) gas 5.
☐ Remove the bags and brush dough with milk. Bake in the oven for about 50 minutes for the large loaf or 20 minutes for the rolls.
☐ Remove from the pots and cool on a wire rack.

Bagels

Makes 16 ☆
Preparation: 30 minutes
Rising: 1¼ hours
Cooking: about 55 minutes

½ teaspoon sugar
2 teaspoons dried yeast
8 fl oz (200ml) hand hot water
1lb (450g) strong white flour
1 teaspoon salt
1oz (25g) margarine
1 egg yolk from a size 2 egg
beaten egg for glazing

To finish:
poppy seeds, sesame seeds, chopped onion

Dissolve the sugar then the yeast in the water as usual.
☐ Sift the flour and salt into a mixing bowl. Rub in the margarine. Add the egg yolk. Stir to mix and knead to make a smooth dough.
☐ Put into an oiled polythene bag and leave to rise for about 1 hour.
☐ Knock back and knead the dough. Divide into 16 pieces. Roll into 5in (13cm) lengths. Shape into rings and place on floured trays.
☐ Place trays in greased polythene bags and leave for 10 minutes.
☐ Bring a large pan of water to the boil. Drop two or three bagels in at a time. Cook for 5 minutes.
☐ Set oven to 350F (180C) gas 4.
☐ Remove bagels with a draining spoon and blot dry with kitchen paper. Place on greased baking trays. Brush with beaten egg and top with seeds or chopped onion.
☐ Bake for 20 minutes until brown.

Baking bread

Generally 400F (200C) gas 6 is the ideal temperature for baking bread in tins or on baking trays. It gives the bread time to bake through before it over-browns and also allows the bread to achieve its maximum rise or 'spring' during this time.

Once baked, it should be well risen and golden. Once removed from the tin, the sides and base should be brown and the loaf sound hollow when tapped on the bottom.

However, when baking in earthenware containers a lower temperature is given because they do not conduct the heat so well and require longer, slower cooking.

Glazes and toppings

This is one way of ringing the changes to a basic bread recipe. Whatever glaze and decoration you use, apply it just before you put the loaf into the oven. In some recipes you may find that the glazing is left until part way through the baking. Brush carefully so as not to let the glaze run into the slashes (see shaping).

● Salt and water: Dissolve ½ teaspoon salt in 2 tablespoons water. Brush over the top of the bread before baking for a soft bloom.

● Milk: Use as above for a brighter, more glossy finish.

● Egg and milk: Shake an egg with 2 tablespoons of milk in a screw-top jar. Brush the tops about 15 minutes before the end of baking to give a rich, deep gloss and good colour.

● Seeds: Poppy, sesame, cardamom or caraway seeds can be sprinkled on to the bread after glazing to give a nutty texture and added flavour to the crust.

● Kibbled wheat: Sprinkle over the loaf after glazing.

● Crushed salt: Use as above.

Storing bread

Good homemade bread is at its very best the day it is made. Loss of sponginess and softening of the crust are a natural part of staling, and there is no known way to prevent these changes. Bread which is made with a dough that contains as much liquid as the flour will take remains palatable longer than a drier dough. Brown breads will last longer than white. Store in a covered container in a cool place. Avoid the fridge. Low temperatures cause rapid staling.

❄ Freezing bread

Except for emergency supplies or for a very short time, freezing is not recommended for homemade bread. If it is frozen for much more than a week the crust separates, or 'shells', away from the crumb. However, if you do want to make more than one loaf at a time and keep a reserve on hand, use the following method: Cool the bread. Wrap it immediately in foil and freeze quickly. Allow to thaw in the foil in a cool place.

Making bread in a mixer

An electric mixer with a large bowl and a dough hook is very useful for mixing and kneading bread dough. Dissolve the yeast in the liquid in the mixer bowl and allow to froth. Add the flour and mix for a minute or two on the lowest speed. Increase the speed by 1 or 2 settings and work for a further 3 minutes. Cover the bowl and leave the dough to rise. Turn to the lowest setting for 1 minute for the knocking back stage. Continue as recipe instructs.

Making the bread in the food processor

Put the flour and salt into the processor bowl. Add the fat, if any, and process for a few seconds. Dissolve the yeast in the liquid and allow to froth. With the machine running, quickly pour the yeast liquid through the feeder tube. A ball of dough will form in about 15 seconds. Process for 1 minute. Remove dough, place on a work surface and knead briefly with the hands to make a smooth ball. Put into an oiled plastic bag and leave to rise until it has doubled in size. Continue as individual recipe instructs.

Flower Pot bread and rolls

Any risen dough may be baked in this way but why not try using half granary flour and half white for a change. If you don't have enough tiny flower pots for making the rolls, small dariole moulds are almost the same shape and may be used instead.
If the sides of the bread are not brown when you remove it from the pot, place the loaf directly on the oven rack and bake for about 5 minutes.

Aftercare

Wipe flower pots or earthenware containers with a damp cloth after baking.

Steps to making Pizza Napolitana.

Pizza Napolitana

Makes 2 pizzas ☆☆☆
Preparation: 15 minutes
Baking: 25-30 minutes

---

about 1¾lb (800g) risen Bread Dough
olive oil to brush
¼ recipe Tomato Sauce (page 431)
7oz (200g) Mozzarella cheese
1¾oz (50g) can anchovy fillets
few black olives

Set oven to 400F (200C) gas 6.
☐ Knock back and knead the
dough. Divide in half. Roll and pat
each piece to a round about 8in
(20cm) diameter. Place on to greased
baking trays or into greased
sandwich tins of the same size.
☐ Brush the dough well with oil.
Spread with Tomato Sauce to
within a thumb's width of the edges.
☐ Bake for 20-25 minutes.
☐ Meanwhile cut the cheese in
strips and cut the anchovies in half
lengthways. Halve the olives and
remove the stones.
☐ Remove the pizzas from the oven
and arrange the cheese, anchovies
and olives over top. Bake for a
further 5 minutes to melt the cheese.
☐ Serve immediately.
Tip: An olive stoner will make the
job a lot easier.

Calzone

Serves 4 ☆☆☆
Preparation: 20 minutes
Baking: about 20 minutes

---

about 1¾lb (800g) risen Bread Dough
olive oil to brush

The filling:
4oz (100g) Prosciutto ham, shredded
4oz (100g) salame, shredded
4oz (100g) Mozzarella cheese, cubed

The glaze:
3 tablespoons cold water
½ teaspoon salt

Knock back and knead the dough.
Set oven to 425F (220C) gas 7.
Divide in half. Roll each piece to a
10in (25cm) circle.
☐ Brush the dough with oil to
within a thumb's width of the edge.
Divide the ham, salame and cheese
between one half of each circle.
☐ Brush the edges of the dough
with water then fold the free half of
dough over filling. Pinch firmly
around the edges to seal.
☐ Place on a baking tray and slash
the tops in two places. Mix the
water and salt together. Brush over
the dough.
☐ Bake for about 20 minutes to
brown. Cut in half to serve.

✳ For freezing pizzas
Cover the dough with Tomato Sauce, bake
for 20 minutes, cool. Wrap in foil and store in
the freezer for up to 2 months.
To thaw
Unwrap and place on baking trays.
Put into the oven pre-heated to 400F (200C)
Gas 6 for 15 minutes. Add topping and bake
for a further 5 minutes. Alternatively
completely finish the pizzas, cool and freeze.
Then, unwrap and place on baking trays.
Put into the oven pre-heated to 400F (200C)
gas 6 for about 20 minutes.

Enriched Yeast

Many European countries have their own and quite distinctive speciality breads. These are made with an enriched yeast dough which has butter and eggs added to a basic recipe. Another variation is where dried or candied fruit is added, with sugar and spices, to plain bread dough. Often these breads are made in a traditional shape either by moulding in a tin, or shaping in a particular way.

Kugelhopf

Serves 12 ☆
Preparation: 20 minutes
Rising: about 2 hours
Baking: 30-35 minutes

The yeast batter:
7 fl oz + 1 tablespoon (200ml + 2 tablespoons) milk and water mixed
½ teaspoon sugar
1 tablespoon dried yeast
12oz (350g) strong white flour
1 teaspoon salt
1 egg, size 2, lightly whisked

The dough:
1oz (25g) caster sugar
2 eggs, size 2
3oz (75g) butter, melted
3oz (75g) raisins or sultanas
1oz (25g) red and green glacé cherries
3 tablespoons white rum
melted butter for greasing
icing sugar to dust

First make the batter: Heat the milk and water until just beginning to bubble around the edge. Pour into a jug and stir in the sugar to dissolve. Sprinkle the yeast on top and leave for about 10 minutes until thick and foamy.

☐ Meanwhile, sift the flour and salt into a large mixing bowl. Stir in the egg to make a stiff batter. Scrape down mixture from sides and cover. Leave in a warm place to rise for 1-1¼ hours until well risen and very bubbly.

☐ Prepare the dough: Add the sugar, eggs and melted butter to the yeast batter and beat well with a wooden spoon or one hand. There will be large bubbles on the surface.

☐ Grease a Kugelhopf tin with melted butter (see sidelines page 360).

☐ Add the fruit and rum to the dough and beat well. Turn the mixture into the prepared tin. Place tin in an oiled polythene bag and put in a warm place. Leave to prove for about 40 minutes until the mixture comes to within a thumb's width of the rim.

☐ Set oven at 375F (190C) gas 5.

☐ Remove tin from the bag and bake for 30-35 minutes until well browned and springy to the touch. Invert on to a wire rack and leave for a few minutes.

☐ Carefully remove the tin and allow cake to cool. To serve: Sprinkle well with icing sugar and cut in wedges.

The Kugelhopf and the traditional tin in which it is baked.

Danish Pastries

Makes 12 ☆☆
Preparation: 1½ hours
Rising: about 1¾ hours
Baking: about 20 minutes

The dough:
¼ pint (150ml) milk
2oz (50g) caster sugar
1 tablespoon dried yeast
12oz (350g) strong white flour
½ teaspoon salt
9oz (250g) butter
1 egg, size 2, lightly beaten
egg for glazing
apricot and strawberry jam
sugar and cinnamon for dusting
chopped almonds and icing sugar to finish

The almond filling:
1oz (25g) ground almonds
1oz (25g) caster sugar
1 egg white from size 2 egg

The apple filling:
2oz (50g) apple purée
1 tablespoon soft brown sugar
½ teaspoon ground cinnamon

First make the dough: Heat the milk until it begins to bubble around the edge. Put into a jug and stir in ½ teaspoon of the sugar to dissolve. Sprinkle the yeast on top and leave for about 10 minutes until thick and foamy.

☐ Meanwhile, sift the flour, salt and remaining sugar into a mixing bowl. Cut 2oz (50g) of the butter into small cubes and rub in finely.

☐ Add the yeast liquid and the egg and mix well with a wooden spoon or one hand. Turn out on to the work surface and knead for a few minutes to make a smooth silky dough.

☐ Put dough in a lightly oiled polythene bag. Leave in a warm place for about 1½ hours until the dough is puffy and springy to the touch.

☐ Meanwhile, cut the remaining butter into two and place each piece on greaseproof paper. Divide each piece into an equal number of pieces of about 1in (2.5cm). Flatten pieces of butter with a palette knife.

☐ When dough has risen, knock back and knead to remove the air bubbles. Roll out to a 16in × 8in (40cm × 20cm) rectangle.

☐ Dot one section of butter pieces evenly over the top two-thirds of the dough, leaving a thumb's width free around the edges. Fold the bottom third of dough up and fold the top third down.

☐ Press around the edges with the rolling pin to seal. Wrap in foil and

---

Kugelhopf

This delicious yeast cake appears in slightly different forms in Germany, Austria and in Alsace. In some places it is made with just currants and almonds but the mixture of sultanas and coloured cherries is also good.

Preparing the Kugelhopf tin

To prepare the tin for baking: Wash well, then dry in the oven pre-heated to 375F (190C) gas 5 for 10-15 minutes. Brush all over inside around the indentations and the centre tube with melted butter. The tube allows the heat to penetrate better to the centre of the mixture.

chill for about 15 minutes.

☐ Place the dough on a lightly floured surface with the fold on the left. Roll to the original dimensions. Repeat with the remaining butter, folding as before. Chill again.

☐ Re-roll and fold twice more, chilling in between and chill for a final half hour before using. If preferred leave in the fridge for half a day.

● Windmills: Roll about one quarter of the dough into a 15in × 5in (38cm × 13cm) rectangle about ⅛in (3mm) thick. Cut into three equal squares with a sharp knife. Slash each square at the 4 corners from the outside towards the centre to within about 1in (2.5cm). Brush the tips of the triangles formed in this way with egg glaze. Put a teaspoonful of apricot jam in the centre of each. Turn alternate corners into the centre, overlapping and pressing to hold in place.

● Pinwheels: With about one quarter of the dough, roll a rectangle 10in × 5in (25cm × 13cm). Sprinkle with sugar and dust with cinnamon. Roll up like a Swiss Roll. Cut into three slices and flatten each slightly with a palette knife.

● Cocks' combs: With about one quarter of the dough roll a rectangle 12in × 5in (30cm × 13cm) and cut into three equal pieces. Mix the almond filling ingredients together adding sufficient beaten egg white to form a thick paste. Spread a little filling along the centre of each piece. Brush the edges with egg glaze and

fold in half. Press edges together and slash at ½in (1cm) intervals along the sealed edge. Bend each pastry back to open the cuts. Sprinkle with chopped nuts if liked.

● Crescents: Roll the rest of the dough into a 10in (25cm) diameter circle. Cut into 6 equal wedges. Mix the apple filling ingredients and put a little in the centre of the wide edge. Brush the sides with egg, and roll up from the wide end to the tip. Shape into crescents.

To bake the shaped pastries: Set oven to 400F (200C) gas 6. Transfer to baking trays. For a spongy pastry leave uncovered to prove for ½ hour before glazing and baking for 20 minutes until golden brown. For a crisp, crunchy result glaze and bake after shaping without proving. Cool on a wire rack.

☐ To finish: Put a little red jam in the centre of the Windmills. Mix sufficient icing sugar and water together to make a piping consistency. Spoon into a paper forcing bag and cut off the tip. Pipe a coil of icing on each Pinwheel. Dust the Crescents with icing sugar.

✻ To freeze: Wrap the dough in foil after its final rolling, then freeze. Thaw overnight in the fridge then proceed as for fresh dough. To freeze baked pastries, omit any icing and pack carefully into rigid containers. Cover tightly and freeze. Remove from the container and thaw on cooling racks for 1-2 hours before serving. Add the icing just before serving.

Danish Pastries

You can make simple filled Danish Pastries by rolling out all the dough and cutting into 4in × 4in (10cm × 10cm) squares. Place a little almond or apple filling, jam or poached fruit in the centre of each square and fold in the four corners. Glaze and bake as for other Danish Pastries.

Fashioning Windmills

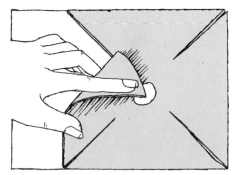

Turn in alternate corners and press on to the filling.

Making Cocks' Combs

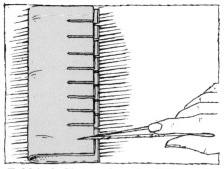

Fold in half to enclose the filling and slash along the open side.

Gently pull each pastry to open the serrations.

Making Brioches

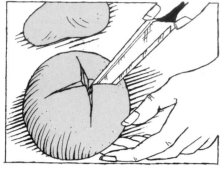

Make a ball and a pear-shaped piece of dough. Cut a cross in the top of the ball of dough and insert the dough peg into it.

Brioche

This continental bread makes a delightful change from toast at breakfast time. Serve with homemade preserves or honey.

Makes 1 large brioche ☆
Preparation: 15 minutes
Rising: about 2½ hours
Baking: 30 minutes

The dough:
½ teaspoon sugar
2 tablespoons hand hot water
2 teaspoons dried yeast
8oz (225g) strong white flour
1 tablespoon caster sugar
½ teaspoon salt
2 eggs, size 2, lightly whisked
2oz (50g) butter, melted

butter for greasing
beaten egg for glazing

Stir the sugar into the water to dissolve. Sprinkle the yeast on top and leave for about 10 minutes until thick and foamy.

☐ Sift the flour, sugar and salt into a mixing bowl. Make a well in the centre. Add the eggs, butter and yeast liquid. Stir well with a wooden spoon to form into a soft dough.

☐ Turn out on to a lightly floured surface and knead for about 5 minutes until smooth and silky. Put dough in an oiled polythene bag and leave in a warm place for 1¼-1½ hours until very puffy and well risen. Remove the dough from the bag.

☐ Knock back and knead the dough. Cut into two pieces, the larger about 3 times the weight of the smaller. Shape into 2 neat balls. Drop the larger piece of dough into a 2 pint (1.2 litre) buttered brioche mould.

☐ Draw one side of the small piece of dough out into a peg, so the whole piece looks like a large pear. With a sharp knife cut a cross on top of the dough in the tin and spread the cuts apart. Brush the centre and around the top of the hole with beaten egg. Insert the dough peg into the cavity and gently but firmly press the two pieces together without misshaping them.

☐ Place the mould in a polythene bag and leave to prove in a warm place for 1-1¼ hours until well risen.

☐ Set oven to 350F (180C) gas 4.

☐ Remove the dough from the bag and bake the brioche for 15 minutes until set. Remove from oven and brush with egg glaze. Bake the brioche for a further 15 minutes until it is well risen and brown.

☐ Turn out on to a wire rack and leave to cool for a few minutes before serving.

Variation: Small Brioches can be made in the same way. Let the dough rise for 1 hour. Knock back and knead. Divide the dough into 12 equal pieces. Cut each into 2 pieces, one about 3 times the weight of the other. Shape into neat balls. Put the larger piece into buttered individual brioche moulds or bun tins.

☐ Cut crosses on the top of the large balls. Shape the smaller balls into a pear shape as for the large Brioche. Brush the inside of the cuts with butter and insert the small shapes.

☐ Prove for about 45 minutes. Glaze the little Brioches before baking. Bake for 10-15 minutes at the same temperature.

☐ Serve hot while fresh or freeze in the same way as the large Brioche. Thaw and reheat in the oven for about 5 minutes.

Variation: Savoury Filled Brioche. When the large Brioche is baked and cooled, carefully cut out the top ball. Scoop out some of the crumbs. Whip together 8oz (225g) soft chicken liver pâté with 2 tablespoons brandy and 2 tablespoons double cream. Fill the cavity and replace the top.

❇ To freeze: Cool completely. Put in a polythene bag and store in the freezer for up to 6 weeks. Remove from the bag and set on a baking tray in the oven preheated to 400F (200C) gas 6 for 10-15 minutes.

Savarin aux Framboises

Serves 4 ☆☆☆
Preparation: 35 minutes
Rising: about 1 hour
Baking: about 20 minutes

butter for greasing

The yeast batter:
½ teaspoon sugar
3 tablespoons hand-hot milk
1½ teaspoons dried yeast
1oz (25g) strong white flour

The dough:
3oz (75g) strong white flour
¼ teaspoon salt
1 tablespoon sugar
2oz (50g) butter, softened
2 eggs, size 3, lightly whisked

The syrup:
8oz (225g) caster sugar
9 fl oz (275ml) water
3 tablespoons kirsch

To serve:
8oz (225g) raspberries
¼ pint (150ml) double cream, whipped

First prepare a 1¼-1½ pint (750-900ml) savarin mould by heating in a moderate oven for about 10 minutes. Cool and butter well.

☐ Make the yeast batter: Dissolve the sugar in the milk. Sprinkle the yeast on top and leave for 10 minutes until thick and foamy.

☐ Put the flour in a bowl and beat in the yeast mixture. Scrape the mixture down into the bowl. Cover and leave for about 20 minutes until puffy and bubbly.

☐ Make the dough: Add the flour, salt, sugar, butter and eggs and beat well to make a thick pouring consistency.

☐ Pour into the prepared mould. Place in a lightly oiled polythene bag and leave to rise in a warm place for 35-40 minutes.

☐ Set oven to 400F (200C) gas 6.

☐ Remove tin from the bag and bake for about 20 minutes until well browned. Invert on to a cooling rack and leave for a few minutes. Loosen around the edges and the centre with the tip of a sharp knife. Shake out on to the rack.

☐ Meanwhile, make the syrup: In a saucepan, dissolve the sugar with the water on a moderate heat. Simmer for 10 minutes. Stir in the kirsch.

☐ Set a tray under the cooling rack and spoon syrup over savarin until all is absorbed. Cool. Fill with raspberries and whipped cream and serve.

Variation: Fill the cavity of the Savarin with any seasonal fruit.

How high?
The batter will take around 35-40 minutes to rise to about one thumb's width below the top.

Glazing the Savarin
Syrup will soak through the sponge and on to the tray beneath the cooling rack. Keep spooning this syrup over the sponge until it is all absorbed.

❋ Freezing a Savarin
After cooling, put the savarin in a plastic bag and store in the freezer for up to 1 month. To serve: remove from the bag and thaw on a wire rack at room temperature for about 3 hours. Fill with fruit of your choice and serve with whipped cream.

Brioche and Savarin aux Framboises.

Saucisse en Brioche

It is important to warm the sausage before wrapping in the brioche dough so they hold together during baking. The sausage is heated sufficiently if it is placed in the oven for 15 minutes while the oven is preheating. If the sausage is too long for the piece of dough, trim a little off one end of the sausage, so it can be completely closed inside the dough.

Brioche Goubaud

This exciting French recipe is like a fruit tart which rises during baking to look rather like a chef's hat. To tell when it's baked, tap the top. It should sound hollow.

Lardy Cake

The cake may also be made by folding and rolling the lard, sugar, fruit and spices between layers of plain dough. This traditional English yeast bread is more commonly made in a square tin.

Rolling croissant dough

Keep the butter at the temperature at which it will roll easily—do not allow it to become soft and oily. If the butter does soften, return it to the fridge and remove when chilled.

✳ Freezing croissants and brioche

These little breads can be frozen and reheated in a few minutes to serve at breakfast. They are best not stored for too long in the freezer, as they may lose their flaky crusts.

Saucisse en Brioche

Serves 8-10 ☆ ☆ ☆
Preparation: 20 minutes
Rising: about 2½ hours
Baking: 20 minutes

1 × Brioche Dough
12oz (350g) piece of garlic sausage about 2in (5cm) diameter
milk for glazing
butter for greasing

Prepare the dough and let rise for 1½ hours in an oiled polythene bag. Knock back and knead. Return to the bag and let prove for about 50 minutes in a warm place.
☐ Meanwhile snip the sausage casing and pull off. Put the sausage on to a baking tray and place in a cold oven. Set oven at 375F (190C) gas 5, 15 minutes before the dough has finished proving.
☐ When ready turn the dough out on to a lightly floured sheet of greaseproof paper. Roll to a 12in × 9in (30cm × 23cm) rectangle. Lay the hot sausage lengthways along the dough. Brush along one side and the ends with milk. Roll the dough around the sausage to encase it completely.
☐ Roll the log backwards and forwards, smoothing with the hands to fit the dough closely to the sausage. Close the ends over the sausage and press to seal.
☐ Roll the log of brioche over on to a greased baking tray, seam side under. Glaze with milk and bake at the same temperature for about 20 minutes until well risen and golden brown.
☐ Serve hot, cut in slices as a first course or a snack.

Brioche Goubaud

Makes 8 portions ☆
Preparation: 15 minutes
Rising: 2½ hours
Baking: about 35 minutes

1 × Brioche Dough
butter for greasing

The filling:
8oz (225g) crystallized fruits
3 tablespoons orange liqueur

The glaze:
2 tablespoons apricot jam
1 tablespoon water

Prepare the dough and let rise for 1½ hours in an oiled polythene bag. Meanwhile, chop the fruits and mix with the liqueur. Leave to macerate for 1 hour.
☐ Remove the dough from the bag. Knock back and knead the dough until smooth. Divide into 2 equal pieces and form each into an 8in (20cm) circle.
☐ Butter a sandwich tin the same diameter as the dough. Press one piece on to the base and spread the macerated fruits over the surface. Cut the second circle of dough across into 8 wedges. Reassemble the pieces on top of the fruit.
☐ Leave the tin in a polythene bag in a warm place for about 1 hour until puffy.
☐ Set oven at 400F (200C) gas 6.
☐ Remove the tin from the bag and bake dough for about 35 minutes until golden brown. Turn out to cool.
☐ Warm the jam and water together and sieve over the top of the tart. Serve fresh, cut in wedges.

Lardy Cake

Makes 8-10 portions ☆ ☆ ☆
Preparation: 20 minutes
Rising: 1-1¼ hours
Baking: 45 minutes

1lb 14oz (850g) risen bread dough
4oz (125g) lard
4oz (125g) caster sugar
4oz (125g) currants
2 teaspoons mixed spice
butter for greasing

To finish:
a little melted lard
caster sugar

Divide the dough into 3 equal pieces. On a lightly floured work surface, shape each one into an 8in (20cm) disc. Press one disc into the bottom of a greased 3in (7.5cm) deep cake tin of the same diameter.

☐ Cut the lard into small flakes. Use half to dot over the dough and sprinkle with half the sugar and fruit. Dust with spice.

☐ Layer the remaining pieces of dough, sugar, fruit and spices finishing with dough. Press around the edge of the tin to seal the dough together.

☐ Put the tin into an oiled polythene bag and leave in a warm place to prove for about 1-1¼ hours until well risen and springy.

☐ Set oven at 375F (190C) gas 5.

☐ Remove cake from the bag. Score the top of the cake into diamonds with a sharp knife. Bake for 30 minutes. Brush with melted lard and sprinkle with sugar. Bake for a further 15 minutes until well browned.

☐ Leave in the tin for a few minutes before turning out to cool. Serve cut in wedges and spread with butter.

✳ To freeze: Freeze in a polythene bag for up to 2 months. Remove from bag and thaw at room temperature for 2-3 hours. Bake in preheated oven 400F (200C) gas 6 for about 10 minutes.

Croissants

Makes 12 ☆☆
Preparation: 3 hours
Rising: 9 hours
Baking: about 15 minutes

½ teaspoon sugar
7 fl oz (200ml) hand hot water
1 tablespoon dried yeast
14oz (400g) strong white flour
1 teaspoon salt
9oz (250g) butter
1 egg, size 2, lightly whisked

To finish:
beaten egg to glaze

Fresh croissants and brioches are delicious to serve for breakfast or tea.

Prepare the yeast: Stir the sugar into the water. Sprinkle the yeast on top. Leave for about 10 minutes until foamy.

☐ Sift the flour and salt into a mixing bowl. Cut 1oz (25g) of the butter into cubes and rub well into the flour.

☐ Make a well in the centre and pour in the yeast liquid and the egg. Mix to a dough with a wooden spoon or by hand. Turn out and knead for 3-4 minutes until silky and smooth.

☐ Put the dough in a lightly oiled polythene bag and place in the fridge.

☐ Divide the remaining butter into 3 equal portions and place on pieces of greaseproof paper. Put two portions in the fridge. Cut the third piece of butter into 12 equal pieces. Flatten each piece with a palette knife.

☐ Remove dough from fridge and roll to a rectangle of 20in × 8in (50cm × 20cm). Dot the 12 pieces of butter over the top two-thirds of the dough, leaving a thumb's width free around the edges.

☐ Fold the bottom third of dough up and the top third down over the top. Press along the edges with the

rolling pin to seal. Wrap in foil and refrigerate for ½ hour.

☐ Roll and fold the dough with the 2 remaining portions of butter, chilling between rollings. Roll, fold, and chill 3 more times. Wrap in foil and refrigerate for about 8 hours.

☐ Work with half the dough and leave the rest in the fridge. Roll each piece to an 18in × 6in (45cm × 15cm) rectangle. Cut into 3 equal squares and then diagonally to form 2 triangles.

☐ Brush the triangles with beaten egg and roll up from the wide end towards the tip. Place on greased baking trays, shaping into crescents by drawing the tips in towards each other.

☐ Place the trays in polythene bags and leave to rise at room temperature for about 1 hour until puffy and resilient to the touch. Brush with beaten egg.

☐ Set oven to 425F (220C) gas 7.

☐ Remove trays from polythene bags and bake for about 15 minutes until croissants are crisp and brown. Cool on a wire rack. Serve fresh with homemade preserve or honey.

Fruit Streusel Cake

Serves 8-10 ☆☆
Preparation: 30 minutes
Rising: about 1¾ hours
Baking: 40-45 minutes

The dough:
¼ pint (150ml) milk
1 teaspoon sugar
2 teaspoons dried yeast
9oz (250g) strong white flour
1 teaspoon salt
1oz (25g) butter, softened
2 egg yolks from size 2 eggs

The filling:
2lb (900g) apples or plums
2 tablespoons caster sugar

The topping:
4oz (125g) plain flour
4oz (125g) caster sugar
4oz (125g) butter, cubed

Prepare the dough: Heat the milk until just beginning to bubble around the edges. Pour into a jug and stir in the sugar to dissolve. Sprinkle the yeast on top and leave for about 10 minutes until thick and foamy.

☐ Sift the flour and salt into a large bowl and make a well in the centre. Pour in the yeast liquid. Add the butter and the egg yolks. Mix well with a wooden spoon or one hand to form a dough. Turn out on to a lightly floured board and knead until smooth and silky. Put into an oiled polythene bag and leave in a warm place for about 1 hour until well risen and puffy.

☐ Knock back and knead dough. Roll to a circle about 12in (30cm) in diameter. Grease a 10in (25cm) deep, round cake tin. Fit the circle of dough into the base.

☐ Prepare the filling: Peel, core and slice the apples or cut plums in half and remove the stones. Arrange the fruit over the dough and sprinkle with the sugar.

☐ Make the topping: Mix together the flour and sugar and rub in the butter. Sprinkle topping over the fruit. Put the dish into a polythene bag and leave in a warm place for

45-50 minutes until dough is puffy and springy to the touch.

☐ Set oven to 400F (200C) gas 6.

☐ Remove cake from the polythene bag and place on a baking tray. Bake for 40-45 minutes until well risen, brown around the edges and with the topping crisp.

☐ Serve hot or cold.

Variations: Other fruits which are good to use in this cake are red or blackcurrants, blackberries, kiwi fruit, apricots or a mixture of fruits in season.

● For a different topping, mix together 3oz (75g) each of flour, soft brown sugar, chopped walnuts and butter with 2 teaspoons cinnamon.

Hot Cross Buns

Traditionally, these buns are served on Good Friday but they are really too good to bake just once a year. Serve hot as a teatime treat.

Makes 14 buns ☆
Preparation: about 40 minutes
Rising: about 2½ hours
Baking: 15 minutes

The yeast batter:
½ teaspoon caster sugar
7 fl oz (200ml) hand hot water
2 teaspoons dried yeast
5oz (150g) strong white flour

The dough:
1 egg, size 2
1oz (25g) butter, melted
7oz (200g) strong white flour
1 teaspoon salt
1 teaspoon mixed spice
1oz (25g) caster sugar
3oz (75g) currants
1oz (25g) chopped mixed peel

butter for greasing

The crosses:
4 tablespoons flour
2 tablespoons cold water

The glaze:
2 tablespoons caster sugar
2 tablespoons milk

Prepare the yeast batter: Dissolve the sugar in the water. Sprinkle the yeast on top and leave for about 10 minutes until thick and foamy.

☐ Put the flour in a bowl and stir in the yeast mixture. Cover and leave for 20 minutes until puffy.

☐ To make the dough: Add the egg and melted butter to the batter. Sift in the flour, salt, spice and sugar and mix well to make a soft, sticky dough.

☐ Turn dough out on to a lightly floured surface and flatten with the hands. Spread half the fruit over the dough and fold in the edges. Shape into a ball.

☐ Flatten again, sprinkle with the rest of the fruit and form into a ball again. Work lightly with the hands to mix the fruit through the dough evenly.

☐ Put into a polythene bag and leave in a warm place to rise for about 1½ hours until well risen and puffy.

☐ Knock back and knead on a lightly floured surface to remove the air bubbles. Divide into 14 equal pieces. Shape into neat balls and place on lightly greased baking trays.

☐ Place trays in oiled polythene bags and leave in a warm place to prove for 50-60 minutes until well risen.

☐ Meanwhile make the crosses: Mix together the flour and water to make a smooth paste. Have ready a paper forcing bag.

☐ Set oven to 425F (220C) gas 7.

☐ When the buns are risen, remove tin from the polythene bag. Put the paste into the forcing bag and snip off the end. Pipe a cross of paste on top of each bun. Bake for 15 minutes until well browned.

☐ Meanwhile make the glaze: Dissolve the sugar in the milk over a low heat. Boil for 3 minutes. Transfer buns to wire racks and brush with the milk glaze. Allow to cool a little before serving fresh with butter.

Variation: Use rolled shortcrust pastry for the crosses if preferred. Roll thinly and cut ¼in (5mm) wide strips. Brush buns with a little milk and lay the strips on before baking.

Fruit Loaf

Makes 1 large loaf ☆
Preparation: 30 minutes
Rising: about 2½ hours
Baking: about 1½ hours

The fruit mixture:
18oz (500g) mixed dried fruit
grated rind of 1 lemon
grated rind of 1 orange
¼ pint (150ml) cold black tea

The yeast batter:
7 fl oz (200ml) milk
1 teaspoon sugar
1 tablespoon dried yeast

The dough:
18oz (500g) strong white flour
2 teaspoons salt
3oz (75g) caster sugar
3oz (75g) butter, cubed
1 egg, size 2, lightly whisked

Put the dried fruit, grated rinds and tea in a pan on a low heat. Bring to the boil, remove from the heat and allow to cool. Drain the fruit and blot dry.

☐ Make the batter: Heat the milk until it just bubbles. Do not boil. Put in a jug and stir in the sugar. Sprinkle in the yeast and leave for about 10 minutes until thick and foamy.

☐ Sift the flour, salt and sugar into a large bowl. Rub in the butter, add the yeast liquid and egg. Mix to a soft dough.

☐ Turn out on to a lightly floured surface and knead until smooth. Place in an oiled polythene bag. Leave in a warm place for about 1½ hours until well risen and puffy. Remove from bag, knock back and knead dough well on a floured board. Shape into a rectangle. Spread some of the fruit over the surface of the dough and press in.

☐ Fold one-third of the dough over and cover with more fruit; press in. Fold the remaining third of dough over. Flatten dough out to its original size and sprinkle over and press in the remaining fruit. Roll up like a Swiss Roll.

☐ Grease a 2½ pint (1.4 litre) loaf tin or use two smaller tins. Place the dough inside. Place tin in an oiled polythene bag and leave to prove in a warm place for about 50 minutes.

☐ Set oven to 350F (180C) gas 4. Remove tin from bag and bake for about 1½ hours. Remove from the tin and cool on a wire rack. Serve sliced and buttered.

Steps in the making of a Fruit Loaf.

MAKING PRESERVES

Pickling
Preserving in salt and alcohol
Jam and marmalade-making

Pickling.....the right way

A shelf full of colourful homemade pickles is a most satisfying sight. The flavours are far superior to those from commercially produced recipes and though their appearance is exotic, they are made from the combination of quite basic ingredients. All types of pickle – and these include raw or cooked vegetables, sweet vegetables or fruit – are preserved in vinegar. Depending on the different spices added, various flavours are achieved to enhance the basic ingredients. Vegetables are soaked in a salt brine to draw out as much water as possible and remove any bitter flavour. They can then be packed into jars straightaway or, in the case of some varieties, blanched first before covering with vinegar and spices. Fruits do not require salting and are cooked in the spiced vinegar. Once in jars they must be sealed tightly to prevent evaporation and should be stored in a cool, dark place to protect the colour. They will keep for months and in fact should be left for at least 2 months to mature before use. Traditionally, pickling was a way of preserving excess food grown during the summer for use in the winter. For those with large gardens this may still be so, but it is quite possible to make small quantities with shop-bought ingredients.

Pickling equipment
The most important rule for successful pickling is never to use utensils made of copper or brass. This is because the vinegar will react on them and taint the flavour of the pickle. Only use stainless steel, aluminium or enamel pans, wooden spoons and nylon sieves.

How much vinegar?

It is important to have enough spiced vinegar to fill the jars to overflowing. To be sure you allow enough, fill the jars right to the top with water and measure the volume.
If you find you do not have enough vinegar, just top up the jar with unflavoured vinegar from the bottle. During storage, it will mix with the rest and absorb the flavours.

Sizes of jars

A jar of about 14 fl oz (400ml) will hold about 8oz (225g) of food and ½ pint (300ml) vinegar.

Storing

Always wash the outside of the jars before putting them away. Sticky jars are not pleasant to pick up and dirt can settle on them if they are not clean.
To finish off, label jars with the name of the pickle and the date it was bottled.

Making the brine

The flavour of vegetables is greatly improved by being immersed in a salt and water solution. Dissolve the salt then add the vegetables. It is best to use coarse or block salt because table salt contains chemicals which may cloud the vinegar.

The right foods Most fruits and vegetables can be pickled. For recipes which require the ingredients to be left whole or cut in pieces, choose firm foods in peak condition. For pickles in sauces where the ingredients are cut small, you can use soft or over-ripe fruit and vegetables but be sure to remove any blemishes or mould. Always deal with the ingredients when they are perfectly fresh.

The spices Whole spices are generally used for pickles prepared in clear vinegar. This is because ground spices produce a cloudy effect. Whole spices such as seeds of mustard and celery, peppercorns, allspice, fennel, and dill are all popular and look attractive in the jar. Fresh or dried bay leaves, fresh celery leaves, fennel or dill fern add colour and flavour.

The vinegar Use a vinegar that is specifically for pickling or is called 'distilled'. Some of the wine and flavoured vinegars are not always strong enough to preserve food and their delicate flavour is lost when mixed with the pickles.

If the recipe calls for it, cut fruit and vegetables into bite-size pieces or smaller as neatly as possible. Discard or cut away any mould or bruised spots. Pickle immediately. Once you have started with a batch of ingredients continue at the stated intervals. Blot ingredients dry to avoid diluting the vinegar.

The containers Conventional preserving jars may be more suitable if you have a large family; where smaller amounts are preferred, use old pickle or jam jars if the lids are sound. Use lids lined with waxed paper or cling film to prevent them from coming into contact with the vinegar. Always wash the jars thoroughly in hot, soapy water. Rinse well and invert on to a tray. Dry in an oven set at 200F (100C) gas low. Wash and rinse the lids well but do not put them in the oven if they have rubber or plastic bands inside.

Filling and sealing jars
Pack the food loosely in the jars, allowing space for the vinegar to surround all the pieces. If whole spices are to be used, intersperse them with the pieces of vegetables or fruits as you fill the jar.

White vinegar may be preferred for light-coloured foods such as cauliflower or the tiny silver-skinned onions, though brown vinegar is traditional for pickled onions. Check the bottles to see if the brown vinegar has already been spiced. If not it can be spiced in one of the following ways:
● Add spices to the cold vinegar in a screw top jar. Shake occasionally. Prepare up to two months in advance.
● In a large saucepan bring the vinegar and the spices to the boil. Remove from the heat and cool immediately. If allowed to boil for too long the strength of the vinegar is reduced.
● Add the whole spices to the jar with the vegetables or fruits and just pour the vinegar over. As the pickles mature, the flavours spread without the vinegar diminishing.

Preparation of fruits and vegetables Wash them all thoroughly, with the exception of cherries, crab apples and sometimes pears, and remove stems and flowers. Skins are not always removed, but instructions are given in individual recipes.

Fill jars completely to overflowing with the vinegar. This is to ensure there is no trapped air.

For vinegar pickles only, use a tight screw cap. When closed, invert the jar to be sure there is no escaping liquid.

For more solid pickles (e.g. those in a thick sauce), seal jars with cling film or waxed paper. Or melt white wax and pour on top of the cooled pickles, then cover with cling film, greaseproof paper or fabric.

Finishing touches Homemade pickles make good gifts and useful items on bazaar stalls. Cut decorative covers for the top with scraps of fabric and tie with coloured string or wool.

Pickled Onions

Makes: 4 × 14 fl oz (400ml) jars
Preparation: about 30 minutes plus
2 days soaking

2lb (1kg) pickling onions

The brine:
8oz (225g) salt
4 pints (2.25 litres) cold water

The spiced vinegar:
2 small red chillis, halved
4 small bay leaves
4 small blades of mace
1 teaspoon mustard seeds
2 pints (1.15 litres) vinegar

Put unpeeled onions in a bowl.
☐ Make up brine in a bowl with half the ingredients. Add onions, cover with a plate and weight down to keep onions submerged.
☐ Cover bowl and leave for 24 hours. Drain onions, rinse with cold water, and remove skins.
☐ Repeat brining procedure. Leave for 24 hours.
☐ Drain onions. Bring to the boil in a large pan of cold water. Drain and blot dry.
☐ Divide onions between jars. Add spices. Pour in vinegar until it runs over the edge. Screw on lid.
☐ Wipe jars. Store for 2-3 months.

The steps in preparing Pickled Onions.

Cooking beetroot
Young beetroot cook much more quickly than those bought in the winter. To tell when they are cooked, rub the surface with the back of a fork. If ready, the skin will rub off easily.

Dry salting
This is recommended for vegetables such as cucumbers and marrows as they contain a large proportion of water anyway.

Keep cool
During the salting or brining stage keep the bowl in a cool place out of direct sunlight. Use a clean tea towel or piece of muslin to cover.

Pickled Cucumbers and Pickled Beets with some of the ingredients you can add for flavouring.

Pickled Cucumbers

Makes: 4 × ½ pint (300ml) jars
Preparation: about 20 minutes plus 2 days soaking

2lb (1kg) cucumbers, washed and trimmed
3oz (75g) onion, coarsely chopped
4 red chillis
2 tablespoons salt
4 small bay leaves
4 branches fennel fern
2 teaspoons mustard seeds
2in (5cm) piece root ginger, peeled and sliced in 4
about 1 pint (550ml) vinegar

Cut cucumbers into 1in (2.5cm) slices about a thumb's width thick. Cut each slice into quarters.
☐ Put cucumber in a bowl with the onion and chillis. Sprinkle with salt and stir. Cover bowl and leave for 2 days.
☐ Drain vegetables and rinse in cold water. Blot dry.
☐ Divide the vegetables between the jars. Push a chilli, bay leaf and branch of fennel inside each jar. Sprinkle over mustard seeds. Add ginger.
☐ Bring the vinegar to the boil. Ladle into the prepared jars until it just runs over the sides.
☐ Screw lids on tightly. Wipe jars and store for 2-3 months.
Variation: Use pickling onions cut in slices in place of chopped onions.

Pickled Beets

Makes: 1 × 1¼ pints (750ml) jar
Preparation: 15 minutes plus 40 minutes cooking

1lb (450g) beetroot, washed
salt

The spiced vinegar:
1 small onion, coarsely chopped
6 peppercorns
2 bay leaves
6 whole cloves
½ teaspoon salt
about 14 fl oz (400ml) vinegar

Cook beetroot in boiling salted water for 40 minutes. Drain and cool.
☐ Skin the beetroot and cut into ½in (1cm) cubes. Spoon into prepared jar.
☐ Put the spiced vinegar ingredients into a saucepan. Bring to the boil. Simmer for 3 minutes.
☐ Ladle vinegar and spices over the beetroot to cover.
☐ Screw lids on tightly. Wipe jar and store for 2-3 months.
Variation: For a pickle that can be eaten immediately, slice the beetroot thinly instead of dicing. Pour over cold spiced vinegar. Store in the fridge and eat within 2-3 weeks.

Mixed Pickles

Makes: 4 × 14 fl oz (400ml) jars
Preparation: about 45 minutes plus
2 days soaking

2lb (1kg) mixed vegetables:
pickling onions, fresh peas, celery, broccoli
    and cauliflower

The brine:
4oz (125g) salt
2 pints (1.15 litres) cold water

The spiced vinegar:
1 teaspoon celery seeds
2 blades mace
8 allspice berries
8 whole cloves
1in (2.5cm) piece of cinnamon stick
1 bay leaf
2 pints (1.15 litres) vinegar

Wash and prepare the vegetables.
☐ Make the brine and add the
vegetables. Cover with a plate and
weight down to keep vegetables
submerged. Cover the bowl and
leave in a cool place for 2 days.
☐ Drain the vegetables. Rinse and
drain again. Remove the onions and
blanch them.
☐ Blot all the vegetables dry.
☐ Make a Spice Bag and put in a
saucepan with the vinegar. Bring
slowly to the boil.
☐ Remove from the heat and cool.
Remove Spice Bag. Arrange the
vegetables loosely in jars. Ladle
vinegar until it runs over.
☐ Screw lids on tightly. Wipe jars
and store for 2-3 months.

Sweet Mixed Pickles

Makes: 4 × 14 fl oz (400ml) jars
Preparation: about 45 minutes plus
2 days soaking

2lb (1kg) mixed vegetables:
green, yellow and red peppers,
pickling onions, green beans,
    young carrots and broccoli

The brine:
4oz (125g) salt
2 pints (1.15 litres) cold water

The spiced vinegar:
6oz (175g) caster sugar
2 pints (1.15 litres) vinegar
2 mace blades
8 allspice berries
8 whole cloves
1in (2.5cm) piece of cinnamon stick
1 teaspoon coriander seeds
few celery leaves to finish

Wash and prepare vegetables.
☐ Soak the vegetables in the brine
and drain as for Mixed Pickles.
☐ Blanch the peppers, onions, and
carrots. Drain and rinse in cold
water.
☐ Blot all the vegetables dry.
☐ For the spiced vinegar, dissolve
the sugar with the vinegar in a pan.
Add the Spice Bag. Bring to the boil
and cool before discarding the bag.
☐ Fill jars with vegetables and a
few leaves of celery. Ladle in the
vinegar until it just runs over. Screw
the lids on tightly. Wipe the jars and
store for 2-3 months.

Blanching vegetables
It is usually best to blanch (briefly boil)
peppers, onions and carrots to make them
more tender.

Making a Spice Bag
Put all the spices into a small piece of clean
muslin and tie together tightly at the top with
string or thread.

Preparing vegetables
Wash vegetables in cold water. Trim,
remove seeds and stalks, and cut into neat
pieces—peppers in $\frac{1}{2}$in (1cm) squares, beans
and carrots into 1in (2.5cm) lengths;
cauliflower and broccoli into small florets.
Peel onions unless otherwise stated, shell
peas and slice celery.

Old-fashioned Dill Pickles

The best type of cucumbers for this recipe is the variety called 'ridge' cucumbers. They must be picked while small and crisp. Try to use ones not more than about 4in (10cm) long. This type of cucumber has little prickles over the surface which should be scrubbed off in cold water.

The best jars to use are the old-fashioned stone jars with wide tops. Lids of plastic pots can be used to hold a weight from your scales or a can of food to press the cucumbers under the brine.

Crisp Cucumber Slices

Ice cubes are used as a means of keeping the cucumbers cold if there isn't room in the fridge. As they melt the water dissolves the salt.

Pickled Chilli Peppers

You can easily pickle small red chillis to serve with Italian antipasti, or Indian food. Wash the chillis, put into small jars and cover with spiced vinegar. Cover with tight fitting lid and store in a cool dark place for 2-3 months before using.

Sweet Sour Peppers

Makes: 4 × ½ pint (300ml) jars
Preparation: 45 minutes

---

4 red peppers, seeded
4 green peppers, seeded
3 medium onions, peeled
1oz (25g) salt
¼ pint (150ml) white vinegar
4oz (100g) caster sugar

Finely chop peppers and onions and put in a saucepan.

☐ Cover with boiling water and leave for 15 minutes. Drain well.

☐ Return vegetables to the pan. Add the salt and enough water to cover. Bring to the boil and simmer for 5 minutes. Drain well.

☐ Return the vegetables to pan and add the vinegar and sugar. Bring to the boil, and simmer for 10 minutes. Stir occasionally.

☐ Ladle into prepared jars and fill to the top. Cover tightly with cling film and a screw top lid.

☐ Wipe jars. Store for 1 month.

Tip: This recipe is very good added to meat sauces and served with pasta.

Crisp Cucumber Slices

Makes: 2-3 × 1 pint (550ml) jars
Preparation: 20 minutes plus 3 hours soaking

2lb (1kg) cucumbers
4 onions, peeled
1 small green pepper, seeded
2oz (50g) salt
ice cubes
1 pint (550ml) white vinegar
½lb (225g) caster sugar
1½ teaspoons ground turmeric
1½ teaspoons mustard seeds
4 small red chillis

Trim and wash cucumbers in cold water. Slice into ⅛in (3mm) slices.

☐ Slice the onions to the same thickness and cut the pepper into narrow strips.

☐ Put all the vegetables into a large bowl. Sprinkle with salt and cover with ice cubes. Stir.

☐ Cover the bowl with a cloth and leave in a cool place for 3 hours. Drain well.

☐ Heat the vinegar and sugar in a large pan to dissolve the sugar. Add the spices and drained vegetables. Bring to the boil.

☐ Remove from the heat and ladle to top of jars. Cover with tight-fitting lids.

☐ Wipe jars and store for 2-3 months.

Old-fashioned Dill Pickles

No specific quantities are required for this recipe, but do ensure that you keep the ratio of salt to vinegar and water as given. The size of the recipe depends on the number and size of cucumbers you have and on the size of jar you use.

---

small, well-shaped cucumbers
whole sprays of dill with stalks, fern and seeds

The brine:
4oz (100g) salt
½ pint (300ml) white vinegar
4 pints (2.25 litres) water

Wash and place a layer of whole cucumbers in the bottom of a large jar. Cover with a layer of dill sprays.

☐ Continue with layers until the jar is full. Do not press too tightly at this stage.

☐ Mix the salt, vinegar and water together and pour over the cucumbers. Make up more if required. Cover with a plastic lid just smaller than the top of the jar. Weight down. Cover with tight-fitting lid.

☐ Store for 3-4 weeks until the cucumbers have become an olive green and are firm and crisp. They are then ready to serve.

Tip: You can add 1 clove of chopped garlic to each layer. If the dill does not have seed heads on it, sprinkle bought dill seeds in with each layer.

Piccalilli

Makes: 2 × 14oz (400ml) jars
Preparation: 15 minutes
plus 2 days soaking

The brine:
2oz (50g) salt
1 pint (550ml) water

4oz (125g) green beans
4oz (125g) cauliflower trimmed
4oz (125g) silverskin onions
1 pint (550ml) vinegar
2 teaspoons powdered mustard
$\frac{1}{2}$ teaspoon ground ginger
2oz (50g) caster sugar
1 teaspoon ground turmeric
2 tablespoons cornflour
about 2 tablespoons cold water

Make the brine in a large bowl. Prepare the vegetables as for Mixed Pickles. Soak them in the brine for 2 days.

☐ Drain vegetables, rinse and blot dry.

☐ Put the vegetables in a saucepan with the vinegar. Bring to the boil and simmer for 3 minutes. Remove vegetables with a draining spoon.

☐ Put mustard, ginger, sugar, turmeric and cornflour in a bowl. Mix to a smooth paste with cold water. Stir in the hot vinegar.

☐ Return mixture to the saucepan. Simmer, stirring constantly for 3-4 minutes until thick. Stir in the vegetables.

☐ Divide mixture between jars. Seal tightly. Wipe jars and store for 2-3 months.

Pickles in sauces
There are many interesting pickles in which the vinegar is thickened with flour and powdered spices. Both fruits and vegetables can be done this way and the flavour is easily varied by using different spices.

Piccalilli
Other vegetables such as small cubes of peeled cucumber, red or green pepper or broccoli can also be used.

The picture shows some of the vegetables which are good to use in Piccalilli.

To preserve horseradish

Fresh horseradish is not available all the year round but is easily pickled. Wash and peel roots and grate immediately. Fill small jars two-thirds full and add ½ teaspoon salt and ¼ teaspoon of sugar to each. Cover horseradish with white vinegar and cover with waxed paper and a tight fitting lid. Use drained for pickle recipes or for making horseradish sauce.

Filling jars

Unless otherwise stated, pickles should be filled to the very top of the jar. This excludes the air which can cause discoloration and encourage the growth of mould.

Pickled Carrots and Onions

Makes: 4 × ½ pint (300ml) jars
Preparation: 45 minutes
plus 4 days soaking

The brine:
4oz (100g) salt
1½ pints (900ml) water

1lb (450g) silverskin onions
1½lb (675g) large carrots, peeled
1 tablespoon fennel seeds
6 peppercorns
1 bay leaf
1¼ pints (750ml) white vinegar
4 tablespoons flour
2oz (50g) sugar
2 tablespoons cold water
salt to taste

Dissolve 2oz (50g) of the salt with ¾ pint (450ml) of the water in a large bowl. Add the unpeeled onions. Cover with a small plate and weight down. Cover the bowl with a clean tea towel and leave in a cool, dark place for 2 days.

☐ Drain and peel the onions. Make a fresh brine with the remaining salt and water. Add the onions. Weight down, cover and leave for 2 days. Drain.

☐ With a melon scoop, make carrot balls the same size as the onions.

☐ Make a Spice Bag with the fennel seeds, peppercorns and bay leaf.

☐ Put bag in a saucepan with the vinegar. Simmer for 5 minutes.

☐ Mix the flour and sugar to a smooth paste with cold water. Stir in the hot vinegar. Return to the saucepan. Simmer for 3 minutes, stirring constantly.

☐ Add the onions and carrots and simmer for a minute before removing the Spice Bag.

☐ Divide the vegetables and sauce evenly between the jars. Cover with cling film and screw lids on tightly.

☐ Wipe jars and store for 2 months.
Variation: Add shelled fresh peas to the brine for added colour.
Tip: Use the vegetables in casseroles having first drained them and then soaked them in water for 1 hour.

Beetroot Relish

Makes: 4 × ½ pint (300ml) jars
Preparation: about 1 hour

2lb (1kg) beetroot, cooked and skinned
3oz (75g) piece of horseradish, peeled
1 pint (550ml) white vinegar
4oz (125g) caster sugar
3 tablespoons flour
about 2 tablespoons cold water
½ teaspoon salt
freshly ground black pepper

Mince or process the beetroot and the horseradish finely.

☐ Heat the vinegar in a saucepan. Mix the sugar and flour to a smooth paste with the cold water. Stir in the hot vinegar.

☐ Return mixture to pan and bring to the boil. Stir in the beetroot. Simmer for 5 minutes, stirring occasionally until thick. Season with salt and pepper.

☐ Ladle into prepared jars. Fill to within ¼in (5mm) of rim. Cool.

☐ Place discs of wax paper on top of the relish and cover the jars tightly with either metal lids or cling film.

☐ Store for 1 month.

☐ Serve hot or cold with cold meats, burgers or in sandwiches.
Variation: For Cucumber Relish, dice 1lb (450g) peeled cucumbers and 1 large onion. Make a brine with 2oz (50g) salt and 1 pint (550ml) water. Soak vegetables overnight and drain. Rinse in cold water and drain again. Put ¾ pint (450ml) white vinegar in a pan with 1 teaspoon of celery seeds. Bring to the boil. Make a paste with 2 tablespoons of flour, 2 tablespoons of sugar, ½ teaspoon powdered turmeric and 2 tablespoons of cold water. Stir in the hot vinegar.

☐ Return mixture to the pan and bring to the boil. Stir in the vegetables and simmer for 5 minutes stirring occasionally until thick. Season with salt and pepper. Ladle the relish into prepared jars and pot as usual.

Chutneys

This traditional type of pickle with its careful blending of spices is made from a mixture of chopped fruits and vegetables, cooked with sugar and vinegar, to achieve the desired consistency. Some recipes are simmered for a short while and the ingredients remain recognizable – others are cooked to a rich pulp.

Mixed Fruit Chutney

Makes: about 3 × ½ pint (300ml) jars
Preparation: about 45 minutes
Cooking: about 45 minutes

1lb (450g) ripe tomatoes, peeled
1 large peach, peeled
1 large pear, peeled
1 medium onion, peeled
1 small red pepper, seeded
½ teaspoon salt
¼ pint (150ml) wine vinegar
4oz (125g) soft brown sugar
6 whole cloves
4 allspice berries
1in (2.5cm) piece of cinnamon

Chop the tomatoes, fruits, onions and pepper. Put in a saucepan on a low heat. Cover and simmer for 20 minutes, stirring occasionally.
☐ Add the salt, vinegar, and sugar. Make a Spice Bag and add to the pan.
☐ Simmer uncovered for 20-25 minutes, stirring occasionally until thick. Remove Spice Bag.
☐ Ladle into the jars. Place a disc of greaseproof paper on top of the chutney. Cover the jars tightly with lids and wipe with a clean wet cloth. Store in a cool dark place for about 2 months before serving.

Plum Chutney

Makes: 3 × ½ pint (300ml) jars
Preparation: about 15 minutes
Cooking: 15 minutes

10oz (275g) stoned plums, cubed
4oz (125g) cored apples, cubed
1 clove garlic, peeled and crushed
1 medium onion, peeled and chopped
4oz (125g) sultanas
¼ teaspoon ground ginger
¼ teaspoon allspice
pinch each of cayenne, ground cloves and grated nutmeg
1 teaspoon salt
½ pint (300ml) wine vinegar

Put all the ingredients in a saucepan and bring slowly to the boil. Simmer for 15 minutes until the fruit is tender but still holding its shape.
☐ Ladle into prepared jars and cover with discs of greaseproof paper. Seal jars tightly with lids and wipe with a clean wet cloth. Store in a cool dark place for about 2 months before serving.

Jars for chutneys
You do not require special jars but be sure the ones you use are tight fitting to prevent evaporation of the vinegar. This makes the chutney dry out and shrink. Screw-top lids are best, and if metal, they should be lined with cling film. As with all bottled pickles and preserves, pot chutney in clean, warm jars while hot.

Storing chutney
Most will improve in flavour the longer they are kept, and if they have been covered tightly and stored in a cool, dry, dark place, they should remain in good condition for up to 3 years.

Equipment
As for pickling but the pan used for cooking the chutney should be heavy-based stainless steel or aluminium.

Plum Chutney can be made with any plums in season.

Spicy Cucumbers

Makes: 3 × 1 pint (600ml) jars
Preparation: ½ hour
plus 3 hours soaking

about 4lb (1.75kg) cucumbers
2oz (50g) salt
2 pints (1.15 litres) water
1 clove garlic, crushed
2oz (50g) preserved ginger, sliced
14 fl oz (400ml) pickling vinegar
1lb (450g) dark brown sugar
2 tablespoons ginger syrup
2 teaspoons mustard seeds
2 teaspoons coriander seeds
½ teaspoon cardamon seeds
¼ teaspoon ground cayenne

Wash the cucumbers, then cut in half lengthways.
☐ Scoop out seeds and discard. Cut cucumbers into batons.
☐ Dissolve salt in the water in a bowl. Add cucumbers, cover and weight down. Leave for 3 hours.
☐ Drain. Rinse in cold water. Put into a large clean cloth. Shake gently to dry.
☐ Put remaining ingredients into a large saucepan. Set on a moderate heat. Bring to the boil, stirring, to dissolve sugar.
☐ Add the cucumbers. Bring back to the boil. Remove from heat.
☐ Ladle into jars. Cover tightly, wipe jars and store.

Steps in the preparation of Spicy Cucumbers.

Pear Chutney

Makes: 4 × ½ pint (300ml) jars
Preparation: 20 minutes
Cooking: about 1¼ hours

2lb (1kg) pears, peeled
8oz (225g) tomatoes, peeled
8oz (225g) onions, peeled
8oz (225g) soft brown sugar
1 teaspoon salt
¼ teaspoon ground cloves
½ teaspoon ground cinnamon
pinch of cayenne pepper
14 fl oz (400ml) pickling vinegar

Core the pears. Quarter the tomatoes. Put the pears and onions through a mincer, or chop very finely.
☐ Put pears, onions, and tomatoes in a large saucepan on a low heat. Simmer for 15-20 minutes, stirring occasionally.
☐ Add the remaining ingredients and cook very gently, uncovered and with frequent stirring, for about 1 hour until chutney is thick.
☐ Ladle into prepared jars and cover tightly. Wipe with a clean wet cloth and store.

Green Tomato Chutney

Makes: 3 × ½ pint (300ml) jars
Preparation: about 20 minutes
plus 45 minutes soaking
Cooking: about 1 hour

1lb (450g) green tomatoes
1 tablespoon salt
12oz (350g) cooking apples
8oz (225g) onions
2 large cloves garlic
14 fl oz (400ml) pickling vinegar
½ teaspoon ground cloves
½ teaspoon ground cinnamon
½ teaspoon black pepper
8oz (225g) soft brown sugar

Chop the tomatoes and put in a bowl. Sprinkle with the salt and stir. Leave for 45 minutes.
☐ Peel and core the apples. Peel the onions and garlic. Chop very finely.
☐ Drain tomatoes but do not rinse. Put in a heavy saucepan with the

remaining ingredients.

☐ Place on low heat and bring slowly to boil. Simmer, uncovered with frequent stirring, for about 1 hour until chutney is thick.

☐ Pot, cover tightly and store.

Apricot Chutney

Makes: about $4 \times \frac{1}{2}$ pint (300ml) jars
Preparation: 20 minutes plus overnight soaking
Cooking: about 1 hour

8oz (225g) dried apricots
8oz (225g) onions
12oz (350g) cooking apples
grated rind of 1 orange
2 cloves garlic, crushed
2 teaspoons ground ginger
1 teaspoon salt
1 pint (550ml) pickling vinegar
8oz (225g) seeded raisins
8oz (225g) soft brown sugar
2oz (50g) walnuts, chopped

Put the apricots in a bowl with enough cold water to cover. Leave to stand overnight. Drain, and discard the water.

☐ Peel the onions and peel and core the apples. Coarsely chop the apricots, onions, and apples.

☐ Put the chopped ingredients in a large saucepan with the orange rind, garlic, ginger, salt, vinegar, raisins and sugar.

☐ Set on a low heat and bring slowly to the boil, stirring, until the sugar has dissolved.

☐ Cook gently, uncovered with frequent stirring, for about 1 hour until the ingredients are tender and thickened to the desired consistency. There should be no moisture remaining on the surface.

☐ Stir in the chopped walnuts. Ladle into prepared jars and cover tightly.

☐ Wipe with a clean wet cloth and store in a cool dark place for about 2 months before serving.

Variation: Omit the chopped walnuts completely or use blanched sliced or chopped almonds.

Apple and Blackberry Chutney

Makes: about $3 \times \frac{1}{2}$ pint (300ml) jars
Preparation: about 15 minutes
Cooking: about 1 hour

1lb (450g) cooking apples
1lb (450g) blackberries
1lb (450g) onions
grated rind and juice of 1 lemon
1 teaspoon mixed spice
1 teaspoon salt
2 tablespoons chopped mint
1 pint (550ml) red wine vinegar
1lb (450g) granulated sugar

Peel, core and chop the apples. Peel and chop the onions.

☐ Put the apples, onions and blackberries in a large pan with the rind and juice of the lemon, mixed spice, salt, chopped mint, wine vinegar and sugar.

☐ Stir over a low heat until the sugar has dissolved. Bring to the boil and then reduce heat. Simmer, uncovered with frequent stirring, for about 1 hour until the chutney is sufficiently thick and no liquid remains on the surface.

☐ Ladle into prepared jars and seal tightly. Wipe with a clean wet cloth and store in a cool dark place for 2 months before serving.

The picture shows some of the chutneys you can make when there is an abundance of fruit.

Cooking fruit chutneys
Cooking time will vary with the quantity of fruit in relation to the pan you use. The longer you can cook the chutney the better so use a heavy pan and keep the heat low. Stir frequently to prevent sticking.

Green Tomato Chutney
This is a good chutney to make when you have an excess of tomatoes in the garden at the end of the season. Soaking them in salt for a little while reduces the sharpness.

Pickled Fruits

Many of the firm fruits are suitable for pickling. The half sweet, half sour flavour makes them delicious to serve with roast or grilled meats, and they make an attractive garnish. You can strain off the vinegar and thicken it to use as a sauce to serve with meat or game.

Sweet and Sour Fruit Salad

Makes: 2 × 1 pint (550ml) jars
Preparation: 30 minutes
Cooking: about 20 minutes

14 fl oz (400ml) cider vinegar
12oz (350g) caster sugar
3 whole cloves
½ teaspoon allspice berries
1¼in (3.5cm) cinnamon stick
1½lb (700g) firm melon
2 dessert apples
6oz (175g) cherries

Put the vinegar and sugar in a saucepan on a low heat. Stir until the sugar has dissolved.

☐ Make a bag of the spices and add to pan. Bring to the boil and simmer for 5 minutes.

☐ Cut the melon in half and discard the seeds. Cut the flesh into balls with a melon scoop. Peel and core the apples. Cut into cubes. Remove the stones from the cherries, and blot them dry with kitchen towel.

☐ Add melon and apples to pan. Bring to the boil and reduce heat. Simmer for 5 minutes.

☐ Add the cherries and bring back to the boil. Remove pan from the heat, cover and allow to stand for 10 minutes.

☐ Discard the Spice Bag. Ladle the fruit and its syrup into prepared jars. Fill to overflowing with extra vinegar if necessary.

☐ Cover jars tightly, wipe with a clean wet cloth and store.

The steps in making Sweet and Sour Fruit Salad.

Pickled Cherries

Makes: 2 × ½ pint (300ml) jars
Preparation: 15 minutes
Cooking: about 15 minutes

12oz (350g) cherries
6oz (175g) caster sugar
2 × 1in (2.5cm) pieces cinnamon stick
8 whole cloves
about ¼ pint (150ml) wine vinegar

Wash the cherries, drain well and blot dry. Cut off all but about 1in (2.5cm) of the stems.
☐ Put the sugar, spices, and vinegar into a small saucepan. Bring to the boil, stirring continuously, until the sugar has dissolved.
☐ Add the cherries. Bring back to the boil and simmer for about 10 minutes until tender.
☐ Ladle the fruit and vinegar into the prepared jars. Divide the spices between the jars and, if necessary, add a little extra vinegar, filling to overflowing.
☐ Cover the jars tightly. Wipe with a clean wet cloth and store.

Pickled Damsons

Makes: 3 × ½ pint (300ml) jars
Preparation: 15 minutes
Cooking: 3-4 minutes
plus 4 days soaking

1lb (450g) damsons
2 × 1in (2.5cm) sticks of cinnamon
2 mace blades
¼ teaspoon allspice berries
about 9 fl oz (250ml) wine vinegar
8oz (225g) soft brown sugar

Wash the damsons in cold water. Drain and blot dry with kitchen paper. Prick each fruit in 2 or 3 places with a skewer and put in a large bowl.
☐ Put the spices in a saucepan with the vinegar. Bring to the boil and pour over the damsons.
☐ Cover the bowl with a plate and leave to stand for 2 days. Strain the vinegar into a saucepan. Bring to the boil and pour over the fruit. Leave for 2 days.
☐ Put the fruit and vinegar in a saucepan and add the sugar. Heat gently, stirring continuously, until sugar has dissolved.
☐ Bring to the boil and simmer for 3 minutes.
☐ Ladle into prepared jars. Add extra vinegar, filling to overflowing if necessary. Divide the spices between the jars.
☐ Cover tightly, wipe jars with a clean wet cloth and store.

Pears with Ginger

Makes: 3 × ¾ pint (450ml) jars
Preparation: 10 minutes
Cooking: 5-15 minutes

2lb (900g) firm cooking pears
1in (2.5cm) piece of root ginger
a strip of lemon rind
1lb (450g) caster sugar
¼ pint (300ml) cider vinegar

Peel, core and cut the pears into eighths. Thinly peel the ginger and chop finely.
☐ Put the lemon rind, sugar, and vinegar into a saucepan on a low heat. Stir until the sugar has dissolved.
☐ Add the pears and ginger to the pan and bring to the boil. Reduce the heat and simmer until tender.
☐ With a draining spoon, carefully place the pears in the prepared jars. Discard the lemon peel and pour the vinegar and ginger over the fruit. Add extra vinegar, filling to overflowing if necessary.
☐ Cover the jars tightly, wipe with a clean wet cloth and store.
Variation: For pickled peaches, halve and stone fruit. Stud each peach half with a whole clove. Make a vinegar and sugar syrup in the same way as for pears, adding a strip of orange peel instead of lemon. Cook and bottle in the same way as pears. Store for 2-3 months before serving. Delicious served with sliced cold meats.

Pickled Cherries
Red cherries of the morello type are best for this recipe. Part of the stems are left on for picking them up to eat.

Pears and peaches
Simmer in the sweetened vinegar until just tender. The time can vary greatly depending on the variety of fruit and how ripe it is.

Sweetened vinegar
It's a good idea to keep a little in reserve in a jar to top up the pickled fruits if they shrink during standing.

Pickled Damsons
This method is used to keep the fruit whole. They can be stored in the same way as pickled cherries but the skins are more likely to burst.

Salting beans

Be sure to choose very fresh, tender beans for salting. Don't let them become wilted before you prepare them.

An easy way to remove the strings from the sides of runner beans is just to cut off a thin strip with a swivelling vegetable parer. If the beans shrink down in the jar too much you can add a few more but not after the first day or so. Newly added beans will not have the same amount of maturing as the first. When blotting the beans dry, work with a few at a time, and always use a clean dry cloth. To weight the beans down, set a can of food on top of the plastic lid.

The right container

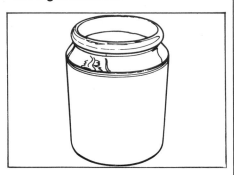

Earthenware jars such as this are ideal for dry salting and vegetables.

Preserving in salt

For those with ample cellar space for storage and a large crop of beans from the garden, dry salting is one way to preserve them for winter use. In Normandy it is traditional on the farms to serve salted beans from the summer on Christmas day.

Equipment

You need large glass or earthenware jars with wide tops, a plastic lid or saucer to fit down inside the jar for pressing and suitable covers. Choose cork, glass, plastic or wood but not metal or aluminium foil which reacts with the salt.

Small pickle jars can be used as long as they are broad enough to take a disc or lid which will support a weight for pressing the beans down.

Ratio of salt to use

The right quantity of salt in relation to the food is most important. It draws moisture from the food to form a concentrated brine and prevents growth of certain bacteria. If you don't use enough salt, the food will become slimy and have to be discarded. Too much salt will make the beans inedible.

A general rule is 1 part salt to 4 parts prepared vegetables or 1 part salt to 3 parts unprepared vegetables. This can vary however with different vegetables.

Salt Beans

___

about 1¾lb (700g) fresh beans, French
   or runner
½lb (225g) salt

___

Wash beans well in cold water. Put in a large clean cloth and shake gently to blot dry.

☐ Top and tail and if runner beans are used, cut a thin strip down each side to remove the string. Leave small French beans whole, but cut runner beans across into ½in (1cm)

slices. Put into a large mixing bowl.

☐ Put a layer of salt in the bottom of a 1½ pint (900ml) jar. Set aside about 2oz (50g) of the salt. Sprinkle the rest over the beans. Stir to coat lightly.

☐ Pack the beans into the jar. Put a plastic lid or similar on top of the beans and press down firmly. Place a weight on top and leave overnight. Add the last of the salt in a layer on top, adding more if necessary to cover the beans completely.

☐ Cover the top of the jar with cling wrap and a tight metal, glass or cork lid. Store in a cool dark place. They will keep for several months.

To use: Remove the beans from the jar. Put into a large colander and rinse very thoroughly with cold water. Continue until a raw bean tastes suitable for eating. Put into a large mixing bowl. Cover with tepid water and leave for 2 hours. Throw away the soaking water. Cook in boiling water – do not add salt – for 25-30 minutes until tender.

Salted Turnips

Very fresh, tender young turnips can be treated in the same way as the beans. Choose small turnips which are very crisp. Scrub well in cold water. Pare very thinly. Cut into cubes about ½in (1cm). Rinse well and blot dry in a clean cloth. Pack into jars in the same way as the beans using the same ratio of salt to prepared food. To serve, rinse and soak then cook in boiling water without salt until tender. Serve in cubes or mash and sprinkle well with coarsely ground black pepper and lots of butter.

Salting is an ancient method of preserving. Select only the best quality produce and prepare as you would for cooking. Beans salted in the summer can be eaten well into the winter months.

Preserving in alcohol

Bottled fruits in alcohol are very expensive to buy in the shops, but they are easy to make for yourself, especially if you have bottles of spirit brought back from foreign holidays.

Like the Rumtopf, the best jars to use are earthenware which keeps out the light and preserves the colour of the fruit. However, glass jars are attractive for showing the fruit and can be used successfully if they are stored in the dark.

Fruits preserved in this way can be used in many ways. You can serve them straight from the jar with cream, mixed into fruit salads, or made up into many different recipes.

Small jars of fruit in alcohol also make pretty gifts, and are unusual additions to bring-and-buy sales.

The simplest method to preserve fruits in alcohol is to cover the raw fruit with sugar and undiluted alcohol. Use a wide-necked jar so a lid or saucer may be placed on top of the fruit to hold it below the surface of the liquid. A more economical way is to poach the fruit in a sugar syrup then add a proportion of spirit. Fruit done this way must be sealed tightly to exclude all the air.

Containers: If using raw fruit and just alcohol, an air-tight seal is not necessary and jars covered with cling film secured with an elastic band or a cork are sufficient. For poached fruit, use jars which you can seal with tight-fitting rubber rings and glass lids.

Storage: Store all preserved fruits in a cool, very dark place to prevent fading or discoloration.

Exotic Pineapple and Bananas in Rum and Tangerines in Brandy are both delicious.

Rumtopf

The traditional German 'rum pot' consists of layers of seasonal fruits and sugar, covered in rum and left to mature.

To prepare the fruits: Wash and dry firm fruits. Remove cores and stems and cut larger fruits into segments. Plums and apricots need only be halved and stoned. Remove the stems from cherries but leave the stones in.

Soft fruits such as strawberries and raspberries should never be washed. Just remove the stalks and hulls.

The equipment: Tall jars with tight covers are all you will need. Earthenware is best for excluding the light, but if you use glass, store the filled jars in black plastic bags in a cool dark place.

The proportions: Allow about 8oz (225g) caster sugar to every 1lb (450g) prepared fruit and enough rum to cover. Use white rum for the light fruits and dark rum for the red. Be sure rum is full 40 per cent strength.

To make the Rumtopf: Put a layer of prepared fruit in the base of a clean jar. Sprinkle with the appropriate amount of sugar. Stir with a fork to coat all the fruit. Cover the jar and leave in a cool dark place overnight.

Add enough rum to completely cover the fruit. Press a plastic lid on to the fruit and weight down with a can or a scale weight. Cover the jar tightly and store.

As different fruits become available, add more layers with more sugar and more rum until the jar is full. Store for about 1 month before using. Check occasionally and top up with more rum if necessary.

Rumtopf with fruits in season.

Dried fruits in alcohol

Pitted prunes in ruby port, or dried apricots in brandy can be done in the same way as Figs in Madeira. Use fruits which are edible without soaking for best results. Be sure to cook until well puffed and tender, otherwise they will continue to absorb liquid during storage, leaving air pockets in the jars.

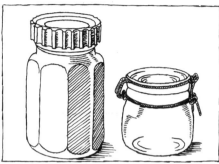

Some of the types of jars you can use for preserving fruits in alcohol. Le Parfait and Kilner jars should be used if the fruits are preserved partly in syrup.

Tangerines in Brandy

Makes: 1 × 1¾ pint (1 litre) jar
Preparation: 15 minutes

6 tangerines, peeled
8oz (225g) caster sugar
about 12 fl oz (350ml) brandy

Divide one tangerine into segments for filling gaps in the jar.
☐ Pack fruit in prepared jar and sprinkle with the sugar.
☐ Add the brandy to within 1in (2.5cm) of the top. Cover firmly with cling film and invert the jar. Repeat two or three times to ensure the fruit is submerged.
☐ Leave in a cool dark place, turning occasionally over the next day or two, until the sugar is completely dissolved.
☐ Top up the jar with a little more brandy. Cover with cling film and then with a lid. Store for 6-8 weeks before serving.

Figs in Madeira

Makes: 2 × ½ pint (300ml) jars
Preparation: about 40 minutes
Cooking: about 30 minutes

8oz (225g) dried figs
½ pint (300ml) cold water
2oz (50g) caster sugar
a strip orange rind, shredded
7 fl oz (200ml) Madeira

Put the figs in a saucepan with water to cover. Bring to the boil and simmer for 15 minutes until tender.
☐ Strain off the liquid and make up to ¼ pint (150ml) with water. Return to the pan with the sugar and orange rind.
☐ Stir over low heat to dissolve the sugar. Simmer for 5 minutes.
☐ Remove the fruit with a draining spoon and pack loosely into prepared jars. Divide the syrup evenly between the jars. Fill to the brim with Madeira.

☐ Seal well. Wipe jars with a clean wet cloth and store. Turn the jars once a week for three weeks.

Pineapple and Bananas in Rum

Makes: 1 × 2¾ pint (1.5 litres) jar
Preparation: about 40 minutes

3¼lb (1.5kg) fresh pineapple
6 large bananas
juice of 1 lemon
1lb (450g) caster sugar
about ¾ pint (450ml) white rum

Peel the pineapple and remove all the eyes. Cut into slices about ¾in (1.75cm) thick. Discard hard core. Cut rings in wedges.
☐ Peel the bananas. Cut in slices the same thickness as the pineapple. Put in a bowl with the lemon juice. Stir lightly with a fork to coat the bananas.
☐ Put a layer of pineapple in the prepared jar and sprinkle with sugar. Add a layer of bananas and sprinkle with sugar.
☐ Continue in this way until you have used all the fruit and sugar. Pour the rum over the fruit to cover completely. Cover the jar tightly.
☐ Store in a cool dark place. Turn the jar over gently, holding the lid on firmly, once or twice a day to dissolve the sugar.
☐ Use after about 3 days in trifle, with ice cream or cream.
Tip: If you want the fruit to keep for a month, use pineapple on its own. It will fade in colour but the flavour becomes better as it absorbs more rum.
● Bananas treated in this way become very soft after about 3 days. However, if you pack them on their own in rum and sugar they are very good for turning into a purée to use in a banana fool or banana ice cream. Stir the purée into an equal quantity of thick custard or whipped cream. Serve straight away or freeze in a plastic container. Remove from freezer 30 minutes before serving.

Jam and marmalade-making

Making jams and marmalades is one of the tastiest and most satisfying ways of preserving fruit. It is not terribly difficult but it does require an understanding of certain basic principles in order to achieve bright, well set results. Once these are mastered, you can turn your hand to experimenting with flavour combinations – providing an endless source of new recipes.

How it works

When fruit is boiled with the right proportion of sugar, for the correct time, a substance called pectin is released from the fruit. This is what makes the jam set and gives it the characteristic spreading consistency. To make the pectin work, it is nec-essary to have a certain amount of acid present. This may be found naturally in the fruit itself or you may have to add it in the form of lemon juice, orange juice or commercially pre-pared pectin.

Choose your fruits

High in pectin–cooking apples, blackcurrants and redcurrants, gooseberries, damsons, firm plums, quince, cranberries and all citrus fruits.
Medium–apricots, blackberries, soft plums, raspberries and loganberries.
Low–strawberries, cherries, pears, peaches, pineapple, rhubarb, melon and marrow.

When fruits are medium rich or low in pectin the amount of pectin will need to be increased. This can be done by combining high pectin fruits with the lower pectin fruits.

Commercially prepared pectin

This is available in bottles from grocers and chemists–follow the instructions carefully.

The ingredients for making Strawberry Jam.

Pans to use

Broad shallow preserving pans are best so that the evaporation of liquid is achieved as quickly as possible. If using large saucepans, work in small batches so the pan is not too full. To help prevent sticking, brush the inside of the pan with a little oil before adding the fruit.

Preparing jars

Any jars can be used for jams and marmalades. Wash jars well in hot soapy water and rinse well. Set on oven trays and place in the oven pre-heated to 200F (100C) gas low for a few minutes to sterilize them and prepare them for potting the jam.

Quantities

As a guide 3lb (1.5kg) fruit will make about 3 pints (1.75 litres) jam. Measure the capacity of your jars with water before commencing so you will have sufficient ready when you want to pot the jam.

For a good set

Strawberries are low in pectin and acid and require the addition of lemon juice for a good set. Redcurrant or gooseberry juice could also be used but their flavour is rather dominant.

Cool it

Strawberry jam is left to cool slightly before it is stirred. This helps to keep the fruit suspended throughout the jam.

Opposite: A luscious selection of fruits ready for jam-making.

Choosing and preparing fruit

Fresh, under-ripe fruit will help ensure a good set as over-ripe fruit contains less pectin. Wash, drain well and remove stalks, stems, cores, peel and stones.

Softening fruit

First cook in little or no water depending on the fruit. This softens the skins and helps release the pectin.

Adding the sugar

When the fruit becomes a pulp the sugar is added. Any type of sugar may be used but special preserving sugar dissolves quickly and helps reduce the amount of scum that forms on the top as the fruit boils. The fruit is simmered over a gentle heat until the sugar dissolves, then the heat is increased and the jam boiled until setting point is reached.

Testing for setting

● Dip a wooden spoon in the boiling jam and lift out.
● Hold horizontally over the pan and allow drips of jam to run together and form a large blob which will hang from the spoon before dropping. A second test is to put a little jam on a cold, dry saucer and allow to cool. If the surface of the jam sets and crinkles when pushed with a finger it is ready to pot.

Potting and covering

Most jams are potted immediately into hot, clean jars then covered with waxed paper discs (wax side down). Cover top with clear cellophane secured with an elastic band. Stick on a label with the type of jam and date it was made.

Storage

Keep covered and cleaned jars in a cool dark place to prevent mould forming due to dampness or shrinkage from heat. Check dates on jars and use oldest first.

Strawberry Jam

Makes: about 3 pints (1.75 litres) ○
Preparation: 10 minutes
Cooking: 40-45 minutes
plus cooling

3½lb (1.5kg) strawberries
juice of 1 large lemon
3lb (1.5kg) preserving sugar

Only wash the fruit if any soil is clinging to it. Remove the hulls and cut large berries in half.

□ Put fruit in a large saucepan with the lemon juice. Cook gently, stirring frequently for 25-30 minutes until very soft.

□ Add the sugar and stir until dissolved. Increase the heat and boil rapidly for 10 minutes. Begin testing at this point. Cook to setting stage.

□ Remove from the heat and cool until a skin forms on the surface. Stir and ladle into warm jars. Cover jam with waxed paper discs.

□ Moisten one side of the clear covers with cold water. Place over the jars, wet side up. Fix in place with elastic bands.

□ Cool. Wipe the jars and store in a cool dark place.

Variation: Strawberry and Orange Jam. Wash and thinly peel the rind from 2lb (1kg) oranges. Cut the rind into shreds. Remove the pith from the oranges and reserve. Cut the orange segments from the membrane, reserving the pips. Put the pith, pips and membrane in a muslin bag. Put the orange rind, lemon rind and juice in a saucepan with 1 pint (550ml) of water. Add the muslin bag and bring contents of the pan to the boil. Reduce heat, cover and simmer for 45 minutes. Remove muslin bag, pressing it against the side of the pan to extract the juice. Add the orange segments and 2lb (1kg) hulled strawberries. Cook for a further 10 minutes before adding 3lb (1.5kg) sugar. Stir until sugar has dissolved. Continue as for Strawberry Jam.

Apples, blackberries and raspberries make wonderful jams.

Blackberry and Apple Jam

Both of these fruits require the addition of extra pectin. Apples and blackberries, like raspberries and redcurrants, are in season at the same time, and so have become traditional companions in jam-making.

Makes: about 4 pints (2.25 litres) ○
Preparation: about 15 minutes
Cooking: about 35 minutes
plus cooling

3lb (1.5kg) blackberries
1¾lb (700g) cooking apples
7 fl oz (200ml) water
4lb (1.75kg) preserving sugar

Wash and hull the blackberries. Put in pan with half the water. Simmer until soft.

☐ Peel and core apples. Cut in thin slices and put in second pan with remaining water. Simmer until reduced to a pulp.

☐ Mix blackberries with the apple pulp. Add the sugar and stir until dissolved. Increase the heat and boil rapidly, stirring frequently, for 10 minutes.

☐ Start testing at this stage. Cook until setting point is reached.

☐ Remove from the heat and ladle into hot jars immediately. Cover the jam with discs of waxed paper, waxed side down. Let cool for a few minutes.

☐ Moisten one side of the clear covers with cold water. Place over the jars, wet side up. Smooth over the jar tops and fix in place with elastic bands.

☐ Leave to cool completely. Wipe the jars with a clean wet cloth. Store in a cool dark place.

Variation: Blackberry and Elderberry Jam can be made with wild or cultivated fruit. Simmer 3lb (1.5kg) of washed and stemmed elderberries in ½ pint (300ml) water until reduced to a pulp. Sieve to remove seeds. Put the purée with 3lb (1.5kg) washed and hulled blackberries in a pan and simmer for 10 minutes until soft. Add 6lb (3kg) sugar and stir over a low heat until dissolved. Increase the heat and boil for 10 minutes stirring frequently. Continue as recipe.

Raspberry and Redcurrant Jam

Makes: about 2 pints (1.2 litres) ○
Preparation: 30 minutes
Cooking: about 35 minutes
plus cooling

2lb (1kg) raspberries
8oz (225g) redcurrants
2¼lb (1.25kg) preserving sugar

Remove the hulls from the raspberries. Wash the redcurrants and remove all the stems and stalks.

☐ Put the raspberries in a large saucepan and cover. Set on a low heat and cook very gently in the juices which form (do not add water), stirring occasionally. Cook for about 10 minutes.

☐ In a second pan put the redcurrants with enough water to cover. Cook gently for 5 minutes.

☐ Add the raspberries and the sugar to the redcurrants. Stir until the sugar has dissolved. Increase the heat and boil rapidly for 10 minutes.

☐ Start testing at this point. Cook until setting point is reached.

☐ Remove from the heat. Ladle into hot jars immediately. Cover the jam with discs of waxed paper, waxed side down. Cool for a few minutes.

☐ Moisten one side of the clear covers with cold water. Place over the jar tops, wet side up, and fix in place with elastic bands.

☐ Leave the jam to cool completely. Wipe the jars with a clean wet cloth. Store in a cool dark place.

Rose-hip Jam

Makes: about 2½ pints (1.4 litres) ○
Preparation: 30 minutes
Cooking: about 25 minutes
plus cooling

2¼lb (1.25kg) ripe rose-hips
7 fl oz (200ml) water
3 fl oz (100ml) redcurrant juice
2lb (1kg) preserving sugar

Wash rose-hips and remove the stalks. Cut them in half.

☐ In a large saucepan bring the water to the boil. Add the hips, cover the pan and simmer, stirring frequently, for about 10 minutes until fruit is reduced to pulp.

☐ Liquidize or process the pulp and sieve. Put purée, redcurrant juice and sugar in a pan.

☐ Place on a low heat stirring constantly, until the sugar is dissolved. Increase the heat and boil rapidly for 10 minutes. Begin testing at this point. Cook until setting

point is reached.

☐ Remove from the heat. Ladle into hot jars immediately. Cover the jam with discs of waxed paper. Cool for a few minutes.

☐ Moisten one side of the clear covers with cold water. Place over the jars, wet side up. Smooth over the jar tops and fix in place with elastic bands.

☐ Cool, wipe and store jars.

Apricot Jam

Makes: about 3½ pints (1.75 litres) ○
Preparation: about 30 minutes
Cooking: about 1¼ hours
plus cooling

3lb (1.5kg) apricots
juice of 1 lemon
½ pint (300ml) water
3lb (1.5kg) preserving sugar

Wash the apricots in cold water. Cut in half with a sharp knife and remove the stones.

☐ Put the fruit in a large pan with the lemon juice and water. Cover and simmer for about 40 minutes, checking frequently, until the fruit is tender.

☐ Remove the lid and cook for a further 15 minutes until the fruit can be squashed with a fork.

☐ Add the sugar and stir until dissolved. Increase the heat and boil rapidly for 10 minutes. Start testing at this point. Cook until setting point is reached.

☐ Remove from the heat. Ladle in to hot jars immediately. Cover the jam with discs of waxed paper, waxed side down. Cool for a few minutes.

☐ Moisten one side of the clear covers with cold water. Place over the jars, wet side up. Smooth over the jar tops and fix in place with elastic bands.

☐ Leave the jam to cool completely. Wipe the jars with a clean wet cloth. Store in a cool dark place.

Apricot jam for the taste of summer.

Easy to peel

Dipping the oranges in boiling water first softens the skin and will enable you to remove the peel thinly.

Skimming marmalade

Foam forms on top of marmalade which must be skimmed off as soon as it is cooked. If it is left, it is very difficult to remove.

Suspended peel

Cooling and stirring the marmalade is done to ensure the fruit and peel are suspended throughout.

Frozen fruit

Seville oranges make the best marmalade but their season is short—mid-January to the end of February. If you do not have the time then to make marmalade, freeze the oranges whole, and use them at a later date.

The steps in making Seville Orange Marmalade.

Making Marmalade

Marmalade is a jam made from citrus fruits which are high in pectin. Most of the pectin is contained in the pips and pith and the easiest way to extract it is to tie the pips and pith in a muslin bag and boil it with the cut up fruit. In some recipes the pith and membranes are added to the bag while in others only the pips are removed and the whole fruit is sliced to make the main part of the marmalade. In each recipe the rind and the fruit require long cooking to soften the peel and reduce the flesh to a pulp.

Seville Orange Marmalade

Makes: about 3 pints (1.75 litres) ◯
Preparation: 30-40 minutes
Cooking: about 1¾ hours
plus cooling

2lb (1kg) Seville oranges
4 pints (2.25 litres) water
juice of 2 lemons
4lb (1.75kg) preserving sugar

Scrub the oranges well with a clean brush. Dip each orange in turn in a pan of boiling water. Thinly pare off rind and cut in shreds.

☐ Put the peel and half the water in a saucepan. Bring to the boil. Reduce the heat and cover the pan. Simmer for 1½ hours until soft.

☐ Meanwhile, strip off the pith from the oranges. Cut out the segments and chop coarsely. Tie the membranes, pith, and pips loosely in a piece of clean muslin.

☐ Put the chopped flesh, lemon juice, and the muslin bag in a second saucepan with the rest of the water. Cover and cook very gently for about 1½ hours.

☐ Remove the bag, pressing out as much liquid as possible. Add the drained peel. Add the sugar and stir until dissolved.

☐ Increase the heat and boil rapidly for 10 minutes. Start testing at this point. Cook to the setting stage.

☐ Remove from the heat, skim off the foam and leave to cool until a skin forms on the surface. Stir and ladle into warm jars. Cover the marmalade with discs of waxed paper, waxed side down.

☐ Moisten one side of the clear covers with cold water. Place over the jars, wet side up. Smooth over the jar tops and fix in place with elastic bands.

☐ Cool and wipe jars before storing.

Grapefruit Marmalade

Makes: about 4½ pints (2.25 litres) ◯
Preparation: 45 minutes
Cooking: about 1½ hours

3lb (1.5kg) grapefruit
2 small lemons
6 pints (3.5 litres) water
6lb (3kg) preserving sugar

Wash the fruit. Thinly peel the rind from the fruit, cut in thin strips and place in a large pan.

☐ Cut the pith from the grapefruit and reserve. Slice the grapefruit, reserving the pips. Squeeze the juice from the lemon. Add strained juice to pan with grapefruit slices.

☐ Put pith, pips and lemon skins in a muslin bag. Add to the pan with the water. Bring to the boil.

☐ Simmer for 1 hour until fruit is very soft. Remove muslin bag, pressing to extract all the juice.

☐ Add sugar and continue as usual.

Three-Fruit Marmalade

Makes: about 2½ pints (1.4 litres) ◯
Preparation: 30 minutes
Cooking: about 2½ hours
plus cooling

---

2 pints (1.2 litres) water
about 1½lb (700g) frozen citrus fruits: 1 large grapefruit, 2 large lemons, 1 large sweet orange
3lb (1.5kg) preserving sugar

Put the water in a saucepan and bring to the boil. Add the whole frozen fruit and reduce the heat. Simmer, covered, for about 2 hours until the fruit is soft.

☐ Remove fruit with a draining spoon to a chopping board. Slice thinly with a knife and fork.

☐ Separate the pips and return them to the pan. Boil for 3 minutes. Remove the pips and discard.

☐ Add the sliced fruit to the pan. Boil again to make sure the fruit is pulpy and the water has evaporated.

Add the sugar and stir until dissolved.

☐ Increase the heat and boil rapidly for 10 minutes. Start testing at this point. Cook to the setting stage.

☐ Remove from the heat. Leave to cool until a skin forms on the surface. Stir and ladle marmalade into warm jars.

☐ Cover the marmalade with waxed paper discs, waxed side down. Moisten one side of the clear covers with cold water. Place over the tops, wet side up, and secure with elastic bands.

☐ Cool. Wipe the jars with a clean wet cloth. Store in a cool dark place. Keeps for several months.

Variation: Limes can be treated in the same way. They mix very well with grapefruit to make a two-fruit marmalade.

Tip: If time is short, the peel may be minced or liquidized.

Three-Fruit Marmalade made from frozen fruit.

Oven cooking of the frozen fruit

If you have the oven on, you can cook the fruit for marmalade at the same time as another dish. Put the whole frozen fruit into a covered casserole and cook for 4-5 hours until tender. Cooking fruit from the freezer makes it easier to make small batches.

It is very important to do this before the sugar is added to achieve a good clear set.

Poor pectin content — the clot is broken in several small beads.

Medium pectin content — the clot is not very firm and can be broken into two or three.

Good pectin content — a single large clot is formed.

Jelly-making

More fruit is necessary when making jelly because only the juice is used. Wild or cultivated fruits which are available in abundance are popular because they are more economical.

Selecting fruit for jelly
Choose those which are high in acid and pectin. Fruits such as pears, cherries and strawberries need so much pectin to set them that the flavour can be marred unless they are mixed with high-pectin fruits of a suitable flavour. As with jam, under-ripe fruits give the best set; damaged parts should be avoided.

Some good fruits to use for jelly:
- blackberries
- crab apples
- currants
- elderberries
- gooseberries
- loganberries, raspberries
- quinces
- rowanberries

Preparing the fruit
Wash in cold water and discard any blemished fruits and leaves. The juice will be strained so you don't need to remove small stems. Cut larger fruits such as apples and plums into small pieces.

Put fruit in a pan with the correct amount of water. In the case of soft fruits, very little will be needed. Hard fruits, however, will require sufficient water to cover.

Testing for pectin
It is essential to know the quantity of pectin present in the juice before you can estimate the amount of sugar to use. Follow this simple test as soon as the fruit is cooked. Into a small tumbler or cup put 1 teaspoon of the juice from the softened fruit and leave to cool. Add 1 tablespoon of methylated spirit and shake to combine. Leave for 1 minute. Pour onto a saucer as shown in the diagram. If the pectin clot is poor continue simmering fruit to concentrate the juice by evaporation. Test again, and should it still be low add lemon juice, redcurrant juice or commercial pectin following the manufacturer's instructions.

Straining the fruit pulp
Old-fashioned jelly bags made from thick flannel are still available from good kitchen specialists. However, you can make your own by sewing tapes at each corner of a 14in × 16in (35 × 40cm) piece of firmly woven white cotton. Fix the tapes or loops of the bag to the four legs of an upturned kitchen stool or chair.

Place a large bowl or jug beneath. Pour boiling water through to scald the bag. Empty water away, replace the bowl, and ladle in the fruit pulp. Leave to drip for at least 2 hours or overnight but no longer than 24 hours. Do not squeeze the bag as this will result in the jelly being cloudy.

Measuring the juice
When the pulp has stopped dripping, measure the juice from the bowl. Return to a clean pan and bring to the boil. Add the sugar and stir until dissolved. Increase the heat and boil rapidly for 10 minutes and start testing for a setting point as for jam-making.

Filling jars
Once setting point has been reached remove pan from the heat. Dispose of the scum which will have formed on the surface with crumpled kitchen paper. This must be done thoroughly but quickly before the jelly starts to set. Pour into jars prepared as for jam-making but tilting the jar to prevent air bubbles forming. Cover and pot as for jam.

Quantities
The amount of jelly obtained varies with the crop and the amount of juice extracted. But, as a general guide, to each 3lb (1.5kg) sugar you can expect around 5lb (2.25kg).

Blackcurrant Jelly

(*without pectin*)

Makes: about 3½ pints (1.75 litres)○
Preparation: about 20 minutes
Cooking: about 1 hour
Draining: overnight or similar

4lb (1.75kg) blackcurrants
2 pints (1.2 litres) water
preserving sugar

Wash the fruit, put in a large saucepan with the water and bring to the boil. Reduce the heat, cover the pan and simmer for about 45 minutes until the fruit is soft.

☐ Remove from the heat. Mash the blackcurrants and test a little of the juice at this point for pectin.

☐ Ladle the fruit and juices into a prepared jelly bag. Leave to drain until no more juice drips through.

☐ Discard the fruit pulp. Measure the juices and return to the pan. Bring to the boil. For each 1 pint (550ml) of juice add 1lb (450g) preserving sugar. Stir until dissolved.

☐ Increase the heat and boil rapidly for 10 minutes. Start testing at this stage. Cook until setting point is reached.

☐ Remove pan from the heat. Skim and ladle into hot jars. Cover as for jam. Store.

Damson Jelly

(*with pectin*)

Makes: about 2½ pints (1.4 litres) ○
Preparation: 30 minutes
Cooking: about 1 hour
Draining: overnight or similar

3lb (1.5kg) damsons
1 pint (550ml) water
4lb (1.75kg) preserving sugar
the juice of 1 large lemon
4 fl oz (125ml) liquid pectin

Wash and prepare fruit. Put in a saucepan with the water and bring to the boil.

☐ Reduce the heat to simmering. Cover the pan and cook gently for about 45 minutes until the fruit is tender. Test for pectin at this point.

☐ Ladle the fruit and juices into prepared jelly bag. Leave to drain.

☐ Discard the fruit pulp. Measure the juice and make up to 1½ pints (900ml) with water if necessary. Put in a heavy saucepan with the sugar and lemon juice.

☐ Set on a low heat. Stir until the sugar dissolves. Increase the heat and bring to a full boil. Stir in the pectin and boil rapidly for 3 minutes, stirring occasionally.

☐ Remove pan from the heat, skim and ladle into hot jars. Cover as for jam, and store.

Variation: For damson and apple jelly without pectin, use 2lb (1kg) damsons, 2lb (1kg) apples and 2½ pints (1.4 litres) water. Measure juice and add 1lb (450g) sugar to each 1 pint (550ml) of juice.

Tip: For a different flavour add a piece of bruised ginger root or 6 whole cloves to the fruit as it simmers. Powdered spice will give a cloudy result.

Freezing fruit for jelly
If you do not have enough from one picking of fruit or the right combination for the recipe, freeze the fruit for use at a later date.

Do not disturb!
Don't tilt jars until the jelly has set completely as you will disturb the clotting.

Draining fruit through a jelly bag.

Pale jellies

Sugar is usually added to the boiling juice, but if you prefer a very delicate colour when using pale fruits, you can add the sugar to the cold juice and heat them gently together.

Storage

As for jam and marmalade, jellies are best stored in a cool, dry, dark place.

Cloudy jelly

This is usually due to the fact that the juice was disturbed during straining.

Gently does it

It is important to simmer the fruit gently before straining to ensure that the maximum amount of juice has been released.

Blackberry and Apple Jelly

Makes: about 3½ pints (1.75 litres) ○
Preparation: 20 minutes
Cooking: about 1¼ hours
Draining: overnight or similar

3lb (1.5kg) blackberries
1lb (450g) cooking apples
1 tablespoon lemon juice
2 pints (1.2 litres) water
preserving sugar

Wash the blackberries and apples in cold water. Cut apples in eighths, including the cores and pips. Put fruits in a large saucepan with the lemon juice and water.

☐ Bring to the boil. Reduce the heat, cover pan and simmer for about 1 hour until fruit is reduced to a pulp.

☐ Remove from the heat and mash the fruit. Test a little of the juice for pectin at this point.

☐ Ladle the fruit and juices into a prepared jelly bag. Leave to drain until no more juice drips through.

☐ Discard the fruit pulp. Measure the juice and return to the pan. Bring to the boil. For each 1 pint (550ml) of juice add 8oz (225g) preserving sugar. Stir until dissolved.

☐ Increase the heat and boil rapidly for 10 minutes. Start testing at this stage. Cook until setting point is reached.

☐ Remove pan from the heat. Skim and ladle into hot jars. Cover as for jam and store.

Crab Apple Jelly

Makes: about 4 pints (2.25 litres) ○
Preparation: 20 minutes
Cooking: about 1¼ hours
Draining: overnight or similar

6lb (3kg) crab apples
the juice of 1 lemon
4 pints (2.25 litres) water
preserving sugar

Scrub the crab apples well. Pay special attention to the blossom end and remove the stalks.

☐ Cut the fruit in quarters and put in a pan with lemon juice and water.

☐ Bring to the boil and then simmer for about 1 hour until the fruit is completely tender.

☐ Remove from the heat and mash the fruit. Test for pectin at this point.

☐ Ladle the fruit into the prepared jelly bag and leave to drain completely.

☐ Discard the fruit pulp and measure the juice. Return juice to pan and bring to the boil. For each 1 pint (550ml) of juice add 1lb (450g) of sugar. Stir until dissolved.

☐ Increase the heat and boil rapidly for 10 minutes. Start testing at this stage.

☐ Continue as for Blackberry and Apple Jelly.

Gooseberry and Elderflower Jelly

Makes: about 4 pints (2.25 litres) ○
Preparation: 10-15 minutes
Cooking: about 1 hour
Draining: overnight or similar

4lb (1.75kg) gooseberries
2 pints (1.2 litres) water
preserving sugar
4 large elderflower heads

Rinse gooseberries and place in a pan with the water. Bring to the boil and simmer for 40 minutes.

☐ Test for pectin and adjust if necessary. Drain fruit and juice.

☐ Discard fruit and measure juice. Put the juice in a pan and bring to the boil. For each 1 pint (550ml) of juice add 1lb (450g) sugar. Stir until dissolved.

☐ Wash elderflower heads and tie in a muslin bag. Add to pan.

☐ Increase heat and boil rapidly for 10 minutes. Test and cook to setting point.

☐ Continue as for other jellies. Remove flowers before skimming.

The steps to making Lemon Curd.

Lemon Curd

Makes: $3 \times \frac{1}{2}$ pint (300ml) jars
Preparation: 10-15 minutes
Cooking: 20-25 minutes

4 large lemons
1lb (450g) caster sugar
4oz (125g) unsalted butter
4 eggs, size 2

Wash the lemons in cold water. Wipe dry with kitchen towel. Grate the rinds finely.

☐ Put the sugar and butter into a bowl. Squeeze the lemons and add the strained juice to the bowl.

☐ Set bowl over a pan of hot water on a moderate heat. Stir until the butter melts and the sugar dissolves.

☐ Lightly whisk the eggs and add to the bowl with the lemon peel. Cook for about 15 minutes, stirring frequently until the mixture is thick and smooth.

☐ Pot as for jam. Curd will keep for 1 month in fridge.

EXTENDING YOUR REPERTOIRE

Patés, terrines and raised pies
Working with gelatine •Cooking with eggs
Pasta and pasta dishes
Iced desserts

Pâtés, terrines and raised pies

Today, pâtés and terrines are often served as first courses. Like raised pies, they are also very suitable for cold buffets, lunchtime snacks, light suppers and other informal meals such as picnics. Because they benefit from being made in advance and are eaten cold, they are an excellent standby for busy cooks.

The original pâtés and terrines were usually made from pork. They were an economical way of using off-cuts of meat to create delicious dishes in their own right.

Originally, pâtés had a pastry crust; terrines did not but took their name from the earthenware dishes in which they were cooked. Nowadays the two terms are used interchangeably although a 'terrine' often means a mixture which is rougher and coarser in texture. Pâtés are usually, though not always, of a softer, spreading consistency. The old idea of enclosing the mixture in pastry survives in pâtés or terrines 'en croûte' – in a crust.

A particular type of pastry crust – hot water crust – is used to enclose a savoury meat mixture to make raised pies. Fillings for raised pies, like that on page 404, are rather similar to pâtés and may conveniently be prepared at the same time.

Ingredients

Most pâtés and terrines are based on protein foods – meat, poultry, game and fish are the most common, but eggs, cheese and vegetables are used too. Often two or three different meats, fish or vegetables are combined, so that the variety of pâtés is endless. To obtain a close texture, the main ingredients are finely chopped, minced, puréed or liquidized.

Because pâtés are often made from lean meats and are dense mixtures requiring slow cooking, they need to be protected from drying out in the oven. Fat of one sort or another has an important role to play. Diced or minced pork fat, butter or cream is often added to the body of the pâté giving flavour and substance, as well as binding and moistening the mixture. In most pâtés, thin slices of fat are also used to line or cover the dish in which the mixture is cooked. A very good fat to use is 'spec', a pure pork fat. It is sold in some delicatessens and pork butchers. Also very good is streaky bacon which gives extra colour and flavour to the dish.

In lighter, softer pâtés, eggs, cream, cream cheese and white sauce are often used to bind the ingredients together.

Preparing the mixture

Coarse textures can be achieved by shredding cooked meats with forks, as for confits. To give a finer grain, put all the meat through a mincer. To get a very smooth, even finer texture, use your food processor or liquidizer. For extra interest, different foods can be layered, or diced meat, fish or pork fat interspersed through the mixture. When the finished pâté is cut, the slices display a mosaic of colours and textures.

When a recipe says 'season to taste' it can be difficult to know how much to add. Take a small amount of the mixture, roll into a ball and poach or fry for a few minutes. Cool and taste.

Containers

Pâtés which require baking can be cooked in any deep ovenproof dish. Small ramekins, soufflé dishes or custard pots are suitable for individual portions. Casseroles of earthenware, ovenglass or ovenproof porcelain are good for larger quantities which can then be served from the dish. Cake tins and loaf tins are also useful for terrines which are to be sliced. Containers without lids can be covered with foil.

Cooking

Long, slow cooking helps develop the subtle flavours characteristic of pâtés and terrines. It is necessary, too, to ensure complete cooking of the close-textured interior without overcooking the outside. A moderate to slow oven is best, with the terrine set in a pan of hot water.

Cooling and storing

Once cooked, the dish should be set on a wire rack to allow air circulation and quick cooling. Many pâtés yield juices during cooking which must be poured off. It is usual to press some of the firm terrines by weighting them down during cooling. Unopened cans of food or weights from your kitchen scales can be used. Most pâtés will keep for several days in the fridge. Firm types of pâté freeze quite successfully. For quicker thawing, freeze individual portions or slices.

Sealing pâtés

To keep pâtés fresh, you can cover them in a number of ways. A glaze of stock or wine set with gelatine gives an attractive clear top which can be decorated with herbs and berries. Melted butter and pork or poultry fat are also good. Once the covering has been cut into, the pâté should be eaten fairly soon. Such toppings should not be applied if the pâté is to be frozen.

Serving

Soft pâtés are served in individual small pots, or spooned from a larger dish. They are best eaten with a crisp accompaniment such as toast or savoury biscuits. Firmer, coarser types of pâté are cut in slices or wedges. Fresh crusty French bread makes a good foil for these textures.

Duck and Turkey Pâté

Duck and Turkey Pâté

To make a coarse texture, work the meats as little as possible. Mincing is better than processing or liquidizing if you have access to a mincer. The dark meat from the turkey can be used instead of duck for the dark layers if preferred, and chicken breasts may be substituted for turkey breasts.

Partial cooking of the duck makes it easier to remove the flesh from the bones.

Serves 8 ☆☆
Preparation: 1½ hours plus 3-4 hours marinating
Cooking: 1¾ hours plus overnight chilling
Setting: 1 hour

The duck layers:
2¼lb (1kg) duck on the bone (½ large duck)
2oz (50g) onion, peeled and chopped
1 clove garlic, peeled and chopped
¼ pint (150ml) red wine
4oz (125g) chicken livers
4oz (125g) belly pork, cubed
3 tablespoons brandy
juice of 1 orange
salt and freshly ground black pepper

The turkey layer:
12oz (350g) turkey breast meat
1oz (25g) onion, peeled and chopped
1 teaspoon chopped fresh rosemary
salt and freshly ground black pepper
1 egg white from a size 2 egg
3 fl oz (100ml) double cream

The glaze:
¼ pint (150ml) clarified Chicken Stock or white wine
1 teaspoon powdered gelatine
juniper berries and bay leaves

Put the duck into a saucepan with the onions, garlic and wine. Cover and simmer for 30 minutes. Remove from the heat and cool.

☐ Pick all the flesh from the bones of the duck. Wash the chicken livers, drain and blot dry. Liquidize the 3 meats to a coarse paste.

☐ Turn into a container and pour over the cooking juices, brandy and orange juice. Season. Cover and refrigerate for 3-4 hours.

☐ To prepare the turkey layer: Cut the meat into cubes. Liquidize or process with the rest of the ingredients. Work to a coarse paste.

☐ Set oven to 300F (150C) gas 2.

☐ Spread half the duck mixture in a greased 3 pint (1.75 litre) terrine. Spread the turkey mixture over, then the remainder of the duck. Cover the dish with foil or a lid.

☐ Set terrine in a pan of hot water in the oven and cook for 1¾ hours, until firm and the juices are clear.

☐ Remove the terrine and pour off the cooking juices. Set on a rack and cover with foil. Weight down with a can or similar for several hours. Chill overnight.

☐ To make the glaze: Put the stock or wine into a saucepan on a low heat. Sprinkle the gelatine over the surface and whisk to dissolve. Cool until beginning to set. Decorate the pâté with juniper and bay leaves, then pour the jelly over. Chill for 1 hour before serving.

Chicken Liver Pâté

Serves 8-10 ☆☆☆
Preparation: 45 minutes
Cooking: 1¾ hours plus overnight chilling

3oz (75g) brown breadcrumbs
¼ pint (150ml) white wine
2 tablespoons brandy
1lb (450g) chicken livers
8oz (225g) belly pork
12oz (350g) chicken breast fillet
2oz (50g) onion, peeled
1 large clove garlic, peeled and sliced
½ teaspoon dried green peppercorns
6 juniper berries
1 tablespoon fresh thyme leaves
1 egg, size 2
8-10oz (225-275g) streaky bacon rashers or spec

Soak the breadcrumbs in the wine and brandy.

☐ Wash the livers, drain and blot dry with paper towels. Cut the pork, chicken and onions into cubes.

☐ Liquidize or process the meats to a smooth purée. Add the soaked breadcrumbs and all the other ingredients except the bacon and mix until well combined.

☐ Set oven to 350F (180C) gas 4.

☐ Remove the rinds from the bacon, if using, and stretch the rashers with the back of a knife. Use to line a 3 pint (1.75 litre) terrine.

☐ Fill with the pâté mixture. Tuck in the ends of bacon or spec and cover with more bacon or spec if necessary. Cover dish tightly.

☐ Set terrine in a pan of hot water in the oven and cook for 1½ hours or

until firm and the juices are clear. Remove the foil. Cook for 15 minutes to brown the bacon lightly.
☐ Remove to a rack to cool. Cover. Chill overnight. Serve with toast.

Fish Pâté

Serves 8   ☆☆☆
Preparation: 45 minutes plus 1 hour marinating
Cooking: 2½ hours plus overnight chilling

14oz-1lb (400-450g) fresh salmon
3 fl oz (100ml) white wine
1¼lb (700g) haddock fillet
3oz (75g) onion, peeled
6oz (175g) butter, softened
3 eggs, size 2
salt and freshly ground black pepper
5oz (150g) watercress

Fillet and skin the salmon. Cut into long strips about the thickness of the thumb. Lay in a shallow dish and pour wine over. Leave for 1 hour.
☐ Skin the haddock and cut in chunks. Chop the onion coarsely. Liquidize or process the haddock and the onions to a paste.

☐ Gradually work in the butter followed by 2 of the eggs. Drain the liquid from the salmon and work the marinade into the fish mixture. Season with salt and pepper.
☐ Wash the watercress and discard the coarse part of the stems. Put in a colander and hold over the sink. Slowly pour a kettle of boiling water over the watercress. Drain well.
☐ Set aside 1lb (450g) of the fish mixture for the top. Work the remaining egg and the watercress into the rest of the fish.
☐ Set oven to 300F (150C) gas 2.
☐ Spread half the watercress mixture in a greased 3 pint (1.75 litre) terrine. Lay half the strips of salmon on top. Cover with the rest of the watercress mixture, then with the remaining salmon. Finally, spread white fish mixture on top.
☐ Cover the dish with foil or a lid. Set in a pan of hot water in the oven and cook for 1½ hours. Remove the foil. Cook for about 1 hour until the mixture feels firm when a knife is inserted, and the top is set.
☐ Remove to a rack to cool. Pour off the excess juices. Cover. Chill overnight before serving.

Fish Pâté

Use a liquidizer or food processor to work the fish to a purée, then mix in the other ingredients. If your machine is not large enough to take the whole recipe at once, do a little at a time and complete the mixing in a bowl with a wooden spoon.
The juices which come from the fish during cooking make a very good stock which can be stored in the freezer for later use.
❋ This pâté is not suitable for freezing.

Fish Pâté and Chicken Liver Pâté.

Lamb Terrine 'Gérard Pennec'

Serves 12   ★★☆

Preparation: 45 minutes plus 3-4 hours marinating

Cooking: 1¾ hours plus overnight chilling

The smooth mixture:
12oz (350g) lean lamb
7oz (200g) pork fillet
5oz (150g) belly pork
2 eggs, size 2
4 tablespoons brandy
salt and freshly ground black pepper
1 tablespoon fresh thyme leaves

The chunky mixture:
14oz (400g) lean lamb
7oz (200g) cooked gammon or bacon in
    the piece
4 tablespoons brandy
4 tablespoons madeira
6oz (175g) streaky bacon rashers or spec
2 bay leaves
sprig fresh thyme

Prepare the smooth mixture: Cut the 3 meats into cubes. Purée in the liquidizer or processor. Add the eggs, brandy, seasoning and herbs. Work well again to make a very smooth, soft mixture. Refrigerate, in a covered container, for 3-4 hours.

☐ Make the chunky mixture: Dice the meats and place in a covered container with the brandy and madeira. Refrigerate for 3-4 hours.

☐ Set oven to 350F (180C) gas 4.

☐ Mix the two mixtures together by hand. Turn into a greased 3 pint (1.75 litre) terrine.

☐ Remove the rinds from the bacon, if using, and stretch the rashers with the back of a knife. Cover the pâté with the bacon or spec tucking it in at the sides. Arrange the bay leaves and the thyme on top and cover the dish tightly with foil or a lid.

☐ Set in a pan of hot water in the oven and cook for 1½ hours until the pâté is firm and the juices are clear. Remove the cover and bake for 15 minutes to brown bacon lightly.

☐ Cool. Pour off the excess juices. Chill overnight before serving.

Lamb Terrine 'Gérard Pennec'.

Terrine En Croute

Serves 12   ★★☆

Preparation: 1 hour

Cooking: 2 hours

8-10oz (225-275g) streaky bacon rashers
1½lb (700g) belly pork
1lb (450g) lean veal
8oz (225g) pig's liver
3oz (75g) onion, peeled
large sprig of parsley
½ teaspoon ground mace
1 large clove garlic, peeled
few peppercorns
few juniper berries
6 tablespoons madeira
¼ pint (150ml) white wine
1lb (450g) shortcrust pastry
beaten egg for glazing

Remove the rinds from the bacon and stretch the rashers with the back of a knife. Use some to line a 3 pint (1.75 litre) terrine.

☐ Mince together coarsely the meats and put in a bowl. Grind together all the flavourings except for the madeira and wine. Combine the two mixtures and stir in the madeira and white wine.

☐ Set oven to 350F (180C) gas 4.

☐ Pack mixture into the lined terrine. Tuck in the ends of the bacon and use more if necessary.

☐ Cover dish tightly with foil or a lid. Set in a pan of hot water in the oven and cook for about 1½ hours until firm and the juices are clear.

☐ Remove dish to a rack to cool. Pour off the juices and turn out the pâté: Loosen around the sides with a knife and turn out carefully.

☐ Set oven to 425F (220C) gas 7.

☐ Roll the pastry into a 15in (38cm) square. Trim off about 1in (2.5cm) from one side and make into pastry leaves.

☐ Set the cooled terrine in the centre of the pastry. Wrap the pastry around neatly to make a closed parcel, sealing the edges with beaten egg.

☐ Set on a baking tray with the pastry seam underneath. Brush the top with egg and decorate with the pastry leaves. Bake in the oven for about 30 minutes until golden brown.

☐ Cool on a wire rack, then serve cut in slices.

Country Pork Pâté

Serves 10-12, makes ☆☆☆
about 3lb (1.5kg)
Preparation: 30 minutes
Cooking: 2 hours plus chilling

12oz (350g) streaky bacon rashers
8oz (225g) pig's liver
3oz (75g) onions, peeled
4 large cloves garlic, peeled
1lb (450g) pork fillet
8oz (225g) belly pork
salt and freshly ground black pepper
1 tablespoon fresh sage, finely chopped, or
    1 teaspoon dried sage
½ teaspoon ground mace
¼ pint (150ml) double cream
2 eggs, size 2
8oz (225g) pork kidney

Remove the rinds from the bacon and stretch the rashers with the back of a knife. Use to line a deep ovenproof dish of about 2½ pint (1.4 litre) capacity.

☐ Wash the liver. Mince with the onions, garlic, pork fillet and belly pork. Season generously with salt and pepper, then add the sage, mace, cream and eggs. Mix until well combined.

☐ Wash and trim the kidney. Cut into pieces the size of the end of the thumb. Stir gently into the pâté mixture.

☐ Set oven to 325F (160C) gas 3.

☐ Pack the pâté mixture into the lined dish. Wrap the ends of the bacon over the filling. Cover the dish tightly with foil or a lid.

☐ Set in a pan of hot water in the oven and cook for about 2 hours until the juices run clear.

☐ Remove the foil and set the dish on a rack to cool. Pour off the excess juices. Chill for several hours.

☐ Loosen pâté around the sides with a knife. Invert on to a plate, shaking gently to remove.

☐ Serve cut in wedges or slices with garlic bread.

Variation: As an alternative to the kidney, stir cooked, coarsely chopped chestnuts into the pâté before cooking.

✳ *To freeze:* Leave the pâté in the dish and when it is completely cool pour off any excess juices that have collected. Wrap closely in foil and freeze for up to 2 months. To thaw, leave unwrapped in the refrigerator for 24 hours.

Lamb Terrine 'Gérard Pennec'
This is a classic terrine from Provence in which diced meat is marinated in spirit before being mixed into a soft smooth pâté to create an interesting two-textured effect. The principal meat used is lamb and suitable cuts include boned shoulder and leg.

Terrine En Croute
Any of the baked, firm terrines may be enclosed in pastry and re-baked. Terrines made in this way are particularly good to serve with other cold food for a buffet.

Country Pork Pâté
This pâté will keep in the fridge for several days and is excellent for large parties.

Cooking pâtés and terrines
To tell when a pâté is cooked, insert the blade of a sharp knife or metal skewer down into the centre. When the pâté is ready the blade will come out clean, and the juices will run clear, not pink. Save the juices which collect during cooking. They add a delicious flavour to gravies and sauces.

Rashers for wrapping
Streaky bacon adds fat and flavour to a terrine during cooking and can be used as a decoration as well. Leave the rashers to come right over the edge of the dish because they will shrink back during cooking.

Individual pâtés
Recipes for individual pâtés may be found on pages 406-408

Preparing a terrine

Line the bottom and sides of the terrine with strips of streaky bacon.

Spoon the prepared filling into the lined dish.

Cover the dish and place in a pan of hot water in the oven to cook.

Raised Pies

Hinged pie moulds are used to make the so-called 'raised' pies with their characteristic fluting around the deep sides. The purpose of the hinging is not only to make lining with pastry easier, but so that the sides can be removed part way during baking for deeper browning.

Loose-bottomed cake tins can be used very successfully for these pies, too. Lining is done in a different way, but removal of the sides is quite simple. After 1 hour of baking, remove the tin from the oven and loosen the pie around the sides with a knife. Stand the tin on a can of food or similar. The sides of the tin will drop down and can be removed. Return the pie to the oven to finish baking. True raised pies are made by actually raising the pastry up around the outside of a mould. The mould is then removed and the pastry filled with a savoury meat mixture. Traditional fillings include pork and apple, game, lamb or veal and ham.

Hot water crust is the best pastry for making traditional raised pies as it is the simplest to mould and is most suitable for long baking.

Add a teaspoon or so of extra water if necessary to make a pastry which can easily be worked. Keep it well covered when not working with it so it won't dry out, and use it soon after making while it is at its most malleable. If you prefer, you can use your own favourite pastry instead of hot water crust.

Veal and Ham Pie

Serves 8 ☆☆☆
Preparation: 45 minutes
Cooking: about 1¾ hours plus
3 hours chilling

The pastry:
1lb (450g) plain flour
2 teaspoons salt
4oz (125g) lard
about 5 fl oz (150ml) water

The filling:
1½lb (700g) pie veal
8oz (225g) boiling bacon
1oz (25g) onion or shallot
1 large clove garlic
salt and freshly ground black pepper
pinch ground nutmeg
4 tablespoons Veal Stock
3 tablespoons port
1 tablespoon brandy
1 egg, size 2, beaten with 1 tablespoon water for glazing

The jelly:
9 fl oz (275ml) Veal Stock
2 teaspoons powdered gelatine

First make the pastry: Sift the flour and salt into a bowl. Cut the lard into cubes and mix with the water in a saucepan. Heat just until the lard is melted.

☐ Pour over the flour. Mix in well with a wooden spoon. Turn out on to the work surface and knead lightly to a smooth ball. Cover pastry with the bowl and set aside while you make the filling.

☐ For the filling: Cut the veal and the bacon into cubes. Coarsely chop the onions and garlic. Put filling ingredients in a food processor or liquidizer and work to as coarse or fine a mixture as liked. (It may be necessary to process the meat a little at a time.)

☐ Season with salt and pepper, then add the nutmeg, stock, port and brandy. Work briefly to mix evenly.

☐ Set oven to 350F (180C) gas 4.

☐ To shape the pie: Roll about half the pastry at a time and leave the rest covered. Roll to about ¼in (5mm) thick. Cut a piece the size of the base of a pie mould or tin about 7in (18cm) long. Fit neatly into the base, then trim.

☐ Cut 2 bands of pastry the same dimensions as the sides of the mould. Press on to the inside of each side. Brush around the edge of the base with egg glaze. Set the sides in position and secure with the clamps or pins.

☐ Press around the inside of the bottom with the fingers to seal the pastry join.

☐ Brush over the join with egg glaze. (An alternative way to line the tin is to assemble the different parts of the mould or cake tin, if using, and fit the pastry in one piece, pressing down firmly and trimming excess pastry.)

☐ Pack the filling into the lined tin. Brush the pastry edges with egg. Roll the remainder of the pastry and position over the top of the pie. Trim with a knife.

☐ Press around the edge with a fork to seal. Cut a hole in the centre of the pastry lid with the top of a plain forcing pipe. Cut a circle of pastry with the large end of the pipe and remove the centre. Brush with egg and press around the hole.

☐ Brush the top of the pie very lightly with egg and set on a baking tray. Bake for 1 hour. Remove from the oven and remove the sides of the tin.

☐ Brush the pie all over with glaze and bake for another 20 minutes. Glaze again and bake for a further 20-25 minutes until well browned. Cool on a wire rack.

☐ To prepare the jelly: Pour the stock into a saucepan and place on a low heat. Sprinkle the gelatine over the surface and whisk to dissolve. Cool until beginning to set.

☐ Insert a funnel into the hole in the top of the pie. Carefully ladle in the setting jelly. Chill for about 3 hours.

☐ Serve in slices as a first course, or with salad for a light lunch This pie is also very good for picnics.

❋ *To freeze:* Wrap in foil when cool and store in the freezer for up to 2 months. To thaw, leave wrapped in the fridge for 24 hours.

Stages in making a Veal and Ham Pie in a raised mould.

Raising a pie on a jam jar

If you have only one jar of a suitable size, roll only enough pastry to make one shape at a time. Chill to firm. Keep the rest of the pastry covered on the work surface.

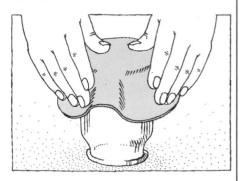

Press the circle of pastry over the upturned jar.

Firmly mould the pastry across the base and down the sides.

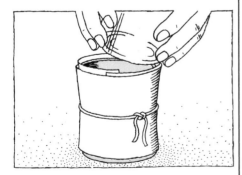

Twist the jar to remove it from the set pastry.

Little Pork Pies

Makes 6 pies   ☆☆
Preparation: 45 minutes
Cooking: about 1¼ hours plus
2 hours chilling

½ × **pastry recipe as Veal and Ham Pie**
1lb (450g) lean pork
2oz (50g) onion
salt and freshly ground black pepper
1 tablespoon leaves of fresh thyme or 1
    teaspoon dried thyme
½ teaspoon ground mace
2 tablespoons Veal Stock
beaten egg for glazing

The jelly:
5 tablespoons Veal Stock
1 tablespoon gelatine

Make the pastry and set aside. Cube pork and onions. Process or liquidize coarsely. Season with salt and pepper, then add thyme and mace. Process or liquidize to a fine paste.

☐ Roll the pastry about ¼in (5mm) thick on a lightly floured board. Cut into 6 circles about 5in (13cm) diameter. Mould each circle over the bottom of an upturned small jar with straight sides. Press into shape. Trim the edges of the pastry to level. Tie a double band of greaseproof paper around each shape to support during baking.

☐ Set on a tray and chill until firm. Roll the remaining pastry and cut circles the size of the tops of the pies. Use the trimmings to make pastry leaves. Lay the lids and leaves on a plate and cover with film to prevent drying. Do not chill.

☐ When pastry shapes are firm, remove jars by twisting gently. Fill pies with prepared filling. Pour a teaspoonful of stock into each.

☐ Set oven to 425F (220C) gas 7.

☐ Brush the edges of the pastry with egg and set the lids in place. Pinch to seal. Glaze the tops and make a hole in the centre of each with the tip of a plain forcing pipe. Decorate with pastry leaves.

☐ Bake for 10 minutes then turn down to 375F (190C) gas 5 for 30 minutes. Remove the paper bands. Glaze the pies all over.

☐ Bake for another 15 minutes. Re-glaze. Bake for a final 10-15 minutes to complete the browning. Cool on a wire rack.

☐ To make jelly: Put stock in a basin with gelatine. Set in a pan of hot water. Whisk to dissolve. Cool until beginning to set. Place tip of a plain forcing pipe in each pie hole in turn and spoon in jelly. Chill for 2 hours to set.

✱ *To freeze:* Wrap in foil when cool and store in the freezer for up to 2 months. To thaw, leave wrapped in the fridge for several hours.

Individual pâtés

It is very convenient to have individual portions of pâtés ready for serving. Soft pâtés and spreads are particularly good and many can be made quickly at the last minute, or stored in the fridge for a few days.

Potted Shellfish Pâté

Serves 6   ☆☆☆
Preparation: 15 minutes plus ½-¾ hour chilling

8oz (225g) crab meat
2oz (50g) shelled prawns
3oz (75g) butter, softened
squeeze of lemon juice
salt and freshly ground black pepper
3 tablespoons double cream
2 tablespoons white vermouth
2oz (50g) clarified butter (optional)
lemon slices and parsley to garnish

Liquidize or process the crab meat and prawns. Add each of the other ingredients in turn and blend to combine well.

☐ Spoon into 6 cocottes. Chill for ½-¾ hour. (If preferred, melt the clarified butter and pour over the top. Refrigerate for up to 2 days.) Garnish with lemon slices and parsley and serve with Melba toast, if liked.

Kipper Pâté

Serves 8   ★★☆
Preparation: 10 minutes plus 1 hour chilling

8oz (225g) kipper fillets, cooked
8oz (225g) unsalted butter, softened
1 egg white from size 2 egg
1 clove garlic, peeled and chopped
grated rind of ½ lime
juice of 1 lime
1 teaspoon finely chopped tarragon
1 tablespoon finely chopped chives
salt and freshly ground black pepper
tarragon leaves and lime peel strips
    to garnish

Remove any skin and bones from kippers. Process kippers with other ingredients to a smooth paste.
☐ Pile into small dishes or one large serving dish. Chill for 1 hour.
☐ Garnish with tarragon leaves and strips of lime peel. Serve with pumpernickel bread.

Duck Confit

Serves 6-8   ★★☆
Preparation: 30 minutes plus
6 hours chilling
Cooking: 2½ hours

---

1 duck, about 4½lb (2kg)
1 onion, peeled and coarsely chopped
1 large sprig fresh rosemary
2 teaspoons salt
strip of thinly pared lemon rind
7 fl oz (200ml) red wine
4 tablespoons raspberry vinegar
1oz (25g) seedless raspberry jelly

Set the oven to 300F (150C) gas 2.
☐ Quarter the duck. Put in an ovenproof pan with all the other ingredients except the jelly. Cover. Cook in the oven for about 2½ hours until very tender.
☐ Strain off juices and fat and set aside. Discard skin and bones. Shred flesh with 2 forks or chop with a knife.
☐ Pack into 6-8 ramekins. Pour the juices into a saucepan with the jelly. Bring to the boil, stirring.

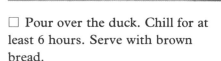

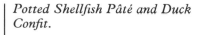

☐ Pour over the duck. Chill for at least 6 hours. Serve with brown bread.

Potted Beef

Serves 4   ★★★
Preparation: 20 minutes plus 1 hour chilling

8oz (225g) fillet steak in one piece
4oz (125g) butter, softened
2oz (50g) onion, peeled and chopped
1 teaspoon green peppercorns
1oz (25g) stoned green olives, chopped
1 teaspoon anchovy paste
2oz (50g) clarified butter, melted
oil for brushing

Brush steak with oil and brown both sides under a hot grill, then cube.
☐ Process or liquidize to a smooth paste with all but the melted butter. Divide between small pots.

☐ Pour the melted butter on top. Chill for 1 hour. Serve with hot toast. (If preferred, refrigerate for 2-3 days.)

Potted Shellfish Pâté and Duck Confit.

Duck Confit
During chilling, some of the fat rises to the top and forms a coating which helps preserve the pâté. This fat can be eaten by those who like rich food or it can be scraped off.
For a less rich pâté, chill the juices so the fat can be separated off before simmering the juices with the jelly.
The confit will keep in the fridge for several days as long as the fat is left on.

Potted Beef
Use rare roast beef in place of fillet if available.

Sardine-stuffed Lemons and Kipper Pâté

Smoked mackerel and smoked eel are good instead of sardines or kippers in these recipes.

Stilton Pâté

Stilton Pâté will keep for several days in the fridge. Packed in attractive jars or pots it makes a pretty gift.

Sardine-stuffed Lemons

Serves 6 ☆☆
Preparation: 30 minutes plus 1 hour chilling

---

3 large lemons
2 × 4½oz (2 × 120g) cans sardines
salt and freshly ground black pepper
2 teaspoons grated horseradish
5 tablespoons white wine
2 teaspoons powdered gelatine
5 tablespoons double cream
lettuce leaves, parsley or chervil to
    decorate

Cut lemons in half lengthways. Cut out flesh. Reserve a few segments and squeeze remainder.

☐ Drain sardines. Mash well with seasoning and horseradish to taste. Add lemon juice.

☐ Put wine and gelatine in a small basin. Set in a saucepan of hot water. Whisk to dissolve the gelatine. Cool.

☐ Mix well into sardines. Stir in cream. Pile into lemon shells. Chill for 1 hour.

☐ Garnish with reserved lemon segments, lettuce leaves and sprigs of fresh parsley or chervil. Serve with brown bread and butter.

Sardine-stuffed Lemons.

Stilton Pâté

Serves 8 ☆☆☆
Preparation: 10 minutes plus 1 hour chilling

8oz (225g) blue Stilton cheese
8oz (225g) cream cheese
2oz (50g) crème fraîche
2oz (50g) butter, softened
½ teaspoon ground nutmeg
4-5 tablespoons dry white vermouth
watercress to garnish

Process or liquidize the cheeses, crème and butter together to a smooth paste. Add the nutmeg and vermouth to taste. Mix in to combine the ingredients well.

☐ Spoon into small pots. Chill for 1 hour. Garnish with watercress and serve with rye or other coarse brown bread cut in chunks.

Variation: Instead of the Stilton use Roquefort or Gorgonzola.

Turkey Liver Pâté

Serves 8 ☆☆
Preparation: 30 minutes plus 1 hour chilling

1oz (25g) butter
2oz (50g) onion, chopped
1 large clove garlic, chopped
1lb (450g) turkey livers
4oz (125g) cream cheese
3 tablespoons whisky
salt and freshly ground black pepper
pinch ground allspice

Put the butter, onions and garlic in a frying pan on a low heat. Cook with occasional stirring for 10 minutes to soften the onions.

☐ Wash the livers in cold water. Blot dry. Chop roughly and add to the pan. Cook, stirring, for 5-7 minutes. Do not overcook.

☐ Liquidize or process to a smooth paste. Add the cheese and whisky and work until well mixed. Season to taste and add allspice.

☐ Turn into 8 small dishes. Chill for 1 hour. Serve with crisp biscuits or toast.

Working with gelatine

Working with gelatine offers endless opportunities for creativity in both sweet and savoury dishes. Over the years it has been used by great chefs for elaborate and extravagant dishes, yet it is equally useful for making a wide variety of simple and everyday recipes, including moulded shapes, mousses, pâtés, whips, and cold soufflés as well as cold soups and clear glazes.

What gelatine is
Gelatine is a protein food refined from the connective tissue of animals. At one time it was almost exclusively available in sheets, or 'leaves', but now it usually comes in powdered form. It may be sold in sachets with sufficient to set 1 pint (600ml) liquid, or loose in cartons and bags.

How to use it
You must first dissolve gelatine in hot liquid. After cooling, it will begin to thicken and eventually set as a firm pale straw-coloured jelly. Because it is almost odourless and tasteless, it is ideal as a base for other flavours and colours.

Principles of gelatine cookery
● Firstly, remember gelatine is not actually 'cooked', as this would only toughen it. It is only necessary to dissolve it.
● Secondly, dissolved gelatine must be given time to cool before it can begin to set. The setting time depends on the amount used, and how it is chilled.
● Thirdly, gelatine dishes will melt and return to their liquid state if allowed to become warm. It is important to keep all gelatine recipes chilled until served.

Tips for using gelatine
● If you are using gelatine, use standard measuring spoons and be sure they are dry. Gelatine absorbs liquid and quickly becomes sticky. Always use standard measuring jugs.
● Some raw fruits such as pineapple and kiwi fruit contain an enzyme which prevents the setting of gelatine. If you use these fruits, cook them first, or use canned ones.
● When adding dissolved gelatine to another mixture, make sure that both the gelatine and the mixture are at the same temperature. If the temperature of dissolved gelatine is reduced too quickly it can form into beads in the dish.
● To make a well-blended mixture for dishes such as mousses and soufflés, let the dissolved gelatine begin to set before folding in the whisked egg or cream.

Moulds to use
Gelatine recipes can be set in dishes or glasses from which they are to be served. But if you wish to turn them out, use metal moulds, bowls or cake tins for the easiest removal. Plastic is sometimes suitable if it is flexible enough to be pulled away from the food for unmoulding. Glass, porcelain and earthenware are not satisfactory for plain jellies but can be used for mousse-type dishes.
To determine the capacity of moulds, fill them with water then measure the volume of the water.

❄ Freezing
Clear gelatine dishes are not suitable for freezing as they become granular, cloudy and do not freeze evenly. However, the creamy mixtures for mousses, soufflés and cheesecakes as well as savoury mixtures can be frozen as the effects mentioned will be masked.

Alternatives
When a very small quantity of liquid is used, put the cold liquid into a bowl and add the gelatine. Place the bowl in a pan of hot water on a low heat and stir until dissolved. Alternatively, put the cold liquid into a saucepan on a low heat and sprinkle the gelatine over the surface. Whisk until completely dissolved. Do not allow to boil.

Get set
To make jelly set more quickly, stand the filled mould in a bowl of ice.

Dissolving gelatine
This is not as difficult as you may have imagined. Measure the hot liquid in a jug and sprinkle the gelatine over the surface. Stir or whisk with a fork to dissolve the gelatine completely.

To turn out mousse-type moulds

Break the set mould away around the edges of the container with the finger. Gently pull the whole mould back to loosen underneath. Invert on to a serving plate and shake to release.

Decorated moulds

The base of the mould can be decorated with sliced olives or strips of cucumber rind if liked. Spread a thin layer of clear jelly on the bottom then place the decoration in it. Allow to set before filling with main mixture. When the main mixture is set, wipe the outside of the mould with a cloth wrung out in hot water then proceed as above. If the mould does not come out immediately, continue to wipe with the hot cloth. Because there is only a thin layer of jelly holding the decoration, it will melt very quickly so care must be taken in turning out such moulds.

Savoury gelatine dishes

Gelatine is used in a wide range of savoury dishes, both for its qualities as a setting agent for holding small pieces of food together, and because it makes an attractive, clear glaze for meat, fish and poultry. This is a particular advantage in preparing dishes for a buffet, as the glaze will not only look very decorative, but also it will keep the food from drying out. Savoury gelatine dishes must always be prepared well in advance to allow for setting time. Serving itself is then very easy, as these dishes require little or no last-minute attention. Many savoury gelatine dishes can be frozen, too, for even greater convenience.

Foods to use

Fresh, frozen or canned foods can be used but, with the exception of cheese, fresh and frozen foods are usually cooked first. They are then mashed, sieved, puréed or chopped before mixing with the dissolved gelatine. Interesting and economical dishes can be made with cheese, eggs, and vegetables, and more expensive dishes can include fish and shellfish, poultry or meat. The liquid used to dissolve the gelatine can be wine, cider, fruit juice, stock, canned soup or milk. Mayonnaise, yogurt and soured cream make good additions to flavour and texture. Herbs, too, are equally important for colour, flavour and variation.

Salmon Mousse

Serves 4-6
Preparation: 20 minutes
Setting: about 4 hours

¼ **pint (150ml) white wine or Fish Stock**
1 sachet powdered gelatine
4oz (125g) smoked, fresh cooked or canned drained salmon
3 tablespoons mayonnaise
4oz (125g) low-fat soft cheese
3 fl oz (100ml) double cream
salt and freshly ground black pepper
1 tablespoon lemon juice

To garnish:
parsley sprigs
lemon twists
cucumber slices

Put wine or stock in a saucepan on a low heat. Sprinkle the gelatine over the surface and whisk to dissolve completely. Do not allow to boil. Cool until beginning to thicken.
☐ Liquidize or process the salmon to make a purée. Mix in the mayonnaise, cheese and double cream.
☐ Season to taste with salt and pepper and lemon juice. Stir in the gelatine.
☐ Put into a 1 pint (600ml) fish mould or equivalent. Chill for about 4 hours to set.
☐ Turn out on to a serving dish. If liked, make an 'eye' for the fish with a slice of stuffed olive. Then garnish with parsley, lemon twists and cucumber slices and serve with brown bread and butter or toast as a first course or with salad as a light lunch or supper dish.

Salmon Mousse makes a good first course, or a light lunch or supper dish.

Vegetable dishes with gelatine

Vegetables set in stock thickened with gelatine make particularly attractive dishes. They may be used on their own or with cheese or egg. Many nutritious and appetizing dishes can be made quite economically with canned, fresh or frozen vegetables.

For more flavour, use the vegetable cooking water, white wine, cider or light stock to dissolve the gelatine. To make the stock clearer, strain it through a coffee filter before use.

Vegetable Medley Flan

Serves 8-10 ☆ ☆ ☆
Preparation: 45 minutes
Setting: about 2 hours

10in (25cm) pastry case, baked

The filling:
½ pint (300ml) Chicken Stock
1 sachet powdered gelatine
1oz (25g) spring onions, finely chopped
1 tablespoon finely chopped parsley
1 tablespoon chopped mustard and cress
12oz (350g) cream cheese

The topping:
12oz (350g) cooked vegetables, such as peas, carrots and French beans
18 fl oz (500ml) clarified Chicken or Vegetable Stock
1 sachet powdered gelatine

First make the filling: Put the stock into a saucepan on a low heat. Sprinkle the gelatine over the surface and whisk to dissolve completely. Do not allow to boil. Cool until beginning to thicken.

☐ Put the onions, parsley, mustard and cress, and cheese into a bowl and beat well together. Gradually beat in the thickening jelly. Spoon into the pastry case.

☐ Chill for about an hour to set.

☐ To decorate: Prepare and cool the vegetables. Use the stock to dissolve the gelatine in the same way as for the filling. Cool until beginning to thicken.

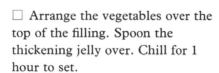

☐ Arrange the vegetables over the top of the filling. Spoon the thickening jelly over. Chill for 1 hour to set.

☐ Serve within 3 hours, cut in wedges, accompanied by salad.

Glazing foods with gelatine

A glaze of gelatine mixed with stock can turn the most ordinary portions and cutlets of fish, poultry or meat into very glamorous dishes.

It is important to use a good clarified stock, although canned consommés can be used. Stock cubes do not make very good stock for glazing because they are cloudy when made up.

Glazed Lamb Cutlets

Serves 4 ☆ ☆
Preparation: 50 minutes
Setting: about 1 hour

8 lamb cutlets, trimmed of fat
¼ pint (150ml) clarified Basic Brown Stock
a sprig of fresh mint
¼ pint (150ml) white wine
1 sachet powdered gelatine

This beautifully arranged Vegetable Medley Flan makes an impressive summer-time dish.

The decoration:
1 canned red pepper or tomato, cut in strips
a few fresh mint leaves

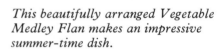

Grill or fry the cutlets. Blot with kitchen paper to remove as much fat as possible. Cool.

☐ Put the stock into a saucepan with the mint on a low heat. Simmer for 30 minutes to extract the mint flavour. Remove the mint.

☐ Sprinkle the gelatine over the surface of the stock. Whisk to dissolve completely. Do not allow to boil.

☐ Remove from the heat and stir in the wine. Cool until beginning to thicken.

☐ Arrange the chops on a serving dish. Decorate with strips of red pepper or tomato and mint leaves. Carefully spoon a little of the glaze over each chop. Chill for a few minutes. Spoon the rest of the glaze over the chops and the dish.

☐ Chill for about 1 hour to set. Serve accompanied by a salad.

To unmould plain jellies

Break the jelly away from the sides of the mould with a finger.

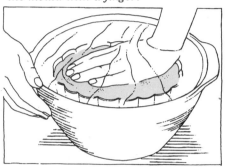

With one hand over top, and one under the mould, slide through tepid water.

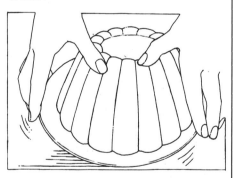

Invert a plate over the mould then turn upside down. Shake gently to loosen and remove mould.

Moulded jellies

To tell when the jelly is ready to turn out use these tests: Gently tip the mould sideways. The jelly should not sag but should stay level. You can also gently draw the bowl of a spoon over the jelly. The spoon should not stick at all.

You can make a variety of attractive and simple desserts by setting fruit juices, milk, coffee, etc. with gelatine. For quicker setting, put the mixture into glasses, individual moulds or dishes.

Citrus Fruit Jelly

Serves 6-8 ◯
Preparation: 10 minutes plus 1½ hours chilling
Setting: 6-8 hours

The grapefruit layer:
14 fl oz (396ml) canned grapefruit juice
1-2 tablespoons caster sugar
1 sachet powdered gelatine

The orange layer:
2 pints (1 litre) orange juice
2 tablespoons caster sugar
2 sachets powdered gelatine

To serve:
thick cream or custard

Put the grapefruit juice into a saucepan on a low heat. Add sugar to taste and stir to dissolve.
☐ Sprinkle the sachet of gelatine over the surface. Whisk to dissolve completely. Do not boil.
☐ Pour into a 2¼-2½ pint (1.25-1.4 litre) metal mould. Cool and chill for about 1½ hours until set on top.
☐ Meanwhile make the orange layer in the same way. Cool. Spoon on top of the grapefruit layer.
☐ Chill in the fridge for 6-8 hours until set firmly. Turn out on to a serving dish. Serve with thick cream or custard, if liked.

Banana Milk Jelly

Serves 3-4 ◯
Preparation: 5 minutes
Setting: 5-6 hours

---

18 fl oz (500ml) bottle of banana flavoured milk
1 sachet powdered gelatine

Put the milk into a saucepan on a low heat. Sprinkle the gelatine over the surface. Whisk to dissolve completely. Do not boil.
☐ Turn into a 1 pint (600ml) metal mould. Cool and chill for 5-6 hours until set firmly.
☐ Turn the jelly out on to a serving dish. Serve with sliced bananas.
Tip: Use strawberry or chocolate flavoured milk in the same way.

Gaelic Coffee Jelly

Serves 4 ☆☆
Preparation: 15 minutes plus chilling
Setting: about 2 hours

---

18 fl oz (500ml) strong coffee
2oz (50g) soft brown sugar
1 sachet powdered gelatine
4 tablespoons whisky
3 fl oz (100ml) double cream whipped, to serve

Put the coffee and sugar into a saucepan on a low heat. Stir to dissolve the sugar.

☐ Sprinkle the gelatine over the surface. Whisk to dissolve completely. Do not boil.

☐ Remove from the heat. Stir in the whisky. Cool.

☐ Pour ¾ of the mixture into 4 glasses. Chill for about 1 hour until set on top.

☐ Put the rest of the jelly mixture into a bowl. Chill in the fridge, whisking occasionally to form a thick froth.

☐ Spoon the foam on top of the plain jelly. Chill for 1 hour to set completely.

☐ Serve with a spoonful of whipped cream on each dessert.

Grape Mould

Serves 4
Preparation: 10 minutes plus chilling
Chilling: 6-7 hours

---

1 pint (600ml) red grape juice
2oz (50g) caster sugar
4 teaspoons powdered gelatine
6oz (175g) black grapes

Put the grape juice and sugar into a saucepan on a low heat. Sprinkle the gelatine over the surface. Whisk to dissolve. Do not boil.

☐ Cool and chill until mixture begins to thicken.

☐ Cut the grapes in half and remove the pips. Put into a bowl and pour the thickening jelly over. Stir gently.

☐ Pour into a 1¼ pint (750ml) metal mould. Chill for 6-7 hours until completely set. Turn out on to a serving dish. Serve with thick cream or custard, if liked.

Variation: Make a striped jelly with a white grape juice layer alternating with the red. Allow each layer to set before commencing with the next.

Tip: If you wedge the container at an angle while it is setting you can create a diagonal striped jelly.

Cheesecakes

Uncooked cheesecakes are made by setting curd, cottage or cream cheese with gelatine. Flavour may be added in the form of fruit purée, fruit juice, coffee or chocolate. The mixture can be very simple, or made richer with eggs and cream. Try some of the low-fat cheeses if you want to keep the calories down: cottage, ricotta or quark are good. Yogurt has a distinctive flavour and may be used in place of cream. For a base, sponge cake is an interesting alternative to the more usual biscuit crumbs.

Fruit Salad Cheesecake

Serves 4-6   ☆☆☆
Preparation: 15 minutes plus chilling
Setting: 3 hours

The filling:
grated rind and juice 2 oranges
1 sachet powdered gelatine
8oz (225g) full-fat soft cheese
5.3oz (150g) natural yogurt
2oz (50g) caster sugar

The crumb mixture:
4oz (125g) gingernut biscuit crumbs
2oz (50g) demerara sugar
1oz (25g) butter, melted

To serve:
3 bananas, peeled and sliced
2 tablespoons lemon juice
3 kiwi fruit, peeled and sliced
¼ pint (150ml) double cream, whipped

First make the filling: Put the rind and orange juice into a saucepan on a low heat. Sprinkle the gelatine over the surface and whisk to dissolve completely. Do not boil. Cool until beginning to thicken.

☐ Whisk together the cheese, yogurt, and sugar. Whisk in the gelatine mixture. Turn into a deep 8in (20cm) sandwich tin. Chill for 1 hour.

☐ Meanwhile make the crumb mixture: Mix together the crumbs, demerara sugar and melted butter. Press on top of the filling. Chill for 3 hours.

☐ Turn out on to a serving plate. Decorate with sliced banana (dipped in lemon juice), kiwi fruit and whipped cream.

To remove cheesecakes from their tins

Break filling away around the edges by pressing gently with the tip of a sharp knife between the filling and the tin.

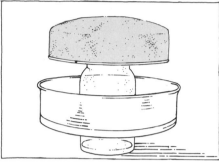

With a loose-bottomed tin, set on top of a jam jar and ease sides down.

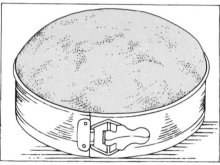

With a spring-form tin, release the clip on the side and carefully lift the sides upwards.

With a deep sandwich tin, invert directly on to a serving plate. Shake gently to release. The crumb mixture will now be on the base.

Praline Cheesecake

Serves 6

Preparation: 45 minutes
Setting: about 4 hours

The base:
4oz (100g) rich tea biscuits
2oz (50g) butter, melted
butter for greasing

The praline:
1oz (25g) blanched almonds
1oz (25g) caster sugar

The filling:
12oz (350g) cream cheese
2oz (50g) caster sugar
½ teaspoon vanilla essence
4 tablespoons water
1 sachet powdered gelatine
¼ pint (150ml) double cream
3 egg whites, from size 2 eggs

Put the biscuits into a polythene bag. Crush to fine crumbs with a rolling pin. Mix with the melted butter.
□ Press firmly into the bottom of an 8in (20cm) diameter loose-bottomed or spring-form cake tin. Chill.
□ Make the praline: Put the almonds and sugar into a small frying pan. Set on a moderate heat to melt the sugar. Stir until lightly browned. Turn out on to a buttered tray and leave to cool.
□ Break into chunks with a rolling pin. Put into a plastic bag and crush coarsely with the pin. Set aside.
□ Make the filling: Beat together the cheese, sugar and essence in a large bowl. Put the water and gelatine into a small bowl and set in a pan of hot water on a low heat. Stir to dissolve completely. Cool.
□ Stir a little of the filling into the gelatine. Pour filling mixture back into the bowl and beat well.
□ Whip the cream to soft peaks. Fold into the cheese. Whisk the egg whites to make soft peaks. Fold into the filling.
□ Spread the filling over the crumb base. Chill for about 4 hours to set. Sprinkle with the praline and serve.
Tip: Keep praline in a screw-top jar in a cool place.

Blackcurrant Cheesecake

Serves 4-6

Preparation: 15 minutes
Setting: 4 hours

8oz (225g) blackcurrants
2oz (50g) caster sugar
4 tablespoons water
1 sachet powdered gelatine
4oz (100g) low-fat soft cheese
one layer sponge cake about 7½ × 1in (19 × 2.5cm)
3oz (75g) blackcurrant jam

To finish:
¼ pint (150ml) double cream, lightly whipped

Put the blackcurrants, sugar and water into a saucepan on a moderate heat. Simmer for 5 minutes. Cool.
□ Liquidize or process fruit to a purée. Return to the saucepan. Sprinkle the gelatine over the surface and whisk to dissolve. Do not allow to boil.
□ Beat the cheese with the purée. Turn into a sandwich tin the same size as the cake. Chill for about 4 hours.
□ Spread the cake with jam. Turn the set filling out on top of the cake, and decorate with whipped cream before serving.

Mousses and cold soufflés

Delicious desserts with a soft foamy texture are made by folding whisked egg whites and whipped cream into gelatine when it's beginning to set. You can use fresh, frozen or canned fruits, citrus fruit juices, coffee or chocolate for these desserts. Adapt a basic recipe by replacing the same amount of liquid or purée with other flavourings of your choice.
✳Recipes of this nature can usually be frozen. Freeze in the mould and thaw for 8-10 hours depending on size. If preferred remove from mould on to a cakeboard, cover with foil and freeze.

Strawberry Soufflé

Serves 6-8 ☆☆☆
Preparation: 45 minutes plus
overnight macerating
Setting: 5-6 hours

1lb (450g) strawberries
4oz (100g) caster sugar
7 fl oz (200ml) red wine
3 tablespoons white rum
2 sachets powdered gelatine
½ pint (300ml) double cream
2 egg whites from size 2 eggs

Prepare a 5in (13cm) diameter
soufflé dish as illustrated.

☐ Set aside 3 of the best
strawberries for decoration. Hull
and slice the rest and put in a dish
and sprinkle with 3oz (75g) of the
sugar. Cover and leave overnight.

☐ Put the wine into a saucepan on a
low heat. Sprinkle the gelatine over
the surface. Whisk to dissolve
completely. Do not boil.

☐ Coarsely chop the strawberries
with their juices and the rum in a
liquidizer or food processor. Mix in
the liquid gelatine mixture. Cool
until beginning to thicken.

☐ Whip the cream to soft peaks.
Whisk the egg whites until opaque.
Add the remaining sugar. Whisk to
form a soft meringue.

☐ Fold first the cream, then the
meringue into the fruit.

☐ Turn into the prepared dish.

Chill for 5-6 hours to set. Carefully
remove the paper collar.

☐ Cut the reserved berries in half
and use to decorate the soufflé.

Variation: If liked, you can pipe
extra whipped cream on top of the
soufflé and decorate with the fruit.

Chocolate Mousse

Serves 6 ☆☆
Preparation: 30 minutes
Setting: about 2 hours

---

3 fl oz (100ml) chocolate flavoured milk
1 sachet powdered gelatine
1 tablespoon cocoa
1 teaspoon vanilla essence
2oz (50g) caster sugar
¼ pint (150ml) double cream
2 egg whites from size 2 eggs

To serve:
pouring cream or Quick Chocolate Sauce

Put the milk and the gelatine in a
bowl. Set over a pan of hot water on
a low heat. Stir to dissolve the
gelatine completely.

☐ Add the cocoa, vanilla and sugar.
Stir until well mixed and the sugar
is dissolved. Remove from the heat
and cool until beginning to thicken.

☐ Whip the cream to soft peaks.
Fold in the chocolate mixture.

☐ Whisk the egg whites to form soft
peaks. Fold into chocolate mixture.

☐ Divide among 6 glasses. Chill for
about 2 hours. Serve with cream.

Preparing a soufflé mould

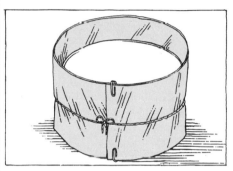

*Encircle a straight-sided soufflé dish
with a double thickness of greaseproof
paper, allowing 2-3in (5-7.5cm) collar
above the edge.*

*Secure the paper with paper clips and
tie around with string.*

*To remove the paper, undo the clips
and string. Use a knife dipped in hot
water to help in peeling the paper
away.*

*Strawberry Soufflé is a very
handsome dessert for special occasions.*

Strawberry Sandwich

Serves 8-10
Preparation: 45 minutes
Setting: 3 hours

---

2 sponge flan cases about 10½in (26cm)
   diameter

The filling:
12oz (350g) strawberries
4oz (100g) caster sugar
¼ pint (150ml) red wine
1 sachet powdered gelatine
1 egg white from size 2 egg
3 fl oz (100ml) double cream

The icing:
1¼lb (575g) icing sugar
about 3 fl oz (100ml) water
few drops red colouring

To finish:
1 teaspoon powdered gelatine
1 teaspoon sugar
3 tablespoons water
3 fl oz (100ml) double cream, whipped
4oz (125g) strawberries

First make the filling: Liquidize or process the fruit with 3oz (75g) of the sugar. Put the wine into a saucepan on a low heat. Sprinkle the gelatine over the surface and whisk to dissolve completely. Do not boil.
☐ Gradually whisk the fruit purée into the gelatine. Cool until beginning to thicken.
☐ Whisk the egg white until opaque. Add the remaining sugar and whisk to form a soft meringue.
☐ Whip the cream to soft peaks. Fold into the fruit purée then fold in the meringue. Spoon into the flan cases and leave in a cool place for 2 hours to set.
☐ Make the icing: Put the icing sugar into a bowl. Gradually stir in water until the icing coats the back of a spoon thickly. Tint pale pink with food colouring.
☐ To finish: Invert one filled sponge on to the other. Set on a wire rack. Spread the icing over the top and sides. Leave to dry for about 1 hour.
☐ Meanwhile put the gelatine, sugar, and water into a small basin. Set over a pan of hot water on a low

heat. Stir to dissolve the gelatine and sugar. Cool until mixture begins to thicken.
☐ Slice the strawberries from top to bottom. Dip one slice at a time into the gelatine then press around the sides of the cake. Pipe cream on top and decorate with strawberries.
☐ Serve as a dessert cut in slices.
Variation: Raspberries may be substituted for the strawberries in the filling mixture.

Strawberry Cakes

Makes: 18 cakes   ☆☆
Preparation: 20 minutes
Setting: 1 hour

---

18 individual sponge flan cases
filling recipe as for Strawberry Sandwich
¼ pint (150ml) double cream, whipped
4oz (125g) strawberries for decoration

Divide the filling mixture between the flan cases. Chill for 1 hour to set.
☐ Put the cream into a forcing bag fitted with a ¼in (5mm) rose pipe. Decorate the cakes with cream and strawberries and chill until required.
Variation: For Strawberry Mousse, spoon the filling mixture into 4 glasses, decorate with cream and strawberries and chill for 1 hour.
Tip: If you do not want to fill that many sponge cases you can freeze the remaining strawberry filling. Spoon into individual dishes or one large dish. If you reserve yogurt or cream cartons and their lids these would be ideal for taking on picnics.

Strawberry Sandwich, Strawberry Cakes and Strawberry Mousse can all be made from the same filling mixture.

Cooking with eggs

No other single food contributes so much to cooking as the egg. When heated egg proteins coagulate to hold a shape, or to help bind other food together. This setting property makes them especially useful in many sauces, cakes, coatings for fried foods, croquettes and in numerous other egg dishes. Eggs can be whisked to take in air and give a puffy texture and impressive volume to omelettes, meringues, soufflés, mousses and cakes. They can also form an emulsion with oil or butter to make some of the great sauces.

How to cook eggs

Eggs can be cooked by all cookery methods – boiling, poaching, frying, baking and even grilling. Their nature will change according to the method chosen.

Eggs are very sensitive to temperature and require relatively little heat for a very short time in order to set. Keep the temperature low for most dishes, or cook the egg dish in a water bath in the oven or over hot water on top of the stove.

Boiling
● Eggs straight from the fridge will crack if put into boiling water so bring them to room temperature for about 20 minutes first. Alternatively, start them in cold water. For boiling times of different egg sizes see page 37.

● If you want to shell the eggs cleanly immediately they are cooked, cool them quickly under running water.

● For uniform cooking, use a large enough pan to allow circulation of the water. Put eggs in a chip basket and lower into the water so all have the same cooking time.

Poaching
● Put boiling water into a frying pan to a depth of 2in (5cm).

Reduce the heat to barely bubbling, then add the eggs. For poaching times see page 53.

Frying
● Use just enough fat to cover the base of the frying pan. Heat until little wavelets show or butter begins to colour. Add the eggs. Cook on low heat to set. Serve basted with the fat, if liked.

● Omelettes: Whisk the eggs lightly. Cook in very hot butter until brown and slightly chewy on the outside, tender and almost runny inside.

● Scrambled eggs: Whisk eggs and cook in butter, stirring, on a low heat.

Baking
● Heat ramekins and the cream or butter being used then add the eggs. Cook in a pan of water in the oven.

The language of eggs

Oeufs au beurre noir – fried eggs with a sauce made by browning the cooking butter and flavouring with vinegar.

Oeufs mollets – soft-boiled eggs garnished in various ways.

Oeufs mornay – hard-boiled eggs topped with a cheese sauce and grated cheese before being browned under the grill.

Oeufs en gelée – soft-boiled eggs set in aspic.

Oeufs brouillés à la forestière – scrambled eggs with chopped mushrooms and bacon.

Oeufs Florentine – poached eggs on a bed of cooked spinach with a hot cheese sauce poured over.

Oeufs sur le plat Bercy – eggs baked in shallow dishes in the oven and served with a tomato sauce and grilled sausages.

Ingredients for making crêpes.

Storing boiled eggs

If you keep soft-boiled eggs in water they will keep their shape better for when you want to serve them.

❄ Freezing

Whole boiled eggs should not be frozen because it makes them tough. If they are finely mashed or sieved, they will freeze satisfactorily.

Oeufs Mollets à l'Indienne

You can prepare all the parts of this dish in advance so that when required it can be assembled in a very few minutes. It is best not to leave mayonnaise open to the air for more than a few minutes because a skin forms on top.

A simple and attractive alternative to this recipe is to coat the eggs with plain mayonnaise and garnish with lumpfish roe.

When baking eggs in the oven, you can cover them or not depending on taste. If you prefer the yolks bright and unclouded, do not cover.

Oeufs Brouillés

If you have a spirit lamp, you can cook the eggs at the table. That way they are served at exactly the right moment without the risk of over-heating and becoming dry.

Oeufs sur le Plat au Mais

In place of the sweetcorn, substitute sliced onions cooked in butter until tender. The dish then becomes Oeufs sur le Plat Soubise.

Oeufs Mollets à l'Indienne

Serves 5

Preparation and cooking: about 20 minutes

5oz (150g) long grain rice
salt
5 eggs, size 2, at room temperature
1 × Curry Mayonnaise
few strips canned red pepper
large bunch watercress

First cook the rice in plenty of salted boiling water until tender (about 12 minutes). Drain and leave to cool completely.

☐ Meanwhile, put the eggs into a chip basket. Lower into a large saucepan of boiling water. Simmer for 6 minutes, stirring gently for the first minute to centre the yolks.

☐ Remove the basket and plunge it into a sink of cold water. Keep running cold water over the eggs until they are completely cold.

☐ Gently crack the shells by tapping them on the work surface. Carefully peel away the shells and the membrane.

☐ To assemble: Arrange the rice on a serving dish. Set the eggs on top. Coat with the mayonnaise and garnish with the strips of red pepper

and the watercress.

Tip: If preparing the dish in advance, store the shelled eggs, covered, in a bowl of cold water. Keep in the fridge for up to 24 hours.

Tarragon Eggs

Serves 4

Preparation and cooking: about 30 minutes

---

4 eggs, size 2
6oz (175g) long grain rice

The mushroom sauce:
12oz (350g) button mushrooms
3oz (75g) butter
2 cloves garlic, finely chopped
2 teaspoons finely chopped tarragon
½ pint (300ml) double cream
squeeze of lemon juice
salt and pepper
2 tablespoons brandy

Cook the eggs in the same way as for Oeufs Mollets à l'Indienne but simmer them for 12 minutes. Meanwhile, cook the rice.

☐ Set the oven to its lowest setting.

☐ Shell the eggs and cut in half lengthways.

☐ Drain the rice and put it in an ovenproof dish. Arrange the eggs on top, cut side down. Cover closely and keep warm in the oven while you make the sauce.

☐ Wipe or wash the mushrooms and blot dry. Trim the stems level with the caps. Leave whole or slice if preferred.

☐ Melt the butter in a large frying pan on a low heat. Add the mushrooms, garlic and tarragon. Cook gently, stirring, for about 5 minutes to soften the mushrooms. Stir in the cream and simmer for about 5 minutes. Season to taste with lemon juice, salt and pepper and stir in the brandy.

☐ Spoon over the eggs and rice. Serve immediately as a light lunch or supper dish.

Oeufs Mollets a l'Indienne

Scrambled Eggs with Mushrooms

Serves 4 ☆☆☆
Preparation: 15 minutes
Cooking: about 5 minutes

4 rounds fresh bread, 3in (7.5cm) diameter
5oz (150g) butter, softened
4 flat mushrooms the same size or slightly
    larger than the bread
4 eggs, size 2
2 tablespoons single cream
salt and pepper

Heat the oven to 300F (150C) gas 2.
☐ Prepare the croûtons first: Spread the bread on one side with a little of the butter. Put a little more butter in a frying pan on a moderate heat.
☐ When the butter begins to turn brown add the bread, plain side down. Fry for a minute or so to brown lightly. Turn the bread and fry the buttered side.
☐ Remove to a serving dish and keep warm in the oven. Put about 1oz (25g) of the butter into the pan on the heat.
☐ Wipe and trim the mushrooms. Add them to the frying pan when the butter begins to brown. Cook the mushrooms gently for about 5 minutes, turning, until tender.
☐ Set one mushroom on top of each round of fried bread and keep warm.
☐ Just before serving, cook the eggs. Melt the remaining 2oz (50g) butter in a sauteuse or similar pan of about 8in (20cm) diameter, on a low heat.
☐ Whisk together the eggs, cream, and a little salt and pepper. Strain into the pan. Stir until the egg begins to form into thick clumps or flakes.
☐ Remove croûtons from oven and spoon a portion of scrambled egg on to each mushroom. Serve immediately.
Variation: Add 2oz (50g) shelled prawns and 1 tablespoon fresh chopped chervil to the pan before scrambling the eggs. Serve with fresh wholemeal bread.

Scrambled Eggs with Mushrooms.

Oeufs sur le Plat au Mais

Serves 4 ☆☆
Preparation: 10 minutes
Cooking: 15 minutes

10oz (283g) can cream-style sweetcorn
¼ pint (150ml) single cream
ground mace
salt and pepper
butter for greasing
4 eggs
1oz (25g) grated cheese

Mix together the corn and cream. Season with mace and salt and pepper. Put mixture in a buttered gratin dish or similar about 10in (25cm) diameter. Place in the oven and turn the setting to 350F (180C) gas 4.
☐ When the oven has reached the right temperature, remove the dish. Make 4 little wells in the corn with the back of a spoon. Break one egg into each well.
☐ Season the eggs with pepper. Return the dish to the oven. Bake for about 10 minutes until the eggs are cooked to taste.
☐ Remove dish from the oven and sprinkle with cheese. Serve immediately.

Oeufs en Cocotte à la Crème

Serves 4 ☆☆☆
Preparation and cooking: about 25 minutes

¼ pint (150ml) double cream
4 eggs, size 2
1oz (25g) butter
salt and pepper

Divide the cream among 4 cocotte dishes. Set in a meat tin and add a little water. Place in the oven and set to 350F (180C) gas 4.
☐ When the oven has reached the right temperature, remove the tin and break an egg into the hot cream in each dish. Dot with butter and season with salt and pepper.
☐ Add more water to the meat tin to come about half way up the dishes. Return to the oven and bake for about 10 minutes until the eggs are set.
☐ Remove the cocottes from the pan and wipe dry. Serve immediately with freshly cooked vegetables or a salad.

✳ **To freeze Smoked Salmon Roll**

Set the filled roulade on a tray. Freeze until firm. Remove from the tray and wrap closely in foil. Store in the freezer for up to 1 month. To thaw, leave in the wrapping at room temperature for about 1½ hours.

Rolling roulades

Trim the edges so the roulade will roll without breaking. Use the greaseproof paper as a cradle to rock back and forth to make a neat roll. If you want to leave the roulade unfilled and fill it later, roll the roulade with the paper inside. Later simply unroll the paper, add filling and re-roll.

Roulades and Soufflés

Roulades and soufflés are related, but are treated differently so that each takes on its own distinctive form. Both are made by folding whisked egg whites into a sauce or purée. The roulade is baked in a shallow tin and is then rolled up like a Swiss Roll. The conventional soufflé is baked in a straight-sided dish above which it rises in a puffy crown. Both roulades and soufflés may be sweet or savoury. One of the useful features of a roulade is that it can be made well in advance. Some freeze quite successfully so they can be made when you have a free moment and kept ready for assembly as a first course, a light supper dish or a rich and delicious dessert. Prepare the baking tin before starting. Grease a Swiss Roll tin well then line with greaseproof paper. Cut diagonally into the four corners of the papers. This enables you to bend the paper into the corners. Grease again. For savoury roulades, dust with flour.

Turkey and Vegetable Roulade

Serves 4 ☆☆☆
Preparation and cooking: 1 hour

The roulade:
2oz (50g) butter
2oz (50g) flour
½ pint (300ml) milk
6oz (175g) mature Cheddar or Red Leicester cheese, grated
3 eggs, size 3, separated
¾ teaspoon dried mixed herbs
salt and pepper
12oz (350g) mixed cooked vegetables (potatoes, carrots, sprouts)
oil for greasing

The filling:
grated rind and juice of ½ lemon
6oz (175g) cooked turkey meat, chopped
2oz (50g) ham, chopped
3½oz (100g) mushrooms, sliced
1 tablespoon chopped parsley or chives
tomato and spring onions to garnish

Grease and line a Swiss Roll tin 9in × 13in (23cm × 33cm).

☐ Set oven to 375F (190C) gas 5.

☐ Melt the butter in a saucepan on a low heat. Stir in the flour to make a smooth paste. Gradually add the milk, stirring continuously, until the mixture is smooth and thick. Stir in the cheese.

☐ Remove from the heat, divide the mixture in half and put half to one side. Allow to cool a little, then stir the egg yolks, herbs and salt and pepper to taste into the remainder.

☐ Blend, process or purée the cooked vegetables together until smooth and stir into the seasoned sauce.

☐ Whisk the egg whites until stiff and fold in using a metal spoon. Spread the mixture in the prepared tin and smooth over. Bake in the oven for 30 minutes.

☐ Meanwhile, prepare the filling: Place the remaining sauce in a large saucepan and stir in the lemon rind and juice, turkey, ham, mushrooms and parsley or chives. Cover and simmer gently for 15 minutes. Season to taste.

☐ Turn the roulade base out on to a clean sheet of parchment paper and remove the lining paper. Spread the filling over and quickly roll up, using the parchment to help. Roll on to a serving plate, garnish with sliced tomato and spring onions and serve immediately.

Smoked Salmon Roll

Serves 6 ☆☆☆

Preparation: 30 minutes
Cooking: 35-40 minutes

2oz (50g) butter
2oz (50g) flour
14 fl oz (400ml) milk
3 eggs, size 2, separated

The filling:
4oz (125g) smoked salmon
squeeze of lemon juice
3oz (75g) cream cheese
¼ pint (150ml) double cream

Melt the butter in a saucepan on a low heat. Stir in the flour until smooth. Gradually add the milk, stirring continuously to make a smooth sauce. Cook for a further

minute, continuing to stir.

☐ Remove from the heat. Add the egg yolks and beat in.

☐ Set oven to 325F (160C) gas 3.

☐ Whisk the egg whites until they make firm peaks. Fold in the hot mixture.

☐ Spoon on to a greased, lined Swiss Roll tin 12in × 8in (30cm × 20cm). Bake in the oven for 35-40 minutes until golden and firm.

☐ Turn out on to a piece of greaseproof paper dusted with flour. Leave to cool while you make the filling.

☐ Liquidize or process the salmon to a paste. Work in the lemon juice and the cheese. Whip the cream to soft peaks then mix in lightly.

☐ Carefully scrape the lining paper from the roulade base. Trim the edges. Spread with filling to within a thumb's width of the edges.

☐ Use the paper to roll up firmly. Cut into slices and place on a serving dish.

Cheese Soufflé

Unlike roulades, soufflés cannot be baked in advance. They must be served immediately they come from the oven. You can, however, prepare the soufflé ready for cooking about 1 hour before and leave it covered in the fridge. It can then go into the oven when required.

Serves 3-4 ☆☆☆

Preparation: 15 minutes
Cooking: about 25 minutes

1oz (25g) butter
1oz (25g) flour
½ teaspoon dry mustard
salt and pepper
8 fl oz (250ml) milk
3 eggs, size 2, separated
1 egg white from a size 2 egg
4oz (125g) grated Cheddar cheese
1 tablespoon grated Gruyère

Melt the butter in a saucepan on a low heat. Stir in the flour, mustard and salt and pepper to taste. Gradually add the milk and cook, stirring constantly, until a smooth

sauce is obtained.

☐ Stir in the egg yolks then the cheese. Remove from the heat as soon as the cheese is melted.

☐ Set oven to 375F (190C) gas 5.

☐ Whisk the 4 egg whites to firm peaks. Whisk a little into the hot sauce. Fold the cheese mixture into the rest of the egg whites lightly and quickly.

☐ Turn into a greased 1½ pint (900ml) soufflé dish and level the top with a palette knife or the back of a spoon.

☐ Cut into the soufflé a thumb's width from the edge with the tip of a sharp knife to form a ring all the way round.

☐ Sprinkle the top with the Gruyère cheese. Bake in the oven for about 25 minutes until well risen.

☐ Serve immediately by cutting into the centre of the soufflé so that each guest samples some of the creamy centre and the outer crust.

Variation: Make the Cheese Soufflé entirely with Swiss cheese and flavour with 2 tablespoons kirsch. Halve and pip 4oz (125g) black grapes. Layer soufflé mixture and grapes alternately in a greased soufflé dish. Bake as for Cheese Soufflé. Serve as a dessert, sprinkled with sugar.

Tips: Cutting a circle in the soufflé mixture near the edge of the dish before baking helps the soufflé to rise evenly to give the traditional 'top hat' effect. If the mixture is just piled into the dish roughly it will rise unevenly. It can be very attractive but tends to fall more quickly.

● In a fan-assisted oven, the soufflé will rise beautifully to an even greater volume than in still heat, but use a lower setting.

● You can vary the flavouring of a savoury soufflé but keep the consistency of the basic sauce the same as for Cheese Soufflé: Use 1oz (25g) butter and 1oz (25g) flour to 8 fl oz (250ml) liquid and 3 eggs plus 1 extra white.

Custard Tart.

Custard Tart
The filling may bake a little more quickly if put into hot pastry. To tell when the custard is baked, insert a thin knife into the centre. It will come out clean when the custard is set. If there is a little too much filling for the pastry case, gradually add the extra as the custard bakes and shrinks.

Petits Pots de Crème
Make the custard mixture as for Crème Caramel. Stir in 1oz (25g) grated plain chocolate. Bake in small ramekins.

Baked custard

Some of the easiest dishes to make are the various forms of baked custard. The preparation is very brief, and the baking straightforward if a little care is taken to control the temperature.

The egg mixture can be baked in dishes as for Crème Caramel or in pastry cases as in savoury or sweet quiches and the old-fashioned Custard Tart. To protect the delicate mixture from too much heat, bake in a moderate oven and stand the dishes in a pan of hot water. The pastry also fulfils the same protective function.

Custard Tart

Serves 4   ☆☆☆
Preparation: 10 minutes
Cooking: about 45 minutes

8in (20cm) baked sweet pastry case

The filling:
14 fl oz (400ml) milk
2 eggs, size 2
1 egg yolk from a size 2 egg
2 tablespoons caster sugar
grated nutmeg

Set the oven to 350F (180C) gas 4.
☐ Put the milk on to heat until just bubbling around the edges. Put the eggs and egg yolk and the sugar into a bowl. Whisk in the hot milk.
☐ Set the pastry case on a baking tray and strain the milk and egg mixture into it. Strain into the baked pastry case. Sprinkle generously with grated nutmeg.
☐ Bake for about 45 minutes.
☐ Serve lukewarm or cold.

Crème Caramel

Serves 4   ☆
Preparation: 15 minutes
Cooking: 45-50 minutes
plus 2-3 hours chilling

The caramel:
2oz (50g) caster sugar
2 tablespoons water

The custard:
2 eggs, size 2
1 egg yolk from a size 2 egg
1 tablespoon sugar
14 fl oz (400ml) milk
1in (2.5cm) piece vanilla pod

To make the caramel: Put the sugar and water into a small saucepan on a low heat. Stir to dissolve the sugar. Heat gently until the sugar melts and turns a pale golden brown.
☐ Pour the syrup immediately into the bottom of 4 individual soufflé dishes or ramekins. Tilt to spread the caramel over the bases.
☐ Set oven to 325F (160C) gas 3.
☐ Whisk eggs and sugar in a bowl. Put milk and the vanilla pod into the caramel saucepan on a low heat. Leave to warm very gently for about 10 minutes to extract the flavour from the vanilla pod. Discard the pod, then whisk the milk into the eggs.
☐ Strain the custard into the dishes. Set in a pan of hot water and place in the oven. Bake for 45-50 minutes.
☐ Remove the dishes to a wire rack and leave to cool. Chill for 2-3 hours. Turn out on to a plate and serve with the caramel sauce around the custards.

Meringue

Meringue is one of the most decorative of all baked foods. It is also the simplest. It is made only of egg whites and sugar whisked together.

It may be made and baked quickly into a soft, delicate foam. Alternatively, it can be whisked more firmly and piped into beautiful shapes and baked until crisp.

In its natural state, meringue is either white or a pale creamy colour – perhaps light golden brown – outside. However, you can tint it a pastel colour with a few drops of appropriate food colouring, or turn it into a coffee or chocolate meringue.

Most commonly, meringue is left unflavoured but if you like, you can easily give added flavour by using brown sugar or by the addition of concentrated essences such as vanilla, almond, strawberry, raspberry or coffee.

A very good flavour is obtained by using sugar which has been stored in a jar with a whole vanilla pod for some days.

The easiest way to shape meringue is by piling it or spreading it lightly with a rubber spatula. You can then form peaks with a fork or palette knife. Two large dessert spoons are good for making oval-shaped meringues or you can pipe the meringue mixture with a plain or rose pipe into swirls, stars, rings and many other decorative shapes.

Soft meringue makes a good contrast to tart citrus fruits, mincemeat, baked apples, and many hot puddings. Crisp dry meringues can be sandwiched with whipped cream, ice cream or Crème Pâtissière.

Soft meringue must be made, baked and served within minutes. Hard meringues will keep in the freezer or in an airtight container in a cool place for at least a month. But be sure to keep them well wrapped and dry because they absorb moisture very readily.

Make meringues whenever you have egg whites left over from a recipe – stored ready in the freezer, they make a most useful standby for elegant desserts. They require no thawing and can be used straight from the freezer!

Making meringue

For both hard and soft meringues, the same rules apply:
● Make sure that all utensils used for making meringue – whisks, measures, basins, and forcing bags and pipes – are completely free of grease.
● Use egg whites which are at room temperature.
● Use 2oz (50g) sugar for each egg white.
● When separating the eggs, take care not to let any particle of the yolk get into the white.
● Whisking by hand can take up to 10 minutes so an electric whisk saves a lot of effort.
● Whisk the whites until opaque and beginning to form peaks, before you whisk in any sugar.

Flavoured, coloured and piped into different shapes, meringue widens the creative cook's decorative repertoire. (See overleaf for instructions on how to make the meringues illustrated.)

Whisking meringue

The firmer the meringue is, the better it will hold its shape, and the harder it will bake. Meringue will never become very firm if there is any fat at all in it either from the egg yolk, or from improperly cleaned utensils. It will also not whisk firmly if the sugar is added too early or too much is whisked in at once.

Egg whites which are too cold do not usually whisk as easily as those at room temperature.

Baking meringues

For very white meringue, use a very slow oven and long baking. The instructions for baking Polonaises serve as a good example. For a slightly softer, creamy-coloured meringue, use the instructions for Meringues Chantilly. When meringue is baked, it will come off the lining paper easily – small ones can be lifted off, larger ones need to be removed with a palette knife.

Basic Meringue Mixture

Makes about 12oz (350g)
Preparation: 12-15 minutes

4 egg whites, from size 2 eggs
8oz (225g) caster sugar

Whisk the egg whites until white, opaque and beginning to hold soft peaks.
☐ Divide the sugar into two equal portions.
☐ From one portion add 1 tablespoon at a time to the meringue, whisking each in well. When all that portion of sugar has been used, whisk until the mixture is stiff.
☐ Sprinkle the second portion of sugar over the meringue. Fold in lightly but thoroughly with a metal spoon or rubber spatula.
☐ Bake immediately.

To shape the meringues illustrated on page 423
Put ½in (1cm) rose pipe into a large forcing bag and fill with meringue:
● For spirals – start with stars of meringue and on them press out the final burst of mixture with a spiralling movement.
● For rings – draw 3in (7.5cm) circles on the lining paper, turn over then follow the marks with the pipe.
● For repeated shells – hold the tube at an angle of 45° to the tray. Press out the meringue, lift the pipe then bring it down towards you in a short jerky movement. Repeat.
● For long reversed scrolls – hold the pipe at an angle of 45° to the tray. Press out the meringue in the shape of a large comma with a long tail then reverse back at the end to start the next 'comma'.
● For mushrooms – use plain ½in (1cm) pipe. Shape fingers of meringue about 1½in (4cm) long, and some small round buttons as caps. When baked, stick the caps on to the stalks with whipped cream.

To flavour meringue:
● coffee flavour – add 3 teaspoons coffee essence after whisking, and fold in the remaining sugar.
● chocolate flavour – add 4 teaspoons cocoa sifted with the second portion of sugar.
● strawberry or raspberry flavour – add ½ teaspoon strawberry or raspberry essence with the second portion of sugar.

Meringues Chantilly

Makes 18
Preparation: 15 minutes plus 10 minutes finishing
Cooking: 50 minutes plus cooling

Basic Meringue Mixture
½ pint (300ml) double cream
a few drops vanilla essence or
**   1 sachet of vanilla sugar**
oil for greasing

Set the oven to 250F (120C) gas ½ and grease 3 baking trays and line them with baking paper.
☐ Make the meringue as directed. Dip 2 dessert spoons in a jug of cold water. Shake off excess water, heap one spoon with meringue and invert the second spoon over it to shape.
☐ Hold the side of the bottom spoon against a prepared tray and scoop the meringue off with the second spoon to form an egg shape.
☐ Shape the rest of the meringue mixture in the same way.
☐ Bake for about 50 minutes until set. Cool on a wire rack.
☐ Whip the cream with the vanilla essence or sugar until it forms soft peaks. Pipe in swirls on half the meringues, or pile it on with a spoon. Set the remaining meringue shells in place on top of the cream.
☐ Serve within an hour.
Variation: Divide the meringue mixture into two batches. Flavour one with vanilla and the other with strawberry or raspberry essence. Made and baked as above, they look spectacular arranged alternately on the serving plate.

Polonaises

Makes 8 ☆☆☆
Preparation: about 20 minutes plus
20 minutes finishing
Cooking: 1 hour

4 egg whites, size 2 eggs
8oz (225g) caster sugar
butter for greasing

The filling:
¾ pint (400ml) double cream
fresh or canned fruit—such as
    pineapple, mandarins, peaches and
    cherries

Set the oven to 200F (100C) gas ¼
and prepare two baking trays: Brush
well with butter. Line with foil or
baking parchment. Butter again.
With a biscuit cutter, mark 24
circles about 3½in (8.5cm) across.
☐ Make the meringue mixture as
directed previously. Put into a
large forcing bag fitted with a
plain ½in (1cm) pipe.
☐ Pipe 8 bases: starting in the
centre and coiling around and
around out to the marked edge.
Then make 16 rings without centres.
☐ Bake for about 1 hour or until
firm. With a palette knife transfer to
wire racks to cool.
☐ Whip the cream until it just
holds in peaks. Put half into a
forcing bag with a plain pipe and the
rest into one with a ½in (1cm) rose
pipe.
☐ Build up the Polonaises in 3
layers. Stack 2 rings on top of each
base by sandwiching each with a
ring of cream. With the rose pipe,
fill with swirls of cream. Just before
serving, decorate with fruit.
Variation: A layer of fruit may be
placed on the bottom of the cases
under the cream. In this case, serve
soon after filling.

The baked meringue shells will store for at
least a month if put into an airtight box and
kept in a cool place.

*The various stages in making
Polonaises. Those skilled in piping
may make them in one operation by
building up the 'walls' using a
continuous spiral up from the
perimeter of the base.*

Hazelnut Torte

Serves 8 ★★☆
Preparation: 20 minutes plus
20 minutes finishing
Cooking: 40-45 minutes

4 egg whites, size 2
6oz (175g) caster sugar
4oz (100g) hazelnuts, ground
2 tablespoons cornflour
oil for greasing

The Coffee Buttercream:
6oz (175g) butter, softened
7oz (200g) icing sugar
1 tablespoon instant coffee
2 teaspoons boiling water
3 tablespoons Tia Maria

To decorate:
3-4oz (100g) toasted hazelnuts, flaked
a few chocolate coffee beans

Set the oven to 300F (150C) gas 2 and prepare 2 baking trays: Grease and line with baking parchment.

Grease the insides of two 9in (23cm) flan rings. Set one on each tray.

☐ Whisk the egg whites until white, opaque and beginning to form soft peaks. Whisk in 4oz (100g) of the sugar to make a stiff, firm meringue.

☐ Sift the rest of the sugar, the ground hazelnuts and the cornflour into the meringue. Fold in lightly but well.

☐ Divide the meringue equally between the 2 flan rings and spread to level.

☐ Bake in the oven for 40-45 minutes until set and lightly browned. Transfer the layers of meringue to wire racks to cool.

☐ Make the Coffee Buttercream: Beat together the butter and enough sugar to make a soft, light cream. Dissolve the coffee in the water, add the liqueur and beat this into the butter mixture.

☐ To finish the torte: Sandwich the meringue layers with some of the coffee filling. Spread the sides with more.

☐ Sprinkle the nuts in a line along the centre of a piece of greaseproof paper. Hold the sandwiched

meringues between the hands, roll along the nuts and then press them on firmly with a palette knife.

☐ Spread the top smoothly with more of the buttercream. Put remainder into a small paper forcing bag.

☐ As if you were writing, hold the bag held at an angle and pipe two parallel rows in a swag effect around the edge of the torte as shown.

☐ To make the dots and flowers, hold the bag upright. Use more or less pressure to make larger or smaller dots.

☐ Decorate with toasted hazelnuts, and chocolate coffee beans. Make the torte a few hours before serving to allow the meringue to mellow.

Variation: Another delicious torte can be made by substituting coconut for the hazelnuts, flavouring the buttercream with vanilla essence and decorating the top with small pieces of pineapple.

Filling and decorating Hazelnut Torte.

Baked Alaska

Baked Alaska is sometimes called 'Norwegian Omelette' or 'Omelette Surprise', the surprise being an interior of solid cold ice cream concealed in a freshly baked crisp meringue shell. The meringue and a sponge base insulate the ice cream from the heat during the short baking time.

Serves 6 ☆☆☆
Preparation: 25 minutes plus cooling
Cooking: 20 minutes

The sponge base:
4oz (100g) self-raising flour
4oz (100g) caster sugar
4oz (100g) butter, softened
2 eggs, size 3
1 tablespoon milk

4 egg whites, size 2
8oz (225g) caster sugar
8oz (225g) vanilla ice cream
6oz (175g) raspberries

First make the sponge flan: Set the oven to 350F (180C) gas 4.

☐ Put the flour, caster sugar and butter into a bowl with the 2 eggs and 1 tablespoon milk. Beat well together.

☐ Fill 5 paper bun cases with mixture (to use excess quantity) and put the rest into a 8in (20cm) sponge flan tin. Bake in the oven for about 15 minutes. Turn out and cool.

☐ Make the meringue as directed on page 424 with the egg whites and sugar. Put into a large forcing bag fitted with a $\frac{1}{2}$in (1cm) rose pipe.

☐ Raise oven to 425F (220C) gas 7.

☐ Set the sponge on a baking tray. Fill with the raspberries then set the ice cream on top. If necessary, cut the ice cream to the size of the central depression in the cake.

☐ Pipe the meringue around and around to cover the whole of it, starting at the edge of the sponge and ensuring that there are no gaps.

☐ Bake in the oven for about 5 minutes, until lightly browned, and serve immediately.

Lemon or Lime Meringue Pie

Serves 8 ☆☆☆
Preparation: 10 minutes plus chilling
Cooking: 5 minutes

8in (20cm) baked Sweet Flan Case
8oz (225g) butter, softened
8oz (225g) sugar
yolks of 3 size 3 eggs
rind and juice of one large orange
rind and juice of one large lemon
**   or lime**
Basic Meringue Mixture

Beat together the butter and sugar until thick and creamy.

☐ Add the egg yolks, citrus rind and strained juices and fold in gently but thoroughly.

☐ Fill the pastry case with the mixture and chill for at least 1 hour.

☐ Pile the meringue on top of the filling. Roughly swirl with a palette knife to form peaks.

☐ Bake as for Baked Alaska.

Variation: Try this topping with your favourite pie fillings – but increase the sugar content slightly.

Poached meringue
Another exciting way to cook soft meringue is to poach it. Gently ease spoonfuls of Basic Meringue Mixture into a large pan of water or milk just under the boil. Cook for about 3 minutes on one side. Carefully turn and cook the second side in the same way. Remove with a slotted spoon and drain on crumpled kitchen paper.
Serve with fresh fruit salad or with pouring custard.

Baked Alaska
The depression in the centre of a sponge flan tin means it requires an awkward amount of cake mixture – use the excess to make 5 small buns.

Whipping cream
Double cream is the best type to use if you want to pipe it. Take care not to over-whip it or it will separate and not pipe well. Keep testing it as you whip – it is ready when it forms peaks which *just* fold over.
Another test is to tip the basin – if the cream stays in position it is firm enough.

Use whipped cream as soon as possible after whipping. It is liable to separate on standing.

Baked Alaska makes a memorable dinner-party dessert that never fails to impress.

Raspberry Meringue Cream Gâteau is the perfect centrepiece for a summer party table.

For a pretty effect, add a few drops of pink food colouring to the meringue mixture to tint it pink. Or, colour half the meringue mixture for the small meringues only, then arrange them in alternate colours around the sides of the gâteau.

Raspberry Meringue Cream Gâteau

Serves 8 ☆☆☆
Preparation: 15 minutes
plus 20 minutes assembly
Cooking: about 50 minutes

9in (23cm) baked Basic Whisked Sponge
Basic Meringue Mixture
oil for greasing
$\frac{3}{4}$ pint (400ml) double cream
$\frac{3}{4}$lb (350g) fresh raspberries

Set the oven to 250F (120C) gas $\frac{1}{2}$ and grease and line 3 baking trays with baking paper. On one tray, mark a circle about 8$\frac{1}{2}$in (21cm) across.

☐ Put the meringue mixture into a forcing bag fitted with a $\frac{1}{2}$in(1cm) plain pipe and make about 20 small shapes of meringue on each of the trays. Spread the rest of the meringue just inside the marked circle on the third tray.

☐ Bake the meringues in the oven for about 40 minutes for the small meringues and 50 minutes for the large one. Cool them all on wire racks.

☐ Cut the sponge cake across in half. Whip the cream until it forms peaks which just flop over and the cream stays level if the bowl is tilted to one side.

☐ Reserve about 24 of the best berries for decoration. Spread the rest over the bottom layer of sponge. Set the large disc of meringue on top. Spread with some of the cream, and carefully set the second layer of sponge in place over that.

☐ Coat the sides and top of the gâteau with more cream. Press the small meringues around the sides as shown. Put the gâteau on a serving plate.

☐ Put the rest of the whipped cream into a large forcing bag fitted with a plain $\frac{1}{2}$in (1cm) nozzle. Pipe a lattice effect on top of the gâteau and fill the lattice with the reserved berries.

Tip: A pair of sandwich sponges may be used instead of a large sponge cake cut in half.

Variations: This simple showpiece lends itself to endless adaptations. Try any of the following:
● Strawberries, stoned and halved cherries or chocolate buttons instead of the raspberries.
● Flavour the cream with vanilla, chestnut essence or brandy or fruit liqueur.
● Colour all or half of the small meringue shapes.

Pasta and pasta dishes

Fresh pasta is really delicious and also quite simple to make—by hand or with a machine. The basic ingredients are bread flour and water but egg, spinach purée or tomato purée can be substituted for some of the liquid to give pasta a different colour and taste. Served simply with olive oil, pepper and grated Parmesan cheese, or more elaborately with any number of tasty sauces, pasta can be used as a first course or for a main meal. Once the basic techniques of pasta-making are mastered you can go on to create a vast variety of dishes, together with a wide range of sauces.

Cooking pasta

Pasta should be cooked in plenty of boiling salted water.

Instructions are given with each recipe for fresh pasta but there are one or two rules which should be followed for cooking pasta successfully.

● Use a large saucepan to allow free movement of the pasta in the water which prevents it sticking together.

● Allow 1¾ pints (1 litre) of water for every 4oz (125g) pasta.

● Add pasta to fast boiling water with 1 teaspoon salt to each 1 pint (600ml).

● Add all the pasta at once, sprinkling small shapes over the surface and coiling long, raw pasta around as it gradually softens. Stir once.

● Allow water to return to the boil and reduce heat. The water should bubble gently throughout cooking without boiling over and to ensure this, the pan is kept uncovered.

Fresh pasta should be cooked for no more than 2-3 minutes. Whichever pasta you are cooking, start testing at the minimum time given in each recipe. Just take a piece of pasta from the pan with a fork and bite between the teeth. It should feel firm to the bite or what the Italians call 'al dente'.

How much?
Allow 4oz (125g) fresh pasta per person for a starter and 6oz (175g) for a main course.

Meal-in-a-bowl
Add cooked pasta to soups for a more substantial dish. In some stock-based recipes, the pasta can be added raw towards the end of cooking thus saving on saucepans.

A hand-operated pasta machine.

Pasta Dough

Pasta dough is easy to make, and you'll find your skills improving with practice. Aim to work in as much flour as you can for every egg used because the firmer the dough the better the pasta. Until you become practised, it is wise to work with a small piece of dough at first. To achieve thin pasta, roll the dough the width of the pin — but no wider.

Makes: 1lb (450g) ☆

10oz (275g) bread flour
3 eggs, size 2
a little olive oil

Put the flour into a large mixing bowl. Make a well in the centre. Whisk the eggs and pour into the centre of the flour.
☐ With the hand, keep turning the flour into the egg until a dough is formed.

Steps to making your own pasta.

□ Turn out on to the work surface, kneading and stretching with the palm of the hand to make a smooth elastic dough. Add up to 1oz (25g) extra flour if necessary.

□ Put the dough into a polythene bag and fasten. Leave to rest for 30 minutes or store it in the fridge for up to 24 hours.

□ Rub the rolling pin well with a little olive oil. Cut off about one-third of the dough and keep the rest inside the bag. On a clean work surface, roll the piece of dough into a long oval. Continue to roll and smooth out with the hands until it is thin enough to see through to the work surface. (Work as quickly as possible because the dough will dry out and become unusable.)

□ Allow pasta to dry for 15 minutes hung over the back of a chair or rail. (This will enable it to dry out sufficiently to prevent sticking together at the next step.)

□ For spaghetti or noodles: Roll up the dough like a Swiss Roll. Slice off as thinly or thickly as required with a sharp knife. Unroll the strips and cook as required.

□ For stuffed pasta: Do not allow the dough to dry at all but use immediately as directed.

How to serve pasta

In some parts of Italy pasta may be served at two meals a day. It forms an integral part of family meals or, for more elaborate menus, it will become a whole course on its own. Pasta must be cooked and served fresh: if you try to keep it hot it loses much of its quality and sticks together. Once cooked, drain the pasta in a colander and turn into a hot serving dish. As an accompaniment to a large meal it will need no more than a little olive oil or cubes of butter, a sprinkling of Parmesan cheese and freshly ground black pepper. Chopped fresh herbs and a little cream will also taste delicious. For a more substantial lunch or supper dish you can add a meat or fish sauce.

Sauces for pasta

Italian sauces for pasta are easier to make than the French ones. The basis of many is either a thick tomato purée, a Béchamel Sauce or finely minced meat, fish or vegetables. Sauces can be simple or more exotic with herbs, nuts and spices. You can keep a supply of basic sauces in the freezer for quickly putting together a wide variety of pasta dishes. The following sauce recipes are all suitable for freezing and those served hot can all be thawed in a saucepan over a low heat.

Tomato Sauce

Serves 4   ☆☆
Preparation: 15 minutes
Cooking: 1 hour 45 minutes

1 medium onion
2 large cloves garlic
1 medium carrot
1 small red pepper
1 stick celery
2lb (900g) tomatoes
3-4 tablespoons olive oil
1 teaspoon dried oregano
pinch of sugar
salt and freshly ground black pepper

Peel the onions, garlic and carrot. Remove the seeds from the red pepper. Chop all the vegetables coarsely.

□ Put the oil into a large heavy pan on a low heat. Add the onions and garlic. Cook, stirring occasionally, for about 10 minutes until soft.

□ Add the remaining vegetables and oregano. Cover and cook very gently for 1½ hours, stirring occasionally. Add the sugar and season to taste.

□ Remove from the heat and cool. Liquidize or process to a thick pulp. Return to saucepan and reheat. Serve with freshly cooked pasta. Store in the fridge for up to 3 days, or freeze in a covered rigid container for up to 4 months. To serve, allow to thaw gently in a pan over a gentle heat.

Rolling out pasta dough

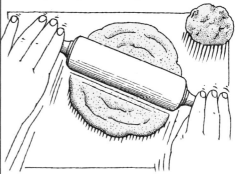

Roll the dough until it is thin enough to see through to the work surface. Allow to dry for 15 minutes.

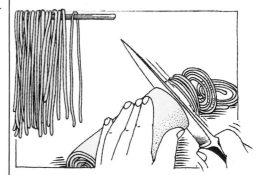

Roll up the partly-dried pasta and slice to the desired width.

Cutting pasta

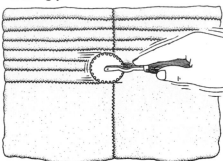

Pappardelle are wide ribbon noodles cut with a serrated wheel.

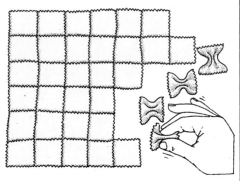

To make farfalle, cut squares of pasta with the wheel then pinch together at the centre to make small bows.

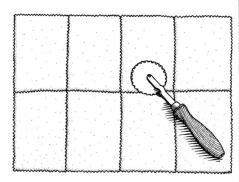

The broad flat strips of pasta called lasagne may be cut with the wheel or a large sharp knife. Rolled up with filling inside they become cannelloni.

Ragú or Bolognese Sauce

Serves 4 ☆☆
Preparation: 30 minutes
Cooking: about 1½ hours

---

4 tablespoons olive oil
1 medium onion, finely chopped
1 stick celery, finely chopped
1 medium carrot, grated
¾lb (350g) trimmed lean beef, minced
9 fl oz (250ml) red wine
14oz (396g) can tomatoes
freshly grated nutmeg
salt to taste

Put the oil into a large heavy pan on a low heat. Add the onions and cook, stirring occasionally, for 10 minutes until soft. Add the celery and carrot and cook for 5 minutes.

☐ Add the meat a little at a time, stirring to break up the lumps. Cook for 10 minutes, stirring.

☐ Stir in the wine and the tomatoes. Add a little nutmeg and salt. Cover and simmer gently for about 1½ hours stirring frequently.

☐ Adjust the seasoning. Serve at once with freshly cooked pasta, or cool and freeze for up to 3 months.

Pesto Sauce

Serves 4 ☆☆☆
Preparation: 5 minutes

4oz (125g) fresh basil leaves
¼ pint (150ml) olive oil
1oz (25g) pine nuts
3 large cloves garlic, peeled
3oz (75g) grated Parmesan cheese
2oz (50g) grated pecorino cheese
2oz (50g) butter, softened

Put the basil, oil, nuts and garlic in a liquidizer or food processor. Work until mixed to a paste.

☐ Beat in the cheese and butter.

☐ Serve with freshly cooked pasta. Refrigerate for up to 3 days or freeze in small pots.

✱To use: Thaw at room temperature for 3-4 hours or in the fridge for 24 hours.

Puttanesca Sauce

Serves 4 ☆☆☆
Preparation: 10 minutes
Cooking: 25 minutes

1¾oz (50g) can anchovy fillets
2 cloves garlic, crushed
4 tablespoons olive oil
3oz (75g) butter
2 tablespoons capers
5oz (150g) black olives
14oz (396g) can tomatoes
salt and freshly ground black pepper

Drain and chop the anchovies. Put in a pan with the garlic, oil and butter. Cook over a low heat until the garlic browns.

☐ Rinse the capers in cold water. Stone and halve the olives. Add the capers and olives with the tomatoes to the pan. Mash the tomatoes lightly with a fork. Stir well and bring to the boil.

☐ Reduce heat, cover pan with a lid and simmer for 20 minutes, stirring occasionally.

☐ Season to taste and serve with freshly cooked pasta.

Mushroom Sauce

Serves 4 ☆☆☆
Preparation: 10 minutes
Cooking: 15 minutes

8oz (225g) mushrooms, cleaned
2oz (50g) butter
salt and freshly ground black pepper
4 tablespoons white wine
a squeeze of lemon juice
½ pint (284ml) carton double cream
1 tablespoon freshly chopped parsley

Chop the mushrooms. Melt butter in a pan and add the mushrooms. Season with salt and pepper and cook gently for 10 minutes.

☐ Add the wine and lemon juice and cook for 2 minutes.

☐ Add the cream and bring to the boil. Stir for 3 minutes until sauce has thickened slightly.

☐ Serve with freshly cooked pasta.

Electric pasta machines will do all the mixing, kneading, rolling and cutting of the dough. Different attachments enable you to produce lasagne, tagliatelle and spaghetti as well as other short-cut shapes.

Useful equipment

Special spaghetti tongs have large teeth which grip the pasta and make serving easier. Ordinary kitchen tongs will do just as well. Wooden spaghetti spoons are flat and fitted with small pegs which help to stir the pasta during cooking.

Pasta-making equipment

Different pasta-making machines have their own particular refinements but in principle they all work in the same way. In addition to the raviolatore and the round pasta cutter there is other equipment available.

Electric pasta machine—this is a large machine with a very powerful motor similar to a food processor. The flour, egg, water or flavouring is placed in a drum at the top and the machine switched on. After the dough has been mixed thoroughly and is of the correct consistency it is extruded, with great force, through the attachment that is being used. The machine will also make bread and biscuit dough.

Hand operated machines—these are obviously less expensive and will do the rolling and cutting process just as well. Available from kitchen shops, they are usually made of steel with a clamp-base fitting. A handle turns the rollers which pass the dough on through the chosen cutter to produce the cut pasta. Different attachments are available for making spaghetti and ravioli, as well as the standard cutters for tagliatelle and lasagne strips.

For hand rolling—a special rolling pin for pasta can be bought from specialist kitchen shops. It is longer than the usual pin without handles. The ends are tapered and this helps to ensure that the centre area of the pin is concentrated on the pasta and it is easier to roll with quick and even strokes.

Whichever method is chosen one should remember that it is a technique that is quite specialized and may take a little time to master. However the finished result is quite unmistakable.

Pasta Parcels with Mushroom Sauce

Serves 6 ☆☆☆

Preparation: 1 hour
Cooking: 40-45 minutes

1lb (450g) Pasta Dough

The filling:
6oz (175g) monkfish, skinned
3oz (75g) button mushrooms, sliced
9 fl oz (250ml) milk
2oz (50g) butter
2oz (50g) streaky bacon, chopped
1 small onion, finely chopped
3 tablespoons flour
salt and freshly ground black pepper
a squeeze of lemon juice
2 tablespoons brandy
1 tablespoon chopped chives
butter for greasing
olive oil to brush

The sauce:
1oz (25g) butter
3oz (75g) button mushrooms, sliced
2 tablespoons flour
9 fl oz (250ml) milk and cream mixed
salt and freshly ground black pepper
pinch of ground mace

To make the filling: Wash the fish and blot dry with a paper towel. Cut into small cubes.

☐ Put the fish and mushrooms into a saucepan with the milk. Set on a low heat. Cook very gently for about 10 minutes while you prepare the rest of the filling.

☐ Melt the butter in a pan on a moderate heat. Add the bacon and onions. Cook, stirring occasionally, for about 5 minutes until the onions become translucent. Stir in the flour.

☐ Remove the saucepan from the heat and strain off the liquid from the fish. Stir into the bacon and onion mixture gradually. Cook for 3-5 minutes until thickened. Stir in the fish and mushrooms. Season to taste with salt and pepper. Add the lemon juice and brandy. Finally, stir in the herbs. Set aside to cool.

☐ Roll out the pasta very thinly. Cut 6in (15cm) circles using a small plate as a guide. Cook one at a time in a large pan of boiling salted water. When the pasta disc comes to the surface, lift out with a draining spoon. Place discs flat on kitchen paper. Cool.

☐ Place discs on work surface and smooth flat with your hand. Place teaspoons of filling in the centre of each disc. Draw up the edges to the centre to cover the filling. Pinch together at the top and secure with a cocktail stick.

☐ Set oven at 425F (220C) gas 7.

☐ Re-roll the pasta trimmings. Cut into ribbons the width of the little finger. Cook for 2 minutes in the same boiling water. Drain and cool. Wrap one around the neck of each parcel as a string.

☐ Set the parcels on greased baking trays. Brush with olive oil and bake for 12-15 minutes to brown.

☐ Meanwhile make the sauce: Melt the butter in a small saucepan on a moderate heat. Add the mushrooms and cook, stirring, for about 3 minutes to soften. Stir in the flour.

☐ Gradually stir in the milk and cream and cook for 3-5 minutes, stirring, until thickened. Season to taste with salt and pepper and a pinch of ground mace.

☐ Serve the parcels immediately with the sauce.

Tortellini in Broth

Serves 6 ☆

Preparation: 20 minutes plus drying
Cooking: about 10 minutes

1lb (450g) Pasta Dough
salt
4 pints (2.25 litres) chicken broth
chopped basil, chives or parsley or grated
**   Parmesan cheese to serve**

The filling:
2oz (50g) ricotta cheese
2oz (50g) cooked, drained spinach
grated nutmeg

Mix the filling ingredients together in a liquidizer or food processor until smooth.

☐ Roll out the pasta very thinly and cut out 1½in (3.5cm) circles using a

pastry cutter. Put a little filling on one side of each circle.

☐ Fold over the free sides of the pasta to form semi-circles and press around the edges to seal. Fold each filled pasta around the finger to form a little hoop and squeeze ends gently together.

☐ Lay tortellini in a single layer on lightly floured trays. Leave to dry for 1 hour.

☐ Cook in a large saucepan of boiling salted water for 5-7 minutes or until they rise to the surface. Drain.

☐ Heat the broth. Add the tortellini and bring to the boil. Serve immediately with a little chopped herbs or grated Parmesan cheese.

Spinach Roll with Tomato Sauce

Serves 6   ☆ ☆ ☆
Preparation: 30 minutes
Cooking: about 25 minutes

6oz (175g) Pasta Dough
Tomato Sauce (page 431)
2oz (50g) grated Parmesan cheese

The filling:
1oz (25g) butter
1 medium onion, finely chopped
8oz (225g) cooked, drained spinach
3 tablespoons flour

2 tablespoons milk
4oz (125g) ricotta cheese
1 egg, size 2, beaten
2 tablespoons chopped fresh basil
salt and freshly ground black pepper
milk for brushing

Melt the butter in a saucepan and cook the onions gently for about 10 minutes until softened.

☐ Add the spinach. Sprinkle on the flour. Gradually stir in the milk. Cook for 3-5 minutes until thickened.

☐ Mix together the ricotta cheese and the egg. Add to the spinach mixture with the basil. Season to taste with salt and pepper. Remove from the heat and cool.

☐ Meanwhile roll the pasta dough on a sheet of greaseproof paper to a 8in × 13in (20cm × 33cm) rectangle. Spread the filling over, leaving a strip a thumb's width all around.

☐ Fold in the edges to cover the filling. Brush edges with milk.

☐ Using the paper to help, roll up the pasta like a Swiss Roll to make a log about 12in (30cm) long.

☐ Dust a clean piece of muslin about 16in (40cm) square with a

little flour. Lay the pasta roll in the centre and roll up firmly, wrapping the cloth around the pasta several times. Tie the ends with string, like a cracker.

☐ Place in a long pan of boiling salted water to cover the roll completely. (A fish kettle would be ideal.) Cook for about 25 minutes.

☐ Heat the Tomato Sauce in a pan.

☐ Remove the pasta roll from the water, unwrap muslin and cut roll into ½in (1.5cm) thick slices. Arrange on a hot serving dish and spoon the Tomato Sauce over. Sprinkle with cheese and serve at once.

Classic Italian dishes: from left to right, Pasta Parcels with Mushroom Sauce, Tortellini in Broth, Spinach Roll with Tomato Sauce.

Make Ravioli either in a raviolatore (above) or simply cut it out with a ravioli cutter (above and below) or sharp knife. Try different fillings and sauces like the ones shown.

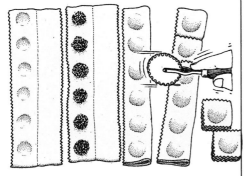

Traditional Ravioli can be made in several ways. Here the filling is placed at intervals along one side of the pasta strip and the other side folded over. The wheel cuts between the mounds to make squares.

Using a raviolatore

A raviolatore consists of a tray made of moulded aluminium about 12in × 4½in (30cm × 11cm). It contains 24 square indentations which are divided by a saw-tooth raised border.

● To use, brush the indentations with olive oil. Coat with a generous dusting of flour. Invert and tap to remove the excess flour.

● Wrap a rectangle of thinly rolled pasta around the pin which comes with the raviolatore. Unroll loosely over the tray. Dip your fingers into a little flour and press down all the indentations.

● Drop a little prepared filling into each cavity. Spread flat with a palette knife. Brush around the edges of the pasta with water.

● Unroll a second strip of pasta over the flattened filling and press lightly around each indentation to seal. Using the small rolling pin, roll over the squares. The jagged teeth will cut through the excess dough and you can remove the trimmings.

● Invert the tray over a work surface. Tap to release the ravioli. Prise out any which stick with the tip of a sharp knife. If your kitchen is very warm, chill tray briefly.

Ravioli with Spinach Filling

Serves 6
Preparation: 1 hour
Cooking: 5-10 minutes

1lb (450g) Pasta Dough

The filling:
8oz (225g) cooked spinach, drained
5-6 basil leaves, chopped
4oz (125g) ricotta cheese
2oz (50g) grated Parmesan cheese
1 egg yolk from size 2 egg
salt and freshly ground black pepper
pinch of ground nutmeg
flour for dusting

The sauce:
9 fl oz (250ml) double cream
3oz (75g) grated Parmesan cheese

Cut the dough in half. Roll each half to a rectangle thin enough to see through to the work surface. Cover each piece with cling film and make the filling.

☐ Mix together the spinach, basil, ricotta and Parmesan cheese with the egg yolk to make a smooth mixture. Season generously with salt, pepper and nutmeg.

☐ Place teaspoons of filling at 1½in (3.5cm) intervals down one side of each piece of dough. Brush around filling with water.

☐ Fold the clear half of dough over the filling. Press to seal the dough between the mounds of filling. Cut out as shown.

☐ Lay the ravioli on a tray lined with greaseproof paper in a single layer. Dust lightly with flour. Leave for 10 minutes.

☐ To cook: Drop half the ravioli, one at a time, into a large pan of boiling salted water. Cook without a lid for about 5 minutes. (When cooked, the ravioli will rise to the surface and the pasta will become translucent.) Remove with a draining spoon. Keep warm while you cook remaining ravioli.

☐ To make the sauce: Heat the cream and grated cheese in a small pan on a low heat until melted. Pour over the ravioli and serve.

Ravioli with Chicken Filling

Serves 6　　　　　　☆☆
Preparation: 1 hour
Cooking: 5-10 minutes

1lb (450g) Pasta Dough

The filling:
5 fl oz (150ml) thick white sauce, cold
7oz (200g) cooked chicken, finely minced
2 tablespoons tomato purée
salt and freshly ground black pepper
ground mace

The sauce:
Tomato Sauce (page 431)
2 tablespoons finely chopped fresh chives, basil or oregano

Roll the pasta as for Ravioli with Spinach Filling.

☐ Mix all the filling ingredients together. Continue as for Ravioli with Spinach Filling.

☐ Serve hot with Tomato Sauce sprinkled with chopped herbs.
Tip: You can make ravioli up to one day before they are to be cooked. Spread shapes on kitchen paper. Turn them from time to time until they are dry on both sides.

Pigeon Lasagne

Serves 4　　　　　　☆☆☆
Preparation: about 1 hour
Cooking: 25-30 minutes

3 pigeons
10oz (275g) dessert apples, peeled, cored and thickly sliced
¼ pint (150ml) cider
¼ pint (150ml) Game Stock
8oz (225g) fresh lasagne
salt and freshly ground black pepper
butter for greasing

The cheese sauce:
1oz (25g) butter
5 teaspoons flour
7 fl oz (200ml) milk
7 fl oz (200ml) single cream
3oz (75g) grated Cheddar cheese

The brown sauce:
1oz (25g) butter
1 tablespoon flour
¼ teaspoon ground allspice

Set the oven to 300F (150C) gas 2. Put the pigeons in an oven dish with the apples, cider and stock. Cover and cook for 30 minutes until pigeons are tender. Cool.

☐ Meanwhile cook the pasta.

☐ Cut the meat from the pigeons and slice thinly. Remove the apples with a draining spoon and reserve the stock.

☐ Make the cheese sauce: Melt the butter in a pan and stir in the flour. Gradually stir in the milk and cream. Bring to the boil. Season and mix in the cheese.

☐ Make the brown sauce: Melt the butter in a pan and stir in the flour. Gradually stir in ¼ pint (150ml) of reserved stock. Season with salt and allspice.

☐ Set oven to 375F (190C) gas 5.

☐ Butter a 3 pint (1.75 litre) casserole. Spread a layer of cheese sauce over the bottom. Arrange half the cooked lasagne over the sauce.

☐ Make a layer with half the sliced pigeon. Spread the brown sauce and the apples over this.

☐ Repeat layers finishing with the cheese sauce.

☐ Cook for 25-30 minutes.

No-cook pasta?
It is possible to use specially manufactured raw lasagne for dishes that are layered with sauces. Follow the packet instructions for recipes with more liquid sauces which will be absorbed by the pasta during cooking.

Cooking Lasagne
Cook lasagne sheets a few at a time to prevent sticking. Bring a large pan of salted water to the boil. Add the lasagne and as soon as the water returns to the boil remove with a slotted spoon. Rinse with cold water and lay out flat on a work surface while you continue with the remaining pasta.

Fresh pasta of different colours can be easily made at home. Serve with Ragú or a sauce of your choice.

Ring the changes

Change the colour of your pasta by replacing one of the eggs with 2-3 tablespoons of tomato purée for pink pasta or 2-3 tablespoons of cooked, well drained and liquidized spinach for green.

Large shells

Conchiglie or large raw pasta shells are available from Italian delicatessen shops. They will hold a variety of fillings.

Pasta Bolognese

This recipe is ideal to serve when you have a crowd of people to feed. The sauce can be made in advance and heated through at the last minute. The pasta should be cooked just before serving. The combination makes perfect party food.

Serves 4 ☆☆☆
Preparation and cooking: 10 minutes

1½lb (700g) fresh tagliatelle of 3 assorted
    flavours: plain egg, spinach and tomato
2-3 tablespoons olive oil
Ragú Sauce
grated Parmesan cheese to serve (optional)

Cook the tagliatelle as directed. Drain. Mix with the olive oil.
☐ Heat the sauce to boiling, then spread over the bottom of a serving dish. Arrange the tagliatelle over the top. Serve immediately. Sprinkle with grated Parmesan cheese, if liked.
Tip: Tagliatelle or spaghetti are also good with Pesto Sauce (page 432) or Tomato Sauce (page 431). For the best appearance, serve the pasta on top of the sauce and then mix together if liked, or leave the guests to stir or not as they wish.

Tagliatelle with Bacon

Serves 4 ☆☆☆
Preparation and cooking: 20 minutes

1lb (450g) Pasta Dough
    cut as tagliatelle
4oz (125g) streaky bacon, chopped
2oz (50g) pine nuts
salt
3 eggs, size 2
¼ pint (150ml) single cream

Put the bacon and nuts in a saucepan on a moderate heat. Cook, stirring occasionally, for about 10 minutes until the bacon is crisp. Pour off the fat.
☐ Cook the tagliatelle in boiling salted water for 2-3 minutes until 'al dente'. Drain. Stir into the bacon.
☐ Whisk together the eggs and cream. Stir into the pan with the tagliatelle and cook 2-3 minutes until the eggs are set. Serve immediately.

Stuffed Conchiglie

Serves 4 ☆☆☆
Preparation: 10 minutes
Cooking: 15 minutes

8 very large shells of pasta
salt
16 prepared mussels—freshly cooked or
    bottled
6oz (175g) mozzarella cheese
Tomato Sauce (page 431) or Cheese Sauce
    (page 437)

Cook the pasta shells in boiling salted water. Drain. Put 2 mussels into each shell.
☐ Cut the cheese into strips and place in the shells.
☐ Put the sauce into a shallow ovenproof dish. Set the shells on top. Cover the dish loosely with foil.
☐ Cook in the oven preheated to 375F (190C) gas 5 for about 15 minutes.
Tip: This dish can be prepared in advance and cooked when required.

Iced desserts

Homemade iced desserts are exciting and rewarding to make, and above all delicious to eat! They are quick to prepare and freeze, with only the occasional stir or whisk required to create the right texture. Once made they can remain in the freezer for 6 to 8 weeks. Having grasped the basic principles of iced dessert making, you will have endless pleasure trying out different combinations and building up a good selection of flavours – greatly extending your dessert repertoire.

A variety of ices which can be made in your freezer – ice cream served as a sundae, redcurrant sorbet, orange sorbet in the orange shell, liqueur-flavoured or butterscotch ice cream with whipped cream and grated chocolate, coffee parfait with meringues and whipped cream, and vanilla ice cream on a bed of apricot purée and decorated with crisp wafers.

Iced desserts

They can be divided into two categories although they may be known by different names.

Cream ices

These are generally more complicated to make with more ingredients added in various ways to make a wide range of desserts. They are smoother and richer than water ices.

Custard ices: The most varied, they can be made with custard powder, or cornflour and any fruit or flavouring. (With the traditional egg mixture, acid fruit are not used because the custard may curdle.) The combination of milk and cream gives them a smooth texture. Milk on its own gives a crunchy texture.

Iced creams: Traditionally a mixture of cream and fruit purée, which is frozen. This recipe has been adapted over the years to become the more familiar dessert we know today with the inclusion of various flavourings. One variety is soft scoop ice cream which, because it never freezes very hard, can be served straight from the freezer.

Iced mousses: The method for this dessert is to add whipped cream to a rich custard made with egg yolks alone or sometimes with the whisked whites added as well. When frozen in a mould and turned out to serve they are called 'parfaits'.

Iced soufflés: This is the combination of a sugar syrup, whipped cream, egg whites and flavourings. It is quite an economical method of making a frozen dessert because of the large amount of whisked egg whites.

Water ices

These are basically sugar syrups flavoured with fruit juices or purées; they are stirred several times during freezing. They are very refreshing.

Sorbet: A water ice which has whisked egg white added halfway through the freezing stage. The finished consistency is smooth and firm.

Sherbet: Used to describe different desserts in different countries but generally a water ice which has whipped cream added to it.

Granita: The simplest of all water ices as it is frozen without beating. They are stirred just before serving to produce a 'mushy' mixture.

Useful equipment:
● An electric blender or food processor to make fruit purées, chop nuts and beat sorbets.
● A sugar thermometer for making syrups.
● A nylon sieve, spatula and wooden spoon for making fruit purées. Do not use metal utensils as these can impart a metallic taste to the fruit.

Hints for success:
● Start with all the ingredients and bowls, whisks and spatulas well chilled. The quicker the mixture is put in the freezer, the better it will taste.
● To cool mixtures quickly, stand bowl in a container of ice cubes or cold water.
● Sugar is a most important part of ices: too much keeps it from freezing, too little makes very hard ices. Follow the recipes given to give you the guidelines when you experiment.
● Foil containers are good for freezing as they help to speed the freezing time.
● Too much alcohol will stop the mixture freezing successfully.
● Remember to set your freezer to the 'Quick Freeze' setting or the compartment in your fridge to its coldest setting at least 30 minutes before you use it.

Equipment

If you are making iced desserts for the first time, it is unnecessary to purchase special equipment. However such equipment is now widely available, and includes ice cream makers and sorbetières like those shown in the photographs. These operate on the principle of continuous stirring of the contents, and are just metal boxes with paddles fitted inside the lid which operate inside the freezer. They run from an ordinary 13-amp socket and the cord fits easily between the door or lid of the freezer and the frame. When the ice cream is set, the machine switches itself off automatically. The paddles are then removed and the box of ice cream is left in the freezer until required.

Another type of electrically-operated ice cream maker consists of a refrigerated box similar in size and design to a food processor. The whole machine works automatically and the paddles stop when the ice is set.

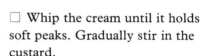

Vanilla Ice Cream

Serves 6   ☆☆☆
Preparation: 30 minutes
Freezing: 4 hours

---

9 fl oz (275ml) milk
1 vanilla pod
3 eggs, size 2
3oz (75g) caster sugar
½ pint (300ml) double cream

Put the milk and vanilla pod into a saucepan over a low heat for about 2 minutes until steaming. Remove from heat and infuse for 8 minutes. Strain through a nylon sieve.
☐ Whisk the eggs and sugar together until light and fluffy. Whisk in a little of the hot milk, then stir egg mixture into the pan.
☐ Stir constantly over a low heat for 3-4 minutes until slightly thickened. Remove from the heat and plunge the base of the pan into cold water. Leave to cool.

☐ Whip the cream until it holds soft peaks. Gradually stir in the custard.
☐ Turn into a 1½ pint (900ml) polythene container and freeze for four hours.
☐ To serve: Transfer ice cream to the fridge 1 hour before required.
Variation: For Coffee Ice Cream, dissolve 1 teaspoon instant coffee in the milk. Make in the same way as Vanilla Ice Cream.

Syrup Soft Scoop

This recipe is very easy to make, and the result is velvety smooth. It will not freeze very hard so it is ready to serve straight from the freezer.

Serves 4   ☆☆☆
Preparation: 5 minutes
Freezing: about 3 hours

5oz (125g) golden syrup
½ teaspoon vanilla essence
7 fl oz (200ml) double cream
1oz (25g) walnuts, chopped

Stir the syrup, vanilla essence and 2 tablespoons of the cream together.

☐ Whip the remaining cream to soft peaks and stir in the syrup mixture and the nuts.

☐ Turn into a 1 pint (600ml) polythene container and freeze.

Chocolate Ice Cream

Serves 4   ☆☆☆
Preparation: 20 minutes
Freezing: about 3 hours

---

3 tablespoons cocoa powder
3 tablespoons cornflour
4oz (125g) caster sugar
14 fl oz (400ml) milk
2 teaspoons powdered gelatine
$\frac{1}{2}$ teaspoon vanilla essence
$\frac{1}{4}$ pint (150ml) double cream
1 egg, size 2

Mix the cocoa, cornflour, sugar and 2-3 tablespoons of milk.

☐ Heat the remaining milk in a saucepan over moderate heat. When the bubbles appear around the edge stir in the cocoa mixture. Return to the saucepan and continue to cook, stirring until thick and smooth.

☐ Remove from the heat. Whisk in the gelatine and the essence. Cool. Whip the cream to soft peaks. Beat the egg. Fold in the cream and egg.

☐ Turn into a 1 pint (600ml) container. Freeze for 3 hours. Transfer to fridge 1 hour before required.

Variation: When you fold in the cream add one of the following
● 2oz (50g) ground hazelnuts
● 2oz (50g) chopped fudge
● 2oz (50g) chocolate chips
● 2oz (50g) chopped preserved ginger

Tip: Serve single scoops of ice cream in chocolate cups. Melt cooking chocolate and brush over the inside of cake cases. Allow to dry before repeating with more chocolate to build up a thick wall. Allow to set firm before peeling off the paper.

Stages in making Vanilla Ice Cream in an ice cream maker.

Bombes and scoops

In a bombe mould, layers of different flavoured ice cream can be built up, each layer being frozen before the next is added. (A pudding basin could be used instead of the mould). Ice cream scoops, made of stainless steel, are available from many kitchen shops. Dip the head of the scoop into cold water after each ball of ice cream is shaped. Alternatively, use a melon baller and several different flavours of ice cream.

Full of flavour

Vanilla pod gives the best vanilla flavour but there are also good vanilla essences in specialist food shops. Make your own vanilla sugar by storing a vanilla pod in a jar of caster sugar.

Making egg custard

If you feel worried about cooking egg custard in a saucepan, put the mixture in a bowl and cook over a pan of hot water.

Accompaniments for iced desserts

For that really professional look serve your iced desserts with wafers, sweet biscuits, meringues, fresh fruit, nuts and chocolate.

Ice cream machines

All the recipes can be made in an electric ice cream maker but for individual recipes check manufacturers' instructions for specific times.

The big freeze

Generally speaking both cream and water ices are ready to serve after 2½-3 hours. However, the flavour improves if they are kept for 24 hours before serving.

Adding gelatine to ice cream helps make it smoother. Be sure to whisk it well into hot custard. Custards made with gelatine do not form thick skins so can just be stirred when cold.

Taking ice cream on picnics

If you don't have an insulated hamper, place frozen picnic ice packs on either side of the tin of ice cream. Wrap tightly in several thicknesses of newspaper.

Fruit Ripple

More economical ice creams can be made with a cornflour or custard powder base and make good desserts for children. These ices freeze much harder than other types so are good for taking on picnics.

Serves 4   ☆☆☆
Preparation: about 1 hour
Freezing: 3 hours

2 tablespoons cornflour or custard
    powder
3oz (75g) caster sugar
14 fl oz (400ml) milk
2 teaspoons powdered gelatine
few drops of vanilla essence
¼ pint (150ml) double cream
1 egg, size 2
3oz (75g) jam, sieved

Mix the cornflour or custard powder to a smooth paste with the sugar and 2-3 tablespoons of the milk. Heat the remaining milk in a saucepan over a moderate heat.
☐ When bubbles appear around the edge stir into cornflour mixture.
☐ Return to the saucepan and continue to cook, stirring constantly for about 3 minutes until thick and smooth. Remove from the heat.
☐ Whisk the gelatine into the custard. Stir in the vanilla essence and leave to cool.
☐ Whip the cream to soft peaks. Beat the egg until it is light and foamy. Fold the cream into the custard and then the beaten egg.
☐ Put about one-third of the custard into a 1½ pint (900ml) loaf tin. Place in the freezer for 20 minutes to set.
☐ Dribble half the jam over the surface and cover with a third more custard. Return to the freezer for a further 20 minutes.
☐ Dribble the remaining jam over the custard and cover with the remaining custard. With the handle of a wooden spoon, stir the contents of the tin lightly to achieve the ripple effect. Return to the freezer and freeze for 3 hours.

☐ To serve: Transfer ice cream to the fridge 1 hour before required. Spoon or scoop into glasses. Decorate with fresh fruit and serve with wafers.
Tip: Blackcurrant, raspberry, or strawberry jams are particularly good. If the jam is too stiff, stir in 1 tablespoon warm water, then leave to cool before adding. Decorate the ice cream with fresh fruit in season.

Iced Rum and Raisin Mousse

Although this recipe is called a mousse, do not be tempted to thaw it and serve as an unfrozen dessert as it will separate.

Serves 6-8   ☆☆☆
Preparation: 20 minutes plus macerating
Freezing: 4 hours

4oz (125g) seedless raisins
4 tablespoons rum
4 eggs, size 2, separated
4oz (125g) icing sugar
9 fl oz (275ml) double cream

Put raisins and rum into a screw-top jar. Leave for 4 hours, shaking occasionally.
☐ Whisk the egg whites until foamy. Gradually whisk in half the sugar to make a soft meringue.
☐ Whisk yolks with remaining sugar until pale and creamy. Whip cream to soft peaks.
☐ Fold the yolks into the cream. Stir in the raisins. Finally, fold in the meringue.
☐ Put in a 1½ pint (900ml) foil container. Freeze for 4 hours.
To serve: Transfer to the fridge about 30 minutes before required.
Tip: Line a bombe mould or pudding basin with vanilla or chocolate ice cream and freeze. Fill the centre with Rum and Raisin Mousse and freeze.
Variation: Make a tutti-frutti ice by adding chopped glacé fruits such as cherries, pineapple and angelica. Serve with maple syrup.

Peach Iced Cream

Serves 4 ☆☆☆
Preparation: 30 minutes
Freezing: 4-5 hours

6 large fresh peaches
1 teaspoon lemon juice
4oz (125g) caster sugar
3 tablespoons Cointreau
7 fl oz (200ml) double cream

Remove the skin and stones from the peaches. Put the flesh into a food processor or liquidizer with the lemon juice, sugar and Cointreau. Process to a purée.

☐ Whip the cream to soft peaks. Fold into the fruit purée. Transfer to ice cream maker if using. When stirring has finished remove blades and freeze. Alternatively, turn mixture into a 1¾ pint (1 litre) metal mould or container. Freeze for 4-5 hours until firm.

☐ To serve: 30-40 minutes before required, turn ice out of mould on to serving dish. Return to the fridge. Serve with a little Cointreau poured over the ice cream.

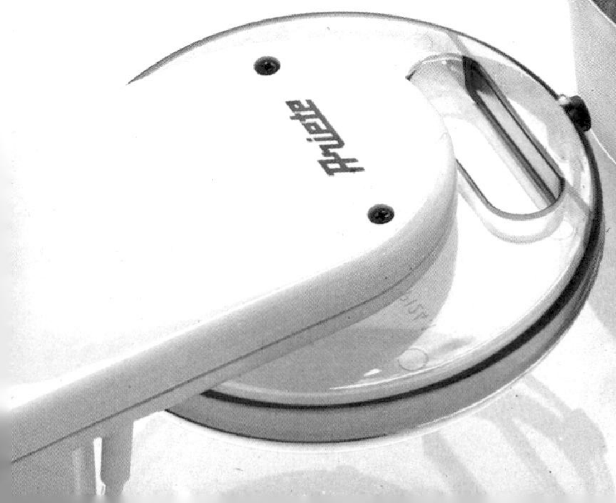

The steps in making Peach Iced Cream.

Preparing peaches

Use ripe freestone peaches for easier peeling and removal of the stones. Peel them as thinly as possible with a sharp knife. Hold peaches over a bowl to catch all the juices. It is better not to blanch peaches in hot water unless they are very large and very good quality as you are liable to partially cook the flesh. For this recipe you will require 1lb (500g) peach flesh.

Grapefruit Sorbet

Serves 6
Preparation: 20 minutes
Freezing: 4½ hours

3 large grapefruit
6oz (175g) sugar
8 fl oz (250ml) white wine
3 egg whites from size 2 eggs
fresh mint leaves to decorate

Cut the grapefruit in half and remove the flesh. Liquidize the flesh from 2 of the grapefruit. Use the remainder in another recipe.
☐ Discard the membranes from the shell and wash well. Pat dry and place in the freezer until required.
☐ Put the sugar and wine in a saucepan over low heat. Stir until the sugar dissolves to make a clear liquid. Simmer for 3 minutes and remove from the heat.
☐ Add the grapefruit purée and pour into a 1¼ pint (750ml) aluminium foil container. Cool.
☐ Place in the freezer and leave for 45 minutes. Stir. Freeze again for 35-40 minutes until mushy.
☐ Turn the mixture into a large bowl and break the crystals down with a fork.
☐ Whisk egg whites to soft peaks and fold into the grapefruit mixture. Pour back into the aluminium foil container, cover with cling film and return to the freezer. Freeze for 3 hours.
☐ To serve, place scoops of sorbet into the grapefruit shells and decorate with fresh mint leaves.
Variation: Add a handful of mint leaves to the sugar and wine syrup when you remove it from the heat. Cover and allow to infuse for 20 minutes. Strain the syrup and proceed with recipe. Experiment with different varieties of mint such as lemon mint.
Tip: Serve scoops of grapefruit sorbet as a dessert or between courses of a very rich meal. The refreshing tang helps to clear the palate before the next dish arrives.

Pineapple Sorbet

Serves 4
Preparation: 10 minutes
Freezing: 4½ hours

7oz (200g) caster sugar
¼ pint (150ml) water
14 fl oz (400ml) pineapple juice
3 tablespoons lemon juice
2 egg whites from size 2 eggs

Dissolve sugar in water. Boil for 3 minutes. Stir in the pineapple and lemon juice. Continue in same way as Grapefruit Sorbet.
Tip: This recipe looks quite spectacular if it is served in a fresh pineapple shell. Remove leafy tuft 1in (2.5cm) down from top. Cut a thin slice from the base if it does not sit straight. Scoop out flesh and use for another recipe. Chill empty shell and fill with sorbet to serve.

Melon Sorbet

Serves 6
Preparation: 15 minutes
Freezing: 4½ hours

2½-3lb (1.25-1.5kg) green-fleshed melon
4oz (125g) caster sugar
8 fl oz (250ml) white wine
juice of ½ lemon
2 egg whites from size 2 eggs
3oz (75g) seedless green grapes, halved

Halve the melon and discard the seeds.
☐ Scoop out the flesh from the melon and liquidize or process to a purée with the sugar. Mix in the wine and lemon juice.
☐ Whisk the egg whites to soft peaks. Add the grapes to the melon and wine purée. Fold in the egg whites. Put into a 1 pint (600ml) aluminium foil container. Freeze in the same way as Grapefruit Sorbet.
Tip: Experiment with different types of melon like galia or ogen. Watermelon does not have such a strong flavour but the pink flesh makes a very pretty sorbet.

Orange Sorbet

Serves 4 ○
Preparation: 10 minutes
Freezing: 4½-5½ hours

---

3 fl oz (100ml) water
6oz (175g) caster sugar
strip of thinly pared orange rind
14 fl oz (400ml) orange juice
juice of 1 lemon
2 egg whites from size 2 eggs

Put the water, sugar and rind in a saucepan over low heat. Stir until sugar dissolves. Simmer for 3 minutes. Remove from heat.
☐ Strain in the fruit juices. Pour into a 1¼ pint (750ml) foil container. Cool.
☐ Place in the freezer. Leave for about 45 minutes. Stir. Freeze again for 35-40 minutes.
☐ Turn mixture into a bowl. Break down the crystals with a fork. Whisk egg whites to soft peaks. Fold into the frozen mixture.
☐ Return to the container. Cover with cling film. Freeze for 3-4 hours.
Variations: For Lemon Sorbet, make in the same way using 7 fl oz (200ml) water, 10oz (275g) caster sugar, strip of thinly pared lemon rind, ½ pint (300ml) lemon juice and 2 egg whites.
● For Redcurrant Sorbet mix 1lb (500g) puréed redcurrants with 6oz (175g) caster sugar, the juice of ½ lemon and 2 egg whites.

From left to right: Orange Sorbet, Lemon Sorbet, Redcurrant Sorbet.

Flavouring water ices
Most recipes are for fruit flavoured water ices but they are equally delicious made with coffee, perfumed tea such as Earl Grey, or wine. Experiment to achieve the flavour you prefer.

Cooling quickly
To cool the sugar syrup quickly before completing the sorbet, plunge the pan into a bowl of cold water or ice cubes.

Freezing for the creative cook

Freezer ownership adds enormously to the range of possibilities open to the keen cook. Not only does it allow you to store a range of foods of your choice, including foods which normally have a limited season. It also enables you to make the most effective use of the cooking time at your disposal. Often, it takes little more time to prepare a quantity of food for the freezer than to cook a single dish; while entertaining and getting ready for busy times like Christmas become far more rewarding once you are able to plan ahead with the help of the freezer.

What to freeze

Freezing fruits and vegetables at the height of the season, whole or part carcasses of meat, or freshly caught fish adds economy and variety to your table all the year round. In addition to these basic foods, many recipes can be frozen at a stage where much or all of the time-consuming preparation has been done. Moreover, foods which would otherwise have been thrown away can be kept for use in recipes at a later date.

Whole, made-up dishes are marvellous to have in the freezer. Instructions for freezing suitable recipes will be found elsewhere in *The Creative Cook*.

Some tips for freezing

Most food flavours are better if the dishes are not stored for too long so keep a check on storage times for made-up dishes. Baked foods can sometimes take on the taste of plastic so again don't store them for too long.
● Wrap everything closely in heavy-weight freezerwrap, foil or freezer bags. Frozen foods quickly become dried out and show 'freezer burns' unless precautions are taken.
● Store heavy foods under fragile ones. Pretty edges on pastry can be partly protected by leaving in the dish in which they were made but handle them gently in the freezer. Leave delicate cakes in their baking containers for safety.
● If foods are frozen in glass, porcelain or pottery, allow them to come to room temperature for an hour or so before reheating or the temperature shock may crack the dish.

Stock and stock-making

Stock stores very well in the freezer. Pack the stock in small containers to have ready for adding to soups, sauces or stews. It is also quite convenient to freeze stock in ice-cube trays, transferring the frozen cubes of stock to polythene bags for storage.
● Wash and chop bits of left-over vegetables such as onions, carrots, celery, parsnips and swedes. Store in plastic bags ready for soup or stock-making. Use from frozen.
● Wrap carcasses and bones from cooked meat or poultry in freezerwrap and put into plastic bags. As they take up space, freeze for a short time only. Use for stock-making.

Sauces

When cooking a sauce, make a little extra when you have spare milk or cream to use up and freeze it. If you make a thick sauce it can be adapted for use in croquettes, which require a very stiff mixture, or thinned on reheating for various other recipes. Store in small plastic containers. To thaw, put frozen block into a saucepan on a low heat. Cover and stir frequently. It will take about 10 minutes to thaw ½ pint (300ml) of sauce. Stir in milk, cream, wine or stock to give the desired consistency.
● Fruit or vegetable purées are also useful to freeze. Store in small plastic containers. Thaw slowly in a saucepan if served hot, in the fridge overnight or at room temperature for 3 hours if served cold. Use as they are for sauces or thicken with cornflour.

Fish fillets

If you have a ready supply of fresh fish – such as sole or trout – available you can freeze them for later use. Clean, skin and fillet the fish, then wrap each fillet separately in freezer-wrap and store in flat packages of foil for quick freezing and thawing. Ready-prepared fillets are excellent for making a variety of fish dishes where strips or cubes of fish are needed.

Pastry

Pastry can be stored in the freezer in several forms. The rubbed-in mixture of short or sweet pastry can be put into plastic bags. It will require no thawing and can be mixed straight-away. Any of the short or sweet pastry doughs also freeze well. If you do not have enough time to completely prepare puff or flaky pastry, freeze them at any stage. Freeze in blocks not more than 1in (2.5cm) thick. Thaw at room temperature then proceed with the next step.
● Baked pastry freezes well too. In addition to baked flan cases frozen in their serving dishes, you can bake tart shells. Open freeze them and then pack with greaseproof paper between them. Pack in rigid containers.
● Many attractive sweet and savoury

dishes can be made at the last minute, if you freeze rectangular sheets of cooked pastry about 6in (15cm) wide and 12in (30cm) long. Open freeze on a tray and wrap each piece separately in cling film. Stack on a piece of cardboard or a thin cake board the same size to prevent cracking. Over-wrap again in freezerwrap film or cling film. Thaw and fill with hot savoury fillings or whipped cream and fruit.

Casseroles

One of the most valuable things to have in the freezer is a good casserole or stew. A complete course can be thawed beforehand and heated while you prepare the rest of the meal.

● Freezing may cause thickened sauces to separate a little when thawed. It is important to reheat very gently. Certain recipes may be thickened after thawing to prevent this problem.

● Flavours tend to fade during long freezer storage. Store highly seasoned casseroles for not more than 6 weeks.

Boiled rice

Spread in a thin layer on a tray lined with greaseproof paper and open freeze. This prevents the rice sticking together. Transfer and freeze in a plastic bag. Use from frozen in soups and made-up dishes, croquettes, stuffing and so on.

Sponge cakes and puddings

Sponge cakes and puddings freeze very well as the high sugar and fat content keeps them moist and they will retain their flavour for up to 2 months. Cakes are best thawed at room temperature and as this may take some time, serving must be anticipated well in advance. Their icing and decorating is better left until after thawing, although it is possible to freeze cakes complete with whipped cream or butter cream. It is also better to add jam and other runny fillings after thawing. Sponge pud-dings can conveniently be reheated from frozen.

Cakes and crumbs

Cut sponge cake into fingers and lay on a tray. Open freeze then pack in a plastic bag. Thaw on a tray for 30 minutes at room temperature. Use for making trifles and charlottes.

● Make cake crumbs and store in a plastic bag. Thaw for a few minutes before coating sweet foods to be fried.

● Mix crumbs with half their weight of desiccated coconut and rub in half the total weight of butter. Store in a plastic bag and use to top custard or milk puddings. Brown under grill.

Bread and crumbs

Trim the crusts from left-over bread. Wrap the slices separately in foil or film and pack together in a plastic bag. When needed, you can peel off as many slices as you require. To thaw, lay out the slices in a single layer on the work surface for about ½ hour. Use for making bread and butter pudding, or fried bread.

● Prepare and sieve crumbs. Store in a plastic bag. Use without thawing for stuffings and croquettes.

● Cut small shapes from thinly sliced bread and store in polythene bags. Use for croûtons to serve with soup.

● Mix equal weights of grated cheese and crumbs and rub in half the total weight of butter. Store in a polythene bag and use for topping gratin dishes.

Lemons and oranges

Pare thinly to avoid the bitter pith. Cut peel into thin shreds or shapes with cutters. Store in a small plastic box. Use to flavour and garnish soups, sauces, caramelized fruit, crêpe dishes and so on.

● Lemons grate faster and more easily when frozen. It is also worth freezing lemon slices so that they are always available for drinks.

Herbs

Fresh herbs can be frozen in small quantities for later addition to soups, sauces and casseroles. They can also be chopped and added to butter, and pats of the frozen butter can then be used to garnish grilled meats.

Thawing and reheating

If you have the time, thawing in the fridge is the best way. If you pack casserole recipes in shallow polythene or foil containers to freeze, they will thaw overnight. Deeper containers with a more solid block of food may take as much as 24 hours. Lids should be left on and bags kept sealed during thawing.

Cooking ahead

It should be remembered that freezing need not be just for long-term storage. It can be very helpful to prepare a casserole one week for the next and the most convenient way to do this is to freeze it in the dish in which it was cooked and in which it will be served.

❄ Freezing and thawing cakes

Less rich cakes are best frozen for a short time only and can be thawed in their wrapping to keep them moist. Fatless sponges are best frozen in their baking tin or dish. They are very fragile and benefit by being protected from heavier foods in the freezer. They should be unwrapped and removed from the container while still frozen to avoid tearing the delicate skin.

Filling polythene bags with liquid

Stand the bag in a tall jug and fold the top back like a cuff. Spoon or pour liquid into the bag. Twist the neck of the bag to close, allowing a little space for expansion during freezing. Seal with freezer tape ties.

Filling containers

Plastic boxes can be filled to the top with soup if you are going to remove the frozen soup before storing. Line the box with a polythene bag and fill with the soup. Freeze uncovered then gently pull out the sides of the boxes and pull out the block of soup. If you are going to store the soup in boxes, leave at least 1in (2.5cm) space for expansion. Cover and freeze. If you run out of rigid containers use empty milk or juice cartons. They are waxed inside and are ideal for soups and sauces.

10 rules for freezing cooked dishes

● Food intended for the freezer should be kept very clean and handled as little as possible. It should also be kept covered. (This is because freezing prevents germs from multiplying but does not kill them.)

● Ingredients should be fresh and of good quality.

● The taste of salt and pepper is intensified after freezing, so made-up dishes should only be lightly seasoned. More seasoning may be added later if needed.

● If possible, slightly undercook dishes intended for the freezer, as they will cook a little more when they are reheated after thawing.

● Garnishes are best added before serving, rather than before freezing.

● Hot foods should be cooled rapidly before freezing, for instance by standing containers in iced water. All foods should be at room temperature or below before being put in the freezer, to avoid raising the temperature of food already there.

● Food should be frozen as quickly as possible, either by using a fast-freeze switch if a number of dishes are involved, or, if a single item is being frozen, placing it against the sides or base of the freezer. Allow about 2 hours for freezing made-up dishes.

● When packaging it is important to exclude as much air as possible to prevent evaporation. However, when freezing liquid foods some room should be left in the container to allow for expansion. Storing food in convenient portions makes it easier to remove the amount required.

● Label carefully, with the date when frozen, number of portions and a reminder of any additions and adjustments to be made when the dish is served.

● Cooked food must never be refrozen once thawed.

Problem foods

Most cooked dishes will freeze well but there are some exceptions.

● Egg-based sauces such as custard will curdle on thawing.

● Dishes containing hard-boiled egg, as this becomes rubbery when frozen.

● Dishes with a high gelatine content, such as jellies and aspic. On thawing the texture becomes granular, there is some loss of water and the clearness of the jelly is spoilt.

● Icings such as royal and glacé icing may crack when thawed.

● Strong-tasting foods must be well packaged. A short storage time is recommended.

● Cooked onions, garlic, spices and herbs sometimes give a musty flavour to cooked dishes which have been frozen. Quantities should therefore be reduced and adjusted on reheating.

● Sauces tend to thicken on freezing, so they should be made slightly thinner than usual.

Food storage time	Preparation	Packaging	Thawing and serving
Plain unrisen yeast dough (1-2 months)	As freezing tends to destroy yeast cells, extra yeast may be used. Freeze after first kneading.	In loosely tied, oiled polythene bag, or bag dusted with flour.	Loosen bag and leave to rise for 5-6 hours at room temperature or overnight in fridge. Knock back and continue as usual.
Plain risen yeast dough (2 weeks)	Allow dough to rise in polythene bag. Turn out and knead lightly.	Repack in polythene bag and seal.	Leave to thaw as for unrisen dough, then continue as usual.
Home-baked bread (1 month)	Freeze quickly when freshly baked and cooled.	Wrap in polythene bag or foil.	Thaw in packaging at room temperature for 3-6 hours.
Cakes (2 months)	Cut down amount of flavouring used.	Pack undecorated cakes in polythene bags. Open freeze decorated cakes, then wrap in polythene and pack in rigid containers. Also wrap sponges after freezing to avoid damaging surface.	Thaw undecorated cakes in wrappings at room temperature for 1-3 hours, according to size. Remove wrappings from decorated cakes before thawing for 2-4 hours.
Uncooked biscuits (6 months)	Prepare dough and shape into rolls the width of finished biscuit. Alternatively, shape dough into biscuits and open freeze.	Wrap in polythene or foil.	Leave roll of dough in packaging at room temperature until soft enough to cut into rounds. Bake as usual. Bake shaped biscuits from frozen, allowing 4-5 minutes longer than usual.
Uncooked shortcrust pastry (3 months)	Prepare and roll dough as usual.	Wrap in polythene or foil. For flan cases, line plates and open freeze, then remove pastry and wrap in polythene or foil. Place in rigid container for protection.	Leave 3 hours at room temperature or overnight in fridge. Unwrap flan cases and cook from frozen, adding 5 minutes to usual baking time. Or unwrap and leave at room temperature for 30 minutes before filling and baking.

Food storage time	Preparation	Packaging	Thawing and serving
Cooked pies (3-4 months for meat pies, 6 months for fruit pies)	Bake in foil plates and cool.	Wrap carefully in polythene or foil, and rigid container for protection.	Thaw at room temperature for 2-4 hours. Make steam vents in top and reheat in oven.
Uncooked flaky and puff pastry (6 months)	Prepare up to last rolling, and form into blocks not more than 1in (2.5cm) thick.	Wrap in polythene or foil. For vol-au-vent cases, open freeze, then wrap in polythene or foil and place in rigid container for protection.	Thaw at room temperature for 3-4 hours or overnight in fridge. May be cooked from frozen at 450F (230C) gas 8 for 15 minutes.
Uncooked choux pastry (3 months)	Shape pastry and open freeze.	Wrap in polythene or foil.	Bake from frozen at 400F (200C) gas 6, allowing 5 minutes longer than usual.
Cooked choux pastry (2 months)	Split sides of pastry and allow to dry out and cool. Open freeze.	Wrap in polythene or foil.	Leave wrapped at room temperature for about 1 hour, then remove wrappings and crisp for a few minutes in oven at 350F (180C) gas 4.
Pancakes (2 months)	Cook as usual and cool on a wire tray.	Stack in layers between foil or greaseproof paper. Wrap each stack in foil.	Leave wrapped at room temperature for 2-3 hours, or overnight in fridge. To thaw quickly, unwrap, separate pancakes and leave at room temperature for 15-20 minutes. Heat in oven at 350F (180C) gas 4 for 10 minutes.
Uncooked pizzas (3 months)	Prepare to baking stage. Do not garnish.	Wrap in polythene or foil, freeze and overwrap.	Bake from frozen at 450F (230C) gas 8 for 30-35 minutes.
Cooked pizzas (2 months)	Bake pizza and cool. Do not garnish.	Wrap in polythene or foil, freeze and overwrap.	Unwrap and heat at 400F (200C) gas 6 for 15-20 minutes.
Pasta (2 months)	Leftover pasta may be cooled under cold running water and blotted dry.	Wrap in polythene bag.	Reheat in boiling water.
Sweet and savoury mousses (1 month)	Prepare but do not garnish.	May be frozen in freezerproof serving dishes. Alternatively, line dish with foil, freeze mousse, remove from container and store in polythene bag.	Thaw at room temperature for 2-3 hours, or in fridge for 6-8 hours.
Pâtés and terrines (1 month)	Reduce seasoning and spices.	Freeze in tin or mould, remove and wrap in polythene.	Thaw in wrappings at room temperature for 6-8 hours or overnight in fridge.
Stews, casseroles and other meat dishes (2 months)	Reduce seasoning and other flavourings. Cook for slightly less time than usual.	Pack in rigid containers. Alternatively, freeze in foil-lined casserole, remove when solid and pack in polythene bag.	May be reheated from frozen. Make sure food comes to the boil, then simmer gently.
Soups (3-6 months)	Reduce seasoning. Omit any cream and add on reheating. Soups may be reduced before freezing to save freezer space.	Pack in rigid container, allowing some space for expansion. Alternatively, line container with polythene bag, remove soup when frozen and seal.	Heat from frozen, adding more liquid if required.
Stocks (2-3 months)	May be reduced before freezing.	Pack as for soups.	As for soups.
Sauces (2-3 months)	Using cornflour in place of flour will help minimize separation on thawing. Add cream or eggs on reheating rather than before freezing.	Pack as for soups.	Reheat gently from frozen, over boiling water if possible, stirring constantly.

Microwaving for the creative cook

Microwave ovens are the most recent development in cooking technology. Their advantages include speed, cleanliness, economy and versatility. However, to use this new cooking aid most effectively and creatively, it is helpful to understand what happens when you microwave food, and the kinds of tasks a microwave oven performs best.

So far in this book we have considered the various ways of cooking by heat transference in a normal gas or electric oven. But in a microwave oven there is just one basic cooking method. The food to be cooked is simply placed in the oven, in a suitable container, for the required length of time. Invisible microwaves then bombard the food, causing the moisture molecules within it to vibrate very fast. This creates friction, which in turn generates heat within the food. While the food gets hot, the oven itself remains cool. So cakes and roasts cooked in a microwave won't brown, unless special 'browning' elements and dishes are used. The speed at which the food cooks is another factor preventing browning.

Due to the intense heat produced within the food, it will continue to cook even after it has been taken out of the oven. Time is therefore allowed for this, known as standing time.

The microwaves do not cause any changes in the food apart from cooking it through. For this reason microwaving is particularly suitable for foods such as fish, vegetables and fruit which are flavoursome in themselves and merely need to be lightly cooked.

It takes about one-fifth to one-quarter of the time to cook by microwave as it does using more conventional methods. However, timing will be influenced by the amount of food to be cooked – two baked potatoes will take one and a half times as long as a single potato. Therefore, if large quantities of food need to be cooked it may be more practicable to use a conventional oven.

Microwaves will only penetrate to about 1.5in (4cm) from the outside. Food which is thicker than 3in (7.5cm) will therefore cook by conduction of heat from this outer layer rather than by direct microwave action. Special attention has to be paid to the shape of cooking containers and the positioning of food so that it cooks as evenly as possible. Dishes should preferably be straight-sided and evenly shaped — round or ring-shaped containers are best, while square ones may cause problems.

The fat and sugar content of food also has to be taken into consideration. The presence of either will make food cook faster in a microwave oven, so that, for instance, fat meat will be ready sooner than lean. Food containing a good deal of moisture will take longer, however.

It is possible to cook most kinds of food in a microwave oven. However, it will not deep-fry or shallow-fry and is not suitable for foods like soufflés and batters, which require hot air around them in order to rise, though it is well adapted to cooking dishes which are steamed, casseroled or cooked in a sauce or liquid. Some things a microwave oven does admirably, and the creative cook will probably choose to concentrate on these, treating the microwave as a useful adjunct to the conventional oven rather than as a replacement. Suggestions for using the microwave oven to advantage follow. Remember always to take the manufacturer's instruction book as a guide when using a microwave oven, as models vary quite considerably.

Fish

Fish cooks very well in a microwave oven, staying moist and retaining its natural flavour and nutritional value. Microwaving is ideal for fish dishes which would normally be poached, baked or steamed, though not suitable for cooking fried fish or fish in batter.

● Cook fillets, steaks or whole fish covered, leaving a small hole for steam to escape. Brush the skin with melted butter or fat.

● When cooking fillets, overlap the thin tail ends and place these towards the centre of the dish for more even cooking. Any sauce should be added halfway through cooking.

● Wrap small pieces of foil around the heads and tails of whole fish for part of the cooking time to protect them. Be sure the foil doesn't touch the sides of the oven.

● Cook fish until just firm and leave to stand for a few minutes.

Vegetables

Most vegetables cook extremely well in a microwave oven. Being quickly cooked in a small amount of water, or sometimes none at all, they retain their texture, flavour, fresh colour and nutritional value.

● When preparing fresh vegetables, try to ensure pieces are of even size. Cooking times will be affected by the age and freshness of the vegetables.

● Add just a little water to the container – roughly 4-8 tablespoons per lb (450g). Root vegetables will need less, mushrooms and tomatoes none at all.

● Add salt after cooking according to taste.

- Guard against overcooking. If possible, allow vegetables to stand for a short while after removing them from the oven.
- Jacket potatoes cook very well in a microwave oven. Scrub, prick well and set on kitchen paper.

Fruit

Similarly, fruit cooked in a microwave oven retains its fresh taste, texture, shape and nutrients. Generally, less sugar is needed when fruit is cooked in this way – another health benefit.

The same rules apply as for cooking vegetables. The container should be covered, leaving a small opening for steam to escape. Little additional water or sugar syrup is needed, but the skin of the fruit should be pierced or cut to prevent any spattering.

Soups and sauces

The advantage of cooking these in a microwave oven is that they do not stick to the sides or base of the container, so a smoother result is achieved. Also, it is often convenient to be able to heat the soup or sauce in the container in which it is to be served.
- Cook uncovered, and stir during cooking, preferably with a wire whisk.
- Soups containing milk, cream or eggs tend to boil more quickly than water-based soups. Thick soups will take longer to heat than clear ones.

Low-fat cooking

One advantage of microwave cooking that will recommend it to slimmers and the health-conscious is that often less fat is required.

Defrosting

Used in combination with a freezer, microwaves can bring a wonderful degree of flexibility and freedom to meal preparation. Fast defrosting by microwave makes the contents of the freezer immediately accessible, so that cooking for the freezer becomes more worthwhile.
- Home frozen food will take longer to thaw than commercially frozen, as it contains larger ice crystals.
- Defrosting must be followed by standing time, which will vary according to what is being defrosted. Solid items like pies, for instance, need a good standing time.
- A defrost button ensures even thawing.
- Remember that foil trays and metal tags used in packing food for the freezer must not be put into a microwave oven.
- Casseroles and liquid foods should be stirred, so that any frozen lumps are moved to the side of the container. A large block of frozen liquid will, however, thaw more quickly in a pan on the stove.
- Frozen bread, buns and croissants are quickly ready to eat.

Reheating

Another useful feature of the microwave oven is that it reheats so well, without drying up the food or altering flavours.
- Cover food to be reheated, distributing larger items around the outside of the container. Stir liquid foods during reheating, and again on removal.
- Stand bread, pizzas, flans and similar foods on kitchen paper to reheat. Do not cover.

Kitchen chores

A microwave oven can make the cook's work easier by taking over such chores as softening butter and heating small amounts of liquid quickly.
- Citrus fruit and peaches become easier to peel when they are first warmed in the oven. Remember to make a small slit in the skin first.
- Chocolate melts easily in a microwave oven. Put the broken pieces into a bowl and heat for a minute at a time, stirring every minute, and removing the chocolate when it is smooth and liquid.
- To brown almonds in a microwave oven, spread them on a heavy dish and shake this every $1\frac{1}{2}$ minutes until the nuts are sufficiently brown.

Planning

Remember that cooking by microwave is a very 'busy' method. The cooking is often so rapid that there is no time to do anything else before the food requires attention. Plan meals so that part is cooked by conventional methods and part in the microwave oven.

A cool kitchen

There is no heat generated by microwaves, except the heat from the food itself, so the kitchen stays cool. However, you may want to have the conventional oven on low to keep plates warm or food hot.

Timing

Food can be over-cooked and dry out very rapidly, so it's always wise to check at an even earlier stage than recommended. Slight under-cooking is usually better, as the food can always be returned to the oven for a little longer if necessary. Timing will also be influenced by the make of cooker and the requirements of individual recipes.

Containers

Save time by cooking or heating food in the dish in which it is to be served. Always check that dishes are a suitable size for the food and that there is no metal content such as gold trim on a plate.

Foil

As a general rule metal foil should not be used in a microwave oven, though small pieces may be wrapped for protection over sections of food which might otherwise be in danger of over-cooking. The foil must never be allowed to touch the sides of the oven, but should be held close to the food with, for example, an overwrapping of cling wrap.

Covering food

This prevents splashing, retains moisture and helps food heat more evenly. Cling wrap makes a good covering but should always be pierced to allow steam to escape.
Foods such as bread, cakes and pastry should not be covered. Instead, stand on kitchen paper.

Cooking meat and poultry

Roasting meat

Personal preferences vary greatly, and so do ovens and individual joints, but the information given here provides a general guide to roasting times.

● Joints should be placed fat side up on a rack in a shallow tin and set in the centre of a preheated oven. If the joint is very lean, add fat and baste during cooking.

● All meat joints may be cooked successfully by the so-called 'slow' method, which reduces shrinkage, results in a tender roast and is suitable for all cuts. The joint is put into a preheated oven and cooked at 350F (180C) gas 4. However, sometimes a joint may be 'sealed' by putting it into a hot oven at 450F (230C) gas 8 for 5-10 minutes to sear the surface, before lowering the heat to 350F (180C) gas 4 and cooking as usual.

● Joints cooked 'on the bone' take slightly less time, as bone is a good conductor of heat.

● As joints vary considerably in size and shape, the most accurate way of checking that meat is properly cooked is with a meat thermometer. This should be inserted into the centre of the meat when the joint appears to be almost ready.

● After cooking a large joint should be allowed to 'rest' before it is carved. This waiting time enables the fibres to soften and relax, and the juices to be distributed more evenly throughout the meat.

Roasting times for meat

Meat	Cooking time in oven preheated to 350F (180C) gas 4	Meat thermometer reading
Beef		
On the bone (medium-done)	15 min per lb (450g) +15 min	160F (71C)
On the bone (well-done)	25 min per lb (450g) +25 min	
Off the bone (medium-done)	20 min per lb (450g) +20 min	174F (79C)
Off the bone (well-done)	30 min per lb (450g) +30 min	
Stuffed joints	add 5-10 min per lb (450g)	
Veal		
On the bone	25 min per lb (450g) +25 min	180F (82C)
Boned and stuffed joints	30 min per lb (450g) +30 min	
Pork		
On the bone	30 min per lb (450g) +30 min	190F (88C)
Boned and stuffed joints	add 5-10 min per lb (450g)	
Lamb		
On the bone (medium-done)	25 min per lb (450g) +25 min	180F (82C)
On the bone (well-done)	30 min per lb (450g) +30 min	
Boned and stuffed joints	40 min per lb (450g)	

Roasting times for poultry

All poultry should be well-thawed before cooking, and cooked to reach an internal temperature of 190F (88C).

Bird	Cooking temperature	Cooking time
Chicken		
Unstuffed	375F (190C) gas 5	20 min per lb (450g) +20 min
Stuffed, or cooked in foil or roasting bag	375F (190C) gas 5	25 min per lb (450g) +25 min
Poussin	375F (190C) gas 5	20 min per lb (450g) +20 min
Turkey		
5-8lb (2.25-3.6kg)	350F (180C) gas 4	2-2½ hours (foil-wrapped 2½-3½ hours)
8-11lb (3.6-5kg)	350F (180C) gas 4	2½-3¼ hours (foil-wrapped 3½-4 hours)
11-15lb (5-6.7kg)	350F (180C) gas 4	3¼-3¾ hours (foil-wrapped 4-5 hours)
15-20lb (6.7-9kg)	350F (180C) gas 4	3¾-4¼ hours (foil-wrapped 5-5½ hours)
25-30lb (11.25-13.5kg)	350F (180C) gas 4	4¾-5½ hours (don't foil-wrap)
Duck	425F (220C) gas 7, then reduce to 350F (180C) gas 4 after 20 min	20 min per lb (450g)
Goose	425F (220C) gas 7, then reduce to 325F (160C) gas 3 after 20 min	20 min per lb (450g)

Roasting times for game

Feathered game
Only young birds are really suitable for roasting. Place a knob of butter inside bird to prevent dryness and lay streaky bacon over the breast. Remove bacon 15 minutes before end of cooking time to allow breast to brown, and sprinkle lightly with flour. Baste often during cooking.

A partridge, pigeon, snipe, woodcock, widgeon or teal will normally serve 1 person; a grouse or quail 1-2 people; a mallard or guinea fowl 2-3 people; a pheasant 3-4 people.

Bird	Cooking temperature	Cooking time
Grouse	375F (190C) gas 5	45 min
Partridge	400F (200C) gas 6	30-45 min
Pheasant	375F (190C) gas 5	50-60 min
Pigeon	400F (200C) gas 6	25-35 min
Quail	425F (220C) gas 7	20 min
Snipe	425F (220C) gas 7	20 min
Woodcock	425F (220C) gas 7	20 min
Mallard	425F (220C) gas 7	30-45 min
Teal	425F (220C) gas 7	20 min
Widgeon	425F (220C) gas 7	30 min
Guinea fowl*	375F (190C) gas 5	60-80 min

*treat as feathered game

Venison
As venison is a dry meat it benefits from marinating and is better served slightly underdone. Brush with oil, wrap in foil and roast in oven preheated to 375F (190C) gas 5 for 35 min per lb (450g). Remove foil 20 minutes before end of cooking time to allow joint to brown.

Hare and rabbit
Only young hares are suitable for roasting. To cook without stuffing, baste well, lay streaky bacon over back and roast in oven preheated to 325F (160F) gas 3 for $1\frac{1}{2}$ hours. Remove bacon 15 minutes before end of cooking time.

To cook stuffed hare or rabbit, insert stuffing, sew up and lay streaky bacon over back. Roast in oven preheated to 350F (180C) gas 4 for about $1\frac{1}{2}$ hours, basting frequently. Remove bacon 15 minutes before end of cooking time.

Boiling meat and poultry

Boiling is suitable for less tender cuts and for salted meats. Use just enough cooking liquid to cover the joint, which should fit the pan fairly snugly. The cooking liquid may afterwards be used in stocks or soups, if not too salt.

Fresh meat is cooked in salted water, salt meat such as ham in water without any salt. The cooking time is calculated from the moment the water reaches boiling point. However, the meat should simmer rather than boil hard, as this toughens it and makes it shrink. Remove any scum which appears after the water has come to the boil.

Meat to be served cold may be left to cool in the cooking liquid.

Meat	Cooking time	Suitable additions	Note
Fresh beef	20 min per lb (450g) +20 min	onion, carrot, bouquet garni, salt	Serve with boiled vegetables and dumplings added to the pot for cooking.
Salt beef	25 min per lb (450g) +25 min	onion, carrot, bay leaf, peppercorns, allspice	
Ham and bacon	25 min per lb (450g) +25 min	bay leaf, peppercorns	If very salty, soak before cooking. Weigh after soaking.
Mutton	20 min per lb (450g) +20 min	onion, carrot, bouquet garni, salt	Serve with a sauce, e.g. caper sauce, onion sauce.
Ox tongue	about $3-3\frac{1}{2}$ hours	onion, carrot, bay leaf, peppercorns, salt	Blanch before cooking. Put in a pan, cover with cold water and bring to boil. Discard water and rinse tongue. Serve with Cumberland sauce.
Rabbit	about $1\frac{1}{2}$ hours	onion, carrot, peppercorns, salt	Blanch before cooking. Put in a pan, cover with cold water and bring to boil. Remove rabbit and put in cold water for a few minutes.
Boiling fowl	2-3 hours	onion, carrot, bouquet garni, giblets, garlic, salt	Serve with a sauce, e.g. parsley sauce, tomato sauce.

Boiling and steaming vegetables

Vegetables should, wherever possible, be prepared immediately before they are to be cooked. The chart gives details, together with times for boiling and steaming.

Although when boiling tough, starchy roots and tubers, such as turnips and potatoes, it is better to start them in cold salted water, most other vegetables should be put into salted water that has already been brought to the boil. Steaming will take slightly longer but is particularly appropriate for the more delicate vegetables. Put the food to be steamed into a suitable container set above fast boiling water and cover tightly. Do not allow to boil dry.

Vegetable	Preparation	Boiling Start in cold (C) or boiling water (B)		Steaming
Artichoke (globe)	Cut off stalk and discoloured scales.	B	20-40 min	50-60 min
Asparagus	Rinse and trim bases. Pare stalks thinly.	B	5-10 min	12-15 min
Beans, broad	Shell. Peel older beans.	B	10-12 min	—
French	Top, tail and rinse.	B	2-10 min	
runner	Top, tail and string. Wash and cut in sections.	B	5-8 min	
Beetroot	Clean carefully in cold water without breaking surface.	B	small 20-30 min large 45-50 min	—
Broccoli	Wash, trim away ends and woody stalks.	B	5-10 min	10-12 min
Brussels sprouts	Remove damaged leaves. Wash and cut cross in stem end.	B	5-8 min	8-10 min
Cabbage, green	Remove outer leaves. Quarter and core. Wash and drain, leave in quarters or shred.	B	quarters 10 min shreds 3-4 min	20-25 min 10-15 min
red		B	shreds 10-15 min	—
white		B	quarters 10 min shreds 3-4 min	20-25 min 10-15 min
spring greens	Wash well and remove tough stalks.	B	15 min	—
Cardoons	Cut off base and outer stalks. Separate stalks, scrub and cut in pieces.	B	20 min	30 min
Carrots	Top, tail, scrape lightly and wash. Trim and wash baby carrots.	B	baby 10 min large 20 min slices 7-10 min	20-30 min
Cauliflower	Remove green leaves and woody base. Wash. Leave whole or divide in florets.	B	whole 15 min florets 5-8 min	15 min
Celeriac	Peel thickly and cut out woody centre. Slice or dice.	B	slices 10 min whole 35 min	—
Celery	Separate stalks. Trim away base and leaves. String and scrub.	B	pieces 10-15 min	20-30 min
Chard	Cut stalks away from leaves. String stalks. Wash stalks and leaves.	B	leaves 1-2 min stalks 10-12 min	7-8 min 15-20 min
Chicory	Trim away base and core. Discard damaged leaves.	B	whole 10-12 min slices 5 min	20-30 min 10 min
Chinese leaves	Separate leaves. Wash well and trim bases. Shred.	B	10-12 min	15 min

Note: all boiling times are estimated from the moment the water comes to the boil (C) or returns to the boil (B).

Vegetable	Preparation	Boiling Start in cold (C) or boiling water (B)		Steaming
Courgettes	Top, tail and wash.	B	whole 8 min	—
			slices 2-3 min	10 min
Cucumber	Peel for cooking, cut in chunks.	B	lengths 2-3 min	7 min
Endive	Discard damaged leaves. Trim base. Rinse well in bowl of cold water.	B	shreds 8 min	—
Fennel	Trim away base of root, leaves and little stems. String outer leaves. Wash. Halve, quarter or slice.	B	quarters 10 min	—
			slices 8 min	
Jerusalem artichoke	Scrub well and rub off skin after cooking or peel first.	C	10 min	20-30 min
Kale, curly	Wash leaves, cut away tough stems and ribs.	B	chopped 25-30 min	—
sea	Wash leaves. Trim off roots and tops of stalks and wash.	B	leaves 15 min	10-12 min
			stalks 25 min	
Kohlrabi	Cut away stalks. Peel older kohlrabi, scrub young ones. Quarter or slice.	B	whole 30-40 min	—
			quarters 20 min	
			slices 10-12 min	
Leeks	Trim off roots and green tops. Cut in lengths and wash well or partly slit and soak whole.	B	lengths 5 min	10 min
			whole 15-20 min	25 min
Mangetout peas	Top, tail and wash.	B	4-5 min	—
Marrow	Peel, cut in chunks, removing seeds.	B	15 min	10-20 min
Mooli	Peel and slice.	B	10-12 min	—
Mushrooms	Wipe and trim base of stalks.	B	small 3 min	20 min
Onions	Trim ends and discard outer skins.	B	small 10 min	30 min
Parsnips	Top, tail and pare. Leave whole, cut in chunks or slice.	C	small 20 min	20-30 min
			slices 10 min	
Peas	Shell fresh peas.	B	1 min	25 min
Potatoes	Peel or scrub well. Leave new potatoes unpeeled.	C old	15 min	30 min
		B new		
Pumpkin	Peel, remove seeds and fibrous tissue and cut in chunks.	B	10-15 min	30 min
Salsify	Scrape and wash.	B	25-30 min	—
Scorzonera	Scrub thoroughly.	B	25-30 min	—
Spinach	Wash thoroughly, discard tough stems.	B	2 min	7-8 min
Squash	Peel, cut in chunks, discarding seeds.	B	whole 30 min	20-40 min
			pieces 10-15 min	
Swedes	Peel, cut in chunks and slice.	C	whole 30-40 min	45-50 min
			chunks 20 min	20-30 min
Sweet potatoes	Peel, slice or cut in pieces.	C	25 min	—
Sweetcorn	Discard husks and silk. Cook as cobs or cut off kernels with a sharp knife.	B	whole 5-7 min	—
			kernels 2-5 min	
Turnips	Scrub young turnips, peel older ones. Slice or cut in chunks.	C	whole 20-30 min	20-30 min
			slices 10-12 min	
Yam	Peel, slice or cut in chunks.	C	20 min	—

Pulses and grains: soaking and cooking times

Some packaged pulses may not need soaking in which case follow the label instructions. Canned beans are ready-cooked and only need heating.

It is important to cook beans—especially kidney and soya beans—at a rolling boil for the first 10 minutes to destroy any harmful substances.

Simmer pulses in fresh water, not in their soaking water.

Both soaking and cooking will take longer if the pulses are old.

Pulses	Quick* soak	Long** soak	Cooking time
Adzuki beans	1 hour	1 hour	1-1½ hours
Black beans	3 hours	7-8 hours	1-2 hours
Black-eyed beans	1 hour	7-8 hours	1-1½ hours
Borlotti beans	1-2 hours	7-8 hours	1-2 hours
Broad beans	3 hours	7-8 hours	1-2 hours
Brown beans (Dutch)	1-2 hours	7-8 hours	1-2 hours
Brown beans (Egyptian)	1-2 hours	7-8 hours	1-2 hours
Butter beans	3 hours	7-8 hours	1-2 hours
Cannellini beans	3 hours	7-8 hours	1-2 hours
Chick peas	3 hours	7-8 hours	2-3 hours
Flageolet beans	3 hours	7-8 hours	1-2 hours
Haricot beans	2 hours	7-8 hours	1-2 hours
Lentils (beige)	—	—	45 min
Lentils (green)	—	—	45 min
Lentils (red split)	—	—	25 min

Pulses	Quick* soak	Long** soak	Cooking time
Mung beans	1 hour	1 hour	1 hour
Peas (green or yellow)			
whole	1 hour	7-8 hours	1-1½ hours
split	30-45 min	1 hour	45-60 min
Pinto beans	1 hour	7-8 hours	1-2 hours
Red kidney beans	2 hours	7-8 hours	1-2 hours
Soya beans	1 hour	7-8 hours	45-60 min

Grains	Quick* soak	Long** soak	Cooking time
Brown rice	—	—	40-45 min
Couscous (to steam)	—	—	20 min
Pasta, dried	—	—	8-12 min
fresh	—	—	3-5 min
White rice	—	—	15-18 min

*Put in cold water, bring slowly to boil, turn off heat and leave to soak.   **Put in cold water and leave to soak.

Oven temperatures

	Electricity °F	°C	Gas mark
Very cool	150	70	
	175	80	
	200	100	
	225	110	¼
	250	120	½
Cool	275	140	1
	300	150	2
Moderate	325	160	3
	350	180	4

	Electricity °F	°C	Gas mark
Moderately hot	375	190	5
	400	200	6
Hot	425	220	7
	450	230	8
Very hot	475	240	9
	500	260	
	525	270	
	550	290	

Basic recipes

For easy reference, here is a list of some basic recipes you are often likely to need.

Index

The recipes in this index have been grouped by main ingredient. So if you plan to cook chicken, for instance, look up 'Chicken' and you will find all the chicken recipes in *The Creative Cook* listed alphabetically. Other entries such as 'boiling', 'flavouring joints', 'roasting' and 'stuffing' show where information on cooking methods for chicken may be found.

● For your convenience recipes may be further listed according to type. Hence 'Simple chicken casserole' also appears under the heading 'Casseroles and stews' and 'Cream of chicken soup' under 'Soups'.

● In addition, those recipes with names which may not be immediately self-explanatory e.g. 'Poulet Normande' will be given separate entries.

● If a recipe title mentions two main ingredients, that particular recipe will be listed under both. So 'Banana and kiwi cake' appears under both 'Banana' and 'Kiwi fruit' as well as 'Cake'.

Note: *Recipes are shown in italics.*

A

ACKNOWLEDGEMENTS

The following also supplied photographs: Anthony Blake (279); BPCC/Aldus Archives (418, 422); British Chicken Ltd. (181); British Meat (110); Eric Carter (353); Corning Ltd. (321, 337); Danish Dairy Board (360); Davis Gelatine (408, 411, 412, 415, 416); Egg Information Bureau (417); Flour Advisory Bureau (318, 342, 354); Food Services Press Ltd. (407); Good Housekeeping Magazine & Bryce Attwell (428); Good Housekeeping Magazine & Anthony Blake (339); Good Housekeeping Magazine & Robert Golden (427); ICTC Electrical Ltd. (433); Kraft (413); McDougalls Flour (365); Mushroom Growers Association (419); National Dairy Council (410, 420); New Zealand Meat Producers (178); Sarsons (379); W.L. Housewares (429).

Thanks are due to the following for their help in loaning kitchen equipment and tableware: The French Kitchen Shop; ICTC Electrical Ltd; David Mellor (4 Sloane Square, London SW1); Russell Hobbs.